MORE PRAISE FOR
THE GOD PROBLEM

"*The God Problem* is the next paradigm. It doesn't take you down the proverbial 'rabbit hole'—it will take you to a place from which you will never reemerge, a brand-new universe in the same skin as the one you now unknowingly inhabit."
—Heinz Insu Fenkl, director of the State University of
New York's Interstitial Studies Institute

"Bloom's greatest talent is his ability to deliver mind-bending concepts in beautifully accessible prose. The breadth and scope of his knowledge is utterly extraordinary, and *The God Problem* is enormously engaging. It truly manages to get beyond the usual divisions between science and belief, and it offers an arresting and original take on the question of how a universe designs itself."
—Matt Thorne, Encore Award–winning novelist

"Absolutely sparkling with ideas."
—David Christian, founder of the International Big
History Association and author of *Maps of Time*

"Part scientific history lesson, part meditation on the foundations of cosmic evolution, *The God Problem* is the work of a rare thinker willing to face directly into one of the great unsung mysteries of science: the stupendous creativity of the universe. At once entertaining, irreverent, and erudite, *The God Problem* brilliantly dances around the edges of physics, biology, and philosophy, showing us what may be the next staging ground in the advance of truth."
—Carter Phipps, author of *Evolutionaries*

"[An] entertaining, suspenseful, rigorous, and thoroughly mathematical survey of the complexity of cosmic (and human) nature."
—Martin Bojowald, author of
Once Before Time: A Whole Story of the Universe
and professor of physics,
Institute for Gravitation and the Cosmos, Penn State

"*The God Problem* is what James Joyce's *Ulysses* might have been like had he written about science. It's an intellectual history no one has put together before. It's like a James Bond martini—shaken, not stirred. It rearranges your thoughts and opens the doors of perception. And it's fun. *The God Problem* is urgent. It's entangled with the Mortality Problem, and the Mortality Problem looms ever larger in the lives of 70 million baby boomers. Many of us have abandoned conventional religion in favor of a deeper inquiry into spirituality. Some of us have looked to the East without finding everything we sought. Some of us have looked to the pagan past with some success. But when you look into the face of modern science in all its glory you'll find many of the pieces we've all been missing. And revealing those missing pieces is what *The God Problem* is all about. Don't let anyone undersell this."

—Steve Hovland, video maker

"A work of genius. In one book, more history, science, and philosophy than I have encountered in a lifetime of learning. This book stomps mud tracks across disciplines and slashes with a razor, rendering the death of a thousand cuts to the complacency of status-quo thinking. What some call heresy others will certainly call genius. A paradigm/mind-set/game changer."

—Robert Steele, number one
Amazon.com reviewer for nonfiction

"An ebullient, enthralling piece of intellectual detective work, bursting with original insight. Bloom brings his kaleidoscopic mind to bear in unraveling the cosmic mysteries of creativity."

—Alex Wright, author of
Glut: Mastering Information through the Ages

"Bloom takes us on a magic carpet ride of ideas about . . . well, about everything. And it turns out that everything we knew about everything is probably wrong. Howard Bloom is the absolute master polymath, and his book is an intellectual cave of wonders made more wonderful by the tales of the lives of the people behind the ideas. Don't start this book late at night, for it will banish sleep."

—Robin Fox, author of *The Tribal Imagination* and
former director of research for the
Harry Frank Guggenheim Foundation

"A gleeful intellectual romp through the farthest reaches of science and philosophy in search of the answer to the ultimate question. And in the end we find that it's bagels all the way down."

—Nova Spivack, serial entrepreneur
and CEO of Bottlenose

"Is *The God Problem* a great book . . . like Darwin's *The Origin of Species,* Lyell's *Principles of Geology,* or Newton's *Principia Mathematica?* . . . [R]are is the book that ever evokes such thoughts as these. Books and ideas that matter have to open up ideas. . . . *The God Problem* is a book that makes connections [and] makes its readers make connections. . . . It is also Bloom's best book yet, a sweeping narrative of divergent ideas brought under one umbrella through a Keatsian demiurge."

—Dan Schneider, founder of Cosmoetica.com

"It's a blast of clean energy! Exalted! Glorious! Astounding."

—Nancy Weber, author of *The Life Swap*

"*The God Problem* is thrilling. The way Bloom tells the story, you can't stop reading until the end."

—Hector Zenil, Institut d'Histoire et de
Philosophie des Sciences et des Technique

"*The God Problem* is a sacred secular masterpiece. Divine. An act of astonishing genius. Bloom has created the ultimate scientific detective story. I pray with all the neutrinos in my soul that it will become the adjunct Bible of the future."

—Mark Lamonica, winner of the Southern California
Booksellers Association nonfiction award

"A crowning achievement by one of the deepest thinkers of our time. A page-turner, something you almost never see in a subject this profound."

—Walter Putnam, dean of communications at the
Kepler Space Institute

"An incandescent exploration of the most intractable scientific enigmas, with the most cogent and surprising critique of the second law of thermodynamics since the invention of the steam engine. It shakes out like shining from shook foil and oozes to a greatness."

—George Gilder, author of *The Israel Test* and
Wealth and Poverty and winner of the White House
Award for Entrepreneurial Excellence

"A must-read for those wanting great literature delving into the greatest mysteries."

—Edgar Mitchell, sixth astronaut on the moon

"Terrific. I am stupefied by the amount of work Bloom has put in. Bloom is an authentic genius."

—Jean Paul Baquiast, Institut d'Etudes Politiques de Paris

"*The God Problem* will change your life."

—David Swindle, associate editor, PJ Media

"I can't stop reading *The God Problem*—it's infectious."

—Mark Lupisella, NASA Goddard Space Flight Center

"An enjoyment shot through with things you never knew."

—Allen Johnson, author of
The Evolution of Human Societies

"A profound and extraordinary look into the history of human thought."

—Yuri Ozhigov, chair of quantum informatics,
Moscow State University

"Boy, what a book! I haven't gotten this much pleasure from science since James Gleick's *Chaos* in 1988. Bloom's *The God Problem* is the most thrilling thinking matter of our time."

—Pascal Jouxtel, author of *Comment les systèmes pondent,
une introduction à la mémétique*

"Great book, a huge scope, a delicious intellectual buffet, a fantastic effort to corral a conundrum. The range of scholarship is extraordinary and the unfolding of the story is magnificent."

—Sean O'Reilly, editor at large, Traveler's Tales

"Howard Bloom has never shied away from tackling BIG issues. Within *The God Problem* he takes on the biggest yet and does so with an eminently engaging style that makes the central illuminations glow."

—Robert B. Cialdini, author of *Influence*

"My face was hurting from smiling, contemplating, reading until my eyes hurt. Bloom has managed to make my heart swell with pride and my head hurt in amazement that no one before him has strung together these theories, observations, mistakes, and explanations of, well, ALL THINGS science in such an entertaining way! Great read!"

—Shy'Ann Jie, Colby Research Group,
University of Delaware

"This is the antidote to nihilism. It is Chicken Soup for the Collective Soul of the Global Brain. Bloom's content, pace, and style will rivet you, which is what happens when someone suggests an entire paradigm shift!"

—David Tamm, author of *Universal History and the Telos of Human Progress*

"An eye opener. An alternative language for discussing the origins of the universe. Bloom's clarity and accessibility allows almost anyone entry into the mystery of how mathematics became the language of science. *The God Problem* is a romp."

—Steve Miller, artist, faculty member
at the School of Visual Arts

"Another Magnificent Bloom Opus! I adore Bloom's storytelling of our intellectual history. It is SUCH fun to read, making it feel like a play whose hero is you."

—Elisabet Sahtouris, author of
Earth Dance: Living Systems in Evolution

"A fascinating bunch of stuff about a live issue. Always something unexpected and interesting around the next narrative corner."

—Bill Benzon, author of
Beethoven's Anvil: Music in Mind and Culture

"Breathtaking."

—Michael Mendizza, founder of Touch the Future

"Brilliant. Filled with things I didn't know and thoughts I wouldn't think without Bloom. I love the moral and positive exhortation at the end and the rare optimism about a social order in a time of crisis."

—Danny Goldberg, author of *Bumping into Geniuses: My Life inside the Rock and Roll Business*

ALSO BY HOWARD BLOOM

The Genius of the Beast: A Radical Re-Vision of Capitalism

HOWARD BLOOM

THE

GOD

PROBLEM

HOW A GODLESS
COSMOS CREATES

New foreword by BARBARA EHRENREICH

 Prometheus Books

59 John Glenn Drive
Amherst, New York 14228

Published 2016 by Prometheus Books

Cover image © 2012 Media Bakery, Inc.
Cover design by Nicole Sommer-Lecht

Inquiries should be addressed to
Prometheus Books
59 John Glenn Drive
Amherst, New York 14228
VOICE: 716–691–0133
FAX: 716–691–0137
WWW.PROMETHEUSBOOKS.COM

20 19 18 17 16   5 4 3 2 1

Library of Congress Cataloging-in-Publication Data

Bloom, Howard K., 1943-
    The God problem : how a godless cosmos creates / by Howard Bloom.
        pages cm
    Originally published: 2012.
    Includes bibliographical references and index.
    ISBN 978-1-63388-142-6 (pbk.) — ISBN 978-1-63388-143-3 (e-book)
    1. Science—Social aspects. 2. Religion and science. 3. Cosmology—Miscellanea.
I. Title.

Q175.5.B57 2016
500—dc23

                                                                            2015034984

Printed in the United States of America

CONTENTS

FOREWORD
BY BARBARA EHRENREICH

I t's easy to see how Howard Bloom has eluded the acclaim he so richly deserves. He's an intellectual outlier, unclassifiable and maniacally curious about everything from the nano to the cosmological scale. An autodidact, he has no graduate degrees and no cozy university or institute to house him. He refuses to specialize or take on modest byte-size projects, instead hopping around between physics and space travel, war and the nature of human community.

So for those of us who admire him, or at least enjoy being challenged by him, he is a sort of secret treasure—audacious in philosophical reach, rambunctious and witty in his manner of presentation. Better yet, his unaccountability to any scientific or intellectual establishment often puts him ahead of the curve, where he can pinpoint issues and trends that are barely discernible from the mainstream. That was the case with his 2000 book, *Global Brain*, on the emergence of a collective human consciousness, and even more so with this audacious volume, which challenges the philosophical underpinnings of science and shows how they will have to evolve to keep up with empirical reality.

To put *The God Problem* in the sweeping historical context it deserves: For the last few hundred years, the assumption of Western science has been that the universe, or physical world, is dead, meaning that anything that goes on it can be ultimately reduced to the interactions of inert bits of matter. An amoeba, for example, doesn't move because it "wants" to, but because of attractions and repulsions between molecules on its surface and chemicals within its environment.

In practice, this has meant that science is on a mission to crush all forms of *agency*, which I mean in the philosophical sense as the capacity for

1

action. Scientists never allowed, as Bloom playfully suggests, that hydrogen atoms might lust after oxygen atoms or that living creatures might swim and run and fly for the fun of it. The goal of science was always to replace agency—or whim or desire—with deterministic mechanisms: Atoms are *compelled* to unite by their configurations of electrons. Birds fly to find food or escape from predators, and the ones that fail to do so would be eliminated by natural selection. Whatever moved or flew or otherwise acted was itself inert, moving only in obedience to unseen forces or the "laws of nature," although the source of these laws was never explained. Animals, as Descartes and generations of scientists insisted, were machines for consumption and reproduction; only humans were set apart by their capacity for consciousness and will.

I was educated in this scientific tradition, ending up in cell biology, which proposed that you cannot understand, say, the flight of a humming-bird until you have killed the bird, cut its wing muscles into slices a few microns thick, and subjected them to electron microscopy. Thus a kind of unacknowledged necrophilia runs through modern laboratory biology: to study something you first have to kill it. You know you have "understood" it when you arrive at a theoretical description that contains no hint of agency—just a series of mechanisms involving organelles, which you have isolated through high-speed centrifugation, and molecules, identified by a series of fractionation processes. The hummingbird's speed and grace is explained by the density of mitochondria in its wing muscles, leading to an abundant flow of ATP to the myosin. All notions of play or agency or will are banished.

As for humans, individual scientists usually hedge on the subject of whether humans possess free will, but the long-term trend has been to extinguish it to an occasional flicker. Twentieth-century psychology, for example, postulated that humans act in response to instincts, like animals, or that they are driven by "drives." Economics, if it can be called a science, sees human action springing from rational calculations that are performed to fulfill biological needs, which themselves arise from the buzz of atoms and the jostling of macromolecules. No one, then, is free. Everything happens "for a reason" as part of some vast, insensate, cosmic mechanism. Insofar as human consciousness survives the gaze of mechanistic biology, it is a solitary beacon in an otherwise dead world. As the great molecular biologist Jacques Monod observed, as if surveying the wreckage: "Man at last knows he is alone in the unfeeling immensity of the universe."[1]

But science itself has been changing, and not because of any philosophical unease about the paradox of "man's" existence in an otherwise dead world. It was simply overwhelmed by new empirical evidence, starting with studies of the photoelectric effect that led, in the early twentieth century, to quantum mechanics and the shocking realization that electrons move as if by chance or, to risk the dread charge of anthropomorphism, by choice. Then came, late in the twentieth century, the equally paradigm-challenging formulations of nonlinear dynamics—or, as it is more sensationally termed, chaos theory. Put simply, very small differences in starting conditions can lead to huge differences in effects, which is why, among other things, we cannot hope to predict the weather with total confidence. Biological systems also turn out to be mathematically nonlinear and better described by algorithms than by static (and effectively deterministic) equations. It turns out that patterns can arise out of muddle; microscopic events can synchronize to produce macroscopic effects.

On a less theoretical level, science finally seems to be acknowledging the existence of nonhuman agency, at least in the case of nonhuman animals. Here, too, the empirical evidence is decisive: despite our Cartesian brainwashing, we can all observe that animals do not always perform according to mechanistic expectations—that, among other things, they play. Only in the last few decades, claims that animals have consciousness, emotions, and intelligence have ceased to be heretical. Ethologists have found nonhuman animals using tools, developing local cultures, and even producing art. But we have yet to hear a retraction or, better yet, an apology, from the biologists who for so long declared them to be unthinking *things*.

However grudgingly, the scientific worldview is being reanimated, which is not to say the world is being re-"enchanted." No deities, spirits, or vitalistic forces—and certainly no "bearded and bathrobed god," as Bloom puts it—are required to explain this pulsating, ever-surprising universe, which seethes with activity at the smallest level and, through a mere quantum fluctuation, may be able to bud off an entirely new baby universe. Agency, meaning also desire and will, is, in some form, everywhere, from inchworms to electrons, and it is time for science to recognize that everything is, in some not merely metaphorical sense, alive.

The God Problem, in other words, is an invitation to an entirely new philosophical paradigm, one that is thoroughly rational but also open to the existence of forms of consciousness other than our own. Potentially, it changes everything.

ADVENTURE THAT TAKES YOUR BREATH AWAY

I'm the author of *The God Problem*, so I should be decorous and humble. But I swear by all the pebbles on the pink-brown plains of Mars that if you dip into *The God Problem*, you will have one of the greatest intellectual adventures of your life. *The God Problem* will swizzle, twizzle, and soar you. It will give you radically new ways to think and see. Or, as one commenter on *The God Problem* puts it,

> "The most enjoyable reading I've done in a very long time. An enJOY-ment—a simultaneous stimulation of intellect and emotion—that would fry the brains of a lesser mind.... This may sound weird, but the closest I can come to describing the FEELING of reading *The God Problem* is how I felt when I read Dr. Seuss as a child.
>
> *The God Problem* is the next paradigm. It doesn't take you down the proverbial 'rabbit hole'—it will take you to a place from which you will never reemerge, a brand-new universe in the same skin as the one you now unknowingly inhabit."
>
> —Heinz Insu Fenkl, director, Interstitial Studies Institute, SUNY

Or, as Francis Pryor, president of the Council for British Archaeology, says,

> "Bloody Hell.... What a truly extraordinary book. I'm gobsmacked."

The God Problem is a book of surprises. There's a reason. Researching *The God Problem* was one of the greatest intellectual adventures of my life. Nearly every discovery came as a shock.

It all began with an idea about cosmic creativity, a concept I called "corollary generator theory," a theory I'd come up with after taking a very strange math course at Reed College in Portland, Oregon, in 1961. It was a course that shoved us students—students with the highest SAT scores in the country, higher than the test scores at Harvard, MIT, and Caltech—into an almost impossible task. Our job for two full semesters? Derive the entire natural number system from 165 words. Derive eight elementary-school textbooks' worth of math—the system of basic arithmetic—from five rules. The way that you probably were forced to derive Euclid's geometry from a handful of "givens," axioms, in high school.

After that course in the fall, winter, and spring of 1961 and 1962, it hit me that maybe the cosmos had done what we overwhelmed students at Reed had struggled through. Maybe at the instant of the big bang, nature had started with a handful of simple rules, simple axioms. Then nature, evolution, and the universe had derived the implications of those rules second by second, year by year, Planck instant by Planck instant, for 13.7 billion years. In other words, maybe you and I are the result of 13.7 billion years of homework.

By the time I sat down to write *The God Problem*, fifty years had passed since the opening day of that whale of a math course at Reed. I remembered the course vividly. But I did not remember the name of the 165 magic words from which we'd derived the basics of arithmetic. So my assistant tracked down the one remaining math professor at Reed who remembered the course and could tell us what those 165 very strange words had been. "Peano's axioms," said the prof. Sometimes known by the more alliterative moniker "Peano's postulates."

But when I tunneled into arcane books and found a few copies of Peano's axioms, all in slightly different wordings, there was one small problem. They were incomprehensible. Utterly and completely beyond understanding. I was stunned that I'd been able to grasp them when I was nineteen.

Now here's the trick. I work for you. My job is to take the most incomprehensible of things and make them not only clear but also a delight to read. My job is to feed you a dessert tray for the intellect. But I'm not here simply to bedazzle you with pastries. My task is to feed you sweets with an insidious power—the power to utterly change the way you see. To utterly upshift the way you perceive everything around you and everything inside of you. Permanently.

You are abnormally bright. But there was no way in the craggy corridors of heaven or hell that I could explain Peano's Impossibilities to you. So I took another approach. I decided to tell you the tale of how those axioms had come to be. Often by telling you a story I can get at the gist, the heart, and the muscle of something incredibly complex.

To pry open an entrance to the saga of Peano's axioms, I first wanted to tell you where the very concept of an axiom had come from. So I went on a hunt. A hunt that lasted over a year. A hunt that would blast open the origin of many a scientific cliché . . . and would reveal those clichés' Achilles' heels.

In the very beginning of this expedition, I ran into an unexpected problem. I wanted to give you one short, sharp chapter summarizing the history of math. And all the standard sources on the history of math from Bertrand Russell's *History of Western Philosophy* to the *Encyclopædia Britannica* agreed on one thing: The Mesopotamians had invented angles and the 360-degree way of measuring them.

So I wanted to put you in the sandals of a Mesopotamian 2,700 years ago using this new invention, the angle. To do it, I wanted you to feel the protractor—the tool that measures angles—in your hands. And to give you that touch in your fingertips, your palm, and the muscles of your arm, I needed to know what a Mesopotamian protractor was made of. Was it wood, clay, or copper? For a month, I combed obscure books and even more obscure journals to find the raw material from which Mesopotamian protractors were made, the substance that would determine the heft and feel of a protractor in your hand. For a month, I kicked myself in the butt, accusing myself of wasting time on such a petty matter when, if I were sane and serious about delivering a finished book to you, I should simply skip the puzzle and move on. But I couldn't stop.

When I'd spent four weeks on the raw material of Mesopotamian protractors and was still empty-handed, a thought hit me. Maybe I couldn't find even the slightest hint of a Mesopotamian protractor because—are you ready for this—there was no such thing. And maybe there was no such thing as a Mesopotamian protractor because all the books and reference sources were wrong. Maybe the Mesopotamians had not invented the angle. Sounds petty, right?

But thus began an adventure into the origin of ideas that you and I take for granted every day. Ideas at the very foundations of logic and reason. Your logic and reason and mine. Thus began an adventure that led to heresies. Five heresies, to be precise. Heresies that seem outrageous. And thus began the wild ride into tradition-overturning thought that you are about to take.

One more tiny confession: This is a book about metaphysics. But if I told you that, you would never read it. So I tried to give you metaphysics in a form that would be irresistibly delicious. A story with a plot. A story with suspense. But if you are an author, when you finish writing a book, you have this sense of dread. You are haunted by the possibility that what you tried to achieve simply did not work. I mean, after all, you are human.

So it was an amazement when one of the people I admire most on planet Earth, James Burke, the creator of an entirely new form of video literature with his BBC/PBS series *Connections* and *The Day the Universe Changed*, wrote this:

> "Enthralling. Astonishing. Written with the panache of the Great Blondin turning somersaults on the rope above Niagara. Profound, extraordinarily eclectic, and crazy. The most exciting cliff-hanger of a book I can remember reading."

May you soar these cliffs with delight.

And when you're finished, tell me how it went.

APPETIZERS, CANAPÉS, AND SNACKS

INTRODUCTION: I DARE YOU—
THE WEIRDEST RIDE IN THE UNIVERSE

The year was 1961. A dozen freshmen sat around a broad conference table at Reed College in Portland, Oregon. Statistics said they were the brightest class of college students in the country. Their median SAT scores were higher than those of the entering classes at Harvard, MIT, and Caltech. Yet what was about to come was a shock. A shock and an almost impossible challenge.

Little did these students know that the math course whose opening session they were about to undergo would dare them to grow an ornately complex and powerful tangle from nearly nothing. It would demand that they grow a vine big enough to house a tribe of giants from a handful of magic beans. It would challenge them to an act of secular sorcery.

And despite their brainpower, only one in ten would be able to handle the task. Only one in ten would be able to extract the entire system of natural numbers from just 165 words mimeographed in blue on a sheet of paper. Only one in ten would be able to find multiplication, addition, subtraction, negative numbers, positive numbers, and rational numbers in just five simple statements, five simple rules that occupied less than twelve lines of space.

But those who were able to successfully tackle this peculiar yearlong homework assignment would win two prizes. They would monopolize the attention of the girls in the class, girls desperate for help with their homework. And that 10 percent of achievers would do something more. They'd uncover a key to a brand-new way of understanding the naked creativity of a very peculiar cosmos.

***

God's war crimes, Aristotle's sneaky tricks, Galileo's creationism, Newton's intelligent design, entropy's errors, Einstein's pajamas, John Conway's game of loneliness, information theory's blind spot, Stephen Wolfram's new kind of science, and six monkeys at six typewriters getting it wrong. What do these have to do with the birth of a universe and with your need for meaning? Everything, as you're about to see.

How does the cosmos do something it has long been thought only gods could achieve? How does an inanimate universe generate stunning new forms and unbelievable new powers without a creator? How does the cosmos create? That's the central question of *The God Problem*.

In *The God Problem* you'll take a scientific expedition into the secret heart of a cosmos you've never seen. An electrifyingly inventive cosmos. An obsessive-compulsive cosmos. A driven, ambitious cosmos. A cosmos of colossal shocks. A cosmos of screaming, stunning surprise. A cosmos that's the biggest invention engine—the biggest breakthrough maker, the biggest creator—of all time.

For 350 years, science has dodged one of the biggest mysteries in the universe—the God Problem. The God Problem is the simple riddle of how the cosmos hatches explosive novelties, the riddle of how the cosmos creates. How does the universe do what only bearded deities, divine designers, and holy minds in the sky have been thought to do? How does the universe invent a big bang? How does she fashion the first quarks? How does she come up with stars and galaxies? And how does she produce the biggest puzzle of all—the life, the consciousness, and the passion that make your hundred trillion cells you, and my hundred trillion cells me?

How does the universe invent astonishments? And why does a material universe, a universe of mere forces, things, and laws, have creativity at all? That, too, is the God Problem, the problem that the creationists and the intelligent design advocates are trying to rub our noses in. It's the problem that scientific atheists like Richard Dawkins, Daniel Dennett, Christopher Hitchens, and Sam Harris have all too often dodged.

How does a cosmos of elementary particles and gravity turn the impossible into the real, the real into the ordinary, and the ordinary into the raw material of new inventions, new breakthroughs, new astonishments, and new impossibilities? How does the cosmos pull off the act of genesis over and over again? Without a creator?

That's the puzzle of the cosmos into whose heart you are about to dive, the cosmos of which you are a crucial part. It's the mystery of the universe as an invention engine out to surpass herself, setting off new bombshells that shatter every norm. It's the riddle of a cosmos that uses you and me to dream, to fantasize, and to reengineer the very nature of reality.

***

To tackle the God Problem, we'll thread our way through an enchanted forest of brain teasers. Why is this a profoundly social cosmos? A cosmos of stimulus and response? A conversational cosmos? A cosmos that outgoogles Google? A cosmos in search of her identity?

Why does this cosmos break some of the most cherished laws of physics? In this universe one plus one does not equal two, x does not equal x, and A does not equal A. Why? Why does this cosmos break the second law of thermodynamics—entropy? Over and over again?

Why does the cosmos shun randomness and laugh at the notion of six monkeys at six typewriters accidentally thumping out the works of Shakespeare, accidentally pounding out stars and galaxies? What does the answer tell us about how the cosmos outengineers human engineers when she generates amazements?

And how does overturning the basic assumptions of science without mercy help us peephole the naked workings of an ingenuity whose secrets this cosmos resolutely hides?

The God Problem will take you on a tour of corollary generator theory—an astonishingly simple way to understand the basics of nature's inventive itch without equations. *The God Problem* will put you on a train from Poland escaping the threat of Hitler to the questionable safety of Paris with eleven-year-old Benoît Mandelbrot, the father of fractals, and show you how even Mandelbrot was unwittingly following the simple rules of cosmic creativity.

The God Problem will tell you the tale of another thwackingly simple theory that explains the past and future of the universe, including mysteries like dark energy. That theory is the Big Bagel—the toroidal model of the cosmos.

The God Problem will put you smack in the middle of the minds of some of the most interesting humans ever to grace the earth. *The God Problem* will take you on a journey that covers six thousand years of riddles, puzzles, and paradoxes; six thousand years of bizarre ways of thought; six thousand years of invention and breakthroughs; six thousand years of zigs and zags that reveal how the rules of cosmic creativity work their wonders in human beings. Six thousand years of riddle-solving that have given you and me the tools with which we think every day. And in the process, *The God Problem* will give you six new thinking tools you've never had before.

The God Problem will show you humanity's ultimate challenge—to save the cosmos that gave us birth. To squeeze all our passion and all our knowledge into one ball and roll it with what the poet Andrew Marvell called "rough strife through the iron gates of life."[1] But this time the iron gateway is the black hole at the end of the universe.

So strap yourself in. If the muses are with us, this will be one of the wildest scientific rides of all time.

But first, a demonstration you can do without leaving your couch. Try poking your right finger through the palm of your left hand. Did your finger go through the skin and bone and come out on the other side? No? Now for a question. How old are you? If you gave a figure under 150, you're wrong. Why? For the answer, try another question: Why didn't your finger go through your palm and come out on the other side of your hand? It's because you're solid, right? And what makes you solid?

The answer is protons. How old are those protons? They're 13.73

billion years old. They were burped forth in the first 10^{-32} second,[2] the first nanosliver of a second, of the big bang.

Is what makes you solid a part of you? If the answer is yes, then you are as old as the universe. If the answer is yes, then you are a child of the big bang and a descendant of explosions, collisions, catastrophes, stars, and galaxies.

The protons in your hand have been through every slam, every bash, every disaster, and every creative crash this cosmos has ever managed to throw their way. And there have been smashups, bashups, and disasters galore. But here's a little secret. The story of those cosmic calamities and material miracles is your biography. The story of the universe—from protons and suns to curiosity—is your history. And the God Problem is the riddle of how you came to be.

THE CAFÉ TABLE AT THE BEGINNING OF THE UNIVERSE

At heart this is a book about shape shock and the riddle of the supersized surprise. What is shape shock and what is the riddle of the supersized surprise? Everything—as you're about to see.

You and I are seated at a café table in the nothingness before the big bang. You are a wildly imaginative visionary and I am a crusty conservative. You have extraordinary visions, and I am a stick-in-the-mud, a crust of toast committed to logic and to common sense. You and I have nothing better to do, so we've been sitting here at our outdoor table sipping one coffee after another ever since the nothingness began.

Absolutely nothing is happening, right? Why? Because there is nothing, no thing, no action, no space, no time, no form, no substance, no shadow, no sunshine, no squirrels, no trees, no planets, no sticks, no stones, no bones, not a single solitary thing. And there never has been.

Suddenly you perk up. You have a nutty vision, an insane daydream. You point to a spot in the blackness a few feet away from our table. And you tell me that if I watch very carefully, I will see a pinprick infinitely smaller than a pinprick smash abruptly from the nothingness, then expand at super-speed. Blowing up like a hyperkinetic balloon. A speed-rush sheet, a manifold, of raw space and time.

The boredom must have gotten to you, I tell you. What you're claiming is loony. What's more, it's impossible. And it defies the laws of logic. I've been sitting here across the table from you for a good long time. I've kept my eyes peeled. And there has never been a pinprick of any kind. What's more, this wacky stuff you call space and time has never existed either. Nor will it ever exist. Why? Because nothing comes from nothing. Zero plus zero equals zero. The idea that this basic fact could ever change is wild-eyed fantasy. And it defies the first law of thermodynamics, the law of the conservation of matter and energy, a law so basic that every respectable twenty-first-century scientist will someday declare it thoroughly and completely right.

While I, in exasperation, am trying to get simple logic across to you, wham, a pinprick infinitely smaller than a pinprick suddenly shows its head. It's what physicists like Stephen Hawking and Roger Penrose will someday call a singularity.[3] I am stunned. This simply does not make sense. But you stay cool and act as if nothing is happening. Meanwhile, that pinprick blows up so fast that it makes me dizzy. And sure enough, it has three properties that have never existed before. Three properties that, if common sense prevailed, should not exist. Those properties are time, space, and speed—time, space, and energy. How in the world did you know this would happen? And how in the nonexistent world did the nothingness pull this off?

The pinprick whooshes outward like the rubber sheet of a trampoline on a growth binge, unfurling as a superspeed space-time manifold. I am stunned. What the heck is space? What in the world is time? And what is powering all this speed? Who in the world invented these peculiar things? And if they weren't invented, how the hell did the utter emptiness burp them out?

While I'm sitting there with my jaw dropping, you are as cool as a scoop of gelato in a block of ice. Finally you open your mouth again. And you make another of your wacky predictions. That unfurling sheet, that giant sail of space and time, you say, is about to produce something called "things." And those things are going to precipitate from the sheet of space, time, and speed the way that raindrops precipitate from a storm cloud.

Now I know you've lost it. You got me with your prediction about the pinprick. But that was beginner's luck—and dumb luck of that kind does not strike twice. Now listen to me very carefully, I tell you. There is no such thing as "things." There have never been things. And there never will be things. That sheet speeding open a few feet away from us has only three properties: space, time, and energy. And those are bizarre enough all on their own. Let's get logical. Everyone knows that one plus one equals two. Add space, time, and speed and what do you get? You get space, time, and speed—period!

Then, far less than a second into the existence of your blasted space-time-speed manifold, there comes a rain, a hail storm, a blizzard. Of what? Of things. Gazillions of them. Roughly 10^{87} to be a bit more precise. What are they? They're elementary particles—quarks. All popping simultaneously from a mere whoosh.[4] And it makes no sense. In fact, it is impossible. So why in the world have you been right twice? And why is my down-to-earth logic, my sturdy and sober rationality, my clear and sensible thinking, all wrong?

Things will soon get worse. This peculiar rule-breaking and massively innovating cosmos that you and I have been watching from our café table will churn out galaxies, stars, molecules, cells, and DNA. Not to mention thinkers, talkers, lollypops, common sense, croissants, cannibals, café tables, and you and me. But how?

That is the God Problem. But how in the world did the God Problem come to be?

THE PROBLEM WITH GOD:
THE TALE OF A TWISTED CONFESSION

Imagine this. You are a twelve-year-old in a godforsaken steel town that once helped suture the Great Lakes to the Atlantic coast of North America and Europe. A city that, for you, is a desert—a wasteland without other minds that welcome you. Buffalo, New York.

Your bar mitzvah is coming up. (Congratulations—you are Jewish for a day.) And you are avoiding a huge confession. One that will utterly change your life. A confession about one of the biggest superstars of human history. God.

You are not a popular kid. In fact, other kids either ignore you or try with all their might to keep you from getting anywhere near their backyard play sessions, their baseball diamonds, their clubs, and their parties. When they do pay attention to you, it's to take aim. They kick soccer balls in your face. They grab your hat and play toss with it over your head while you run back and forth trying to yank it out of the heights above your reach. Or they pry your textbooks from your arms and throw them on a lawn covered with dog droppings.

No one your age wants you in Buffalo, New York.

But at the age of ten you discover a clique that *does* welcome you. Why? It's a clique of dead men. And dead men have no choice. The two heroes you glue yourself to, two heroes not in a position to object if you tag along and join them in their games, are Galileo and Anton van Leeuwenhoek. These are men who shuffled off this mortal coil roughly three hundred years ago. But they put you on a quest, a mission, an adventure that will last you a lifetime.

Your task? To pursue the truth at any price, including the price of your life. To find things right under your nose, things that you, your parents, and all the kids who shun you take for granted. To look at these everyday things as if you've never seen them before. To look for hidden assumptions and to overturn them. To look for really big questions then to zero in on them. Even if the answers will not arrive in your lifetime.

Why do this? Because your dead companions have lured you into science. And the first two rules of science are:

1. The truth at any price including the price of your life.
2. Look at things right under your nose as if you've never seen them before, then proceed from there.

What's more, in science the next big question can be more important than the next big answer. New questions can produce new scientific leaps. They can tiddlywink new flips of insight and understanding. Big ones. Paradigm shifts.

New questions can even show the people who've rejected you how to think in whole new ways. And that is your mission. Finding the questions that will produce the next big perception shift. Finding the unseen vantage points that will allow others to radically reperceive.

So how does God get into the picture? Remember, you are twelve. Your bar mitzvah is coming up. Your dad is going to throw a party for all the kids you know—for all the kids who humiliate you at Public School 64. And this time you are invited. Yes, your bar mitzvah is the very first time that you will be allowed to attend a celebration with your peers. And it gets better. The center of attention will be, guess who? You.

But something is rumbling through your mind. Something you refuse to register. Something that could cancel your bar mitzvah. You've read the arguments that Bertrand Russell has made about God. These arguments hit home with you. God, in Russell's opinion, is a silly idea. If it took a God to create a universe, then a thing as complex and as powerful as a God would need a creator, too. And who or what created God?[5]

In other words, the notion of a God doesn't make sense. And it doesn't appeal to your emotions, either. So the confession that you are dodging is this: You are about to become a stone-cold atheist. But if you admit that to yourself right now, you will blow your bar mitzvah.

The result? The question of whether there is a God stays safely hidden in your subconscious. You never put it in words, even to yourself. But that's just the beginning.

The party happens—a bowling party. It isn't what you expected. The other kids show up. But they do what they've always done. They ignore you. You are left out even at your own shindig. Thank God the dead guys of science still welcome you. But the heap of presents is extraordinary.

Then it's confession time. There is no God. You are as certain of that as you are that a bus slamming into you and your bicycle at thirty miles per hour at the corner of Colvin Avenue and Amherst Street could do you serious damage. And if there were a deity hanging around in the skies, what kind of God could he be? A monster, a pervert, and a serial killer? A demented and addicted murderer of plants, animals, and entire species? A torturer and slayer of creatures made in his own image, a mass murderer of human beings?

You've read the Bible from cover to cover, and one story in particular bothers you. The story of Job. Job is a good man, a man whom God has made successful and rich. And a man who believes profoundly in his maker. But God is sitting around heaven one Saturday afternoon with the Accuser—God's chief prosecutor: a combination of security chief, head of Earth's domestic spy agency,[6] and district attorney.[7] There is no Super Bowl and no TV. So what do two very macho guys, two guys on a power trip, do when they are forced to amuse themselves? They compete over who can do the best job of guessing the future. They make bets. (Why we humans and the gods that we imagine get a kick out of testing our prediction powers—and competing over them—is a subject for another time.)

Here's how your twelve-year-old mind recalls the tale. The Accuser bets God that humans only believe in the Deity-in-Chief so long as he delivers the goods. God, the divine attorney implies, suckers humans into belief by paying them off, by putting them on the payroll. Cancel the flow of bribes, says the quibbling public prosecutor of the heavens, make life miserable enough for the greatest believer, and even the most pious human will turn on God and curse his very name. You're on, says God. I'll take that bet.

To prove his point, God puts Job in the crosshairs of a demonstration project. Wealth, in these biblical times, is based on the number of four-legged animals you own. And because God has been generous to Job, his flocks of animals are abundant—seven thousand sheep, three thousand camels, a thousand oxen, and five hundred "she-asses" to be precise.[8] So God kills the sheep, the camels, the oxen, and the asses. He wipes out Job's savings.[9] He turns Job from a rich man to a poor man overnight.

Does this make Job turn on God? Not a bit. Strip Job of his fortune and he still swears his belief in his creator. So God takes the demonstration a step further. God has been good to Job in the fertility department, and Job and his wife have ten kids—three daughters and a whopping seven sons. So God kills the children. All ten of them. Does Job curse God? Not one bit. He hangs on tight to his belief.

God takes things even further. He takes aim at the one thing Job has left, his body. He turns Job's very skin into a torture chamber. He gives Job boils whose pains produce an infinite hell minute by minute and second by second. Job sits in a pile of ashes and covers himself with them, trying to stop the agony. But does Job say screw you to the big guy in the sky? Does he curse God? Not one bit. He prays to God, he begs for God's aid, and he sticks to God through thick and thin.

The bet is over. God wins. Then God, who is praised for his compassion but should be condemned for his mean streak, gives Job ten new children and a slew of new sheep.

In other words, God is a mass murderer. He has no compunctions about killing Job's children. And he acts as if a new family will make amends for the kids whose lives he has snuffed. Why does God kill so casually? In this case, just to win a bet. What's worse, God makes mass murder ordinary. He makes massacre an everyday reality. How? When you and I were born, only one thing was certain about the rest of our lives: that you and I would someday die. Just as billions of humans and over a trillion, trillion, trillion (10^{36}) microorganisms, animals, and plants have died before us. Yes, God kills creatures by the trillions of trillions of trillions. In fact, trillions of trillions of trillions is an undercount.

A God who slaughters is no God at all. Or if he is, he is a God who has to be opposed. He is a God whose cruelty cannot be allowed to continue. He is a God who must be stopped.

Or, to put it in the words of the mid-twentieth-century American poet Archibald MacLeish, "If God is God, he is not good. If God is good, he is not God."[10] If God is all powerful, if God is omnipotent, then his brutality is outrageous. And if God is not the creator and the controller of violence, then God is not omnipotent. He is not all powerful. He is not God.

Your bar mitzvah takes place on your birthday, so you are now a grown-up thirteen. And you've finally confessed your atheism. But you see the dilemma of deity—the problem of Job, the problem of good and evil—in terms of another biblical story, the tale of Jacob. Jacob wants to climb to the heavens and palaver with God, to negotiate with him face to face. God plays this scene as if he were Al Pacino in *The Godfather*. He has a thug, an angel, guarding the ladder to heaven. You imagine this as a ladder about eight feet high leading to a heaven that hovers over the earth at roughly the height of a low-hanging tree house. When Jacob reaches the foot of the tree house ladder, the holy bouncer refuses to let him touch even the first rung. Jacob objects. Strenuously. The two—Jacob and the angel—get into a nasty fight, wrestling their biceps off. Jacob loses.

As you see it, it's your job to do what Jacob failed to accomplish. It's your job to toss the bouncer aside as if he were a crumpled candy wrapper. It's your job to climb that ladder, to barge into God's living room, to grab the little sucker by the collar of his robe, and to tell him that either he shapes up or we humans will have to take over. Why? Because it's your job to do something we still have not learned how to do—to stop the massacre, to stop the new Holocausts and the new Rwanda's. To stop death in its tracks. To stop the vicious little bastard we call God.

The first rule of science is the truth at any price including the price of your life. That rule also applies to morality. You have to stop torture, pain, and death even if doing so endangers you. Which means if mass murder is taking place, you and I have to stop it. Even if we risk losing our lives.

But the nonexistence of god and the cruelty of the cosmos is not the really big revelation. It is not the insight that leads you to a massive challenge for science—and to a massive challenge for you and me. The crucial bolt of lightning that hits you is this. You are still thirteen. A mere ten weeks after your bar mitzvah and your confession of atheism, the Jewish High Holidays arrive. Your parents believe in God so deeply that they literally try to outdo God's bouncer—they wrestle you into a car to take you to Temple Beth El on Richmond Avenue. Why? Because High Holiday services are the most important services in the Jewish year. But when it's time to leave the car, you refuse. So your mom and dad literally grab you by the ankles and try to drag you from their blue, four-door Frazer while you hold on to the rear right doorframe for all you're worth. Or at least that's the way you remember it.

What's more, by then you've been in science for a whopping 23 percent of your life. Since the age of ten. So you've read a considerable amount of anthropology. And every tribe you've ever read about agrees with your parents. Every tribe believes that there is some sort of god, some sort of supernatural power. Yes, the gods of each of these strange clans scattered across the face of the earth and sprinkled through history have been different—gods who create, gods who keep things running, gods who destroy, gods with faces on the fronts and backs of their heads, gods with a third eye, gods who hold lightning bolts in their hands, gods who hold fistfuls of snakes, dog goddesses, gods of civilization, gods of music, Earth goddesses, gods and goddesses of death, goddesses of light, monkey gods, emperor gods, gods of jade, gods who handle heaven's paperwork, gods who file reports on your behavior, gods with elephant trunks, goddesses with eight arms, gods with the heads of jackals, goddesses with the heads of cats, and gods with the heads of hawks. Nearly every tribe and nearly every human being has gods. Belief in gods is all over the place. It's universal. It squeaks and squoozes from every pore of humanity.

So if there are no gods in the sky, on the mountaintops, or in rivers, rocks, and underworlds, where are they? The second rule of science tells you to look at things right under your nose as if you've never seen them before, then to proceed from there. The most obvious thing right under your nose turns out not to be under your nose at all. It turns out to be behind your nose. The gods are in our imaginations. The gods are in our emotions and in our passions. The gods are in our hearts and minds.

But take God out of the skies, put him in the minds, guts, and gonads of human beings, and you're left with a massive question. How does a Godless cosmos pull off the tricks that every genesis myth tries to grasp? Back to your café table in the nothing before the birth of the universe. If you believe the big bang theory—and the story of what the big bang theory means for you and me is about to come—then once upon a time there was a nothing. From that *no thing* came the first *some thing*, the big bang. And it wasn't just any something. It wasn't just an undifferentiated mass like a black hole. It was a speed rush of time and space that had within it the seeds of an entire universe. The seeds of atoms, suns, planets, and galactic superclusters. The seeds of algae, cabbages, flamingos, termites, and trees. The seeds of you and me.

That's a colossal act of creativity, a stupendous act of genesis and invention. How did it happen? Why did it happen? If there is no creator, no engineer, no omniscient and omnipotent consciousness presiding over the start of everything, no sleazy little bastard in the sky making bets with his buddy the public prosecutor, then how did this rush of time and space come to be? How did the universe create something so unlikely, something so surprising, something that broke every previous rule? Something that made brand new rules of its own? How did the cosmos create time and space? And why?

But there's more. In the first 10^{-32} seconds of this cosmos's existence, as you and I saw from our café table at the beginning of the universe, the space-time sheet popped forth the very first things—quarks. Then it showered protons and neutrons. But that was just the opening act. The cosmos shaped the flickers and flits of photons and electrons. It crafted the lumpy nanoballs called atoms, the giant sweepings of dust and gas called galaxies, the massive clench and screaming crunch of stars. The cosmos birthed giant ropes of molecules able to seduce each other into dances beyond the dreams of human choreographers into the most peculiar molecule dance of them all, life.

How in the world did the cosmos pull this off?

How does a godless cosmos make a heaven and an earth? How does she make crocodiles, crusaders, continents, and Milky Ways? How does a godless cosmos cough up insight and emotion? How does it burp forth you and me?

That becomes the quest of a lifetime for you. It's the quest you will begin in 1956. It's the mission that you will pursue for over half a century. It's the question whose answer can change the way that hundreds of millions of others see. It's the question that can help us utterly reperceive.

How does the cosmos create?

That's not just any question, it's THE question.

It's the God Problem.

2

A TASTE OF SIN

BRACE YOURSELF: THE FIVE HERESIES

Before we probe for clues to the God Problem, we need to equip ourselves with five tools—the five heresies. Remember the second rule of science: look at things right under your nose as if you've never seen them before, then proceed from there. Question your assumptions. To question your assumptions, you have to find them. And that's the really hard part. But here are five assumptions conveniently overturned for your edification and delight. Five heresies we'll use to crack the code of cosmic creativity.

1. *A* does not equal *A*.
2. One plus one does not equal two.
3. The second law of thermodynamics, that all things tend toward disorder, that all things tend toward entropy, is wrong.
4. The concept of randomness is a mistake. These days randomness goes under the fancy name of *stochasticity*. But no matter how it slicks itself up with arcane terminology, there is far less randomness in this universe than today's science believes. And far less randomness than you and I often think.
5. Information theory is not really about information. Its equations cover only a tiny sliver of what the theory claims. The real core of communication is what information theory's founder Claude Shannon calls "meaning." And "meaning," believe it or not, is not covered in information theory. Why is that a big mistake? Meaning is

central to the cosmos. Central to quarks, protons, photons, galaxies, stars, lizards, lobsters, puppies, bees, and human beings.

And here are a few of the concepts we'll use to peel open the robes with which nature hides the secret curves of her creativity, concepts we'll use to probe the implications of the five heresies:

- Ur patterns, deep structures of the cosmos, patterns the cosmos repeats over and over again.
- Repetition. Better known in mathematics as iteration. When you repeat an old pattern in a new location, you sometimes make something new.
- Which leads to the concept of translation. Translation is just another word for repeating something old in a new medium. Or is it?
- Corollary generator theory. From a few basic rules you can generate a cosmos. Some call these basic rules axioms. Some call them algorithms. But don't let the fancy names fool you. They're just simple rules.
- Implicit versus explicit realities. Here's a question for you: If you can generate an entire mathematical system from just a few simple rules (and you can), was that mathematical system implicit in the rules from the beginning? Was it hidden in some spooky way? Is the future hovering in your vicinity at this very minute, immanent and ghostly but just out of reach? Does every blockbuster invention that the cosmos— and that we—will someday conceive exist in a possibility space just outside the bounds of reality?
- Opposites are joined at the hip. Night and day, poisons and pleasures, innovation and destruction are usually different facets of the very same thing. Despite the battle they wage with each other, they are Siamese twins, children of the same parents, children that have taken slightly different paths. Opposites work together in the very opposite of the way they seem—not tearing each other to bits or threatening to annihilate each other. Opposites are like the right and the left end of a football defensive line. They work together in teams.

- The bottom line? Sociality. This is a profoundly social cosmos. A profoundly conversational cosmos. In a social cosmos, a talking cosmos, a muttering, whispering, singing, wooing, and order-shouting cosmos, relationships count. Things can't exist without each other. And the ways things relate to each other can make them radically different from their fellow things. Got that? No? Believe me, as we move forward, you will. And if the muses are with us, you'll enjoy the ride.

HERESY NUMBER ONE: WHY *A* DOES NOT EQUAL *A*

"*A* is *A*" is one of the most important assumptions underlying Western culture. Logic,[1] reason, algebra,[2] calculus,[3] and trigonometry[4] are based on the notion that *A* is *A*. Every equation in math has an equal sign. And every equal sign is a statement that one thing is the same as another. Every equal sign is a testament to the ubiquity of $A = A$.

The calculations of Newtonian science,[5] of Einsteinian science, and of quantum mechanics[6] are based on *A* is *A*. So is the software that runs medical equipment like MRI scanners. And the software that helps drug researchers sort through chemical combinations looking for cures to problems like AIDS and cancer.[7] $A = A$ has taken science and mathematics a long way. A very long way indeed. Every one of the 560 active satellites in orbit around the earth today owes the precision of its placement to *A* is *A*. And the manufacture of the microchips in your laptop, your iPad®, and your cell phone is also a testament to the power of *A* is *A*.[8] But what if *A* does *not* equal *A*?

One of the strangest uses of $A = A$ is in pop philosophy. The followers of Russian American novelist and philosophical thinker Ayn Rand, author of *Atlas Shrugged* and *The Fountainhead*, have adopted $A = A$ as their slogan. These "objectivists" chant "*A* is *A*" like a mantra to ward off evil thoughts. For good reason. Says Rand in her most famous book, her emotionally compelling, 1,168-page *Atlas Shrugged*, published in 1959: "*A* is *A*. Or, if you wish it stated in simpler language: You cannot have your cake and eat it, too."[9] Says Rand, *A* is *A* is not just an airy idea in the abstract realm of wizened graybeards speaking the incomprehensible language of academic philosophy.

Ignoring the fact that *A* is *A*, insists Rand, is the source of "all the secret evil you dread to face." What's more, Rand shouts in your face that "all the disasters that have wrecked your world, came from your leaders' attempt to evade the fact that A is A."

Got that? Every catastrophe on the planet has come from dodging *A* is *A*.

But not all philosophers and mathematicians are as enthusiastic about *A* is *A* as Ayn Rand. Barry Mazur, the Gerhard Gade University Professor of Mathematics at Harvard University, asks, "When is one thing equal to some other thing?" The answer should be simple, right? Not really. In fact, Mazur says that, "One can't do mathematics for more than ten minutes without grappling, in some way or other, with the slippery notion of equality." Why slippery? Because each *A*, each "thing," is presented to us in a different context, says Mazur. Each *A* is at the heart of a different network of relationships. And the very quality of *A*-ness is the result of an act of distortion. A violent act of reality abuse. An act of abstraction. Says Mazur, "The general question of abstraction . . . is neatly packaged in the Greek verb *aphairein*, as interpreted by Aristotle in the later books of the *Metaphysics* to mean simply separation: if it is whiteness we want to think about, we must somehow separate it from white horse, white house, white hose, and all the other white things that it invariably must come along with."[10] But have you ever seen a whiteness that is not attached to some thing? To some piece of paper, to some little white house with its neat white picket fence, to a neatly pressed and folded white dress shirt, or to an albino rhinoceros? In all probability, never. So abstracting whiteness is an extremely useful trick. But it can mislead us about the nature of reality.

Mazur wrote a twenty-four-page paper on the problems with $A = A$. But Terence Parsons, professor of philosophy and linguistics at UCLA, was even more bugged about $A = A$. He wrote an entire book on the subject, *Indeterminate Identity: Metaphysics and Semantics*. Parsons puts the problem of *A* is *A* like this:

> Suppose a ship sets sail, and while at sea it is completely rebuilt, plank by plank; is the resulting ship with new parts the ship that originally set sail? What if the discarded pieces of the original ship are assembled into a ship; is *that* the ship that originally set sail?[11]

Think about this for a minute. Imagine that you are an ancient Greek ship captain. You plan a one-year voyage from the port of Piraeus near Athens to get the rarest and most expensive commodities from the Spanish colony of Empúries roughly 1,164 miles away. Because the voyage will be long, you take lumber to replace any planks of your ship that become worm-eaten or waterlogged. And you budget enough coins to pay for more lumber along the way. You have been at sea for a month when, in fact, some planks become water sogged. So you replace them. Then you put the waterlogged planks on the deck in the sun to dry out. When they are nice and dry, you cover them with pitch to waterproof them. And when you have enough of these recycled planks, you begin to build a second ship. By the time you've been gone a year, you are no longer sailing just one ship. You are sailing two. The first ship is the one whose planks you've been replacing. And by now, you've replaced every single plank. Ship two, the ship you're towing behind you, is built from the planks you've dried out and recycled.

Now here's the puzzle. Which $A = A$?

When the two ships return to their home port, which ship is the original? Which is the ship you set sail in? Remember, the empty ship that you're towing is really the old ship in disguise. It has every single worn-down board and plank of the original. And the ship your crew is hunkered down in has all new planks. It's new from stem to stern. But your crew has never stopped sailing in it, sleeping in it, and eating in it. So is the ship with all new parts the original? Or is the original the ship you are towing on a rope behind you? Which ship is the real deal? Which $A = A$? Then Parsons poses another A is A mind twister.

> If a person has a brain transplant, or a memory transplant . . . is the resulting person the same person who antedated the operation, or has the old person ceased to exist, to be replaced by another?[12]

Parsons says that philosophers have "puzzled over questions of identity" like this "throughout history." In fact, the puzzle of the ship that is repaired en route so many times that it's totally rebuilt is called the Ship of Theseus dilemma. It goes all the way back to the Greek historian Plutarch, who wrote up a version of it in roughly 100 CE.[13]

What Parsons calls these "puzzles" of "*A* is *A*" cry out for solutions. So why have nearly two thousand years of pondering led to no answer? Because, says Parsons, "There is no answer." "There is no answer at all." Yes, those are Parson's words: "no answer at all." How could that possibly be? "Because," says Parsons, "of the way the world is."[14] Because abstractions may be indispensable. But they don't accurately reflect reality.

Twentieth-century über-philosopher Bertrand Russell, the man whose writings helped shoehorn you into atheism, was tortured by the paradoxes of *A* is *A* in his 1903 book *The Principles of Mathematics*. He puzzled over whether the relationships called "=" and "is" even exist. He twisted and turned over the question, as he put it, of "whether there is such a concept at all."[15] In fact, Russell said, "It may be said, identity cannot be a relation."[16] It can't represent something that exists in the real world. But we have to use it. Why? It's handy as all get out. Up to a point.

Bertrand Russell had a "friend" at Cambridge who was seventeen years his junior. A friend whose three brothers had committed suicide, leaving him and his one remaining brother to question life profoundly. In Russell's opinion, that friend was "the most perfect example I have ever known of genius."[17] The friend's name was Ludwig Wittgenstein. And Wittgenstein would become the airy and incomprehensible god of twentieth-century philosophy. But even Wittgenstein had his doubts about *A* is *A*. In his usual elliptical and indecipherable manner, Wittgenstein put *A* is *A* at the head of the list of "word-formations with which we feel not fully at ease." He said this lack of ease

> manifests itself, e.g., in our always having found the proposition A = A to be something strange and profoundly mysterious. If we are shown a way of not coming up against this proposition, if we are offered a notation that excludes it, then we are prepared straightaway to welcome this and to abandon the law of identity, this putative foundation of the whole of logic.[18]

Can we help Wittgenstein out? Can we help him escape from $A = A$? Can we show him "a way of not coming up against this . . . putative foundation of the whole of logic?" Yes.

But why in the world does one *A not* equal another *A*? If we clone you and get an identical copy, why are you not your clone? Location, location, location. Location in time. Location in space. Location in a big picture. And your place in many smaller pictures nested within that big picture. Not to mention that each of the two yous is composed of different raw materials. And that each of you sets off on a different set of adventures. Being you triggers one mesh of chemical and electron flows in your brain. Looking at your clone triggers another. The two of you are not the same because of what you might call the law of separation. Because of what you might call the law of differentiation. And because of the laws of sociality, the laws of the talking cosmos, the laws of the conversational cosmos. Which leads us to the man who founded $A = A$: Aristotle.

WHEN IS A FROG A RIVER?
ARISTOTLE WRESTLES HERACLITUS

If A is A, a philosopher should equal a philosopher. But that's not the way the cosmos works. Similar things set themselves apart from each other. And that includes philosophers. What's more, opposites are joined at the hip. Einstein says that most creative acts come from opposition. They come from pitting yourself against someone with another point of view. They come from the law of differentiation. And that was true of Aristotle and his law of identity, his law of noncontradiction,[19] his construction of the base for A is A.

Aristotle came up with the idea behind A is A[20] to fling a finger in the face of another philosopher, a philosopher who, in his words, saw "the whole of this visible nature in motion."[21] Who was Aristotle's straw man, the thesis maker against whom Aristotle aimed his antithesis? Aristotle developed his ideas in opposition to Heraclitus, the founder of the school of perpetual transformation. Heraclitus was responsible for turning change into what Aristotle called a "dogma." And a pernicious dogma at that. Or at least that's the way Aristotle saw it.

Location often leads to differentiation. Athens was the home base of the Lyceum, the school that Aristotle founded in 335 BCE and ran. But Heraclitus was a philosopher from the city of Ephesus, on the opposite shore of the Aegean Sea. And Heraclitus was obsessed with the shifting nature of things. "What was scattered gathers," he said, "What was gathered blows apart." Heraclitus tried to get that message across in slightly different terms in his best-known phrase, "You cannot step twice into the same river."[22] What did Heraclitus mean? The river is always changing. The water into which you put your foot the first time is no longer there the second time you dip your toes into the flow. The swirl of liquid you felt surging around your calves is now somewhere downstream. And in all probability even the patterns of the water that caressed your leg have changed as they've moved a few yards further toward the sea, shifting from the spiral swirl you felt around your calves to a streamlined, straight, "laminar" flow.

Heraclitus proved his proposition that all things change in a rather abrupt way. He died ninety-one years before Aristotle was born, his flesh scattered just as he'd implied it would be. However, location in time is another source of differentiation. And there was a ninety-one-year gap between Heraclitus and Aristotle. But like a whirlpool in a stream, Heraclitus's ideas survived. In fact, they thrived. Heraclitus's concepts were so pervasive that another Athenian philosopher, Cratylus, took Heraclitus's notion of perpetual, second-by-second change a step further.[23] According to University of Pennsylvania philosopher Charles H. Kahn, "Cratylus denied that you could even step in the river once, since you are changing too."[24]

The result, says Aristotle, was that the "most extreme"[25] followers of Heraclitus said it was impossible to fix a name to anything. Is this little green creature hopping across your kitchen table after your trip to a summer pond a frog? According to the Heraclitan change zealots, you can't say yes or no. Why? In Aristotle's words, the Heraclitans "considered that verification was not a thing that is possible."[26] OK, but once again, why? Because the frog is changing. A year ago it was an egg. Two weeks ago it was a tadpole. And by the end of the summer it could well be digested into the muscles and bones of your frog-eating dog. This, says Aristotle, led to an "extreme opinion" among some of the change enthusiasts—the opinion that "one ought to speak of nothing." Cratylus was the change extremist who Aristotle used as a prime example. And Aristotle says that Cratylus "was of [the] opinion that one ought to speak of nothing, but moved merely his finger."[27] In other words, Cratylus reduced all philosophy to helpless hand waving. Or, as Aristotle put it, the change-obsessives' argument meant that you couldn't even consider things "as existing."

This was intolerable for the hard-minded Aristotle. He wanted things to stand still and stay the same long enough to allow him to use reason on them. He was sufficiently generous of mind to admit "that there is some foundation in reason"[28] for the dogma of change. But Aristotle wanted to trounce it nonetheless. The result? Aristotle put forth a principle that would remain fundamental to philosophy, mathematics, and logic for the next 2,300 years. Formally it's called "the law of noncontradiction."[29] Here's how Aristotle put it in his *Metaphysics*: "The same attribute cannot at the same time belong and not belong to the same subject and in the same respect."[30]

Like much of the language of philosophy, Aristotle's law of noncontradiction was in dire need of simplification. It needed an interpreter with a gift for straight talk. And that's what it got. Two thousand years later. In the form of a diplomat for the royal family of Hanover, Germany,[31] a man who helped Hanover's George I become king of England in 1714. A man who met in Hanover with Russia's six-foot-six-inch tsar Peter the Great. A man who also dropped in on the philosopher Spinoza, who became a collaborator with one of the fathers of the wave theory of light, Christian Huygens, and a man who spent time with the father of the microscope, Anton van Leeuwenhoek. In 1673, a hundred years before the American Revolution, this multitalent was sent on a geopolitical mission to England. While he was there, he showed off a calculating machine he had invented to Britain's Royal Society, and he was promptly made a member. Meanwhile, he came up with another breakthrough: calculus. Then he had his reputation smeared by Sir Isaac Newton, who wanted total credit for the invention of calculus for himself.

The man we're talking about is Gottfried Wilhelm Leibniz. And Leibniz became the great simplifier of Aristotle's concept of noncontradiction. Aristotle told us that "the same attribute cannot at the same lime belong and not belong to the same subject and in the same respect."[32] That's a nearly incomprehensible statement. But Leibniz put it a bit more clearly. He came up with "*A* is *A*."[33] Either "*A* is *A*" or it is not "*A*."[34] There is no

Mister In-Between. Much easier to understand. Right?

However you phrase it, Aristotle put the law of noncontradiction, the law of identity—*A* is *A*—at the very center of his philosophy and at the very heart of something else that Aristotle tried to codify[35]—logic. Aristotle promoted identity as the most basic and incontrovertible law in this cosmos. Here are a few of the things that the philosopher to beat all philosophers, Aristotle, said about the law of noncontradiction, his precursor to *A* is *A*: It is "the most certain principle of all things."[36] It is a principle "regarding which it is impossible to be mistaken." It is "the best known" of all principles. It is not just a guess. It is absolutely "nonhypothetical." It is "a principle which everyone must have who understands anything that is." Why? Because of all the principles on the planet, this one is the topper, "the most certain of all." Look, says Aristotle, let's be frank, "It is impossible for anyone to believe the same thing to be and not to be."[37]

So what about Heraclitus, whose principles, says Aristotle, seem to imply that opposites can coexist—that *A* can be *A* and *not A* all at once? Heraclitus's principles imply that a frog can be a former tadpole, a terrific jumper, and a future doggie dinner all at the same time. They imply that if you looked closely for a week or two, you'd see the frog change before your very eyes. Heraclitus may have said things of this sort, Aristotle says, but "what a man says, he does not necessarily believe."[38] Heraclitus, in Aristotle's opinion, could not possibly have really felt deep down that *A* is sometimes not *A*. Why? Because it is "impossible for the same man at the same time to believe the same thing to be and not to be." Case closed.

Well, not quite entirely closed. Look, says Aristotle, "if a man" were foolish enough to claim that *A* is not *A*, "he would have contrary opinions at the same time."[39] And, says Aristotle, no sensible man would walk around denying his own claims and making himself seem idiotic. Right?

The result? Aristotle says that *A* is *A*, the law of noncontradiction, is the most fundamental of all the propositions in philosophy and in daily life. It is "the starting point even for all the other axioms." According to Aristotle's way of thinking, *A* is *A* is a notion that we take for granted every time we open our mouth to say, "What are we going to feed this frog? And whose bedroom is it going to sleep in?" (Note that in those two sentences we just took it for granted that the bewildered beast is a frog. And that it will be the same frog no matter who it sleeps with.) *A* is *A* is an assumption that we take for granted every time we grab the frog and put it back in its shoebox. Our decision to reach out our hand and gently grip a blob of green shows that we believe the frog is actually there. And that the frog we manage to get our hands around is the same frog we'll see the next morning when we open the shoebox again. What's more, we assert that *A* is *A* every time we google "frog food" and take it for granted that we can feed this frog the same sorts of things that our quick Internet search shows other amphibian lovers have fed theirs.

***

A = *A* is fundamental to logic. It is fundamental to mathematics. It is fundamental to science. And it is fundamental to the care and feeding of frogs. But I have sorry news to report. *A* = *A* is false. It is sometimes a good approximation. But in the end, it's not 100 percent true. Why? Because Aristotle was right. But so was Heraclitus. Opposites *can* be true simultaneously. In fact, they usually are.

It all goes back to location, location, location. It all goes back to differentiation.

Try this bit of reasoning.

A does not equal *A* because of location. For example, location in time. The letter *a* printed by your computer on a page at 9 a.m. is not the same as the second *a* your printer zips out at 9:01. Electrons have shifted positions in their shells, heat has moved entire empires of molecules around. The lighting of your room has shifted as the sun has changed position outside your window. The printer desk on which the *a* rides has moved over seventeen miles around earth's axis, has sped 556 miles around the sun, and has jack-rabbited 864.3273285 miles around the core of our galaxy. No way are the two *a*'s printed at slightly different times the same.

A is not simply a shape represented by ink on the mulched and pressed tree pulp we know as paper or on the pixels of a computer screen. And it is not just a logical abstraction. *A* is a complex social interaction. It's an interaction between your eye and a patch of pixels or an ink shape. It's an interaction of your *brain* with that pixel or ink shape. And it's an interaction of the culture embedded in your brain with the squiggles on the screen or on the page. Your culture is the product of 2.5 million years of accumulated thought— the accumulation of insights, emotions, questions, answers, and tools like language. Tools like the alphabet. Tools like *a*, *b*, *c*, and *d*. Your culture is the product of built-in, instinctual instructions in your brain, instructions like those that linguist Noam Chomsky[40] and his pupil Steven Pinker refer to as your linguistic deep structures and your language instinct.[41]

All these things—neurons, synapses, synaptic senders, synaptic receivers, and the facets of culture in the cloud of your mind, a cloud that shifts from second to second—change between the reading of one *A* and another. Your mind is like Heraclitus's river. Your mind, in fact, is like nineteenth-century father of psychology William James's "stream of consciousness,"[42] a bubbling, babbling brook. Your mind constantly produces different currents of associations, different swirls of thought, and different moods.

Then there is the change that location makes in the network of relationships that comes to mind around each *A*. The location of each *A* is different in a gestalt, different in a large-scale structure. Try this big-picture structure to get a feel for how different the mesh of relationships can be mere fractions of an inch apart:

> When, in disgrace with fortune and men's eyes,
>   I all alone beweep my outcast state
> And trouble deaf heaven with my bootless cries
>   And look upon myself and curse my fate,

There are twelve *a*'s in this well-known snippet of Shakespeare. Each one is pronounced differently. That means each *a* has to be tossed from the primary visual cortex in the back of your head to the temporal and frontal lobes up front, where some sense of what in the world it is begins to become clear.[43] Then the *a* is thrown to your motor cortex, which figures out how to send a blast of signals to billions of muscle cells in your larynx[44] and your tongue so that those muscles can contract and relax in a way that produces a sound that others will recognize as part of a word. Or so your motor cortex can "say" each *a* silently in your head. That's a staggering web of relationships. And it is *different* for each *a* that you pronounce.

Each *a* involves a different team of axons, dendrites, electrons, and muscles. If you speak the lines of Shakespeare out loud, each *a* sets up a different wave blast in the air, the wave blast we call sound. And, most important, each *a* has a very different meaning. Take a look at just this super-short phrase, a phrase with two *a*'s in very different contexts doing very different jobs:

all alone

Small as this phrase is, large-scale structure, big-picture structure, gives each *a* a radically different role. And large-scale structure makes each *a* a part of a very different team. The three-letter *all* team makes a very different sound and meaning than the five letter team of *alone*.

Let's shift $A = A$ to physics for a second. A proton = a proton, right? Two protons are identical, *n'est-ce pas?* Not quite. Like the letter *a* in a Shakespearean sonnet, every proton has a unique place in big-picture structures. And that place in the big picture changes the proton's role in the cosmos. Protons are participants in social processes. And those social processes help generate the radical differences between the swatches of space and the clumps of matter in this universe. In the minutes after the big bang, all protons were almost equal. But not quite. Some clumped together in dense zones, zones in which they bounced around, colliding head on and ricocheting at manic speed. Others were just a tad more spread out. And just a tad more leisurely in their crash, smash, slam, and bang. The great *UN*equalizer was what Nobel Prize–winning astrophysicist George Smoot calls "quantum mechanical fluctuations—tiny wrinkles in space-time."[45] Smoot should know. He's the man who headed the team of one hundred scientists on the COBE project, the cosmic background radiation project that discovered the modern traces of these primordial quantum-mechanical wrinkles, wrinkles that stretched and pinched the space-time manifold into a spotty pattern like the patches of color on a spotted cow's back. Just how different were these patches of newborn space-time from each other?

Sufficiently different, in the words of the Department of Energy Office of Science News and Information, to form the "the primordial seed from which, over billions of years, the galaxies and large structures of the present-day universe grew."[46]

Let's go back to our café table at the beginning of the universe. From the big bang to roughly 300,000 years ABB (after the big bang), protons were part of a hot soup, a plasma. But that plasma surged with pressure waves like a stormy sea. And each proton played a different role. If you were a proton, you might be bunching shoulder to shoulder with other protons to make a peak in the pressure wave. I might be off somewhere doing the opposite, putting distance between myself and my neighbors to make one of the pressure wave's dips and gullies, one of the pressure wave's troughs. In addition, you might be participating in the formation of a dense patch of space-time and matter from which a galaxy would eventually grow. And I might be part of the more widely separated slam dance of protons that would someday produce the lacey macramé of empty space between gangs of galaxies. I might be dancing out the early shapes of the spacing pattern that makes the universe on a very large scale look like a lace, like the tracery of a dish-washing detergent foam.

A billion years down the line, you might be surrounded by the spherical surge of a moving electron. You might be the nucleus of a hydrogen atom. And you might be captured by an evolving star. You might be forced to emit light as your electron is excited then is left alone to calm down again, or as your electron is stripped away. Your electron might be turned into a photon that goes on a multi-light-year trip as a kind of sentence, a kind of sonnet—in a very distinct set of frequencies, the unique visual cry of distressed hydrogen.

Meanwhile, if I were a proton, I might be part of a molecule of water, freezing with a mass of my fellow water molecules into a spicule of ice way out in the cold darkness of space.

Both of us would be protons, right? *A* is *A*. *A* = *A*. But we'd each be different. Like the *a*'s in a Shakespearian sonnet, we'd play different roles even if we were side by side. Just as you and I can be side by side in a poker game but each play a different hand, and each play a very different part in the social drama of the night. Big-picture structure counts. Your unique place in the social mesh changes your role. So does mine. And big-picture structure and positioning in the social mesh are location. Or, to put it in real estate terms, big-picture structure and positioning are location, location, location. And in the end, location, location, location gives every fleck and fiber of this cosmos a different role in a massive weave, a massively shifting, changing, and self-upgrading tapestry.

***

There's a bit more to this business of my frog is not equal to your frog. Yes, your frog and mine both eat the same kind of food. And they look very much the same. But each one is unique. Each has a different life history and a different future. Each is composed of different molecules of raw material, and each has a different place in your home and mine. Generalizations about frogs, generalizations that my frog = your frog, are extremely useful. Without them the vet would not be able to operate on your frog or mine. Without them, books on the care and feeding of frogs would be useless. But $A = A$ is a generalization. It is not precise. It is half a truth. The whole truth? A is A. But each A is different. Aristotle was right. And so was Heraclitus. Opposites are joined at the hip.

***

Now let's go back to thinking like physicists and mathematicians for a second. To simplify things, we will strip away the context of the cosmos, its galaxies, its photon floods, and its gamma rays. We will strip away the context of language. We will strip away the context of the human brain. We will strip away the passage of time and its impact on the movement of atoms, molecules, the aging of paper, the aging of ink, and the flow of fresh electron messages through the pixels of your laptop, your iPad, your Kindle®, and your brain.

We will strip away the 3.85 billion years of evolution it took to make a human being. And we will strip away culture and the 2.5 million years or so of evolution it has taken to make language and the use of breath that makes the sound of *a* rich in meaning. We'll ignore your change in moods and associations as you move from reading one word to reading another. And we'll also strip away the phonetic alphabet and its history and evolution.

If, indeed, there is no cosmos, no evolution, no humans, no culture, and if time stands still or is reversible, then *A* may equal *A*. But without the history of the cosmos, without evolution, without humans, without the brain, and especially without language, there is no *A* at all. None!

So *A* = *A* is a simplification, one so radical that it sometimes utterly distorts reality. It skins reality alive. Is *A* = *A* useful? Does logic come in handy? Is math a magnificent symbolic system with which to comprehend what's around us? And is math based on *A* = *A*? Yes. Absolutely. But math and logic are just that—very, very simplified representations. Symbolic systems with massive powers. But symbolic systems that sometimes do enormous injustice to the richness of that which they attempt to represent. Symbol systems that sometimes do enormous injustice to science's greatest mystery, cosmic creativity.

***

One frog is never identical to another frog. And the very same frog is a slightly different frog ten minutes from now. Aristotle and Heraclitus were both right. A equals A. But A does not equal A.

HERESY NUMBER TWO:
WHY ONE PLUS ONE DOES NOT EQUAL TWO

Put two apples together on your desk, and what do you have? Two apples. Twice as many apples as just one. And nothing more. One plus one equals two. Right? Sometimes yes. And sometimes no. Sometimes very emphatically no.

Let's go back to our café table at the beginning of the universe. And let's dial back to the very beginning. Once again, you are the wild-eyed visionary. I am the sober voice of reason. Quarks have just come blizzarding from the expanding sheet of space and time. Quarks by the gazillions. You predicted them. You predicted that these very first things would form themselves using the raw material of the speeding space-time sheet. It was an absurd idea. But you were right. And I was flummoxed and frustrated.

Now you tell me that quarks are going to come together in groups of three. And that one plus one plus one will not merely equal three. Not at all. Once the trios of quarks get together, you say, they will change character and give birth to something utterly new, something far more surprising than mere quark three musketeers. And once again, I know the rules of logic and the rules of arithmetic. You were right about a cosmos flickering from nothing. You were right about the precipitation of quarks. But that was just a fluke. I know with every bit of reason in my bones that this time you are wrong. Wrong as wrong can be. One plus one equals two. And one plus one plus one equals three.

Is this nutcase prediction of yours right? You give me a little demonstration. You lay out groups of three quarks on the café table in front of my nose. And you ask a few questions.

What happens if you introduce two up quarks to one down quark? Do you get just three quarks? Just three times as much quarkdom? Far from it, you claim. In fact, you predict a radical transformation. You predict something the cosmos has never seen before. You predict something with impossible properties. And with inconceivable future possibilities. Something that you tell me will someday make the solidity of my hand, the substance of my brain, and the churning hearts of the stars above my head. You tell me to grab two up quarks and one down quark from the middle of the table and let them loose on my dinner plate. Whammo. The three bunch so tightly that it's impossible to tell they were ever three individual quarks at all. And the result is something so galumphulous that this cosmos has never seen its like before. What is the bizarre beast that the three quarks on my dinner plate have transformed into? You explain that it's a proton. This is downright weird. It's the equivalent of laying out three apples on your dinner plate and getting a woolly mammoth.

But you've got another quiz question for me. What happens if you get me to present one up quark to two down quarks? Three friggin' godforsaken quarks, I answer angrily, still stung by your proton trick. Let's be logical. Quarks in, quarks out. But, no. You predict an equally impossible new whomp. An equally unlikely bit of future shock. So I grab one up quark and two down quarks to prove a point—that one quark plus one quark plus one quark equals THREE miserable quarks. But when I let the quarks loose on my bread platter, they rush toward each other and entwine, making yet another absurd abruptness this cosmos has never seen before. Something so strange it baffles me utterly. You try not to look smug. And you tell me it's called a neutron. That's like putting three pats of butter on a bread plate and ending up with a dancing whale.

What the hell is going on here? Cosmic creativity. Raw and unadorned cosmic creativity. A creativity in which *A* does not equal *A* and one plus one does not equal two. The creativity at the heart and soul of the God Problem.

HERESY NUMBER THREE: PREPARE TO BE BURNED AT THE STAKE (THE SECOND LAW OF THERMODYNAMICS— WHY ENTROPY IS AN OUTRAGE)

> *The central issue . . . is whether the surprising—one might even say unreasonable—propensity for matter and energy to self-organize "against the odds" can be explained using the known laws of physics, or whether completely new fundamental principles are required. In practice, attempts to explain complexity and self-organization using the basic laws of physics have met with little success.*[47]
>
> —Paul Davies

The second law of thermodynamics shows up in nearly every major and minor science: physics, chemistry, biology, astronomy, cosmology, and far, far more. What is this indispensable and incontrovertible law, the law without which many scientists would feel utterly naked? Where did the second law of thermodynamics come from? A central metaphor. The steam engine. And that's one reason it is wrong. The cosmos is not a steam engine.

But let's skip steam engines and get right down to the nitty-gritty—the second law of thermodynamics itself, a law that's holy, sacred, and revered. What is the second law? All things tend toward disorder. All things fall apart. All things tend toward the random scramble of formlessness and meaninglessness called entropy.

What in the world is entropy? The standard example of entropy is this. Take a sugar cube. There's a bowl of them in the middle of our café table at the beginning of the universe. Pick up the cube and take a close look at this little wonder of sweetness. Nice geometric form, right? Six perfectly square sides. Sharp edges made just a little bit jagged by the sugar crystals. Impressively consistent white coloring. Now feel it with your fingertips. Interesting roughness on the square surfaces, right? And an interesting variation on that roughness on the edges. What's the point? This sugar cube is a nice example of form. A nice example of structure. And a nice example of a big picture. A big picture? Really? Yes. That sugar cube between your thumb and forefinger is the product of roughly 2.5 million years of technological evolution. The tall, reedy, and green sugar cane it came from was raised on a massive plantation, a monocropping farm, an estate probably located on the northeast coast of Brazil. The cane was cut from its roots by a low-paid migrant laborer bent over nearly double grabbing the base of the plant and hacking at the cane with a machete. The cane was transported to a mill by railroad or truck, washed, soaked with water, crushed, and chopped to produce a thin liquid runoff.[48] Then the liquid was put through a centrifuge and boiled away several times in a mill and again in a sugar refinery. Eventually, only small, white sugar crystals were left. Finally a heap of crystals less than half the size of your thumb was pressed into a cube, wrapped in paper, and sent from Brazil[49] through a complex chain of wholesalers and retailers to your café at the beginning of the universe.

Quite an accomplishment. A lot of work has gone into this cube of tasty stuff. All with the goal of pumping pleasure into your taste buds as you drink your sweetened coffee.

Now drop the sugar cube into your water glass. Your full water glass. And watch. Be patient. Give it some time. Or tell me some more of your absurd ideas to pass the time. Take a look again in a quarter of an hour. What do you see? Clear water. No sugar cube. Nothing but liquid transparency. What happened? Entropy. All things tend toward disorder. The molecules of sugar in your glass went from a highly ordered state to a random whizzle of glucose and fructose molecules evenly distributed through the water in your glass.

And that, says the second law of thermodynamics, is the fate of everything in the universe. A fate so inevitable that the cosmos will end in an extreme of lethargy, a catastrophe called "heat death." The cosmos will come apart in a random whoozle just like the sugar cube did. The notion of heat death is a belief so widespread that it was enunciated by Lord Kelvin in 1851 and has hung around like a catechism. Do a search for it in Google Scholar™ and you'll find 4,350 articles focused on "heat death."

But is the second law of thermodynamics true? Do all things tend to disorder? Is the universe in a steady state of decline? Is it moving step by step to randomness? Are form and structure steadily stumbling down the stairway of form into the chaos of a wispy gas?

No. In fact, the very opposite is true. The universe is steadily climbing up. It is steadily becoming more form filled and more structure rich. Huh? How could that possibly be true? Everyone knows that the second law of thermodynamics is gospel. Including everybody who is anybody in the world of physics, chemistry, and even complexity theory.

Let's review what we've seen at our café table at the beginning of the universe. First a something came from a nothing—that something was the pinprick, the singularity, at the beginning of the big bang. That infinitesimal blip turned out to be a rush of time, space, and speed. A time-space manifold unfurling like the biggest bedsheet this universe has ever seen. Then the sheet of nothing but time, space, and speed precipitated like a storm cloud, raining, pouring, hailing, and showering the very first things: quarks. Quarks by the gazillions. Quarks in only six different forms.[50] With gazillions of identical copies of each of these six forms. Precisely identical copies. No matter where they appeared. And all of these precise clones appearing at exactly the same instant. Precipitating with astonishing simultaneity. With mind-boggling synchrony.

Were these quarks formless? Far from it. All came complete with a social rulebook built into their very essence. All knew precisely which other quarks to evade and which other quarks to embrace. And all followed these rules of quark courtesy and protocol with precision, forming instant duos (mesons) and trios (baryons). Most of the trios, the quark threesomes, settled into one of two forms—the proton or the neutron. But here's the deal. Protons and neutrons were so radically different from quarkdom, so eye-buggingly new, that they shocked the digestive solids out of the arch skeptic at the table, me. Is this a tendency toward formlessness? Is this a dissolving sugar cube? Is this a universe tumbling down the staircase of structure? No. This is a universe stepping up. A universe sprinting steadily up toward new structure and new ways of doing things. A universe inching, jumping, loping, and cart-wheeling upward on a staircase of amazements.

When protons and neutrons became the new holy trinities of the material world—elementary particles—I, the down-to-earth grump, was stunned. In fact, I'm still getting over the shock. But I know my logic. When you've got a mess of particles slamming, banging, and bouncing,[51] you are going to run into the second law of thermodynamics. You are going to end up with a random soup. That's it. All things tend toward entropy. All things tend to disorder. Or, to put it differently, all things fall apart. What's more, science has proved this in over a hundred years of research. Right?

But you have something far wackier in mind. Yes, the brand-new cosmos looks like randomness and entropy—it looks like the liquid that was once a sugar cube. But looks can be deceiving, you say. Squint and take a look at the big picture, you tell me, and you'll see something that makes randomness and disorder look ridiculous. Squint and use your extra peripheral vision, you tell me, and you'll see order on a level that defies belief. I follow your orders, squint, and try to get a handle on the cosmos as a whole. At first, all I see is a mixed up, random flurry of protons and neutrons jittering maniacally in the scalding soup of a plasma. All I see is elementary particles slamming and smashing into each other, then ricocheting away at speeds that make the collision of bullets slamming head-on look like gentle slow-motion kisses. And I'm about to tell you that what's in front of my nose has proven you radically wrong. But then I take in the macroscale. And something very different is happening. These gazillions of crashing particles are cooperating in the formation of waves and troughs. Waves and troughs that ripple from one end of the cosmos to the other. The slam-banging, bump-em-car particles are collaborating the way that molecules of water in ocean waves work together. They are rippling as coherently as ropes of clay, ropes that stretch across the cosmos for hundreds of light-years, waves that roll protons and neutrons in tight synchrony, waves that retain their identity until they reach distant corners of the cosmos hundreds of thousands of light-years from the point where they began.

These particle tsunamis are the pressure waves we twizzled into a few minutes ago. And they are so regularly and harmoniously—yes, harmoniously—spaced that cosmologists call them musical.[52] Thanks to social behavior on the grandest scale, astrophysicists say this early cosmos and its plasma rang like a massive gong.[53] Or, to put it in the words of the most prestigious peer-reviewed journal in North America, *Science*, "The big bang had set the entire cosmos ringing like a bell."[54]

In other words, the plasma shows a form of coordinated social behavior that defies belief. Any rational, logical thinker would know that a cosmos of elementary particles descended from nothing would swish and swivel at random. But randomness, a concept whose gaffs, gaps, and gashes we'll soon see, fails to materialize. Thanks to large-scale structure, big-picture structure, and social behavior, the particles of this cosmos rock and roll to their own self-generated beat. They defy the rules of arithmetic. Protons plus neutrons does not just equal protons plus neutrons. It equals music. A primitive precursor of the music that you and I listen to on iPod®s and Pandora®. Now this is positively spooky. It's like adding a zillion apples and oranges and getting a hurricane—a spiral twist of air that retains its geometric shape and identity as it picks up cars, cows, and rooftops. It's like adding a zillion water molecules and getting the massively coordinated swells and troughs of a tidal wave in the sea.

Is this harmony of pressure waves, this symphonic spacing of universe-spanning ripples, this mass choreography of elementary-particle pulses, entropy? Is it a tendency toward disorder? Is it what a turn-of-the-twenty-first-century thermodynamics critic, Professor Emeritus of Chemistry at Los Angeles's Occidental College Frank L. Lambert, calls mere "energy dispersal"?[55] Is this entropy at work? No. Bear with me while I repeat—it's large-scale structure. It's a strange big picture. And it's social behavior. Social behavior riddled with shape shock, riddled with form. And it's so antientropic that those in the scientific world who are trying desperately to rescue entropy from the ubiquity of form and structure call it "negentropy."[56]

Remember the first two rules of science: the truth at any price including the price of your life and look at things right under your nose as if you've never seen them before, then proceed from there. Question your assumptions! Entropy is a very big assumption.

But why in the world is it so far off the mark?

HERESY NUMBER FOUR: RANDOMNESS IS WRONG—
THE SIX MONKEYS AT SIX TYPEWRITERS ERROR

> *The chances that merely by chance they [DNA molecules] should have become arranged in the meaningful ways in which they are arranged are beyond much doubt less than the chances that a pile of rocks rolling down a hillside will arrange themselves by chance on a railway embankment in such a way as to spell out in English the name of the town where the embankment is.*
> —Michael Polanyi, Fellow of the Royal Society[57]

We are at our café table at the beginning of the universe. And we are bored. Painfully bored. I'm playing with a swizzle stick. You are building pyramids of sugar cubes. Why are things so dull? For over 370,000 years we've watched the cosmos shimmy with a sizzling-hot musical plasma. We've watched the particles of the cosmos doing a dance that makes Olympic synchronized swimmers look disorganized and spastic. But, frankly, it is getting a bit worn. Then, after 379,000 years of this same old same old, you drop your cube twiddling, wave a hand in front of my dazed eyes to get me out of my coma, and pipe up again with something I haven't seen in eons—enthusiasm. You have a funny feeling. It just hit you that another cosmic act of one plus one does not equal two is about to happen. And, as usual, your idea is goofy as hell. The bump-em-car smashup of the plasma, you are certain, is about to slow down. And when the plasma's particles slow, one proton plus one electron is going to equal something far more than just a proton and an electron rattling around at random in the vacuum of space. Actually, at this point there is no empty space, no wide-open vacuum. The slam and bang of particles is too tightly packed. However, you are convinced that entropy is about to look ridiculous.

And you are eerily right. At roughly the 380,000-year mark after the big bang, the particles in the plasma slow down. We call that deceleration "cooling." The skittering protons, neutrons, and electrons separate, and give each other more space.[58] But more space does not mean solitude. It does not mean time off from social gatherings. And it does not mean randomness. In fact, it means the very opposite. The puny particles called electrons discover for the first time in their 380,000-year existence that they are not satisfied on their own. Whizzing in their vicinity are particles 1,837 times more massive than they are.[59] Hulking giants. At least relatively speaking. These galumphulous Gargantuas are protons. And the tiny flits called electrons find that they have an electromagnetic hunger, an electromagnetic craving for a sort of coziness this universe has never known before. What's more, the hulking giants of the new cosmos, protons, discover that they, too, feel they are missing something. They discover that they, too, have an electromagnetic longing at their core.

This is so illogical it's absurd. Look, I explain to you, if you picture a proton as the size of the Empire State Building, an electron is the size of your fist. Let me repeat, a proton is more than 1,837 times more massive than an electron. So any rational and sober thinker can see that there is no way in hell that protons and electrons are going to develop electromagnetic lusts. And there's no way that electrons, which are, relatively speaking, the size of your pinkie, are going to flirt with protons that are, relatively speaking, one hundred dragons high. Look, even if one proton *did* manage to hook up with one electron somewhere in this cosmos, it would be a freak event, a fluke, a one-time-only perversion that could not and would not ever happen again. But you are not sober and rational. You have strange visions, visions of a universe that glories in rule breaking. You have visions of a universe that reinvents itself. You have visions of a cosmos that is profoundly and peculiarly social. But once again, you are about to be on target and I am about to be dead wrong. Why? Reason has deceived me.

Hold on to your seat. Roughly 380,000 years after the big bang, electrons discover that their needs fit the longings of protons perfectly. No matter where the electron is and no matter what its life history, pick any proton in this universe at random, flip it an electron from anywhere you please, and they embrace. What's more, their fit is more precise than anything that even the makers of the ultimate high-precision scientific device, CERN's Large Hadron Collider,[60] have ever been able to achieve.

If this were a truly random universe, this fit simply should not be. The metaphor that most often explains randomness in pop culture and in informal discussion among scientists is the image of six monkeys at six typewriters. Monkeys do not know how to type. But the beasts occasionally bump an elbow, a foot, or a chin on the keyboard, bapping out a thoroughly haphazard letter of the alphabet. Give them a few billion years, says the six-monkeys model of randomness, and the illiterate beasts will eventually type out the works of Shakespeare. Give them a bit more time, and they'll randomly peck out the evolution of the cosmos. From utter disorder, order can emerge through an accumulation, a pileup of arbitrary accidents.

Let's ponder this notion of arbitrary accident for a second. If this is a six-monkeys-at-six-typewriters universe, a random universe, zillions of particles jostling and jolting around each other should come up with zillions of different ways to be together, zillions of different ways to date, mate, marry, and combine. Or they should find no way to socialize at all, no way to connect. They should be so radically different that they mismatch each other like pieces taken from very different jigsaw puzzles or like shards taken from different shattered teacups. But the random universe exists only in our imagination. Things are not infinitely varied. Things are not riddled, crinkled, patterned, and punched with an infinite zoo of wildly wangling differences. Elementary particles don't come in sizes from infinitesimal to the size of black holes. Particles are not rhomboid, rumpled, corduroyed, uglied up with noses on sixteen sides, wriggling with tentacles, or writhing with jelly-fish-like shapes. Instead of a random mix of permutations and combinations, elementary particles have astonishing uniformity. The total number of different kinds of elementary particles in the cosmos comes to less than four hundred.[61] Only four hundred kinds of nanobits in a cosmos of 10^{87} particles. And the kinds of teams these particles make when they first mingle and mate are even smaller. That is utterly shocking.

So it turns out that the last thing you'd expect does indeed happen. Electrons do indeed discover that their inanimate lusts match the loneliness of protons perfectly. And electrons and protons do glump together. They do pair up in proton-electron twosomes. What's worse, when electrons discover how naturally they fit around protons, the result is a radically new set of properties. Radically new, but radically *few*. It's the handful of properties we call an atom: hardness, durability, and the ability to play with others in the sandbox of space, to team up in ways this cosmos has never seen before. How many kinds of atoms does a cosmos of zillions of particles sliding into each other's arms produce? If things were really random, the species of newly born atoms should be wacky, crazed, and without end. But our universe does not blat out more than a zillion to the zillionth power new forms of atoms, as the probabilistic equations of randomness would imply. Far from it. It produces just three rigidly constrained species of atoms. One is called hydrogen. One is called helium. And the third is called lithium. Only three different kinds of these new astonishments, these new particle teams, these atoms, in a universe of zillions of particles? And all of these atoms appearing pretty much at the same time? With astonishing supersynchrony? That doesn't make any sense. It doesn't follow the rules of randomness.

Look, even just two cubes tossed around in a cup, dice, have thirty-six possible outcomes. How can an entire cosmos seething with more protons, neutrons, and electrons than we have words to describe, how can a universe of nearly infinite dice and nearly infinite tosses, produce just three varieties of atoms? This is staggering conformity and self-control. It is not mere trial and error. It is not mere mix and match or blunder and chance. It is not six monkeys at six typewriters. So what is it? It's the paradox of the supersized surprise. It's the mind snarler at the core of cosmic creativity. It is the question at the heart of the God Problem.

A BRIEF HISTORY OF THE GOD PROBLEM:
WERE KEPLER, GALILEO, AND NEWTON CREATIONISTS?

The God Problem—the problem of how the cosmos creates—is not as old as you might imagine. Why? Because most of the fathers of modern science felt the answer was obvious. Kepler, Galileo, and Newton believed in God. They believed in an intelligent designer. In fact, the greats of early science were creationists. They believed in the biblical account of the creation of the world. With a few minor modifications.

Early in the 1600s, Johannes Kepler, an intense-looking mathematics teacher at a religious seminary in Graz, Austria, got the chance of a lifetime. He was offered a job as mathematician to the Holy Roman emperor in Prague. He took it. Then he squeezed out extra time to pursue an obsession. He worked as assistant to one of the most phenomenal astronomers and compilers of data on stars and planets of all time. That phenom was a Dane acting as the imperial astronomer in Prague,[62] an astronomer who had replaced a nose he'd lost in a duel with a bionic nose made of silver and gold[63]: Tycho Brahe. Meanwhile, Kepler invented a new kind of refracting telescope, watched the stars and the planets at night, wrote down his observations, puzzled over their mysteries, scraped away at Brahe's ever-growing mass of data on the pinpricks of light in the nighttime sky, and wrote letters to another man obsessed with the same puzzles in the distant Italian city of Pisa: Galileo Galilei.

Kepler kept this up for decades. What did he get for his years and years of pattern seeking? He discovered that the orbits of the planets were elliptical. And he stripped bare the three laws of planetary motion.[64] Kepler pulled off this glimpse of nature's inner workings by using one of the most intriguing tools of science, a tool that would still be crucial to Albert Einstein three hundred years later—geometry. To be specific, Kepler worked out the infernally tricky patterns of the five known planets of the day—the loops and wiggles traced in the sky by Jupiter, Mars, Saturn, and Venus, plus the movements of Earth around the sun—by squeezing geometrically shaped boxes into what he thought might be the planets' orbits. By squeezing geometric shapes into the planets' "spheres." Why did Kepler try to solve what he called "the mystery of the cosmos"[65] with geometric shapes? Because, said Kepler, "Geometry . . . is God himself."[66]

Did Kepler puzzle over the God Problem? Did he ask how the cosmos creates without a hulking, bearded king of heaven in a bathrobe? No, Kepler was a creationist and a believer in an intelligent designer.

In the beginning, said Kepler, there was nothing but God. And God had geometry at his heart. God had curves, straight lines, triangles, squares, and circles in every inch of his immeasurable consciousness. "Why waste words," wrote Kepler in his 1619 *Harmonices Mundi*, his *Harmony of the World*, "Geometry, which was before the origin of things was coeternal with the divine mind and is God himself."[67]

So Kepler's God mapped out the heavens using guess what? Geometry. With geometry, God created. But Kepler missed out on the heart of the God Problem—how does the cosmos create *itself*? Kepler calculated with absolute precision that in 3993 BCE, during the summer solstice, *God* had created.[68] Created what? The universe, presumably cranking out the entire thing in seven days, just like the Bible said.[69] And how, in Kepler's view, did the creator God pull this off? He used the same geometry that the Greek mathematician Euclid had perfected in Alexandria, Egypt, over two thousand years ago in 300 BCE. Geometry, said Kepler, "supplied God with the patterns for the creation of the world."[70] Presumably God made light, the sun, the stars, the plants, the animals, and the Garden of Eden pretty much as the Bible claimed. But he did it with a compass and a straightedge. He did it with geometry.

Then, says Kepler, God made man in his own image. He made Adam. Needless to say, Adam, in Kepler's view, was shaped, seized, and shaken by geometry. So geometry, said Kepler, "passed over to Man along with the image of God."[71]

The result? Said Kepler, the ability to grasp mathematics and geometry was built into the very foundation of the human mind. Or, to put it in Kepler's words, man's math skill, "the recognition of quantities . . . is innate in the mind."[72] Math is riveted from birth into your thinking machinery and mine. If you struggled in agony to grasp math in high school and college, you might disagree. But Kepler believed that geometry is central to the way that you see the book in front of your eyes, the ceiling above your head, the walls on either side of you, and everything else from the curls in the tails of chipmunks to the curves of girls in tight skirts and to the hip-shoulder ratio of men who work out more than you and I do. Says Kepler, "the recognition of quantities ... dictates what the nature of the eye must be."[73] Yes, even your eyeball was built by math, built by geometry.

In studying the newest data coming in from the astronomy of Tycho Brahe and from his own observations, then puzzling out their patterns with geometry and writing up his results in sixteen books, what did Kepler feel he was accomplishing? He was presenting his reports, his dispatches, his bulletins, what he called his "*envoi* on the work of God the Creator."[74] He was reading God's mind. And he was peeping through the cracks of the material world to see something Kepler felt that God himself wanted man to discover. Kepler was scoping out what he called the "patterns for the creation of the world,"[75] the deep structures that God had used to create sticks and stones, bones and beasts, dust, dirt, dramas, and dreams. But most important, Kepler was groping for the patterns and deep structures that the creator had used to craft the heavens and their mirror,[76] the thoughts of human beings.

Every scientist who makes breakthroughs does it with the use of a tool, a central metaphor. What was Kepler's central metaphor? Circles, triangles, and the five Platonic solids. Geometry. And why does metaphor work? How do things you can draw with pen and paper, things you can sketch with the fluorescent pixels of a computer screen, or things you can imagine with the three pounds of meat we call a brain, how do these things manage to crack the codes of slowly moving dots of light in the heavens and of jittering particles on the earth? The mystery of metaphor will prove vital to the secret heart of the God Problem. So will deep structures. But we'll save the role of metaphor for later.

What was Kepler's contribution to solving the God Problem? He passed down the concept that the cosmos is based on very simple patterns, Kepler's "patterns for the creation of the world." Repeated patterns. Patterns that can be grasped by drawing pictures. Patterns you can get a grip on by making wooden models of things with four sides, six sides, twelve sides, and even twenty sides: the tetrahedron, the cube, the dodecahedron, and the icosahedron.

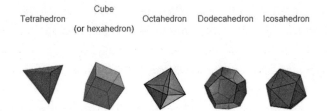

The five Platonic solids. *Courtesy of DTR, Wikimedia Commons.*

Would Kepler prove to be right?

GALILEO'S NATURE FETISH: POKING THE POPE

Meanwhile, 422 miles away in the Italian city-state of Pisa, lived the most important thinker and inventor with whom Kepler swapped letters—Galileo Galilei, the chairman of the mathematics department at the University of Pisa.[77] The man who master physicist Stephen Hawking says "more than any other single person, was responsible for the birth of modern science."[78] What was Galileo's take on the God Problem? How did he think the cosmos creates? Galileo seemed more concerned with how God runs the world on a day-to-day basis than with how it all came to be.

In fact, in Galileo's opinion, the problem of cosmic creativity did not exist. Why? Because "God placed the sun at the center of heaven and . . . therefore He brings about the ordered motions of the moon and the other wandering stars by making it turn around itself like a wheel."[79] It's very simple. God put together a cosmos. He crafted it the way a wheelwright crafts a wagon wheel. There is no further question. No mystery. There is no God Problem.

Meanwhile, Galileo was up against a God Problem of his own. The Inquisition was on his tail. And the Inquisitors had made a big name for themselves by arresting an astronomer who believed that the heavenly bodies are worlds like ours and that they house life. The Inquisitorial executioners had "stopped the tongue" of this astronomical speculator "with a leather gag" on February 17, 1600,[80] and had burned him alive in a public square,

Rome's Campo de' Fiori—the ironically named Field of Flowers. That roasted, charred, and martyred astronomer was Giordano Bruno. Galileo did not want to follow in Bruno's fried and sizzled footsteps. So he wrote to a woman with pull, a woman he hoped would help him dodge the blaze of the Inquisitors' bonfire, the Grand Duchess Christina of Tuscany, daughter of Catherine de Medici and wife of another Medici, the grand duke of Tuscany.

And Galileo argued for ignoring holy books. Why? There was a better way to get to God. The writers of the Bible, Galileo said, had manipulated the details to produce mass appeal. Explained Galileo, "To accommodate the understanding of the common people it is appropriate for Scripture to say many things that are different (in appearance and in regard to the literal meaning of the words) from the absolute truth." To understand God, he said, don't be fooled by the creator's propaganda. Don't look at holy writ. Look at the world God has created.

Nature, said Galileo, is the real holy deal. She follows God's laws to the last jot and tittle. Back to Galileo: "Nature is inexorable and immutable, [she] never violates the terms and the laws imposed upon her, and does not care whether or not her recondite reasons and ways of operating are disclosed to human understanding."[81] Holy books may get God's intentions wrong. But nature always gets them right.

Said Galileo, to read the mind of God, open your eyes and look at what's under your nose. "In disputes about natural phenomena," Galileo wrote, "one must begin not with the authority of scriptural passages but with sensory experience and necessary demonstrations." Why? Because, Galileo explained, "the Holy Scripture and nature derive equally from the Godhead." In other words, holy scripture is "the dictation of the Holy Spirit" and the natural world is "the most obedient executrix of God's orders." Nature is absolutely scrupulous about sticking to the divine commandments, the commandments that make stars wheel and that make cannonballs fall.

The bottom line? "God reveals Himself to us no less excellently in the effects of nature than in the sacred words of scripture."[82]

So what did Galileo contribute to a secular and godless solution to the grand question of how the universe creates? He insisted that you and I must not slip into airy reasoning and abandon the realities right under our noses.

If you want to know the patterns with which God or cosmic creativity runs the world, if you want to know the rules and laws of our earth and of the heavens above, you have to open your eyes. Facts count more than theory. And "demonstrations," real-world experiments, reveal more than any letter from St. Paul or biblical account of the life of Isaiah.

In Austria, Johannes Kepler was using geometry as his central metaphor. Galileo, too, relied on a central metaphor, one that had been used for close to three thousand years—laws. Laws dictated by a central authority, a Lord. And Galileo used a second metaphor. He imagined that if he carried out what he called an "experiment"[83] on a table top, his strangely limited test could reveal the principles underlying the motions of avalanches, raindrops, bullets,[84] and the moons of Jupiter.[85] He imagined that when he rolled a ball down a tilted plank with a ruler mounted below it, measured its movement with that ruler,[86] timed the ball's journey by singing a marching tune,[87] then worked out the math of the ball's motion, that same math would fit the motions of all things on heaven and earth. He imagined that the metaphor of a ball on a table could reveal the rules by which God maintained his dictatorial powers over the entire cosmos.

This was a big, big stretch. A stretch into the mystery of metaphor. Why should rolling a ball on a table-top gizmo tell you anything about something vastly different: a star, a dot of light in the sky? Why should something you do between four walls down here on earth, down here in Galileo's house in Pisa or in his other house in Padua, have any relation to the nighttime darkness above your head? But that wasn't the end of Galileo's big stretches. He imagined that the Lord's rules popped forth from workroom[88] experiments with particular clarity when he probed the things in front of his eyes with another metaphorical tool, geometry.[89]

The "grand book [of] the Universe," Galileo said, "is written in the language of mathematics."[90] But Galileo's mathematics had very few numbers. And it had no formulae, no equations.[91] What did it have? Explained Galileo, "Triangles, circles, and other geometrical figures."[92] Things you could picture. Things you could draw. Why geometrical figures? Because the only respectable math among intellectuals in Galileo's day was geometry. Geometry and simple ratios between numbers. Arithmetic was something employed by lowly merchants in the streets. And the West as yet had no algebraic equations of the kind we would recognize today. The equal sign had been invented in 1557 by Oxford's Robert Recorde.[93] But it had not yet come into fashion. "The language of mathematics," Galileo explained, is written in characters, and those characters are "triangles, circles, and other geometrical figures." Without those "geometrical figures," he warned, "it is impossible to understand a single word of it."[94] A single word of what? A single word of the "grand book [of the] universe."[95]

That's a lot of metaphors. A lot of comparisons. The universe is a book. The cosmos is written in a language. The characters of that language are the triangles, circles, and other figures of geometry. That's a lot of highly improbable leaps. Why in the world was Galileo resorting to metaphor?

Three peculiar assumptions were Galileo's contribution to the God Problem:

(1) That the universe is governed by laws like the laws that governed Galileo's three hometowns, Padua, Pisa, and Florence.[96]

(2) That an experiment in a home workroom could say something meaningful about the strangest and most distant of things, things whose size might dwarf that of the balls Galileo experimented on.[97] And

(3) That the essence of the experiment could be caught in geometry. In other words, that mathematical scratches of ink on pieces of mashed tree pulp—paper—could express the essence both of tabletop experiments and of heavenly things.

Did Galileo's strange assumptions work? Would they pass the test of time? And, most important to the God Problem, if they did work, why?

***

Isaac Newton started his scientific career thirty-five years after Kepler and Galileo. And, like Kepler and Galileo, Newton was a creationist and a believer in intelligent design. God is "the Maker and Lord of all things,"[98] Newton said. What's more, "He constitutes duration and space."[99] And "duration and space" were two of the central mysteries that Newton-the-scientist explored. Said Newton, God is the reason things have come to be. He is the source of all creation.[100] So how, in Newton's view, does God create?

It's back to the metaphor of God the authority figure, a God who is in Newton's words "the divine legislator,"[101] a God who "governs all things."[102] For Newton, God was not an abstraction. He was not a mere figure of speech. He was nearly as human as you and me. God, said Newton, is "a living, intelligent, and powerful being."[103] God, Newton added, is "supreme . . . most perfect . . . eternal and infinite, omnipotent, and omniscient."[104] And Newton declared in his culture-changing masterpiece, his 1687 *Philosophiae Naturalis Principia Mathematica*, better known as the *Principia*, that "this most beautiful system of the Sun, planets, and comets, could only proceed, from the counsel and dominion of an intelligent and powerful Being."[105] What's more, God came up with utter amazements and laid them out before us by extremely human means. By quasi-governmental means: again, by command and by "like wise counsel."[106] What in the world is "like wise counsel?"

Counsels—groups of men who gather to give advice, clusters of consultants—were normal for the highest lords of Newton's day—emperors and kings. But they are a peculiar proposition for a cosmos, a strange way for an all-powerful God to go about the business of creation. Who did Newton think God consulted? Who did he think the Great Omniscience bounced ideas around with before he crafted the ultimate immensity? Newton's heaven was wildly unscientific. It was teeming with God's courtiers. Before the beginning there was what Newton described as "the Perfect Trinity . . . Father, Son, and Holy Ghost."[107] Eventually they were joined by "the prophetic Angel Gabriel." And later, long after the expulsion from the Garden of Eden, the "Saints" and "the forty Martyrs . . . [who were the] most powerful ambassadors to God." What's more, Newton implies that there are mobs of holy warriors, the "hosts." "Christ" is not only "the Prince of Princes," but "the Prince of Hosts."[108] Christ is the leader of vast armies. So Newton's heaven was a densely populated neighborhood. And the "Son" and the "Holy Ghost" were probably in on the divine consultations at the beginning of the universe. But the basic mechanism of creation was a flat-out do-this-or-else, an executive order.

Not a very creative solution to the problem of how the cosmos creates. To Newton, the cosmos is as it is because of the biggest jack-in-the-box in history. The ultimate *deus ex machina*—God.[109] God said it, so it was so. Yes, Newton used the God Copout.

But Newton also contributed a more down-to-earth metaphor to our understanding of the creativity of the cosmos. It was an anthropomorphic metaphor, but one you could wrap your hands around. Literally. "We know him [God]," Newton said, "only by his most wise and excellent contrivances of things, and final causes."[110] Newton gave us God the contriver. God the engineer in chief. God the maker of machines. Why was the cosmos such an astonishing place? Because it was an invention. An incredibly precise gadget fitted together by God. And what did Newton think of when he used a word like "contrive"? What did he himself contrive?

Newton was obsessed with the precision machinery of his age. When he was a kid, he had his own set of tools, which he used to make two instruments that translated the physical motion of mere matter into a measure of time—a water clock and a sundial. In fact, he made many dials. And those dials were among the very first precision measuring instruments in human history. Measuring instruments of a kind that the Babylonians, the Greeks, and even Kepler never had.

In his childhood, Newton also worked out a simple way to measure wind power. He jumped and measured how far the wind carried him. Then he spent hours and days watching workmen build a new-technology windmill near his family's farm on the manor of Woolsthorpe near the town of Colsterworth.[111] Young Isaac watched the mill when it was working, examined it when the wind died and when its internal wheels stopped turning, and finally, when he was fifteen years old, built a perfect working model, one whose linen blades turned when he blew on them or when he blasted them with air from a bellows. Newton's model windmill even crushed grains of wheat and turned them into flour. Then Newton translated the windmill into another medium, into the use of a new power source—a mouse running on a treadmill.[112] To top it all off, Newton invented his own form of mechanized transport—"a mechanical carriage—having four wheels, and put in motion with a handle worked by the person sitting inside."[113]

The great American novelist Nathaniel Hawthorne, writing up Newton's childhood obsession with machinery in 1869, said that as a kid, Newton "showed a capacity to translate something ephemeral into a more solid language."[114] Measuring the distance the wind carried you when you tried to jump straight up and down, then using that measure to gauge the wind's strength and speed was an act of translation. Turning the power of the wind into the motion of a grinding stone was an act of translation. And turning grains of wheat into flour was yet another act of translation. Translation is yet another clue to the God Problem.

But there were more acts of translation to come in Newton's life. And more uses of metaphor. Let's inch back to what Newton imagined God the Contriver might be. What other gadgets were fresh in Newton's mind when he wrote his central book, the *Principia*? Newton used the example of the pendulum clock,[115] of yet another pendulum-powered gizmo, a pendulum hung over a ruler,[116] and of "machines." What machines did Newton have in mind? We all know about Newton's interest in the inner workings of "clocks and such like instruments." But Newton did not see clocks the way that you and I do. The word "gear" for a wheel with teeth had not yet been invented.[117] So Newton perceived clocks as machines "made up from a combination of wheels." More important to Newton were devices that amplified the power of your arms and hands: "The pulley, or . . . a combination of pulleys. . . . The force of the screw [think of a drill] to press a body. . . [via] the hand that turns the handles. . . . And the wedge [that] presses or drives the two parts of wood it cleaves . . . [thanks to] the mallet," thanks to the hammer.[118]

What's the trick to the pulley, the screw, the drill, and the wedge? For example, what's the secret to the wedge that's used to split a tree trunk into planks? Translation. All of them translate one kind of movement into another, one kind of force into another. Says Newton, "The power and use of machines consist only in this, that by diminishing the velocity we may augment the force."[119] The screw, the pulley, the drill, and the wedge translate speed into slamming or piercing strength. They turn speed into power. Or, in the case of clockwork, Newton's "machines" translate the motion of a pendulum and a spring into the turning of hands that the neural synapses of our brain then translate into the strange concepts we call hours and minutes.

Newton's machines, to use Nathaniel Hawthorne's words, "show a capacity to translate something ephemeral into a more solid language."[120]

Newton's metaphor of the machine maker and of the contrivance crafter's creation—a mechanism—would stick like glue. Today, scientists are obsessed with finding an explanatory "mechanism" to open the mysteries they are trying to pierce. Without a mechanism, they often won't accept a new idea. For example, as we'll see a bit later, Charles Darwin was not the man who first proposed the idea of evolution. His grandfather Erasmus had laid out the concept of evolution sixty-two years before the publication of Darwin's *Origin of Species*. So why is Darwin the god of evolutionary theory? Because he provided a mechanism—natural selection.

But the concept of mechanism is a metaphor. It's based on Newton's pulleys, wedges, windmills, and clocks. And it involves a huge stretch—imagining that the patterns of our tools and of our contraptions can tell us something profound about the stars in the skies and about the workings of our minds and eyes. Is that assumption true?

***

To Newton, the problem of cosmic creativity had a simple solution: God. God was the great contriver in the sky. God was the heavenly mechanic crafting a universe that worked like a machine. But many in the scientific community are getting antsy about the limitations of Newton's machine metaphor. They are roiling with discontent over the shortcomings of the mechanistic approach. And they are right. It may be time to challenge the machine model of how the cosmos creates. And it may be time to explore the value of that other Newtonian achievement, translation. Translation and the limitations of the machine metaphor will provide yet more clues to the solution of the God Problem.

***

Remember, Newton was a creationist. So were Kepler and Galileo. In fact, until 1950, very few if any major thinkers would pose the God Problem the way you are posing it. But there is a list of people who would come up with clues to cosmic creativity: Gottfried Leibniz, Georg Hegel, Karl Ernst von Baer, George Boole, Hans Driesch, and Herbert Spencer. Not to mention George Henry Lewes, Bertrand Russell, and Giuseppe Peano. Each of these men (and, alas, they are all men, not women) would come at the God Problem from a different point of view. But like the five blind men trying to figure out the elephant, each of them would be right. Each of them would see the problem in a different way, each of them would use different tools to solve the God Problem, and, in the process, each of them would come up with another facet of a multifaceted truth, another piece of the elephant. And yet all their answers would miss something. Something very big. What?

All of these men would feel that they could discover some of the core tricks that a creator God or a godless nature uses to run the cosmos. And all would feel that if they tried with all their might and dedicated their lives to the task, they could do it by using the tools of science. But, in reality, none of them would ask the question of how the cosmos creates in quite the way that you are asking it. Why? Because until the 1950s, they would be missing something vital to a step-by-step tale of how a cosmos of nothing lifts itself into a something, and a pretty elaborate something at that. They would be missing a big picture, a narrative thread. They would be missing a story of how the cosmos began. They would be missing the big bang.

GAMOW VERSUS HOYLE:
THE WAR BETWEEN BIG BANG AND STEADY STATE

How do we crack the code of what Immanuel Kant in 1755 called the "essential capacities in the natures of things to raise themselves to order and perfection"?[121] How do we crack the code of cosmic creativity? How do we solve the God Problem? We start with a primary power tool of explanation: a narrative, a big picture, a story. A story that was in its infancy when you entered science at the age of ten in 1953. A story that was at the heart of a battle. That story fighting for its right to be was called the big bang.

How did the big bang get into this? And how did you get into the big bang? Let's shuffle backward in time for a minute. Let's skediddle to the year before your bar mitzvah. You are twelve years old. And, alas, you do not feel particularly smart. You were late to learn to read. And you were so slow at doing paperwork that your first-grade teacher thought you were mentally retarded. In fact, she sent you off for psychological testing to prove it. But you teach yourself to play chess. Why? Because it's something that intelligent people do. And, since you cannot play baseball, party, date, play poker, or do anything normal, you are hoping for acceptance in at least one category on this feeble little planet. You are hoping to be intelligent. Intelligent people play chess.

Your mom has tried to help you escape from the kids who've been using you as a football and from the teachers who have been bullying you at PS 64. So she has put you in a new grammar school, an experimental school at Buffalo State Teachers College, an educational "School of Practice" in which kids from every extreme, kids who are vandals and kids who are loftily bright, have been assembled as guinea pigs for new teaching methods. And you have finally met a few people more or less your age who are bright as laser beams, kids of staggeringly high intelligence. These prodigies come over to your big bedroom overlooking the trees of Delaware Park and you play chess with each one of them. They beat you. Humiliatingly. In roughly five to seven moves. Game after game after game.

One of these ultrabrainy new friends even tells you that he can checkmate you without looking at the board. He lays on one of the two double beds in your room and stares up at the ceiling plaster while you set up the chessboard on the tan, shag-looped carpet where he can't see it. You sit on the rug next to the chessboard, and you announce the position to which you are moving your pawns and knights. Your friend, Michael Wolfberg, can't see the pieces and can't see the board. But he beats you in five to seven moves. Several years later, Wolfberg will go off to MIT.

But you? To your credit we must say at least one thing. You never give up. You keep on trying. But when it comes to standard marks of intelligence like playing chess, you are a loser.

Your mom thinks otherwise. When you fixate on the work of Anton van Leeuwenhoek at the age of ten, she takes you to a store that sells used lab equipment to med school students at the local university, the University of Buffalo. And she lets you pick out a gorgeous 1930s professional microscope with Zeiss lenses and a brass barrel. It is hard to operate, but ever since then you've been raising microorganisms in a five-gallon pickle jar that you've stashed in the back of your bedroom closet. Why shut single-celled pond creatures in your closet? You are now reading two books a day. And the books you've chewed your way through on microscopy and microbiology have told you that microorganisms—protozoa, protists—love to multiply in the dark. Don't we all!

When you salivate over an Edmund Scientific ad for a mail-order build-it-yourself computer kit in a magazine, your mom hops in again. Despite the fact that your parents will not indulge you in toys, your mom turns over enough cash to buy the kit. She hands the moolah over instantly, without forcing you to whine and beg. Computers in that era are the size of your house. Your entire house! When the kit arrives it is not a computer in any normal sense of the word. It isn't even digital. It doesn't operate on a binary system—ons and offs, ones and zeros. What is it? A Boolean algebra machine. A device with wheels and wires that performs calculations in symbolic logic, figuring out formulae in which the connectors are not pluses and minuses. Calculating the results of formulae with connectors like AND, OR, NOT, and IF/THEN. Those formulae will someday prove vital to the operation of something that does not exist when you are twelve years old—search engines. And the metaphor of the search engine will someday yield clues to the God Problem.

What's more, at the age of twelve you coconceive a game-playing computer with Wolfberg—the chess genius. He constructs it and later wins a few local science-fair prizes with it. And thanks to your mom, you have private weekly coaching sessions in the principles of out-of-the-box thinking with the head of research and development for the Moog Valve Company,[122] a company that makes super-hi-tech valves for advanced rocket engines.[123] Like the engine of the Bell X-1, the first experimental airplane to break the sound barrier. An airplane made by Bell Aircraft, a company based in Buffalo.

Now your mom goes even further. She twists arms at the University of Buffalo and wrangles you a meeting with the head of the university's graduate physics department. Yes, when you are twelve! She has balls. The last thing a busy man like this wants to waste his time with is a preadolescent kid. A preadolescent kid who can't even play chess!

Your mom pops you into her big Buick and drives you over to the green-lawn-and-tree-dominated university campus, a campus you love. Once you enter the ivy-covered building of the graduate physics department, why does the august and cerebral department head keep you in his office for over an hour instead of the five minutes he has probably scheduled? Because the two of you brainstorm on the hot topic of the day. The one that Kepler, Galileo, and Newton would have salivated over. The one that opens doors to the God Problem. That topic? The evolution of the cosmos: the battle over the big bang versus the steady state theory of the origin of the universe. The battle between George Gamow and Fred Hoyle.

***

From the late 1940s to the mid-1960s, the battle of big bang versus steady state was the biggest slamdown in the physics community. It was a mud wrestling match between two competing stories. A scientific battle for possession of a territory long held exclusively by religion, a battle to be *the* story of the origin of everything in sight, a battle to replace the biblical book of Genesis. And it was a battle between two metaphors, two big pictures.

Fred Hoyle's steady state theory said that the cosmos churned out new matter constantly. Hoyle's steady state also declared that aside from a cycle of expansion and contraction, the universe had remained pretty much the same forever. And it would stay pretty much the same in an infinite future. Big bang theory was very different. It said the cosmos was limited. It had a beginning. It had been spat from nothing in an all-powerful whomp. Then the newborn universe had evolved. It had coughed out particles, plasmas, atoms, gasses, galaxies, stars, and human beings. It had self-assembled. It had pulled off an act of secular genesis.

The slamdown of big bang versus steady state was not a battle between mere schlumps. On one side was a six-foot-three-inch,[124] hard-drinking, hard-thinking Russian American with a fabulous sense of humor and an equally fabulous scientific background, George Gamow. Gamow was a physicist, cosmologist, and mathematician who had successfully escaped the Soviet Union at a time when defection was punished by death. His first escape attempt had been a failure. He had gotten into an inflatable rubber boat with his wife in the middle of the night in 1933[125] and tried to paddle across the Black Sea from the Crimea to Turkey,[126] but he had been caught by the authorities. It wasn't an escape attempt, he'd told the border police. It was a science experiment. But his second effort to get out succeeded.

Gamow had worked out the mystery of radioactive decay. He had explained something radically new—quantum tunneling—how a particle slips through energy barriers that should not let it pass.[127] He had worked on the question of how new elements are generated in the hearts of stars. He had perfected equations that predicted the life course of newborn galaxies. He had worked in England with one of the greatest and most headline-making scientists of the early twentieth century, Nobel Prize–winner Ernest Rutherford, the father of nuclear physics. He had worked in Denmark on quantum physics with the field's founder,[128] Niels Bohr, at the Institute for Theoretical Physics in Copenhagen, the city that gave quantum physics its dominant form—the Copenhagen interpretation. But that's not all. Gamow had also come up with a mathematical explanation of why the universe is 99 percent[129] hydrogen and helium.[130] He'd been the youngest scientist ever elected to the Academy of Sciences of the USSR. What's more, he was the man who had given James Watson and Francis Crick—the discoverers of DNA—a central clue to the language of the double helix, a central clue to the genetic code. And he'd helped name the thermonuclear reactions that led to the atomic bomb.[131]

On the other side of the big bang versus steady state debate was the English scientific megatalent Fred Hoyle, a man who would one day be knighted by the queen for his scientific contributions. Hoyle was the director of Cambridge University's Institute of Astronomy. He was a mathematician who had gone even further than Gamow in explaining the synthesis of new elements in the hearts of dying stars. While Gamow was contributing ideas that would lead to the atomic bomb in the United States in World War II, Hoyle had been working on another radical new military technology, radar.[132] Hoyle had won the Mayhew Prize, the Smith's Prize, and he would go on to win the Gold Medal of the Astronomical Society, the Bruce Medal, the Royal Medal, the Klumpke-Roberts Award, and the Crafoord Prize. Hoyle's work on nucleosynthesis would eventually win one of his collaborators a Nobel Prize. And the scientific community would wonder why that prize had not gone to the man most responsible for the research it honored, to Hoyle himself.

The battle between Hoyle and Gamow, the battle between the steady state and big bang theories, was not restricted to science. Religion would hover just out of sight. The struggle would eventually turn Hoyle from a staunch atheist into a believer in God. And it would bring a strange ally to the side of Gamow, a man who hovered between agnosticism and atheism.[133] That unexpected supporter was, of all people, the pope.[134] Yikes.

The story of big bang's battle with steady state began, says Fred Hoyle, in late 1946 or early 1947, when you were a mere three years old. Says Hoyle, "the steady-state theory may be said to have begun on the night" when the thirty-two-year-old Hoyle went to the movies in Cambridge, England, with two of his friends, his colleagues in astronomy, physics, and mathematics, Hermann Bondi and Tommy Gold.[135] Recalls Hoyle, "The picture, if I remember rightly, was called *The Dead of Night*. It was a sequence of four ghost stories, seemingly disconnected as told by the several characters in the film, but with the interesting property that the end of the fourth story connected unexpectedly with the beginning of the first, thereby setting-up the potential for a never-ending cycle. When the three of us returned that evening to Bondi's rooms in Trinity College, Gold suddenly said: 'What if the Universe is like that?'"

Like what? Says Hoyle, "a never-ending cycle!" Could a cycle be the secret to the tale of the cosmos? Could it account for the new evidence coming in from radio astronomy? Could it account for facts that had been piling up for seventeen years hinting strongly that the universe was expanding? Hinting so strongly that astronomers were forced to conclude that, indeed, the universe above our heads is blowing up like a balloon?

When they left the movie theater and went back to their digs in Cambridge, Hoyle, Bondi, and Gold brainstormed madly into the night. World War II had just ended a year earlier. Men released from the military back into civilian life had time to hang around together and talk ideas until the sunrise. Says Hoyle, "These were the days, late 1946 or early 1947, when anything that anybody suggested was avidly discussed, before everybody became bowed down with committees and other forms of unproductive administrative work."[136] After that post-movie night of exhilarating idea tossing, there came a year of hard work and silence. Bondi and Gold focused on what Hoyle describes as "problems different from those in which I had become interested." Just what *had* Hoyle become interested in? A vital clue to cosmic creativity: "the synthesis of elements in stars." Then, says Hoyle, skipping many a tantalizing detail, "From February to May 1948 our paths converged to a considerable extent . . . in what became the published versions of the steady-state theory."[137]

And what is steady state theory? The universe has no beginning and no end. It just keeps chugging along, expanding and contracting, then expanding again.[138] OK, if the universe is in a holding pattern, in a loop, then why is it expanding? Because, says Hoyle's steady state theory, the cosmos is continuously churning out new matter. Old light is losing energy. It's getting "tired."[139] Because old light has less energy, when you run the light of old and distant stars through a prism and break it up into its basic colors, it turns out to be shifted into the low-energy zone, the red zone, the zone of long, lazy wavelengths. That's the redshift, the Doppler effect. Run distant, old starlight through your prism and you get the lines you normally expect from the hydrogen, helium, carbon, and sodium in the star. But those lines aren't where you normally expect to see them. They are shifted over to the red zone. Hence the term "redshift." And the redshift's interpretation is one of the hottest topics of debate of 1955, the year when you have your meeting with the head of the University of Buffalo's graduate physics department.

Yes, according to Hoyle, old light loses energy and runs down. That's one key to steady state theory. But the first law of thermodynamics says that the amount of energy in the cosmos is conserved. It always stays the same. So how does the cosmos make up for the loss of energy in tired old light? It generates new matter, new particles, the particles that combine to make protons and neutrons.[140] And new hydrogen. Yes, the cosmos churns out brand new matter, matter that never existed before. But that's not all. The cosmos is also spewing out new energy. And that energy is powering the expansion of space.[141] Hence an expanding universe. In Hoyle's steady state theory, cosmic creativity is a nonstop process. The cosmos is perpetually churning nothing into something like a commercial dairy machine churning milk into butter. And the universe is doing this act of genesis on its own. But how? How does the cosmos create new matter from mere emptiness?

Hoyle never really answers that question. In his last book, written in 2000 and titled *A Different Approach to Cosmology*, a book that emerged the year before Hoyle died, Sir Fred confronts the question and answers it like this: "Where do new particles come from if not from some previously existing particle? Our answer conceptually is from the basic fabric of space time."[142] But how is space-time twisted into knots of matter? Hoyle basically takes a pass. He says, "Everything is made out of nothing, despite the saying attributed to Lucretius that only nothing can be created out of nothing."[143] OK, one plus one does not equal two in this universe. Add nothing to nothing and you don't get nothing. In fact, you get something. Interesting idea. But once again, how? And why?

Hoyle hypothesizes the existence of a "C-field," a creative field with negative energy.[144] And how does negative energy crank out its astonishing inventions—Planck particles,[145] quarks, and the three forms of atoms we call hydrogen, helium, and lithium? Hoyle did not know.

But back to 1951, long before Fred Hoyle's final book. You were a mere eight years old when the spit hit the fan in England. It began when Martin Ryle, an Oxford-educated astronomer, did something supremely nasty to Hoyle's Cambridge friend Tommy Gold. Tommy Gold was a superb radio astronomer. When the chairman of Cambridge's Cavendish Radio Astronomy Group left and his job was up for grabs, Hoyle and Gold assumed that Gold would get it. Instead, Martin Ryle snatched the position. The result was a nasty grudge match. A grudge match so bitter that Ryle blackballed Gold from the Radio Astronomy Group at Cambridge. Yes, Ryle banished Gold from the Radio Astronomy Group that was his natural home. Gold's academic position was in Cambridge's Cavendish lab. But he was not even allowed to approach the offices where the Cavendish Radio Astronomy Group was located.

Radio astronomy was a hot new field. It had begun in 1933 when a Bell Labs physicist and radio engineer tried to get a handle on the static that bedeviled intercontinental phone calls and built an antenna a hundred feet across and twenty feet tall, an antenna that looked like a spider on its back with its legs sticking straight up into the air. The engineer, Karl Jansky, mounted this monster antenna on four Ford Model T tires so the behemoth could rotate, then he let it rip. He got three types of static.

Two of these statics were easy to pin down. One came from thunderstorms in the neighborhood and the other came from thunderstorms far away. But there was another form of static, a hiss, whose origin Jansky couldn't pin down. Then Jansky realized that this static had a pattern. A pattern that cycled every twenty-three hours and fifty-six minutes. Twenty-three hours and fifty-six minutes is the "sidereal day." It's the period in which the stars and planets seem to rotate above your head. Aha, perhaps the source of the mystery static was in the heavens. Jansky scoured star maps and came to the conclusion that the biggest source of his mystery hiss was the massive cluster of stars known as the Milky Way and that the most potent hiss came from the very center of the Milky Way, the star cluster known as Sagittarius. Thus was radio astronomy born.

Radio astronomy, a field a mere eighteen years old in 1951, would prove vital to people like Fred Hoyle and George Gamow, vital to understanding the story of the cosmos and the tale of how the cosmos creates.

Then things with Martin Ryle, the Oxford astronomer who had "stolen" Tommy Gold's chair, got even nastier. In 1951 at a conference in London—the Massey Conference—Hoyle gave what he thought of as a perfectly normal paper, a "paper on the technical problem of the conductivity of an ionized gas in a general electromagnetic field." Controversy, says Hoyle, was the last thing on his mind. But Ryle stood up and slammed both Hoyle's paper and a paper by Tommy Gold. And he did it with venom. Recalls Hoyle, "If my mouth was open when Ryle began speaking, it must have closed immediately with an audible snap." Hoyle explained that "there is all the difference in the world between a critic saying 'I don't agree with you' or 'I get a different answer' and Ryle's habit of flat denunciation." After the conference, Hoyle and Gold piled into Gold's $250 Hillman automobile and consoled themselves with "chips-with-something at midnight at Jack's Cafe, situated on a hilltop on the ancient A1 road from London to Edinburgh, about halfway between the towns of Stevenage and Baldock." Thus, says Hoyle, "began an attack that was to persist for almost two decades."[146]

Meanwhile, in the United States, George Gamow was developing the theory of the big bang.

Here's where the redshift and radio astronomy came in. Steady state theory said that the redshift came from the exhaustion of geriatric light. Big bang theory said that the redshift came from the expansion of a universe that had begun as an exploding pinprick and had been whuffling outward ever since. And there was no way these two views would ever meet.

Gamow was the uncontested leader of the big bang crowd. But when it came to battling Hoyle, Gamow let Martin Ryle handle the heavy artillery. Ryle was bitter, hostile, and nasty. But whenever Gamow met Hoyle, the big Russian was remarkably friendly. A conference was set up in the mid-1950s in which the organizer hoped to see sparks fly between Gamow and Hoyle. No dice. The two refused to hiss, scream, and claw at each other.[147]

But Gamow *did* want to debate. He just wanted to do it privately. Fred Hoyle took a leave without salary from Cambridge in the autumn of 1956 to spend a few months in Pasadena, California, at Caltech, MIT's West Coast rival. Gamow was 250 miles away at the Scripps Institute in La Jolla, California, where he was being paid a high fee per day as consultant to the submarine and aircraft maker General Dynamics.[148] Gamow didn't dare break away for a few days to visit Hoyle. He couldn't afford to lose even one day's consulting fees. He'd already spent every cent. But he telephoned Hoyle over and over again pleading with the British astronomer to come down to Pasadena for a visit.

Hoyle was ready to go in for the kill. Says he, "The stage was set" for the final deathblow to big bang theory. Why? Hoyle felt the evidence that would topple big bang and Gamow was piling up. He writes, "Because of the variabilities of composition that were appearing in stars, the stage was set in 1956 for a rejection." A rejection of the big bang. Hoyle tells the story of what happened next using the vocabulary of war: "George Gamow tried a rearguard action, something connected with manganese, 'mangan' as George always called it." But there was nothing sneaky about Gamow's "rearguard action." George Gamow wanted to debate the matter with Fred Hoyle face to face.

Recalls Hoyle, "He kept telephoning to Caltech from La Jolla, eventually suggesting that . . . I should go down there for a general discussion."[149]

Hoyle accepted the invitation and headed down to La Jolla. When he got to the wooden huts of the Scripps Institute, Hoyle says, Gamow continued to be more than just civil. The Russian was warm and convivial. Recalls Hoyle, he'd "blown every penny of his still-to-be-earned" consulting money, "most of it in the purchase of an enormous white Cadillac convertible." Hoyle continues, "I recall George driving me around in the white Cadillac, explaining his conviction that the Universe must have a microwave background, and I recall my telling George that it was impossible for the Universe to have a microwave background with a temperature as high as he was claiming."[150] Nine years later, that microwave background whose temperature Hoyle and Gamow debated would demolish steady state theory. Shatter it and bury it. Despite the fact that, ironically, Fred Hoyle's prediction of the temperature of that background radiation would prove to be on target and George Gamow's would not. The background radiation, one source of radio astronomy's hiss, would be interpreted as leftover energy from the big bang. Certain evidence that, indeed, a big bang had taken place.

But in the early 1950s,[151] Ryle was the flamethrower in the war of big bang versus steady state. Gamow, the trickster and joker, summed that war up like this:

"Your years of toil"
Said Ryle to Hoyle
Are wasted years, believe me
The steady state
is out of date
unless my eyes deceive me

My telescope
has dashed your hope;
Your tenets are refuted
Let me be terse:
Our Universe
Grows daily more diluted!"

Said Hoyle, "You quote
Lemaître, I note
And Gamow, well, forget them!
That errant gang
And their Big bang
Why aid them and abet them?

You see, my friend
It has no end
And there was no beginning
As Bondi, Gold
And I will hold
Until your hair is thinning!"

"Not so!" cried Ryle
With rising bile
And straining at the tether;
"Far galaxies
Are, as one sees,
More tightly packed together!"

"You make me boil!"
Exploded Hoyle,
His statement rearranging
"New matter is born
Each night and morn.
The picture is unchanging!"

"Come off it, Hoyle!
I aim to foil
You yet (The Fun commences)
And in a while,"
Continued Ryle,
"I'll bring you to your senses!"[152]

But Fred Hoyle's ride through the hills around La Jolla, California, in George Gamow's white Cadillac was in 1956. You were brainstorming big bang versus steady state theory 2,195 miles away at the University of Buffalo in New York State in 1955, early in the big bang versus steady state battle. And big bang theory, the side of the battle that you picked at the age of twelve, would provide a vital tool. It would provide a big picture. A narrative frame. It would pull together the story that unfolds before you and me at our café table at the beginning of the universe.

***

But a narrative frame only answers one question—*what* happened. It fails to answer an even bigger puzzle, the puzzle of how and why.

THE TALE OF THE TERMITES

The clues to the God Problem are in a peculiar epic. A six-thousand-year story. A saga of mind tools that we humans have been honing for three hundred generations. A tale of mind tools invented by Aristotle then evolved in ways that would have left Aristotle in a state of shock. A tale in which much of what you and I have been taught turns out to be wrong. A tale that leads, among other things, to the history—and the mystery—of the 165 words from which you extracted a massive mathematical system at Reed College. And a tale that ends in surprising new ways to solve the puzzle of cosmic creativity. Not to mention your creativity and mine.

But there's one clue to keep in mind before we begin the detective story of the God Problem. That clue is a riddle, the riddle of simple rules.

***

In India and Africa, humans use cow dung as everything from the tiling for the floors of their huts to fuel for their cooking stoves. Termite dung and termite spitballs are even more useful than cow patties.[153] They come out in tidy, round pellets or in rod-shaped bricks. Why is relieving yourself in a geometric form handy? Because there's a simple rule that obsesses termites: clean up the mess![154] When you find a lone brick of dung littering a passageway, pick it up and look for a neat pile of bricks on which you can put it. When you see a lump of dirt messing up the corridor, dig it out, chew it into a sphere, and saturate it with your cement-like saliva. Saliva that's laced with the chemicals of attraction, laced with social perfumes, laced with pheromones. Next, look for the pile with the greatest height and the greatest social magnetism. The pile that has attracted the most attention. The pile with the greatest popularity. The pile whose pheromonal odor is the hardest to resist. Look for the tallest pile around. And neatly deposit your pellet of termite dung on top of the pile. There, now doesn't the corridor look better?

What's the result of thousands of repeated acts of termite tidiness? What's the result of your obsessive-compulsiveness? What's the result of what mathematicians call "iteration"? What's the result of repeating a rule—clean up the mess—over and over again on the heaps that your rule itself has produced? Towering pillar after pillar of termite dung.

Then comes the second rule of termite neatness. When two piles of dung bricks or spitballs rise high enough, climb on top with your cargo of litter and deposit your new contribution so it protrudes beyond the edge of the column's circumference. Build the top of the column outward. Outward in the direction of another towering column. In other words, build the tops of dung or spitball-brick towers so that their peaks reach out and touch each other. What does this simple second rule of repetition generate? Gothic arches. And massive walls.

The termite itch for cleanliness results in an architectural master-piece—a termite hive eighteen feet high with a basement six feet deep. A termite hive 972 times the height of the average termite—the equivalent of a 640-story human building over a mile and a half high and four miles wide. A hive topped with spires or domes. A hive with air conditioning that ups the level of moisture in the room the workers use to farm the fungus they feed on. A hive whose air ducts tweak the level of carbon dioxide and keep the temperature at a steady eighty-six degrees in the chamber of the queen and in the brood chambers no matter what the outside conditions might be. A hive whose airshafts process one thousand liters of air each day. A hive that houses two million inhabitants.

From tiny obsessions and trivial fixations great things can grow.

Is there a termite blueprint for this intricate structure? No. So how does this spectacular termite city arise? From the simple rule of termite obsession—pick up the mess and stack it neatly on the biggest pile around. From another basic rule: attraction and repulsion. From repulsion against mess and from attraction toward the tallest pile in the neighborhood. From iteration—from the repetition of a rule upon itself. From the repetition of a rule with obsessive persistence. From the repetition of a rule twenty-six billion times or more.

Think of it this way: the termite's simple rule is an assumption. And the termite's assumption turns out to map onto reality. A reality that does not exist until the termite makes it. A reality no single termite can make. A reality that only tens of thousands of termites can build. A reality that pulls an impossibility into existence. The termite's assumption is a rule that makes walls where there were no walls and towers where there were no towers. For the termite's assumption plugs into a world that isn't there. The world of what is not but what could be. The termite's assumption, its rule, pick up the mess, is something with a peculiar sorcery. It is an axiom.

3

THE SAGA OF A SCRATCH MARK

THE MYSTERY OF THE MAGIC BEANS:
WHAT THE HELL IS AN AXIOM?

> *Different collections of mathematical equations are different universes.*
>
> —**Brian Greene**[1]

What is an axiom?

Your first clue to the God Problem came at Reed College in 1961. It arrived on that peculiar day when the math professor walked into a room of freshmen who'd just sat down around a table together for the very first time, a room of students who had no idea of what was coming. In the professor's hand was a stack of sheets of paper that exuded the pungent, sweet smell of mimeograph chemicals. The prof asked the student on her right to pass the papers around.

The 165 words on those papers contained the magic beans that would grow what physicists call a "toy universe."[2] Those 165 words contained a set of simple rules you'd never heard of before. They contained the five simple rules known as Peano's postulates. Otherwise known as Peano's axioms. And every week for the next nine months you were told to derive a new corollary from those axioms. You were told to pull a new implication from those simple rules. It wasn't easy. In fact, it was barely doable. But what came spilling from Peano's axioms was amazing: addition, subtraction, multiplication, division, squares, square roots, and rational numbers. The entire mathematical system that it had taken you eight years of grammar school and more than eight math textbooks to learn. All the complex and powerful twists of arithmetic and more were present from the beginning in the half page of Peano's axioms. But how?

What are Peano's axioms? They're mind-numbingly tough brain crushers. They may be short, but they are difficult as hell. Here's how one advanced introductory book of mathematics puts them. Don't be surprised if you can't understand a word.

Peano 1: There is a nonempty set with a distinguished element 1. The set will be henceforth denoted N.

Peano 2: For each $x \in N$ there exists one and only one element x'. The element x' will be from now on called the successor of x.

Peano 3: $x' \neq 1$ for every $x \in N$.

Peano 4: If $x' = y'$ then $x = y$.

Peano 5: If M is a subset of N with the following properties
(i) $1 \in M$, and
(ii) $n \in M \rightarrow (n + 1) \in M$ for every $n \in M$,
then $M = N$.[3]

Wikipedia, which often does a far better job of summarizing than it's given credit for, puts Peano's axioms in easier words. But even this is close to impossible to understand.

There is a natural number 0.

Every natural number a has a successor, denoted by $S(a)$.

There is no natural number whose successor is 0.

Distinct natural numbers have distinct successors: if $a \neq b$, then $S(a) \neq S(b)$.

> If a property is possessed by 0 and also by the successor
> of every natural number it is possessed by, then it is
> possessed by all natural numbers.[4]

If you find this a bit dense, you are not alone. Remember, your class at Reed had the highest median SATs in the country. Yet only one out of ten students could do their homework assignments. Only one in ten could understand Peano's axioms well enough to extract their implications. Thanks to some accident of grace, you were one of that tiny elite able to handle the task. But Lord knows how you did it. Remember, you were hopeless at the game of the intelligent. You were a failure at chess.

Actually, you were able to crack the code of this homework because you'd learned to make up for the limitations of your brain with another quality: persistence. You were accustomed to enduring mental torture and to plowing ahead no matter how painful the job seemed. In other words, you were accustomed to a practice that stood the termites in good stead. You were accustomed to what mathematicians call iteration. Persistence. And iterative persistence is one key to the way in which the cosmos creates.

When all the wonders of math came spilling forth from five axioms, you came up with a theory: corollary generator theory. Corollaries were what your teacher insisted you extract week after week. In the words of the *Oxford English Dictionary*, a corollary is "a proposition appended to another . . . following immediately from it without new proof; hence . . . an immediate inference, deduction, consequence." Corollary generator theory is very simple. It says that perhaps this universe started with a handful of rules, a handful of axioms, just like you did at Reed. And just like the termite. And perhaps the universe has been doing her homework ever since. Perhaps she has been yanking the implications of those simple rules from their hiding place. Perhaps she has been extracting the starting rules' corollaries. Perhaps she has been figuring out what new forms and functions are consistent with those starting rules. And perhaps she has been holding on to what fits and tossing out what does not.

But if you're going to get serious about corollary generator theory, you're going to have to understand something basic: How did Peano's axioms come to be? What are axioms? And what can the history of axioms tell us about the God Problem?

***

In 1900, Giuseppe Peano left his home in Italy to attend the International Congress of Philosophy in Paris. It was a cusp-of-history, full-sky fireworks moment. The International Universal Exposition of 1900 in Paris was in full swing. A new century was opening, and the exposition's goals were massive: the "general enlightenment of the world … breaking down national prejudices and unifying and civilizing all nations and peoples." But there was more in the kit bag of the exposition's goals. To "concentrate at the French metropolis" the biggest gee-whiz "products of human invention, industry, and achievement in all parts of the world." And, to put a maraschino cherry on the frosting, "to attract there and bring into contact and cooperation the men, the talents, and the ideas of all nations."[5] In other words, to pull together the greatest thinkers on the planet. And to help them gestate the ideas that would rip open the piñata of a new century.

More than 105 international congresses took place at the exposition,[6] including the First International Congress of Physics,[7] the Fourth International Congress of Applied Chemistry,[8] a thirty-five-nation International Socialist Congress, and nearly forty congresses that one official 143-page report, published in 1901 by the US Bureau of Education and titled *Sociology at the Paris Exhibition*, classified as "sociological." In fact, the International Association for the Advancement of Science, Arts, and Education was born at the exhibition. Its Anglo-American, French, Russian, and German groups organized themselves on the exposition's grounds and headquartered at the exposition's *Palais des congrès* for the entire six months of the exposition. The US government found the event so monumental that it appointed a "Commissioner-General for the United States to the International Universal Exposition." A Commissioner-General who maintained official offices in three cities—New York, Chicago, and Paris—and who accounted for his activities with a 396-page report.[9]

One of the more than 105 congresses was the International Congress of

Mathematicians, the very first math conference of the twentieth century, a conference of mathematicians intent on leaving the old math of the nineteenth century behind and on pulling off a revolution in their field. And despite the debut of an entirely new art form, art nouveaux,[10] despite the unveiling of the biggest telescope in human history, despite the showing of a startling new invention, talking films, despite Rudolf Diesel's display of an entirely new kind of engine, his diesel engine (and a diesel engine running on peanut oil at that), despite extravagant buildings erected by Belgium, Bosnia and Herzegovina, Finland, Germany, Greece, Hungary, Italy, Russia, Switzerland, Turkey, and the United States, despite the extraordinary industrial displays and the assembled intellectual fire power, at least one attendee thought that the man who stole the show was an Italian named Giuseppe Peano. Who was that attendee thunderstruck by Giuseppe Peano? He was a Euclidean geometry addict from Britain, a man whose atheism, pacifism, and sexuality would spark scandals. He was a philosophical superstar in the making. He was the twenty-eight-year-old Bertrand Russell.

Yes, Bertrand Russell, the man who influenced your atheism, was transfixed when he heard Giuseppe Peano's ideas.[11] Actually, his word was "intoxicated."[12] Peano's concepts were what Russell had been looking for all his life. And Russell was so electrified that he asked Peano for his writings— all of them. Then he left the conference, went home to Fernhurst[13] in West Sussex, and for six weeks did just one thing—studied "quietly every word written by him and his disciples."[14] And on the basis of Peano's work, Russell declared the year 1900 to be "the most important year of my intellectual life."[15] Why? In part, because Giuseppe Peano had pulled off the ultimate in axiomatization.[16]

What's axiomatization? What is the Great Axiom Hunt? And how does its strange tale give us clues to the way the cosmos creates?

BARLEY, BRICKS, AND BABYLONIANS:
THE BIRTH OF MATH

The story of the Great Axiom Hunt goes back six thousand years. It all started with the building of one of the very first examples of a brand new invention, a town. That town was built eleven thousand years ago. Its name was Jericho. And it was built by pushing, pulling, and tugging a bunch of seemingly useless boulders to a central location; flattening their tops, bottoms, and sides with stone tools; and heaping them systematically on top of each other the way termites heap their turds. Logically, this should have been an outrageous waste of time. One boulder plus another boulder equals two boulders. And that is it. Yet the result was staggering: something old hat to social insects, but brand new to human beings. The first man-made walls.[17]

But not the kind of walls you have on either side of you right now. The walls of Jericho and of the buildings within them were curved. Why? The citizens of Jericho built round structures. So the people who built Jericho gave us the circle. And yet they did not give us the circle. Why? The denizens of Jericho put the circle into everyday life. But they did not put the circle into the human mind. They did not have the modern concept of the circle. At all. The idea as we know it did not exist.

Two thousand years later,[18] a people to the northwest of Jericho, a people in what is today Turkey, came up with another daffy idea. Living through the rainy season was rough. The footpaths turned into a muck so high that it came up to your knees and made it nearly impossible to walk. If you were old and weak or young and weak, you could be exhausted by this stuff, sink into it, and never escape. That life-threatening muck was mud. Absolutely normal mud. Then some wild-eyed dreamer proposed a lunatic fantasy. Turn a toxic waste into a resource. Take the mud. Pat it into something no elementary particle, star, four-legged animal, or human had ever seen—rectangles. Perfect rectangles. Giant Lego blocks roughly the size of shoeboxes. Leave the rectangles of mush in the sun to dry.[19] Then put over ten million of these rectangles together. What result did these dreamers have in mind? Something that must have seemed utterly impossible at the time. Brick buildings. Garden apartment complexes. Complexes with roughly two thousand three-room, single-family apartments.

This was the very first city of brick, a city that radically changed the way that you and I think. It was Catalhöyük. And Catalhöyük's apartment complexes gave you and me something as radically new as the circles of Jericho: straight lines, right angles, and flat surfaces. Straight lines, right angles, and flat surfaces—planes—were all things that no human had ever seen before. In fact, they were things that the cosmos had never before belched forth. Straight lines, right angles, and planes were astonishingly new to a universe that gathers matter into balls, that clumps stuff into spheres, and that sets them alight as stars. A universe that fashions planets and moons in just one shape—round.

The people of Catalhöyük did not let their acres of flat space go to waste. They took advantage of their walls to harness their fantasies and to exercise their minds. They went artistic. They painted more square feet of artwork on the inner walls of their apartment bedrooms, kitchens, and worship rooms than all the art in the Louvre. And one-third of their painted walls were an attempt to get a handle on the world using symbols. They were translations from one medium to another. They were paintings of goddesses giving birth among wild animals, paintings of stick-figure men hunting red deer with bow and arrow, and paintings of dead Catalhöyük citizens being consumed by vultures—the sacred way to dispose of bodies. One out of every three apartments in Catalhöyük was a worship room. And in the sacred chambers the painted walls stabbed and jabbed at you in 3-D. Plaster-molded breasts poked at you from the flatness. And massive, threatening horns of bulls stabbed at you from the walls.

Through the line, the right angle, the flat surface, and paintings, the people of Catalhöyük gave the cosmos a whole new way to iterate. A whole new way to repeat herself in a new medium. But, like the citizens of Jericho, the builders of Catalhöyük did and did not give us the plane, the straight line, and the right angle. Why? They inserted lines and planes into our daily lives, but did not insert them into our minds. And, indeed, the circle and the line would remain implicit for a very long time. It would take thousands of years before we humans would turn the circle and the line into concepts, into mental tools, into explicit realities.

How did we go from having the straight line, the circle, and the plane staring us in the face to having the straight line, the circle, and the plane in our tool kit of ideas? How did we get the straight line, the circle, and the plane uploaded to our brain? And how did Peano and his axioms get into this act? That's the question whose answer we are stalking.

***

Four thousand years after the founding of Catalhöyük there arose one of the first civilizations to build city-states and empires, a civilization nestled between the Tigris and Euphrates rivers in what is now called Iraq. That civilization was the culture of the Mesopotamians—the Sumerians and the Babylonians. The year was roughly 3200 BCE.[20] That's more than two thousand years *before* the founding of the city of Rome. Yet metropolitan bustle and its gifts were rising in the thirty-one cities of Sumer—the urban web that called itself "The Land of the Lords of Brightness."[21] And the Sumerians and Babylonians would be among the first to make at least one implicit legacy of Catalhöyük, the line, explicit. But they would never quite get the circle. And in their failure to invent the concept of the circle lies a tale.

In his definitive book, *The History of Western Philosophy*, Bertrand Russell says about one group of Mesopotamians, namely the Babylonians, that "we owe to the Babylonians the division of the right angle into ninety degrees, and of the degree into sixty minutes"[22] This claim is repeated wherever you look, from popular online educational sources like the Internet's Wonder*Quest*[23] to the Notes and Queries section of Britain's newspaper the *Guardian*.[24] Not to mention books like Graham Faiella's *The Technology of Mesopotamia*.[25] But it's wrong. Dead wrong.[26] And the real story is even more interesting. The Babylonians never invented the concept of the angle.[27] They had no word at all for a right angle. And they never divided a circle into 360 degrees. The way they *did* think is utterly alien to us. And sometimes it's valuable to step into an alien mind. Why? To get a perspective on the tools of thought that we take for granted.

What mind tools did the Sumerians and the Babylonians *really* invent? Massive breakthroughs.[28] Breakthroughs that laid the groundwork for math, for modern science, and for axioms. In roughly 2600 BCE the priests of the city of Sumer,[29] the city that introduced irrigation and monocropping, came up with a brand-new way of counting things,[30] a mathematical system to tote up the sacrifices of oats, barley, chickens, fish, and sheep that you, a normal citizen, offered to your gods.[31] The holy prelates created a system to keep track of your sacrifices of grain right down to the last seed of barley, to the last barleycorn. Counting and keeping track of sacrifices was so important that the Mesopotamians had a goddess of writing, Nisaba. And Nisaba was also the goddess of another indispensable treasure: grain.

But Sumer's priests and gods were not the only ones who counted things. The Sumerians were long-distance traders. They swapped cloth, food, jewelry, weapons, and tools with customers in Asia Minor and Iran, bringing home wood, metals, and stone. To simplify this long-distance trade, they developed a balance, a scale, and standard weights.[32] And they invented markings to keep track of just how much your bag of barleycorns really weighed.[33] Those markings and the markings of businessmen and priests were the first numbers. What's more, in 2100 BCE, 4,100 years ago, the Sumerians required that you keep records of the figures involved in your commercial trades, that you not toss out those business records when the trades were done. That record keeping would someday lead to science.

How did Sumerian numbers work? Let's switch points of view. You're no longer a trader or an average citizen. Imagine that you're a Sumerian record keeper: a priest and scribe. Your writing surface is a moist, squishy tablet made of the same raw material as the brick walls of the buildings around you, mud. Specifically, your writing pad is made of the form of mineral-charged, phyllosilicate mud known as clay. And your clay tablet is one of the first handheld calculators. It's roughly the length and breadth of your hand and it's an easy-to-hold inch thick. That clay tablet is your empty word processor screen and your blank sheet of paper.

Then there's your writing instrument—a reed with a point chiseled down to a wedge-shape that makes triangular markings. You stab a single vertical marking into the clay to get a Y. That Y is your first numeral, a one. In fact, it may be the first number in history. How do you represent four? You make four ones, four Y's—YYYY. And how do you make the number eight? Eight ones: YYYYYYYY. Now stop making vertical markings. Make a horizontal mark. Point the triangular head of your reed to the left: <. That horizontal stab, that arrowhead pointing sideways, <, is your ten. So here's how you mark eleven:

< Y

One ten mark, <, and one one mark, Y.

Then came a giant leap of imagination. The Sumerians came up with ways to apply the numbers that tallied sacrifices of barleycorns, fish, and sheep to figure out the sizes of farm fields. Why translate the sizes of farm fields into stab marks on clay? Why turn expanses of land into symbols, into numbers? Why iterate the realities of daily life in a whole new medium? Because you have a bureaucracy, a vast gaggle of priestly scribes like you who write things down. And that bureaucracy needs barley, chickens, fish, and sheep to keep running. It needs food to feed its horde of bureaucrats. What's more, you have another expensive piece of public overhead—a "big man," a king.[34] So you invent the property tax. Which leaves you with a problem. How do you tax fields?[35] How do you find their sizes? How do you calculate which landholders owe what to the temple and to the state?

Can you somehow apply the numbers with which you've counted barleycorns and chickens to this problem? The answer at first seems obvious. Absolutely not. A chicken and a field are two radically different things. A plot of earth has nothing to do with a tally of feathers and fish. A patch of earth and scratches on a smartphone-sized tablet of mud have nothing in common but the mud they are made of. Or do they? Are there underlying patterns so deeply engrained in this peculiar cosmos of ours that scratch marks and land can, in fact, match each other somehow? The answer is yes.

The solution to the problem of turning land into numbers, into Y's and <'s, is something strange. It's the secret of the termite: iteration. Repeat a number upon itself. Use a number as two things simultaneously. For example, you can use thirteen as a count, a tally, a way of keeping track of the sacrifice I've just brought you, as in thirteen chickens. And you can use thirteen as a simple rule, an algorithm, a thou shalt. As in "thou shalt add thirteen chickens to thirteen chickens thirteen times." Writing the number thirteen down thirteen times. Then adding up the result: 169. We call that repeated form of addition "multiplication." And it comes in handy for a priest or a merchant. Why?

Suppose you are a priest and I am a farmer. I bring you a load of barley.[36] You open the sack I've given you and count the barleycorns out. It takes you fifteen hours. I'm not kidding. Fifteen miserable, painful hours. Why? There are roughly 10,800 kernels of barley in my load. You write your final total, 10,800, down on your hand-tablet of clay. Then I go home and get you another load of barley. You are tired of counting barleycorns. In fact, you never want to count another barleycorn in your life. What do you do to save yourself time? And to save your sanity? You do something that's damnably close to sympathetic magic. Something that smacks of what the great early-twentieth-century anthropological synthesizer Sir James George Frazier called "the mistake of assuming that things which resemble each other are the same."[37] And you do it with things that do not resemble each other in the least—you use magical manipulations of the scratches in your clay hand tablet, the scratches that you claim stand for grain and animals. You figure that my two loads of barleycorns are roughly the same size. So you work out a simplified rule, a rule of iteration. You come up with a timesaver based on $A = A$. An assumption. An assumption that works brilliantly. You figure that every load I bring you is roughly 10,800 barleycorns.

Then, in Mesopotamian terms, you "heap" two 10,800s together. Not by dumping the loads of barleycorns out on the floor and counting them. You heap them symbolically. On your mud tablet. You ignore the real-world barleycorns and you work with something else—abstractions. Symbols. Numbers. You play around with your Y's and <'s. You add the two 10,800s up. You invent addition. And in one svelte scoop you discover that I've given you 21,600 barleycorns. Holy Marduk. You've just saved fifteen hours of counting time. Then I go home and come back with a third load of barley-corns. Once again, you assume that $A = A$. You assume that two loads of barley are the same. And you "heap" the number 10,800 on itself. You "heap" my third load on your running total and determine that I've given you a total of 32,400 barleycorns. Give or take a few hundred. You wicked wiz, you—you've just saved yourself a total of forty-five hours of counting.

Then comes the next farmer. He brings you nine loads. There is no way in Ea's torture chambers that you want to count his first load. So you figure that his batch is about the same as mine. You turn a "load" into more than just a guesstimate for the loads I bring you. You figure that every "man-load" is 10,800 barleycorns. No matter who it comes from. Congratulations. You've just invented a new standard measure. And you call it a "gu."[38] No kidding, a gu. In the English translation of the Bible, gus show up all over the place. But the King James Bible calls a gu a "talent." The meaning of a talent? One load!

By the end of the day, your new supplicant has repeated his delivery process nine times. He's brought you nine loads of barley. Nine gus. And you've noted one gu nine times, crediting the worshipper by name. The pious man making a sacrifice finally tells you that he's finished. He's done his duty by the gods. He is going home to get some rest over a nice meal of barley. Then you add his gus up. This new worshipper has brought you nine gus. A gu is 10,800 barleycorns. You "heap" 10,800 barleycorns nine times. You use nine not just as a count but as a command, a rule, a verb, a process, a thou shalt, an algorithm. You add 10,800 to 10,800 nine times. And you get a total of 97,200 barleycorns. Wow, this guy has beat my 32,400 barleycorns hands down. And hands will turn out to be very important in this process of implication extraction, this process of corollary generation. But let's get back from hands to the really important subject, you.

Manipulating numbers instead of counting barleycorns has now saved you a total of 180 hours on just two worshippers. Amazing. But there's another *nimsahara* in the ointment (that's Old Babylonian for fly).[39] Adding up and multiplying numbers is faster than counting barley seeds. But, frankly, it is tedious as all get out. How in the world can you speed it up and ease the burden? Can you possibly yank a few more implicit properties— a few more hidden patterns—from mud, a reed, and scratch marks? From your translation of barleycorns and chickens into the medium of Y's and <'s? From numbers? Is there another invention lurking in the twilight zone of implicit order waiting for you to pull it from possibility to reality, from fantasy to fact? Yes. It's called the table. And you use it for the kind of auto-mated "heaping," the kind of multiple addition, that counting load after load calls for. You write

1	gu	10,800 barleycorns
2	gu	21,600 barleycorns
3	gu	32,400 barleycorns
4	gu	43,200 barleycorns
5	gu	54,000 barleycorns
6	gu	64,800 barleycorns

And you keep going, for gu after gu after gu. You are amazing. You've just automated counting. You've just invented the multiplication table. You've done it by iteration. By repeating numbers upon each other. By using numbers in two ways:

- as counts
- as rules

For example, the simple phrase "heap six gus" means add one gu to itself six times. But now you can skip counting and adding. You can look up the result on your palm-sized tablet, on your clay cheat sheet, on your new bit of personal technology, your new extracranial mind empowerer. That bit of extracranial smarts tells you instantly that six gus are equal to 64,800 barleycorns. Congratulations. You've just invented a new mind tool. You've just invented the multiplication table.

Multiplication is a huge time saver when you use your table. In just one workday it can allow you to accomplish one hundred workdays of counting. Yes, multiplication can empower you to do one hundred workdays of counting between dawn and dusk of a single day! Not bad for scratches in clay.

Your next move of implicit order extraction? Your next act of sorcery and pattern discovery? It's another act of translation. Another act of moving patterns from one medium to another. Another act of a kind that often makes new things. You've already followed the example of Catalhöyük and you've extracted amazing implicit properties from mud—bricks, walls, sleeping platforms,[40] kitchen areas with domed ovens,[41] protective fortifications, flat surfaces, and the strange sort of corners at which flat walls meet. Now comes the time to extract more implicit properties, this time from something else right under your nose, from reeds. And from something else. Your body. From fingers, arms, and feet. The problem you apply these to? The question we started with. How do you measure the size of my field? How do you translate the area that my property occupies into numbers? And how do you do it for property that I want but that I do not yet have, the fields of my father?

It's roughly 2050 BCE in the Old Babylonian city of Nippur.[42] It's four thousand years ago. I come to you with a predicament. My father has just died. I have three brothers.[43] By law, we all inherit equal shares of dad's property. That property includes a house, a shrine table, eleven sheep, one ox, two cows, three bushels of bitumen tar, two and a half shekels of silver, a share in the revenues of the city's Great Gate, pottery, two grindstones, a wooden door, a wicker door, three palm rib doors, a sanctuary gate, two wagons—an old wagon and one whose construction is not quite complete—plus a field next to the house of one of my brothers, a field next to the property of Igmilum the butcher, and another field next to the property of Sin-lidis, the leather worker. This problem is for real. It happened to four brothers—Sallurum, Apiyatum, Ziyatum, and Lugatum. The only thing we'll simplify is the field. In the real case, there were several plots of land in different locations, some of them fertile and some of them listed as waste ground.

To divide these goodies up, all of these things had to be translated into scratch marks on clay. Yes, translated. And all of them had to be reduced to some sort of common unit of measure. No matter how artificial and distorted that unit of measure might be. In other words, all of them had to be homogenized with an equal sign. All of them had to be expressed in some form of *A* equals *A*. Why? Why did we need what Aristotle would later call a law of identity? So the land, wagons, doors, shares in the revenues of a city gate, and shrine table could be heaped and cut up into portions with what you've just invented—scratch marks. Indentations in clay. Tally signs for chickens, fish, sheep, and barley. Translations.

Back to your dilemma. Can you tell my brothers and me how to divide the land up fairly? Can you do it using your scratches on palm-sized mud tablets? The logical answer should be no. *A* equals *A*. A scratch is a scratch is a scratch. Frazer would tell you to watch out for the pitfall of "sympathetic magic." Watch out for "the mistake of assuming that things which resemble each other are the same."[44]

But you, you clever devil, will add a few new tools to your kit. A few new apps. You will find a new use for your fingers, your arms, a rope, and your walking stick—your reed. You will use your reed, a rope, your fingers, and your arms to count space.

Counting space? Surely that's absurd. A scratch mark in wet clay cannot "be" an expanse of dirt. But you will trump absurdity by inventing "lengths" and "fronts"—breadth and depth.[45] Space and distance. And you will show the power of translation by using more than reeds, ropes, fingers, and arms. You will show the power of translation by using—are you ready? Barleycorns and bricks. Here's how. You will lay a bunch of barleycorns side by side in a straight line until they reach the width of one of your fingers. Yes, the width. That distance of less than an inch from one side of your finger to the other. The distance from left to right across one of your finger joints. How many barleycorns does that take? Your finger is roughly 0.65 inches wide. (At least that's the width the Mesopotamians turned into a standard.) So you peg the number of barleycorns in a finger's breadth at seven.

Barleycorns equal fingers? That's silly. Or is it? Now you've got your barleycorn (a "se") and your seven-barleycorn finger-width (a "su-si") as units of length. But you go a few steps further. You've just translated barleycorns into fingers; now you translate fingers into arms. You use the width of a finger of your right hand to measure your left arm from your elbow to your fingertips. When the Babylonians did this, they got twenty-four. So twenty-four finger-widths equal one forearm, one cubit, one "kus." You are now set up to translate forearms into, brace yourself, barleycorns. Since one arm is twenty four finger-widths, and one finger-width equals seven barleycorns, one arm length equals 168 barleycorns. You get that figure by using one of your new inventions: the multiplication table. Are you still with me?

Frankly, if you're going to measure farm plots, measuring in barleycorns, finger-widths, or arms will be time consuming. Laying out a line of barleycorns from one end of my dad's property to another and counting each grain will take forever. And bending over, putting your forearm on the ground, and forearming the plot of land over and over again from one end of my father's field to the other will break your back. What's more, you've learned from counting loads of barleycorns at the temple that the bigger your measure, the more time you save. So you look for another measuring device. A longer one. And what do you find? Those bulrushes that grow in the local swamps. The bulrushes that tower over your head. The rushes from whose shoots you make your equivalent of pens, your cuneiform markers. And from which you make your walking sticks. You find reeds. You measure a full-grown reed in forearm lengths, in cubits. And you establish another standard: one reed is equal to seven forearms. One reed is equal to seven cubits.[46] One "gi" is equal to seven kus. Again, one bulrush is equal to seven forearms. And, since everything comes down to the size of a barley seed, one reed equals 1,176 barleycorns. Well done!

The idea that barleycorns in a bushel basket can equal your sacrifice to the gods, your evening meal, and the length of a field may seem like a gross violation of sanity. Or like superstition and sorcery. But it fits perfectly with another of your mathematical inventions, another of your radical break-throughs, the table. Here's how length measured in barleycorns and reeds might look in table form:

1 reed	7 forearms (cubits)	168 fingers	1,176 barleycorns
2 reeds	14 forearms (cubits)	336 fingers	2,352 barleycorns
3 reeds	21 forearms (cubits)	504 fingers	3,528 barleycorns
. . .			
10 reeds	70 arms (cubits)	1,680 fingers	11,760 barleycorns

And you've got all this on a handy tablet of clay no bigger than an iPhone®. Translation is amazing.

But back to your problem . . . dividing my father's land between me and my three brothers. You draw the shape you call a "bull's head"[47] or an "equalsided"[48] on your wet clay slab. You draw a tiny square. You do it using your finger as a measure—you make each side equal to one finger-width. Then you lay out seven barleycorns on each side of the square to show me that this is, indeed, a bull's head all of whose sides are equal. Then what? What does this have to do with my problem? You cagey cuneiform mangler, you fill the entire square with barleycorns. And you make me count the barleycorns to be certain that there's no hocus-pocus going on here. The number? Forty-nine. More or less.

Now you whip one of your clay tablets out of your leather pouch.[49] It's one of your multiplication tables.[50] You make me read the entry for seven heaped on itself seven times. What's the answer on the table? Forty-nine. <<<<YYYYYYYYY. Precisely the number of barleycorns I just counted. In other words, you did it. You used scratches in mud to predict how many barleycorns there are in a square that is one finger wide and one finger deep. You used your multiplication table to find what you Babylonians call the "field" and what moderns would someday call the "area" of the square you drew. You used your table to find the field of a bull's head all of whose fronts measure the same.

You haven't invented the metaphor of "squaring." To you, there's nothing special about the square. A four-sided figure is a four-sided figure is a four-sided figure. But you have invented the process of multiplying a number by itself—four times four or ten times ten. In fact, one of those mud pocket tablets you are carrying in your robe is a table of what moderns will someday call "squares," a table of numbers raised upon themselves. And your clay table is filled with scratches that tell you how many barleycorns you can squeeze into squares that are two fingers, five fingers, fifteen fingers, and forty-five fingers per front. Again, you do not have the metaphor of the square. But even without it, you are pulling off miracles. I hate you.

Then you claim an even bigger distortion of *A* equals *A*. An even bigger act of translation. You claim that the principles of your seven-barleycorn square, your one-finger-by-one-finger square, will work on farm fields. You claim that if we measure a square farm field that's seven reeds on all of its fronts, your multiplication table will still apply. Seven reeds heaped upon themselves seven times will give an answer of forty-nine. Forty-nine what, I ask you in exasperation. Forty-nine "reed-strips," you proclaim with a beaming face.

You wicked thing, you. You have just pulled off an act of secular sorcery, an act of radical translation. You have done something so close to summoning spirits from the ether that it's absurd. You've shown that seven barleycorns heaped seven times summons the number forty-nine and that seven reeds heaped seven times summons, ummm, the same Bel-forsaken[51] number, forty-nine?!? Reed walking sticks and barleycorns summon the same number? This is goofy. But you have shown that radically different things can somehow equal each other. And that your numbers can tap the magic powers of that strange equality. What's more, you have translated an area, a massive expanse of soil and stubble, a field, into barleycorns. Bizarre!

Now you take your reed and your clay tablets out to my farm field. And you bring along another time-saver—your coil of measuring rope. A measuring rope that will give you the length of twenty reeds in one svelte loop.[52] You claim that with the magic wand of your reed and your rope, plus a few arms and fingers, you are going to solve my problem—figuring out how to divide my beloved father's land with my brothers. Fat chance. But you are lucky. Mesopotamian farm fields are crowded up against each other in the sort of straight-line shapes that make starting at one end with your plow and going straight to the other end easy. They're not laid out in hard-to-plow circles, inkblot swatches, or crazy splotches. In fact, they are laid out pretty much in the shape of the bottoms of bricks—in rectangles.[53] They have straight sides like the straight sides of the bull's head you drew for me on your clay tablet. This makes your job a lot easier.

You do not wave your wand like a summoner of ghosts and spirits. Instead, you stretch your rope and lay down your reed as many times as it takes to go from one corner of the field to the nearest corner to your left. You measure the width, the "front" of my dad's land. You explain to me that my father's field is twenty reeds wide. You make a rough sketch of my land on a wet and squishy clay tablet. And you mark down that twenty-reed measure. Now you pick up your rope and your measuring reed again. And you measure the distance to the nearest corner on your right. You measure the length of my dad's field. You get ten reeds. You mark that down on your tablet. According to your measurements and your tablet, my father's land has a "front" of twenty reeds and a "length" of ten reeds. In modern terms, it's twenty reeds long and ten reeds wide. Now comes a huge leap.

You, you ballsy son of an ox, are about to invent yet another something new. You are about to pull yet another rabbit of implicit reality out of your clay, reed, rope, and scratch-mark hat. From two numbers, ten and twenty, you claim that you can calculate what you call the "field"—the area of my father's little patch of real estate. With those two numbers, ten and twenty, you claim that you can answer my problem. You claim that you can figure out how to divvy up my father's land between me and my brothers. Frankly, I don't believe you.

You draw four lines on your clay in the shape of a brick, a rectangle. In the shape of my field. You lay out a "field plan,"[54] a "drawing."[55] This is not a big deal. Our ancestors, yours and mine, started drawing things on cave walls over twenty thousand years ago. And the good folks of Catalhöyük turned out wall drawings by the yard. But your crude sketch is another suspicious bit of sympathetic magic. Another absurd attempt at translation. You claim that it "represents" my land. You make what you call the "front" twenty finger-widths long. You make the "length" ten finger-widths wide. Now you whip out another of your pocket mind extenders and time savers, another one of the tablets that you've made to save yourself months counting barleycorns in the temple, your multiplication table.

You look up ten heaped on itself twenty times, ten times twenty, ten multiplied by twenty. You show me the answer—two hundred. And you tell me that my dad has left two hundred somethings of land. Two hundred somethings of what? I'm ready to throttle you. Two hundred reed-strips. Says who? Says you. And says the king. He's made the reed-strip a standard. So my brothers and I have two hundred reed strips to divide.

How do you divide two hundred reed strips between four brothers? How do you "break" it into four pieces?[56] You whip out another table, a table of reciprocals.[57] (Alas, you haven't invented modern division.) You look up some numbers on your table, and there you have it. It turns out that each of us gets fifty reed strips. And if I don't believe you, we can do the whole calculation all over again. This time in bricks. Yes, in Mesopotamia, the brick is at the bottom of everything. One reed-strip is one hundred and eighty bricks. If I accuse you of nonsense, we can get a load of bricks, use your measuring reed to lay out one reed-strip, cover it with bricks, and count them.

But I will simply have to trust you. So you tell me that the "field" of my dad's property—the area— is thirty-six thousand bricks. And using your table of reciprocals, each of us brothers gets nine thousand bricks of land.

In another real-life example from ancient Babylon, the land shown in a Babylonian field plan called BM 47437 comes to "4 reeds 4 cubits 4 small cubits + I cubit 18 fingers 4 1/2 barley-corns."[58] Yes, barleycorns, bricks, land, fingers, forearms, ropes, scratches on clay, and numbers all equal each other in some radically peculiar way. No wonder the world calls you Mesopotamian math priests Magi—the original magicians.[59]

How have you Babylonians done all of this? By probing the nothingness for implicit opportunities, for implicit realities, for what twentieth-century physicist David Bohm will someday call "implicate properties." By coming up with ideas. By trying a thousand ideas that don't work until you find the one that does. By doing this for roughly thirty-six hundred years. For 180 generations. By writing down what works. By teaching what works to kids who go through tens of thousands of clay tablets doing it wrong before they learn to do it right. (One Babylonian school building was converted to a residence in 1740 BCE, during the reign of Samsu-Iluna, Hammurabi's son. How? The new occupants made floors, walls, and furniture with fourteen hundred clay tablets that the students in the place hadn't disposed of or recycled in the building's soaking-and-reusing facilities. Those tablets were homework and classwork assignments on creative writing, vocabulary, spelling . . . and math.)[60]

You've achieved the impossible. How? By turning what's merely implicit into the explicit. By turning your technologies into ideas. Into new thought tools. Into metaphors. By acts of iteration and translation, acts of translation from one medium to another. By turning a brick from building material and a barleycorn from gruel, transforming them into standard measuring devices. And by turning those standard measuring devices into numbers. By turning mere wisps and imaginings into something hard and fast. By turning everyday things into ideas, concepts, metaphors, and mind tools. By being innovative as all hell. By translating patterns from one medium to another. By translating absurdities—scratch marks—into something that matches your everyday reality . . . and mine. Something that allows you to predict new solidities. Something that gives you instant shortcuts to counting up a million barleycorns.

What does it mean to turn a technology like a brick and a rope into an idea? What does it mean to make the implicit explicit? What does it mean to translate what's right under your nose into a mind tool? The implicit isn't obvious. Far from it. It takes an enormous creative leap. How hard is it to find a concept that works? Take a look at one of the ideas that the Babylonians did *not* get. Thanks to bricks and to the straight walls that bricks make, the Babylonians had walls that met at what we call "right angles." But, despite the protestations of Bertrand Russell, the Babylonians had no concept of the angle.[61] No concept of any form of angle. Not to mention no concept of the right angle. And this was despite the fact that every room they sat in had corners. And despite the fact that the solidity of their buildings depended on getting right angles, well, umm, right. Get the angles wrong and your building might collapse.[62]

Angles are measured with circles. And the Mesopotamians had no idea that a circle could be defined by a radius sweeping out an arc from a center point. No idea that every point on a circle is an equal distance from the circle's center. They had no idea that a circle was a special sort of mathematical entity. As we'll see in a second, they seldom saw the sky as a circle. And they never saw it as a circle measured out in our kind of degrees. Not to mention the fact that they never saw the sky as a hemisphere. Angles, circles, and hemispheres, things that seem to us obvious, did not exist in their vocabulary. Despite the fact that they drew circles. With compasses.

And despite the fact that they used tables of reciprocals to "break" things apart, they didn't invent division. Each of these things would have been a breakthrough. Each was implicit in what the Babylonians had already invented—the brick, the compass, math, and astronomy. And each was obvious. Or was it? If it was so obvious, why did 180 generations of Babylonians working their way through millions of calculations and billions of words and numbers not get it? More important, if the Babylonians didn't get these simple concepts, what concepts are hovering just outside our grasp, outside your grasp and mine, implicit in our technology and in our biology, in our arms, our fingers, our cars, our planes, our cell phones, and our computers? What simple concepts are hovering in the air around us day after day after day? Simple concepts that we don't get. Concepts that we don't grasp because we haven't yet invented the words and the ideas that will capture them. Concepts available if we turn the tools we work with every day, our modern equivalent of bricks, ropes, fingers, barleycorns, and reeds, into metaphors. Concepts available by finding strange equations between things, strange relationships that make radically unequal things equal.

***

In Turkey's Archaeological Museum of Istanbul there's a roughly four-foot-long copper rod shaped like a walking stick. It's called the Nippur Ell. What is it? A tool of translation. A tool for transforming length into words. A tool for translating length into cuneiform markings on clay. A tool for transforming length into numbers. It's a standard that gives the length of eight elementary Sumerian distance markers. Eight standard measures. The slab is four Sumerian "feet" long. As in the two feet you and I walk with. The ones with little pink toes. Four Sumerian feet translate into sixteen Sumerian "hands" in length.[63] Then there are other measures like the ell (as in "elbow"—the arm—the cubit—thirty modern inches), and our constant companion the brick (nineteen modern inches long).[64] The copper rod is not yet a measuring stick or a number line. It is not a modern ruler. It has no number markings. It has no small units that subdivide the rod so you can use it to measure with precision. Again, it's simply a device for translating length into words. It's the sort of thing that you, the Mesopotamian priest, held your rod and rope up to, to make sure their distances were correct. It's the sort of thing you used to make sure your rod and rope matched the standard for reeds and ropes, the standard that was common in your time. Again, this Sumerian rod of copper is not a ruler. But it is a big step forward. And the metaphor of the step, the pace forward when you walk, for the next stage of the solution to a problem is another Babylonian invention.

The bottom line? The Babylonians did a great job of looking right under their noses and seeing everything from their fingers, their elbows, and their feet to the clay they walked on. Yet there was much they didn't see. A fact that may be true for you and me.

SCRATCH MUD AND YOU GET MIND:
THE RISE OF A VIRTUAL REALITY

Now back to you and your scratch-mark magic. You've just convinced me that you are onto something. I'm going to send one of my kids to learn how you've done it. I'm going to send one of my boys to you to be educated as a bureaucrat, a scribe, a mathematician, and a priest.

But there's another bit of magic in all this math stuff. You will teach children like mine the secrets of your clay, your scratches, your tables, your "fields," your multiplication, your "heaping" and your "breaking," your barleycorns, your forearms, your man-loads, and the secrets of measures like the rope and the reed. More important, you will teach my kids the ideas that make sense of it all. And they will teach all that to a younger generation who will, in turn, teach them to another. And somewhere along that line another transformation will occur.

I was leery as all Kur (the Mesopotamian underworld) when you claimed you could answer questions about my inheritance with this strange new system of yours. But when one of my kids grows up and teaches yet more kids the secrets of cuneiform math, farmers like me will no longer question you when you whip out your clay tablets and tell us how to divide up our land. We will take the relationship between scratches on clay and real estate for granted. We will add your numbers to our infrastructure of habit. We will add your scratches and numbers to our symbol stack. We will no longer think of them as fantasies, abstractions, and madness. We will treat them as solid realities.

We will treat them as assumptions. Assumptions whose arbitrariness we will no longer see. Just as four thousand years down the line we moderns will forget that an inch means "a twelfth part," a foot is one of those things our ankles are attached to, and a yard is a walking stick.

Us moderns forget that an inch, a foot, and a yard are based on metaphor and radical abstraction. We forget that they are based on a fantastical relationship between arms, fingers, and ink on paper. We forget that they make an impossible claim—that squiggles on pulped tree stuff or on a computer screen equal farm fields and food. We forget the bizarre claims of the equal sign. The bizarre claims of "equation."

***

You tossed a tangle of ridiculous ideas at me when you popped your notions of new ways to use reed strips, barleycorns, and numbers. But what will happen when your strange phantasms become their own hard and fast realities in the Mesopotamian mind? New kids with new curiosities will invent or extract new implicit patterns and possibilities from the act of counting, from the act of keeping track of counts with scratches in clay, and from the act of iterating in inventive new ways. New generations of kids will extract new implications from the tricks you can play by manipulating numbers step by step by step, repeating numbers over upon themselves in brand-new ways.

They will work out how many workers it takes to harvest a barley field of any size you can imagine. They will calculate how much bread and beer it will take to feed those workers. They will work out an equivalence between barleycorns and something radically unbarleylike—silver (sixty barleycorns equals one shekel of silver). They will invent a measure that leapfrogs the reed strip and the finger strip into a new dimension (one finger strip is a strip one finger wide and one reed long).[65] Yes, they will literally take the reed strip and the finger strip into a new dimension. They will invent 3-D measures like the hinu, the seven-finger-high cube. The Babylonians will also use their 3-D measures of volume to calculate the number of barleycorns that would fit into a container shaped like cylinder (a "log"), a container shaped like a cone, a container shaped like a cone with its point hacked off, and a gaggle of containers of other shapes. And they will figure out how many barleycorns would fit into a granary shaped roughly like a pyramid.

In addition, they will invent strange math games that eventually turn out to have application in reality—applications of the sort that we would handle with binomial and quadratic equations. But their way of solving these problems will be very different from ours. They will pose fanciful math riddles to school kids—if seven houses had seven cats and each of the seven cats caught seven mice and each of the seven mice had eaten seven bags of emmer wheat and each of the seven bags of wheat weighed seven heqat, how many things have I just tossed at you in this riddle? If every ear of barley has seven corns and every ant carts away seven ears and every bird eats seven ants and every person spots seven birds, how many things are in this puzzle?

The Mesopotamians will also use the math of barleycorns and silver, the math of shekels, to invent loans and interest. And they will make tables calculating just how much I'll owe you on a loan after a day, a week, a month, a year, two years, three years, and more. Right down to the last barleycorn of silver. They will also calculate just what kind of jackpot you could hit if you made a really fabulous loan. The strike-it-rich bonanzas of the loan biz will become such obsessive daydreams that they will seduce ordinary Babylonians into doing fantasy calculations of interest on clay over and over again.

Most important, the Mesopotamians will use math to invent one of the most potent forms of magic humankind has ever seen: science. The Sumerians and the Babylonians will keep records for hundreds of years and examine those records to look for repeating patterns, number patterns, the sort of patterns that show up on grids and tables of numbers, tables of symbols for bricks and barleycorns laid out on hand-sized slabs of clay.[66] They will hunt for patterns in the past from which they can predict patterns in the future, patterns from which they can predict things to come. Priests will keep track of the prices in the market of barley, dates, pepper, cress, sesame, and wool—Mesopotamia's key commodities.[67] They will keep track of the prices of these basic staples in precisely the same order century after century. In some "extreme cases" even tracking prices in the morning, at noon, and at the close of day.[68] They will keep these records in a standard order that makes it possible to look for cycles in three hundred years of records or more.[69] They will keep track of the weather and the rise and fall, the griefs and victories, of kings.

And they will find patterns. They will find what experts on Babylonian math call "zigzag" patterns. What we would call "oscillating patterns." Patterns that go back and forth on a table over and over again. Patterns that jerk from side to side. And after seventeen hundred years of math,[70] they will start something new—keeping detailed records of the movements of the sun, the moon, the planets, and the stars. They will invent libraries and will compile hundreds of years of records of the heavens. Hundreds of years of records written in scratch marks and kept on hand tablets of clay. In the heavens they will find echoes of patterns of the seasons, the patterns of the growth of crops in the farm fields, and the patterns of commodity prices in the marketplace. And they will look for the iteration of those patterns in their centuries of cuneiform records of real-world things. With those patterns, zigzag patterns, they will successfully predict eclipses and the movements of dots of light in the night sky, dots of light that have obsessed us humans since we invented the first lunar calendar and wrote it down using scratch marks on bone in the ice ages thirty-two thousand years ago.[71] The Mesopotamians will find that the positions of stars and planets on the horizon change in recurring patterns as the seasons change and as the years roll by. Patterns that repeat. Patterns that iterate. The Mesopotamians will invent astronomy, market analysis, weather prediction, and a mathematical form of political science based on the stars. Their market predictions, their political predictions, and their math-and-star-based guidance for the personal life of the average Mesopotamian citizen will not quite work out. They will miss the mark in "the real world." But they will fit our emotional needs so precisely that they will remain alive today in the practice of astrology.

And many of the Mesopotamian number-based predictions of the patterns of the heavens *will* work out. The Mesopotamian hunt for mathematical patterns of stars, planets, and the sun and moon will lay the base for our astrosciences. In the distant twenty-first century, we will still consult the Mesopotamians' astronomical tablets, the tablets that record hundreds of years of events in the heavens. And in the end, what does this all come down to? Mere dents in the surface of clay.

But those Mesopotamian dents in clay will offer yet one more clue to the mystery of the God Problem, the mystery of how the cosmos creates. They will prove that there are many ways to get to a common destination. Many ways to find a deep structure, an underlying pattern. Many ways to translate that pattern into new and strange soups, goops, raw matter, symbol sets, and languages. Many ways to see corresponding patterns in everything from stars to mud patted together in a tablet of clay.

THE SORCERY OF CORNERS

Remember, the Babylonians have no word for the right angle and no concept of the angle at all. Yet they will find one of the strangest secrets that the right angle possesses—one of the strangest implicit properties of the corner angle so vital to their architecture. And with that peculiar discovery, they will build yet one more stage on the ziggurat of ideas, one more story on the tower of translations that will lead up the giant staircase to Peano's axioms. They will extract this implicit pattern from the givens of their land measurements, their reeds, their arms, and their Y's and <'s. They will unfold a pattern that's mistakenly named for a Greek—Pythagoras. It's called the pattern of Pythagorean triples. But Pythagorean triples are Mesopotamian through and through. And like multiplication, the powers of these triples are so close to summoning spirits from the ether that it's ridiculous.

Here's the story. The year is 1781 BCE, nearly four thousand years ago. It's close to a thousand years before the founding of Rome, and there's a political catastrophe. Shamshi-Adad, an Assyrian king who has pulled together an empire that holds much of Mesopotamia, Syria, and Asia Minor in its fist, dies. His death is a disaster. To quote historian William James Hamblin, "Six rival kings jockeyed for position, aiding, betraying, and attacking each other in dizzying turnabouts."[72] And it's even messier than it seems. Eight city-states and at least three nomadic tribes are tussling for control. But a clever Babylonian snatches the falling Mesopotamian marbles and takes control of the game. He takes control of twenty-four of the cities of the Land of the Lords of Brightness.[73] He is Hammurabi, ruler of Babylon. And he turns all of Mesopotamia into one of those things that's implicit in the invention of the city, an empire: the Babylonian Empire.

One of Hammurabi's most important technologies is the scratch mark in a hand tablet of clay. But Hammurabi translates that scratch mark to a new medium, stone. Then using the scratch mark on a stone monument or two, Hammurabi standardizes something far more elusive than measurements. He standardizes human behavior. He translates human actions and punishments into units of their own kind. He puts together one of the first written codes of law. And under Hammurabi's laws, Mesopotamian city life flourishes.

One of the things that flourishes is architecture.[74] Another thing that booms is the math that helps architects do their thing. What thing is that? To get a sense of the Babylonian achievement, let's take a sidestep to another people. Yours. The Hebrews. (Remember, you are Jewish for a day.) There are two creation myths in the Bible. In one, God is a wind whuffling over the sea and the open landscape, a god who makes grass as his very first life-form.[75] He is a god of nomadic sheep herders. Nomadic sheep herders like the man Abraham, the father of the Jews. In that first creation myth, God is a wind, a breath, who speaks things into existence. Language is his central technology. Language—a human invention—is the first creation myth's central metaphor. Language is something a nomad constantly moving his tent to a new location, a nomad who has to avoid heavy burdens, can carry with ease. God says four words, "Let there be light,"[76] and there is light. Words have power.

But Abraham was originally a townie, not a wanderer. He was born in roughly 1812 BCE in Ur,[77] a sister city to Babylon. And in the other creation myth of Genesis, God is very much like the owner of a house in a city, a city of the "elohim"—a city of "the gods." God's technology in this second bib-lical myth is based on mud, the source of Babylon's bricks and of its kitchen pottery.[78] Not to mention the source of its writing pads. God has a garden, the Garden of Eden. And he wants a servant to relieve him of caring for the plants himself. What's more, God is cheap. Instead of paying a gardener,[79] he makes a laborer out of the least expensive thing around. "The dust of the ground"[80]—mud. That homemade servant is the first human being. His name comes from the stuff he's made of—Adam, from the word *adamah*, Hebrew for "earth." So another human invention—the technology of pottery and of brickmaking—is the central metaphor of the second creation myth.

Why does the city god of one creation myth in the Hebrew Bible use something Mesopotamian, mud, and in the other use the ultimate por-table technology, the word? The Jews believed that their founding father, Abraham, had left the city life of Ur in roughly 1782 BCE and had become a shepherd, a wanderer. So in one creation myth, God is a "roo-ach," a drifting wind. And in the other, God has a Mesopotamian lifestyle.

Mesopotamians, like the Babylonians, got their basic unit of construction from the innovators of Catalhöyük. They built with brick. Even the Babylonians' three giant rings of defensive walls, walls over thirty-two feet wide (wide enough for a chariot to drive on their tops) and over seven stories high,[81] walls that Nebuchadnezzar himself bragged were "mountain high,"[82] were made of bricks. Hundreds of millions of them. And bricks are a form of iteration. Iteration of a basic rule—pat mud together and put it out to dry in the sun. Iteration? What in the world am I talking about? If you are a Babylonian brickmaker, you will repeat the rule of scooping up mud and patting it into a standardized mud rectangle nineteen inches long hundreds of thousands of times before you die. If you are a Babylonian bricklayer, you will repeat the rules of laying a mud brick hundreds of thousands of times, too. And if you are a Babylonian architect, your job will be to invent new ways to use the old rules of the brickmaker and the bricklayer. Your job will be to invent new ways to use old tools and old techniques. New ways to use what the bricklayers of Catalhöyük began. New ways to use the repetition of the brick to go utterly beyond the two-story Catalhöyük apartment complex creators' dreams. New ways to build walls of height and thickness that defy belief. New ways to build townhouses, temples, towers, hanging gardens, and ziggurats—towering step pyramids up to seven stories high. New ways to erect buildings that threaten the gods by reaching to the skies. New ways to build the way a termite builds. New ways to catch up with the achievements of an insect. New ways to translate old rules—old patterns—into a new medium.

Let's go back to God the city dweller. God who lives in a city of gods, a city of elohim. In the myths of the Bible, God got nervous when the Babylonians built their first skyscraper, their first ziggurat, the Tower of Babel, a building roughly one hundred and sixty feet high—sixteen stories.[83] The book of Genesis gives the impression that God, the homeowner in a city like Babylon, lived in an exclusive community in the sky, a high-class gated neighborhood hovering at the height of your average low-hanging cloud.[84] Height was apparently one of the few things that allowed the gods to lord it over humankind. The Semitic word for a god, "al"—as in "elohim" and "Allah"—is associated with height and the sky. And the Babylonians were about to break the gods' monopoly on altitude. So the Lord got the other gods on his block together and said let's stop those pesky humans before they become as mighty as we are. Why? Because, said God, "now nothing will be restrained from them, which they have imagined to do."[85] So together the mighty ones of heaven—the elohim, the gods—toppled the Babylonians' tower and split men into separate language groups, forcing them to babble incomprehensibly so they would never have the power to unite and threaten the sky giants again.

It didn't work. The Babylonians kept building ziggurats. And translation from one language to another, from one medium to another, remained a tool of genesis, a tool of creation. A tool of creation that made gods obsolete.

***

Translation and repetition of old rules in a new medium, iteration, are tools of genesis, tools of creation? Bloom, come off it. What do you think you are talking about? OK, imagine that you are a Babylonian architect. As an architect, your job is to create buildings so awesome that they will become the subject of myth. Buildings that will make their way into books like the Bible. Your job is to create buildings that will terrify other peoples' gods. Buildings whose fame will echo 155 generations down the line. Buildings so utterly beyond belief that they will make passersby stop in their tracks. Structures so astonishing that they will attract gawkers like the Greek historian Herodotus from 1,220 miles away. Structures that will express the majesty of Babylon. To fashion amazements, you, the architect, will have to extract new implicit meanings from brickwork, new implicit possibilities from the iteration of old rules in brand-new ways.

Your job will be to do what termites do. To create buildings that grab attention. How do you get a termite's attention? With the trick of the gods. With height. When a termite is walking down a corridor in the hive and sees a stray turd littering the floor, she picks it up compulsively, then looks for a nice, neat place to put it. An irresistibly attractive place. What attracts her? Height. Yes, height is a sign of the accumulated attention of others, the accumulated obsession. Height is a sign of popularity. And popularity, believe it or not, is an organizer. Piles compete for the termite's attention.

Which one wins? The tallest. For termites and for humans, height is the trigger of a recruitment strategy.

As an architect, you will be a master of recruitment strategies. A master of what the Bible is talking about when it explains that the Tower of Babel's planners said "let us make us a name" for ourselves.[86] You will be a master of the power of attraction. A master at reshaping old rules in new ways. A master at using iteration to achieve creative breakthroughs. And you will be something more: a master of the big picture. A master of vision. A master of imagination. A master at conceiving the new dreamscraper into which bricks can fit. To take those dreams from fantasy to reality, you will invent new ways of putting together the teamwork of brickmakers, bricklayers, and the bricks themselves. New ways of organizing repetition. New ways of extracting complexities from the implicit possibilities of the rectangle and of numbers. New ways of extracting amazements from mud. New ways to do what your city's astrologers—your fellow masters of height—managed to pull off. You will be a master of new ways to grab the attention not just of your neighbors, but of humans thousands of years down the line.

You will invent new ways to work out the corollaries of an axiom—the brick. You will invent new ways to work out the corollaries of yet another axiom—the magnetism of attention. And in the process, you will give a clue to cosmic creativity.

***

But to startle foreigners, to make strange gods' knees quake, and to awe your own citizens, you will have to make sure that your walls are straight. And you will have to make sure that your walls meet at something you don't have a word for—perfect right angles. Imagine that you are building a ziggurat of the kind that made God nervous. If the corners of your walls do not meet at precise right angles, you are in big trouble. If the angle at which your walls meet is off by even a bit, you will build an unstable structure, a crooked tower. But you don't have the concept of an angle. Any kind of angle. And you don't have a word for a "right angle." What's more, you are over fourteen hundred years away from the notion of ninety degrees.[87] So how do you make sure that you've got your corner angle, your right angle right? You do it with scratch marks in clay. You do it with numbers. Naked numbers. And with the strange patterns that numbers summon forth.

Here's how. Take two bricks. Lay them out at what looks to you like a right angle. So far, so good. But you have a problem. How do you make sure that your corner angle is perfect? How do you make sure that when you extend it fifty reeds to your left and fifty reeds to your right and that when two hundred workers spend two hundred days putting bricks in place, your building won't be crooked?

Here's the trick you've discovered. Extend the lines of the wannabe right angle of bricks at your feet. Make one line of bricks three bricks long. Make the other line four bricks long. Now use a string of gut to measure the diagonal between the farthest tips of your two lines of bricks. And move your lines of bricks until the diagonal is precisely five bricks long. Got that? One line three bricks long, one line four bricks long, and one line five bricks long. Forming a triangle. Now step back and take a look at what you've accomplished. Amazing. The result is a perfect right angle. What's more, you math-obsessed priests and scribes have discovered that this three to four to five relationship holds up for right angles whether you're making a right angle with tiny lines a few fingers long, a right angle with medium lines a few forearms long, or a right angle with massive lines a few hundred reeds or ropes long. But why?

Why are the number relationships of things only a few fingers long just like the number relationships of things a few arms, a few ropes, or a few Babylonian miles long? (A "Babylonian mile" is seven of our miles.[88]) Surely in a random universe of six monkeys at six typewriters such peculiar forms of sympathetic magic should not apply.

No matter what its answer, the fact is that you Babylonians have discovered that this 3:4:5 relationship is just the beginning of a series of magic number relationships that match up with perfect right angles. Even though you don't have a word for right angles. In Columbia University's Plimpton collection is a Babylonian tablet from 1700 BCE. On its face is a table of fifteen numbers,[89] fifteen of what we today call Pythagorean triples. They should really be called Babylonian triples. Pythagoras would not appear on the scene for another 1,130 years. The peculiar trios of numbers are triples like these:

3:4:5
5:12:13
8:15:17

All of these numbers match up with perfect right angles. All of these are products of the implicit properties that emerge when you translate a shape, a right angle, into a radically different medium—scratch marks on clay, numbers. And all of them come from the magic of an implicit property that your mathematicians have teased from two thousand years of number practice and from two thousand years of number play.

But where in the world do such relationships come from? And how in the world have they come to be?

CELEBRITIES IN THE HEAVENS: HOW TO INVENT ASTRONOMY

How do humans create? One answer—we look for patterns. Every once in a while we invent a new pattern-finding tool. We derive it from a hunch, from a deep feel for the way we think it will work. Then we go through a Darwinian process. We try it out a million times to test its "fitness." More accurately, to see if it fits. To see if it fits the real world.

And how do we know whether it fits? We test its power to predict. For example, we test it to see if it helps us build a house, a temple, a palace, or a ziggurat with perfect right-angle corners. If our hunch proves to be on target, why in the world does our wisp of mind stuff and gut instinct work? Perhaps because it taps into an underlying pattern, a deep structure of the cosmos we live in. Perhaps because it repeats that pattern in a whole new way. And perhaps because it reflects one of the ways in which the cosmos herself creates.

To see how, let's look at one more implicit possibility that the Babylonians derived from scratch marks on clay . . . astronomy.

Remember, Bertrand Russell says in his *History of Western Philosophy* that you Babylonians have the notion of a 360-degree circle. But Russell is wrong. So are educational sources like Wonder*Quest*, professional wisemen like the folks who run the Notes and Queries section of the *Guardian*, and writers about Mesopotamian technology like Graham Faiella. How did so many experts get it wrong? Once more with feeling: *the implicit isn't obvious.* Far from it. To the best of our knowledge you Babylonians have no circles[90] measured out in identical units, no curved measuring devices, no protractors or measuring dials. Some texts say that you Babylonians have "astrolabes"—measuring devices that help you find angles on a dial. It's not true. Yes, over a thousand years down the line you will make two clay circles summing up your zodiac. Two round tablets out of hundreds of rectangular tablets of clay concerning the heavens.[91] But even those two circles are cross-hatches, charts, and tables. They are wobbly and crudely drawn. And they are not measuring devices. The fact is that you Babylonians see things in lines. Like the line of the horizon. And like the line on a chart of numbers. But even a line looks different to you than it will to moderns four thousand years down the, bear with me, line. Why?

You have no rulers. No measuring devices marked out in smaller units. Remember, that big copper standard of length called the Nippur Ell has no small precision markings within its big units, its feet, hands, and elbows. So you Babylonians see the sky in terms of a crude line. The line of the horizon. And when you're trying to make sense of the heavenly bodies, you don't bother to look up at the sky. Why? You want to see where the heavenly bodies are when they cross the line of the horizon. But without a precision measuring tool, how will you note where the heavenly bodies rise and fall?

The human brain is a pattern recognition machine. And one key tool in our arsenal of pattern recognition devices is the story. You are a Babylonian priest. How do you make sense of the pinpricks of light in the sky? You view the heavens as a connect-the-dots puzzle. And you see planets and clusters of stars as animals, women, and men. You call constellations "the Viper, the Raging Serpent, the dragon Lakhamu, the Great Lion, the Gruesome Hound, [and] the Scorpion-man."[92] Not to mention the tuft of hair, the bull of heaven, the faithful shepherd of heaven, the charioteer, the scimitar, the great twins, the lion, the goat-fish, the scorpion, and the great swallow.

OK, now you've translated the stars into the patterns you understand the best. Human and animal patterns. What's next? You watch the heavenly bodies' social relationships. You watch carefully to see when two stars, planets, or constellations come together or separate as they rise or fall on the horizon. You also watch to see when stars and planets enter the tiny zone of the horizon where the sun and the moon blip their way into the sky in the morning or where the sun and moon slip from the ceiling of the sky at night. (Yes, the sky is a ceiling and a roof, a flat roof, as flat as a tablet of clay—we'll see why in a minute). You also specify the space between two heavenly bodies in the sky in terms of the constellations within which they rise and fall when they cross the horizon and enter the sky.

Yes, Bertrand Russell and others say, you specify the distance between two stars in the same "house" of a constellation in "degrees." And, yes, you have a love affair with the number 360. It is part of a special system your math moves into when you hit the number sixty. From that point on, you count in multiples of sixty—120, 180, 240, 360, 420, etc. And six sixties is 360. But your degrees are more social than numerical. Why? You never come up with the clincher that makes the measurement of angles possible—the circular precision measuring device marked out in 360 equal units. Instead, you use a pattern recognition tool far more compelling than numbers—you use myth.

Zoom back to 1728 BCE, when Babylon grabbed the whole bag of game pieces and rose to power over all the rest of the thirty-one Mesopotamian city-states. To show they were on top, the Babylonians wanted their god to rule over the gods of all the other cities. They wanted their giant in the heavens to top the pecking order of the sky. The central Babylonian god was Marduk. And up until then Marduk had been a rather insignificant deity. That insignificance had to end. So, in the words of Rupert Gleadow, a mid-twentieth-century sidereal astrologer who wrote a history of something vital in his field, *The Origin of the Zodiac*, the scribes of Babylon engineered a crisis. A sea monsteress arose and threatened creation. That monsteress of bitter waves and of salt water flooding, that monsteress of the tsunami, was Tiamut. So terrifying was Tiamut, says Gleadow, that "even Anu, the original creator, fled before her."[93]

One brave petty god volunteered to do battle with this female

Mesopotamian Godzilla. He was Marduk, the god of the Babylonians. But Marduk wanted something in exchange. If he battled Tiamut and won, he wanted a promotion. He wanted to be counted among the big guys of the sky, the great gods. Marduk did more than challenge and stop the encroaching bitter water monster. He tore Tiamut, the monsteress, in half. And from those two halves "heaven and Earth were made." But Tiamut was not alone. She had eleven other monsters on her team. When these monsters tried to flee in terror, Marduk snagged them in a net and "set the eleven demons in heaven as constellations . . . the Viper, the Raging Serpent, the dragon Lakhamu, the Great Lion, the Gruesome Hound" and more.[94] The monsters of Tiamut were accompanied in the heaven by a ragged handful of other constellations—Tiamut herself, "her husband Kingu, and the constellation Hydra, representing an unfortunate dragon."[95] Eventually eighteen constellations would be whittled down to twelve. The twelve constellations of what the Greeks would later organize in a very different way and would call the zodiac. So when it came to the Babylonians' first attempts to understand the sky, anthropomorphism ruled. The early pattern recognition tool was the story. The myth. Math came next.

Here's the really hard thing to understand. You've heard me say it before, but it bears repeating. The Babylonians would make huge strides in grasping their world with math. But they would do it with lines. The Babylonians did not have what we call geometry. The sphere was not in the tool kit of the Babylonian mind. The circle was not a standard tool of Babylonian math. It seldom if ever appeared in the Babylonian mathematical and astronomical vocabulary. To the Babylonians, the sky was not a circle. It was not a part of a sphere. It was not a hemisphere. It was a roof.

For the tale of that roof, let's return the spotlight to the battle between Marduk, the god of Babylon, and Tiamut, the salt-sea monsteress of chaos. Remember, when Marduk conquers Tiamut, he splits her in half to make heaven and earth. Says the Enûma Eliš, the Babylonian creation myth: "He split her open like a mussel into two (parts); Half of her he set in place and formed the sky (therewith) as a roof."[96] Mussel shells are curved. But the sky Marduk makes from Tiamut's body is apparently not. Marduk erects gates on the east and the west, the gate on the east from which the sun and the moon will later emerge each morning at dawn, and the gate on the west through which the sun and the moon will exit the sky at dusk and blip into the underworld. Then Marduk sets the upper half of Tiamut as a roof between the pillars of these gates. A flat roof. When Marduk wants to make sure his roof of sky will stay in place, he buttresses Tiamut with the sort of structure used in flat-roof architecture. "He fixed the crossbar."[97] And he "made strong the bolt on the left side and on the right."[98] Marduk turns Tiamut into the sort of ceiling that is standard in the most impressive buildings of Babylon. Flat roofs of cedar that are "adorned," as the neo-Babylonian king Nebuchadnezzar put it, on the "under side with gold and precious stones . . . adorned like the stars of the heavens."[99] But in the case of Marduk's ceiling, the stars are for real.

That's why Robert Harry Gent of the University of Utrecht's Institute for History and Foundations of Science, says, "The earliest Ancient Near Eastern views on the cosmos imagined it to be box- or cylinder-shaped."[100] Boxes have a flat top and a flat bottom. So do cylinders. Think of the top and bottom of a can. Perfectly flat. And flatness lends itself perfectly to the primary Babylonian tool for making sense of the world—the flat clay tablet with scratch marks. The result? The Babylonians tried to crack the code of the movements of the sun, the moon, the planets, and the stars using tables. Using the sort of two-dimensional tables you inscribe in clay, the sort of two-dimensional clay tables on which you tally the numbers of chickens and fish that farmers like me bring to you as a sacrifice. The sort of two-dimensional clay tablets on which you scratch multiplication tables.

Yes, you Babylonians feel that you can crack the secrets of the skies by ignoring the black, starry ceiling above your head. You have something more precise to work with: a simple line, the very edge of the sky, the horizon. You call the horizon a "cattle pen."[101] And you keep track of where the sun rises on the outer rim of the roof of sky.[102]

Each day the sun rises in a slightly different place. And each night the sky is different. Why? Roughly once a month a new constellation rises on the horizon. In fact, a new constellation rises in a very significant spot on the horizon—it surrounds the swatch of sky from which the sun will rise roughly twelve hours later. It surrounds the cattle pen of the sun. Here's how it works in the terms we humans understand most easily—in terms of tales of beings like you and me but beings with a few extra privileges—gods.

We normal upper-middle-class Babylonians are lucky if we own one house. But things are different for the super rich. Especially for super-rich rulers. They can have multiple residences. The sun god, Shamash, is richer than super rich. He has twelve houses. And each of his houses comes complete with a throne.[103] These twelve houses are the twelve key constellations. A new one of these constellations appears on the horizon just before sunrise each month. It bumps and budges from the same vicinity in the cattle pen of the eastern sky's edge from which the sun will emerge at dawn. And each constellation provides Shamash the sun god with a different house. Which means that each month at sunrise, Shamash, the god of the sun, steps from his throne in a different one of his palaces. He emerges from the house provided for him by a different constellation. His guards, the Scorpion, the Mad Dog, and the Bison Man (all of whom are star clusters—constellations) open his palace door.[104] His charioteer waits for him outside. He mounts the chariot carrying his tool—a pruning saw, a saw for pruning date trees.[105] A "directing god,"[106] a messenger, a scout briefs Shamash and his driver on the path for the day and on any obstacles they face, then opens the bolt of the doors of heaven. And Shamash the sun god crosses the boundary of the cattle pen outside his house, exits from the horizon, and sets forth on his straight-line passage across the flat roof of the sky. Your sky and mine.

That's the mythic element of the Babylonian explanation system. That's how the Babylonians applied the tool of storytelling. And the story is a key instrument of sense making and of pattern finding. The story is a key tool with which to pull implicit patterns from the chaos of the real world.

But there was more. The Babylonians turned the sky into a tic-tac-toe–like cross-hatch of lines, a chart. A timekeeping chart, the kind of timekeeping chart we still use today, a calendar. They did it by using the twelve "houses" of Shamash, the twelve palatial residences of the sun. Remember, every month another constellation appears at dusk on the line of the horizon from which the sun will emerge in the morning. Every month another constellation takes possession of that key line of the eastern sky from which roughly twelve hours later the sun will push forth like a bull bolting from the gate of a pen or like a chariot charging from a gate. The Babylonians coupled these shifts in the constellations with changes in the phases of the moon. And they used those changes of the moon to cut their year into twelve parts—twelve moon-ths, twelve *mon*ths. What's more, the Babylonians invented what the Greeks would call the "circle of little animals,"[107] the zodiac. But their zodiac was very different from ours.

To the Babylonians, the zodiac was not an animal zoo. And it was not a circle. Why? Again, circles and spheres scarcely existed in the Babylonian mind. They were not structures of Babylonian pattern recognition. What mattered to the Babylonians was the same sort of pattern-imposition device that periodically pulled the cities of Mesopotamia into an empire—the question of who rules over whom. The question of how the dominant power assigns places to those who've been subordinated. The sort of question best sussed out with story, with mythology.

The Babylonians called the zodiac "Shupuk shame," "the piling up of heaven."[108] To them, the relationship between the constellations and the line of the horizon was originally a mess. It took a god to set it straight. And how did that god make order out of the sky's chaotic piles? By establishing a social pecking order. A pecking order you could represent on the grid of a clay tablet. Said one Babylonian inscription, "When the order of the world was threatened by hostile powers, the sun, moon, and Venus were set by Bel to rule over the Shupuk shame,"[109] to rule over "the piling up of heaven," to rule over the celestial sloth.

Who was Bel? And how did he get into this? Bel was one of the names of Enlil,[110] Lord of the Air, "god of Earth, wind and spirit."[111] Yes, it's confusing, but hang in with me. To the Babylonians it looked as if the sun, the moon, and the constellations all rose from the spot on the horizon dominated by one mountain on the east. It looked as if the sun, the moon, and the constellations literally came from this mountain and entered the sky. Bel was the god of this "Great Mountain." He was the god of the mountain in the east from which the sun rose. Which means that Bel was "the sacred mountain on which the gods are born."[112]

But giving birth to the gods in the sky wasn't enough for Bel. He was also the "God of the lands."[113] A god who presumably laid out the territories of city-states and nations, a god who presumably laid out the boundaries of those territories as if they were farm plots. A god like the priests who used the straight lines of their measuring reeds. And Bel was presumably a god who used right angles, not circles. How do we know? Bel, an inscription from the Mesopotamian ruler Sargon tells us, "sets the foundation of all things."[114] And the foundations of a Babylonian building start with a right angle. But forget right angles. Remember, the Babylonians used them but didn't have a word for them. In fact, as you'll recall, the Babylonians had no angles at all.[115] Everything that mattered to a Babylonian was a rectangle. A rectangle like a farm field . . . or like a tablet of clay.

So "when the order of the world was threatened by hostile powers," how did Bel "set . . . the sun, moon, and Venus . . . to rule over the Shupuk shame?" How do you make mathematical sense out of a social hierarchy? If you are a Babylonian, you do the same thing you've done to predict the market prices of barley, dates, pepper, cress, sesame, and wool.[116] You get out your moist iPhone®-shaped hand-tablet of clay and draw a table.

Making sense of the heavens with a grid, a table.
Reprinted from Alfred Jeremias, The Old Testament in the Light of the Ancient East, *vol. 1 (London: Williams and Northgate, 1911), p. 11.*

On a boundary stone from 1300 BCE you can see the Babylonian cross-hatched table format blown up big time. Across the top are divisions for the sun, the moon, and Venus,[117] the heavenly bodies that rule over the twelve constellations of the zodiac, just like Bel ordered them to. Which means the sun, the moon, and Venus cut the stone into three vertical columns. Below the sun, moon, and Venus are the animals they rule. And each animal symbolizes a constellation.

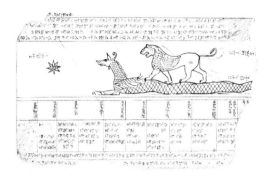

Even this Old Babylonian prayer to the Gods of Night from 200 BCE is laid out as a grid—a table—with columns for ten stars and constellations. *From Robert Harry van Gent, Webpages on the History of Astronomy, http://www.staff .science.uu.nl/~gent0113/ (accessed December 29, 2011), originally published in Alfred Jeremias,* Handbuch der altorientalischen Geisteskultur *(Leipzig: JC Hinrichs, 1913).*

This is where math and mythology cross paths. What did the Babylonians find using their clay charts and tables? Ways to figure out the time of night. Ways to predict eclipses of the moon. Ways to predict the month, the day of the month, and the part of the moon that would be eclipsed. Plus the direction from which the shadow eclipsing the moon would strike, and "whether the moon rises while already eclipsed or sets while still eclipsed."[118] Why was this relevant? Because you could use these observations to read the forces of history. You could use them to predict the sorts of ups and downs the king would need to take into account to make his decisions for the day, the month, and the year. You could use your charts of the sun, moon, planets, and stars to give your ruler a heads up on the sorts of cyclical patterns that Shakespeare would someday characterize with a metaphor of another chartable pattern that links heaven and earth, another chartable up-and-down that couples the moon and the sea: "There is a tide in the affairs of men."

Here's the sort of advice that the Babylonian priests derived from the horizon crossings of the heavenly bodies and that these clerics passed on to the king in the days from 1595 to 648 BCE.[119]

> If the moon becomes visible on the first day: reliable speech; the land will be happy.
>
> If the day reaches its normal length: a reign of long days.
>
> If the moon at its appearance wears a crown: the king will reach the highest rank.[120]

But that's not all. Even farm animals—the wealth[121] of the Babylonians—got into the picture.

> the cattle of [Akkad] will lie in
> the steppe undisturbed. If the moon and Sun are in opposition:
> the king of the land will widen his understanding.[122]

The priest who figured all this out by reading his charts of the horizon signed his predictions

> From!
> RaSil the elder, servant of the king.[123]

WHAT'S THE ANGLE? BLINDNESS IN BABYLON

All of this was an act of translation from one medium to another. From sky to clay to mind. It was an attempt to interpret recurring regularities, an attempt to uncover iterative rules and deep structures of the sky, using the pattern-recognition tool of anthropomorphism. We don't know if any of its human predictions came true. But there was a spinoff in another realm. In the realm of math.

The Babylonian priests who worked century after century to ferret out the patterns of the sky found something we've already mentioned. They discovered what those who study Mesopotamian clay tablets on astronomy and astrology call "zigzag" patterns.[124] Without circles the Babylonians discovered something we only see in terms of circular things—cycles. Cycle, as you know, is a word that comes from the circle. But, as you and I also know, circles did not exist in the math and mind of Babylon. The Babylonians understood their zigs and zags as number series. Number series that reach a boundary then reverse, reach another boundary, then reverse again. Like reaching the boundary of a farm field with your plow and reversing direction or like reaching the left-hand edge of a path, then continuing to plod ahead but reversing your cross-wise wobble and zagging ever so slowly to the path's other side. With only lines and numbers, the Babylonians discovered a primal pattern, the wobble between opposites, the wobble between extremes. They discovered the oscillating pattern of a sun that budges from the bullpen of the sky a bit farther to the north each day of spring, then reverses direction and pushes its way into the ceiling of the heavens a bit more to the south each day of the fall. They discovered the oscillating pattern of the monthly changes of the moon, which starts as a sliver-thin crescent of silver, then fills out to a round disc and narrows to a sliver again.

And they discovered the oscillating relationship between two different kinds of years. One year—the lunar year—was determined by the oscillating patterns of the moon, moon changes you can use to carve time into twelve months, twenty-eight to thirty days per month,[125] and a year of 354 to 355 days.[126] The other strangely different year—the solar year—was determined by the oscillating patterns of the sun, a zigzag that carves the year into roughly 365 days, 5 hours, and 48 minutes. What's more, the Babylonians found a cycle of 18.03 years that brings the wobbling years of the sun and of the moon back together again.[127] They discovered an 18.03-year cycle that can help you figure out when to toss an extra month into your calendar to bring your moon-based calendar and your sun-based calendar back into sync. In other words, they discovered an 18.03-year cycle that can help you correct your calendar when a spring month, a planting month like Nissanu, the first month of the Babylonian year, threatens to wander into the harvest season of the fall.

The Mesopotamians did what you did in math class when you extracted implicit properties from the 165 words of Peano's axioms. You worked out the corollaries. You worked out the hidden potential in a set of simple rules. So did the Mesopotamians. They invented the hat, then pulled rabbits from it. The Mesopotamians—the Sumerians, the Assyrians, and the Babylonians— genuinely pulled new order, new patterns, new realities, from the nothingness of implicit order. Or, to put it differently, the Babylonians invented tools this universe had never seen before then tested them against the threats and opportunities, the perils and the pleasures, of reality. And in the process, the Mesopotamians became a part of the process with which the cosmos creates.

***

Lurking in the wings or hovering over the heads of the Babylonians was a flock of implicit properties they simply didn't see. Properties they didn't recognize because they lacked the tools that would have made those properties clear—the ruler and the circle marked in 360 units, or the sort of semicircle we use today to translate angles into numbers—the protractor. They lacked the sort of numbered dial, the full 360-degree circle, or the 180-degree half circle we use in things like speedometers. Just around the corner was the sort of implicit property that a simple 360-degree dial would have helped the Babylonians invent, think up, yank from the realm of possibility, pull from possibility space, or corollary-extract. But the Babylonians never saw it.

What *did* they have? One more device I haven't mentioned. Their water clocks. But those clocks would have seemed very strange to you and me. They had no dials. No measuring circles. Instead, they translated time into, hang on to your socks, bricks. A Babylonian water clock was a jar with carefully calibrated markings on the inside and a hole in the bottom.[128] You measured time by the weight of the water that had run from the hole. What unit did you use for your measurements? The "mina."[129] You measured time in units of, of all things, weight. Weight—the heft you can feel in your hands, arms, and shoulders when you pick up something. The sort of thing you'd been measuring for centuries in the market with a scale and with standard weights. The sort of thing you used to measure groceries. And you could convert the unit of weight you measured time with, the mina, to, of all things, the weight of bricks. Yes, if you wanted to, you could translate the time that hangs heavy on your hands into sun-dried blocks of mud.

Talk about translation from one medium to another.

***

The Babylonians left us a day divided into hours and a counting system from which we've derived our sixty-second minute, our sixty-minute hour, and our twenty-four-hour day—all a gift of their charts, their water clocks, and their obsession with multiples of sixty. But how did the Babylonians get so far with so little? How did they find so much of what we now know without the tools we have today? Why can you translate the patterns of nature into so many different symbol systems and so many different substances? Why can you translate from a vast expanse of land to scratches on a cell-phone–sized piece of clay? Why can you translate distance and silver into barleycorns? Why do the numbers you invented to count chickens, fish, sacrifices, swaps, and trades give you the 18.03-year patterns of the sun, the moon, and the dots of light that move across the sky? Why do a Y, a <, and the width of a finger equal the stuff you can hog in a cylindrical storing "log"? Why do they also translate to the number of bricks you need to build a ziggurat? Why do numbers apply to ants, rats, birds, cats, and stars? Why can scratches on clay tablets help the king's bureaucrats calculate how many barley loads will fit into a public granary, how many bricks they will need to build the city walls, how many workers they will need to put those bricks in place, how much bread and beer they'll need to feed that crew, and how much copper they'll need to give a brick city wall hi-tech shielding?[130]

And why in Ishtar's name can wispy mind stuff, the whorl in what William James would someday call the bubbling, babbling "stream" of thought and feeling, grasp the patterns of a real world? Why does the sympathetic magic of the mind and its tools, from clay and reeds to supercomputers, so often work? Why do central metaphors work? Why does math work? There is a giant equal sign at the core of our logic. But why?

***

And one postscript: What new ideas and tools do you and I have to invent so that kids a hundred years down the line can take them for granted as hard and fast realities?

WHY KNOT? THE EGYPTIAN ROPE TRICK

What are axioms? And what do they mean to the God Problem? The next step in the answer to that question would come from a people eight hundred miles to Babylon's southwest. The people who would unfold the next implications from the simple rules of Mesopotamian math were the Egyptians. And their contribution would be based on a tiny advance with mighty consequences. The Egyptians would invent the first precision tool of measurement. The first tool of measurement marked off in smaller units. The first ruler. The Babylonians had long ago used ropes to measure distances of twenty reeds. But the new Egyptian tool would be a rope that was marked off. Marked off in twelve cubits—marked off in twelve forearms. Marked off with twelve knots.

How did Egypt come to be? Through a massive act of reperceiving what's under your nose. Through seeing the potential for riches in a disaster. From 8500 to 5300 BCE[131] the Sahara desert was green and lush. On its eastern edge was a long and skinny valley. A valley watered by the longest river in the world. Overwatered. A valley in a land of rain. A valley swamped and flooded. Not a good place to live. Those who tried it didn't last long. They died a violent death at the hands of their neighbors. Archaeologists who've found the graves where the damaged bones of these victims of murder and conflict lie believe the mayhem in the Nile valley was caused by battles "for land and food"[132] in the hideous conditions of a water-overdosed land.

Then, in 5300 BCE, the monsoon rains pulled back and the lush and leafy green of the Sahara desert turned to brown. A parched, ferociously hot and sandy brown with dunes a hundred miles long and temperatures that rocketed up to 120 degrees.[133] The retreat of the monsoons that dried out the Sahara also dried the river valley.[134] And humans rushed into that valley from the newly parched desert. But the Nile River valley had a problem. For over half of the year it was dry as a bone. Then the Nile spilled over its banks, and the valley was flooded. Flooded not just for a week or two, but inundated by what would become known as "the flood of a hundred days."[135] Inundated year after year, from June until September.[136] That's when, in roughly 5200 BCE, the shapers of an innovative culture turned the curse of the Nile's flooding into a blessing. How? They built their villages on elevated lands, lands the surging waters normally did not reach. They ensured the immunity of their homes to the floodwaters by building mud dikes. Then they sat back and let the Nile do its worst.

In that worst was a bonanza. When it flooded and pulled back again, the Nile deposited a new coat of soil on the land. It deposited the rich earth it had picked up on its four thousand–mile journey from its source. And it carried away the toxic salts that could destroy the land's fertility. When the waters returned to their banks, the dry desert air cracked the mud open and aerated the soil. That's when the inhabitants planted seed for barley and wheat in the cracks riddling the rich new coat of earth. The people who worked out this scheme for disaster taming and catastrophe riding were the Egyptians. And every year when the flood came, the Egyptian farmers retreated to their villages on high ground and made way for the overflowing waters again. But predicting the Nile's flooding was crucial to this scheme. So, like the Babylonians, the Egyptians needed calendars. And like the Babylonians, they needed land surveyors. Why? Because in the Nile's flood, the boundary markers of their fields were washed away.[137]

That's where the knotted measuring rope came in to the picture. After the annual flooding of the Nile subsided, the government sent out "rope stretchers," harpedonapts.[138] Their job? To take out their clubs, to pound stakes into the corners of your land, and to use their knotted ropes to measure the length and breadth of your property. The rope stretchers helped you figure out where your neighbor's property ended and where yours began. In the process, they measured the size of your land, its area. Why? To calculate your taxes. To figure out what payments you owed to the pharaoh. How very much like Mesopotamia.

At the center of the knot counter's work were right angles—the right angles at the corner of your property. Right angles and the hidden properties—the implicit properties—of a knotted rope twelve units long. For there was a magic in the twelve-knot rope. An unexpected property. A property exceedingly close to sorcery. Like the Babylonians, the Egyptians discovered that if you tug and pull at the simple rules of a right-angle tri-angle—just three straight lines and one perfect right angle—you can milk the udder of number. And they discovered that the emergent properties, the corollaries, the implicit patterns that you can pull from a twelve-unit knotted rope are astonishing.

The most astonishing corollary the rope stretchers put to work every day was an implicit property that they extracted using a tool they shared with the Babylonians. That tool? The magic number series the Babylonians had discovered—the radically misnamed Pythagorean triples. In particular, the number series 3, 4, 5.

To see how they did it, put yourself in the knot counter's place. It's 2580 BCE. Pharaoh Khufu and his vizier Hemon have just put their faith in you to lay out the lines of a perfect right-angle foundation for a new pyramid at Giza. It's going to be the biggest ever—forty-eight modern stories tall. Two hundred and eighty arm-lengths high, two hundred and eighty Egyptian cubits. The height of roughly one hundred peasants' huts piled on top of each other.[139] The height of nearly seven ziggurats. The success or failure of a twenty-year-long building project will depend on the precision of your work. You will be respon-sible for the triumph or collapse of a building process that will require over 2.3 million blocks of stone. Yes, million. Blocks of stone whose smallest will be two and a half tons and whose biggest will max out at thirteen tons. You will be responsible for the success or failure of a building process that will involve more than eight thousand workers living in huge government barracks and villages.[140] Villages that some researchers believe included "bakers, butchers, brewers, granaries, houses, cemeteries, and probably even some sorts of health-care facilities."[141] Villages to which unemployed peasants with free time on their hands during the hundred days of the Nile's flooding may have willingly come to do their bit to perpetuate "the glory of Egypt," to quote a speculation from a team of archaeologists underwritten by National Geographic.[142]

If you're going to build a pyramid that pleases Khufu, your life is on the line. Your right angle is going to have to be exact. Crooked pyramids won't stand the rigors of time. They won't win you Khufu's praise. And they won't keep you safe from the vizier's punishments.

As the pharaoh Sneferu's architects will discover just forty years down the line, a pyramid whose angles have been miscalculated[143] will rapidly start cracking up.[144] What's more, crooked pyramids like the "Bent Pyramid" that Sneferu's minions built will not pull off the termite trick. They will not snag admiration for thousands of years to come. They will not retain their majesty. They will not make enemies tremble. They will not awe your pharaoh's allies. They will not punch past the bounds of the impossible. They will not express the key characteristic that makes humans thrill: an awesome height. So how do you make sure that the right angle at your first corner is exact? How do you get the angle of the pyramid's first corner absolutely 100 percent perfect? Without the concept of an angle. You turn your twelve-cubit-long knotted rope into a right-angle triangle. How?

Stick with me here. This is easy to show with animation but hard to get across with words. Club one of your pegs into the ground at the point where you want your pyramid's walls to meet. Now stretch your twelve-knot rope out straight in the direction you want your first wall to go. Use the rope to measure out a line three knots long. Hammer in a second peg at that three-knot point. Go back to the point where you want your walls to meet. Do your best to approximate a right angle. Measure out another line where you want your second wall to be. Make this one four knots long. Pound another of your harpedonapt stakes into the ground at the four-knot length. You now have three pegs in the earth, one at your corner, one three knots away from your corner, and one four knots away from your corner. Are you with me so far?

Now comes the heart and soul of the trick. The technique with which you translate numbers into a shape. The trick with which you transform a linear series—a straight knotted rope—into a form. Anchor the end of your rope to one of your stakes. Now stretch your rope to loop around the two other stakes. Loosely. If you've done your job well, you now have your rope stretched out in a triangular shape. One leg is three knots long. The other leg is four knots long. And the catty corner rope, the rope across the diagonal at the gaping mouth of the right angle, is roughly five.

Now for the pièce de résistance. The part that makes you as clever as Isis.[145] Leave your corner stake in place. But adjust your other two stakes until your measuring rope is as taught as the strings of a ben,[146] an Egyptian harp.[147] Make sure the stakes land perfectly on the three, four, and five points of your rope. Congratulations. You've just completed a triangle. A triangle with a perfect right angle at its corner. It's that Babylonian discovery called a 3:4:5 triangle. A Babylonian discovery that helps translate numbers into a shape. Three plus four plus five equals guess what? Twelve.

But this is jarringly peculiar. How does a twelve-unit-long, perfectly straight, and easily coilable knotted rope bear within its length the secret of a right-angle triangle? A perfect right-angle triangle? A right angle so reliable you can base a pyramid on it?

The Egyptian twelve-knot rope and its magic: it makes a right angle. *Courtesy of the late Bryan Dye, http://www.mathsnet.net.*

How does a twelve-unit line bear hidden within it, implicit within it, the certified, guaranteed right-angle[148] first corner for the Great Pyramid at Giza, a pyramid that will be the world's tallest building for the next thirty-eight hundred years?

Thanks in part to your perfect right angle, your handiwork at Giza will be admired by humans for thousands of years to come. But there's another audience to please. The gods. And to keep them happy you have to build temples. When it comes to temple building, you, the harpedonapt, the rope-stretcher, will have to go further than mere lines and angles. You will have to make sure that your angles are laid out pointing north[149] by using astronomical landmarks like the seven-star constellation called the Thigh of the Ox, Meshtiu.[150] And guess how you will do it? You will use the secrets of knotted ropes to synchronize your architecture with the heavens. Laying out your perfect right angle for the temple's corner and aligning it with the stars is so important that when you do it, you, the rope stretcher, will be the focus of all eyes in a religious ceremony called "stretching the cord."[151]

Rope counting, surveying, turning a patch of land into numbers then translating those numbers into a fraction of a peasant's grain or into the straight line of a temple wall that links the heavens and the earth, all of this is so crucial that the pharaoh sometimes appears in Egyptian art carrying the club that you, the harpedonapt, use to hammer in the stakes that make right angles and that measure fields of mud. Says the goddess Sesheta to Pharaoh Seti I in an inscription on the Temple of Abydos, a temple that Seti rebuilt in roughly 1445 BCE, eight hundred years before Greece's mathematical thinkers would enter the scene,

> The hammering club in my hand was of gold. I struck the peg with it. Thou wast with me in thy capacity of Harpedonapt. Thy hand held the spade during the fixing of the temple's four corners with accuracy by the four supports of heaven.[152]

The technology that turned land into numbers had been crucially important to the Babylonians. So important that even the gods of the Babylonians carried surveying tools. In the Babylonian case, the creator god, the moon god, and the battle goddess Inanna all carried "the rod and the ring."[153] What were the rod and the ring? A measuring rod two reeds long. And a loop, a ring, of rope. A measuring rope. A rope twenty reeds long. But the Egyptian gods had a big advantage over the Babylonian gods. Twelve Egyptian gods were called gods of the measuring rope, "those who hold the cord."[154] But their ropes were knotted.

***

Egypt's measuring knots drive home a message: the message of the termites, the message of modularity. The message of building things from simple components. The message of building by repeating simple rules. The message of repetition. The message that three thousand years down the line would be known as iteration.

HOW TO HYPNOTIZE A GREEK:
MATH AS A TOURIST ATTRACTION

How intensely did the Egyptians build on the art of rope stretching, piling together complex things from simple units, and hunting for number patterns, for deep structures? How obsessively did the Egyptians pursue the arts that would lead to axioms? In roughly 1800 BCE, over thirteen hundred years before the writing of the Bible, the Egyptians issued one of their first books of practical mathematical problems and solutions. It was the Rhind Mathematical Papyrus, "written during . . . the 12th dynasty [the reign of] King Amenemhet III (ca. 1844–1797 BCE)."[155] The copy now in the British Museum was made by a scribe named Ahmose.[156] For centuries other scribes would continue cranking out new copies of the Rhind Papyrus.[157]And other Egyptian writers would produce yet more books of arithmetic: the Moscow Mathematical Papyrus, the Kahun Mathematical Fragments, the Berlin Papyrus, the Mathematical Leather Roll (now in the British Museum), and the Reisner Papyrus.[158] These were papyrus rolls riddled with real-life arithmetic problems. They were texts bulging with a Babylonian invention, tables. Tables to speed the calculations of down-to-earth specialists like "the accountant, surveyor, tax assessor, builder, baker, brewer," barn builder,[159] and architect.[160]

One papyrus roll written four thousand years ago claimed to be a work "for acquiring the knowledge of all obscure matters." It claimed to be a document revealing the invisible patterns of the real world. But the mysteries it probed were remarkably down to earth. Its chapters promised things like a "rule for estimating a round barn" and a "rule for computing fields."[161]

The Egyptians had another practical use for numbers. They loved keeping track of the things they owned. Like Mesopotamia's priest-scribes, they wanted to count "possessions, products . . . and prisoners."[162] So they became obsessed with clever ways you could use numbers to calculate imagined possessions, possessions of your daydreams—cutting things in half, doubling them, multiplying them by ten, "multiplying fractions by each other, finding unknowns, computing the areas and volumes of figures, [and] calculating the slopes of triangles." The Egyptians were solving the sort of problems that today are solved by algebra.[163] Thorny, complex problems. But they were doing it without algebra. They were doing it with methods that accomplish the same thing by different means. Which leads back to the problem of translation. Why can radically different systems accomplish the same ends?

Like the Babylonians, the ancient Egyptians worked out ways to calculate the volume of everyday storage vessels, round containers, cylindrical containers, and rectangular containers. The kinds of storage vessels merchants used. And the kind of oversized storage vessel a pharaoh would someday use to help him in the underworld—the building with a square base and a triangular peak, the pyramid. But the Egyptians went further. They invented ways to mathematically transform one shape into another, using lines to answer questions about curves[164]—an approach that would eventually result in the calculus of Newton and Leibniz. They also invented the idea of a proof[165]—going backward from the answer to prove that it solves the problem you started with. An idea that would soon be vital to the evolution of guess what? The axiom.

Meanwhile, Egyptian math was so intricate and powerful that Democritus, the Greek philosopher who came up with the notion of the atom, bragged that he had spent five years with the rope-stretching harpedonapts, learning their practices. Five years implies a lot of knowledge. A lot of knowledge in what Democritus calls "the construction of lines with demonstration."[166] A lot of knowledge in the roots of what would soon be called "geometry."

But Democritus was not the only Greek thinker fascinated by the mathematical mysteries of the harpedonapts. In roughly 552 BCE, over twelve hundred years after the Egyptians wrote their first compendium of arithmetic problems and solutions, Pythagoras also took a trip to Egypt to learn the secrets of the harpedonapts. When he got back to Greece, he unfolded yet another implicit property, another secret that was hidden implicitly in the right-angle triangle. And the implicit property that Pythagoras unfolded from the realm of the invisible, from the dark landscape of possibility space, would forever change the course of Western thought. Including your thought and mine.

***

Who was Pythagoras? One of Pythagoras's modern biographers, Christoph Riedwig, asserts that if you and I were to meet Pythagoras, we might not regard him as a legitimate thinker.[167] In fact, we'd see him as a madman with exhibitionist tendencies. Why? Pythagoras's way of presenting himself smacked not of reason, but of show business. He was tall, charming, and strange. His robe was a startling white. And unlike your everyday Greek man of intellect, under his robes he wore an outrageous violation of the fashion of the day—a contribution to couture from the horse-riding barbarian warriors of the steppes to the northeast, the Scythians. Trousers.

Pythagoras crowned himself with a halo—he wore a gold wreath on his head. And he spread wild tales about himself. He leaked the rumor that he had a "golden thigh," a claim you could not check because those Scythian trousers rendered his legs unavailable for inspection. A golden thigh was the sort of thing reserved for the earthly children of gods—men whose fathers were gods and whose mothers were mortals. Pythagoras also claimed that he had gone to the ends of the earth and had met a mythical people called the Hyperboreans. When he'd spoken with the priest of the Hyperboreans, Pythagoras had proclaimed himself "the Hyperborean Apollo"—the Hyperborean sun god. Pythagoras implied that the priest had believed him. There was only one problem. There were no Hyperboreans. Pythagoras was building himself up by telling tall tales.

What's more, Pythagoras's followers claimed he could produce miracles. A bear was ravaging the neighborhood of Daunia, mauling the people it passed on its way to the garbage heaps. It was said that Pythagoras went out to confront it, grabbed it, petted it, fed it "barley and fruits," and made it promise to calm down and "never again to touch a living creature."[168] The bear apparently made good on his promise.

Beans were sacred to Pythagoras. Beans, he said, had been born from mud at the same time as man.[169] (Yes, that Mesopotamian mud fetish again.) Pythagoras would not allow his followers to swallow a single legume. But word had it that one day in Tarentum, Pythagoras spotted an ox browsing on beans and asked the herdsman to get the ox to eat something a little bit less holy. The cattle herder apparently thought this peculiarly dressed man was crazy and made fun of him. So Pythagoras, dressed in white with his halo on his head, went over to the ox, whispered in its ear, and the ox never nibbled a bean again.[170]

What's more, it was said that Pythagoras had appeared in two towns simultaneously, two towns separated by a body of water. How did he pull off this violation of the laws of nature? He was able to scoot between the two towns by walking on water, quick-stepping across the H_2O between the two hamlets.[171] This was five hundred years before the same claim was made for Jesus. Who spread these wild stories? There's a good chance that they came directly from Pythagoras himself. All of this smacks of hype, not philosophy. And certainly not science. Yet Bertrand Russell in his *History of Western Philosophy* says about Pythagoras, "I do not know of any other man who has been as influential as he was in the sphere of thought."[172]

Why? Pythagoras grew up in the Greek island city of Samos, a city, like most Greek cities, on the sea: the North Aegean Sea. He was a precocious child. When he was ten years old, he gave speeches on philosophy. And many of the wisest elders of Samos showed up to listen. What's more, they treated him with "honor" and "reverence."[173] Then, when Pythagoras was eighteen[174] years old, Samos indulged in a nearly universal human sport, war.[175] War meant rowing the oars of a war galley, a long, thin craft designed to ram and sink other galleys. And rowing did not appeal to Pythagoras. Nor did being killed in combat. So he fled. It was the beginning of thirty-eight years of travel—and of data gathering.

Many think that Pythagoras's first trip was across the Aegean Sea to a Greek trading city perched on the edge of Persian territory, Miletus. The eighteen-year-old Pythagoras, legend says, wanted to meet a celebrity of the day. A celebrity of thought. Thales of Miletus. Why did Pythagoras make a pilgrimage to Thales the first stop on his trip? Why did he use Thales as the entry point for nearly half a century of travel and of soaking up foreign ideas? What was so compelling about Thales?

Remember, there are millions of ideas floated by the sea of human beings. Trillions. And only a few stick. To get ideas to last, you have to build a termite column, a ziggurat, a monument that will have attentional magnetism. One way to do it? The name game. Piling up associations with those who already have fame. And Thales was famous. So famous that it was said that the lawgiver of Sparta, Lycurgus,[176] had visited him when Lycurgus was trying to come up with a way to reorganize his hometown. That's heady fame—visits from not just a head of state, but from a new state maker. Another reason Thales was on Pythagoras's trip map? Pythagoras wanted his ideas to stick. So he had to build upon the tallest column in sight. And in the world of the mind, Thales was that column.

But when it came to math and mysteries, who were the most famous thinkers of all? They were the ones who advertised their powers with another version of the termite trick—the ones who promoted themselves with pyramids. The ones who showed off the heights to which they could go. Literally. The Egyptians. Thales had gone to Egypt to study the mathematical mysteries of the rope stretchers and of the priests who used the rope stretchers' mathematical legacy. In fact, Thales had picked up the Egyptian elements of solving practical problems with shapes and numbers, but had transformed what he'd received. He'd translated the math concepts of the Egyptians in a way that would alter them utterly. Thales had stopped thinking about triangles, pyramids, and cylinders in terms of clay tablets, knotted ropes, and slabs of stone. He had stopped using numbers to find the size of farming plots and to count the grain in a sack[177] or in a silo.[178] Instead, he'd turned the Egyptians' down-to-earth mathematical ideas into abstractions.

In the process, Thales had created a new field in which the mind could roam and play. A new field in which the mind could use the Babylonian and Egyptian legacy in whole new ways. Thales had created geometry.[179]

But that's not all. Thales had also given us a new way to explain things. The Babylonians and the Egyptians had accounted for unexpected events in two ways—

with math and correlations, with science;

and by looking for anthropomorphic patterns and blaming the battles of the gods.

Thales dismissed the gods from the realm of explanation and concentrated on god-less patterns. Patterns you could grasp by pondering Egyptian math.

Patterns you could grab hold of by applying that math to the realm of perfect shapes—shapes that existed in a virtual world, a world of imagination, in the realm of abstraction. Shapes that existed in the airy realm of reason. And Thales had given this new way of explaining things a name: philosophy.[180] In other words, Thales had found the tallest column around, added to it, then claimed it as his own.

Now Pythagoras was out to take over that column. And he would pull it off. But in the process Pythagoras would build on Thales's base in ways that would permanently expand the tool kit of Western thought. In 536 BCE, after his stopover in Miletus to see Thales, Pythagoras took off for Egypt to study firsthand the secrets of the rope stretchers.[181] He headed for Egypt to tap the wisdom of twenty-five hundred years of Egyptian arithmetic. And twenty-five hundred years of fame. In his travels, he also is said to have visited Mesopotamia,[182] the first home of numbers and of mathematical tables in clay. And it's said that Pythagoras also visited the Persian Empire[183] and India.[184] In India, too, there was a hidden harvest of new mathematical ideas.

After more than a third of a century of travel and of idea absorption, Pythagoras headed back north and returned to his island home of Samos. With nearly four decades of exotic knowledge under his belt, he expected a hefty welcome. And he got it. He established a school of public affairs. And, says Iamblichus, scholars flocked from all over the Greek world—a world that extended from Spain to the Ukraine—to learn from him. But Pythagoras was *too* popular. Says Iamblichus, "His fellow-citizens insisted on employing him in all their embassies, and compelling him to take part in the administration of public affairs." Politics and international relations were not Pythagoras's goal in life. Not at all. Pythagoras wanted to think. Says Iamblichus, Pythagoras "fashioned a cave, adapted to the practices of his philosophy, in which he spent the greater part of day and night, ever busied with scientific research, and meditating."[185] In that cave, says Iamblichus, Pythagoras pulled together all he had learned and "unfolded a complete science of the celestial orbs, founding it on arithmetical and geometrical demonstrations."[186] Pythagoras put his jumble of mathematical ideas from Egypt, from Mesopotamia, and possibly from India, into coherent form. Into the sort of form that would suit a master builder of his own fame and celebrity. Into a big picture. Into a religion. A religion of math. A religion whose motto would be, "Number is the essence of things. Everything is Number."[187] And advancing that philosophy, that secular religion, was Pythagoras's aim.

SEDUCE 'EM WITH NUMBERS:
HOW TO DO A PYTHAGORAS

With a fully developed big picture, a fully developed worldview based on numbers under his belt, Pythagoras traveled 713 miles west to Italy, and settled in the Greek colony of Magna Græcia in the city of Croton. In 530 BCE, Pythagoras began to recruit followers.[188] Followers so anxious to be with him that they went through five painful years of initiation rites to be close to him.[189] If you wanted to become an acolyte, you had to go through five years without talking. Not a word. And you had to demonstrate utter submission. Utter submission to Pythagoras.

Was there a valid idea at the heart of this egomania? Something worth pondering for a thousand years or two? Yes. And it was a concept that would shape the thoughts of every major Western thinker from Plato to Peano. Not to mention Bertrand Russell. Through Peano, it would reach out even to you at Reed College in 1961. Here's how one of those influenced by the ideas at the heart of Pythagoras's cult building put it. That man whose thinking was sculpted by Pythagorean ideas was Aristotle, arguably the greatest Western philosopher of all time. Said Aristotle, the Pythagoreans

> maintained that Number was the beginning of things, the cause of their material existence.[190]

Want to know how the universe began? Look to numbers. Want to know how the universe creates new things? The answer, again, is in numbers. Want to know why things are shifting and changing around you at this very moment? It's all numbers.

What a peculiar distortion of sanity. What strange drugs had Pythagoras been taking?

But there's more. Let's turn over the microphone once again to Aristotle.

The elements of Number are odd and even. The odd is finite, the even infinite. Unity, the one, partakes of both these, and is both odd and even. All Number is derived from the one.

Pythagoras said that you can do a Peano. You can extract an entire universe from just two things, from odd and even, from one and two. Not to mention an entire number system. Actually, according to Pythagoras you can extract an entire cosmos from just the number one. In his view, a primal unity—a one—differentiates. It buds. It splits into two. Into two opposites. And those two opposites spawn a system that goes all the way to the infinite. To Pythagoras numbers *are* the cosmos. Numbers are you and me. Aristotle explains the Pythagorean beliefs like this:

The heavens, as we said before, are composed of numbers. . . . The finite, the infinite, and the one, they [the Pythagoreans] maintained to be not separate existences, such as are fire, water, etc.; but the abstract infinite and the abstract one are respectively the substance of the things of which they are predicated, and hence, too, Number is the substance of all things.[191]

Reality is a mask. It is a cover-up. Like the rubber human face on a cyborg. Behind it is another reality. A more profound reality. A reality of simple rules. A reality of ideal shapes and ratios. Shapes and ratios that determine every event and every visible thing around us. But for Pythagoras, the real hidden driver, shaper, and creator is number. Number creates a something from a nothing. It is "the beginning of things." Number generates the mystery of opposites joined at the hip—the unity of the odd and the even, the wedding of the finite and the infinite. Number is behind the movement of the heavens. Why? Because the heavens are literally made of numbers. Yes, says Aristotle, to the Pythagoreans "the heavens . . . are composed of numbers."[192] Number is the raw stuff of everything from sandals to salamanders.

Think about it. The idea that "Number is the substance of all things" is stranger than at first it looks. There is a surface appearance and a deeper reality. An "abstract" reality. That reality is hooked, hauled to the surface, and made visible by the sort of scratch mark on clay that the Babylonians invented to count chickens, fish, land, and barleycorns. It is captured and made visible by the strange and inexplicable relationships those scratch marks generate—relationships like the triples generated by the sides of right-angle triangles. It is captured and made visible by relationships that allow you to use a knotted rope twelve forearms long to make a perfect right angle, a perfect corner for a temple or a pyramid. It is hauled from invisibility to the surface by relationships like the number cycles that predict the return of the stars and the planets in the skies to their previous positions. It is hauled from a hidden realm by relationships like the number cycles behind a miracle device for predicting seasonal changes—that chart, that grid we still use—the calendar.

Three thousand five hundred years before Pythagoras, in the days before math, it had been a huge stretch to imagine that markings used to count loads of grain and to tally offerings of chickens and fish could also apply to sizing up plots of land, to measuring fields, and to building foundations, walls, and ceilings. It had been a ridiculous leap to claim that the numbers tracking sacrifices, swaps, and trades could also apply to shapes. And it had seemed positively absurd to claim that the numbers designed to count chickens, fish, barley, and sheep could predict the movements of the sun, the moon, and the stars, the movements of the heavens.

But Pythagoras took these absurd stretches past the point of impossibility. He claimed that all of the visible world is a manifestation of an invisible world, an unseen world of the sort captured by Mesopotamian markings on clay or by squiggles of ink on an Egyptian papyrus. And he implied that the qualities seized by those scratches and squiggles were more real than the reality that you and I see before our eyes. What led Pythagoras to this strange conclusion? Two things. An invisible reality, an implicit order that Pythagoras pulled from the right-angle triangle. And a bizarre relationship that Pythagoras discovered hidden in music.

***

Music? Remember, numbers began as simple ways to keep track of things like the fish you offered as a sacrifice to the priests at your temple in Sumer. And fish are things you can see. Things you can touch. Things you can catch in a net and slap down on a Mesopotamian kitchen table or hand over to a priest. But music is a nothing. You can't see it, touch it, pile it up, carry it around in a bag, or hand it over to a priest. While you or some expert friend sing it and strum it on your seven-stringed kithara,[193] it hovers in the air. But then it disappears. It shifts your moods, cheering you or saddening you. But in a sense, it scarcely exists. So how did Pythagoras manage to find math hidden in music's invisible folds? How did he find one immaterial pattern, the pattern of number, in yet another immaterial pattern, the pattern of rhythm and melody? How did he pull an implicit property from something as unseeable and as insubstantial as implicit order itself? And why in the world should such a pattern even exist?

Iamblichus is one of the leading ancient biographers of Pythagoras. He wrote in the fourth century BCE, eight hundred years after Pythagoras's death.[194] Iamblichus's account is said to include some highly questionable components, but it gets across the general idea. According to Iamblichus, Pythagoras was ambling down a street, probably in Croton. The philosopher with the halo and the trousers was deep in thought, pondering how instruments like the compass, the straight edge, and surveyors' tools had added precision to the powers of sight and how the scale and standard weights had turned something we feel with our sense of touch into numbers.

How, thought Pythagoras, could you use numbers and measuring tools to find the underlying patterns of the things we hear? Or, as Iamblichus put it, Pythagoras "was intently considering music, and reasoning with himself whether it would be possible to devise some instrumental assistance to the sense of hearing so as to systematize it, as sight is made precise by the compass, rule, and telescope, or touch is made reckonable by balance and measures."[195] Pythagoras was pondering a basic problem of translation. A problem of translation from one medium to another.

As he pondered, Pythagoras passed the shop of a metalworker, a blacksmith. The sound of the craftsman hammering out his sheets of iron on the anvil caught Pythagoras's ear. Says Iamblichus, all the "sounds . . . harmonized, except one." Music was extremely important in the Greece of Pythagoras's day. Greek intellectuals were obsessed with it. Eventually, says Eli Maor, music would rank in importance with math and astronomy in the

Greek educational system. But that was in the future. Pythagoras was one of those who put music on its intellectual pedestal.[196] The point? Pythagoras had what we'd call an educated ear. A very educated ear. Iamblichus says that "he recognized in these sounds the concord of the octave, the fifth, and the fourth." He heard musical harmonies.

Pythagoras was curious about what, precisely, had generated this harmony in the smithy's shop. He rushed in and apparently persuaded the blacksmith to help him figure out what had produced the musical notes and their delicious concordance. The two looked over the shape, the size, and the position of the iron sheets on the anvil. They tried out a variety of hammer blows and ruled out everything but the weight and heft, the "magnitude . . . the weights and the swing of the hammers." Aha. Weight. This was something you could measure. This was something you could express in numbers.

So Pythagoras rushed home and set up an experimental apparatus. Says Iamblichus, he hammered a stake into his wall. From the stake he hung four strings of gut, four strings that were as close as possible to identical, strings of identical strength and identical length. Pythagoras attached a measuring weight to the bottom of each string. Then Pythagoras "struck" the strings two at a time. When he hit the string from which a six-pound weight dangled and the string from which a twelve-pound weight hung, he got an octave. He got a higher and lower version of the same note. Like playing two different C's at the same time on the piano. Like playing one C eight notes higher than the other. Bingo. A six-pound weight and a twelve-pound weight. Six and twelve. This was a number relationship. The sound of the same two notes at different places on the musical scale, one high and one low, came from a ratio, a doubling, a relationship of one to two, $6:12 = 1:2$.

Pythagoras then hammered at the string from which his eight-pound weight hung and simultaneously whacked the string from which his twelve-pound weight dangled. He got the strange harmony known as a fifth. What does the ratio of twelve to eight boil down to? $8:12 = 2:3$. So a 2:3 relationship of weights also produces a musical sound. Then Pythagoras struck his twelve-pound cord and the cord from which his nine-pound measuring weight hung. He got another sound pleasing to the ear. Another sound that appeared in the music of his time and still appears in ours. He got the chord known as a fourth. And once again, what happens if you do a bit of arithmetic with the numbers of the weights involved in the harmony of a fourth? Is there a relationship between twelve and nine that can be reduced to another primal fraction, to a ratio? $12:9 = 4:3$. Yup, another simple ratio.

So ratio equals harmony. Ratio equals beauty. Ratio equals music. And what is ratio? The relationship between numbers. Conclusion? Numbers equal cords. Numbers equal beauty. Numbers equal whatever in the human spirit is roused by music. Music equals something deep in your emotional structure and mine. To put it in terms of $A = A$, math = emotion = numbers. So math and emotion operate on the basis of some sort of shared deep structures. Deep structures that we are literally tuned into. A very strange conclusion.

But according to Iamblichus, Pythagoras took things a step further. He attached his strings to a musical instrument he called "a string stretcher." Explains Iamblichus, "by the aid of pegs he produced a tension of the strings analogous to that effected by the weights." What did Pythagoras get? A musical instrument with just one string. An instrument called a monochord.

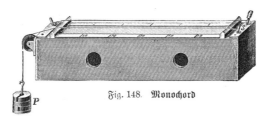

Fig. 148. Monochord

Pythagoras's one-stringed musical instrument, the monochord. *Courtesy of Wikimedia Commons, from* Bibliothek allgemeinen und praktischen Wissens für Militäranwärter Band III *(Berlin: Deutsches Verlaghaus Bong & Co., 1905).*

And what are the pegs of a stringed instrument? Tension makers that ape the impact of Pythagoras's weights. Number = music = weight = tension. What an amazing chain of radically different A's that equal each other.

But Pythagoras went even further. He showed that

music = numbers = harmony = beauty = emotions = hammers = weights = strings.

He even showed that a blacksmith's blows equal musical notes and that mechanical pegs stretching a monochord's string equal weights dangling from a wall. How in the world do such equalities exist? How do such weird permutations of Aristotle's law of identity occur? How do things that do not by any stretch of the imagination equal each other echo each other anyway?

But this was not enough for Pythagoras. According to Iamblichus, he "extended the experiment to other instruments, namely, the striking of pans, to pipes and to monochords [and] triangles." And what did Pythagoras discover? Implicit properties. Iteration. Translation. Repetition of the same thing in a new medium. Number. Ratio. "He found the same ratio of numbers to obtain." As Iamblichus puts it, "He discovered the harmonic progression." And what is the harmonic progression? "A certain physical necessity," to quote Iamblichus. A pattern so stubborn that it makes its own rules and asserts them with absolute authority. A pattern like the 3:4:5 rope trick that makes right angles. A pattern that materializes as if by magic. A pattern that is hidden but waiting to be found. A pattern that is invisible until 175 generations of thinkers taking wild stabs in the dark finally find it lurking like a trout beneath a rock in a stream. A pattern that is invisible until a human or a cluster of humans invents the right mind tool with which to fish it out. An implicit pattern. An implicit property.

Pythagoras had cracked the code of music with number. He'd found what seemed to be a deep structure. But was it?

From there Pythagoras went on to build an elaborate musical theory. He named some sounds "tonic," others "dominant" or "subdominant." He played with octaves, "tetrachords," "pentachords," "octochords," semitones, tones, and pitches and "filled up the middle spaces with . . . sounds in diatonic order." He "progressed to the chromatic and enharmonic orders." Concludes Iamblichus, "This is the way in which music was said to have been discovered by Pythagoras." But that was by no means the end of Pythagoras's deep dive into the math of music. Iamblichus says that "having reduced it to a system, he delivered it to his disciples as being subservient to everything that is most beautiful."[197]

And Iamblichus does mean everything. Having spotted a deep structure in music, a number structure, a chicken-fish-sheep-and-scratch-mark
structure, Pythagoras hunted for that same structure in everything above and
everything below. He looked for the rules of musical harmony in the hearts,
souls, moods, and bodies of humans like you and me. He made number the
base for a new system of nutrition, medicine, and psychotherapy. But that was
just the beginning. To show just how high these deep structures of harmony
went, Pythagoras took a giant leap of generalization. He climbed to the very
heavens. He claimed to prove that the ratios of music and number made sense
of the mysteries of the heavens. He claimed that the patterns ruling music also
govern the sky. How in Hecate's name did Pythagoras pull this off?

The record is fuzzy, and it takes a bit of guesswork, but the answer
involves a simple but crucial step beyond the astronomy of the Babylonians
and the Egyptians. It involves a shape that the Babylonians never tackled.[198]
A shape that the Egyptians may have toyed with but never explored with
intensity.[199] That shape is a sphere. And the sphere would provide a radical
upgrade to the tool kit of humanity, a radical upgrade to the tool kit of ideas.

***

Why is the introduction of a sphere so shocking? Because, again, to the
Babylonians and the Egyptians the sky was flat. You already know the story of
how Marduk defeated Tiamut, the monsteress of the salt sea, by tearing her
in half, then turning her top half into a flat roof. The Egyptians also saw the
sky as a flat roof over their heads. Or as the flat belly and chest of a sky goddess
arching over the earth like a dog or like a female marine doing push-ups with
her feet on one horizon and her hands on the other. So where did the idea that
the sky was the visible portion of a sphere come from? Where did the idea
come from that the sun, the moon, the planets, and the stars all have their own
individual spheres, their own transparent globes in the sky? How did the notion
that the earth is surrounded by concentric spheres, perfect spheres, arise?

Well, it's obvious, you might say. The ancient Babylonians, Egyptians,
and Greeks were surrounded by spherical things—apples, oranges, grapes,
eggs, the sun, and the moon. But the obvious is never as obvious as it seems.

Unfolding an implication takes an act of extraordinary invention. A creative act. An act of radical reperception. An act that follows the second rule of science: look at things right under your nose as if you've never seen them before, then proceed from there. The source of the sphere was not the Egyptians. The old Egyptian papyruses contain at least one problem that scholars think may refer to a spherical shape. The Egyptians referred to it as an "egg" and a "basket."[200] But the best translations are irritably vague. And it's not what you and I have in mind when the word sphere crops up. It's not a globe, a glass ball, a Christmas ornament, or a fishbowl. None of these things existed in the ancient Egyptian world. What's worse, if all of these man-made things *had* existed, the Egyptians and Babylonians still might have missed the central feature that we think holds globes, Christmas tree ornaments, oranges, grapes, and the sun together. They might easily have missed the fact that if you anchored a string at the center of a sphere, a string that reached from the center to any point at all in the sphere's shell, that string would precisely reach every other point in the shell. In other words, every point on the surface of a sphere is an equal distance from the center.

The idea of the sphere had not yet been conceived. And without ideas, we are often blind. We do not see.

***

Which leads back to a question. How did the invention of the sphere arise? And how did we manage to picture spheres in the heavens? Spheres in the skies? Step one was the perception of the sky as a circle. From the time of Homer in roughly 800 BCE to Thales in 600 BCE, the Greeks saw the world as what Jamie James in his book *The Music of the Spheres: Music, Science, and the Natural Order of the Universe* calls "a round island floating on the cosmic ocean."[201] Roundness counts. Why? Because the Egyptians and the Babylonians did not have the modern mathematical concept of the circle, despite the fact that they invented a math that could handle the contents of round containers.[202]

Then came the Greek philosopher Anaximander who invented something new, space.[203] Who was Anaximander? A citizen of Miletus born in 610 BCE, forty years before Pythagoras. He was a student of a youngster who was fourteen years younger than he was. He was a student of Thales. A student of the man Pythagoras sought out as the very first destination of his travels. By the time Pythagoras hit Miletus to visit Thales, Anaximander was an old man of sixty and still on the learning track. But Anaximander had introduced a new twist that Thales never tried. He was the first philosopher to write up his ideas. According to Themistius, Anaximander was "first of the known Greeks to publish a written document on nature."[204]

And how did Anaximander see nature? What tools of thought, what images, what metaphors, did he use? Remember, the Egyptians had used round things with straight sides to hold up the roofs of their temples. Those round things with straight sides were columns. Our ideas often come from reperceiving things right under our noses. So for Anaximander, the earth was the round, flat top of a column "floating in air."[205] Actually, it was more like the top of an enormous hockey puck. For Anaximander, the earth was two dimensional. And the column on which it rode was squat and fat; it was three times as wide as it was high. This sort of flat earth was popular among Greece's great thinkers. Says Plutarch, when it comes to describing this world, "Anaximenes [says] that it hath the shape of a table. Leucippus, of a drum. Democritus, that it is like a quoit [a round, flat game piece with a hole in the middle] in its surface, and hollow in the middle."[206]

OK, so the earth is a round, flat thing. And at first glance it looks as if Anaximander's metaphors for the sky might be flat as well. But no. Says Plutarch, Anaximander latched on to the circle, the wheel, and an object used in plumbing and in music—the pipe. As Plutarch tells it, "Anaximander says, that the Sun is a circle eight and twenty times bigger than the Earth." OK, the sun is twenty-eight times the size of Earth. An astonishing leap. But more important, the sun is a circle. Plutarch gives more of Anaximander's views. The sun, he says, "has a circumference which very much resembles that of a chariot-wheel, which is hollow and full of fire; the fire of which appears to us through its mouth, as by a hole in a pipe."[207] Adds English philosopher Alan Musgrave, "For Anaximander the planetary spheres became rotating wheels filled with fire, and the Sun, moon and planets merely holes in the wheels through which the fire shines out."[208] If Plutarch and Musgrave are right, Anaximander used three metaphors: the circle, the wheel, and the pipe. All things whose circles are flat—including the circles at the two ends of a pipe.

Anaximander's rotating wheels in the sky are a good start. They are a very useful new metaphor. They carry oodles of implicit mathematical properties. They provide a new way to understand the strange motions of the stars and planets. But they are not the really big jump in metaphor. They are not spheres.

Plutarch believes that Thales, Anaximander's teacher, kicked off the ultimate breakthrough. "Thales," he writes, says the earth is "globular."[209] Aha, a globe. At last. But that's just the earth. What about the sky? Plutarch thinks that's where Anaximander came in once again. Anaximander, says Plutarch, declared that the stars and planets "are moved by those circles and spheres on which they are placed."[210] Yes, that magic word, that magic image, that magic metaphor, the sphere. What's more, Diogenes Laertius credits Anaximander with making a model of his new system of the heavens. Building it, crafting it, or paying a metalworker to put it together for him. What was this strange device, this model of the heavens? A σφαίρα. A ball.[211] The sort of ball that Greeks used in games. The sort of padded iron ball that Greek boxers used to superpower their punches. The sort of shape you see when you're making war and gouging out eyeballs. What other translations are there for σφαίρα? A sphere, a globe. Jackpot.

Back to the fact that metaphor often comes from reperceiving what's under your nose. And what's under your nose is frequently a man-made thing. What's under your nose is frequently a gift of technology. Here's the trick. Balls were not under the noses of the Babylonians and the Egyptians. The Babylonians do not appear to have had ball games. At best, they kicked around stones. The Egyptians did play ball games during the festival of Osiris—a November holiday that took place after the Nile's floods had receded, after the rope stretchers had reestablished the boundaries of your land, a holiday that took place when the time had come for you to plant your seed in the rich, cracked mud that the floods had left behind.[212] But ball games were a very minor part of Egyptian life. Why?

As a Babylonian or Egyptian of middle rank, you had to work for a living. But the Greeks used slaves to do their manual labor. So their lives were daily celebrations of leisure. And ball games became a focal activity in Greek cities like Athens. Ball games with small balls you could toss. Ball games with bigger balls you could kick and bounce. In fact, one funerary vase in the National Museum of Athens features a naked Greek athlete showing off to a little boy by balancing a soccer-sized ball on his knee.[213] Another shows an athletic coach in Greek robes teaching the fine points of a tossing game to two naked boys, two young athletes. In this game, the catcher rides piggyback on the shoulders of his mate and has to snag the ball while maintaining a precarious balance.

But, again, the obvious is far less obvious than you and I think. It can take a long time to turn what's right under your nose into a metaphor. The wheel had been around for roughly two thousand years before Anaximander applied it to the heavens.[214] And the pipe—a flute with holes—was an instrument that had been in use for more than thirty-two thousand years.[215] It took a long time to upload these gizmos, the flute and the wheel, from the real world into the world of the mind. Into the world of metaphor. It takes a tremendous leap of insight, an inventive leap, to turn the everyday into a tool of thought. You can live with something like the sphere and not "see" it for thousands of years. The Greeks were the first to reinvent the game ball as a geometric object. They were the first to come up with the *idea* of the sphere. They were the first to add the sphere to the tool kit of the mind.

What's more, Anaximander introduced the idea that the circles of the heavens were measurable . . . and that they were huge. Reports Plutarch, "Anaximander says, that the Sun itself in greatness is equal to the Earth, but that the circle from whence it receives its respiration and in which it is moved is seven and twenty times larger than the Earth."[216] But much as Anaximander may have introduced space and the sphere to our view of the heavens, he was not as modern as you and I might think. Plutarch says this: "Anaximander concluded that the stars were heavenly Deities."[217] Back to anthropomorphism. Back to myth.

Where does the sphere enter the God Problem? Thanks to his walk past the metalworker's shop and his experiments with weighted gut strings, in roughly 520 BCE Pythagoras had figured out that the relationship between musical notes was mathematical. And he'd figured out that musical relationships are based on ratios. So this ephemeral mover of the heart, this invisible force called music, could be translated to number. Music was number come alive. And number, concluded Pythagoras, was everything. To prove it, he set out to prove that number is the secret of the heavens. And not just any number. The number sequence that made music harmonious. What a horse-choking stretch. What a hard-to-swallow leap of translation. What a jaw-hanging act of equation. How did Pythagoras pull this off? With the metaphor of the sphere developed by Thales and Anaximander.

There is no existing account of where Pythagoras was when this music-and-cosmos brainstorm clobbered him. Or of what set it off. But Pliny the Elder hints that by the time of Pythagoras's musical revelation, the spherical notion had taken off. The flat sky of the Babylonians and the Egyptians had been banished. What had replaced it? The idea that the sun was on one sphere and the moon on another. The idea that each of the five planets—planets then known by the names Phainon (Saturn), Phaethon (Jupiter), Pyroeis (Mars), Stilbon (Mercury), and Phosphorus (Venus)[218]—were on individual spheres of their own. The idea that the fixed stars were on an outer shell, an outer sphere.

There has been a debate about whether the Pythagoreans believed that these shells rotated around the earth or the sun.[219] But the big question in Pythagoras's day seems to have been just how far away each of these shells, these spheres, was from the earth. Says Pliny,

> Many persons have attempted to discover the distance of the stars from the Earth, and they have published as the result, that the Sun is nine-teen times as far from the moon, as the moon herself is from the Earth. Pythagoras, who was a man of a very sagacious mind, computed the distance from the Earth to the moon to be 126,000 furlongs, that from her to the Sun is double this distance, and that it is three times this distance to the twelve signs [the twelve constellations of the zodiac].[220]

Pythagoras claimed there was a peculiar property to these distances. They followed the ratios, the number intervals, of music. How? To quote Pliny the Elder,

> Pythagoras, employing the terms that are used in music, sometimes names the distance between the Earth and the Moon a tone; from her to Mercury

he supposes to be half this space, and about the same from him to Venus. From her to the Sun is a tone and a half; from the Sun to Mars is a tone, the same as from the Earth to the Moon; from him there is half a tone to Jupiter, from Jupiter to Saturn also half a tone, and thence a tone and a half to the zodiac [the fixed stars].[221]

The spheres of the heavens were spaced out like the frets of notes on a one-stringed guitar, or like the fingering for notes on Pythagoras's monochord. How Pythagoras proved this proposition, we do not know. But Pliny says that Pythagoras was not content to find the ratios of musical notes in the heavens. He saw the whole musical system that he'd worked out with gut strings repeating itself in the skies.

Hence there are seven tones, which he terms the diapason harmony, meaning the whole compass of the notes. In this, Saturn is said to move in the Doric time, Jupiter in the Phrygian, and so forth of the rest.[222]

Yikes. Pythagoras saw and heard even the standard Doric and Phrygian time signature of Greece's ancient music in the skies. Pliny calls Pythagoras's system "the harmony of the stars."[223] We know it as the music of the spheres. And the inventor of the concept was Pythagoras.

***

In fact, Pythagoras saw the numbers behind music as the hidden pattern behind far, far more than just heavenly bodies. He felt that number relationships were so deeply embedded in the world on high and in the world below that numbers were the secret to everything, every stone, plant, animal, and human being. Everything you and I see around us, Pythagoras felt, was a translation of basic number ratios into a new medium. Philolaus says that Pythagoras believed that even "the soul is introduced and associated with the body by number." Number knit your soul into your body when you were born. Number holds your body and soul together. And, says Philolaus, to Pythagoras the number relationship that weaves your body and your soul together is musical. It is "a harmony simultaneously immortal and incorporeal."[224]

Number was also behind every social relationship. It was behind community itself. Why? Even the stars have sociality. Even the heavens have community. Look at the number one. Says the third-century-BCE Greek biographer of Pythagoras, Porphyry, one is more than a tally for counting a single chicken or a lone barleycorn. Far more. One is "unity, Identity, Equality, the purpose of friendship, sympathy, and conservation of the Universe."[225] The force of the number one is literally what keeps the cosmos together. It is "persistence in Sameness." How does one pull this off? "Unity in the details harmonizes all the parts of a whole."[226] And more. The number one echoes the creative force that got this cosmos up and running in the very beginning. The harmonies of one echo "the participation of the First Cause."[227]

Then there's two. Two is the great separator. The great competition creator. "The principle of dichotomy."[228] The principle of change. One holds things together and keeps their identities solid. Two tears things apart and makes them grow, morph, and fade. So where does three come in? Three tosses time into the picture. It gives things an envelope of birth, maturity, and decay. Three is "a beginning, a middle, and an end."[229] And four, says Jamie James, is the number of points it takes to create something that puts math on a fast track beyond the imaginings of the Babylonians and the Egyptians. Four is the number of points needed to create a pyramid. What's new about a pyramid? The Egyptians had been building them for twenty-five hundred years by the time Pythagoras came along. The newness wasn't the pyramid itself. It's where Pythagoras chose to build his pyramid. He didn't spend twenty years feeding eight thousand workers barley and brewing them beer so they could build a pyramid in the desert. He built his pyramids in his imagination, in his mind. Big deal. A real pyramid is worth far more than one that's nothing but a fairy tale. A fantasy. Or is it?

Again, Pythagoras uploaded the pyramid to the land of abstraction. He beamed it up to a territory he seems to have invented. The territory of what Plato would later call "the archetypes." A territory that the Greeks would argue counts far more than a mere pyramid of stone. It is hard to build an absolutely perfect pyramid in reality. But it is easy to build a perfect pyramid in fantasy. It is easy to measure out its properties with numbers and to conclude that it is something new—a "perfect solid."[230] It is easy to use perfect solids and perfect forms to invent the massive leap that would carry us toward Peano's axioms—geometry. Or is it really as easy as it seems?

Pythagoras summed all of this up in what became known as the tetractys.

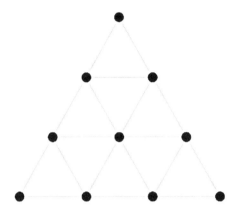

Pythagoras's tetractys. *Courtesy of Jossifresco, Wikimedia Commons.*

One is the start of all things. One is infinite. All begins in unity. Two kicks off the separation into entities and identities. Three puts time into play. And three gives birth to four, the beginning of the world of the perfect mathematical forms. Add them up, and they come to the perfect number, ten. Ten, the number of the "bodies revolving in the heavens"—five planets plus the sun, the moon, the sphere of the fixed stars, topped off with an anti-earth that the Pythagoreans tossed in when the "visible" bodies in the sky only turned out to be nine.[231] Yes, the Pythagoreans cheated to make their numbers fit their theory.

But look at the shape that these numbers make—a pyramid. To get into Pythagoras's cult, you had to swear an oath. An oath of loyalty to Pythagoras. And an oath of loyalty to Pythagoras's big picture. An oath to his picture of a harmony within your body and a harmony within groups that connected with the harmonies of the heavens and the earth. That connected with music. The oath went like this: "I swear by the discoverer of the tetractys, which is the spring of all our wisdom, the perennial fount and root of nature."[232] And the tetractys was all about number.

Pythagoras took the numbers that the Babylonians and the Egyptians attached to grain, fields, sacrifices, architecture, and puzzles about mice and birds to a new dimension. He made the number one a subject of contemplation even if that one was not one anything—it was not one sheep, one goat, one finger, one toe, one brick, one reed, or one rope.[233] Pythagoras translated number into the land of metaphor. Pure metaphor.

And if it was so easy, why had no one done it until Pythagoras came along?

***

Number was it, the core, the essence, and the origin. Number was the deep structure to beat all deep structures. If you understood number, you could accomplish miracles. Reports Iamblichus, Pythagoras said that with number he could "remedy ... human manners and passions."[234] Pythagoras also claimed that he could cure mental illness by restoring "the pristine harmony of the faculties of the soul."[235] And Pythagoras applied number even to medicine. Using ratios, number, and music, Pythagoras "devised medicines calculated to repress and cure the diseases of both bodies and souls."[236] To Pythagoras, healthcare was a matter of bringing "the hot and the cold, the moist and the dry" into harmony.[237] Yes, harmony. As in musical harmony. And as in the harmony of the spheres. Medicine was, in the words of *The Pythagorean Sourcebook and Library* editors David Fideler and Kenneth Sylvan Guthrie, "the perfect harmony of the elements comprising the body."[238] Like music, art, and architecture, health was based on "symmetry."[239] Or, as a young Pythagorean put it when Pythagoras was old and had been preaching his doctrine of numbers for nearly twenty years, health was "the harmonious mixture of the qualities."[240] Health was music! And health was numbers!

Magna Græcia, the part of Italy in which Pythagoras headquartered his cult, was known for its medical school, a fact that may have given Pythagoras's healthcare concepts extra credibility. But one way or the other, says historian of philosophy Robert Sherrick Brumbaugh, Pythagorean medicine stuck around. It had punch, power, and influence. It had status. And status is another word for "height." "Pythagorean ideas combined with older notions to create the Italian-Sicilian medical theory, which was the main Greek rival to the more empirical Hippocratic medicine."[241] Pythagorean medicine was the main competitor to the medicine of the Greek physician and father of medicine Hippocrates, the man who gave us the oath that every modern doctor swears allegiance to, the Hippocratic oath. A smashing triumph for healing by numbers. For healing by math.

To top it all off, the harmonies of numbers and of the spheres were responsible for human creativity. Says Iamblichus, "Pythagoras affirmed that the Nine Muses were constituted by the sounds made by the seven planets, the sphere of the fixed stars, and that which is opposed to our Earth, called the 'counter-earth.'"[242] (It's back to the anti-Earth that Pythagoras had tossed into his system to cheat and get the number ten.)

But you can get across your brilliant insights only if you can remember them. And Pythagoras connected even memory to number and to the heavenly harmonies. Over to Iamblichus's account of Pythagoras's life once again: Pythagoras "called Mnemosyne, or Memory, the composition, symphony and connexion"[243] of all the heavenly bodies, of all the muses, of all the number ratios, and of all the cosmic harmonies crying out to be expressed by human minds.

Pythagoras used his doctrine of number, ratio, and harmony to do one more thing—to rule. Remember, it took a three-year waiting time and five years of self-denial and absolute silence[244] to become an acolyte in Pythagoras's cult, the cult that Pythagoras ruled with an iron fist. Pythagoras used number as the key to a cult of personality and as the key to a totalitarian power. He was tall and handsome. And he had a powerful mind. So he claimed that when it came to the music of the spheres, only he could hear it. In fact, the celestial bodies had taken him into their confidence, they had shared their secrets with him. They had "assimilated" him.[245] And they had done this with no other. Why? Because of the overwhelming hunger of his mind to understand them and because of his utter willingness to imitate the spheres and to obey their lessons. Because he alone had followed an obsession for over forty years. An obsession with numbers. An obsession with the math of the Babylonians and the Egyptians. An obsession with using that math in new ways. And more. Because "his body alone had been well enough conformed thereto by the divinity who had given birth to him."[246] Iamblichus implies that only Pythagoras had a body whose proportions shared the mathematical beauty, the mathematical perfection, the mathematical ratios of music and of the heavens.

The result was a bit peculiar. Peculiar and strangely totalitarian. Pythagoras filled the lives of his acolytes with strictly programmed music. Music he himself performed and sang. Says Iamblichus with a sense of astonishment,

> Here is also, by Zeus, something which deserves to be mentioned above all: namely, that for his disciples he arranged and adjusted what might be called "preparations" and "touchings," divinely contriving mingling of certain diatonic, chromatic, and enharmonic melodies, through which he easily switched and circulated the passions of the soul in a contrary direction, whenever they had accumulated recently, irrationally, or clandestinely—such as sorrow, rage, pity, over-emulation, fear, manifold desires, angers, appetites, pride, collapse or spasms. Each of these he corrected by the rule of virtue, attempering them through appropriate melodies, as through some salutary medicine.[247]

Something far more than the music of Pythagoras's lyre and voice was going on here, says Iamblichus.

> Not through instruments or physical voice-organs did Pythagoras effect this; but by the employment of a certain indescribable divinity, difficult of apprehension, through which he extended his powers of hearing, fixing his intellect on the sublime symphonies of the world, he alone apparently hearing and grasping the universal harmony and consonance of the spheres, and the stars that are moved through them, producing a melody fuller and more intense than anything effected by mortal sounds.[248]

Pythagoras reached the depths of his followers' bodies and souls because he heard the voices of the deep structures of the cosmos. Pythagoras could feel the harmonies of implicit properties in his intellect, his body, and his bones. He could hear the siren call of deep structures aching to be sung, spoken, translated, and expressed.

One result: Pythagoras's cult took off all over the Italian peninsula. It was a cult based on the idea that ethics could be determined by ratio. A cult based on the idea of purifying the soul, then bringing it in line with the harmony of the universe. Pythagoras, says Robert Sherrick Brumbaugh, favored "small communities, in which property was held in common, women given equal opportunities and education, and interest in music and mathematics shared as part of the regular social life."[249] By the time Pythagoras died in 495 BCE, at least eight Italian cities had gone over to the Pythagorean system of rule.[250] A system of rule based on number ratios and harmonies. Like any cult or new system of belief, from Christianity to Mormonism and the Reverend Sun Myung Moon's Unification Church, the Pythagoreans were resented. Those who thought they had no right to exist burned down the house of Milo, the house in which the followers of Pythagoras met.[251] Their goal? To rid Italy of its Pythagorean rulers.

But Pythagoras left a mass of believers, believers who would influence the thinking of the West for the next twenty-five hundred years. Plato adopted and upgraded Pythagoras's idea that perfect forms underlie an imperfect material reality. The early Christians fashioned their mystical doctrine on Pythagorean lines. The Gospel of John begins with the words "In the beginning was the logos—λόγος." What is "logos"? It's a number relationship. It's ratio. Pythagoras's ratio. Logos also translates as "word, thought, and reason." Hence the standard translation of the opening sentence of John is "in the beginning was the word." That translation understates the real meaning. It misses the meat of number.

Pythagoras's ideas penetrated nearly every aspect of life. Polyclitus, the Greek sculptor, put Pythagorean notions of ratios, number ratios, together to measure the "perfect" human body. He created one sculpture as a textbook case to show the perfect ratios of the human form at work. And he wrote up what he'd accomplished by using perfect ratios, perfect proportions. Today Polyclitus's expansion of the Pythagorean legacy is so deeply entrenched in artistic thought that it's called "the canon."[252] The Greeks also applied Pythagorean notions of ratio, harmony, and beauty to their architecture—to buildings like the Parthenon. Ratio and harmony have remained in the artistic ideals of the beautiful body, the beautiful face, and the beautiful building ever since.

What's more, the Pythagoreans were among the first to popularize the word "geometry" and its concepts.[253] And those with a physical bent of mind in Greece explained the peculiarities of matter in terms of tiny basic units, invisible particles, tiny units in the shape of geometry's perfect forms. The particles of earth had the most stubbornly immovable geometric shape—the square. The particles of fire had the "finest" and most flitting, flickering shape, the pyramid. The particles of air were octahedrons—shapes with "eight faces." And water's particles were icosahedrons, geometric shapes "with twenty faces."[254] With that concept, the Pythagoreans kicked off the hunt for the atom. Even Copernicus and Galileo would be influenced by Pythagoras's acolytes, acolytes who would come up with the first sun-centered concepts of the heavens, the first concept of a solar system, a system of orbiting planets, planets circling the sun. And Kepler, Galileo, Newton, and nearly every figure in the history of science would spend their lives fleshing out another Pythagorean legacy—using numbers to feel out the cosmos.

There's one more Pythagorean legacy, a legacy that would be crowded out one hundred and fifty years later by Aristotle. A legacy it's time to bring back to life. A legacy that ties in with the reasons that *A* does not equal *A*, yet *A* does equal *A*. A legacy that ties in with the reason that opposites are often both true.

It's a concept related to the tetractys, the shape that says everything begins with opposites—with unity and division. Everything begins with togetherness and separation. Everything begins with differentiation and integration. The Pythagoreans believed that opposites are joined at the hip, and that the struggle of opposites is built into the bone and marrow of this world. The followers of Pythagoras clung to ten key opposites. Yes, ten, that perfect number again. How basic was this list to the Pythagoreans? Profoundly basic. So basic that Aristotle calls these ten opposites the "ten first principles." Here's how Aristotle lists them in his *Metaphysics*:[255]

Limited	Unlimited
Odd	Even
One	Many
Right	Left
Male	Female
Rest	Motion
Straight	Curved
Light	Dark
Good	Bad
Square	Oblong

To Aristotle, the idea that opposites coexist is irrational. But when Aristotle uses the term "rational," he is using a Pythagorean term. In fact, when you and I use the word "rationality," we are using a Pythagorean term, too. Rationality is a term that comes from the word to which the Pythagoreans gave meaning—"ratio."[256] λόγος. Rational thoughts are thoughts based on mathematical relationships. Relationships between numbers like 2:1 and 2:3. When we use the word "logic," we are also leaning on a Pythagorean notion—the idea that logos, λόγος, underlies everything. And logos, again, is ratio. Pythagorean ratio.[257]

Yet everything Pythagoras did reflected a crazed and thoroughly wacked-out notion: that the scratch marks on wax tablets, Greek numbers, could equal far more than just chickens and pyramids. That they could equal everything from moods and the laws by which cities should be ruled to the shape of kickballs and the movements of dots of light in the sky. This is one of the most absurd stretches in history. How in the world could it possibly be for real? How could scratch marks equal music equal moments of emotional insecurity equal stars? From a crusty and cantankerously conservative point of view, they cannot. Not at all.

Yet one stunningly brilliant twentieth-century author and thinker, Arthur Koestler, sums up Pythagoras's contribution to your daily thought and mine like this:

The sixth century scene evokes the image of an orchestra expectantly tuning up, each player absorbed in his own instrument only, deaf to the caterwaulings of the others. Then there is a dramatic silence, the conductor enters the stage, raps three times with his baton, and harmony emerges from the chaos. The maestro is Pythagoras of Samos, whose influence on the ideas, and thereby on the destiny, of the human race was probably greater than that of any single man before or after him.[258]

SQUARING YOUR WAY TO FAME: PYTHAGORAS'S HOT NEW THEOREM

Pythagoras's discovery of the ratios behind musical beauty was one of humanity's most important attempts to use numbers to grab hold of the hidden properties of an invisible mystery. It was one of humanity's most important attempts to use math to probe a something that is a nothing, a hard and fast thing out there in the real world, but a hard and fast thing that changes every second, a hard and fast thing that the eye cannot see. The Babylonians and the Egyptians had used math to solve the problems of bricks, slabs of stone, rubble, storage containers, and grain. But these were solid things. When Pythagoras used number to grab hold of music, he pinned down the hidden patterns of something ephemeral, something you can sense but that you can't hold in your hand or perceive with your eyes. And that translation was central to Pythagoras's achievement.

But Pythagoras unfolded something else invisible: implicit patterns. And he gained twenty-five hundred years of fame for one last grand demonstration of how you can pull invisible implications from numbers. He gained permanent name value for one final performance on the stage of history, for one more example of how you can enter history's stage with a grand flourish of your robe, your halo, and your trousers, of how you can step into the spotlight and pull things into being from the nothingness, things that in some strange way were there all along. Invisible things, but things tempting and teasing you from just out of sight.

What's the grand demonstration that's kept Pythagoras's name center stage in philosophy, math, and history for 125 generations? It's the feat with which Pythagoras got his name on the right-angle number triples that he did not discover. The right-angle number triples of the Mesopotamians and the Egyptians. The 3:4:5 right-angle triples incorrectly known today as Pythagorean triples. Pythagoras pulled off his most famous act of mathematics and mathe-magic, his greatest flourish of number power, with the Pythagorean theorem. And the Pythagorean theorem's implications are very strange.

***

Let's zip back to the fact that the Babylonians and the Egyptians were masterful builders. To build they needed right-angle triangles. And to guarantee that their buildings would come out straight, they used the magic of the 3:4:5 relationship.

In fact, the Babylonians and Egyptians used an entire table of numbers that resulted in right-angle triangles. Remember the contents of the tablet in Columbia University's Plimpton collection?

3:4:5
5:12:13
8:15:17
20:21:29
12709:13500:18541[259]

These are the Pythagorean triples. But if these triples come to us from the Mesopotamians and the Egyptians, why are they named after Pythagoras?

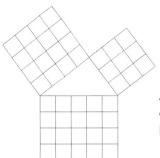

A right-angle triangle breaks out in squares. This is the Pythagorean theorem.
Courtesy of Philippe Kurlapski, Wikimedia Commons.

To see what Pythagoras accomplished, use your Egyptian knotted rope to peg out a right-angle triangle in the dust. Or translate the trick into another medium entirely. Draw a 3:4:5 triangle on your computer screen. Or draw it in the lights of a spectacolor billboard on Times Square. It doesn't matter what medium you pick. And it doesn't matter what size. The Ur pattern, the implicit property that Pythagoras discovered, will pop out nonetheless. Now pick a side. Any side. Let's say your three-unit side. Again, it doesn't matter whether the three-unit side of your triangle is three inches, three fingers, three feet, three forearms, or three stadia. Now draw a square protruding from that three-unit side. A square three units by three units. Then cross hatch your square with a grid of lines spaced equally apart. Checkerboard your square. Turn it into a spitting image of the square checkerboard on which the ancient Greeks played a game they called "pessoi," pebbles.[260] Or a checkerboard like the cross-hatched game board on which the ancient Egyptians played the game of "passing," the game of Senet.

Now draw a square game board popping from each of the two remaining sides of your right-angle triangle. Make sure the sides of each game board are the same length as the side of the triangle from which they grow. You now have a right-angle triangle boxed off by three checkerboards.

Fill the two smaller squares with children's building blocks. Then put all the blocks in a bag. And spill them out into the biggest box of the three. Strange. Very strange. The number of building blocks you pulled out of the two small squares, the two small checkerboards, will fit precisely into the biggest square of the bunch.

Try translating this into a slightly different medium. Take a bag of what the Greeks used for calculating, a bag of stones, pebbles, of equal sizes.[261] Those pebbles are called "calculi" Are you ready to "pebble"? Are you ready to "*calcula*te"? Fill your three-by-three and your four-by-four squares with your equal-sized pebbles, your calculi. Now count up the total number of pebbles in those two squares. Add them together. What will you get? Precisely the number of pebbles it will take to fill the box on the diagonal. Precisely the number of pebbles it will take to fill the square perched on the cattycorner line that the Greeks called the hypotenuse: "the stretching under."[262] Magic.

Or, to translate it once again into another new context. Into the language of mathematics textbooks. How do you find the length of the diagonal side, the longest side, the hypotenuse, the "crossing under," the longest line of a right-angle triangle? Any right-angle triangle at all? You square the two short sides. You add those two squares together. Then you find the square root of the total. That is the Pythagorean theorem.

And that is how Pythagoras invented "squaring." Multiplying numbers by themselves. Three times three is three squared, 3^2. Nine. Four times four is four squared, 4^2. Sixteen. Ten times ten is ten squared, 10^2. Ten times ten is one hundred. But what did Pythagoras really invent? Less than he's given credit for. Yet more. The Egyptians and the Babylonians had the technique of multiplying numbers by themselves. They wrote down table after table of what we call squares. They wrote down table after table of numbers multiplied by themselves. But they lacked something vital. They lacked the crucial tool that captures a deep structure. They lacked the central tool that taps into an implicit property. The Egyptians and the Babylonians were missing the metaphor. They were missing a metaphor that would set multiplying a number by itself apart in the next twenty-three hundred years of math. They were missing the metaphor that would give a tool to Newton and Einstein. The metaphor that would give us $E = mc^2$. They were missing the metaphor that would show up wherever the syllable "quad" appears in math. As in quadratic equations. And in quadrature. They were missing the metaphor added by Pythagoras. The metaphor of the square.

**

But all this leaves a question. Where does the peculiar relationship between triangles, squares, right angles, and Pythagorean triples, number triples, come from? How do implicit properties come to be? And how does Pythagoras's peculiar achievement help explain the creation of Peano's postulates? How does it explain the invention of the axiom?

4

HOW ARISTOTLE
INVENTED THE AXIOM

A TRIP TO PLATO'S CAVE

> *I am only interested in the Platonic essence of a situation,*
> *so that I can weave it into a beautiful mathematical theory,*
> *so that I can lay bare its inner soul.*
>
> —**Gregory Chaitin**[1]

Despite Pythagoras's astonishing accomplishments, another man generally gets the credit for the idea that deep structures underlie the cosmos. That man is Plato. And Plato pulled off this hijack with his concept of archetypes. What are archetypes? Archetypes are perfect forms. Perfect forms of which real things are mere imitations. Archetypes are more real than the things we normally think of as real. The standard example? The chair you're sitting on right now is just an imperfect imitation of an archetypal chair hidden somewhere in the void.

Plato got this across with one of the most famous images in philosophy, his story of the cave. You've learned it. You know it. But the original is a hell of a lot weirder than most of us have ever known. Here's the original way Plato set the scene:

> Imagine a company of men living in a sort of underground cave-like dwelling which has an entrance open to the light of day, long-drawn, and answering in width to the whole of the cave; and in this cave they are

detained from childhood, with their legs and necks so fettered that they cannot change their position and can see only what is in front of them, being unable, by reason of the chains, to turn round their heads.[2]

Got that? It isn't easy going. In essence, it's a thought experiment, a *gedankenexperiment*. Plato imagines people raised in a cave from infancy with their backs to the cave's entrance. Shackled so that they can't turn their heads. Shackled so that all they can see is the back wall of the cave. Shackled so they cannot swivel around to see the cave's opening and that opening's natural light. Back to Plato.

And further, imagine them to have light from a fire which is burning above, and at a distance behind them. Between the fire and the prisoners there rises a roadway along which fancy that you can see a low wall built, like the screen which the jugglers place in front of them, and over which they show their puppets.[3]

In other words, strange things are going on behind the backs of these experimental subjects. Outside the cave's entrance is a setup for a puppet play, complete with the sort of stage behind which puppeteers hide. Behind the stage is a fire built to cast the shadows of what's on the stage all the way to the back wall of the cave. And the only things the poor cave prisoners can see are those shadows. What's the shadows' nature? Brace yourself. Plato's prose is muddier than an olive grove in a rainstorm.

Figure to yourself also a number of people who are carrying behind this wall statues of men and images of various animals, wrought in wood, stone, and in every possible fashion, and other articles of every sort which overtop the wall.... Of these ... they see only the shadows.[4]

Says Plato, the prisoners have a problem. A problem in perception. All sorts of objects are shown on the stage behind their backs—animal statues and miscellaneous idols, for instance. And all of these stage props cast shadows on the cave's back wall. But the cave dwellers think the shadows in front of their eyes are the only reality. Why? Because the shadows are all they can see. All they have ever seen. They are chained so they cannot look over their shoulders or turn around. This is not a cheerful image. Continues Plato:

> If now they could talk together, don't you suppose they would believe that they were naming as the things themselves the figures which they saw passing before them? ... So that in point of fact ... such people would hold nothing to be real except the shadows of the images.[5]

The poor cave prisoners would come to believe that the shadows they've seen all their lives are the only reality.

Then Plato punches home a potent point. He says these prisoners locked tight into a single stiff position by chains in a cave, these prisoners "compelled to keep their heads immovable," these "strange prisoners," are like you and me. They are "like ourselves." We, too, are locked in darkness and illusion. What's more, says Plato, if one of these prisoners were unchained and allowed to turn around and look at the opening directly, the light would blind him. If you tried to assure "him that he had heretofore been looking at illusions, but that now ... he is coming a little closer to reality" he wouldn't believe you. What's more, he "would turn back and take refuge in those things" he had always looked at in the past. In fact, he'd "think them in reality clearer than" the real world he'd glimpsed passing by the cave's entrance.[6] He'd think that the shadows on the back wall of the cave were the real deal and the objects out in the sunlight were phonies.

What's Plato getting at? What's the point of this tangled and tortured metaphor? And why does Plato take up eleven whole pages in one of his most admired books, *The Republic*, to get it across?[7] What is the cave and what is the higher "reality" Plato's talking about?

The cave is the real world that we look at every day. The world you see when you focus on the corner of this open book so you can turn the page. The world you see when you watch your fingers do the page turning. And this world of pages and fingers is just a pale shadow. A pale shadow of what? Of a far more real world. A perfect world. An eternal world.

Elementary philosophy courses usually tell you that Plato used the image of the cave to get across his concept of the archetype. In fact, I just said it. But it's not really true. Plato's main concern in *The Republic* is politics—the question of how the state should be ruled. His point with the story of the cave is that philosophers, men who have stared the sun in the face and who have seen reality, should rule the state. Men like Plato should rule the state. Perhaps even Plato himself should be given the reins of power. Why? When philosophers descend from the world of sunlight to the dark world of the cave, to the benighted world in which you and I live, and when the eyes of these wise men adjust to the nightlike gloom, they "will see ten thousand times better than the inhabitants of the den." And what will they see that you and I miss? "The idea of good."

Plato's "idea of the good" is secular, but Plato makes it sound very much like a god. "The idea of the good" is the sun that illuminates the reality outside of the cave. "The idea of the good" is "the universal author of all things beautiful and right, parent of light and of the lord of light in this visible world, and the immediate source of reason and truth in the intellectual."[8] So a philosopher who has stared "the idea of good" in the face sees a real truth that makes the world of the senses look shabby by comparison. The world illuminated by the Good is one that you and I can penetrate by persistent thought and by using something that owes a debt to Pythagoras—reason, rationality, ratio-nality. With reason, with ratios, number ratios, you, too, can penetrate to what Plato calls "the beautiful and just and good." And you too can see not just pale shadows, you can see the beautiful, the just, and the good "in their truth."

To put it differently, an exit from the cave is "the ascent of the soul to the realm of thought." An ascent into the light of the sun. Again, the sun is the Good.[9] And that sunlike Good is "the source of all things right and beautiful." Including "truth and reason." What additional differences are there between the world of the cave and the world in the sunshine? Why is the world of the cave "the world of becoming"? And why is the realm of the real things beyond the cave "the world of being?"[10] Because the things within the cave will solidify, then decay. But the things outside the cave are "things divine?"[11] They are eternal. They were here before the beginning began. And they will be here forever. They are "the eternal pattern" from which all passing things are copied.[12]

Why can scratch marks on clay or wax equal barleycorns, planets, and stars? Not to mention music and moods? Plato's idea implies an answer. All these things are reflections of deep structures, ideal patterns. The same deep structures. The same patterns. Yes, the same patterns appear in stars, storms, and insecurities. But that's between me and you. That's not Plato.

Back to the fact that in elementary philosophy classes, Plato's eternal patterns are usually called the "archetypes." That's actually a word drawn from another of Plato's books, the *Timaeus*, not from the story of the cave. In the *Timaeus*, Plato uses the phrase "the eternal archetype."[13] But usually Plato simply calls his perfect templates "ideas."[14] One way or the other, whether in the *Timaeus*, the *Republic*, or both, Plato came very close to the notion that the cosmos is based on primal patterns. He came very close to the idea that this is a cosmos with deep structures. A cosmos built from Ur patterns.

But, says Aristotle in all of this, Plato was merely "treading on the heels"[15] of, guess who? Pythagoras.

And how does Aristotle himself fit into all of this? He hit the jackpot. He invented the axiom. And he invented one of the most powerful recruitment strategies in history. He kicked off the twenty-three-hundred-year project that would lead to Peano's postulates. Oh, and Aristotle also kicked off something else. Modern science.

***

What is a recruitment strategy? Richard Dawkins, in his 1976 book *The Selfish Gene*, gave us two powerful ideas: the replicator and the meme. The replicator is an object that can make copies of itself. Says Dawkins, the best known replicator is the gene. In Dawkins's view, a gene is a complex molecule that can make a spitting image of itself. Why bother to call a gene a replicator? Why bother to invent a new term for something we all know is in the reproducing business, the self-copying business? Because the concept helps make sense of something totally ephemeral. It helps make sense of a self-copying something that is not a thing at all. That self-reproducing no-thing is the *idea*. Or, as Dawkins calls it, the meme.

Genes, says Dawkins, make copies of themselves when they are let loose in a rich biochemical goop or soup. For example, nearly four billion years ago they copied themselves frantically in the primordial puddles, pools, undersea vents, and ooze of the early earth.

Memes copy themselves in a very different kind of soup. They copy themselves in puddles of consciousness, in the pools of thought in your brain and mine. What are memes? Words, slogans, poems, pop songs, religions, ideologies, opinions, rallying cries, and pleas for peace. All of these are memes. They slip from molecule to molecule in the brain and from mind to mind. But they are independent of these mere material things. And memes and genes are ambitious. Imperialistic. In Dawkins's word, "greedy." Why?

Those that replicate like blazes will launch their pattern into the future, flooding the landscapes of generations yet to come. And what will happen to those genes and memes that are less ambitious, those that ignore the business of seducing, recruiting, and kidnapping? Those that ignore the game of grabbing clusters of molecules then turning them into temporary doppelgängers, carriers of their pattern? This is a fiercely competitive world, says Dawkins. And those that don't copy themselves obsessively will insure that their pattern dies out. The offspring of the gluttonous, the acquisitive, and the grasping self-replicators will take over the resources and nudge the less piggy memes and genes to the very edge . . . or beyond. Into extinction. To the most compulsive self-copiers go the spoils. Or so Dawkins says.

Dawkins's concepts have worked powerfully as attractors. As memes. Dawkins's phrase the "selfish gene" gets a respectable 330,000 hits on Google. But his word "meme" gets a colossal 38 million. Yes, 38 million hits.

Memes are self-replicators that work without a commitment to any particular team of atoms or molecules, without a commitment to any particular matter. They organize whatever matter of the right kind they run across. They organize a sea of neural tissue, a sea of brain matter, influencing the flow of sodium and potassium that moves a signal down the long, string-like axon of a nerve fiber. They influence the spurts of neurotransmitters at the neuron's tip that transfer a signal from one nerve to the next in line. And they influence the things we say to introduce ourselves to strangers, the positions we take on politics, the vocabulary with which we flirt, the content of the texts and e-mails we send, and even the clichés and stabs at new ideas we weave together when we're making a speech. They influence the words and phrases that gush between you and me.

But memes are not the only insubstantial forms of organization that pull together a swatch of matter for a fleeting second, then leave that matter behind. They are not the only forms of organization that keep their shape, their form, and their identity despite their promiscuous travels from one collection of atoms, molecules, cells, and organisms to another. Memes are not the only recruitment patterns.

Imagine that you and the woman or man of your dreams are flying back to the United States after a quick and totally self-indulgent weekend in London. It's midday. You look out the window of the plane at the Atlantic Ocean below you. What do you see? Waves. If you want, you can lock your eyes on just one wave and follow it for minutes. It has a distinct identity. It trails off to the north and south as far as your eye can see. And its hump seems as well formed as the back of a whale.

Remember when you were a kid and rolled a ball of clay out on a tabletop until it made a long, round clay rope? That's what the wave looks like. But the wave has something in common with the meme. It doesn't exist. What? Of course it exists. If you were in a lazily moving blimp you could follow it for hundreds of miles. You could follow it from the mid-Atlantic for days until it broke on the rocks of the shore of Maine. If you were in the water with a surfboard as the wave approached the shore, you could ride its hump. And if you watched for its arrival on a rocky outcrop of the Maine coast and you tripped or slipped while it was smashing its angry fist against the granite, your body would register the wave's power. The wave, in fact, could roll, mash, mangle, and kill you by merely rearing to a frothy peak and hammering you wrathfully on the stone. As the victims of many a megawave, a tsunami, could attest. That's fairly real. Isn't it?

Yes and no. Imagine that you are a molecule of water in the middle of the Atlantic Ocean. You follow what complexity specialists call "local rules." You do what your neighbors hint that you should do. And what, pray tell, is that? You move in a circle that's anywhere from three feet to 160 feet in circumference. Three feet to 160 feet high. First you circle up to the surface. Then you circle back to the depths. You don't go anywhere. You just keep making the same circular movement over and over again. You iterate. Like the termite and the brickmaker, you repeat a simple rule. But where does your energy come from? It's a translation. A translation of temperature changes and wind into water movement. Into your movement.

The circle under the seagull shows how you, a water molecule, move in place and never leave your home, yet you help generate the long-distance travelers called waves. You simply move in a circle. But your circle may be part of a tsunami that scuds two thousand miles. *Courtesy of the National Weather Service, National Oceanic and Atmospheric Administration.*

But there's more. When you circle to the surface, you participate in the peak of a wave. When you circle toward the bottom of your never-ending loop, you participate in that wave's trough. The next time you circle to the surface you participate in making the peak of yet another wave. Yes, another wave. A wave with yet another distinct identity. A wave that will retain that identity for hundreds or thousands of miles. A wave that will do a heck of a lot of traveling. But do you ever travel? No. You circle up and down, staying in place. And do you have a clue about the distant shore whose rocks the wave will eventually hammer like a giant's fist? Not one whit. Not one crumb, pebble, or hint. All you know is your simple rule. All you know is what your neighbors are doing. All you know is how to rock and roll while you stand in place.

Now look at it from the wave's point of view. You are a wave. What are your corpuscles, your particles, your atoms of being? They change every minute. You are nothing. You are no thing. Your equivalent of cells—your molecules of H_2O—are never the same for more than sixty seconds. You are the very epitome of what Heraclitus spoke of when he said that you can never dip your foot into the same river twice. You are the very essence of what Aristotle was trying to freeze in place with his law of identity, with his $A = A$. And you are the very essence of the abstract realities—the no things more real than reality itself—that Plato hinted at. Yes, you continue to be yourself. But how? The matter that makes you up is constantly changing. From minute to minute, you are reassembling yourself with new ingredients, with new water molecules. You are not a crew of unchanging things, a congregation of unchanging parishioners, a football team with an unchanging roster of players. You are a recruitment pattern that retains its identity despite moving from one temporary team of recruits to another. You are a process. A self-sustaining process. You are a form of organization passing over the landscape like a breeze. You are the wave of a Beethoven or a Beatles chord that travels from a loudspeaker to your ear simply by wiggling an ever-changing collection of molecules of air. You are the very essence of why opposites are joined at the hip. You are the quintessence of why A does not equal A and yet why A *does* equal A all at once. You are a recruitment strategy.

What is a recruitment strategy? A process that keeps its shape second by second by second. A process that imposes its identity insistently even if the matter flowing through it is constantly changing. A pattern that makes matter and energy do a strictly patterned dance. A social dance. Heraclitus's river is a recruitment strategy. The whorl in a trout stream is a recruitment strategy. Theseus's ship is a recruitment strategy. Your body, which replaces over a billion cells a minute[16] yet retains its identity, is a recruitment strategy. Your personality, a rapid-fire flood of changing communiqués between a hundred billion neurons, is a recruitment strategy. So is mine.

A recruitment strategy is both a noun and a verb. It is a process that maintains a shape. It is an action that turns itself into a thing. And it is a thing that turns itself into an action. Above all, a recruitment strategy is social. It seduces other things into its orbit and puts them through a choreography that dictates how they will bow, twirl, and sway with each other. Then it lets them go and moves on to the next batch of recruits. It is a powerful persuader, a choreographer of particles, of forces, and of complex things from asteroids and nebulae to you and me. It is so powerful that it survives despite obstacles and attacks. It is Plato's archetype. But Plato's archetypes are stable and unchanging things. A recruitment strategy is a rider, a glider, and a guider of change. A recruitment pattern is a metabolism on the move. A recruitment strategy is an insistent whirlwind of relationship. And it is often a pattern that appears simultaneously all over the place.

An atom is a recruitment strategy. A galaxy is a recruitment strategy. A star is a recruitment strategy. An atom imposes its spherical pattern of shells within shells on protons, neutrons, and fast-moving electrons. And it does it gazillions of times in gazillions of different locations. It asserts its pattern no matter what the time and place. What's more, it somehow manages to do the same darned thing wherever you look despite the fact that it is not communicating with others of its kind to make sure they are all dancing to the same choreography. Then there's a galaxy. A galaxy inflicts its potato-shaped ellipse and often its spiral arms on ten billion stars or more. What's more, a galaxy imposes its pattern on masses of matter wherever you look in the sky. And a star forces its ball-like shape and its fiery way of crushing atoms on octillions of tons of matter.[17] It does it over and over and over again in thousands of billions of separate locations.[18] Simultaneously. Without communicating with other stars.

Why call these things recruitment *strategies*. Why humanize them? Why give them will? Why give them intention? Because a recruitment strategy is purposeful. It is insistent. It persists. It is not matter. And it is nowhere—no where. It is in no permanent location. Yet a recruitment strategy imposes its shape on matter over and over and over again. It imposes its way of doing things. In location after location after location. If a recruitment strategy is no where and no thing, then what the hell is it? I'm not quite sure. Are you?

But I can tell you this. A crystal of salt is a recruitment strategy. A snow-flake is a recruitment strategy. A genome—a gene team—is a recruitment strategy. A column in a termite nest is a recruitment strategy. A religion is a recruitment strategy. A philosophy is a recruitment strategy. A game is a recruitment strategy. Puzzles, paradoxes, and questions are recruitment strategies. And Aristotle was one of the most potent recruitment strategy crafters in Western history. He was a pattern establisher on a par with religious recruitment strategy crafters like Moses, Buddha, Jesus, St. Paul, and

Mohammed. But, like another great recruitment strategy creator, Confucius, Aristotle was secular. And like Confucius, the recruitment strategy that Aristotle gave birth to changed the human relationship to the invisible world and to the cosmos in ways beyond belief.

What recruitment strategy did Aristotle invent? Modern science. Or, as he called it, "demonstrative science."[19] More specifically, Aristotle invented the modern scientific vocabulary. The modern scientific mindset. He also invented some of the puzzles that modern science would pursue. And some of the key prejudices that modern science would be hobbled by. Aristotle forged one key prejudice in particular—the notion that metaphor is unscientific and that only "analogy" is acceptable. And the notion that the difference between metaphor and analogy is profound.[20]

In the process, Aristotle shaped the lenses through which modern science would see. And he shaped the blinders that sometimes close off modern science's vision mightily. He also established the vocabulary and the assumptions of modern rationality. And Aristotle came up with something else—the recruitment strategy behind Peano's axioms. In fact, Aristotle invented the axiom itself.

ARISTOTLE FIGHTS FOR ATTENTION—
OR ZEROING ZENO

When Aristotle entered philosophy he had a problem. The field was no longer new. It had been around for 220 years, close to the amount of time the United States of America has existed. And philosophy was crowded with greats, with monumental men, with men of towering reputations—Thales, Anaximander, Anaxagoras, Pythagoras, Xenophanes, Heraclitus, Parmenides, Zeno, Empedocles, Leucippus, Protagoras, Gorgias, Thrasymachus, and two megastars, Socrates and Plato. How was Aristotle going to carve out a niche in this overcrowded attention space? How was he going to grab the spotlight of fame? How was he going to turn himself into a star?

This dilemma was not unique to Aristotle. It's a problem that hits all of us, including you and me. It's one of the tools with which the cosmos splits a one into a two and a two into a four. It's one of the sources of a primal pattern—differentiation. And it's one of the secrets to cosmic creativity.

Attention is the oxygen of the human soul. If we get it, we thrive. If we don't get it, we shrivel and die. Without attention our immune system shuts down and brain cells in our hippocampus kill themselves off. So we all compete for a space in the eyes, minds, and hearts of others. We compete with the way we dress, with the gestures we use, with the vocabulary we choose. We compete for attention with the style of our haircut and with the way we slouch, walk, or stand up straight. Or we compete with the way we think. We compete with the way we philosophize.

Frank Sulloway, a former research scholar in the Program in Science, Technology, and Society at MIT and a visiting scholar at UC Berkeley's Institute of Personality and Social Research, wrote a book in 1996 called *Born to Rebel: Birth Order, Family Dynamics, and Creative Lives.*[21] Sulloway's book was about family dynamics. So what did Sulloway's book have to do with Aristotle, a thinker whose life story it never examined? And what did it have to do with the question of how the cosmos creates? Everything.

Sulloway's book contends that the struggle for attention is one of the most fundamental shapers of personality. The first child in the family, Sulloway says, has the stage of parental attention all to herself. So she sparks positive, gleeful attention from her dad and mom by doing something very simple. She does whatever lights up the faces of her parents the most. She does what delights her parents. And in the process, she becomes the good kid in the family.

Then comes infant number two. And infant number two has a dilemma. How will she get attention? Her older sister already holds center stage and knows how to work the spotlight. Her older sister already occupies the good-kid slot. So, says Sulloway, the newcomer in the family goes for attention by finding another niche. She probes for another slot in attention space. That open position? The nonconformist. The rebel.[22] And Sulloway backs this with what he calls "large-scale biographical research."[23] That's an understatement. Sulloway put in twenty-six years of research surveying roughly six million "biographical points of information" on sixty-five hundred individuals.[24] And he performed a computer meta-analysis that included five years as a John D. and Catherine T. MacArthur Foundation

Fellow. So Sulloway's tale of the way we differentiate to grab attention is not just speculation.

Is this pattern of rivalry for attention space peculiar to humans? Not at all.[25] The tendency to microdifferentiate—to split up and become different in order to penetrate new niches—exists among all creatures, big and small, from fruit flies and spiny leg *Tetragnatha* spiders in Hawaii[26] to *Anolis* lizards in the Caribbean[27] and snails on Crete,[28] and from cichlid fish in Africa to *Dolomedes triton* spiders in Ohio. And often the resource these creatures reshape themselves to get is guess what? Attention.

Dolomedes triton are whompingly big water spiders, nearly two and a half inches from leg tip to leg tip. Sometimes called "six-spotted fishing spiders," the *Dolomedes triton* live in North and Central America and hunt tadpoles, small fish, and "anything that cannot get away."[29] Not easy for a mere spider. Reports *Dolomedes* researcher Kelly Kissane,[30] a member of a group you would run in the 1990s, the Group Selection Squad, when two tribes of *Dolomedes triton* water spiders set up camp on different ponds, they rapidly begin to differentiate. They establish different recruitment strategies in order to crack open new resources and to thrive.

And they invent new ways to shine in the spotlight of attention space. How does Kissane know this? Because male *Dolomedes triton* spiders compete for the attention of females by dancing. They wave their forelimbs in the air, stick them out straight, move them to forty-five-degree angles, tap dance, and drum on the surface of the ground or the pond to seduce a fertile female into the act of copulation. And Kissane believes that these water spider dances are a combination of instinctual patterns and of fads and conventions that the cleverest dancers of the past have invented.

What does this have to do with microdifferentiation? When you introduce a male from one pond to a female from another pond and the foreign male dances his little abdomen off to get the local belle to mate with him, the lady turns her back and walks or runs away. Or she shows her distaste for the illegal alien more dramatically. She pounces on the invading male and eats him.

Kissane has not been able to detect any differences in the dances of the spiders from the two nearby ponds. But the females apparently can.

And something in the dance, the demeanor, or the smell of the other-ponders simply does not turn the local girls on. Yes the smell. Different diets produce different body aromas. And the other-ponders may be supping on new items of fast food.

What's more, *Dolomedes triton* water spiders in Alberta, Canada, have very different dances from those of *Dolomedes triton* water spiders in Lynchburg, Virginia, or in Ohio. Measurably different dances. Dances in which they concentrate on the footwork and don't wave their forelegs.

Like the rebel competing with the good kid for attention, groups that settle a new pond subtly take off in a direction that's all their own. To probe their opportunities, new spider groups become new-pattern generators.

This sort of differentiation is all over the place in the realm of living things. In the cells of your eye it shows up in what biologists call "lateral inhibition." The light sensors on your retina compete to be the first to identify an incoming stream of photons—the first to figure out what the incoming bit of light is. Or, in the metaphor of the founder of the Redwood Center for Theoretical Neuroscience—founder of Palm Inc., inventor of the PalmPilot®, and coauthor of an extremely insightful book, *On Intelligence*—Jeff Hawkins, the light sensors in your retina compete to be the first to speak up in a game of *Name That Tune*.[31] How do these visual receptors do it? How do they compete for the attention of higher neural systems? By pattern testing. By a game, a pattern-recognition competition.

Is that fuzzy thing in the distance a line or a shadow? Is it a face or a ski hat on a rack? Is that looming, lumpy dark thing in your bedroom late at night a monster or just a teddy bear? Is that glint at the end of the street a car or a shopping cart? And is it coming at you? How fast? The photosensor that "thinks" it's got the answer nudges its neighbors out of the game. It sends out a signal that tells its closest neighbors on the iris to shut up and let it take over.

By inhibiting its neighbors, the light sensor sets up the equivalent of a trench around itself, a trench that makes it stand out, a trench of silence that radically differentiates it. Standing out—differentiating—by shutting up your neighbors is called "lateral inhibition." Lateral inhibition goes on between the light receptors in your eyes and mine, between the light receptors in the eyes of horseshoe crabs,[32] and even between the touch receptors at the base of the whiskers of rats.[33] Rats use their whiskers to feel their way around the way that you and I use our hands to feel our way around in the dark. To do it, rats rely on the competition between small cylinders of cells in a six-layered clump called the "barrel cortex."[34] Each cylinder is wired to a different whisker. And each cylinder competes for attention. Rats feeling their way around rely on instant cellular differentiation.

What are the light and touch receptors of horseshoe crabs, rats, and humans competing for? Attention. The attention of the higher brain regions to which they send their guesses about what's going on in the world around us. Competition and differentiation turn your sensory neurons and mine into feelers for a search engine, a search engine trying to make sense of the world around us.

Are individual humans—people like Thales, Pythagoras, Aristotle, and you and me—also probes for a search engine of some kind? A search engine of our family, our tribe, our subculture, our nation, our species, or . . . more peculiarly . . . a search engine of the cosmos? That's a question for later. But the fact is that differentiation—like the distance two sisters set up between themselves to get attention—shows up all over the place in human behavior.

What does this have to do with Aristotle? More than you might think. Greece had been a fertile field for microdifferentiation in the 250 years before Aristotle came along. When Thales had started this "philosophy" business in roughly 600 BCE he'd created a new stage on which to attract attention. But would anyone bother to show up in the audience? Would anyone take their eyes off of more established amusements like war, politics, and the Olympics? And would fashion favor this importation of a novelty, the importation of math and its step-by-step patterns of thought, the importation of an invention that the Mesopotamians and the Egyptians had been perfecting for thirty-five hundred years?

Thales had one big thing going for him. He was importing an item that had thirty-five hundred years of stored attention behind it. He was importing an item that had thirty-five hundred years of fame. He was importing thirty-five hundred years of the prestige, power, and mystery cultivated by hundreds of thousands of priest scribes. Priest scribes who had advised the mightiest men of history.

Priest scribes who had proved over and over again that their ability to see the future was more than just an idle claim. Priest scribes whose strange ways of using the scratch marks attached to sacks (*khars*), barrels (*heqats*), jars (*hinus*), and knotted ropes had shown an uncanny ability that you and I know well by now. An ability to predict how many loaves of bread, jars of beer, workmen, blocks of stone, and heaps of gravel it would take to build one of the most unbelievable wonders of the ancient world, a pyramid.

What's the big deal about accurately predicting the supplies of bread and beer for mere heaps of stone? Those heaps were the biggest cooperative projects in human history up until Aristotle's day. And the numbers involved in building them were astronomical. Roughly 175 million loaves of bread, 2.3 million blocks of stone, and over 1.4 billion work hours.[35] The monuments that the predictions of priest scribes had helped build held the Greeks in one of the most potent attentional headlocks on the planet—awe. And by the time of Thales, the reputation of Egyptian and Babylonian priest scribes had washed over Greece for at least two hundred years. In other words, the priest scribes of Babylon and Egypt had established a brilliantly successful recruitment strategy. And they'd done it using the termite trick—height.

Thales did something few sages before him had pulled off. He visited Egypt.[36] More than that, he "practiced philosophy" in Egypt.[37] Then Thales stripped down the Egyptian and Babylonian contribution. He reinvented it. How? By translating it into a radically new medium. Thales tossed away the role of priest, got rid of the Babylonian and Egyptian gods, and forgot about the elaborate bureaucratic structure in which priests were a part. Thales shredded the special relationship between Babylonian and Egyptian mathematical thinkers and the state and crafted something that an individual, an entrepreneur of the mind, could develop and promote on his own—the cult of personality. In Egypt and Babylon, the form of mass attention called fame had been primarily the monopoly of rulers. But Thales built a whole new kind of spectacle and mounted it on the stage of attention. He went after fame for himself and in the process made fame available to mere thinkers. He democratized star power. And in the process, he democratized and secularized the Babylonian and Egyptian knowledge base.

Recruitment strategies are clever. By the time Aristotle came along, says Ohio State University's historian of classical rhetoric James Fredal, Athens had become a "competitive arena" for a nonstop "contest."[38] A nonstop contest for honor, prestige, recognition, reputation, esteem, influence, and renown. A nonstop contest for attention. Especially in philosophy. As Heraclitus put it, "The best men chose one thing rather than all else: everlasting fame."[39] In fact, it appears that a slot had been defined for a leading philosopher of each age.[40] It was a slot that tradition had allotted to Thales, Socrates, and Plato. In other words, the role of the master philosopher of the age had become an attractor. Turn yourself into that leading philosopher and you would have the form of hyperconcentrated attention called immortality. But the competition for that role was fierce.

Competition allows a recruitment strategy to reel in the best and the brightest.[41] And to win the slot of master philosopher of your age, you had to differentiate yourself. How? In the lectures that his followers turned into books, Aristotle took on the greats of philosophy one by one. He spelled out their contributions. And by doing so, he put himself in their league. He played the name game, the game in which you build your own social magnetism by bringing the magnetism of others into your work. The game in which you capitalize on the authority of others. And in his writings, Aristotle defeated each of these long-gone masters. He showed the limitations of their views. And he replaced those views with views of his own. Views he labored hard in his writings to drum into your head. Or views he labored in lecture after lecture to drum into the heads of students at his Lyceum.

In the process Aristotle laid out a whole new vocabulary for the philosophy of the future. And a whole new program. He laid out the new recruitment strategy he called "science." A word he used nearly eighty times in just one book, his *Posterior Analytics*.[42] But first, Aristotle had to prove that he stood out.

***

Aristotle began by declaring that one of his primary ideas was not his at all. He claimed that this notion was obvious to every human with two brain cells to rub together. And he unilaterally declared that it was at the heart of something he called "induction" and "deduction,"[43] a process that later philosophers would call logic.[44] What was this basic notion that Aristotle told you and me we all agree on? A equals A. What later philosophers would call "the principle of identity." What later philosophers would also call "the principle of noncontradiction."[45] Or, as Aristotle put it, "Things which are the same as the same are the same as one another."[46] This fundamental concept, Aristotle declared, had become a battleground in philosophy. Previous philosophers had mounted a conspiracy to trash it. To defeat it. To topple it. "To effect its overthrow,"[47] as one translator of Aristotle put it. The attackers of $A = A$ had not just been ordinary foot soldiers. They had been the superstars of mind. They had been what Aristotle called the "celebrated philosophers."[48]

Now that the stage was set, Aristotle brought on his contestants one by one. First came Heraclitus, the philosopher who said that you can never step into the same river twice. Heraclitus, said Aristotle, had attacked the notion of $A = A$ by declaring "that all nature is in a perpetual flux, so that nothing is in the same state for two successive moments."[49] In other words, every A is in a state of constant change. Which means that the A of this moment does not equal the A of ten minutes ago. This was a sin against the obvious, said Aristotle. It was a sin against $A = A$. So Aristotle dismissed Heraclitus's heresy with a single curt but muddy sentence. "From this it would follow that neither of two contradictories could be predicated with truth of any subject."[50] In other words, if Heraclitus was right, you could not break things down into opposites and test the truth of the opposites with simple either/or questions. And that is just plain silly. Right?

One villain down. Two to go. Next came Anaxagoras. Not Anaximander, the father of the sphere. But Anaxagoras of Clazomenae, the first foreign philosopher to settle in Athens. The friend of Pericles, Athens's leader in the city's golden age.[51] Anaxagoras was the man who said that the moon was a stone and that the sun was a glowing hot ball of iron. What was Anaxagoras's sin against $A = A$? Says Aristotle, he "held that the ultimate elements could never be entirely separated; that nothing in nature was pure or simple."[52] In other words, A had bits of B and C in it. What's worse, every A had elements of its opposite, "opposite elements,"[53] within it. Clearly this was another slander against $A = A$. How did Aristotle defeat Anaxagoras? With another version of the same simple sentence he'd used to clobber Heraclitus. If Anaxagoras is right, "it follows, that neither of two contradictories can be predicated absolutely of any subject."[54] Did Aristotle explain this mind-stumbling pronouncement? Did he offer any further reasoning? Any evidence? No. He made his declaration as an unquestionable truth, then tossed Anaxagoras aside.

What mental wrestler was up next? What superstar of Greek thought? Protagoras. Protagoras was the lawgiver of Thurii, a city established in Italy by the Athenians in the days of Socrates. Protagoras was also the first Greek to charge fees for his private teaching sessions. And he was one of the men to whom Plato had dedicated an entire dialog. He was the man Plato had trashed as a mere "sophist."[55] The man Ugo Zilioli of the University of Pisa calls "Plato's subtlest enemy."[56] And what was Protagoras's crime against $A = A$? Says Aristotle, he "taught that man is the measure of reality."[57] OK, that sounds harmless enough. What's the beef? Says Zilioli, Protagoras sinned with an "ancient" and "robust" form of what we now call relativism. He said that each man perceives A differently. As Aristotle puts it, Protagoras proposed that "the same objects produce different sensations and opinions in different men."[58] Ummm, why does this defy $A = A$? Because it means "that truth may be self-contradictory."[59] And, worse, said Aristotle with venom, it means that "opinion is the criteria of truth."[60] Yikes. We all know, says Aristotle, that $A = A$ is a proposition without a taint, a whiff, or a hint of contradiction. Period. Another great thinker defeated! Another philosophic superstar bites the dust.

Then Aristotle played tag team. He brought in the ultimate ringer— Plato. Not as a heretic, but as a supporter. Plato, he said, took on Heraclitus's doctrine and defeated it. Heraclitus said that all things are in a perpetual state of change. Plato proclaimed the opposite. He claimed that some things are eternal and unchanging. Why? Says Aristotle, "To avoid the consequences of the doctrine of Heraclitus."[61] Says Aristotle, it was to escape the errors of Heraclitus that Plato put forth the concept of the unchanging and eternal patterns, the concept of the exalted archetypes, the concept of the essential forms, the concept of patterns that things of mere matter only imitate. "To avoid the consequences of Heraclitus," says Aristotle, "Plato . . . maintained the existence of the Ideas."[62]

But Aristotle had a problem. A problem that would cause trouble for us today. And it came from his boldness. How did Aristotle present the idea of $A = A$? In opposition to his straw men—the dead greats of philosophy—Aristotle spoke with the voice of a god. He declared that $A = A$ was far more than a mere idea. He declared that $A=A$ was a universal truth. One so basic and so fundamentally woven into the fabric of reality that all men would recognize its obviousness. But this "truth" was, in fact, an opinion. It was a hypothesis. Aristotle dodged his own demand for "demonstration." He made the shady claim that you could prove $A = A$, but that you didn't have to. What later philosophers would call the "principle of identity,"[63] he said, was "a necessary truth and necessarily believed."[64] It was "a principle in things about which we cannot be deceived."[65] It was so obvious that it needed no proof.

Aristotle's presentation of $A = A$ as an absolute bordered on flimflam, fakery, and forgery. But twenty-three hundred years of Western thinkers have fallen for Aristotle's trick.

Why was Aristotle so insistent on the law of identity? Why was he so ferociously focused on the notion that A equals A? Because it was the basis for a whole new system. A system that had its own vocabulary. A system that had its own form of logic. A system with which Aristotle wanted to change the stage-set of attention as profoundly as Thales had done when he had imported Egyptian and Babylonian ideas.

***

From the "pettiness" of egos, massive leaps are sometimes made. And from the need for attention comes repetition of the old in a new context, in a context that sometimes makes old concepts new. Very new indeed.

Aristotle was about to promote a system with which he could establish himself as the next great philosopher after Plato. A system with which Aristotle could put himself center stage under the greatest attentional spotlight of all—the spotlight of history. And the key to Aristotle's entire system was $A = A$.

Philosopher of science David Hull says that there are two kinds of thinkers, the timid and the bold.[66] The timid put forth their ideas in the vocabulary of others. They hide behind others' fame and ride on it. And they try not to step on toes. They eagerly attack the enemies that their sub-culture has targeted as bad guys. But they try hard not to challenge their peers. They try hard not to rouse the wrath of their packmates.

Then there are the bold. The bold have the gonads to put forth entire new systems and vocabularies. And they dare to associate their names and their personalities with their new packages. But boldness is risky. Others take aim at you and try to shoot you down. Others loathe your arrogance. Others hate you for trying to monopolize the stage and for threatening to thrust them into the shadows. They hate you for what the Greeks called your *hubris*—your overweening desire for glory. Your overweening desire for attention.

But Aristotle was the boldest of the bold. He proposed a new logic, a new vocabulary, and an utterly new system. First off, he proposed looking for what he called "elementary laws."[67] "Elementary laws"—that sounds like an automatic, right? A concept that's very old, not radically new. But it was a devastatingly new concept. Look through the collected works of Plato and you will not find it. And Aristotle proposed a system for this hunt for "elementary laws." A system based on what he called "axioms."[68]

How did Aristotle's new system work? Aristotle ordered that you lay out your definitions up front.[69] Then he demanded that you state your "axioms." Next he told you to use something else he called "theorems."[70] Finally, he told you to present something he called your "proof."[71] But that wasn't all. Aristotle handed you the concept of a "hypothesis."[72] He defined a modular nubbin of a whole new kind, a unit—a "unit as an indivisible quantity."[73] And he commanded that you ground your conclusions on "demonstration."[74]

Aristotle did more. He called for dividing things into "genus"[75] and "species."[76] He enunciated what would become the first rule of algebra—"if equals be taken from equals, the remainders are equal." And he called his new package "science."[77] Or, to be more specific, a host of "sciences." Among those sciences were two that Pythagoras had mapped out—arithmetic and geometry. Then there was "zoology," knowledge about animals, a field Aristotle seems to have invented. Says Aristotle, "If the inquiry is zoological"[78] your focus should be on "the characteristics of the whole animal kingdom."[79] And Aristotle's new sciences included many more: "optics . . . physical science . . . [the science of the] physician[80] . . . harmonics[81] . . . mechanics . . . [and] astronomy."[82] Not to mention specialized branches like "stereometry . . . nautical astronomy . . . [and] . . . aesthetical harmonics."[83]

Some of Aristotle's vocabulary was old. He borrowed words like "species," "genus," "science," "hypothesis," and "proof" from Plato. But much of it was stunningly new. Words like "axiom," "theorem," and the "unit as an indivisible quantity" were total innovations. What's more, the use of these words to fashion a methodical system was astonishing.

And Aristotle still wasn't finished. He introduced the opposition between "quantity" and "quality,"[84] the basis of the distinction between merely describing something with words and grasping it mathematically. He laid the base for the prejudice against the "qualitative" and in favor of the "quantitative" that has driven modern science to prize the mathematical and to despise the descriptive. Aristotle also invented a radically new symbol system, a new way to turn ideas about real things into abstractions. It's a method some might praise and others might curse. A method some might find more of a confuser than a clarifier. But it would provide a powerful tool to mathematics. It's the habit of naming what we now call "variables" as A's, B's, C's, and D's. Says Aristotle, "Let A represent animal, B animal characteristics, C D E particular animals, as man or horse. Then A will be the reason why B is predicated of C."[85]

Do you find that at all mind paralyzing? I do. But for those whose minds can handle these things with ease, the technique has been incredibly potent. And fortunately the human enterprise, the grand search engine of which we are all a part, works because of the differences between individual minds. It works because A's, B's, and C's come easily to a small minority of us.

Under Aristotle's application of A's, B's, and C's is a hidden assumption. That assumption? That there are deep structures, underlying patterns, that apply to everything from ears to puffs of air to octopi, not to mention to planets and stars. And, in fact, that's the assumption established by Plato with his story of the cave and reinforced by Aristotle. But remember, it's an assumption. And every assumption is a hypothesis in disguise.

But with A's, B's, and C's, Aristotle's staggering contribution was still not at an end. Aristotle mapped out the key principles of something that you and I use every day: logic. But he didn't call it that. He called it "induction," "deduction," "demonstration,"[86] and "reasoning."[87] And Aristotle's new-fangled "reasoning" was so central to his system that he devoted an entire book to it: the *Organon*.[88] What principles of "reasoning" did Aristotle demand that we follow? The very principles of logic that you and I are challenging right now. Principles that would prove to have enormous power. But principles we will have to carve a path beyond to understand the God Problem.

At the heart of Aristotle's logic were his variations on $A = A$. "Of two contradictories," Aristotle decreed, "one or the other must be true."[89] With those words, Aristotle established the doctrine of dualism. The logic of either/or. The assumption that either A is A or it is not, and there is no compromise. The concept that it's either one thing or the other but not both. Or, as Jonathan Swift would someday put it, the debate over which end of an egg is up.[90] Aristotle called this "dialectical reasoning."[91]

And Aristotle invented another fundamental of modern Western thought—reductionism, breaking things down to their smallest units. "For the attributes of what is compounded of the elementary may be deduced from these."[92] Break things down to their smallest parts, their "elementary members." Why? Because complex things are "compounded of the elementary." And complex things can be explained by the "elementary laws." In fact, the laws were called "elementary" because they were the laws of the smallest units of things, the laws of the "lowest and indivisible classes."[93] The laws of the "elements." But laws of the smallest units would prove blind in one eye to the secrets of cosmic creativity.

Another rule of Aristotle's logic, another rule based on $A = A$: if you find two things of the same kind, look for the laws, the rules that they have in common. More important, "proceed to elicit their peculiar properties." How? By "developing them by means of the common canons." By assuming iteration. If a principle applies to one A it applies to another. If every leaf equals every other leaf and if you find the reason one leaf falls, that reason for falling will apply to all leaves.

In other words, establish which things belong to a common genus or species. To a common type of thing. Then deduce principles that apply to every thing in that category, the principles that apply to the whole "set." (Yes, Aristotle introduced the essential term that would lead to modern math's set theory in the nineteenth century.) Make sure you get your definitions right. If you do, the rules, the "elementary laws," that apply to one A will also apply to another. Stick with $A = A$ and get your A's right, and you will have a guaranteed technique for finding the laws of everything in sight. Including sight itself.

How did Aristotle's system work in reality? Awkwardly. In ways that are foreign to you and me. "The Nile swells at the close of the month," he says, "because the weather is stormy." And why does the weather raise a ruckus at the end of the month? "The weather is stormy because the moon wanes." Today's weather forecasters pay no attention to the moon when they tell you whether to carry your umbrella to work or to douse yourself in sunblock. They do not think that the moon has anything to do with rainy and sunshiny days. So what leads Aristotle to connect storms with the moon? Tradition. Tradition that goes back to the Mesopotamians. And $A = A$.

Or one of $A = A$'s variations. If $a = b$ and $b = c$, then $a = c$. That's Aristotle's key method, the syllogism. If "all men are animals," and if "Socrates is a man; Socrates is an animal."[94] That's a syllogism. How does the syllogism work here? A swelling Nile equals the end of the month. Months equal periods of the moon. So periods of the moon equal the swelling Nile.

What's more, storms come at the end of the month. So periods of the moon equal—hold on to yourself—storms.[95] There's more.

Why do leaves fall? Because they are broad. And because of "coagulation." How can we prove it? By "demonstrative science." And how does "demonstrative science" do its business in Aristotle's hands? By "syllogism and demonstration." Brace yourself once again for the strange:

> Let A be the fall of the leaves, B broadness of the leaves, C the vine. Because A is predicated of B, and B of C, therefore A is predicated of C, and B the intermediate is the cause.[96]

Confusing? You bet. But there's more:

> Again, the broadness of the vine-leaves is deducible from their annual fall. If the fall of leaves is produced by coagulation, wherever there is a fall there must be coagulation, and wherever there is coagulation of sap there must be a fall of leaves.[97]

Leaves fall because they are broad and because of coagulation. Leaves fall because their juices gunk up and stop flowing. So wherever you see leaves dropping you can assume the leaves are broad. You can also assume that coagulation is at work.

This, to Aristotle, was "demonstration." And, he says, "we can scarcely have a knowledge more perfect than demonstration."[98] It would take a considerable evolution of the concept of what "demonstration" is all about to give us the science we recognize today. It would take the development of lab experiments and of forms of math far beyond those of the ancient Greeks. But even that evolution would be hinted at by Aristotle. For Aristotle was wise enough to see that you cannot find the secrets of the universe simply by closing your eyes, shutting out the world, and thinking. You need to add in facts from the real world. You need to add in the evidence of the senses, "sensation." Or, as Aristotle put it, "on Experience . . . ensues the beginning of Art and Science."[99]

Aristotle was not a modern scientist. Much of what he wrote was tangled and muddy. Even worse, much of it was very alien to your way of thought and mine. Aristotle was a Greek thinker immersed in an ancient Greek culture. But he was a thinker who dared to be different. A thinker who defied the inhibitions demanded by the notion of hubris. And his boldness paid off. It won him what he was after: fame. It landed him his place in the spotlight of attention. A place that has endured for twenty-three hundred years.

What's more, Aristotle's program for "science"—his "definitions," "axioms," "theorems," and "proof"—would erect the stage on which modern science would someday strut and fret. So would Aristotle's logic, dualism, A's, B's, C's, categorizing things in genus and species, reducing things to their elements (reductionism), the search for elementary laws, and the demand to look at the evidence of the senses. These would be tools of enormous power. But many would also be blinders shutting out some of the most important secrets of cosmic creativity.

***

Meanwhile, Aristotle's axioms would reach down to Giuseppe Peano. And to your infernally impossible homework at Reed.

HOW EUCLID MAKES ARISTOTLE'S "SCIENCE" STICK

One man would do more than any other human to turn Aristotle's system into a recruitment strategy that would persist for ages. His name was Euclid.

Euclid used Aristotle's new ideas to build a template and a temptation. He used Aristotle's ideas to build a lure that would seduce, kidnap, and recruit the minds of greats far, far beyond his time. Seduction, kidnap, and recruitment are the claws of recruitment strategies. And seduction, kidnap, and recruitment are at the heart of cosmic creativity.

In a sense, Euclid was a man with very few tools. He had a compass, but that compass was apparently merely a string you attached to a centerpoint, stretched out, and swiveled 360 degrees to draw a circle. We don't know if it was a string of gut like Pythagoras's or a string of plant fiber.[100] But we do know that Euclid's string was primitive. It was not knotted in units of length like the ropes of the Egyptians. It couldn't be used to measure. Euclid's tool number two was a straightedge, a device with equally primitive capabilities. Why? The straightedge had no numbers or markings of distance either. The straightedge only helped you do one thing—draw straight lines. Like the compass, it was not a measuring device. In fact, Euclid didn't even have numbers and most of the forms of arithmetic that we take for granted today. Instead of numbers, the Greeks used letters of their alphabet.[101]

But Euclid had a secret weapon. It wasn't hidden in the folds of his tunic, it was hidden in the folds of his brain. He had Aristotle's new system. Euclid had Aristotle's commandments: give your definitions, state your axioms, give your propositions, then lay out your step-by-step proof. Euclid also had Aristotle's new invention of using *A*'s, *B*'s, and *C*'s, the system of using letters to make concepts abstract. Letters may be as gnarly as a tangle of old thread, but they have an advantage. They focus attention on the method and its underlying universals, not on a particular practical problem. Letters focus you on the underlying pattern behind what you are doing. And letters remind you that the pattern you've uncovered can apply to everything from olive pits, rocks, and Greek kick balls to objects in the sky.

We know very little about Euclid the man. He was roughly one generation younger than Aristotle. Geographic distance separated him from Aristotle more than time. Euclid lived in a newly built city on a different continent, the continent of Africa. Specifically, he lived in Egypt. But this was not the Egypt that Thales and Pythagoras had visited. It was an Egypt that had been remade in a Greek image. And Euclid lived in an Egyptian city remade, of all things, in a partially Aristotelian image.

An Aristotelian image? A philosopher influencing the building of a city? Surely that's an exaggeration. But it's not. Remember one basic of cosmic creativity: repeat an old pattern in a new medium and you get something new. Aristotle had been born in Stagira, a Greek city on the borderland between barbarism and civilization. The local barbarians were the Macedonians, a horse-and-war obsessed people to Greece's north. But the barbarian leader, Philip II, the king of the Macedonians, had worked wonders. Says US Army War College military historian Richard Gabriel, Philip was the "unifier of Greece, author of Greece's first federal constitution, founder of the first territorial state with a centralized administrative structure in Europe, forger of the first Western national army, the first great general of the Greek imperial age, and dreamer of great dreams." What's more, he "was one of the greatest captains in the history of the West."[102] Philip fought almost nonstop with the Athenians. And those you fight are often those you learn the most about. Philip had apparently watched the rise of Athens's intellectuals and had imagined what might happen if you were to bring together next-tech weaponry, next-tech tactics, and the outside-the-box perspectives of Athenian philosophy.

Philip was never able to conquer Athens itself. But he had a son who he hoped would take up where he left off. Why could the Athenian way of thought be useful to a military commander? Socrates had established the tradition of questioning your assumptions.[103] And Aristotle was working out a whole new system of analysis. A system based on a brand-new way of thinking that would later be called "logic." A system that Aristotle called "science." Questioning assumptions and logically analyzing what you're up against can help you win battles—and win the world. And even if it fails utterly on the battlefield, it can be a powerful identity tool. A powerful attentional magnet. It can give you status! So Philip hired the greatest Greek mind of the age to tutor his son. That man was Aristotle. In the process Philip made sure that Aristotle would achieve his goal—towering in greatness. Taking center stage in attention space. Achieving lasting fame.

You know who Philip's son was. You've read about him many a time. That mere fact is a testament to the social magnetism he achieved. His name was Alexander. Known later in life as "Alexander the Great."

When Alexander the Great hit the age of twenty-four, he conquered the massive Persian Empire.[104] One of the territories he gathered unto his bosom was a state that Persia had conquered over a hundred years earlier, Egypt.[105] And when Alexander died at the age of thirty-two "in the palace of Nebuchadnezzar II" in the ancient Mesopotamian capital of Babylon,[106] his generals carved up the lands that Alexander had won. One of those generals was named Ptolemy.

Ptolemy and Alexander the Great had been friends since childhood. In fact, as a youth Ptolemy may have studied with Alexander under Aristotle. When Alexander died, Ptolemy did two things. He took over Egypt and he founded a dynasty. The dynasty that three hundred years later would give us Cleopatra. And he added vigor to a city whose foundations Alexander the Great himself had laid out, Alexandria.[107] In Egypt. A city that repeated Athens's patterns in a new location. A city that spread Aristotle's influence. A city that Ptolemy turned into one of the greatest centers of learning the West had ever seen. A city that under Ptolemy built the most famous library in history.[108] A city that drew intellectuals the way that honeycomb, "the sweet food of the gods,"[109] draws ants at an outdoor "symposium," an outdoor drinking party.[110]

One of those Alexandria drew was a mysterious figure, Euclid.[111] And here is nearly everything we know about Euclid,[112] as reported by Proclus, a philosopher and mathematician who came along eight hundred years after Euclid's death, a philosopher who saw Euclid as a dim, mythic figure from the ancient past:

> Euclid . . . put together the *Elements*, collecting many of Eudoxus's theorems, perfecting many of Theaetetus's, and also bringing to irrefragable demonstration the things which were only somewhat loosely proved by his predecessors. This man lived in the time of the first Ptolemy. He is then younger than the pupils of Plato, but older than Eratosthenes and Archimedes, the latter having been contemporaries, as Eratosthenes somewhere says.[113]

Repetition of an old pattern in a new medium often makes something new. Euclid, yes, Euclid the man and the culture he lived in, the culture of Alexandria, provided a radically new medium in which to translate the pattern demanded by Aristotle. And a radically new medium in which to repeat another old pattern, a pattern established by Thales. Geometry.

The Babylonian and the Egyptian math mavens had focused on practical things—taxes, land measurement, and feeding armies of pyramid builders. But not Euclid. The slave culture of Greece and of the new Greek sphere of influence—a sphere of influence that now included Persia and Egypt—made Euclid a man of the mind, a man who despised practicality.

After his first day of class, a new student of Euclid's asked Euclid what practical use he'd be able to make of the geometry he was working so insanely hard to comprehend. Euclid called over "his slave" and said with a tone of airy dismissal, "Give him a coin since he must needs make gain by what he learns."[114] No Babylonian or Egyptian scribe-priest would have said such a thing.

Euclid also had attitude. The Babylonian and Egyptian mathematician-priests were obsequious and obedient around their monarchs. They referred to themselves as their rulers' slaves. But Proclus reported that when Ptolemy I, the general of Alexander who had made himself the new pharaoh, asked if he could get a few quick lessons on this geometry stuff, Euclid was as frigid as an ice storm in a field of barley. "There is," Euclid is reported to have said, "no royal road to geometry."[115] Even a king would have to abase himself and do years of homework to approach the truths of geometry, truths whose laws were far more perfect than the laws of mere politics and power. How very much like the initiation rituals of Pythagoras's acolytes. And how utterly brilliant as a recruitment strategy: to say that your new discipline puts you on a plane far higher than that of mere kings.

Euclid did and yet did not make an original contribution to geometry. Hmmm. Isn't that a statement of opposites, the sort of contradiction that Aristotle said cannot exist? You bet. So what does it mean? In Greece, geometry had been a subject with its own way of looking at the world since Pythagoras in 520 BCE. It had been around for over two hundred years by the time Euclid came around. Geometry had taken the gift of Babylonian and Egyptian math and had added three things that were radically new—the concept of the angle, the concept of the sphere, and the notion of "perfect" geometric figures. Figures you could see with your mind. Figures isolated from all earthly purposes. Figures that no longer were tallies of the number of barleycorns you could fit into a silo. Figures that were now seen as the building blocks of something far bigger than a human heap of stone. Figures that were seen as underlying the cosmos itself. Figures that were imagined to be behind everything from musical harmonies to the powers of earth, wind, and fire. Geometric figures that allegedly repeated their pattern in everything from elementary particles to the spheres of the heavens.

By the time of Euclid, math had grabbed the minds of fans, ambitious careerists, and unwilling students for thirty-seven hundred years. Which means that Euclid stood on the shoulders of giants. And here are some hints as to how these giants were kidnapped, seduced, and recruited by a pattern far larger than themselves. Reports Proclus, when it came to geometry, "Thales was followed by Mamercus, brother of the poet Stesichorus."[116] What's so important about that? Adds Proclus, Mamercus "is recorded to have been zealous about geometry."[117] Zeal: an intense focus, an enjoyment of work, a pleasure that makes work addictive, an obsession that makes work a greater treat than any mere game or party. That is one of the primary tools of a recruitment strategy. Then comes another attractor: the desire for fame. Explains Proclus, "Hippias the Elean has narrated that his reputation was won in Geometry."[118] Reputation implies a fierce competition to be the one who comes out on top, a fierce competition for attention, a fierce competition for renown. Another tool of a recruitment strategy. Then there was the impulse to use math as an excuse for conversation. Intense conversation. The sort of conversation in which each participant vies to be the greatest expert in the room. Or in the city. Or in the era. Reported Proclus, "After Pythagoras, Anaxagoras of Clazomenae discussed many geometrical questions; as also Oenopides of Chios." "Discussed" is a very mild word for what these men did. They were, says Proclus, "renowned" for their "studies."[119] So renowned that Plato mentioned them as his "rivals."[120] Fame, renown, debate, rivalry, and zeal are all tools of a recruitment strategy. Recruitment strategies pull together social movements with a simple tool: the competition for attention.

Which means that these men were intensely competitive. But to compete, they had to cooperate. They had to draw on a common body of work. And they had to add to it. Opposites are joined at the hip. Discussion, competition, fame, and the years of study and thought that feed expert conversation—these are human versions of the sort of termite behavior that builds a hive. These are the hooks of a recruitment strategy. And these are the hooks that turn mere humans into antennas, probes, feelers, and sensory neurons of a search engine. They are the hooks that would turn generation after generation of extraordinary thinkers into new-frontier explorers for you and me.

Again, Euclid did not make an original contribution to geometry. He assembled the ideas of others. Others like Pythagoras, Eudoxus, and Theaetetus. Yet he made the greatest contribution since Pythagoras. How? The secret is in the power of recruitment strategies. The secret is in the power of a persuasive format, a template that vigorously produces copies of itself. Euclid breathed life into the form that Aristotle had sketched out: state your definitions, give your axioms, then proceed to theorems and proof. A form of presentation that Aristotle had conceived, but did not have enough lifetime to achieve. And when Euclid repeated the geometry of Pythagoras, Theaetetus, and Eudoxus in Aristotle's format, he changed geometry utterly.

Again, how did Euclid pull off a paradox? How did he merely repeat the work of two hundred years of predecessors in Greek geometry, yet produce something new? Something with a powerful grip. Something intensely compelling. Like a termite adding to a tower, he iterated something old in a new context. And he generated one of the most potent recruitment strategies that the realm of intellect has ever seen. To repeat, Euclid followed Aristotle's rules for a systematic layout of a science. He started with definitions. He stated his axioms . . . his assumptions.[121] Then he worked out his theorems. And he proved them with logical demonstration.

Even the title of Euclid's work bore the mark of Aristotle's system. Aristotle demanded that you break genus and species down to their most fundamental and unchangeable parts, their "elements."[122] So Euclid's work became known as *The Elements of Euclid*. How does a demand like Aristotle's avoid the fate of most words, the fate of being forgotten? The fate of dwindling into the darkness of obscurity? It survives by building on earlier recruitment strategies.

***

Once Aristotle demanded breaking things down into modular bricks, into elements, many scholars tried to earn their spot on the stage of attention by reducing geometry to its elements. The contestants included Hippocrates, Leon, Eudoxus of Cnidus, Theudius the Magnesian, and Hermotimus of Colophon. So what made Euclid's thirteen books of *Elements* so different from all the rest? Why have Euclid's *Elements* not only survived, but thrived? Why would Euclid's *Elements* play a vital role in shaping modern science and modern philosophy? Why would they lead to Kepler and Einstein? Why would they lead to the tools of your thinking and mine? And why would they prove vital to the God Problem? Or, to put it differently, how did Euclid tap the powers of social magnetism in a way that the others had not? Says Proclus, by "raising to the level of unimpeachable demonstration what had been rather weakly proved by earlier workers."[123] But there must be more to it than that.

Geminus, a first-century-BCE writer, thought he knew the answer to Euclid's success—simplicity. If you've taken a look at *The Elements*, it's very unlikely that you'll agree. Grasping Euclid's *Elements* is like trying to grab two dozen greased Alexandrian garden snakes. That's why the first-day pupil to whom Euclid had his slave give a coin bellyached. And that's why even Egypt's ruler Ptolemy I complained. Yet Euclid's work was apparently a breeze compared to the elements that had come before. And it was perfect for teaching. Says Geminus of those who came before Euclid, many of the previous elements were incomplete. Some had proofs of "an unconscionable length."[124] Some left out vital elements like "proportion."[125] Others started with introductions that did nothing but attack their rivals. But most had too much unnecessary stuff. Ideally, says Geminus, "everything superfluous is to be cut out."[126]

Why? Because what people like Geminus were looking for was the perfect textbook. And too much clutter "might prove an impediment to study."[127] Adds Geminus, the perfect geometry text should use "all that helps forward and contributes to the end in view"—teaching.[128] Passing the knowledge along. Planting it in acres and leagues of new neuronal space. The perfect text should have "a clear and brief exposition."[129] It should avoid the sort of tortured writing that is "painful to our minds."[130] It should minimize "the difficulties experienced by the beginner."[131] Declares Geminus, "In all these respects you will find Euclid's system of Elements to surpass the rest."[132]

Again, why? Because it is complete, "a complete introduction to the theory of the primary figures."[133] And it's just what students need. It goes from the easy to the hard. "The passage from things simpler to things more complex is effected in clear and orderly wise."[134] In other words, Geminus was looking for the perfect recruitment template, the perfect tool for iterating a system in as many minds as possible, the perfect tool for translating geometry into the varied psyches of students with different personalities and with different perspectives, the perfect way to translate a basic pattern into the medium of new minds, the book that could do the most to help teachers garden the ideas of geometry in as many brains as possible. And that's what Euclid's *Elements* turned out to be.

Euclid's *Elements* starts with things we all take for granted, with "common notions,"[135] with axioms, and it shows "the deduction of the theory from accepted ideas,"[136] the deduction of theory from axioms. And, most of all, it uses the plan laid out by a master whose name Geminus doesn't mention: Aristotle.

Over the door of Plato's Academy were written the words "Let no one enter here who is ignorant of geometry."[137] But after Euclid, that phrase was changed to "Let no one come to our school who has not learned the Elements of Euclid."[138]

***

Even to a late-nineteenth-century man like Euclid's Cambridge University translator and editor William Barrett Frankland,[139] Euclid's *Elements* is more than a mere textbook. It is the very epitome of a planter of an old pattern in a new medium. It is a transformer. A remaker. A reshaper. A re-creator of the core of our humanity. In Euclid's *Elements*, Frankland concludes with awe, pleasure, and pride, "Each new geometrical truth is to be another round in the ladder of the soul's ascent to higher things."[140]

And ascents to higher things are vital to the way the cosmos creates.

GALILEO'S DAD AND THE DRUG OF GEOMETRY

In his *Posterior Analytics* Aristotle laid out a new recruitment pattern. And in the *Elements*, Euclid unfurled that pattern's implicit possibilities. Euclid unfolded Aristotle's pattern in a new medium—the medium of geometry. Did Aristotle and Euclid's recruitment strategy work? Did it increase the hold of Aristotle and Euclid on the spotlit center stage of attention space? Did it act as an attractor? Did it seduce, kidnap, and recruit? You bet.

In late-sixteenth-century Italy, the Italy of Galileo's youth, Euclid was so widespread and his recruitment strategy so powerful that the *Elements of Geometry* frightened parents the way that video games frightened the parents of the 1990s. Why? Euclid's geometry was considered addictive. One parent rattled by geometry's threat was Vincenzo Galilei,[141] the father of a kid named Galileo. Galileo's father knew geometry's lure well. He was a musical theorist, a composer, and a player of the lute who is credited with helping to start a revolution that would sideline the madrigal and lead to baroque music.[142] He was also the author of a book called *A Dialog on Ancient and Modern Music,* a work that among other things questioned the story of Pythagoras's musical revelation at the blacksmith shop.[143] But a book that mentioned Pythagoras twenty-three times and called him "divine."[144] And, remember, Pythagoras was more than a thinker about music; he was one of the founders of geometry. So Galileo grew up in the shade of circles, compasses, and heavenly ratios. Yet Galileo had to sneak and connive to learn Euclid. Why? His father wanted him to be able to make a living. His father wanted him to be a doctor. His father wanted that medical career for his son so badly that he forbade Galileo to study geometry. Galileo's dad was convinced that geometry would seduce his son away from a focus on the art of the physician. And he was right. Galileo went behind his father's back and tried to persuade his tutor to teach him the *Elements* of Euclid whether his father wanted it or not. That's attentional magnetism.

When Galileo asked his tutor to slip him geometry on the sly, the tutor knew who was giving him his pay: not Galileo but his father, Vincenzo. So the tutor became as sneaky as young Galileo. He went secretly to Galileo's dad with the news. Galileo's father gave the tutor permission to teach his son the forbidden knowledge of Euclid. But he forbade the tutor to let Galileo know that he'd given a quiet OK. When Galileo took off like a shot and turned out to be a ferociously motivated learner, Galileo's father canceled his approval. But by then it was too late. Galileo had taught himself enough geometry to continue on his own. Writes Galileo's daughter, Polissena, Galileo "had not advanced [with his tutor] so far as the end of the first book of Euclid. He proceeded secretly, wishing to attain at least as far as the forty-seventh proposition, then considered a famous one."[145] Yes, famous. As in "fame." A lure used by a recruitment strategy. And the fame of a geometric proposition means that geometry was in the air. Geometry and its enticements, including its puzzles, its unsolved mysteries.

Like the challenge of proving the forty-seventh proposition, the one that laid out the Pythagorean theorem. The key theorem on right angles. The theorem whose number triples even the Babylonians and the Egyptians had known. The theorem in which you build square game boards on the two short sides of a right-angle triangle, cover the game boards with pebbles, put the pebbles in a bag, shake them up, lay them out on a square drawn on the longest line of the triangle, and discover that your pebbles fit precisely. Or in which you simply count the game board squares on the two short sides, add them up, and get the number of squares in a game board built on side three.

Galileo was seduced by an unholy trio: Pythagoras, Aristotle, and the grand consolidator, Euclid. Galileo was seduced, kidnapped, and reeled in by a recruitment strategy. Galileo was an eager prisoner of geometry.

And he was not alone.

KEPLER: HOW TO TICKLE THE SOUL OF THE EARTH

Aristotle had invented the axiom. And Euclid's use of the axiom in geometry had proven a stunningly successful recruitment strategy. Galileo, who was born over eighteen hundred years after Euclid died, was utterly captivated by what Euclid had left behind. But he was not the only one. Euclid's geometry—and its druglike lure—were infectious. So infectious that Germany's Johannes Kepler, born seven years after Galileo and a full 353 miles away from Galileo's hometown of Pisa, was even more obsessed with Euclid, with geometry, and with axioms than Galileo. And to be more obsessed than Galileo wasn't easy. Just ask Galileo's dad.

Geometry, complete with Aristotle's definitions, axioms, and proofs, would be Johannes Kepler's primary tool for figuring things out. But when we say "figuring things out," do not be deceived. Johannes Kepler's thought process would be so different from yours and mine that we might find it downright Martian. To see how, let's go deep diving in one of the chapters of Johannes Kepler's 1619 book on the *Harmony of the World*, a chapter called "On the Causes of the Influential Configurations, and of Their Degrees in Number and Order."

What's the first step in "science" according to Aristotle? Define your terms. What's the first step that Euclid takes in his *Elements*? Thirty-five definitions.[146] And what's Kepler's first step? An imitation of the method that Aristotle prescribed and that Euclid turned into an action pattern. Kepler's first step is to lay out his definitions. Two of them.

Definition I

The word "configuration" is used for the angle between two rays.[147]

Very interesting. Kepler is using the angle, a concept invented by the Greeks. A concept unknown to the Babylonians and to the Egyptians. A concept that simply didn't exist for the first thirty-six hundred years of mathematical thinking.

As Kepler continues with his first definition, he shows us more of his dependence on the ideas left to him by centuries of others. How? Kepler tells you and me how to determine the angle between the rays from two planets, rays that meet at a point on Earth, by using "the arc of the great circle drawn on the zodiac."[148] Yes, the zodiac. Another invention brought to Kepler, you, and me by over three thousand years of mathematical and astronomical puzzling.

Kepler is not using the flat sky of the Babylonians and the Egyptians. He does not imagine a sky whose constellations are held together and controlled by the sort of harness ropes used on wagon horses in Babylon. The harness ropes that the Mesopotamians believed explained the peculiar movements of the stars.[149] Instead, Kepler imagines a sky of circles. A sky that comes from another metaphor, a use of the technology that comes from cutting lengths of gut or from braiding and twisting fiber filaments into rope and string. He imagines a sky of circles like the circles you can draw with Euclid's string compass. A sky of circles like those that the Greeks took out of the shadows. A sky of the circles that the Greeks used to radically reinvent the scheme for the key constellations.

Remember, the Babylonians saw the sky in terms of their hottest hi-tech device—the chart drawn on clay. They saw the sky as a grid like a tic-tac-toe board. So they saw the twelve key constellations within a system of straight lines, cross-hatched straight lines. Yes, they had reduced their sixteen key constellations to twelve.[150] And they had associated those constellations with the twelve months of their year. But the Mesopotamian constellations were in a "Shupuk shame,"[151] a pileup. A mess. A mess that had been straightened out by imposing a hierarchical grid. By putting the sun to rule over one column, the moon to rule over another, and Venus to rule over a third.

Then the Greeks had radically reperceived the sky. They saw the sky in terms of their new tool of thought—the circle. And the Greeks used their circle to reorganize the twelve key constellations. They remade those constellations from a piled-up grid, a chart, to a circle. And they called their new twelve-slice-of-pizza circular sky a "circle of little animals," a "zodiac."[152]

So far so good. But here's where things get strange. In laying out his Euclidean definitions and axioms, Kepler goes back to an idea that the Babylonians and Aristotle took for granted, but that you and I do not. He goes back to the notion that the planets control the weather. The idea that you can predict storms and sunny skies by looking at the dots of light in the night sky. "The formation of an angle [between the planets] at the Earth is followed by an effect on the Earth," Kepler asserts. What is that effect? Tickling the Earth into exhaling. Tweaking the Earth into breathing out "the material of rains."[153] And tickling the Earth into breathing out the materials "of other occurrences in the sky."[154]

Wait a minute. "Tickling" the Earth into exhaling? Surely this is taking literary license too far. Kepler could not possibly have tickling in mind. He cannot possibly be saying that angles between planets, mere angles, as in the corners of triangles, wiggle a finger of some sort in the Earth's sensitive zones, her soft spots, her equivalent of armpits, tummies, and sexual centers. Or could he?

Yes, that's exactly what Kepler is saying. The angles between planets change the weather by working on something deep within the Earth. Something "in the Earth itself."[155] What in the world does Kepler mean? He answers that question very quickly. He lays out definition number two. And in definition number two of an "influential"[156]angle of the planets, Kepler says that the angle between "the rays of a pair of planets . . . stimulate sublunary Nature."[157]

The angle between planets also stimulates "the inferior faculties of animate beings to be more active."[158] Animate beings like you and me. A mere angle between planets "stimulates" the nature down here on Earth, down here in the "sublunary" zone, down here beneath the moon? And a mere angle between planets kicks you and me into motion? You've got to be kidding. Not at all. But let's leave you and me out of it and get down to this "sublunary nature" idea. For in it lies weirdness. And Plato.

The "foolish herd," Kepler says, imagine that the rains fall from the planets themselves. And scholars believe that the planets impact the weather by rousing "vapors." But this, says Kepler,

> is absurd, and like a joke or a flight of poetic fancy, to suppose that from the coming together harmonically of a pair of rays, as if from the coupling of a man and a woman, a vapor is conceived as the material for wind or rain.[159]

Note that phrase: "the coupling of a man and a woman." Yes, Kepler brings sex into this, not me. He says that "the bowels of the earth" operate "in the manner of a pregnant woman."[160] But rays, Kepler says, do not copulate or writhe in a bed to generate sexual juices. Rays do not work up a sexual sweat to "conceive" vapors. For Kepler the confluence of rays is Pythagorean. It is musical. It is based on ratios.

OK, but do the angles of the planets really influence the weather down here on Earth? You bet. And how do they do it? It's time to cut the primitive foolishness, says Kepler. The foolishness of the "common herd." It's time for reason to speak. But one age's reason is another age's insanity. Here's what Kepler thought reasonable in 1600: The Earth has a soul. And the angles of the planets move that soul. That's how the angles of the planets generate the weather. And that's how "the seat of the cause which sets in motion occurrences in the sky ... is not in either one planet or the other, nor in any empty place in the world, but in the Earth itself."[161]

"The sublunary soul of Nature," says Kepler emphatically, is "moved or stimulated by the aspect" of the planets, by the "looks" of "onlookers,"[162] by the stares from the face of the planets. Then,

> reminded of itself, [it] stirs itself up to draw out from the bowels of the Earth the material for every kind of weather.[163]

Got that, you dummies of the common herd? The planets don't influence the weather by stirring vapors. They churn and mix the weather by waking up the soul of the Earth, "the sublunary soul of Nature," and by reminding her of herself. Isn't that a wacky idea, that the world has a soul? That a planet has a core of emotions, passions, and spirit? No, to Kepler the concept of the soul of the Earth is rock solid. Why? The idea of a "world soul" comes from the best of all possible sources, the most believable, the most unimpeachable, the man who left the shadows of the cave behind and stared the sun of truth in the face—Plato.

But here's another surprise: even Plato was a creationist. He didn't have the Bible and its creation in seven days to go on. The Bible was from a people that the Greeks of Plato's day paid no attention to, a people in a land unworthy of attention, Israel. The creation in seven days came from a people Plato probably never heard of, the Jews. But Plato believed in a "Creator." And during the Creation

> the world became a living creature truly endowed with soul and intelligence by the providence of God.[164]

Those are Plato's very words. Plato's words in his book *The Timaeus*. The "world" is a "living creature." And Plato's notion of a living Earth hung in there, wriggling and writhing nineteen hundred years later in the mind of Johannes Kepler.

But that's not all Plato left to Kepler. Plato was steeped in Pythagoras's number mysticism. According to University of Pennsylvania ancient philosophy specialist Charles H. Kahn, Plato's *Timaeus*, the book in which Plato laid out the idea of the world soul, "is particularly rich in Pythagorean numbers and cosmic geometry."[165] So to Plato, the world soul is both a seat of passion and a center of musical harmonies. Remember, musical harmonies are number ratios. So music equals numbers. And music equals emotion equals soul. Which means that numbers equal emotion. Yes, numbers equal emotion.

This has a strange implication for Plato's idea of a world soul. And for Kepler's. The world soul is generated by numbers. And the world soul is stirred by numbers. The world soul is stirred by what Kepler calls harmonic angles. Yes, "harmonic," as in "harmonies." In other words, the world soul is stirred by music. Just like you and me. And it gets weirder. Explains Kahn, in Plato

> the world soul, from which the human soul is eventually derived, is constructed by a series of odd and even integers beginning with 2 and 3, the

first even and odd numbers, and proceeding through their squares (4 and 9) and cubes (8 and 27).[166]

That, believe it or not, makes the world soul both number and sound, both number and polyphony. How? Continues Kahn, "This construction" of the world soul "is completed by inserting intervals corresponding to the harmonic . . . means."[167]

And why does a soul—a world soul or your soul—resonate to the harmonies of numbers? Kepler has the answer. Just as Pythagoras implied, says Kepler, "circles are potentially the actual souls."[168] Yes, you read it right. Circles may be souls. And souls may be circles. That's why circles "are moved by the aspects," that's why circles are "moved" by the angles with which the faces of the planets—faces like yours and mine—look at the Earth and look at you and me.

What's more, "Nature perceives the quantity of an angle, which two rays form at the Earth." Yes, "Nature perceives." And nature's taste in angles, like your taste in music and mine, is finicky. Geometrically finicky. Nature, says Kepler, "can . . . perceive the fitness of that angle, along with the others, for congruence."[169] Nature hears the "consonances" of angles.[170] What in the world are consonances? Brace yourself. "Consonances . . . are sounds."[171] They are harmonies. They are music. Real music. The sort of music you can get, says Kepler, "by the striking of strings." "Strings" that are "stretched out."[172] The sort of music you can get from the sound of Pythagoras's strings of animal gut stretched by dangling weights.

Nature has an aesthetic sensibility. Nature has a sensuality. Nature has a sensuality that is visceral. (Remember, to Kepler, the Earth has "bowels.") That's why "the sublunary soul of Nature" is moved by angles. That's why nature is stirred by the angles at which the faces of the planets rivet their eyes on the Earth and give the Earth's soul something very human, the oxygen of the human soul, attention.

But there's more. Hang on to your seat. Consonances are the fabled "music of the spheres." And that is not merely a stock phrase. At least not to Kepler. Kepler dedicated the entire book from which this chapter "On the Causes of the Influential Configurations" comes, his *Harmony of the World*, to figuring out the geometry of the universe through one basic technique, a technique that looks utterly daft to you and me. That technique? Puzzling out the patterns of the music that the cosmos makes. If you riddle out the patterns of that music, Kepler was convinced, you could find "the distances of the planets from the Sun by a new form of calculation never tried before by anyone."[173] Why? Because music is one of the most powerful manifestations of geometry, says Kepler. And the cosmos is geometric.[174] The cosmos is geometry incarnate. We all know that. Don't we?

Very strange ideas. Very strange indeed. At least to you and me. Circles are souls. Circles can be tickled by angles between the planets. The Earth has a soul. A soul that exhales. A soul that's a connoisseur of musical harmonies. A soul that can be "reminded of itself." A soul you can sometimes think of in sexual terms. But these ideas are the very opposite of strange to Kepler. Why? Because in all of this, Kepler is standing on the shoulders of Pythagoras and Plato. What's more, Kepler lays out his conclusions using the "scientific" techniques of Aristotle and Euclid—definition, axiom, and proof. Which means that the pile Kepler stands on has social magnetism. It has the kind of attentional magnetism that stokes the enthusiasm of termites, that gets termites to pile on hard, and that motivates termites to build a column in a larger structure. The pile Kepler stands on is a recruitment strategy. A recruitment strategy that by Kepler's day had hung in there for nineteen hundred years. And a recruitment strategy that is about to hang in even tighter.

KEPLER'S BOXES AND BALLS:
YES, KEPLER'S FREAKY MATH

Johannes Kepler's Earth with a soul that savors the music of angles would not be the only bit of his science that we would find odd. If Kepler's astrology came from Mars, his math and his astronomy would come from Venus. It would be strange as strange could be. Why? Because like Galileo, Kepler loved geometry. But that was all he had. The standard tool of today's science, the equation, was still a thing of the future. So how in the world do you probe the heavens with nothing but a string compass and a straightedge? And how do you probe the dots of light in the sky when you are missing something else vital—the angle?

What? Kepler missing the angle? Surely you jest. You just told me that Kepler had angles all over the place. Yes, but Kepler's "angle" was not our angle. Why? Because one key trick that we take for granted was not a part of Kepler's vocabulary. One key technology. We mark off the circle in 360 equal units. And we number the markings. In other words, we turn a circle into a dial. We turn a circle into a protractor. Then we use the 360 numbered markings on the circle to measure. We use those markings to determine whether an angle is two degrees, twenty degrees, or one hundred and twenty degrees. But that sort of marking had not yet been invented in Kepler's time. What did exist?

For Kepler, you measured an angle by drawing a series of geometric solids in a circle to see which solid matched the width of the angle. For example, you drew a square inside your circle to measure what we would call a right angle. If that didn't match the angle, Kepler recommended that you try another geometric shape: "After that the . . . hexagon, the pentagon with the ten-angled star, the octagon with the eight-angled star, the decagon with the five-angled star, and the dodecagon with the twelve-angled star."[175] Draw each of these inside a circle one at a time until you get something that matches the angle you're trying to measure.

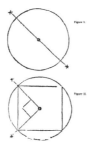

Kepler measures angles by fitting geometric figures into circles. Here Kepler draws a square to measure what we would call a "right angle." *Drawing by Johannes Kepler, from* The Harmony of the World *(1619).*

More of Kepler's use of geometry to translate an angle into math. *Drawing by Johannes Kepler, from* The Harmony of the World *(1619).*

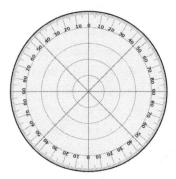

The protractor, the magic modern instrument that the Babylonians, the Egyptians, the Greeks, and Kepler did NOT have. *Courtesy of Georges Khaznadar, Wikimedia Commons.*

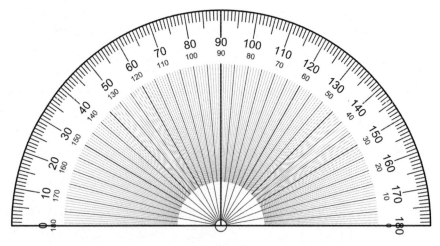

A version of the protractor that may look more familiar. *Courtesy of Scientif38, Wikimedia Commons.*

Why would this primitive way of determining angles be relevant to you and me? Because Kepler was one of those who gave us the solar system we live with every day. The solar system we imagine to be a firm and obvious truth. In Kepler's day, that truth—the truth of the solar system—was still a struggling hypothesis. (Thank you, Aristotle, for that word.) It was a new idea trying to rise high in the competition between termite piles. It was a new concept struggling to become a pillar and a wall of your perception and mine.

Kepler put some indispensable bricks on that pile. But without math as we know it, how in the world did he pull this off? Remember, it was Johannes Kepler who gave us the idea that the orbits of the planets were elliptical. Why is that a big deal? Because once the Greeks had uploaded the circle from a daily fact of grapes, the moon, the sun, and coins to an idea, once they had turned the circle into a mind tool, they'd gone overboard. Aristotle, the ultimate expert on science, had said that circles were perfect. And obviously the heavens were perfect. We all know that, right? So the heavens were clearly built from circles. And the use of circles to explain the heavens had become dogma. Any deviation got you in trouble.

But circles failed to explain the actual movements of the dots in the sky. So Kepler gave us the idea that the orbits of the planets were egg shaped. He gave us the idea that those ellipses could be measured mathematically. And he gave us the three laws of planetary motion.[176] The laws that offer a mathematical description of how the planets slow in their motion when they swing toward the end of the egg away from the sun. And the laws that explain how the planets speed up again when they turn the egg's far end and head back toward the sun again. The laws that make it possible to predict the strange backward and forward movements of the planets in the sky. But, again, Kepler did not do any of this with a math we would recognize.[177] He did it all with Euclid. He did it all with geometry's pictures. And with geometry's shapes. He did it with a compass and a straightedge. Not with a ruler, a protractor, and equations.

But there's more. For Kepler, the real trick was not just to predict the movements of pinpricks of light. He wanted to find the deep structures of the cosmos. And he wanted to find those patterns by using the legacy of Pythagoras and Euclid—geometry. Kepler wanted to find the Ur patterns, the simple patterns, that would explain the distances of the planets from the sun. The patterns that would explain his own meticulous astronomical observations and the even more intense observations of his coresearcher, the great cataloguer of the movements of the dots in the sky—Tycho Brahe. The man with the silver and gold artificial nose.

How would Kepler go about finding the distances between the planets? How would he solve what in one of his book titles he called *The Mystery of the Cosmos?* The tool was obvious. Pythagoras had left it hiding in plain sight. Crack the code of the music of the spheres. Find the distances between the equivalents of frets on a guitar string. And that quest shows just how very different Johannes Kepler's tools of mind were from yours and mine. Prepare for an excursion into the strange.

First, put yourself in Kepler's place. You want to find the distance between the heavenly spheres—the spheres on which the five planets and the Earth revolve around the Sun. How would you manage it? Step one: spheres are balls. So your job is to find the distances between six hollow balls. Six hollow balls nested inside each other. Nested around the core of the sun. Six hollow balls of the universe.

Let's look at your axioms. Let's look at what you can be sure of. Music equals number equals the universe. Really? Yes, absolutely. Why? Geometry and music are one and the same. Geometry is the cosmos. Harmony is astronomy. God thinks in terms of ratios. And God is perfect. Perfection is beauty. Music is the most beautiful thing around. And since beauty is perfection and perfection is God, God and beauty are one. God and music are one. Which means that reason, music, and beauty are joined at the hip. And God is a maker of the most perfect music of all. Especially in his construction of the heavens. So God made a cosmos that's beautiful. A cosmos that hums. A cosmos that sings.

Which means that clue number one to the distances between the orbits of the planets around the Sun is music.

Clue number two? God is geometry. God thinks, eats, and breathes geometry. And God is perfection. What's perfect in geometry? Two things. The circle and its alter ego, the sphere. And the Platonic solids. The tetrahedron, the cube, the octahedron, the dodecahedron, and the icosahedron.

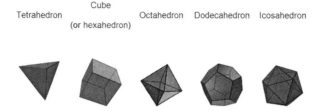

Tetrahedron   Cube (or hexahedron)   Octahedron   Dodecahedron   Icosahedron

Courtesy of DTR, Wikimedia Commons

Clue number three? There are five planets. And there are five Platonic solids. Surely this is no coincidence. Surely this is a clue to God's thinking.

And you have one more hint, one more working assumption. You solve problems by drawing things like triangles and boxes inside of circles. And when you're trying to solve a really tough problem, you can end up with more than forty triangles crisscrossing inside one circle. That's a mess.

Kepler solves a complex mathematical problem using a compass and a straight edge, the tools of geometry. *Drawing by Johannes Kepler, from* The Harmony of the World *(1619).*

And like a termite, it's your job to clean up the mess. It's your job to come up with a simple solution. Why? God is beauty. God uses deep structures—he uses Plato's ideas. And God built the universe. More important, God is not a pig. God is not slovenly. So the universe is not messy.

OK, once again, your goal is to find the distances between six nested balls—the six orbits, the six spheres, of the planets. And your challenge is to find the distances that will match the ratios that make music. Can you think of a way to use God's five profoundly basic things, the five basic boxes of Plato—the five perfect Platonic solids—to do it? Can you come up with a way to use these five strangely shaped boxes to find the ratios of the distances of the planets from each other and from the Sun?

You do it by being extremely clever.

Here's how Kepler straightened out the mess. By fitting boxes inside of hollow balls and hollow balls inside of boxes.

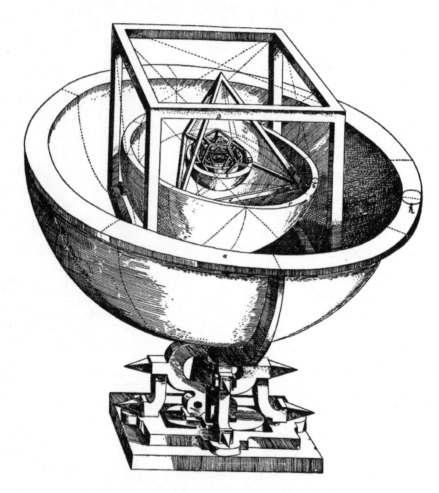

The Kepler Cockup. Kepler's boxes within balls and balls within boxes. The brilliant solution to the solar system. The solution that didn't work. *Drawing by Johannes Kepler, from* The Harmony of the World *(1619).*

To follow Kepler's solution, his answer to the Rubik's Cube® of the cosmos, take a globe. A sphere. A hollow ball. A big one. Sphere number one. Call that the sphere of Saturn. Call it the sphere on which Saturn rides around the sun. Now fit a cube inside of Saturn's sphere. Size the cube carefully so that all of its corners meet the inner surface of the sphere. Precisely. Got it? You now have a box inside a hollow ball. A cubic box fitted tightly inside of a very big ball.

Now fit sphere number two, hollow ball number two, a smaller ball, inside the box that's inside your biggest ball. Yes, fit a sphere inside your cube. You've got it, a sphere inside the cube. A hollow ball inside the cube-shaped box that you've tucked inside of Saturn's sphere. That new ball, ball number two, is the sphere of Jupiter.

This isn't easy, so stick with me. You are fitting boxes inside of hollow balls and hollow balls inside of boxes. Like tucking the grain inside the rat inside the cat inside the house that Jack built. Your hollow balls are your six spheres. They are the spheres of the five planets plus the Earth. Well, the spheres of the planets' orbits, to be more specific. They are the spheres that Kepler was certain carried the planets around the sun. And your boxes are the five Platonic solids.

But I digress. Kepler is not finished with his solution to the mystery of the cosmos. Nor are you. To see the rest of Kepler's solution, fit a tetrahedron—a pyramid with four faces, four triangular faces—into sphere number two, the sphere of Jupiter, the sphere that's nested inside your cube. Make sure all the tetrahedron's corners hit the surface of the sphere, sphere number two, perfectly. Now fit sphere number three inside the tetrahedron. What have you accomplished? You've found the sphere of Mars. You've solved the problem of Mars's orbit and its distance from the sun. Remarkable. But you are not finished.

Now fit a dodecahedron into the sphere of Mars. In other words, tuck a box in the form of the twelve-sided perfect Platonic solid into your Mars sphere. And pack hollow ball number four inside of it. What have you got now? You have three boxes inside of four balls. And, you brilliant thing, you, you have come up with a mathematical solution to the orbit of the Earth. You've come up with the sphere on which the Earth's orbit rides around the

Sun. Only two steps to go and you've got an answer to the puzzle of Kepler's cosmos, a solution to the puzzle of the solar system. And a solution to the puzzle of the music of the spheres.

Inside the sphere of the Earth, stuff an icosahedron, a box with twenty sides, twenty triangular sides. And do the usual. Fit hollow sphere number five into your icosahedron. Tired? You've almost got the whole thing. In this case, you have found the sphere of Venus. For your grand finale, tuck an octahedron into the sphere of Venus. That's an eight-sided box whose eight faces are triangles. Equilateral triangles. And stuff your final sphere, sphere number six, into your octahedron so that it fits perfectly. *Voila*. You've got the sphere of Mercury. You've built six spheres. And with those six spheres you've found the distances of the five planets plus the Earth from the sun. And you've pulled this off with a geometry that makes musical harmonies. Surround the whole thing with "the sphere of the fixed stars"[178] and you've got a universe.

This solution worked only very roughly for the distances between the planets. Too roughly to be of use to science. And Kepler, a careful observer of the heavens, knew it. But it remained his favorite solution to the problem of the planets. It remained the one accomplishment he was most proud of in his entire life. Why? Because it boiled everything down to five perfect geometric shapes, shapes from the very mind of God himself. And because it showed deep structures at work in the cosmos. Alas, it showed that some deep structures can be dead wrong. Many patterns satisfy the human mind. Many are compelling ideas. But not all patterns are really Ur patterns. Not all patterns really reflect the workings of the universe. That's the Kepler cockup—finding patterns that look gorgeous but prove to be wrong.

Which leads to a question. Are simple patterns just a product of the way that we see things? Are they simply fantasies we use to simplify life for ourselves? Are they just a product of a human need to clean up the mess? Or are simple patterns really out there beyond us, above us, and down there below us? Are simple patterns really patterns of reality? And where do axioms and corollary generator theory fit into all of this? The answer would come three hundred years later. But only after the development of a few new mind tools.

***

How potent was the method of definition, axiom, proposition, and proof? How seductive was the Aristotle-and-Euclid method as a recruitment strategy? Under everything Kepler did was a method. A method he assumed was *it*, the one and only technique when it came to science. Lay out your definitions. Give your axioms. Show the world your propositions. Then go for it. Prove them.

Galileo, Kepler's contemporary in Italy, was also in the grip of definition, axiom, proposition, and proof. His *Mathematical Discourses Concerning Two New Sciences Relating to Mechanicks and Local Motion* begins with one definition and four axioms.

And René Descartes, who was just a tad younger than Kepler and Galileo, used definition, axiom, proposition, and proof for the best known of his achievements: *Cogito ergo sum*, "I think therefore I am." What does "I think therefore I am" have to do with the method of Aristotle and Euclid? Everything. Descartes was a French intellectual who had adventured all over Europe as a soldier in the Thirty Years' War.[179] He had joined the hostilities out of anthropological curiosity, "to study the customs of men."[180] But Descartes had another obsession—the axiom. Not just any old axiom. *The* axiom. He was obsessed with finding the single most basic axiom of them all. And $A = A$ did not satisfy him. So in 1628[181] Descartes started a series of trips to a foreign country, Holland, where he secluded himself in a room on an upper story[182] of a house in the middle of Amsterdam and tried to strip away everything in his life[183] to find one truth so basic that you could not deny it. He tried to find the one axiom beyond all axioms. The one thing that was "perfectly certain and evident."[184] The one thing left when everything else was gone.

What was left at the end of Descartes's experiment on himself? The fact that he was thinking. That's how Descartes found *Cogito ergo sum*—"I think therefore I am." What was "I think therefore I am"? The ultimate given. The ultimate undeniable fact. The ultimate truth so basic that all men share it. The ultimate axiom. Or that's how Descartes saw it. For Descartes was in the grip of Aristotle and Euclid. Descartes was in the grip of a recruitment strategy. Descartes was in the grip of the axiom.

Perhaps Descartes should have added a second axiom: "I reproduce therefore I am." Renee's aim was to isolate himself completely from humanity so that he could see what remained. And one thing that remained with extreme stubbornness was sex. Descartes made the woman who cleaned his "isolated" room in Amsterdam pregnant.[185] But that's beside the point. Or is it?

Fifty-three years later, in 1683 at Cambridge University, Isaac Newton, too, was in the grip of the definition, axiom, proposition, and proof game.[186] He kicked off his central book, the *Principia*, with "Definitions." Then, a mere eleven pages into the book, he presented his "Axioms," the insights that would change the nature of physics and science, his "Laws of Motion."[187] For Newton, it was all a matter of definition, axiom, proposition, and proof.

In fact, Aristotle and Euclid were a part of the basic education of every literate thinker in the West,[188] including political philosophers like England's Thomas Hobbes, who ran across an open copy of Euclid's *Elements* on a stopover at "a gentleman's library" on his way to Paris,[189] fell in love with it, then went off to visit another man who thought in terms of definitions and axioms, Galileo, in 1636.[190] Hobbes wrote a simple explanation of Euclid for the masses in his 1655 book, *On Bodies*. What's more, he called Euclid's *Elements* an indispensable "guide to the art of reasoning."[191] So Hobbes injected axioms and propositions into political reasoning. And he influenced a crew of later political ponderers—the Founding Fathers of the United States.

Yes, even the Founding Fathers of the American republic used the definition, axiom, proposition, and proof method. Where? In the Declaration of Independence. Remember these words? "We hold these truths to be self-evident, that all men are created equal, that they are endowed by their Creator with certain unalienable Rights, that among these are Life, Liberty and the pursuit of Happiness." Starting a document with your "self-evident" truths is starting with your axioms. And Ben Franklin, who suggested this wording to Thomas Jefferson, knew it.[192]

But the real big break for axioms came in the nineteenth century. The century of Giuseppe Peano and the century of the Great Axiom Hunt—the grand movement for axiomatization. The grand movement to solve all of the world's most fundamental problems with axioms. The grand movement to use axioms to get at deep structures. And the grand movement that would raise a question: are deep structures and axioms figments of the human imagination or reflections of reality?

5

EVERYBODY DO THE FLIP

GUILLOTINING AN AXIOM:
SEVERING THE NECK OF PARALLEL LINES

L ess than forty-four years after the Founding Fathers of the United States laid down their primary axiom, their "we hold these truths to be self-evident," the community of mathematicians and philosophers would still be doing the homework assignment that Aristotle had given them, the homework assignment for which Euclid had created the template. In 1820, mathematicians and philosophers would still be trying to boil everything down to definitions, axioms, propositions, and proofs. They would still be in the grip of Aristotle and Euclid's recruitment strategy. Then would come a vital twist in the tale of the axiom.

Take an old thing, repeat it in a new context, and you have something new. Sometimes something radically new. Remember, in the days of Euclid, there had been no rulers to measure, no number line with which to comprehend numbers, no algebra, and no calculus. There had been no telescopes, no telegraphs, no railroads. And there had been no one to challenge Euclid's basic assumptions, Euclid's axioms.

But there had been a restless dissatisfaction with one of Euclid's most fundamental axioms for roughly seventeen hundred years. That troublesome axiom is called the parallel proposition. Euclid mires his description of the parallel postulate in abstruse terms. Clarity is not his strong point. In fact, as you know, he was proud of how hard it was to grasp what he taught. Here's how he phrases the parallel postulate:

If a straight line meets two straight lines, so as to make the two interior angles on the same side of it taken together less than two right angles, these straight lines, being continually produced, shall at length meet on that side on which are the angles which are less than two right angles.[1]

Utterly incomprehensible, right? For the sake of simplicity, here's how one Yale scholar, William Withers, sums up Euclid's parallel postulate in his 1905 PhD thesis titled "Euclid's Parallel Postulate: Its Nature, Validity, and Place in Geometrical Systems":

Parallel lines are straight lines which lie in the same plane and will not meet however far produced.[2]

We know this better in the phrase that "two parallel lines will never meet."

The problem was in the words "will never meet." The lines will never meet no matter how far they go? Extend two lines to the stars and beyond and you are making a pretty lofty claim. A claim that's very hard to check. And a claim that leads to a question. If you really were to draw two parallel lines to the very ends of the universe, would they still defiantly maintain their separateness?

Euclid had demonstrated one way to answer this question. Use a step-by-step process to show that a concept is consistent with the starting axioms. Start with your proposition, your hunch that two lines will never meet, and go backward. Reach back to show that the proposition is logically consistent with your axioms. Then assume that if it's consistent, it's a logical necessity unfolding from the axioms. That was the technique Euclid used for the propositions in his *Elements*. Go backward.

Then there was another potential technique. Go forward. Go outward. Check your proposition against reality. See if the real world, the world of sailing ships and stars, backs up your claim.

Less than two hundred years after Euclid's death, a polymath in Euclid's hometown, Alexandria, Egypt, the intellectual center of the late Greek world and of the Roman Empire, was unhappy with the parallel postulate. His name was Ptolemy, and he gave us the system of spheres carrying planets and stars around the earth, the system that prevailed in science for fifteen hundred years, the system that Kepler tried to update. So Ptolemy was a man of powerful importance.

Ptolemy set out to prove what seemed obvious. That two parallel lines will never meet, even if you draw them from a wax tablet all the way to the sphere of the fixed stars. And guess what? Ptolemy, one of those intellects whose brainpower only comes along once in a century, failed. He failed miserably. And he was not alone. Over time, many another man of intellectual force and power tried to prove the parallel postulate. Every one of them tripped, stumbled, and fell. Every one of them failed. For example, Albrecht Durer, the fifteenth-century German genius from Nuremberg, was a phenomenal artist and expert in perspective, a field that uses geometry every day. In fact, perspective uses both parallel lines and the way that parallel lines appear to converge in the distance. In other words, perspective is all about the paradoxes of parallel lines. So in 1525 Durer wrote an entire book on geometry, the *Doctrine of Measurement*,[3] and took a crack at solving the parallel postulate problem by twiddling with something that Aristotle and Euclid had made essential in science—the definition. Durer changed the definition of parallel lines to "straight lines which are everywhere equidistant."[4] So by definition, by Durer's definition, parallel lines never meet. They stay the same distance apart no matter how far they travel. But is that true? Or is it a false assumption? Durer couldn't say.

Seventy-nine years later, in 1604,[5] our friend Johannes Kepler tackled the parallel axiom problem. He solved it by redefining two parallel lines as lines that *do* "have a common point at infinity."[6] A truly rebellious notion. But is that notion true? Is it true in the world below and in the heavens above? Is it true in the world of watermills and popes? Is it true in the world of planets and stars, the world of the heavens that Kepler spent a good deal of his time observing? Do parallel lines really meet at infinity? Kepler couldn't prove it one way or the other.

In late-sixteenth- and early-seventeenth-century England, Sir Henry Savile, the warden of Oxford's Merton College, did two major things for the puzzles of geometry. He founded two chairs of geometry at Oxford—the Savilian chairs. And he became the tutor of mathematics and Greek to Queen Elizabeth.[7] But something in Euclid's masterpiece *The Elements* bugged Sir Henry mightily. In 1621 he wrote, "In the most fair frame of geometry there are two defects, two blots." Historian of geometry William Barrett Frankland explains that "one of these blots was the parallel-axiom."[8]

As late as 1733, experts were still trying to prove that the parallel postulate was not a problem and that Euclid was perfect. In Milan, a Jesuit professor of mathematics named Girolamo Saccheri wrote a book in Latin called *Euclid Cleared from Every Blot*. It was a direct challenge to Sir Henry Savile's claim 112 years earlier that geometry was blotted and blighted.[9] Blotted and blighted by the problem of the parallel postulate. And thirty-three years later, in 1766, Johann Heinrich Lambert in Germany took the problem even more forcefully by the horns. In a book called *The Theory of Parallel Lines*, he did what Saccheri had done. He tried to show that the parallel postulate was absolutely necessary to Euclidean geometry. In fact, both Saccheri and Lambert used the same method to drive their point home. They showed the nightmare that would ensue if you were to toss the parallel postulate aside or fiddle with it.[10] What they didn't realize is that one generation's nightmare is another generation's delight.

***

The parallel postulate controversy lurched forward from century to century. By 1833, says John William Withers, "Perronet Thompson of Cambridge published a book in which he brilliantly demonstrates the insufficiency of twenty-one different attempts to dispose of the Parallel postulate."[11] Twenty-one attempts to dislodge the parallel postulate. That's a respectable number. But five years later, in 1838, the German *Encyclopädie der Wissenschaften und Künste*, the *Encyclopedia of Science and Arts*, one-upped that achievement. The *Encyclopädie* reported on "ninety-two authors who had dealt with the problem."[12] And L. A. Sohncke, the writer of that encyclopedia article and the author of a German *History of Geometry*, wrote that "in Mathematics there is nothing over which so much has been spoken, written and striven"[13] as the parallel postulate. What's worse, all the sound and fury about the parallel postulate had resulted in nothing. Said Sohncke, these efforts had been expended "all so far without reaching a definite result and decision." Did parallel lines meet at infinity as Kepler surmised? Or did they remain a fixed distance apart even if they traveled beyond the hearts of the stars? No one knew.

Only one thing was certain. Through the paradox of the parallel postulate and its pull, the recruitment strategy that Aristotle and Euclid had kicked into motion was once again showing its seductive power.

Then, in the nineteenth century, a few brave souls decided to see what would happen if Euclid was wrong and Kepler was right. What would happen if you were to challenge a basic assumption and turn it on its head? What would happen if you were to flip the parallel postulate and assume that parallel lines *do* meet somewhere? The result of this deliberate axiom flipping? This deliberate upending of an assumption? The axiom flippers gave us a radically new universe. A universe that would turn out to be, guess what? Ours. And these pioneers of assumption flipping did something else. They showed a very different facet of axioms. One that had been implicit ever since the days of Aristotle. But one that had never been proven before. The assumption flippers proved that with new axioms you can unfold new universes and impossible new worlds. An insight that would prove vital to the God Problem.

***

Yes, in the nineteenth century, a handful of pioneers changed geometry, changed the concept of the axiom, and changed the universe. In the process, they laid a foundation for a new approach to the God Problem. They did it by turning the parallel postulate on its head. And they did it by following the second rule of science. Rule number one: the truth at any price including the price of your life. Rule number two: look at things right under your nose as if you've never seen them before, then proceed from there. In fact, William Barrett Frankland, the nineteenth-century author of one of the many books on the story of the parallel postulate, *Theories of Parallelism: An Historical Critique*, says that there was a spirit of intellectual rebellion in the air at the turn of the nineteenth century.[14] A spirit of assumption flipping. That spirit arose in the years around 1800. And the years around 1800 were the hinge point that ended one way of looking at the world and began another.

***

In 1800, the word "revolution" had gained a new meaning. Two great revolutions—the American Revolutionary War of 1775 and the French Revolution of 1789—had changed the knot of associations that the word "revolution" yanked together. Revolution had initially meant the rolling of something, the turnaround. Like the swiveling of a planet circling the sun.[15] By 1800, the word had picked up a more muscular and dangerous meaning. Revolution now meant overturning old systems and replacing them with something new. Revolution now meant bloodbaths like the eight-year war with which the Americans had expelled the British at the cost of twenty-five thousand lives. Revolution meant bloodbaths like the wholesale guillotining of close to forty thousand aristocrats and other "enemies of the revolution" in the streets of Paris from 1793 to 1794.

In science there was no violence. But "that great and vital impulse, which throbbed throughout Europe at the turn of the century,"[16] to quote Frankland, called for the reexamination of old ideas. In fact, the spirit of the time called for more than mere reexamination. It called for overthrow and upheaval. It called, as Frankland says, for "spurning dead forms."[17] And it called for challenging old "formulae and formalities"[18] with "the regenerating pulse which was making old things new."[19] Yes, making old things new. Who said so? William Barrett Frankland.

Frankland did not have the concept of iteration in his vocabulary. He did not know about the creative power of repeating something old in a new environment. He did not know iteration's nature as one of the secrets to cosmic creativity. But that creative power is what he was alluding to. And he was alluding to the way in which the next corollary unfolding from the simple rules of the universe creates breakthroughs. He was alluding to the way in which the next implicit property goes from nothingness to reality. He was alluding to the way the cosmos, like a math student at Reed College, does her homework. He was alluding to the ideas at the heart of corollary generator theory.

When a new corollary is ripe and ready to be unfolded, it rises from the mire in more minds than just one. Why? It is in the *zeitgeist*. It is in the collective unconscious. It is in the spirit of the times. *Zeit* means time. And *Geist* means spirit. Or ghost. *Zeitgeist.* Time's push to unfold new corollaries hovers like a ghost just out of sight. And the *zeitgeist* of the 1800s called for challenging old assumptions. It called for challenging antique intellectual hand-me-downs. And one antique axiom stood out in geometry. The one that had bothered geometers since the days of Ptolemy in roughly 150 CE.[20] It was the parallel postulate.

Challenging the parallel postulate would do two things: It would utterly change the way we see the universe. And it would answer a basic question. When we march off to the land of pure reason and deal with abstract ideas, are we simply wasting our time? Or does the pursuit of purely imaginary forms and incomprehensible complications get at a deep structure of reality?

***

For twenty-two hundred years men had been trying to burnish the reputation of Euclid and to demonstrate that the old Alexandrian-Greek teacher of geometry was the ultimate expert. For twenty-two hundred years scholars had been trying to prove that Euclid could do no wrong. That Euclid was infallible. But the geometry devotees of the late-eighteenth and early-nineteenth centuries were more audacious. They did not want to guillotine Euclid. It was a bit late for that. But they were willing to turn him upside down.

First came Carl Friedrich Gauss, a brickmaker's son from Brunswick in Germany. Ahhh, bricks. The ultimate repeaters. The ultimate iterators. They keep cropping up. Gauss was a bright lad. So bright that the Duke of Brunswick, the highest ruler in Gauss's home territory, spotted Carl when he was only eleven years old[21] and made sure that he got a top-notch education.[22] The duke was on target. Gauss would stun the world with his mathematical genius. He would stun it so powerfully that he would earn a title: "The Prince of Mathematics."[23] And he would stun it so permanently that today the most advanced users of math—the quants on Wall Street, math fanatics who have shifted from university careers in cutting-edge mathematics and physics to stock, bond, currency, commodity, and derivative trading—use Carl Friedrich Gauss's math nearly every minute of their workday. But that is by no means the end of Gauss's achievements. Gauss used his math to "rediscover the first minor Planet, Ceres,"[24] in 1801, when he was only twenty-four years old, a triumph that one of his biographers, M. B. W. Trent, says "made Gauss famous worldwide overnight." And that was just a start.

Gauss was made professor of astronomy in 1807 at Gottingen University and director of the university's observatory.[25] Gauss—who was now thirty years old—didn't just take over the observatory. He eventually moved into it. He made it his home. So Gauss's science literally became his life. In 1833 Gauss and a younger collaborator invented one of the first electromagnetic telegraphs[26]—a device that would pull the world together in a whole new way. And speaking of the world, Gauss mapped the Earth's magnetic field.

Gauss also pulled off a plethora of achievements that only a math wiz would understand. He proved the fundamental theorem for quadratic residues, worked on binary quadratic forms, developed a method of "least squares"[27] (yes, squares, those things Pythagoras gave us), and far, far more. In addition, Gauss's research on matters like electricity and magnetism was so basic that in 1832 he was given a rare dual appointment—as professor of physics at Gottingen and as dean of the philosophical faculty. In addition, Gauss studied Sanskrit, came up with advances in spherical trigonometry, catalyzed an international organization of observatories focused on charting the Earth's magnetism, the Magnetic Union, and founded the union's journal.[28] One result? Despite the fact that he was a German, Gauss won the oldest award given by the British Royal Society, the Copley Medal, in 1838. He won that award along with Michael Faraday. Why? The two were cited for their vital contributions to a new art—turning magnetism into electricity. The art that would trigger the electrification of the world. More important for the God Problem, Gauss sowed the seeds of the nineteenth century's new math. He sowed the seeds of a math that would turn an axiom upside down. How?

Gauss taught two men who would help change math profoundly: Richard Dedekind, whose work on axioms would parallel that of Peano, and Georg Cantor, who would establish set theory. Yes, set theory. A basic that would make the logic of men like Aristotle easier to understand. A tool that would make it possible to manipulate logic with the step-by-step procedures of math. A tool that would make it possible to manipulate logic with the sort of step-by-step procedures that would later give a new invention its brainpower—the computer.[29]

But there's more. Lots more. Seventy-four contributions to math and physics continue to carry Gauss's name.

Karl Friedrich Gauss was clearly a man through whom the cosmos unfolds corollaries and implicit properties aching to be born. Gauss was clearly a man through whom recruitment strategies repeated themselves in a new medium. In Gauss's case, that new medium was an era in which time, space, information, and ideas were silly-puttied into new form by railroads, chemistry, physics, and the new astronomy, a new astronomy ushered in by high-precision refracting telescopes mounted on automated, clock-driven equatorial mountings.[30]

But Gauss says that since 1792, when he was a mere fifteen years old, something else had been nagging him. Poking and prodding from the back of his mind. A problem. A twenty-two-hundred-year-old problem. The problem of the parallel postulate. And something else was twisting and teasing him. The notion that an entirely new geometry might ensue if you turned the parallel postulate on its head. The notion that an entirely new geometry would spill forth if parallel lines did not stay the same distance apart forever.

Remember, Gauss was born one year after the beginning of the American Revolution. He was twelve when the French Revolution unfolded only 429 miles away from his home. He was sixteen when the French began to load France's elegant aristocrats into carts as if they were animals and to trundle those carts to a slicing machine in a public square, a square that had once been called the Place de Louis Quinze, the square of Louis the XV, and was now known as the Place de la Révolution.[31] The carts transported these epitomes of elegance to the guillotine, a high-tech machine that thwacked necks clear through, severing heads from their bodies, and leaving those heads to tumble into baskets like melons. Heads still grimacing with the facial expressions fixed by the emotions of their last second of life.

Which means that assumption flipping was in the air. In the *zeitgeist*. A corollary was calling out to men of genius. A very strange corollary. And Gauss was one of these geniuses, one of the men who hears the call of the impossible aching to become reality. Back to 1799, when Gauss was questioning the parallel postulate, when he was skeptically poking the idea that two parallel lines stay the same distance apart no matter how far they advance toward the infinite. "Most people would regard this as an axiom,"[32] he wrote in a letter to a friend, "I do not." Gauss published 144 books and articles in his lifetime.[33] But he never sat down and put the implications of parallel postulate flipping on paper. Forty years later, he'd regret this oversight. Why? Because non-Euclidean geometry would make a splash. And Gauss wanted to be more than merely wetted by the wave of non-Euclidean fame. He wanted to be soaked. Soaked by attention. And soaked by attention he would be.

Gauss had social magnetism. In 1797, when Gauss was only nineteen years old, Germany had a visitor—and so did Gauss. A voracious twenty-two-year-old violin-playing former child prodigy from an ancient Magyar aristocratic family[34] trudged and rode from the village of Bolya in the principality of Transylvania to Germany with an older mentor, Baron Simon Kemeny. His aim? To tour Germany's universities on a learning quest. The Transylvanian visitor's interests were omnivorous—he loved Shakespeare and the hot new modern German poet Schiller. But his main mission in visiting Germany was to chow down as much math as he could. What's more, he adored geometry. And he was fascinated by the parallel axiom—the parallel postulate—an axiom whose puzzle continued to demonstrate its power to kidnap, seduce, and recruit. The visitor from Transylvania was Farkas Bólyai.

When the Transylvanian youth and Gauss met at the University of Gottingen, they became friends for life. What pulled the two together? Wrote Bólyai, "The passion for mathematics . . . and our moral agreement." But there was more. Gauss felt that Bólyai was the only one who truly understood "his views on the foundation of mathematics."[35] In fact, Gauss called Bólyai a "genius." The two walked the fifty-eight miles from Gottingen to Brunswick together to visit Gauss's parents. And when Gauss was out of the room, Gauss's mother asked Bólyai whether her son "would amount to anything." Bólyai told Gauss's mom that her son would become "the first mathematician in Europe." And she "burst into tears."[36] No wonder the two swore an oath of "brotherhood and the banner of truth."[37]

Then Bólyai went back home to Transylvania and parked himself at the Reformed University in the Transylvanian town of Maros-Vasarhely, where seven years later he would become a professor of math.[38] In 1799, Bólyai received a letter from Gauss in Gottingen about what Gauss called "the iniquitous parallel-axiom."[39] In Gauss's letter appeared the words you've seen above: "Most people would regard this as an axiom. I do not."[40]

What does all this have to do with the God Problem? What does it have to do with Aristotle's invention, the axiom, as a recruitment strategy?

In 1832, thirty-three years after Gauss's letter heaping doubt on the parallel postulate, Gauss's Transylvanian friend Farkas Bólyai published a two-volume book, *An Attempt to Introduce Youth to the Fundamentals of Pure Science, Elementary and Advanced, by a Clear and Proper Method.* The book was in Latin—but math's relationship to universal languages like Latin is a subject for later. The real surprise came at the book's end. It was an "Appendix Showing the Absolutely True Science of Space."[41]

The appendix was an attempt to work out a geometry that would hold true whether the parallel axiom were true or not. And the "Appendix Showing the Absolutely True Science of Space" included a geometry of the sort of universe you'd get if the parallel axiom were false and if parallel lines did, indeed, meet. It was a rather surprising new geometry. Hyperbolic geometry.[42] But the real surprise was not just this alternative geometry. It was the appendix's author. Not Farkas Bólyai. But his son. Thirty-year-old János Bólyai. And János Bólyai was an unlikely thirty-year-old.

János had been given a scholarship to the Vienna Academy of Military Engineers. On graduation he had signed up with the Hungarian military, had become an officer, an "Imperial and Royal Military Engineer,"[43] and had been billeted with thirteen other officers, probably in Temesvár[44] in Romania. Somehow he had managed to get on his fellow officers' nerves. In fact, he had irritated his roommates so severely that every single one of them challenged him to a duel. All thirteen of them. János accepted the challenge. He would duel all thirteen one by one in a single afternoon. But he laid down a condition. After every other duel, he would be allowed to play his violin. The challengers accepted his terms. And the younger Bólyai won thirteen duels in a row. In between fiddling.[45]

Yes, fiddling. As in music—a very Pythagorean interest.

But the fact that János Bólyai could raise such a ruckus made him a liability to the Hungarian military. An officer who can't get along with his teammates is destructive to discipline. If war comes, he could be a one-man disaster. So the military authorities made a deal with János. Accept a promotion, then retire from the military ASAP. Or? The answer was left dangling. But the implication was clear.

Geometry was as powerful a drug to young Bólyai as it had been to Galileo. The pull of the parallel axiom was so strong for János that his father viewed it as an addiction. Wrote Farkas Bólyai to his son, "For God's sake! I entreat you leave parallels alone, abhor them like indecent talk, they may deprive you (just like me) from your time, health, tranquility, and the happiness of your life." In Farkas's view, the parallel axiom would make life an indescribable hell. How did he know? "I have traversed this bottomless night, which extinguished all light and joy of my life." But this was not mere abstract moralizing. The father tried to reveal to his son just how devastating the parallel-axiom addiction had been to his own life. He said, "That bottomless darkness may devour a thousand of tall towers of Newton and it will never brighten up in the Earth." But that's not all: "I thought I would sacrifice myself for the sake of the truth. I was ready to become a martyr who would remove the flaw from geometry and return it purified to mankind. I accomplished monstrous, enormous labors . . . and yet . . . I turned back when I saw that no man can reach the bottom of this night. I turned back unconsoled, pitying myself and all mankind."[46] Some recruitment strategies have hooks as powerful as morphine.

But János got something extremely important in exchange for his enslavement to the puzzles of the parallel axiom. He wrote to his father with excitement, "Out of nothing I have created a strange new universe."[47] By altering one axiom, János Bólyai had pulled off an act that looked eerily like genesis.[48] He had created a cosmos, a parallel world. And he had stumbled across what would become an increasingly vital clue to the God Problem.

***

In reality, János Bólyai hadn't quite created his "strange new universe." He'd found it. How do we know? Others found it too.

"ONE MAN DESERVES THE CREDIT, ONE MAN DESERVES THE BLAME, AND NICOLAI IVANOVICH LOBACHEVSKY IS HIS NAME"

While János Bólyai was fiddling, Aristotle, Euclid, and the puzzle of the parallel axiom continued to suck in new recruits. New recruits to the process of making the implicit explicit. New recruits who would uncover yet more clues to a secular form of genesis.

In 1804, when Carl Friedrich Gauss was twenty-seven years old, when Farkas Bólyai was twenty-nine, and when János Bólyai was only two, the fascination with math was spreading like an infection. Or like a highly successful, six-thousand-year-old recruitment strategy. The Russians established a chair of math at the University of Kazan, the city from which the Mongol-led Golden Horde had ruled and bullied the captive population of Russia for three hundred years.[49] But advanced math of the sort that the Russians wanted to import was not native to Russia. It was heating up like a ferment in Germany. Especially in the vicinity of Gauss, who was less than thirty but whose fame from his discovery of the dwarf planet Ceres[50] was only three years old and was still smoking. Gauss was already known as the "giant mathematician." So the Russians imported a German math professor whose claim to fame was his tight friendship with Gauss the Giant. Gauss, the "Titan" of mathematics.

Yes, Gauss's titanic stature was about to reach out to Russia. But before we see how, let's dive into another indication of the power of the recruitment strategy on whose behalf Gauss labored. Let's dive into a song. A song about mathematics. One of the silliest songs about math ever written.

***

When you were fourteen years old, you fell in love with a tune and its lyrics. It was a nonsense tune written and sung by an unlikely excuse for a pop musician, Tom Lehrer. Tom Lehrer was a Harvard doctoral candidate in math who taught at Harvard and MIT, worked at Los Alamos National Lab and the National Security Agency, and wrote satirical songs in his spare time. Lehrer would go on to perform those songs in nightclubs and on TV. One day in January 1953, he found a recording studio in the Boston yellow pages, went in, paid fifteen dollars for an hour of time,[51] and recorded twelve songs in one fell swoop. In his words, it was a recording debut in which "every expense was spared."[52] You were ten years old at the time. Five years earlier,[53] the only way to sell a dozen recorded songs was to put two songs on a 78 r.p.m. disk, put six disks together, and package them in a multisleeve, multipage, booklike hunk of stiff paper and cardboard called an "album." But in 1953, the vinyl LP—the long-playing record—had just been invented. So for the first time, a singer could cram a dozen songs onto just one disk. Lehrer pressed four hundred copies of his LP and sold them for three dollars and fifty cents on the Harvard campus. Over the next few years Lehrer became a sensation. At least among science nerds. The towering science fiction author and graduate of the Bronx High School of Science Isaac Asimov, for example, was one of Lehrer's biggest fans. (So was Princess Margaret.) You read Asimov's books voraciously. And you loved Tom Lehrer.

Here were the lyrics to one of the Tom Lehrer songs, a song that you sang with great enthusiasm on the bus to and from high school in Buffalo, New York.

> Who made me the genius I am today,
> The mathematician that others all quote,
> Who's the professor that made me that way?
> The greatest that ever got chalk on his coat.
> One man deserves the credit,
> One man deserves the blame,
> And Nicolai Ivanovich Lobachevsky is his name.
> Hi!

Nicolai Ivanovich Lobachevsky is his name.

I am never forget the day I first meet the great Lobachevsky.

In one word he told me secret of success in mathematics:

Plagiarize!

Plagiarize,

Let no one else's work evade your eyes,

Remember why the good Lord made your eyes,

So don't shade your eyes,

But plagiarize, plagiarize, plagiarize —

Only be sure always to call it please 'research.'

And ever since I meet this man

My life is not the same,

And Nicolai Ivanovich Lobachevsky is his name.

Hi!

Nicolai Ivanovich Lobachevsky is his name.

I am never forget the day I am given first original paper

to write. It was on analytic and algebraic topology of

locally Euclidean parameterization of infinitely differentiable

Riemannian manifold.

Bozhe moi!

This I know from nothing.

What-I'm going-to do.

But I think of great Lobachevsky and get idea - ahah!

I have a friend in Minsk,

Who has a friend in Pinsk,

Whose friend in Omsk

Has friend in Tomsk

With friend in Akmolinsk.

His friend in Alexandrovsk

Has friend in Petropavlovsk,

Whose friend somehow

Is solving now

The problem in Dnepropetrovsk.

And when his work is done —

Ha ha!—begins the fun.
From Dnepropetrovsk
To Petropavlovsk,
By way of Iliysk,
And Novorossiysk,
To Alexandrovsk to Akmolinsk
To Tomsk to Omsk
To Pinsk to Minsk
To me the news will run,
Yes, to me the news will run!
And then I write
By morning, night,
And afternoon,
And pretty soon
My name in Dnepropetrovsk is cursed,
When he finds out I publish first!
And who made me a big success
And brought me wealth and fame?
Nicolai Ivanovich Lobachevsky is his name.
Hi!
Nicolai Ivanovich Lobachevsky is his name.
I am never forget the day my first book is published.
Every chapter I stole from somewhere else.
Index I copy from old Vladivostok telephone directory.
This book was sensational!
Pravda—well, Pravda—Pravda said: "Zhil-bil korol kogda-to,
pree nyom blokha zhila"
It stinks.
But Izvestia! Izvestia said: "Ya idoo kuda sam czar idyot peshkom!"
It stinks.
Metro-Goldwyn-Moskva buys movie rights for six million rubles,
Changing title to "The Eternal Triangle,"
With Ingrid Bergman playing part of hypotenuse.
And who deserves the credit?

And who deserves the blame?
Nicolai Ivanovich Lobachevsky is his name.
Hi![54]

Who in the world was Nikolai Ivanovich Lobachevsky?

***

Nikolai Ivanovich Lobachevsky was the son of a man who used geometry every day of the working week. Nikolai's father was a surveyor in Nizhny Novgorod, one of Russia's four biggest cities, the fortress town from which Russia's princes had defended Muscovy against the Tatars, against the descendants of Genghis Khan's Golden Hordes. Nikolai's father died when he was eight. So his mother took little Nikolai and moved to Kazan, the city from which the Tatars had humiliated, bullied, and extracted tribute from the Russians for three hundred years. Kazan established a new university when Lobachevsky was twelve. The math professor was the friend and former teacher of Gauss who the city fathers had recruited from Germany to occupy the chair of math. Yes, the friend of Gauss the Giant, Gauss the Titan. (The friend's name was J. M. C. Bartels.) Lobachevsky entered Kazan's new university at the age of fifteen. At the age of nineteen, he emerged with a master's degree in two fields—physics and mathematics. And at the age of twenty he became a professor in three fields, fields intimately twisted together since the days of the Babylonians—math, physics, and astronomy. At the age of twenty-five, Lobachevsky became the University of Kazan's rector. Five years later, he married and had a remarkable eighteen children. Then he went blind, lost his ability to walk, and died in poverty at the relatively young age of fifty-four.

But long before his blindness and poverty, Lobachevsky tossed away the parallel postulate. He deep-sixed one axiom and replaced it with another. Two lines, he assumed, *could* meet. And they could do the opposite. They could fly away from each other. They could diverge. When Lobachevsky used logic to work out the implications of this new geometry, what did he get? Saddleback geometry. The geometry of the hyperbolic paraboloid.

And in Lobachevsky's method was a vital step toward answering the God Problem. To work out the logic of his new geometry, Lobachevsky had to reverse the process used by Euclid. Euclid took propositions then worked his way backward. He took what seemed to be facts in geometry, then worked back to the axioms and tried to prove step by step that his propositions, his notions, were consistent with the axioms. Euclid already knew his answers in advance. But if this is a cosmos that starts from nothing then unfolds something, and an elaborate something at that, Euclid's approach has got it backward. Is there a math that works its way forward? A math that works from a handful of axioms forward into the unknown? A math that unfolds structures without cheating? A math that can explain the cosmos's creativity? The beauty of flipping the parallel postulate, the beauty of changing the parallel axiom, was that you worked your way into the unknown. You imitated the universe.

In Lobachevsky's case, you used the rules of logic to find the implicit properties of a mini-universe. And what did Lobachevsky find? His saddle-back geometry.[55] Formally known as hyperbolic geometry,[56] a.k.a., negatively curved space.

Lobachevsky's geometry. Change one axiom of Euclid's system and you get a strangely curved universe. *Courtesy of Wikimedia Commons.*

Lobachevsky found a universe in which parallel lines crossed in one direction and fled from each other, growing farther and farther apart, in the other direction.

Was Tom Lehrer right? Did Nikolai Lobachevsky plagiarize from János Bólyai? Or was something else pushing Nikolai and János to make the same discoveries at nearly the same time? Was some sort of common force prodding Nikolai and János's minds? János Bólyai came out with his work ditching the parallel postulate—the parallel axiom—in 1832. But Bólyai had become obsessed with the parallel axiom as a teenager and had begun to develop his anti-parallel-axiom geometry by the time he was twenty-one years old. In 1823, Bólyai had posted his letter to his father, the geometer Farkas Bólyai, explaining with excitement that he had "created a new, another world out of nothing."[57]

János Bólyai had developed and written up his new geometry by 1825.[58] First he'd sent a manuscript on the new geometry to one of his former teachers. Then he'd gone home from his posting at the Directorate of Fortification in the Romanian city of Temesvár to Maros-Vasarhely in Transylvania and had given the details to his father.[59] János Bólyai was enthusiastic about what he'd come up with. His father was not. It took six years for János's father to get the message. Six years to realize the importance of what his son had done. Meanwhile, volume one of Nikolai Lobachevsky's *Geometrical Investigations on the Theory of Parallel Lines*[60] came out in 1832, seven suspicious-looking years after Bólyai had tried to get his father to pay serious attention to his new geometry.

So back to the question. And to Tom Lehrer's musical accusation. Did Lobachevsky plagiarize János Bólyai's work? No, says Leonard Berlin in a journal article called "Plagiarism, Salami Slicing, and Lobachevsky,"[61] an article that starts out with Tom Lehrer's lyrics. The proof? Lobachevsky's book was based on a lecture he'd given just a short time after János pitched his father on the new geometry. A lecture Lobachevsky had given in February 1826.[62]

So what happened? Why did two works—János Bólyai's and Nikolai Lobachevsky's—so closely, well, ummm, parallel each other? Because of the same phenomenon that produces 10^{87} identical quarks simultaneously. Because of the phenomenon that produces a million billion stars all doing pretty much the same thing at pretty much the same time. Because of two things: manic mass production and supersynchrony. Because non-Euclidean geometry was not the product of a single genius lunging outside the box. It was in the air. It was a corollary ripe to pop. It was an implicit property bulging in a pregnant *zeitgeist*, an implication aching to emerge. It was a recruitment strategy on the prowl. It was a hungry pattern pulling minds together in a multigenerational enterprise. Non-Euclidean geometry was an implicit property of Euclid's work. A rebel property. A previously unseen property. A property aching to move from possibility space to reality. And like its parent, non-

Euclidean geometry, too, was a recruitment pattern. A recruitment pattern struggling to be born. Struggling for a secular form of genesis.

***

Through Karl Friedrich Gauss, János Bólyai, and Nikolai Lobachevsky, a group mind, not just an individual mind, was unfolding corollaries from axioms. A multigenerational group mind. And what, in the big picture, in the really big picture, is a group mind? It's a tool that the cosmos uses to feel out her implicit possibilities. It's a tool the cosmos uses to probe her potential. It's a tool the cosmos uses to create.

BARE-NAKED MATH: PEANO STRIPS IT DOWN

Non-Euclidean geometry changed everything. Including the concept of an axiom. And Giuseppe Peano was at the core of that change.

Giuseppe Peano was one of those who sought attention by doing everything right.[63] At least in the beginning. Giuseppe was born in 1858, over twenty years after János Bólyai and Nikolai Lobachevsky published their non-Euclidean heresies. Peano grew up on a farm outside the village of Spinetta—a town "in northeastern Italy, halfway between the industrial center of Turin to the north" and the beach-resort cum city-state that provides a playground and a gambling haven for the superrich, "Monaco on the Mediterranean coast to the south."[64] Spinetta wasn't much of a town. It consisted only of a few buildings at a crossroads. And Peano's family was one of very modest means. The farmhouse in which Peano grew up had a mere four rooms. You entered through the kitchen. You climbed a few stairs to the living room. Behind that was one bedroom. A small bedroom that you and I might well envy. A bedroom equipped with a balcony that overlooked a garden and a stream. And in the living room was a "steep stairway" that led to the attic. Giuseppe slept in the attic. The house may have been tiny, but Giuseppe Peano's father did not see himself as a peasant tilling the land. He saw himself as a proud landowner. A member of the propertied class.

Giuseppe was the second child in a family of four brothers and a sister. According to Frank Sulloway, the birth-order researcher, that should have made Peano a rebel. But it didn't. Why? Giuseppe's older brother was seven years older, too old to be competition for a toddler. In fact, old enough to beam at the sight of an obedient baby brother. So Giuseppe dealt with the difficulties of nineteenth-century farm life by being the good kid. The supergood kid. In winter, Spinetta's local school required that every child come each day with a stick of wood for the stove that kept the schoolhouse warm. Giuseppe did. He also did well in his schoolwork. Very well. And he was competitive. He loved to get the attention and admiration of his elders. He loved to win prizes. So it is not surprising that when he grew up Giuseppe Peano would take as his own a homework assignment that had been handed down for twenty-three hundred years—reducing everything in math and science to axioms.

How do we know that Peano was a "good kid," one who was out to please his parents and any nearby authority figures? His parents were intent on getting him an exceptional education. They pulled strings with Giuseppe's uncle, an educated priest, to get their son into good schools. And they moved from the country into town when they had to, to make Giuseppe's schooling easier. Their efforts paid off. At eighteen years old, as a room-and-board-scholarship college student at the University of Turin's Collegio delle Provincie, Peano worked hard to get perfect grades. Sometimes he missed and only got an eight out of nine points in one of his classes, spoiling the run of nines he'd achieved in his other subjects. But then Peano worked to eradicate the mere eights. And he succeeded. He often got straight nines, a perfect score, an absolutely perfect grade. What's more, starting when he was still a newcomer to the university and one of its youngest students, Peano competed year after year for the Collegio's cash prizes, "two 'Balbo' awards per year and three annual 'Bricco e Martini' awards."[65] Even when Giuseppe didn't win, he came out with honorable mentions—something few others in his class of freshmen and sophomores were able to achieve.

Again, some people are trailblazers, carving paths through the wilderness. Others are trail pavers, tamping down and widening the paths that the blazers have carved out. The real indication that Peano was a trail paver, not a trailblazer, was the fact that his first publications were not original lunges for personal recognition. Instead, they furthered the research and the stature of his professors. Peano's first book, for example, took the classroom lectures of his calculus teacher and put them in book form.

Like a perpetual good kid, Peano followed a path carved for him by his elders. But the biggest elders of all were Aristotle and Euclid. So Peano turned his attention to a heritage from these two greats, a key building block of the Aristotelian method, the axiom. And Giuseppe pulled off one of the biggest acts of axiomatization in history—one of the biggest acts of reducing an entire system to a thimbleful of core concepts.

How did Giuseppe Peano pull off this phenomenal act of axiomatization? How did he come up with Peano's axioms, with the five axioms commonly known as Peano's postulates?

When Peano graduated from the University of Turin, he didn't strike out for new territory. He was still a good kid. So he became a math professor at the university he'd been studying in for four years. And in the 1880s, when Peano was in his twenties, he went on a hunt. A hunt for the simple axioms from which you could unfold the entire system of natural numbers. And eventually he found them.[66] Or he derived them. Or he invented them. Depending on how you look at it. Peano boiled all of basic math down to just nine axioms. Then he realized that he could boil five of those axioms down to just one—Aristotle's principle of identity. He realized he could scootch five of his nine axioms down to the idea that A equals A. That brought Peano's nine axioms down to a mere five. Splendid.

Here's one version of the famous five, Peano's axioms, Peano's postulates, this time without Peano's new language of logical notation. This time in simple English. Well, not so simple.

1. Zero is a number.
2. The successor of any number is another number.
3. There are no two numbers with the same successor.
4. Zero is not the successor of a number.
5. Every property of zero, which belongs to the successor of every number with this property, belongs to all numbers.[67]

Axiom number one—zero is a number—is an idea that would have startled Pythagoras and Plato. There was no such thing as a zero in the mainstream mathematics of the ancient Greeks.[68] The concept was not invented until 400 CE, seven hundred years after Aristotle. It was invented by the Indians. What did it represent? "An empty column on a counting board."[69] So the idea that zero is a number would have startled not only Pythagoras and Plato. It would have startled you and me if we'd thought about it for a bit. If we'd looked at what's under our nose as if we've never seen it before, then proceeded from there. What is zero? It's what the Indians invented: a piece of bare wood. It's a representation of an empty space on a counting board.

But the symbol of an empty space was eventually reinvented as something new in the history of counting, a placeholder. A very strange innovation. In the number ten, the one means that there is a one in the counting board's ten column and an empty space in the ones column. In the number 101, the first one means there is one in the hundreds column, an empty space in the tens column, and a one in the ones column.

Bear with me here. We're adventuring into the sort of territory that makes the eyes of most humans glaze over. Zero is a blank space on a counting board. A nothing. So how does a nothing become a number? How does an empty bit of wood become an abstraction, a symbol, a concept, an idea? How does an empty bit of wood become a virtual reality? How does it become a bona fide part of the string of scratch marks used to count chickens, fish, and sheep? How does it enter a number system invented by Mesopotamians who often had no way to mark when a number was missing from one of their columns—no way to tell a 101 from an 11 or a 201 from a 21? How does it go from the Indian *sunya*[70]—the counting board place holder—to the Latin *zephirum* first used by an Italian merchant in 1202 CE, to the word "zero" that finally appears for the first time in English in 1604?[71] And how does it become a digit, a counter, a tally mark, the start of the standard string of modern numbers—0, 1, 2, 3? That's a good question. And the answer fills entire books. Books like *Zero: The Biography of a Dangerous Idea*[72] by Charles Seife and *The Nothing That Is: A Natural History of Zero*[73] by Robert Kaplan and Ellen Kaplan.

Peano's axiom number two: one number comes after another. In fact, Peano's axioms two through four are all ways of saying that one number comes after another. And axiom number five, for all of its impossible language, is simple: all numbers share a tiny kernel of common properties. You can write numbers down. All of them. You can manipulate numbers with arithmetic. All of them. Numbers are not clouds, clods, or dancing octopi. They are a form of animal, mineral, and vegetable unto themselves. Seven and seven million may be very different from each other. But when you compare them to cups of chai latte, volcanoes, light bulbs, and lamas, it's obvious that seven million and seven belong to the same species. It's obvious that all numbers share common characteristics. That's it. Peano's axioms. Peano's basics we can all agree on.

But there was a problem. How do you know that you can extract the entire number system—addition, multiplication, division, and much more—from Peano's axioms? How do you know that you can extract eight elementary school textbooks worth of math from Peano's five postulates? Well, *you* know because you did it. That's how you spent eight months at Reed College in 1961 and 1962 when you were eighteen years old. That's how you got the attention of girls who normally wouldn't give you a first look. That's how you ended up with some of the loveliest women you'd ever seen asking you to help them with their homework. You derived the entire natural number system from 165 words on a sheet of mimeograph paper. You derived the entire number system from Peano's axioms. Yes, the girls abandoned you the minute you finished helping them with their math. They went out to find real men. But Peano's axioms and their lessons never left you.

And your wrestling match with Peano's axioms is where you got the notion that the universe might be doing what you were forced to do at Reed. That's where you got the idea that the universe might simply be doing her homework—advancing one Planck step of time after another—10^{43} steps per second.[74] That's where you got the idea that the cosmos might be working from a handful of magic beans, from a handful of simple rules, from a handful of axioms. That's where you got the idea that the universe might be unfolding what American physicist David Bohm would later call "implicate"[75] properties. That's where you got what you called "corollary generator theory." That's where you got the notion that the acts of genesis this cosmos pulls off are extractions of the implicit properties hidden in her starting rules. Hidden in her starting axioms.

And that's where you got the idea that the cosmos proceeds by translation. That's where you got the idea that the cosmos creates by threading old patterns together in new ways. That's where you got the idea that a new weave of old ideas knit together in vast multitudes produces a new medium. A new kind of sea in which to swim. A new sort of tapestry into which you can weave old stitches and produce surprise. A new kind of atmosphere in which to fly. A new big picture. That's where you got the idea that the cosmos creates by knitting old patterns into each new medium she generates. And that's where you got the idea that when the cosmos belches forth old patterns in a new medium, those old patterns sometimes become new things. Very new things. That's where you got the idea that translation can sometimes be more than it seems. Far more. That's where you got the idea that translation can sometimes be transformation in disguise.

***

Algebra is essentially a language."

—**Eli Maor**[76]

Translation turned Giuseppe Peano's last three decades of life into a challenge.[77] Why? Translation turned Giuseppe Peano from a good kid to a rebel. Translation turned Peano into an outsider, an explorer, and a heretic. In 1903, fourteen years after he published his first version of his axioms, Peano turned his attention to something that seemed to have nothing to do with math. Nothing whatsoever.

Peano became obsessed with translation and language. At first, that obsession stayed within the accepted boundaries of mathematics. In 1888, twelve years into his fifty-six-year stint teaching at the university where he'd gotten his education, the University of Turin, Peano invented a geometrical calculus. And he took his first chance on being attacked and torn apart by his fellow mathematicians. How? By demonstrating ego and daring. By entering the forbidden zone that philosopher of science David Hull says opens you to attack. By calling his geometrical calculus a "new science." Yes, an entirely new science.

What did Peano's new science do? Translation. With his geometric calculus, Peano translated Euclid's geometry into a new medium. Into the language that Galileo and Kepler did *not* have. The language of equations. Peano translated the kind of complex manipulations of squares, tetrahedrons, icosahedrons, spheres, triangles, and circles that Kepler had loved into nice, neat, easy-to-deal with algebraic formulae. At least he translated geometry into formulae that are easy to deal with for the tiny number of humans on the planet who are adept at equation juggling. Equations that are daunting to most of the rest of us.

But Peano's geometrical calculus did more than just turn geometrical shapes—circles, triangles, rectangles, and multisided polygons bristling with corners—into algebra-style formulae. Peano's geometrical calculus also turned geometrical propositions—geometrical *hypotheses*, geometrical guesses—into equations. And here's the nut of the matter, the real killer app: Peano's geometric calculus turned even proofs—even logical demonstrations—into what Peano calls "the transformations of equations." Yes, Peano turned even logic into a form of algebra. What does all of this come down to? Once again with feeling. It comes down to translation. And translation of an old pattern into a new medium produces something new.

Giuseppe Peano's interest in translation was more than a passing fancy. It was an obsession. An obsession that grew as he got older. Once he'd completed his axioms and his geometric calculus, Peano turned his attention to something that seemed utterly unrelated: a universal language. He called it a "Latin without grammar." He began to write his papers in this newly conceived universal language. He wrote one of his most important books, "the fifth and final edition of his *Formulario Mathematico*,"[78] in Latin without grammar. He went to math and philosophy conventions and even tried to give his lectures in Latin without grammar. At the International Congress of Mathematics at Cambridge in 1912, he insisted on lecturing in this obscure "international auxiliary language"[79] and was forced to drop the idea. What's more, when a group that had been established to spread a competing universal language collapsed, Peano took it over and used it to promote his own universal language, his Latin without grammar.

Peano increasingly took up class time with his students teaching them another of his languages, the symbolic logic[80] to which he had tried to reduce all of math in his book the *Formulario Mathematico*.[81] Peano's fellow math professors were not pleased. They claimed that Peano had ceased teaching real math[82] and had become utterly incomprehensible, "his students quite properly complaining that they could not understand a word of what the hoarse, excitable old man was saying."[83] More than that, one of his "detractors" called Peano a "sub-proletarian . . . idiot."[84] His opponents tried over and over again to get him fired. But legally, Giuseppe Peano was entitled to hold on to his post no matter what. Meanwhile, Peano held another teaching position, a position with a military academy across the street from the University of Turin. His insistence on teaching symbolic logic got him ejected from his military-academy post. But Peano's opponents never succeeded in tossing him out of his seat at the University of Turin.

Peano spent the last twenty-nine years of his life shifting from an exclusive focus on math to the promotion of Latin without grammar. And in those last decades of life, Peano went from the perpetual good kid to the outsider, making a splash at mathematical and philosophical conferences with his universal language, with his notation for logic, and with his postulates, his axioms. Making a splash with tools of translation. And rousing resentment on his home campus. For example, at the International Congress of Philosophy of 1900 in Paris, Peano made that huge impression we talked about before on Bertrand Russell. A life-changing impression.[85] The impression that led Russell to say that "the most important year of my intellectual life was 1900."[86] Here's how Russell describes it:

> The Congress was a turning point in my intellectual life, because I there met Peano. I already knew him by name and had seen some of his work, but had not taken the trouble to master his [logical] notation. In discussions at the Congress I observed that he was always more precise than anyone else, and that he invariably got the better of any argument upon which he embarked. As the days went by, I decided that this must be owing

to his mathematical logic. I therefore got him to give me all his works, and as soon as the Congress was over I retired to Fernhurst [Russell's home] to study quietly every word written by him and his disciples. It became clear to me that his notation afforded an instrument of logical analysis such as I had been seeking for years, and that by studying him I was acquiring a new and powerful technique for the work that I had long wanted to do.[87]

What work was Russell talking about? The quest to show that math and logic are just two different ways of expressing the same thing.[88] Two translations of something primal into a different medium. Two different languages with which to express what Russell called "primitive ideas"— underlying patterns, deep structures, Ur patterns. And where did Russell get the phrase "primitive ideas?" From Peano.[89] Russell was primarily concerned about these basic patterns as abstractions. Not as real-world things.[90] But he was hunting for the underlying logic that Kepler, Galileo, and Newton were sure that God himself had used to build the universe.

Becoming one of Bertrand Russell's favorite thinkers didn't help Peano back home in Turin, where he held on to his professorship by the skin of his teeth. Why did the authorities and his fellow professors plot to get rid of him? Translation, universal languages, and symbolic logic did not belong in math. Translation and bizarre new symbols were alien matters. They were not mathematics. At least that was the opinion of Peano's attackers. But were those attackers right? Or was Peano on to something?

Was Peano's obsession with translation and with the reduction of everything in sight to universal languages—from Latin without grammar and geometrical calculus to logical notation—really irrelevant to math? And is math really irrelevant to the language that you and I use every day? Even more important, was Peano's translation obsession irrelevant to the God Problem?

We shall have to see.

TED COONS, DANCING WONDER:
A TALE OF TWO TRANSLATIONS

Iteration is translation. And translation of the old into a new medium, into a new language, can be transformation. Translation can be an act of creation. Now reverse that. Retro-engineer it. When you find something radically new, dissect it. If you do, you will often discover that the staggeringly new is something old in disguise. You will often find a simple rule at work, a rule repeating itself in unexpected ways. You will often find a simple basic pattern at work. You will often find a deep structure. You will often find an Ur pattern.

In 1967, when you were twenty-four years old, you would acquire a mentor in neurobiology, Ted Coons. And in Coons's life would be a clue to the power of translation, a clue to the nature of deep structures, a clue to the magic of recruitment strategies, and a clue to the God Problem.

When he was fifteen years old, Ted Coons danced with legendary movie star Rita Hayworth, the greatest sex symbol of the 1940s. Coons had been a musical stage performer since the age of six. So when he was seventeen years old, Coons went off to college to major in musical composition. And when he was twenty-seven years old, Coons wired up the brain of a rat and discovered the role of a brain region that had baffled scientists since the second century CE days of Galen[91]—the hypothalamus.

What's more, from his youth until his eighties, Coons was fascinated by Bell numbers,[92] a puzzling mathematical series that unfolds wonders from a handful of simple rules.

$$1$$
$$1\ 2$$
$$2\ 3\ 5$$
$$5\ 7\ 10\ 15$$
$$15\ 20\ 27\ 37\ 52$$

What, if anything, do all these interests share in common?

Coons's life poses a crucial puzzle to the scientific expedition that you and I are on. That puzzle: what connects dance, music, and the arts to science? Born in 1928, Ted Coons grew up in the Oklahoma town of Texhoma, a community of less than a thousand inhabitants where the Wild West was still alive and where rodeo was king. In fact, Coons would eventually become a horseback riding ace. But when he was a mere nubbin of only five years old, music was what really grabbed him. He heard songs like Tommy Dorsey's hit "The Music Goes Round and Round" on the radio. And he insisted on singing them . . . and dancing them . . . himself. Dancing them in what he calls "a soft-shoe and tap routine à la Fred Astaire." In fact, Ted was so uncannily good at it, that when he was six, his mom booked performance dates for him onstage at the Roxy Theater in his hometown. When those performances went over promisingly she booked him even more, putting him on the road as a professional performer in Oklahoma and Texas. But the capital of the sort of entertainment Coons did so well was Hollywood. That was the town that could make you a national—and an international—star.

So that's where his mom took Ted Coons next. And one day, when Coons was in a Hollywood Spanish dance class, Rita Hayworth, one of the greatest glamour queens and sex symbols of the era, popped in. Why? She was the dance teacher's niece. And what student did that teacher pick to dance with Hayworth? The smoothest dancer in the room: Ted Coons.

Then Coons went to Colorado College to major in musical composition. His teachers included two towering figures of twentieth-century music, Virgil Thomson and Paul Hindemith. But, Coons says, "a former student of Hindemith, David Kraehenbuehl, was my greatest influence."[93] Kraehenbuehl and Coons spent as much time discussing what Coons calls "the relationship between musical form and feeling" as they did going over the basics of music theory. And Coons became curious. Music had an astonishing power to stir emotions. But where did those emotions come from? And, in Coons's words, "how was form and its mathematics involved?" That question became more important to Coons than music.

So Coons went off to Yale to study the seat of the emotions, the brain, with the amazing Neal Miller, a pioneer who was doing two things:

(1) Fusing robotic behavioral approaches toward psychology with inward-looking psychoanalytic concepts and

(2) Demonstrating how psychological drives power the forces of history.[94]

Yale is where Coons wired up the brain of a rat, put two electrodes into the hypothalamus, and discovered what that organ seated deep in the lower regions, the animal regions, of the brain does. What does the hypothalamus do? Coons discovered that it's the brain's "hunger center."[95] The hypothalamus tells you "how to regulate" your intake of food, water, and, ahem, sex. Sex, the hunger that made Rita Hayworth a star.

By 1965, Ted Coons was a professor in the graduate and undergraduate psychology department at New York University, in a town where he could indulge his musical interests to the max. Near NYU was a converted Polish center that was the epitome of hi-tech psychedelia. It was four townhouses joined together to provide a huge interior space, a space lit with the next-generation lasers and an army of audio-video equipment of a kind that few had ever seen before. As *Wikipedia* describes it, "Flame throwing jugglers and trapeze artists performed between musical sets, strobe lights flashed over a huge dance floor, and multiple projectors flashed images and footage from home movies."[96]

Coons used the Electric Circus to the hilt. In 1967 he pulled together an Electric Circus performance that paired the rock group Circus Maximus with electronic music pioneering composer Morton Subotnick. Then Coons helped put together a Carnegie Hall concert in conjunction with the Electric Circus and the Pro Musica medieval music performers, a concert called "An Electric Christmas at Carnegie Hall." The Electric Circus made such a splash that it was reviewed in *Time* magazine. For his next act, Coons helped found a multimedia concert series called the Electric Ear. And forty years later, Coons would still be stirring up the music scene. He would involve himself intensely in the American Festival of Microtonal Music's project to complete and perform legendary modernist composer Charles Ives's magnum opus, "The Universe Symphony." Why did Coons throw himself into the completion of Ives's musical take on the entire cosmos? "Out of conviction with Ives and the early Greeks," he says, "that music is in some way the image of the universe."[97] Kepler would have been pleased. So would Pythagoras.

You were one of Coons's students. And Coons's performances in his class on physiological psychology—the field now known as neurobiology—were unforgettable. When he was explaining the animal instincts that we share with lab rats, Coons imitated the rat scratching its ear with its hind leg. OK, he cheated. He used his hands, not his feet. But the way he dug, poked, and squiggled a finger into his auditory canal, the waxy tunnel of the ear, was priceless. Then the way he acted out putting his waxy fingertip twelve inches in front of his face and giving it a good examination, and the way he got across the fact that when no one is looking you and I do this rat thing too, was unforgettable. So was the message: our elaborate psyche is built on the same simple rules that guide the rat.

Thirteen years later, when Coons began to make a regular practice of coming to your brownstone in Park Slope, Brooklyn, to brainstorm, he brought with him the story of his life . . . and he brought Bell's numbers, a series of numbers whose rules can be summed up in thirty-eight almost incomprehensible words, words so tricky that if I were to try to explain them to you, they would drive you crazy. But still, a whole, ornate mathematical system emerging from just thirty-eight words was a wonder. And an even bigger mystery emerged from the tale of Ted's life—the puzzle of why Ted's obsessions with music, math, emotion, and the brain fit together. The puzzle of how dancing with Rita Hayworth at the age of fifteen fit in with a life in science, with the study of animal behavior, and with the patterns of the brain.

Here's how that connection looked to you. There was more than $A = A$ to Aristotle. There was the basic Aristotelian syllogism, the one that's a cornerstone of logic: if $a = b$ and $b = c$, then $a = c$. If all men are mortal and if Socrates is a man, then Socrates is mortal. In Ted Coons's case, the syllogism went something like this. If math = music, if music = emotion, and if math = the cosmos, then emotion = the cosmos. Or

$$emotion = music = math = the\ cosmos.$$

Which means, bear with me, this needs emphasis: *emotion equals the cosmos!* Notice any resemblance to the ideas of Pythagoras?

Pythagoras or not, the idea that emotion equals math, that emotion equals the cosmos, and that music equals all three—emotion, math, and the cosmos—is rather hard to believe. A churn of feelings equals stars and planets? Your upset when you have a fight with your mate somehow equals galaxies? Or, worse, your depression when no person of the opposite sex shows any interest in you somehow reflects the darkness of the space between the stars? Come off it. This is not science. It is nonsense. How in the world did your brainstorming with Ted Coons reach this peculiar conclusion? And how would the product of that brainstorming fit into solving the God Problem?

The answer would lie in two things: Ur patterns and translation.

***

One more perspective on the importance of if $a = b$ and $b = c$, then $a = c$. And one more story. Then we'll get back to the saga of Peano, the axiom, the evolution of science, and the puzzle of how the cosmos creates.

The year was 2001. Ted Coons was visiting you roughly twice a year. And you had just acquired a ten-year-old stepson, Walter the Wonder. He was an adorable kid, with his sandy bangs, his bright, dark eyes, and his curious face. As a new stepfather, you felt it was your job to impart wisdom. So you gave Walter a lecture on what you called "frames of reference." When you run into something interesting, try putting it into another frame of reference and see what happens, you said. Try putting it into another medium. Then you tried to explain what you meant.

Draw a square on a piece of paper. You've just put that square into one frame of reference—the frame of reference of the pencil's graphite and of the paper's bleached wood pulp. Now grab your computer mouse and draw the same square on the computer monitor. You've just translated your square into at least three more frames of reference. Three more mediums. Three? Yes, three . . . and more. You've just translated the square into the muscle movements of your hand on the mouse. The mouse has translated those muscle movements into electrical currents flowing to the computer's microprocessor. The microprocessor has translated the electrical currents from the mouse into commands in a computer program. And the commands in a computer program have translated the electric currents of the microprocessor into lines on an LED monitor. Which means the movements of your hand have been translated into the ons and offs of roughly 786,432 tiny lights on a screen. Those tiny lights, in turn, have sent out a small flood of photons—a flood of particles of light. The particles have hit your retina. In the retina, they have been translated into a burst of electrochemical signals. Those electrochemical signals have traveled to your optic nerve and have been compressed into yet another electrochemical dialect, a shorthand.[98] The optic nerve has carried that compressed signal to your thalamus.

There the signal has been divided up and passed to thirty different brain centers,[99] optic centers, vision centers. Thirty! Each center has turned the electrochemical signal into a unique pattern of its own, analyzing it to find lines, shadows, three-dimensional shapes, colors, and familiar things like faces and geometric shapes. Each center has translated the signals representing the square into a language of its own. Yes, translated! The way that Giuseppe Peano translated geometry into algebra, algebra into logic, and everything he could into Latin without grammar. Then the thirty centers have combined their signals into yet another electrochemical language that's produced an illusion in your brain. The illusion we call "vision" and "sight." The illusion that we are looking directly at the square, not reading an electrochemical pattern put together in the dark prison of the skull. How many frames of reference has the square gone through? How many different languages has the square been translated into? How many different mediums?

Now go online and e-mail the square you've drawn to yourself. Has the square traveled through the air from your computer to your Wi-Fi router? If it has, why didn't you see it? And if you could have seen it, would you have recognized the signal as a square? If you could see the signal traveling on fiber-optic cables to the servers of the worldwide web, would you recognize them as a square? In reality, *are* these signals a square? If they are, why are they so unrecognizable? Why are they scrambled in a form that would look like nonsense if you *could* see them?

Does the square you draw with pencil and paper equal the square you draw with your keyboard and your mouse? Does the signal your mouse sends to your microprocessor equal the square you drew on paper? And does the square you send to your Wi-Fi router equal the square you see on your monitor? What in the world does "equal" really mean?

If you'd been the first person on the planet to send a square to a wireless router on its way to the Internet, would the signal you were sending have been something that's been around in this cosmos for a long time? Or would it have been something new? New not just to computer users, but new to the universe that gave computer users birth? And if your square translated to Wi-Fi signals is new, does it open a path to new possibilities? To entire new kinds of things and processes? To entire new kinds of entities? Beyond that, does it open opportunities to new recruitment strategies? And just how new would those entities and self-sustaining strategies really be?

When the Internet was started in 1982, did it bring forth any things this cosmos had never seen before? Like Google, Amazon®, Twitter®, and Facebook®? And did Google, Amazon, Twitter, and Facebook in any way change the world around them?

Topping it all off, how does Ted Coons's mystery of

$$emotion = music = math = the\ cosmos$$

relate to

a square on paper =
a square drawn by the muscle movements of fingers =
the programming commands to draw a square in your computer =
the square picked out by the LEDs of your monitor =
the square that goes through the air to your router?

When one *A* is seemingly so different from another *A*, how does *A* still equal *A*? And why?

***

Once you'd given this speech, you wondered where in the world it had come from. But your new stepson managed to feign interest all the way through. And when you finished, his eyes were still bright. The bottom line? Translation from one medium to another plays a role in the God Problem. So does the role of translation as transformation. Peano, with his translation obsession, was on to something. But what?

PRESTO, CHANGE-O: TRANSLATION'S LITTLE SECRET

Translation is a very peculiar business. How in the world can a circle equal a string of *A*'s, *B*'s, and symbols? How can the shape of a brick building, of a stone pyramid, of a granary, and of a city wall equal scratch marks on clay? And how can logic, too, equal math? How can logic equal formulas inked on paper? Logic, remember, is something that the brain does. It's something that the brain translates from chemical flows and electron exchanges into words. The brain translates chemicals, electrons, and the brainwide webbing of axons and dendrites into Aristotle's streams of logical argument.

Logic uses words. And what are words? Sounds that we make with our tongue. Sounds that take on their meaning from their positioning in a network of networks—their positioning in the network of a sentence, a sentence that's nestled in the network of a paragraph, a paragraph that's nestled in the network of a complete thought, a complete thought that's nestled in the network of a culture, and a culture that's nestled in an era of history, a culture that's networked into a historical period in whose context the words make sense. Not to mention a historical period that's nestled in the evolution of a universe, nestled within the creative process of a cosmos, nestled like Kepler's boxes nestled in balls and balls nestled within boxes.

But that's just a single strand in the network of translation that makes words. Words are stirrings in the motor cortex of the brain. Stirrings that are translated into movements of the tongue and lips. Movements that are translated into puffs of air. Puffs of air that are translated into oscillations, into wobbles of molecules in a gas. How can these wobbles of gas molecules be captured by a menagerie of symbols? Symbols made by mere finger movements? Symbols made of wedge marks in clay, ink on papyrus, scratches on wax, ink on paper, or flashing diodes on a laptop screen? Symbols that the eye absorbs via beams of light? Symbols that the eye translates from photons into chemical and electron flows?

How in the world can puffs of air and flows in five billion nerve cells or more be captured by written squiggles like the ones you're reading right now? How can they be translated into symbols like the words and sentences in Peano's 231 written works?[100] For that matter, why can Peano's Italian be translated into your English and mine? Then there's the real mystery. Are Bertrand Russell and Peano right? Does logic = math? And if so, why? Why do so many symbol systems equal each other?

Remember heresy number one: *A* does not equal *A*. So how can so many radically different things be equal? Is translation a step in the process of creation? And if it is, why?

***

Looked at from another point of view, Giuseppe Peano's obsession with translation was an obsession with boiling things down. What sorts of things? Numbers, calculus, algebra, formulae, geometry, logic, and language. Symbol systems. Boiling them all down to a central core of underlying patterns. Translating a vast mass of things into a handful of "primitive"[101] statements. Translating a vast mass of things. Translating them into a handful of magic beans.

In a sense, Peano's quest was a repetition of a basic idea from Plato. It was another manifestation of Plato's conviction that behind the jungle of concepts we deal with, behind the wild variety of the things that we see and believe, there are a handful of universals, a handful of basics, a handful of ideas, a handful of archetypes, a handful of deep structures, a handful of Ur patterns. But is that ancient suspicion true? By boiling things down, can you find the bricks with which the cosmos builds things up? The elements, the patterns, or the processes with which the cosmos creates from nothing? The starting recruitment strategies of the cosmos?

And there's another really big question, the question that Giuseppe Peano seemed to sense. Do our symbol systems, all of our symbol systems, equal each other for a simple reason? Do they equal each other because all of them equal something even more basic? Reality? Not to mention the universe?

Is translation just a human trick? Or is it a tool in the trick bag of cosmic creativity?

THE DAY YOU UPLOADED YOUR SELF: TRANSLATION SAVES YOUR LIFE

> *I believe that nature uses the same small set of ideas over and over.*
> —Joseph Polchinski, Kavli Institute for Theoretical Physics, University of California, Santa Barbara[102]

> *I would not give a fig for the simplicity this side of complexity, but I would give my life for the simplicity on the other side of complexity.*
> —Oliver Wendell Holmes

Why can we humans translate geometry, calculus, and algebra into formulae? Why can we translate mathematics into logic, logic into language, and language back into formulae? Why can humans like Giuseppe Peano and Bertrand Russell imagine that math equals logic? And why can they suspect, along with Kepler, Galileo, and Newton, that math and logic equal the fundamental rules of the universe?

What's more, why can you and I sometimes translate the thoughts of wretchedly difficult thinkers like Giuseppe Peano and Bertrand Russell into terms that even we, with our limited brainpower, can understand? One answer is the notion of isomorphic symbol sets. Isomorphic symbol sets and their cousins, Ur patterns. You already have a sense of Ur patterns. I've been slipping them into your reading matter like liquid vitamins into a kid's soda pop. But what are isomorphic symbol sets?

The year was 1995. You had been stuck in bed for seven years with a serious illness—chronic fatigue syndrome. For five of those years you had been too weak to talk. Too weak to power up your larynx to get out a single syllable. And too weak to walk the twenty feet to your own kitchen. You were in the process of losing your wife of thirty-two years. It is very hard for a wife to take care of her husband when that husband is so weak that no one else can enter his bedroom. It's brutally punishing for her to try to sustain you when you are so fragile that the mere sound of a newspaper page turning rips through you like a cannonball. In fact, studies show that the stress of caretaking takes years off of a healthy spouse's life.[103] The result: your wife was escaping the savage envelope of stress by moving to upstate New York and divorcing you. So what did you do? Translation!

You translated yourself into a new medium. You had two computers set up next to your bed. You devised a system that would allow you to control the two of them with a single monitor and keyboard. And you taped a big foam wedge wrapped in silver gaffer's tape—a wedge made of the kind of foam used to make mattresses and bolsters—to the back of your keyboard to prop it up at a sharp angle so you could see the keys when the keyboard was perched on your lap and when you were laid flat with your head propped on a pillow. Then you took advantage of a new kind of space, a space you could move through with only tiny flicks of your fingers on a touchpad or the keys. You translated yourself, your self—your being and your identity—into a new medium. Into a flick-of-the-fingertip world. You ventured into cyberspace. You plunged into a relatively new thing called the Internet and made friends. Friends who didn't care that you were too weak to talk as long as you could type. As long as you could e-mail and IM. As long as you could write colorfully. Which you tried with all your heart and soul to do. Why? Because your sanity depended on attracting cyberfriends. Your sanity depended on a benign use of the ability to seduce, recruit, and kidnap. Your sanity depended on your ability to surf the waves of recruitment strategies.

And you did something more than mere friend seeking. You founded two international scientific groups. Online. Via the Internet. Groups that met every day. Intercontinentally. Conversing day and night from Australia and the United States to Holland, England, Israel, and Russia and back again. And you used those two groups to pursue some questions. One of the biggest of those questions was a puzzle of translation. You were certain that in some underlying way, art, poetry, religion, and science were the same. It was one of those things you knew in your bones. But you couldn't figure out how and why. Did science really equal art? And if so, why?

The Group Selection Squad—the cyberorganization you founded in 1995—was dedicated to overthrowing the scientific tyranny of individual selection—the idea that evolution is a battleground between selfish genes and selfish individuals. There was another view, group selection. Group selection said that individuals both compete and cooperate. They cooperate in groups. And the success or failure of those groups has an impact on genes. For example, the leading champion of group selection, an evolutionary biologist named David Sloan Wilson, argued that if you are a member of a tribe in South America or Africa that has chosen a weak form of social organization and you go up against a tribe whose organizational structure is strong, you will lose.[104] And if you lose, you will lose your property and your women. Even if you don't lose your life, you will lose the right to reproduce. Your conquerors, the folks whose culture has favored the genes of complex social cohesion, will thrive. The conquerors will get your women. And the conquerors will get sexual privileges with those women. Sex leads to children. And children nourish and spread genes. Not to mention the fact that genes nourish and spread children. The genes of the winning group will thrive. The genes of the losing groups will die. Yes, groups.

Or, to put it differently, the best cooperators make the strongest competitors.

Members of the Group Selection Squad included Wilson, who was the only scientist regularly getting pro-group-selection articles into major journals despite the chokehold individual selectionists had on almost every editorial board. Another of your stalwart supporters was Christopher Boehm, director of the Jane Goodall Research Institute at UCLA, author of books like *Hierarchy in the Forest: The Evolution of Egalitarian Behavior* and *Blood Revenge: The Enactment and Management of Conflict in Montenegro and Other Tribal Societies*. The Group Selection Squad included forty other evolutionary biologists and evolutionary psychologists scattered over thirteen thousand miles from Australia to Amsterdam. And the group won its battle. Within a year, you had used the ammunition the group had given you to help place David Sloan Wilson on the front page of the *New York Times* science section.[105] The story was huge. It was a six-column feature, a feature story occupying the entire bottom half of the front page. That front-page story made group selection legitimate overnight.

Then you spotted another hole in science. Another cause. You were working on a new book, the second you would write and publish from your bed—*Global Brain: The Evolution of Mass Mind from the Big Bang to the 21st Century*.[106] And you were frustrated. When physicists talked about elementary particles or stars, they tended to talk about these particles as if each particle existed in isolation. And you were convinced that no particle, no atom, no planet, and no star exists in a vacuum. What's more, you were convinced that every one of these things exists in a network, a web, a crowd, a mob, or a society. In short, you felt that even elementary particles exist in groups.

What's worse, when paleontologists discovered a new prehistoric bird or dinosaur, they tried to reassemble a prototypical individual. They reconstructed that dinosaur's musculature and its stance—upright or four-legged. They even tried to find clues to its coloring. But in the 1990s, paleontologists didn't look for evidence of that individual's group behavior. For example, in 1993 an amateur paleontologist in Beijing, Zhang He, took a fossil he'd found to a local flea market and hit pay dirt. He ran into two full-time paleontologists from Beijing's Institute of Vertebrate Paleontology and Paleoanthropology. These two paleontologists soon discovered that farmers were digging up hundreds of these specimens of ancient birds with feathers and with something no previous bird had possessed—a beak.[107] They named the new bird species after China's greatest sage, Confucius: *Confuciusornis*. Teams of paleornithologists wrote journal articles telling you why they thought *Confuciusornis* lived in trees, why they thought it had evolved its flight mechanism independently from other birds, when it lived, and what its discovery contributed to the big controversy of the day—the debate over whether birds evolved from dinosaurs or from pre-dinosaurian reptiles. The debate over whether birds were dinosaurs who took to the skies and flew.

But here's the twist. Hundreds of the fossils were found together at the margin of an ancient Chinese lake.[108] The paleontologists acknowledged that this might have something to do with "avian social behavior" and "some sort of communal life-style."[109] But did these scientists use their findings to try to reconstruct *Confuciusornis's* group behavior? Not on your life. When you were strong enough to speak, you called them to fill in facts for *Global Brain*. And they were helpful as could be. But avian sociality was not on their radar.

So you founded yet another online group—The International Paleo-psychology Project. Its goal? "To trace the evolution of sociality, mentation, cognition, and emotion from the big bang to the twenty-first century." To find out whether group behavior exists among quarks, atoms, photons, molecules, galaxies, and stars. And to see when and how the patterns we know as emotion and perception entered the evolutionary picture. Yes, the question sounds strange. But should it? Didn't Ted Coons inadvertently tell you that emotion = the cosmos?

The International Paleopsychology Project, like the Group Selection Squad, attracted some amazing minds—paleontologists, entomologists, physicists, computer scientists, evolutionary psychologists, and neurobiologists. Among them was condensed matter physicist Eshel ben-Jacob, president of the Israeli society of physicists—the Israel Physical Society. Eshel was head of the Department of Condensed Matter Physics at the University of Tel Aviv, holder of the Maguy-Glass Chair in Physics of Complex Systems, and a man whose work on, of all things, bacterial group intelligence, bacterial group IQ, took up the entire cover of *Scientific American* in October 1998, when Eshel and his wife came from Israel out to your brownstone in Park Slope, Brooklyn, to visit you in your bedroom.

Ben Jacob's work was riddled with clues to the God Problem. Riddled with investigations of structures that repeat. Structures that repeat on radically different levels of evolution. What had pulled ben-Jacob, a condensed matter physicist, into microbiology? He'd noticed that bacterial colonies in petri dishes spread out in fractal patterns. Patterns like the patterns you see in rocks in museum shops, rocks cut in half and polished to show their gorgeous internal structures, circles, sunbursts, and concentric rings. Ben-Jacob was curious. Did the same forces forge these extraordinary patterns in both dead things—rocks—and in living things, bacterial colonies? Or was something additional at work in the bacteria? Did life repeat the fractal patterns of rocks for reasons that went beyond the mere physics of stone and crystals? In other words, Eshel was on the hunt for underlying patterns, deep structures. And for their translation into a new medium—the medium of life.

Then there was Eshel's friend Joel Isaacson, Professor Emeritus of Computer Science at Washington University. Isaacson's work was supported by NASA, The National Institutes of Health, and a dozen other prestige scientific institutions. Isaacson had devised a mathematical gamelike system, a cellular automata, that accounted for the evolution of the elementary particles called "the baryon octet."[110] He'd done it using nothing but a tiny number of simple starting rules. Rules you might call deep structures. Fundamental patterns. Founding axioms. Ur patterns. What was Isaacson's most intriguing primary rule? A something exists as a something in part because of the space that separates it from something else. An empty space helps give things their identity.

But one of your most important clues to the God Problem—one of your most crucial clues to the problem of how a cosmos without a god pulls off acts of genesis, acts of supersized surprise—not to mention how the same fractal sunburst pattern crops up in rocks and bacterial colonies—came from an incredibly bright graduate student of chemistry at Harvard University, Reed Konsler.

6

IS METAPHOR A CRIME?

THE HUNGER OF THE STUTTERING FORMS:
ISOMORPHIC SYMBOL SETS

In 1998, Reed Konsler injected three words into the discussions of the International Paleopsychology Project. Three words that would offer a clue to the mystery of translation. Three words that would help explain why metaphor works. Three words that would hint at the inner tricks of cosmic creativity. Konsler inserted the phrase "isomorphic symbol sets."

Konsler swears he got "isomorphic symbol sets" from Douglas Hofstadter, the mathematical and scientific deep thinker and author of the Pulitzer Prize–winning 1979 book *Gödel, Escher, Bach*. But that's not where Konsler found it. The concept, perhaps. After all, Hofstadter's 1996 book, *Metamagical Themas,* is subtitled "Questing for the Essence of Mind and Pattern." But search Hofstadter's works and you won't find the phrase "iso-morphic symbol sets." Anywhere. The phrase is Konsler's.

What are isomorphic symbol sets? Symbol sets that look very different, but that match up in some strange way. Symbol sets that explore the world in different terms but that correspond to each other.[1] Symbol sets that can be translated into each other. The way that Giuseppe Peano translated geometry into calculus and algebra. The way that Peano, Bertrand Russell, and another nineteenth-century thinker, George Boole, translated logic into equations. The way that Peano boiled down all of the natural number system to nine axioms. The way that Peano then realized that five of those axioms all equaled just one of Aristotle's ideas, $A = A$. The way that Peano then translated his nine axioms to five. And the way he showed that these axioms could be translated back again. Back to numbers, addition, multiplication, division, and a whole lot more.

Isomorphic symbol sets equal each other. But how and why? Aristotle, Euclid, Kepler, Galileo, Newton, and the Founding Fathers had used different symbol sets. But they had used those symbol sets to explore different manifestations of the same thing—the real world. So had the Babylonians and the Egyptians. They had used different mathematical and verbal languages to grasp the same outer world. And to make predictions about it. To measure the size of a farm field. To calculate the number of barleycorns in a pyramidal silo with a flat top and sloping sides. To lay out perfect right angles for their temples, their pyramids, and their homes. Right angles that would withstand the test of time. To predict the movements of the stars and the planets. To predict the weather.

The Babylonians, the Egyptians, Aristotle, and the Founding Fathers had used symbol sets to predict what next move a king, an emperor, or a Congress would have to make to stay in power. To predict the moves a ruler would have to make to ensure that his farmers had bountiful harvests. To predict the strategies he'd have to use to make sure that his state was not absorbed by another ravenously ambitious empire. And to predict the patterns that the creators of a constitution would have to harness to produce a foundation for a new nation conceived in liberty and dedicated to the proposition that all men are created equal. A nation that would last. The Babylonians, the Egyptians, Aristotle, and the Founding Fathers had used symbol sets to predict the patterns of history. And to surf them!

They had put symbol sets through a Darwinian obstacle course. The isomorphic symbol sets that produced the biggest payoff thrived. Some payoffs were purely social. Some symbol sets made you feel good. Some symbol sets helped you hold a tribe, a city, or an empire together. In which case accuracy didn't count. Astrology is a good example. Religion is another. But many symbol sets and their quirks hung on and grew because they had prediction power. The power to isomorph the real world.

How many of these languages are synonymous—the language of math, the language of logic, the language of politics, the language of science, the language of visual art, and the language of fiction and poetry? Is Pythagoras right—is music synonymous with all of these in some strange and as-yet-unknown way? And what about religion? Is that another synonymous language, another language that in some distant way is the same? How many of these are truly isomorphic symbol sets? If so, why? In what way do they match each other? And more important, why?

***

The answer to that question is in the tale of why metaphor works. But to tell that story, let's go back to Aristotle. Aristotle not only dictated a method for science. He dictated one of our scientific prejudices. The prejudice against metaphor. "Metaphorical reasoning is unscientific,"[2] he said in his *Posterior Analytics*, the book in which he laid out his procedure for science. But was Aristotle right? Is the use of metaphor unscientific? And what does metaphor have to do with translation? What does metaphor have to do with repeating a pattern like a square in finger movements, pencil marks, and the moves of a mouse, not to mention in computer programming code and the pixels on a screen? What does metaphor have to do with the idea that the cosmos equals math, math equals music, music equals emotion, and emotion should in some strange way equal the cosmos? And what does metaphor have to do with the way a godless cosmos creates?

LEONARDO'S STONES: WHY METAPHOR WORKS

Light, says current physics, is simultaneously a wave and a particle. And guess what? Though Aristotle says that "metaphorical reasoning is unscientific," a wave is a metaphor. So is a particle.

How did the highest of the modern sciences—physics—get the notion that light is both a wave and a particle? From metaphors. The tale begins nearly six hundred years ago on the western shores of Italy near the city of Piombino with Leonardo da Vinci and the detailed observations he writes down in his notebooks, the famous notebooks in which he writes his ideas backward so only he can read them. In those notebooks, Leonardo is fascinated by water. And by waves. More than fascinated. He observes waves in riveting detail. Little does he know it, but he's observing a primal recruitment pattern at work.

Since his adolescence, Leonardo has been obsessed with canals. He has constantly drawn schemes for canal construction and improvement.[3] As an adult, Leonardo applies this interest. He helps build so many canals that he will be credited by Stendhal for carrying "water into every corner of the Milanese territory."[4] Understanding water is crucial to his work. And his work gives him a chance to see how water behaves in the stillness and narrowness of a channel.

But that's not enough to satisfy Leonardo's curiosity. He goes to the shore where the Ligurian Sea and the Tyrrhenian Sea meet. It's not the sea's quiet throb alone that interests him. He sticks around to take in the details of a storm. He jots down what he sees in his notebook:

> The air was dark from the heavy rain which was falling slantwise bent by the cross current of the winds and formed itself in waves in the air, like those one sees formed by the dust, the only difference being that these drifts were furrowed by the lines made by the drops of the falling water.[5]

Leonardo sees a common pattern repeating in three different mediums: rain, dust, and air. And he says the air

> was tinged by the colour of the fire produced by the thunderbolts wherewith the clouds were rent and torn asunder, the flashes from which smote and tore open the vast waters of the flooded valleys, and as these lay open there were revealed in their depths the bowed summits of the trees.[6]

But Leonardo is not here just for the thrills, much as he loves them. He keeps his eye peeled for the details. He makes verbal sketches of the "waves of the sea at Piombino," waves "all of foaming water." He observes "the waves of the sea that beats against the shelving base of the mountains which confine it, rush foaming in speed up to the ridge of these same hills, and in turning back meet the onset of the succeeding wave, and after loud roaring return in a mighty flood to the sea from whence they came." The waves pounding the ridges of the hills oscillate. They go in and out, back and forth. Leonardo watches as the "great number of the inhabitants, men and different animals, may be seen driven by the rising of the deluge up towards the summits of the hills which border on the said waters." He sees how "water...leaps up...where the great masses fall and strike the waters."[7] Water makes vast and fleeting walls in the air, walls of splash, when a man, an animal, or a house falls into it. He imagines what it might be like if this were the ultimate deluge, the ultimate flood where "men and birds might be seen together crowded upon the tops of the tall trees which over-topped the swollen waters forming hills which surround the great abysses."[8] Then it's back to reality. Leonardo observes the "eddies of wind and of rain." When it's over and the sky clears, he watches the water slosh as the boats are emptied of "the rain water."[9]

In his less extreme moments, Leonardo also watches how water evaporates. How it flows and how it feels in "a sponge squeezed in the hand, which is held under water, since the water flows away from it in every direction with equal movement through the openings that come between the fingers of the hand within which it is squeezed."[10] He goes for a muscular understanding.

Leonardo imagines how water plays its role in the grand scheme of things. He hypothesizes that, thanks to the heat of the sun,

> the damp vapours, the thick mists and dense clouds . . . are given off by the seas and other lakes and rivers and marshy valleys. And drawing these little by little up to the cold region.[11]

He guesses that the cold transforms these vapors, causing them to join

> together one to another [to] form thick and dark clouds. And these are often swept away and carried by the winds from one region to another, until at last their density gives them such weight that they fall in thick rain.[12]

OK, that explains the weather systems that produce rain. And the transport mechanism that takes water from the seas, lakes, rivers, and marshes, evaporates it into the air, condenses it into clouds, puts those clouds into the atmospheric circulatory system, transports them "from one region to another," then translates the clouds into "thick rain," and waters the fields of distant farms. But what about snow and hail? Speculates Leonardo:

> If the heat of the Sun is added to the power of the element of fire, the clouds are drawn up higher, and come to more intense cold, and there become frozen, and so produce hailstorms.[13]

This is remarkable guesswork. Derived from remarkable powers of observation. But it is just one way in which Leonardo is hunting for underlying patterns in the behavior of water.

Over a hundred years before Galileo would begin writing about "force,"[14] Leonardo notes that the size of a wave depends on the power of the "stroke"[15] that produces it. A wave, he says is a form of "recoil."[16] What's more, the contours of the seabed over which a wave travels make a wave far more complex than you might think. Far more social. "A wave is never found alone," writes Leonardo, "but is mingled with . . . other waves."[17] And the mingling of waves has a surprising pattern. "At one and the same time there will be moving over the greatest wave of a sea innumerable other waves proceeding in different directions."[18] The broad back of a wave will be rippled, dimpled, and cross-hatched by other waves riding upon it. What's more, even the depth, direction, and texture of the shore will determine the wave's cross-hatches, the wave's complexities. How does Leonardo know? He's done some experimenting. He says, "If you throw a stone into a sea with various shores, all the waves which strike against these shores are thrown back towards where the stone has struck."[19] Waves do something strange. They translate. They translate a "stroke" or a shoreline into a language of intersecting ripples. But that's me speaking, not Leonardo. Let's get back to the great Leonardo da Vinci.

What happens when the waves he's watching collide with each other? Do they destroy each other? Does the intersection of two different waves result in a chaos, in a muddle? Does it result in entropy? Not at all. The waves retain their identities. Writes Leonardo, they "can penetrate one another without being destroyed."[20] What's more, "they never interrupt each other's course." Again, Leonardo is writing one hundred years before Galileo will focus attention on terms like "experiment" and "force."[21] But Leonardo is already thinking in those terms. And he's thinking in terms of something else that will be crucial to science. He's thinking in terms of the old Greek concept of the angle. "Waves of equal volume, velocity, and power," he notes, "when they encounter each other in opposite motion, recoil at equal angles, the one from the stroke of the other." And Leonardo thinks in terms of another basic of science—measurability. Remember, the ruler and protractor have not yet been invented. Leonardo does not think in terms of inches, feet, or millimeters. He thinks in terms of Pythagoras's brand of mathematical measurement. He thinks in terms of ratio and proportion. And he thinks in terms of Aristotle's demand—define your terms. But in Leonardo's case, those terms will be measurable. Leonardo jots down the following note to himself: "Define first of all what is height and depth."[22] And he notes, "that wave will be of greater elevation, which is created by the greater stroke." Translation!

Again, he sees that waves bounce off of what they encounter. They hit a barrier and don't disintegrate. Instead, they reverse direction. And in doing so, they pull off an astonishment. They stay intact. To repeat, they hang on to their identity. "The wave produced in small tracts of water," writes Leonardo, the wave produced in narrow canals or small puddles and pools, "will go and return many times from the spot which has been struck." In other words, the wave won't break up. It will bounce. It will reflect. And the number of times the wave will bounce back and forth isn't arbitrary. Not at all. It follows a pattern. The pattern of a rule that Leonardo seems to have determined by strict observation. "The wave goes and returns so many more times in proportion as the sea which produces it contains a less quantity of water, and so conversely." The less water, the more times the wave bounces back and forth. The shallower the water the more the wave reflects off the shore. But if you add more water, the number of bounces shrinks. Give waves enough water, give them enough depth and enough room in which to move and they stop bouncing back and forth altogether. They go in straight lines. How does Leonardo know this? He watches waves in ponds, pools, and runnels. And he watches waves in the sea. Waves in the sea, he notices, do not bounce back and forth the way they do in pools, puddles, and canals. "Only on the high sea," Leonardo writes, "do the waves advance without ever turning in recoil."[23]

What's more, Leonard says, a wave carries an "impression." It carries information about something that has acted on it. It carries a kind of memory, a kind of translation, of what has thrust it into existence—whether that something is an oar, a stone, or the wind. And a wave of water is not alone in retaining this sort of memory. Says Leonardo, "Amongst the [other] cases of impressions being preserved in various bodies we may also instance the wave, the eddies of the water, the winds in the air." Then Leonardo hits on a metaphor, on a translation into another medium, on an example of an object that carries an impression and does something else crucial. It waggles back and forth. It oscillates. Says Leonardo, another body that preserves an impression is "a knife stuck into a table, which, on being bent in one direction and then released, retains for a long time a quivering movement, all its movements being reciprocal one of another, and all may be said to be approaching towards the perpendicular of the surface where the knife is fixed by its point."[24]

In listing three very different things that carry an impression—water, "the winds in the air," and the knife—Leonardo is hunting for objects with common properties. He is hunting for what Aristotle would call "species." Leonardo is hunting for things that are joined by underlying patterns. Patterns that remain the same whether he's talking about waves in water, the winds in the air, or the vibrations of a knife vigorously thrust into a table top. He is looking for translations of a basic pattern from one medium into another. And he finds them. Leonardo also finds yet another thing that seems to share the properties of waves, eddies, winds, and the quivering knife. Sound. The sound we make when we're uttering words. "The voice impresses itself through the air without displacement of air, and strikes upon the objects and returns back to its source." The voice reflects off of objects just like the wave of water in a pond reflects from the bounds of the shore. Both bounce. Both stay intact. And both carry the "impression" of the "stroke," the "concussion" that gave them birth. Even if it's the concussion of your larynx and your tongue. Sound = waves = the patterns of wind = the patterns of dust = the patterns of water = the quiver of a knife. Translation. And equation.

What's more, Leonardo puzzles over "why the thunder lasts for a longer time than that which causes it;—and why, immediately on its creation, the lightning becomes visible to the eye, while the thunder requires time to travel." And he comes to a startling conclusion. A conclusion that will help explain why metaphors work. He concludes that the thunder, too, is behaving "after the manner of a wave."[25]

But that's not all. Leonardo also finds a mystery, the essential mystery of recruitment patterns. A wave may travel enormous distances. But, in fact, nothing—no thing—travels more than a few feet. The water stays in place, simply shimmying under the influence of the wave and passing that shimmy to the water next to it, passing that shimmy to water down the line. Says Leonardo, "The water, though remaining in its position, can easily take this tremor from neighboring parts and pass it on to other adjacent parts."[26] To put it in different terms, Leonardo discovers that a form can travel without substance. A pattern can keep itself alive via a strange process. First it can recruit one sploosh of water, then another. All the while it can retain its process, its appearance, its uniqueness, its identity. Just as you retained your identity when you translated yourself into cyberspace. Or, to put it in God Problem terms, the wave is not a thing. It is a recruitment strategy. One that sustains itself with extraordinary stubbornness.

What's more, Leonardo invents an experiment, one that will become a recruitment strategy in itself. An experiment that will echo down through history. An experiment that will transmit its "impression" like a wave. Leonardo tosses two stones into a still pond at once. He writes:

> If you throw two small stones at the same time onto a sheet of motionless water at some distance from one another, you will see that around those two percussions two separate sets of circles are caused, which will meet as they increase in size and then interpenetrate and intersect one another, while always maintaining as their centers the places struck by the stones.[27]

Waves retain their identity even when they intersect. But how?

There's another clue to the God Problem in this experiment, one that

Leonardo, despite an eye trained by art and science simultaneously, failed to see. It's called interference. But that clue will have to wait another three hundred and fifty years. Meanwhile, back to Italy and Leonardo's big leap. A huge one. Remember, in a pond, many ripples carry the impression of the concussion or stroke that generated them. Right? And even though these waves, these ripples, run across each other, they don't break each other up. Each ripple retains its identity. On the back of a really big wave, many smaller waves can ripple. And each of those smaller waves retains its structure, its shape. So does the master wave on whose back the smaller waves ride.

Now take a look at the light that comes down to us from the sky. We are hit by the light of the sun, the moon, and the stars. All wash over us. And we can see them. Which means that the light from all of these sources converges on our eyes. Surely the more they overlap as they concentrate on the point where we are standing, the more they should blend into a chaos, a muddle, an utter blur. A mere mush of light. Right? But they don't. The light from the sun, the moon, and the stars retains its identity. Despite traveling enormous distances. Despite interpenetrating and intersecting at the lens of your eye or mine. On a cloudless, crisp evening, we're able to stand in a field or on a mountain like Tuscany's Mount Amiata and watch the sun sink and the moon appear. And we're able to see each star clearly. The light from these heavenly bodies doesn't turn into a single smear. It doesn't muddle in a big blur. Could that be because the light from these pricks of brightness in the sky acts like a ripple in water? Could it be because light behaves like a wave in a pond? Not to mention like the sound of a voice or like the knife vibrating in a wooden table top?[28] Could it be because the light from the moon and stars are, in Leonardo's words, "penetrating and intersecting each other," "blending" without losing their identity, merging without losing the "impression" they carry? How very much like ripples in a pond. How very much like waves.

But just to make it clear that this comparison between waves of water, sound, and light is not just a passing figure of speech, Leonardo points out in another passage that sound, light, and ripples in water, are, indeed similar.

> Just as the stone flung into the water becomes the center and cause of
> many circles, and as sound diffuses itself in circles in the air: so any object,

placed in the luminous atmosphere, diffuses itself in circles and fills the surrounding air with infinite images of itself.[29]

How does Leonardo account for this existence of a common pattern seemingly underlying the behavior of ripples, water, sound, the thrumming knife, and, of all things, light? He puts it down to a fundamental handful of rules underpinning all of nature, underlying all of "Necessity." What is that handful of rules? Leonardo says it's called "reason." It's the logic spoken of by Aristotle, Euclid, Peano, and Bertrand Russell. And, says Leonardo, reason controls the pattern of cause and effect. In fact, reason pulls this off with such simplicity that it thrills Leonardo. He nearly sings his awe:

> O marvellous Necessity, thou with supreme reason constrainest all effects
> to be the direct result of their causes, and by a supreme and irrevocable
> law every natural action obeys thee by the shortest possible process![30]

Leonardo uses the metaphor of the sort of thing that the Mesopotamian ruler Hammurabi carved in stone back in 1700 BCE—"law."[31] And a law is a command from an autocrat. A law is a rule. A law is a strict and repeated pattern.

What's more, this repetition of similar rules in such diverse things as water, a knife, sound, and light hints that simple rules run through the entire cosmos, from the biggest to the smallest of things. Back to Leonardo and his amazements:

> Who would believe that so small a space could contain the images of all
> the universe? O mighty process! What talent can avail to penetrate a nature
> such as thine? What tongue will it be that can unfold so great a wonder?
> Verily, none! This it is that guides the human discourse to the considering
> of divine things.[32]

Note that Leonardo does not address himself to an omnipotent creator who can crush worlds in his fist. He sings his praises to something very strange: a "mighty process."

But he's not finished. Leonardo says that even the smallest of things "contain images of all the universe." He implies that the patterns of the heavens repeat themselves on earth. And he implies that the patterns on earth repeat themselves in the wonders of the skies. Leonardo's wonder is over the repetition of simple patterns—a "mighty process"—in new contexts and his awe at the way insubstantial patterns retain their identity—including their impression of what started them.

What's more, Leonardo hits on something else crucial to the God Problem: translation. Translation from one medium to another. Translation from the vast distance of the heavens to the immediacy of the atmosphere. And translation from the atmosphere to "the eye." From the vast "crystalline lens" of the sky to the minuscule "lenses of the eye."[33] And more. Translation from "the instruments of the senses" through "the optic nerve" to "the place where all the senses meet, which is called the common sense."[34] Translation from the skies to the very soul itself. Yes, it was Leonardo who said "the eye is the window of the soul."[35] And he said it while discussing sight and light's underlying pattern, the pattern that light shares with sloshing water, the pattern that light shares with a wave. He said it while using the forbidden tool that Aristotle said had no place in science—metaphor. Yes, metaphor.

Two hundred years later, Isaac Newton disagreed with Leonardo about the nature of light. He, too, pondered the metaphor of the wave for a decade or two. He was tempted by it. He used it a few times. Then he came down with a definitive opinion. Light, he said, was not a wave. Light was not like the water in a pond or like a massive undulation in the sea. Light, he said, was made of "small bodies." In his *Opticks* he said, "Are not the rays of light very small bodies emitted from shining substances?" Not waves. "Very small bodies." The small bodies Newton knew best were bullets,[36] cannonballs,[37] and billiard balls.[38]

Why was light more like a barrage of tiny, solid bits of substance than like a ripple? Why was it more like bullets than like waves of the sea? What was Newton's reasoning? Waves go around obstacles in their path, said Newton. Light does not. Light casts shadows. What else is stopped in its path by obstacles the way light is? "Small bodies." Said Newton about small bodies—bodies like bullets, cannonballs, and billiard balls—"such bodies will pass through uniform mediums in right [straight] lines without bending into the shadow, which is the nature of the rays of light."[39] Try to hide behind a rock to avoid a tidal wave, and you are doomed. But try to hide behind a rock to avoid a barrage of bullets from an approaching army, and those bullets can't reach you. When it comes to bullets, the rock casts the equivalent of a shadow. So light is a particle, not a wave. Makes sense. Right?

In addition, streams of small bodies will be able to "to conserve their properties unchanged in passing through several mediums, which is another condition of the rays of light."[40] As Leonardo had seen, light stubbornly retains its identity. And Newton, too, noted that light retained its identity whether it was traveling through air, water, or glass. But as far as Newton was concerned, the case was closed. Light was not Leonardo's wave. Light was a small body. Light was what you and I call a particle.

And even that term, particle, hides a metaphor. What's a particle? Take a breadcrumb. Mash it with a spoon. Take the smallest bit of mashed bread-crumb you can find. Use a magnifying glass if you have to. Now mash that tiniest bit. Then find the smallest bit that comes from the mashing. And mash, mash, mash even it. A particle is a "little part." It's the smallest bit to which you can mash something. The word comes from the French *partir*—"to part, sunder, to divide, to sever"[41] and from the Latin *pars*—a part.

Is light a wave or a particle? With Leonardo and Newton, the battle of the metaphors for light began. No matter how unscientific Aristotle claims metaphorical thinking is. What's more, this battle of the metaphors would go on for three hundred years. The battle of the metaphor of the wave versus the metaphor of the "little body." The battle of the wave versus the metaphor of the cannonball, the billiard ball, and the bullet. The battle of the wave versus the particle. Why? Because metaphor is the key to human understanding. And metaphor is central to something that Aristotle invented: science.

But why?

PLAID IN THE POOL:
THE EYE DOCTOR WHO GAVE YOU WAVES

One hundred years after Newton, another Englishman would show even more powerfully that Aristotle was dead wrong about metaphor. He would show with even greater force how vital metaphor can be to science.

Thomas Young was perfectly positioned to see vision as translation. He was perfectly positioned to see how light goes from Leonardo's crystalline lens of the skies to the biological lens of the eye and to the common sense and soul on that eye's other side. Why? Thomas Young was an eye doctor. And like many medical men of his time, Young would make a mark on a field often considered far beyond the ken of mere practitioners of healing. He would have a profound impact on physics. And, strangely, Giuseppe Peano's fixation, translation, was how Thomas Young would win his first fame.

When Thomas Young was a mere child in the 1770s and 1780s in the Somerset County town of Milverton south of the River Avon, he was known as "The Phenomenon." Why? He learned a dozen languages, including French, Italian, and eight languages of the Middle East—Hebrew, Chaldean, Syriac, Samaritan, Arabic, Persian, Turkish, and Amharic. Egyptology had been a hot topic in Europe for three hundred years. And the field had a huge unsolved puzzle—what do Egyptian hieroglyphics mean? That was a problem posed by the German Jesuit scholar Athanasius Kircher in the 1650s. And puzzles make waves. Puzzles are recruitment patterns.

When Thomas Young was twenty-six years old, a closet intellectual triggered a major discovery. That closet intellect was Napoleon, who took a portable library[42] on the ship he was about to command, led a fleet of hundreds of vessels,[43] a fleet that Sir Walter Scott said was "at least six leagues in extent,"[44] and invaded Egypt with two armies—an army of soldiers and an army of scholars, an army of experts fascinated by Egypt's mysteries. As fascinated as Democritus and Pythagoras had been. "A few miles to the north of the little town of Rashid which Europeans generally call Rosetta"[45] and thirty miles east of Alexandria in August of 1799, one of Napoleon's soldiers—reportedly an officer of engineers named Bouchard—was using a pick to demolish the wall of a "system of defence works which the Khalifah al-Ashraf Kansu Al-GhurI constructed at Alexandria and Rashid between 1501 and 1516."[46] In the process of cracking the stones of the wall, the Frenchman discovered an ancient black slab of basalt that had been used as building material. It was a chunk of a monument, an ancient Egyptian stele that had been carved in 196 BCE, when Euclid's *Elements* was first taking off in the Egyptian city of Alexandria.

In 1799, when Thomas Young was twenty-six years old, Egyptian hieroglyphics were considered an incomprehensible mystery. There were only the faintest clues to what they meant. Even the scholars with the highest brows and the biggest brains were baffled. But the new stele—the Rosetta Stone—promised to provide a perceptual key. It promised to be a tool of translation. If only someone with massive brainpower could crack its codes. Someone kidnapped, seduced, and recruited by the social magnetism of a highly publicized puzzle.

The Rosetta Stone had three texts in three different writing systems, three different symbol sets—Egyptian hieroglyphs plus yet another unknown Egyptian symbol system, the shorthand script known as demotic (the alphabet of the demes, the writing system of the common people). Below the hieroglyphic and demotic texts was a text in a very well-known language, Greek. A text celebrating the accession of Ptolemy V,[47] who had come to the throne at the tender age of five. The Rosetta Stone declared that Ptolemy V is the ever living god, the beloved of Ptah, and the lord who makes benefactions materialize out of nowhere.[48] It seemed possible—just possible—that the three texts in three different alphabets might be translations of the same words. If so, the Rosetta Stone might be the key to cracking the hieroglyphic code. Not to mention cracking the code of demotic script. But was the Rosetta Stone really what it seemed—the same text in three different symbol sets, three isomorphic symbol sets? No one could tell. No one knew how to decipher the two Egyptian writing systems. At the age of forty-five, Thomas Young threw himself into the problem . . . one of those problems we are told that only geniuses can solve. A problem men and women tackle in order to gain fame, a slot in attention space. A problem of the kind that acts as a recruitment strategy. And after fifteen years of work, Young cracked the code of the Egyptian demotic script, the writing system of Egypt's commoners.

Thomas Young's fame for translating languages became so great that he was asked to write the article on languages in the ultimate reference book, a book series that was by then verging on fifty years old, the *Encyclopedia Britannica*. Young did write that definitive article. And in the process he compared the grammar and vocabulary of four hundred languages. So Young was very aware of the power of translation. Very aware of the power of isomorphic symbol sets.

But Young's biggest contribution to science, legend has it, came from his pleasure walking by the pond at Cambridge University's Emmanuel College, where he was a lecturer. In that pond, it is said, Young saw two ducks swimming side by side. Swimming ducks, like ships in the sea or like speedboats in a lake, churn up a wake, a triangle of ripples that spreads behind them in a V. In the wakes left behind by those ducks, Young saw something that Leonardo had failed to see. Leonardo had only noted one major surprise when the ripples from two stones intersect: that the ripples of the two stones stay intact as they mingle and interpenetrate. The ripples of the two stones, noted Leonardo, maintain their shape, their coherence. They stubbornly maintain their identity. And they maintain their nature as concentric rings, target-like rings, each ring emanating from the spot of the concussion, spreading in circles from the center of the blow, from the site of the force that gave the expanding ripples birth. *A*, saw Leonardo, continues to equal *A*.

Young saw all of this and something more. The waves spreading in a triangle behind the ducks kept their centerline where the force of the duck's breast had plowed through the water. And as the wakes spread, each triangle of waves, each wake, maintained its identity. But only up to a point.

Something else was going on. Where the waves crossed each other, they created something new. They generated something complex and remark-able. What was it? A crazy plaid. A pseudo-Scottish tartan. A geometric gingham, a curved argyle, a moiré pattern. In some spots, the two waves combined to produce a higher wave than the normal ripple. Which made sense. Add one wave to another wave and you should get a bigger wave. One plus one equals two. But in other spots, the impossible occurred. Two waves crossed and left a blank, a nothing, a flat, curved rectangle of water, a curved rectangle in which the surface was unperturbed and level, as if the swatch were not in the middle of a grid of interpenetrating roil, as if it were a tiny, geometric patch of calm. This did not make sense. How could two intersecting lines of turbulence create a calm? How could two crossing and clashing lines of motion make a nothing, an emptiness?[49] And even more, how could two intersecting waves of water make a plaid?

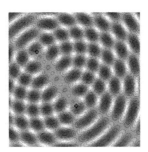

Interference patterns. © 2011 Stephen Wolfram, LLC, http://www.wolframscience.com.

Interference patterns can get creative. *Courtesy of Florian Marquardt, Wikimedia Commons.*

To get at the question with precision, Young invented a device with which to replicate the duck-pond plaid and to examine it with care. He called it a "ripple tank." The ripple tank consisted of a shallow, rectangular basin of water, a basin with a glass bottom. Like a glass-bottomed laundry sink. Young installed a rod on the water's edge. And he mounted a horizontal arm on the rod, an arm that stretched out over the water like the horizontal arm of a construction crane. Hanging from that arm like the cable of a construction crane were two identical wires a foot or two apart with identical weights at their ends. Two weights that could be lowered simultaneously onto the surface of the water—lowered at a precise and measurable location. And at a precise speed. Two weights like the two stones of Leonardo that could be used to literally make waves.[50]

Below the transparent bottom of the basin was a candle—the going form of illumination at the time. And that candle projected the patterns on the water's surface to a screen above. A screen tilted at an angle so that Young could watch it. Or so that Young could take his apparatus to a lecture hall, set up his ripple tank onstage, and show the ripples to his audience. Moving, spreading, genuine real-time ripples.

Using the ripple tank, Young showed precisely what happens when you repeat Da Vinci's experiment and throw two stones into a pond. Yes, as Leonardo noted, the ripples do retain their identity. In the face of considerable opposition. They hold on to their shape despite slamming into each other, a crash that should lead to disintegration. A crash that should lead to entropy. And, yes, they do retain the "impression," to use Leonardo's word, of the force that gave them birth. But the two rings of ripples colliding do something else. Something mathematical. Something that the Babylonians would have called "heaping." The waves perform addition and subtraction. Where two waves meet each other, they add to each other. They do a one plus one equals two. They produce a higher peak than the other peaks in their vicinity. And where a trough meets a peak, they cancel each other out. They do a one plus a "minus one" equals zero. The result? The geometric pattern Young had seen in the duck pond. A moiré. A plaid.

Young was not only a translator, he was a language maker. For example, some claim that Young introduced the term "energy" to physics.[51] But in this case, Young introduced a term he gets full credit for. He called his highly patterned ripple grid and the phenomenon of multiplication and addition that generated it "interference."[52]

Then came the really big stretch. The stretch beyond sanity. The stretch that translates from one medium to another. The stretch that Leonardo made. The stretch to metaphor. The stretch from water to light.

What in the world does an experiment done in a ripple tank in a room on the Oxford University campus have to do with light? What does an experiment in the splash, slosh, and sop of water have to do with the pricks of brightness that come from stars in the nighttime sky? Not to mention with the flood of illumination that comes from the daytime sun? What does a basin of water have to do with the brightness that literally lights up our life? Good question. In 1801,[53] Young answered it by inventing yet another experiment, an experiment that would join the axiom as a basic recruitment strategy. An experiment that would ripple its way into modern quantum physics. Young's "demonstration" (to use Aristotle's,[54] Euclid's,[55] and Galileo's[56] word) is called "the two-slit experiment." How does it work?

Cut two slits in a piece of paper. Two narrow straight up and down openings. Two openings parallel to each other. Take one more piece of paper. Cut just one slit in it. Now light a candle. Put the paper with only one slit in front of the candle. You are using that piece of paper to concentrate candle light in a narrow beam.

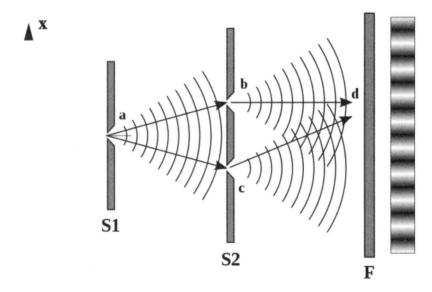

The two-slit experiment. To do the two-slit experiment in the pleasure of your own living room, take two sheets of paper. Put one slit in the first sheet, two slits in the second piece of paper, and use a wall as your screen. Shine a candle (ok, cheat—use a flashlight) through the one-slit screen so you reduce its light to a compact source. Let your compacted light shine through the paper with two slits, and watch the outcome on your wall. You'll see a striped pattern like the one on the far right. Two lights will make a dark. *Courtesy of Francesco Franco, Wikimedia Commons.*

This is not easy to explain in words, so please hang in with me. You now have two sheets of paper. One that's got just one slit. Your light concentrator. And one that has two slits in it. Your light separator. Now set the candle and sheets up so that light from the candle goes through the one-slit sheet and is concentrated, and so the light next goes through the two-slit sheet. Yes, I know it's confusing. But let the light from the two slits shine on the wall. Turn off the lights. What will you get? Logically, you should get a relatively normal wash of light on the wall. You often have two light sources, two candles, two lightbulbs overhead, or two lamps. And a normal wash of light is the result. But a wash of light is not what you see on the wall. Not at all. You see stripes. In fact, you see a lineup of stripes. Why?

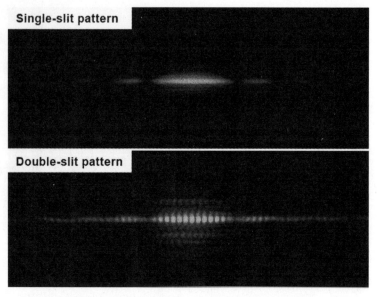

The two-slit experiment. On top is the pattern you get when you shine light through just one slit. Below is the lineup of stripes you get when you shine light through two slits. *Courtesy of Jordgette, Wikimedia Commons.*

Young said that the sideways ladder of stripes was due to the same thing that made the water's moiré—the water's hatched and grid-worked plaid. In other words, Young declared that the stripes of light were made by the same thing that rippled a liquid into a plaid. Said Young, the stripes of light on your wall are due to interference. Where two peaks of light meet, they add to each other. They make lines of brightness. Where two *troughs* meet, they deepen[57] each other. They make lines of darkness. Hence light is not a particle. It is a wave. A wave like the waves in water. Like the waves in Leonardo's pond. Like the waves in the ducks' wake. And like the waves in Young's ripple tank.

Now let's step back and apply the second law of science for a minute. Let's look at things right under our noses—yours and mine—as if we've never seen them before. Two swatches of light overlap and make . . . darkness? This is an absurd notion. It makes absolutely no sense. How can light added to light make light's opposite, a swatch of black? How can one *plus* one equal zero? That's like saying two patches of day make night. But this is not the only bit of absurdity at work in Young's claim. It's not the only piece of outrageousness in Leonardo's—and Young's—idea that light is like water. And it's not the only bit of nonsense in Newton's crazy idea that light—the insubstantial stuff that you can run your hand through, the immaterial flood you walk through every day—Newton's crazy idea that light is a rain of miniature bullets, billiard balls, or cannonballs. These ideas are based on a stark-ravingly ridiculous platform, a lunatic assumption. They are based on the idea that a pattern translates from one medium to another. And they are based on the assumption that despite this violent displacement into soups, goops, vacuums, and solids that seem to bear no relationship to each other, the pattern will stubbornly maintain its identity. That assumption is the bottom line of metaphor. And as Aristotle said, metaphor is unscientific. Right?

Why is metaphor so outrageous? So utterly unbelievable? Let me repeat. In a rational world, light and water are violently different things. There is no reason whatsoever that water and light should be the same. And in truth, every laboratory demonstration, every chemical reaction in a test tube, every act of genetic analysis in a sequencing machine, every experiment on pigeons, rats, or pygmy chimps, every test of drugs on dogs or rabbits, and every social science study based on sampling makes no sense. Every one of these assumes that you can capture a pattern in one small patch of territory, in one manifestation of nature, and blow it up big. What's worse, every one of these assumes that you can grab hold of a pattern in one kind of thing and generalize it to radically different things. Every one of these assumes that you can take a basic pattern and translate it the way Young translated the Rosetta Stone. That you can translate it to something that is grotesquely different. And every one of these carries another hidden assumption. That the real translator, the real duplicator of a basic pattern in radically different mediums, is not you. The hidden assumption is that the real translator is nature.

Yes, Virginia, every act of science makes a vast and peculiar unspoken assumption, a giant leap of faith. It contains a deeply buried axiom. It assumes that scratch marks on clay, wax, or paper can capture the habits of planets and stars. That's absurd! Science assumes that a phenomenon in rabbits, guinea pigs, and pigeons can translate to humans. Another absurdity. Science assumes that a long chain of equations scratched on paper by a Transylvanian artillery[58] officer obsessed with a twenty-two-hundred-year-old Greek notion—the parallel axiom—can reveal a shape hidden behind the mask of the skies. It also assumes that with similar scratch marks that young man—János Bolyai—can summon the properties of a moving four-pound lump of iron and prescribe exactly how to position an artillery piece so it will turn a nest of Russians, Austrians, or Turks[59] into hamburger. Ridiculous.

Science assumes that the cell-and-protein mush of a brain thinking about lines and triangles can feel out the shape of the universe. Yes, science assumes that a scrawl of equations, words, and neurons can imitate, express, grab hold of, and translate a hidden shape of the cosmos. Science also assumes that a minuscule collision in the fifteen-mile circular track of a particle accelerator buried beneath three hundred feet of soil in Switzerland can imitate a smashup in the heart of a star. Or in an interstellar cloud. That is bizarre. A huge, huge stretch. But it pans out. Not all metaphors are valid—remember poor Johannes Kepler's ball-and-box solar system mistake. The Kepler cockup. But some metaphors are on target. And when they are, they pay off big time. Metaphorical thinking works. But why?

The answer is in Reed Konsler's isomorphic symbol sets. The answer is in iteration. The answer is in translation. The answer is in Giuseppe Peano and Bertrand Russell's "primitives." The answer is in Ur patterns.

HOW FORM GOES MANIC—WHAT'S AN UR PATTERN?

"Beauty is truth, truth beauty,"—that is all
Ye know on Earth, and all ye need to know.

—John Keats

What's an Ur pattern? Ur patterns are implicit in the hidden assumptions of science and of everyday life. Ur patterns are what we stab to reach when we do lab experiments. They are what we stab to reach with religion. And they are what we summon to the surface when we do art. They are underlying patterns that we are sure hide behind the realities that assail us. The underlying patterns behind the weather. The underlying patterns behind the seasons. The underlying patterns behind the movements of the sun, the moon, and the stars. The underlying patterns behind the qualities of stones and stallions. The underlying patterns that hide behind floods, tides, invasion, coups, politics, palace intrigue, and tomorrow's grain prices. And the underlying patterns that swirl in Eshel ben Jacob's polished rocks and his bacterial colonies.

Not all patterns are Ur patterns. Not all of them show up in level after level of reality. But sometimes men like the Babylonian mathematicians, the Greek philosophers, the Alexandrian geometers, and Thomas Young are right. Sometimes those patterns are, in fact, for real.

Why call them Ur patterns? Ur in German means the first, the primeval, the essential pattern on which all copies are built. When philologists, language experts, dig down to find a protolanguage, a language from which an entire family of modern languages is derived, they call that primitive font of words and syntaxes an Ur language.[60] When biblical scholars are convinced that the current Bible has its roots in earlier, more primitive works, they call those hidden works Urtexts.[61] When Vladimir Nabokov, the author of *Lolita*, wants to put down groups he thinks are monstrous in 1943, he talks about "the dreadful vulgarity, the Ur-Hitlerism of those ludicrous but vicious organisations."[62] When famed English poet W. H. Auden in 1947 wants to get across the notion that we were born of boredom, and when he wants to conjure up the very first father from whose pattern all other fathers have sprung, he tells us how the "Ur-Papa gave The Primal Yawn that expressed all things."[63] And when Béla Bartók, the form-shattering twentieth-century classical composer, wants to drive home the notion that music is based on primitive patterns, patterns that go way, way back in time, he talks of "the ur-sources of music."[64]

Ur patterns are the most basic patterns we can find. Patterns that appear over and over again in vastly different mediums, in vastly different frames of reference, in vastly different raw materials, and at vastly different levels in the evolution of the cosmos.

There is a good chance that Ur patterns were among the earliest patterns to spin off from the starting rules of the universe. There is a good chance that Ur patterns appeared in the first burst of cosmic creativity—the big bang. And there is a good chance that Ur patterns have been repeating ever since. Repeating in forms that are ever more gaudy and ornate. Reappearing in surprising disguise. When a metaphor works, it's because it taps that basic pattern in a new medium. The way that the interference patterns of water also appear in light. Two different mediums—liquid and brightness. But the same pattern. The same Ur pattern.

And the metaphor of light as a wave appears to work because that wave-like pattern is ambitious, imperious, and insistent. It crops up over and over again, demandingly translating itself into new mediums. We can study it in water, then spot its pattern in very unwaterlike things. In the seismic waves of earthquakes. In sound waves. In shockwaves. In radio waves. In cold waves. In gravitational waves. In the peristaltic waves that carry the bite you just took from an ice cream sandwich down your esophagus and through your gut. In the beta and gamma waves that the guilt or pleasure of that bite arouses in your brain. And in the waves of protein clumping called actin nucleation, waves of round molecules pulling together in strings like the beads of a pearl necklace, then popping apart again as if their thread has broken.[65] What do those waves of actin molecules power? The digestive cells in your gut that absorb the fuel, fat, and nutrients from your ice cream nibble—the tiny hairs, the microvilli, that line your intestinal walls.[66]

If these underlying patterns—Ur patterns—are for real, they may account for Ted Coons's conundrum: they may account for the isomorphism—the parallelism, the synonymousness, the equality, the translatability, the commonality—between music, math, emotion, and metaphor. If they exist, these basic patterns, these Ur patterns, may be deep structures. Some may be more fundamental than others. Some may be delusions. Some may be the products of our eagerness for pattern. Some—like Kepler's geometric balls and boxes—may lead us astray. But some may be the simple rules from which other primal patterns unfold. Some may be the starting rules of everything we know. Some may be the starting axioms of the universe.

What evidence do we have that some of these patterns are real? What evidence do we have that some of these patterns are so basic that they show up on level after level of cosmic evolution? The evidence is the fact that metaphor works. Thomas Young found a single pattern at work in both water and in light, two vastly separated things. And this is flabbergastingly unlikely. Water is a webwork of relationships built on the back of other networks of relationships. Water is a collection of molecules—molecules that contain a trio of atoms, one hydrogen and two oxygen atoms. When gathered in massive groups at just the right temperature range, these molecules make a liquid. And thanks to the webwork of relationships we call liquid, water is a collection of matter that behaves in very peculiar ways. It sloshes, it puddles, it dissolves sugar and salt, it wets leaves, it soaks your clothes. Water is substantial. Yet water is not hard as a rock. You can dip your finger into it, lift your finger, and watch a drop form on your fingertip. Water is an amazement. Water is a mystery.

Light is an amazement, too. Yet it is water's opposite. It has no substance that you can feel at all. You can do cartwheels in the sunshine and the soup of photons will not stop you. What's more, light and water evolved at vastly different times in the cosmos. Photons—the wave/particles of light— appeared in the first instant of the big bang. Water came billions of years later. If you'd been at our café table at the beginning of the universe, it would have taken no wait whatsoever to get your first look at photons. But you'd have been forced to sit around pestering the waiter for more sugar cubes for over a billion years before you caught a glimpse of the first molecule of H_2O. And you'd have been forced to play with your napkin for at least another very slow several billion years before you saw the first puddle of water. You and I would have watched galaxies gather, gravity balls compress, stars catch fire, and the biggest stars burn out. Burning out in as little as a million years.[67] In the deaths of stars, we would have seen new atoms form. You would have predicted this birth of new atomic nuclei from disaster. And I would have told you it was impossible. Logically impossible. But among the atoms birthed from death, birthed in the death of stars, was oxygen. When oxygen and hydrogen first got together as a liquid, we do not know. But it had to be at least two billion years ABB (after the big bang). So light is primeval. But water is two billion years more advanced. Two billion years more complex. If light is as old as the first jellyfish in a very ancient sea, water is as young as your daughter's Montessori teacher. In a universe of six monkeys at six typewriters, in a universe of randomness, the notion that light and water could share anything in common would be preposterous. Grotesque beyond belief.

In other words, water and light are two very different mediums. Vastly and absurdly different. Logically, there should be no relationship between them. But there is. Thomas Young proved it. Thomas Young proved that a primal pattern, an Ur pattern, repeats in two bizarrely separate mediums. And that, ladies and gentlemen, is the essence of metaphor. Finding a pattern in one medium and applying it to another. Finding a pattern in one context and shifting it to another. Making an absurdly gargantuan leap.

But metaphor works. It works because it captures nature. It works because it captures nature's creativity. It works because of deep structures. Hell, it works because there *are* deep structures. It works because of Ur patterns. Is metaphor "unscientific"? Far from it. It is the very core of science.

*****

But Thomas Young was not alone in believing that the same patterns can recur in vastly different mediums. The priest-scribes of Mesopotamia felt that the patterns they grasped with their cuneiform tablets and with their step-by-step math determined the movements of the pinpricks in the sky. Not to mention the weather and the political machinations in the palaces of kings. They were convinced that this world is run by Ur patterns. Plato proposed that everything is based on hidden patterns, the patterns of archetypes. He was certain that all we see is based on Ur patterns. Euclid was sure that the patterns of circles and triangles he outlined in the abstract world of geometry could be applied to the movements of the skies.[68] He, too, was mapping out Ur patterns. Johannes Kepler was absolutely certain that simple patterns unlock the secrets of the cosmos. Those hidden patterns were based on Euclid's geometry and on Platonic solids. Kepler, too, was on a hunt for Ur patterns. Galileo was certain that the "demonstrations" he did on a tabletop, demonstrations of balls rolling down a plane, mirrored the patterns of much bigger balls, the balls he had seen in the heavens with his telescope—the planets and their moons.[69] Galileo was on the prowl for Ur patterns. Isaac Newton, too, generalized the movements of cannonballs, bullets, and billiard balls to the planets and the stars. Today we see what Newton did in a metaphor, the vision of a falling apple. An apple whose fall follows principles that we can generalize to moons and to meteors. Isaac Newton was hunting for Ur patterns. And the non-Euclidean geometers of the nineteenth century, Gauss, Bólyai, and Lobachevsky, were sure that the abstract curved worlds they explored with their math were alive in the cosmos. In fact, Lobachevsky had a telescope with which he searched the skies obsessively to see if his saddleback shape and his parallel-lines-that-meet could be found in the stars. Gauss, Bólyai, and Lobachevsky dedicated their lives to hunting down Ur patterns.

Many of these pattern hunters called Ur patterns "natural laws." Why not simply continue with that simple phrase? Why Ur patterns? The idea of natural law is based on a metaphor that you and I have discussed before. It's the metaphor of a kinglike God commanding a cosmos into being. It's the metaphor of an edict from a dictatorial deity, a divine architect. But we are not hunting down the mind of a creator God. We are hunting down the secret of a cosmos that creates itself. We are not hunting for the creative secrets of a top-down universe. We are hunting for the creative secrets of a universe that built itself up from the bottom. From the start. From the big bang.

Law was not the only metaphor that men like Kepler, Galileo, and Newton relied on to describe the underlying patterns of the cosmos. Their second metaphor was "reason." Their God followed the laws of reason in cobbling together the cosmos. In fact, reason was so powerful that even God was its slave. And reason is a set of simple rules. If the lesson of the termites applies to the cosmos, if this is a cosmos built by repeating simple rules, then the constant iteration of simple rules in new mediums may explain why the same patterns appear over and over again on wildly different levels of cosmic evolution. In wildly different mediums, in wildly different contexts, in wildly different soups, goops, loops, marriages, and weaves. And simple rules, Ur patterns, may explain metaphor.

But how do new goops, loops, marriages, and weaves come to be? Are they innovations that simple rules have woven, carved, molded, and shaped? Is the repetition of simple rules in new mediums really enough to explain how a cosmos pulls itself together in new patterns of relationship, new patterns of organization, new patterns of sociality?

Clues to that riddle would come from a very strange knot of friends in the nineteenth century.

***

But before we dive into this cluster of occasionally scandalous companions, let's dig deeper into the question of where have you and I gone so far and why. We are on a hunt for the reason that *A* does not equal *A*. We are on the prowl for the reason that one plus one does not equal two. And we are seeking the reason that the notion of entropy is wrong. In other words, we are following the spoor of cosmic creativity. We are hunting down the process with which a universe devoid of gods in bathrobes and beards pulls off acts of astonishment, material miracles, acts of secular genesis.

To strip the cosmos's creativity bare, we are probing for the right metaphor. There are two major candidates. The first is the image of a student at Reed College doing her homework. A student extracting an entire mathematical system, an entire eight-years-worth of elementary school textbook stuff, from the 165 words of Peano's axioms. Is the cosmos really like a diligent math pupil unfolding corollaries from a handful of axioms? Does the universe really yank an implicit order from its hiding place and pull it into the light of everyday reality?

Then there's metaphoric candidate number two. The cosmos behaves like a termite accidentally building an edifice. A termite following a simple rule: clean up the mess. A termite unintentionally collaborating with two million others to build an architectural masterpiece. Without an architect.

Both the metaphor of the student and the metaphor of the termite get at the very same thing. The question of whether the material world innovates by extracting the implications from a set of simple starting rules. From a handful of axioms. Which leads to a question: Are ornate complexities really hidden in simple rules waiting to be discovered? And if so, how in the world did they get there? Hints come from metaphor, Ur patterns, recruitment strategies, and translation.

***

Over nine thousand years ago, the citizens of Catalhöyük showed that you could invent a simple module made from mud, the rectangular brick, and extract crazy implications—like an apartment complex housing sixty thousand. From the brick you could unfold something else almost unknown at the time—a city. How very termitelike. And what are brickmaking and bricklaying? Simple rules.

Four thousand years later, the Babylonians showed that if you translate an old rule into a new medium you get something radically new. The Babylonians translated their tallies of barleycorns and bricks into scratches on clay and got mathematics, astronomy, and astrology. What's more, they got a zigzag pattern that seemed to crop up in the back-and-forths of the sun, the moon, and the stars. Not to mention the ups and downs of politics, war, farming, the weather, and the market prices of barley, dates, pepper, cress, sesame, and wool. Had the Babylonians gotten to an Ur pattern? The sort of pattern that makes metaphor work?

Back to the basic question: Are complexities like city walls and ziggurats really "hidden" in simple rules? Or do we invent them? Did bricks recruit the Babylonians? Or did Babylonians invent the brick? The experience of the Egyptians, eight hundred miles to the Babylonians' south, hinted that both answers—invention and extraction—are true. On the one hand, the Egyptians showed how to extract a right angle from a twelve-knot rope. The angle of a perfect corner—the right angle—simply popped out. The implicate form of the right angle was there from the beginning in the relationship between a three, a four, and a five. How do we know that the right angle was hidden in those numbers? The Babylonians discovered it too. But they didn't use a knotted rope. They used another medium: a number chart. When two peoples use different means but arrive at the same thing, it is very likely that what they discover is not a fantasy but a fact. Score one for complexities hidden in simple rules.

But the Egyptians also demonstrated that you could use your knotted rope and your modular blocks of stone to invent. You could create the pyramid. Which left a paradox. When you build a pyramid, to what extent are you inventing and to what extent are you discovering the simple rules that make triangular forms stable? To what extent are you inventing the pyramid and to what extent is a pyramid using you to invent itself? Consider this clue: the Olmecs of Mexico knew nothing about the Egyptians. But they built their first pyramids in roughly 1500 BCE.[70] Despite a separation of 7,700 miles from the Egyptians. And like the masterminds of Catalhöyük, the Mesoamerican Zapotecs invented the city. Without knowing a thing about Catalhöyük. So to what extent did the city use the Zapotecs and the geniuses of Catalhöyük to invent itself? To what extent were the pyramid and the city recruitment strategies? Forms and functions with a life of their own? Here's a hint: insects invented cities, too.

The Greeks provided another clue when Thales, Pythagoras, and Plato looked beyond the bricks and blocks of stone to the patterns that seemed to underlie them. Thales, Pythagoras, Plato, and Euclid showed that you could capture those patterns with yet another form of bizarre translation: translation into the marks on wax tablets that they called "geometry."

In fact, Plato claimed that the abstract forms, the underlying patterns, the patterns of the sort that geometry revealed, were more real than your touchable, squeezable, everyday things. He made a case for what Noam Chomsky would one day call "deep structures," deep structures of the cosmos. A few years later, Aristotle derived yet another form of deep structure. Another distillation of simple rules. He boiled everything down to "logic" and "reason," reason based on something he called "axioms."

In fact, Aristotle went even further. He turned the human pattern hunt into a new kind of recruitment strategy: science. Then Euclid transformed Aristotle's program of definition, axiom, proposition, and proof into an even more powerful recruitment strategy. A recruitment strategy that seduced, kidnapped, and recruited participants the way that waves recruit molecules and the way that stray bits of fecal matter recruit termites. A recruitment strategy that worked its magic for a full twenty-three hundred years.

But were deep structures, simple rules, and axioms the real bricks, mortar, and building stones of the cosmos? Or were they mere human imaginings? The clue that these patterns were in the cosmos came from the power of something that Aristotle had called antiscientific: metaphor. The power of metaphor became obvious eighteen hundred years after Euclid's *Elements*, when Leonardo, Galileo, Kepler, and Newton were seized by Aristotle and Euclid's recruitment strategy and translated its rules into the medium of a new place and time. They turned the simple rules of Euclid and Aristotle into modern science. Yes, modern science followed Aristotle's commands and claimed to despise metaphor. But in reality, it used metaphor over and over again. The metaphor of geometry. The metaphor of the particle. And the metaphor of the wave. But there was more. Modern science in its early centuries also used Aristotle and Euclid's technique—definition, axiom, proposition, and proof. And the early modern scientists, the "natural philosophers"—Leonardo,[71] Galileo, Kepler, and Newton—swore that Nature herself had used the same method. God and His obedient servant, Nature, they were convinced, had been geometers. And God and Nature had used reason to create. Yes, "reason," a word based on Pythagoras's number ratios.

And guess what? The supposition that the cosmos was based on metaphor and the simple rules of reason worked. It helped generate systems that successfully predicted the movements of the planets and the heavens. Chalk up another victory for the notion that simple rules underlie the cosmos. Score another point for the notion that deep structures, Ur patterns, are for real.

But what about the complexities that we pull from simple rules, from axioms? Do we invent them? Or do we discover them? Are they lurking invisibly, waiting to be found? Or do we concoct them? Another clue came in the great age of the axiom, the nineteenth century. János Bolyai and Nikolai Lobachevsky flipped just one of Euclid's axioms and left the rest intact. They flipped the parallel axiom. And what did they find? If you change just one axiom, you get new implicit properties. In fact, you get a different universe. A universe that you did not invent. A universe that took you by surprise. A universe that you found.

So the complex really *was* hidden in the simple. A whole new geometric universe really was hidden in axioms. Then Giuseppe Peano showed the opposite: that the simple was hidden in the complex. Peano demonstrated that you could boil the entire natural number system down to five axioms. In other words, Peano showed that if you dig hard enough, you can find what Plato and Aristotle called "ideas." What Bertrand Russell called "primitives." Dig down to the bedrock and you could uncover what Noam Chomsky would one day call "deep structures."

Meanwhile, a close look at the work of Leonardo da Vinci and Thomas Young would reveal clues that if, indeed, you capture a simple rule at one level, you can sometimes find it repeating in everything from ripples in a pond and waves in the sea to light, sound, and the vibration of a knife stuck in a wooden tabletop. You can sometimes find isomorphic patterns, simple undulations and structures, that look eerily like the translations of a basic pattern into one new medium after another. And, in fact, a close look at Leonardo's and Thomas Young's work would reveal that they rediscovered a pattern so primary that even the Babylonians had tripped across it—the zigzag pattern. But Leonardo and Thomas Young translated that pattern into the idea soup of a new era. They saw the zigzag as a bit more rounded and smoothed. They saw it as an oscillation. They saw it through the lens of a new metaphor: the wave.

What's more, Leonardo and Thomas Young would participate in one of science's longest-lasting metaphor wars: the four-hundred-year-long battle over whether light is a wave or a particle. A battle over two potential deep structures. Meanwhile, you, stewing on all of this, would suggest three reasons that metaphor works. One is the hunger of the stuttering forms. The seeming itch of patterns like the wave to be. To manifest themselves in reality. And the ability of these patterns to operate with a surprising independence from the matter that they grab and bunch. A second is Reed Konsler's "isomorphic symbol sets." And the third is the concept of the Ur pattern. A pattern that repeats itself on level after level of the material world. A pattern that seems to translate itself into everything from the wavelets in a duck pond to the sound of music, and from the light of a candle to the sight of a star in the nighttime sky. But in a sense, Ur patterns, hungry forms, recruitment strategies, and isomorphic symbol sets all boil down to the same thing—simple rules. Simple rules with an itch to manifest themselves in new ways.

This leaves a problem. Wave-and-particle metaphors—primary metaphors of science from the sixteenth to the twentieth centuries—miss something big. Something central to cosmic creativity and to the God Problem. They only scratch the surface of why one plus one sometimes does not equal two. They only hint at why one plus one occasionally equals something so far from two that it jumps off the number line and opens radically new territory. What's more, the metaphors of the wave and the particle barely touch the sort of phenomenon that poses the biggest challenge to the future of science, the embryo.

More clues to the riddle of why one plus one does not equal two and the mystery of the ultimate metaphor—the embryo—would come from one of the most intriguing groups of friends of all time. From a very strange knot of diners, walkers, and brainstormers in the nineteenth century.

REAL ESTATE IN THE EMBRYO: LOCATION, LOCATION, LOCATION— KARL ERNST VON BAER AND HANS ADOLF EDUARD DRIESCH

> *The origin of life, the evolution of increasing biological complexity, and the development of the embryo from a single egg cell, all seem miraculous at first sight, and all remain largely unexplained.*
>
> —physicist Paul Davies[72]

Many others will win a prize. But the palm will be won by the fortunate man for whom it is reserved to trace the formative forces of the animal body back to the general forces that direct the life of the universe.

—**Karl Ernst von Baer**[73]

One of the most important patterns of the cosmos—one of the most important candidates for Ur pattern status—is differentiation. And the tale of differentiation takes us to an ironic destination. Why? Because the metaphor that put differentiation on the map is one missing from most of today's science. It is a metaphor that may have to be reinserted if science is to make sense. It is a metaphor that may have to be faced if science is to take on its ultimate challenge—the challenge of seeing what's right under your nose and mine and explaining it. It is the metaphor of the embryo. That metaphor was at its peak in the nineteenth and early twentieth centuries when two men, Karl Ernst von Baer and Hans Adolf Eduard Driesch, were doing seminal work on embryonic development.

Karl Ernst von Baer was a descendent of a German knight who had participated in a disturbing German conquest. Von Baer's ancestor had joined an army that heeded the call of Pope Celestine III in 1193 to crusade against the "heathen" Slavs on the fringes of the Baltic Sea. These aristocratic Teutonic[74] warriors had spent thirty-four years bloodying the Slavs. Allegedly to convert these primitives to the one true religion, Christianity. The reward? The "glorious" German knights seized the Slavic territories, built German cities in those Slavic lands, German ports, and turned the Baltic Sea into the transportation core of a trading empire, an empire that trafficked in timber, furs, wheat, oats, and ash.[75] Karl Ernst von Baer came from the Slavic end of these Baltic sea paths, the end to the north where raw materials like timber and furs came from. Von Baer was born a knight in the Estonian town of Piibe in 1792, four years after the American Constitution was ratified in the United States. And like Thomas Young, he became a *Wunder Mensch*. A man seemingly capable of everything. He was an adventurer who went to the wilds of Lapland to spot new forms of foliage, new botanical species.[76] He was also a geographer, a geologist, a meteorologist, and a biologist.

A biologist who specialized in watching the development of embryos under a microscope.[77] Among other things, the grumpy-looking, square-faced, but impeccably dressed von Baer was the first to use his scalpel and his microscope to discover that mammals like dogs and women *have* embryos. Von Baer started his career as a college professor at the University of Konigsberg in 1821. Over in England, Thomas Young was demonstrating his ripple tank. And von Baer's work would establish the principle that put another kind of ripple on the map: differentiation.[78]

Von Baer watched through his microscope as an embryo unfolded what von Baer calls one "type of organization"[79] after another. In the beginning, the embryo of a chick is a tiny ball of tissue. It can just as easily become a snail, a sea anemone, or a starfish. Then it differentiates. It takes on the "type of organization" of an all-purpose land vertebrate—a landwalker with a backbone. Next the embryo becomes even more specialized. It avoids the pattern of a mammal and takes on the "type of organization" of a bird. But that is not the end of its branching off on a path of its own. Once again it specializes further. The chick embryo differentiates away from the "type of organization" of ducks and seagulls, from the type of sea birds. It shows the very special pattern, the "type of organization," of a land bird. Finally it parts company with other land birds and takes on the special "type of organization" that will someday make a chicken.[80]

In other words, von Baer watched as embryos went through the process of producing finer and finer distinctions, finer and finer specializations. And more and more unique large-scale structures, more and more unique "types of organization." Von Baer seldom used the word "differentiation."[81] The year 1821 was eighteen years before the rise of cell theory. So, as von Baer explained in his autobiography, "I obviously did not say that what we had here" in the embryo's unfolding, in the embryo's development, "was a cell division process, because the cell theory as well as the idea that animals, too, consisted of cells, was postulated by Schwann only in 1839, and the term 'cell' for elements of animal structures was completely foreign to me."[82] But with or without cells, von Baer came up with Baer's principle: "Development proceeds inexorably from the general to the special."[83] Von Baer's principle would become the core principle of differentiation. And it would gain its meaning from von Baer's greatest accomplishment: putting the embryo on the map, putting the embryo on the menu of metaphor.

Then came Hans Adolf Eduard Driesch, born in the German wine-making town of Bad Kreuznach in 1867, two years after the end of the American Civil War. By the time Driesch was born, von Baer was a seventy-five-year-old busily critiquing Charles Darwin's new theory of evolution, and cell theory had been around for twenty-eight years. At the end of the nineteenth century and the beginning of the twentieth, Driesch turned embryology into a philosophy, a philosophy that dared to challenge Newton's idea of the cosmos as a machine. And a philosophy that dared propose that the embryo provides a far more useful metaphor with which to understand the evolution of the cosmos than the gears (a word, you may remember, that Newton never used—he called them "wheels")[84] in the belly of Newton's windmill.

***

Hans Eduard Driesch was a round-faced man with a stern expression rendered a bit ridiculous by the immense patch of baldness that made his forehead look bigger than his face. But he had a brilliant and audacious mind. At his labs in Germany and in the Marine Biological Station in Naples,[85] during what he called his "long residence in southern Italy,"[86] Driesch turned his microscope on the embryos and on the adult cells of salamanders, sea urchins, sea squirts, land trees, and flowers like the Begonia. The phenomenon that amazed him the most was how developing cells seemed to know the goal they were heading toward. It looked as if sheets and mobs of cells had a sense of their final product, whether that product was an octopus, a tree, or a human being. The cells seemed to have a final big picture as their guide. If you removed a single cell from a developing organism at the right time, it could start all over again from scratch, divide, and make yet another complete organism. "Take the ovary of our sea urchin for instance," Driesch wrote, "and there you have a morphogenetic system every element of which," every cell of which, "is equally capable of performing the same complex morphogenetic course—the production of the whole individual."[87]

What an incredible manifestation of a form aching to be. What an incredible manifestation of a recruitment strategy!

Some sea squirts look like potatoes with tumors. Others look like finger-sized trees with a central trunk and side branches. Cut any part of a branch or a bulge from the sea squirt and that tiny fragment can remake itself into a new, complete, multibranched sea squirt. "The branchial apparatus," Driesch says, "is able to give rise to a complete little organism." And the scrap of sea squirt doesn't even have to bother to make new cells. It can reengineer the cells it's already got. It can repurpose, reassign, and rearrange them as if it had a built-in blueprint, a built in *bauplan.*[88] A blueprint for a sea squirt adult. And that overall big picture seems to orchestrate the individual instructions, the individual marching orders for each cell.

There was a huge mystery here. Driesch called it "form production."[89] And he took on an immense challenge. He tried to hunt down what he called "the laws of form."[90] He probed the unfolding of implicit properties. He looked for the explanation of what "allows that to become real which it has itself held in a state of mere possibility."[91] Driesch looked for the force, for the power that made the possible emerge from nearly nothing.

Whatever that mystery might be, Driesch came up with a name for it, "entelechy."[92] And he challenged Newton. The mystery Driesch sought, he said, was "not a machine."[93] It was not a mechanism like the cogs and wheels in the bowels of Newton's windmill. No machine, Driesch said, could repair itself. No machine could start from one connecting rod and build its other parts, assembling them into a whole as it went along. No screw "knew" where it was going. No gear knew the form it was a part of and knew how to replicate that form. No rotor could build a windmill. No nail could build a house. No spring could assemble a clock. Yet embryonic cells and even some adult cells could build a copy of the organism from which they were wrenched. The entire organism! These cells seemed to contain a sense of the big picture they were laboring to construct.

Driesch felt that this big-picture fixation, this goal-directedness, was not limited to cells. "The universe is an organism or rather is the one organism,"[94] he concluded in 1914 after twenty-five years of work in embryology. And "in evolution all natural becoming is like one great embryology."[95] Yes, to Driesch even the universe, in some strange way, seemed to know where it was going. It seemed to sense the form toward which it was aiming. So did human history. History, said Driesch, is like phylogeny—like the evolutionary process that produces new species—like the process of biological evolution. And history unfolds in a seemingly purposeful way. History, says Driesch, seems driven by "unifying causality,"[96] by an overarching form that aches to be. Driven by an implicit pattern, a big picture, that we have not as yet learned to see. Driven by an entelechy.

***

What's more, Driesch observed that as a system unfolds, its rules change, its laws morph. It seems to reach toward making even higher and previously impossible-to-imagine new orders. It seems to stretch toward big pictures just out of reach. Human history and the cosmos both seem to work as a "system of purposes"[97] to find new kinds of "unity,"[98] new grand unifications. Both the cosmos and history seem to ache to find the next great stair step of implicit order, the next supersized surprise.

Or to translate it in terms of examples from a physics that was not yet available to Driesch, quarks spring together to form impossible new structures: protons and neutrons. Three hundred eighty thousand years later protons and neutrons whump together with electrons to make another inconceivable shock: atoms. Atoms crowd together and nearly a billion years later unfold two more unimaginable forms, galaxies and stars.[99] As mobs get bigger, the forms of cooperation they "invent," the forms of interaction they unfold, get more intricate, more complex. And a few of these interactions turn out to be new shape shocks with rules and surprises all their own.

In the cosmos of six monkeys at six typewriters, in the cosmos of randomness, more things should mean more crazed lunacy, more chaos. But when you get mobs and masses, you don't get entropy. You don't get a confused soup. You get new big pictures. New sanities. New gestalts. To use Driesch's word, you get new "unities." You get new recruitment strategies aching to be. And that is not airy fantasy. It's physics. "More is different,"[100] physicist Philip Anderson would later say in the title of a 1967 University of Cambridge lecture. That lecture would become an article in *Science*. Then it would morph into a "folk theorem" in physics. And finally, it would become a standard part of the physicists' tool kit. Take a look at that name again: "More Is Different." The piece's point? That mobs, masses, and plethora produce emergent properties. Even if those piles, plurals, and plethoras are of absolutely identical things. What's more, Driesch was right. Each layer of emergent properties produces new laws. More than just new laws. Whole new hierarchies of being. Whole new ontologies. In 2010, New York University new-media specialist Clay Shirky, author of *Cognitive Surplus*, would paraphrase Anderson like this: "When you aggregate a lot of something, it behaves in new ways."[101] Sometimes radically new ways.

But back to Driesch in 1914. As an embryo climbs the stairway of implicit order, it unfolds radically new laws. Or, as Driesch put it, "In biological embryology we know that the law of mere cleavage for instance holds good for say ten cell divisions."[102] Then everything changes. Bigger gangs beget bigger structures, higher degrees of the ornate, higher degrees of form and interaction. Higher orders of sociality. Higher orders of choreography. More intricate big pictures. The form that's assumed by a mere ten cell divisions, a mere 1,024 cells, is just a ball. But that "is then followed by the law of organ formation." At 1,024 cells, a whole new law kicks in. A whole new recruitment strategy shows its face. Form itself seems hungry to emerge from possibility space. The form of the head, the heart, the liver, and the arms and legs. All seem eager to gain their opportunities to escape mere implication. Eager to grab the privilege that you and I take for granted every minute of the day. Existence. Form seems eager to be.

For example, the pattern of the eye will do almost anything to be. It will take so many routes to becoming that some experts claim it has evolved separately, yes, on its own, dozens of times in radically different forms and in radically different kinds of life. The eye "wants" to be in as many creatures as possible. And it succeeds. Ninety-five percent of the species on this planet have eyes.[103] Take another example from a radically different realm. The recruitment strategy of a star is so enthusiastic about becoming that it greedily motivates ten billion trillion[104] of its progeny, stars, to yank together raw material, to tear apart the atoms at their hearts, and to blaze with light. The result? The recruitment strategy of the star deliriously dots the skies.

To Driesch, it seemed as if the cosmos and history are not just pushed along by causality. It seemed as if the cosmos and history are not just flicked ahead by their past. It seemed as if they are pulled ahead by their future. As if they are rushing toward a place in a bigger picture. It seemed as if implicit order has a magnetism, as if the implicit has its own form of attraction, its own form of gravity. Formally, the idea that the future pulls us toward itself is called "teleology." And it's one of Aristotle's ideas. Aristotle called it "final cause."[105] Final cause says that the future is as much a cause as is the past. Wheat doesn't just grow because a farmer has planted a seed. It grows because of its destiny—to feed us. In Cambridge in 1700, even Isaac Newton believed in the validity of final cause.[106] Remember, Newton said that "we know God" not just by "his most wise and excellent contrivances of things" but by "final causes."[107] Yes, even Newton believed in the pull of a bigger picture, the pull of a future goal.

But 128 years after Newton's death, the idea of the future as a cause, the idea of teleology, was banished from science.[108] It was banished with the publication in 1855 of a book by a German physiologist and physician, Ludwig Büchner: *Force and Matter or Principles of the Natural Order of the Universe.* That book, *Force and Matter*, got Büchner fired from his position as a professor of medicine at Germany's Tübingen University. But being fired didn't hurt Büchner. Far from it. *Force and Matter* sold hundreds of thousands of copies and became the "Bible of Materialism." And it turned Büchner into an international celebrity. Why? Because there were hundreds of thousands eager to escape the authority of the church and its belief system. Eager for a new creation myth. A creation myth without a dictator in the sky. Without a god. And Büchner told the tale of a cosmos pulled together by gravity, a tale of "worlds and world-systems" that have "evolved by a process of condensation increasing step by step, and have gradually rolled themselves together in compact masses or organized systems."[109] He told the tale of a self-organizing universe. This was the new creation myth that those who wanted to escape the belief system of the church had been waiting for. It was a new creation myth that would be completed four years later with the publication of Charles Darwin's *Origin of Species.*

Meanwhile, Büchner's *Force and Matter* also became the Bible of a new movement, "Free Thinking," otherwise known as atheism.[110]

Büchner did not mince words about the role of the future in shaping the present, about final cause and teleology. Teleology, he said, was "short-sighted," "empty," and "superficial."[111] Not to mention "anthropomorphic." But the role of the future in the present is one of the puzzles that Driesch reopened fifty years after Büchner. Driesch did it with his mystery term "entelechy." Or at least Driesch tried to reopen the subject of the role of the future in pulling the present toward it. But his approach was derided and despised. Should it have been? Were the questions it posed valid?

Nonetheless, von Baer and Driesch put embryology on the map of possible metaphors. Possible metaphors with which to understand how the cosmos creates. And they offered another perspective on the problem that Darwin would soon call "variation." With embryology, von Baer and Driesch brought differentiation front and center. And they implicitly moved the big picture onto center stage—they tried to put the mystery of "form production" in the spotlight.

MASTER OF THE UNIVERSE:
HERBERT SPENCER, GRAND UNIFIER AND FLIRT

One brave synthesizer followed where von Baer and Driesch led: Herbert Spencer. Herbert Spencer is one of the most underrated thinkers of the late-nineteenth century. He was nominated for a Nobel Prize in Literature in 1902. And with good reason. Among other things, he coined the phrases "survival of the fittest" and "theory of evolution"[112]—the two buzzwords used to push Darwin's evolutionary theory into the mainstream. Spencer's books had a profound influence on sociology,[113] economics,[114] education,[115] religion, ethics, biology, and psychology. A largely forgotten influence. How did Spencer become so important in so many fields? He dedicated his life to a grand unified vision, a big picture that would sew all of the sciences together with the threads of a small number of unifying principles. He called that grand vision a "synthetic philosophy."[116]

Spencer married omnivorous curiosity to diligent work. And he was rewarded for his dedication. At least at first. He was not just mildly famous.

He was superfamous. He was the most renowned philosopher of his time in England and Europe. But he was equally revered in a far less familiar place—the non-Western world. His works were translated into the usual languages: German, Italian, Spanish, French, and Russian. But they were also translated into Japanese and Chinese. Over a hundred years ago. Long before Asia made it onto the map of modern states. At a time when the poor of China and India lived in squalid conditions and frequently starved to death. Yet when Herbert Spencer died, the Indian nationalist leader Shyamji Krishna Varma laid out the money to establish a lectureship at Oxford in Spencer's name. And it was Spencer who would apply von Baer's metaphor of the embryo on the grandest of scales.

In fact, Herbert Spencer would use von Baer's work on embryos to derive what may be one of the most fundamental rules of the cosmos. One of the most fundamental rules of "form production." What's more, Spencer's social circle would provide a key word to the mystery of why one plus one often does not equal two. A word that would prove crucial to the riddles raised by Driesch. A word that would prove vital to tracing "the evolution of sociality, mentation, cognition, and emotion from the big bang to the twenty-first century." That word? "Emergence."

Who was Herbert Spencer? Herbert Spencer's life story begins with a man named Darwin. Not Charles Darwin, but Charles Darwin's great grandfather Robert Darwin of Elston. Spencer's life story begins with, umm, a Darwin? Surely you must be kidding. Not at all. To see how, let's go back to 1719, one hundred and one years before Herbert Spencer was born. In the county of Elston there was a local barrister, a lawyer who didn't care much for lawyering. And he didn't have to. He'd inherited an estate, Elston Hall. What's more, in the words of one nineteenth-century account, he "preferred the life of a country gentleman."[117] Country gentlemen love their dogs more than they love their servants. So on May 11, 1719, this perpetually retired attorney had brought a dog into the dining hall of the local bar association. The porter had "offered" to "turn his dog out of the hall." But the barrister with the dog had not cared for this offer. In fact he had "threatened to knock down" and "fling a pot" at the porter who asked him to remove the pooch.[118]

The legal beagle who preferred country gentlemanning was Robert

Darwin, the aforesaid Robert Darwin of Elston. But the dog incident was not Robert Darwin's biggest achievement of 1719. Gentlemen had long collected oddities of stone dug out of the ground—imprints of seashells found on mountain tops and bones of what appeared to be giants and dragons. Were these remains left over from Noah's flood? Or were they objects that would "shock the Scripture-History of the . . . Divines and Philosophers?"[119] Were they growths that had taken hold in the stone from the same seed that produced the first animals themselves? Growths that had never made it all the way from stone to the snarling, whimpering, and whining of life?[120]

Robert Darwin loved finding the sorts of rocks that were at the center of this controversy. And he was in luck. He and, in all probability, his dogs, found a curious slab of rock that had been used to build the "landing place" of a well at Elston. And that stone contained what looked like a very substantial part of a skeleton. Not just any skeleton. The skeleton of a creature unlike any that was currently walking, stalking, or crawling the face of the earth. That slab of rock got Robert Darwin admitted to the high-prestige Vatican of science, the Royal Society in London, at least for a day. The society classified Robert Darwin as a "person of curiosity." Why? The fossil Darwin had found on the landing place of the well at Elston was "the first articulated specimen of a fossil reptile"[121] ever identified. Thus did the Darwin family enter the territory to which Herbert Spencer would later give a name: the theory of evolution. Much, much later on, when the notion that fossils were relics of long-gone evolutionary ages had taken hold, the bones in stone that Robert Darwin had found would be pegged as a plesiosaur from the Jurassic.[122]

But that wasn't the end of the family obsession with evolution. Robert Darwin had more than dogs. He had children. Seven of them. And the youngest was named after a sixteenth-century intellectual who had helped inject humanism into the Renaissance, Erasmus of Rotterdam. Could the young Erasmus Darwin possibly kick off a renaissance of his own? He would give it a try.

Erasmus Darwin went off to Cambridge as a medical student, and when he attempted to establish a medical practice in Nottingham, he just couldn't attract patients. So he moved thirty-five miles away to Lichfield, where his practice flourished. Eventually he'd be asked to act as physician to King

George III. And he'd turn the offer down. Why? In part because he was doing something far more interesting. In 1765[123] when he was thirty-four years old Erasmus Darwin founded a brainstorming group called the Lunar Society.[124] It took its name from the fact that it got together for dinner "every month near the full moon,"[125] a date chosen because there were few streetlights, and the group had to convene on evenings when the moon provided enough light for its members to travel safely through the dark. The Lunar Society included some of the most amazing minds in the brand-new fields of science and technology: Joseph Priestley, the discoverer of oxygen; Mathew Boulton and James Watt, the cocreators and mass producers of the steam engine; and an American correspondent named Benjamin Franklin. The Lunar Society also attracted occasional contributors like Joseph Banks, the botanist to beat all botanists, the scientist who had accompanied Captain Cook on his first trip around the world; and William Herschel, the astronomer who discovered the planet Uranus, its moons, and two moons of Saturn. Herschel's name would become synonymous with astronomy. And his work on nebulae would later help Erasmus Darwin envision the evolution of the universe from a massive explosion in his 1798 book *The Botanic Garden*. But we're getting ahead of ourselves.

In 1782[126] Erasmus Darwin moved twenty-four miles from Lichfield to Derby. And there he founded yet another brainstorming club, the Derby Philosophical Society. This one included people like Josiah Wedgwood,[127] whose father had invented techniques to mass produce imitations of a costly import from China.[128] That import was porcelain ware. It included exquisite knockoffs of Chinese inventions like the teapot, the cup, and the saucer. Because of their original source, these ritual drinking devices were called china. And the Wedgwood name became synonymous with china.

But the forms of industrialization and mass production that young Josiah Wedgwood pioneered were based on the latest science[129] and were radically new. They relied on an exquisite sense of what would later be called "thermodynamics": the production, regulation, and transfer of heat. They also relied on what would later be called "materials science": the transformations that heat could produce, and the materials and chemicals in which just the right amount of heat could produce just the right result. Topping it off,

Josiah Wedgwood's breakthroughs included the invention of something else new called "factories" and the "factory town."[130] All to make mere "china."

Meanwhile, the goods Wedgwood's factories produced were so stunningly gorgeous that Wedgwood's customers included Queen Charlotte of England and Catherine the Great, empress of Russia.[131] And Wedgwood created new forms of lab equipment, new forms of "Philosophical Apparatus,"[132] for fellow Darwin brainstormer Joseph Priestley,[133] the minister of the New Meetinghouse in Birmingham, who discovered oxygen. In turn, Priestley experimented in what he called his "Laboratory" on new materials for Wedgwood.

Then there was Erasmus Darwin's own contribution. In 1794 and 1798 he wrote two books putting forth a new narrative,[134] a new basic story of the rise of life, a new alternative to the Bible's tale of Genesis. A story that began with a big bang, an explosion in which "the whole of Chaos, like grains of gunpowder, was exploded at the same time, and dispersed through infinite space."[135] Erasmus Darwin's new story—his new big picture—would later be called evolution. But Erasmus Darwin himself would only use the word "evolution" six times in these two books. And he wouldn't use it for his grand narrative.

Eighteen years after Erasmus Darwin's death, the man who would coin the term "theory of evolution" would be born into Erasmus Darwin's Derby Philosophical Society. His name? Herbert Spencer. How do you attain the privilege of being born into what may have been the hottest idea-swapping dinner club in the history of science? Herbert Spencer's father, William George Spencer, was the founder of an innovative, individual-centered, progressive school in Derby based on the ideas of a daring Swiss reformer. Spencer's father was also known as a thinker. So it was natural that Spencer's father would become secretary of the Derby Philosophical Society, Erasmus Darwin's "Festive Philosophers,"[136] in 1815. That, alas, was thirteen years after the death of Erasmus Darwin himself. Nonetheless, five years after his ascension to the position of secretary, William George Spencer's first child, Herbert Spencer, the first of nine children and the only one to live, was born.[137]

Herbert exited the womb in 1820, a year that was sizzling with a whole new flare of intellectual energy. Gauss, Bólyai, and Lobachevsky were tilting at the parallel axiom like Don Quixote rushing at a windmill with his old horse trotting and his lance held high. Thomas Young was thirty-seven years old. He had been lecturing about the interference patterns in light for over thirteen years[138] and was giving up his medical practice in the seaside city of Worthing to move to London and dedicate more time to the Royal Society.[139] And Karl Ernst von Baer was twenty-eight and had just postponed a trip to explore the botany of the Arctic Ocean islands of Novaya Zemlya north of Russia in order to get married.[140]

Spencer's education followed his father's philosophy. It was focused on allowing Herbert to range the intellectual landscape like a mountain goat looking for fresh tufts of grass. Spencer was sickly, so his father educated him at home. But Herbert is said to have received his real education from the members of the Derby Philosophical Society. He may have been a mere child, but it was these flashing, flaming intellects with whom he spent his time. And thus it was that his education was rich in Erasmus Darwin's evolutionary ideas. Rich in those evolutionary ideas more than three decades before another Midlands lad eleven years older than Spencer, a Shropshire lad named Charles Darwin, would claim the word "evolution" as his own.

Meanwhile, when he was thirteen, Herbert Spencer was sent off to live with and be educated by his uncle Thomas, a vicar at Charterhouse near Bath. His uncle drilled him in math, physics, free trade, "philosophical radicalism," and skepticism about the state. But Herbert Spencer's education also came from reading. More specifically, from reading the books he agreed with and rapidly tossing aside those he didn't.

Most of the members of the Derby Philosophical Society and of the Lunar Society were religious dissenters. Men who refused the mainstream state religion of England—Episcopalianism. So Herbert Spencer grew up in an environment where questioning assumptions, contesting the normal, and flying over the landscape of all of the sciences looking for big pictures was the norm.

In the educational philosophy of Spencer's father, the care and feeding of the intellect was tailored to fit the individual. The individual was not tailored to fit the academic institution. So when Spencer reached university age, when he reached the age of seventeen, he didn't follow in his father's footsteps and go off to Cambridge. Science was not producing its most spectacular results in the world of academia and the Royal Society. It was producing its most spectacular results in the world of something very new. The world of hi-tech entrepreneurship. The world of radical new game-changers—transport and industry.

A new device had been invented and perfected in the 1780s and 1790s, the decades of the American Constitution and of the French Revolution, the decades twenty years before Herbert Spencer was born. That new device had been developed by two members of Erasmus Darwin's Lunar Society—Matthew Boulton and James Watt. It had been perfected in the Lunar Society's brainstorming sessions, with technically savvy members offering ideas on new tweaks. The new device was the steam engine. And the steam engine would utterly and forever change the world in which humans lived. It would weave a new medium. Literally. In fact, more than one.

By 1820, when Herbert Spencer was born, the steam engine had been attached to milling machines and had been used to dramatically lower the cost of a luxury cloth previously available only to the rich. That cloth was cotton. Until then, the clothes of the poor had been made of wool.[141] Wool shirts and pants could not be laundered.[142] They smelled deplorable. And they housed parasites. Insects whose feasting on your flesh could take decades off of your life. But the steam engine spun the fuzz of a Central American and Asian plant called cotton into thread. Then it wove that thread into a fabric that could be washed over and over again. A fabric that let you launder parasites into oblivion. Steam engines and the machines they drove made once exorbitantly priced cotton clothing cheap.

Meanwhile, two chemists in France used a science still in its birth throes, chemistry, to develop techniques for mass producing the raw ingredients for another miracle product—a product that had previously been made by hand—soap. And soap took the health benefits of laundering to the next level. When two megacelebrities of the decade just before Spencer's birth, Napoleon's first wife, Josephine, and the Duke of Wellington, the man who beat Napoleon at Waterloo, both announced that they bathed daily using soap,[143] they created a revolution. A revolution in hygiene. A revolution enabled by the steam engine, by synthetic chemistry, and by the creation of the factory. A revolution enabled by repeating old patterns in a new medium. The soap and cotton revolution. The revolution that would slowly but dramatically double English lifespans.[144]

And as Herbert Spencer grew from a baby to an adolescent, two other next-generation technologies were changing life in stunning new ways—the telegraph and the use of the steam engine for transportation.

The idea that steam could be used for transport initially seemed absurd. The hugely successful author of historical novels like *Ivanhoe* and *The Lady of the Lake*, "Sir Walter Scott ridiculed the idea of steam being used to propel vessels."[145] But Sir Walter Scott and all the other experts on whose behalf he spoke were wrong. The steam engine was soon harnessed to drive massive vehicles on sea and on land. Vehicles of a size that no human had ever seen.

First steam was harnessed to drive ships. In 1807, when Robert Fulton got his first steamship—the Clermont[146]—to work successfully, his engine allowed the Clermont to plow ahead on its travels from New York to Albany and back when the wind died and enabled the vessel to move against the breezes and the currents with ease. Meanwhile, in the 1780s, Richard Trevithick at the Ding Dong Mines in Cornwall was trying to harness the steam engine to defy the limitations of land travel. He began by building models of something his son, a noted railroad engineer, would later call "the first high pressure locomotive," a fat metal can laid on its side and equipped with wheels. The can was the boiler of a steam engine. Light a spirit lamp that was fixed to the contraption and it "ran round the table, or the room."[147]

The concept of the locomotive was acting suspiciously like a recruitment strategy, like a new form aching to be. Five others were apparently making model locomotives at the same time.[148]

Meanwhile, carriages mounted on rails and drawn by horses were becoming increasingly popular. Yes, horses. But using a steam engine to power one of these land gliders was proving a problem. In 1804, Trevithick put his model-making to work. He built a full-size "steam carriage" that "hauled a train of 10 tons of iron and 70 passengers in five wagons over nine miles."[149] A brilliant success. With one minor problem. It was too heavy for its cast-iron rails. After three trips, it had crushed them. That ended the experiment.

But the advance of technology was creating another radically new medium, a radically new way of seducing, recruiting, and kidnapping dead atoms and bringing them into the grand enterprise of biomass. A radically new way of pulling lifeless molecules into the search engine of the cosmos. And an old pattern was repeating in that new medium. Repeating the way it had when Aristotle had set himself apart from Heraclitus. Repeating the way it does between brothers and sisters competing for the spotlight. Men and women were setting themselves apart to get attention. Their means of doing it? Extracting new implications from the weave emerging around them.

For the next twenty-one years, Britain's engineering geniuses competed to turn the locomotive—the self-mover—into a success. They did it by building one-of-a-kind locomotives where they were needed most—to haul men, equipment, and tons of cargo over short distances[150] at coal fields. And they had a historical accident in their favor. The wars with Napoleon were on, and horses were desperately needed at the front. Which meant that businesses like coal and metal mining, industries that relied on heavy land transport, needed a horse replacement.

In 1814, George Stephenson, an engineer whose father was the fireman for a steam engine that pumped water out of the coal mine of the Wylam Colliery in Northumberland, built one of the first coal-hauling steam locomotives. He named it for the Prussian general who had just helped the English beat Napoleon at Waterloo—the Blucher. And it worked. It could pull thirty tons up a hill. But it did it at four miles per hour, almost as slow as walking speed. Stephenson was not satisfied. He built another locomotive, the "Kilmarnock and Troon." It was a failure. It, too, crushed its rails.[151]

Then came the muscle of real money. Parliament resolved to build a railway—a "plateway"—to carry the coal from inland mines over the twenty-six miles to the port of Stockton, where the coal could be loaded onto ships and sent down the Tees River to the North Sea. It would be called the Stockton and Darlington Railway. At first the plan was to pull the carriages with horses, something that had been common since 1780. But Stephenson was convinced that he finally had a steam locomotive that would work. Just as important, he finally felt he had a form of track that would stand up to the weight of a steam engine on wheels. So he convinced the main financial backer of the project, a wool merchant worth a fortune, to let him cover at least part of the route with what Parliament would call "loco-motive or moveable engines."[152]

By now Stephenson had organized a company. And that company built "Locomotion No. 1," another steam-driven locomotive that looked like a horizontal can on four huge black iron cart wheels. But on the day of its grand opening—the grand opening of the Stockton and Darlington Railway— that can laid flat carried nearly six hundred passengers at a speed of six miles per hour. This was the world's first railroad available to the public.[153] And its twenty primitive "cars" were capable of carrying 5,291 pounds of humans or coal each.[154] Normal runs of the Stockton and Darlington would soon operate at speeds between eight and twelve miles per hour.[155] Experts declared that speeds above twenty miles per hour would suck the wind out of your lungs and kill you. But by 1829, when Herbert Spencer was nine years old, Stephenson had built a locomotive called the "Rocket" that, according to the nineteenth-century's *Civil Engineer and Architect's Journal*, could reach "the extraordinary speed of between twenty and thirty miles an hour."[156] And guess what? No passengers had died of suffocation!

The Stockton and Darlington Railroad had gone into operation a mere one hundred and eleven miles from Herbert Spencer's hometown, Derby, in 1825, when Herbert was five years old. And increasing the span of rail-roads, increasing the speed of the trains, keeping the "tracks" in repair, and reducing or eliminating crashes were among the greatest scientific, tech-nical, and engineering challenges of Spencer's youth.

So instead of going into the armchair field of "natural philosophy," Spencer took the path less traveled and went into railroad engineering. In 1837, when he was seventeen years old,[157] Herbert became an engineer for the London and Birmingham Railway, a line whose track was still under construction and would not open to the public for a year. But that track was a stunning one hundred and twelve miles long and was the first to go from another city to London. What's more, railroads were setting new speed records. They had achieved an unbelievable thirty miles per hour.[158] Ten miles per hour faster than the speed some experts said would suffocate you. A year later Spencer switched jobs, left the London and Birmingham, and became a draftsman for another railway, the Birmingham and Gloucester, a railway designed to connect the growing industrial powerhouse of Birmingham not just to London, but also to the port of Gloucester, thus connecting a major inland factory city to the shipping centers of the sea by steam for the very first time.

The Birmingham and Gloucester Railway was up against an impossible challenge. It would have to use a locomotive to draw a train up the Lickey Ridge, something that the top engineers of the time, including mega-engineering's reigning genius, Isambard Kingdom Brunel, said could not be done. The ridge was just too steep. Steeper than the maximum gradient determined by engineers and scientists. Wrote Francis Whishaw in 1840: "If this is satisfactorily effected, it will throw a new and useful light on the laying out of railways, and will save a vast original outlay in future works."[159] In other words, it will open a jackpot. The experts were betting that the Birmingham and Gloucester's plan to climb the Lickey Ridge would not and could not work. But despite the impossibilities, the railway was completed in 1841.

***

The cosmos hides her creativity by preying on the way we oh-so-quickly become blasé. She covers up her bombshells and her breakthroughs by tricking us into seeing the extraordinary as mundane. Through the Birmingham and Gloucester Railroad, nature had pulled off one of her slickest transformations, using humans to find new shocks in possibility space, new shocks in the realm of the implicit. Nature had used a team of humans to inch toward her next supersized surprise.

But the Birmingham and Gloucester's engineering team had been assembled to handle the problems of construction. And now that the road's construction was finished, that team was no longer needed. So Herbert Spencer was laid off. Where did he go? Back home. Home to Derby. And he began what he called a seven-year "nomadic period."[160]

As he describes it, this lost seven-year period was

a time of scheming and experimenting—mechanical, chemical, electrical . . . and music[al]

Pythagoras would have been pleased. But that wasn't all.

> Then there was political writing, broken by brief efforts to open for myself
> a literary career.[161]

When Spencer speaks of "brief efforts to open for myself a literary career," he means that he tried to make a living by writing. He was, indeed, published. But the money was marginal. And he dabbled in railway ventures—considering a job drawing surveys for a new railroad, a job so trying that it damaged the eyes of one of his friends.

But the twenty-plus Spencer needed a solid home, a base, and a salary. So he tried for a job on "a new weekly journal about to be started," but that didn't pan out.[162] Next, he tried for a job at a brand-new paper that Charles Dickens had just founded in London, the *Daily News*. No luck. Then, Spencer says, "my uncle gave me a letter of introduction to Wilson, the editor of the *Economist*."[163] Wilson was James Wilson, a man who *Blackwood's Magazine* would soon call a "redoubted political economist."[164] James Wilson was five years older than Herbert Spencer and the new editor and new, inexperienced owner of the *Economist*. Wilson's father had been "a thriving man of business, extensively engaged in . . . woolen manufacture"[165] in Wilson's Scottish hometown, Hawick. So Wilson's family did know something about the world of business.

So did James Wilson. At the age of sixteen he had been apprenticed to a hat manufacturer in Hawick. And by the age of nineteen he and a brother had gone to London and with two thousand pounds from their father had set up their own hat manufacturing business. Thirteen years later, Wilson had parlayed his half of two thousand pounds up to twenty-five thousand pounds and had moved with his family into a mansion with large grounds in the Dulwich section of London.[166]

James Wilson had lost that fortune in the crash of 1837. But he'd started writing, writing on the most explosive financial issue of the day, free trade versus a protectionism that was driving up the cost of food in order to benefit rich land owners—the "Corn Laws." Recalls Herbert Spencer, Wilson had "written a work on The Influences of the Corn-laws,"[167] a pamphlet. But it had been a pamphlet with power. Wilson argued for an end to the style of supercharged class-war-mongering debate "declaiming the landowners as selfish, monopolizing law-makers, or the manufacturers as sordid, avaricious beings, grasping at the riches of the great, and treading on the rights of the poor."[168] The Corn Laws, Wilson argued, hurt even the landed classes. The Corn Laws were a national matter, not a class matter. Wilson was new to writing, but his pamphlet bit deep. One newspaper, the *Leeds Mercury*, reprinted all 130 pages of it in installments. It was even quoted in Parliament.[169] James Wilson was so passionate about bringing reason to a debate that sparked class hatred that he wrote up his opinions for the *Manchester Guardian* and the *Examiner*.[170]

Then he got together the money to start a newspaper of his own. Despite the fact that newspapers were money-losing propositions. "Newspapers have been graves to fortunes,"[171] wrote James Wilson's friend and supporter, the famous manufacturer and free-trade politician Richard Cobden. But Wilson took a chance and in 1843 started his publication dedicated to free trade and reasonable debate, the *Economist*.

Starting a new publication in London—a city already flooded with printed matter—was an almost impossible proposition. How would the thirty-three-year-old Wilson pull it off? By making the *Economist* "an organ of the mercantile world."[172] And, as Spencer puts it, by working "on it indefatigably—living at the *Economist* office to devote his full time to it."[173] With his persistence and his sense of what topics mattered most to men in business, James Wilson succeeded. And he succeeded with astonishing rapidity. Says Spencer, with "good business judgment, sufficient literary faculty, and extensive knowledge of commercial and financial matters,"[174] Wilson "soon made" the *Economist* "in course of a relatively short time, a valuable property."[175] What's more, James Wilson pulled off two more miracles. Two more miracles that put him in the very center of the business and political worlds. Explains Spencer, "He had been elected member of Parliament for Westbury [in 1847]; and, subsequently, he had been appointed Secretary of the India Board, or Board of Control [in 1848]—a government department which had for its function to supervise the doings of the East India Company."[176] Concludes Spencer about James Wilson, "He had thus risen in a short time, by sheer force of ability and energy, to a position of considerable wealth and influence."[177] But that was just the beginning of the neophyte publisher's successes when Wilson and Spencer met in the spring of 1848.[178]

Wilson responded to the twenty-eight-year-old Herbert Spencer's letter by inviting him to a Saturday social ritual borrowed from the Chinese and the Japanese. Wilson "invited me to tea at his house on a Saturday evening."[179] It was a night spent discussing the fieriest topic of the time, revolution. Eighteen forty-eight was a year of revolutions. Revolutions in fifty countries. Revolutions that began in France, then spread to Germany, Italy, Austria, and Latin America. Revolutions to repeat an established pattern in new mediums. Revolutions to establish "republics"—democracies like the ones in the United States and in postrevolutionary France.[180] Democracies without kings and without aristocrats. Revolutions to establish a new kind of politics and a new approach to trade. The new approach called "liberalism." And another new approach: "nationalism."[181] The Saturday evening tea at Wilson's house came complete with the daughter of a noble family from France, a noble family that had escaped the guillotine. A woman with nothing but revolution on her mind. First she told tales of the 1789 French Revolution and its bloody aftermath, tales that felt firsthand. For good reason. The Comtesse de Brunetiere's father had been "one of the notables of the first French Revolution." Then came tales of the revolutions happening in Europe at the moment, stories that seemed so real you could feel the blood soaking through your shirt. Again, for good reason. The Comtesse was "intimately acquainted with all the leading politicians of Paris." And Wilson let on that "she had prophesied the leading events of the late revolution two months before they occurred."[182]

What's more, James Wilson, the neophyte founder, editor, and owner of the *Economist*, apparently saw potential in the twenty-eight-year-old Herbert Spencer despite the fact that Spencer lacked the one indispensable thing an intellectual needs to be taken seriously, a degree from Oxford or Cambridge. Or Wilson saw at least a hint of potential. He did not exactly spring at the chance to hire Herbert Spencer.

For three weeks, Spencer heard nothing. Then Spencer called on Wilson at his office on the Strand, this time at a more serious time of day, morning.

Wilson coyly asked if Spencer would be interested in a subeditorship at a London weekly paper. He didn't say which one. But he did ask for Spencer's address. And he did explain that he would be in touch "if an opening should present itself."[183]

Then Spencer took a chance on blowing it. He gave Wilson a copy of one of his political polemics, "The Proper Sphere of Government,"[184] a series of twelve letters published six years earlier in 1842 and 1843 in the *Nonconformist.* A series of letters in which Spencer wrote that the government had virtually no business in the life of the individual. Government's only purpose was to make sure that individuals had rights. "The Proper Sphere of Government" was a radical libertarian screed long before the word libertarian had seen the light of day. In fact, it was giving fresh fuel at that moment to an old British movement that was heatedly opposing a new big-government idea, government-sponsored education.[185] That movement was called "voluntaryism."[186] Radical as Spencer's political statements were, Wilson apparently liked them. But not enough to clutch Spencer to his bosom.

In fact, Spencer had to give up on his London ambitions and go back home to Derbyshire. Once again he was on hold. And once again, his time, he said, was financially "unprofitable." But not mentally unprofitable. He would not allow himself to be inactive. Spencer worked on a book he had in mind. He secured a freelance position writing "a leading article" per week for a new publication, the *Standard of Freedom.* But the *Standard of Freedom* was still just an idea, it still "was not yet launched," reported Spencer, "and even had it been launched the proceeds of one article per week would not have sufficed to meet my expenses in London."[187]

So Spencer did a lot of walking. He walked so he could think out his ideas, something he had a hard time doing when he was sitting alone in a more stationary form of concentration. He walked what he called "the Derbyshire dales" with friends. He took advantage of the fact that the new Midland Railway Company offered a Saturday afternoon excursion train to the countryside. And he tried to understand the scientific explanation of his "long continued repugnance to long-continued attention," the repugnance that made it hard for him to sit still and concentrate but made it easy for him to think while walking outdoors. He tried to figure this hyperactivity out using the latest concepts of biology. The reason, he suspected, was "a physiological one—a want of tone in the vascular system. The vessels lose too soon their normal contractility under stress, and then fail to carry on nervous repair at a rate which keeps pace with nervous waste."[188] A reasonable hypothesis given the state of knowledge of the moment. Then, late in the autumn of 1848, "after five months of uncertainty, there came the offer I had been led to expect."[189]

The opening two words of James Wilson's letter to Herbert Spencer after this five-month gap were not promising. In fact, they were very impersonal, opening with an anonymous "Dear Sir." In his letter, Wilson explained that the position of subeditor had been open "for some time," that it had been filled "temporarily," and that there were seventy applicants for it. In other words, Wilson did not jump up and down with enthusiasm over Herbert Spencer's genius. Enthusiasm or not, the job paid a hundred guineas a year. Spencer saw that sum as "low," but the job also offered a free "room to yourself" at the *Economist* offices complete with the servant "attendance" of "the messenger and his wife," who also "live there."[190]

And Wilson's letter pointed out several more benefits to a writer with ambition, a writer who might like to build his name and fame by publishing articles elsewhere . . . or by writing books. Said Wilson about the subeditorship, "While it requires regular attendance at the office, it does not impose heavy duties." Which means, explained Wilson, "You would have . . . leisure to attend to any other pursuit, such as preparing a work for the press, especially from Friday night until about Wednesday in the following week."[191] Plus, Wilson promised that "if I found that you could contribute leading articles there would be an additional allowance."[192]

What appealed to Herbert Spencer the most was "the light work and abundant leisure." This seemed tailor made for Spencer's ambition to write a book. But Spencer was no more inflamed by enthusiasm than his prospective boss. He says, "No reason for hesitation forthwith presented itself, and I forthwith accepted." He accepted because there were no big drawbacks. Not because it was a fabulous offer.

But the offer from the *Economist was* fabulous. It was astonishing in ways Herbert Spencer failed to foresee. And it put Herbert Spencer smack dab in the middle of things. Smack dab in the middle of things that would contribute clues to the God Problem.

***

The *Economist* offices where Spencer had his room was on the Strand. The Strand was a hot street, vibrant with the sparkling new personal technologies of the age. It was a shopping street with "shoemakers, watchmakers, tailors, wax-chandlers, tobacconists, umbrella-makers, cutlers, linen-drapers, pianoforte-makers, hatmakers, wigmakers, shirtmakers, mapmakers, lozenge manufacturers and sellers of food of all sorts."[193] More important, on the Strand or just around one of the Strand's many corners were the headquarters of thirty newspapers and magazines.

Meeting publishers is a difficult proposition for aspiring authors who have never published a book. But the office of the *Economist* was located in publishing central. In fact, across the street at number 142 on the Strand was the brand-new "large establishment" of a publisher who had outgrown his previous offices on Newgate Street: John Chapman. John Chapman of the firm known as John Chapman Bookseller and Publisher. And John Chapman would change Herbert Spencer's life.

THE SCANDAL OF THE CENTURY: GEORGE ELIOT AND HER APE

Herbert Spencer is about to make the most important friends of his life. Friends who will generate a new concept. A concept vital to the mystery of what Hans Driesch will someday call "form production."[194] The mystery of how new big-picture patterns emerge. The mystery of how the cosmos creates.

It's the spring of 1850.[195] Herbert Spencer is roughly fifteen months into his job with the *Economist*. The modern office building has not yet been invented. So business "establishments" are boarding houses, private entertainment centers, and offices all rolled into one. Which is why Spencer's job comes complete with a bedroom in the *Economist*'s headquarters on London's

Strand. And across the street is another business "establishment" complete with enough bedrooms to house one big family and many guests, the headquarters of publisher John Chapman. John Chapman is one year younger than Herbert Spencer, with strong political views, "liberal" political views, and a determination to get them across. Thomas Carlyle, the social commentator, a man who Spencer will soon get to know, calls John Chapman a "Publisher of Liberalisms." John Chapman is also the epitome of setting yourself apart on the stage of attention space. He is the epitome of differentiation.

John Chapman is handsome, energetic, a radical, a rebel, and a renegade. The novelist William Makepeace Thackeray in 1847, just before Herbert Spencer gets his job at the *Economist*, has coined the term "bohemian" in his novel *Vanity Fair*. And John Chapman is a true bohemian intent on giving a home to other bohemians. Chapman's "large establishment"[196] includes, says Spencer, his "bookselling and publishing business, his family home, and rooms for literary lodgers." Oh, and in addition to Chapman's wife and kids, Chapman's "establishment" includes a room for his mistress. And space for occasional other women. Liberalism, radicalism, and a philosophy called "free love"[197] go hand in hand among 1840s and 1850s London bohemians.

But it isn't John Chapman's women who generate scandal. It is his publishing. In 1846, John Chapman has made a splash by publishing a translation of an outrageous secular German book titled *The Life of Jesus Critically Examined*,[198] a book that strips Christ of his divinity and makes him into a mere historical figure, a mere normal human being. And that book has raised a ruckus. Says the Earl of Shaftesbury, *The Life of Jesus* is "the most pestilential book ever vomited out of the jaws of hell."[199] Score one for John Chapman! He wants to cut the roots of the normal and force a radical reperception. And he's done it. But there's more to come.

John Chapman is a great collector of authors. And a great connector. Once a week, he hosts a soiree for what he feels are some of the brightest young talents of his time. They include two of his houseguests. The American visitor Horace Greeley, the founder of the *New York Tribune*, one of the most influential newspapers of its age in the United States, and the cofounder of America's Liberal Republican Party. Greeley is the man who popularizes the saying, "Go West, young man, go West." And another visitor from the United States, Ralph Waldo Emerson, leader of America's Transcendentalist Movement and one of the greatest essayists and phrase makers in the history of American literature.[200] But these two Americans are only temporary visitors.

The regulars are, if anything, even more smashing: Thomas Henry Huxley, the self-taught comparative anatomist who has recently gone as ship's surgeon on a voyage of discovery to New Guinea and Australia with the HMS *Rattlesnake* and who nearly ten years later will become "Darwin's bulldog"; William Makepeace Thackeray,[201] the author of *Vanity Fair*, who coined the term "Bohemian"; Karl Marx, founder of Marxism; John Stuart Mill, the man who will eventually be heralded by the *Stanford Encyclopedia of Science* as "the most influential English-speaking philosopher of the nineteenth century"; and political radicals fleeing repressive regimes after the failed revolutions of 1848, men like Giuseppe Mazzini, "the spiritual father of the Italian political nation,"[202] and "the 'shining star'[203] of the democratic revolutions of 1848,"[204] the Italian nationalist who helps reunite his nation and whose work influences revolutionary movements in Latin America, the Middle East, India, and China.[205] Not to mention a host of writers whose names we no longer know. One of these forgotten names is Mary Ann Evans. And her name is forgotten for good reason. She doesn't use it.

A few years earlier, in 1846, "Miss Evans," as Spencer calls Mary Ann, has translated the aforesaid scandal-making *Life of Jesus* from the German. Then, in 1851, Chapman buys the *Westminster Review*, a crusading, antiestablishment quarterly magazine founded thirty years earlier by philosopher and social reformer Jeremy Bentham, a magazine that the author of the book *142 Strand*[206]—a history of John Chapman's social circle—says "represented a challenge to conservatism in all its forms."[207]

Chapman has brought Mary Ann Evans[208] from her home in Coventry and has given her a room in his office cum household so she can be the *Westminster Review*'s assistant editor. With the exception of a brief period in which Mary Ann falls in love with Chapman and indulges in a short affair with him, there is no hanky-panky.[209] Rooming at the Chapman establishment is the standard business arrangement of the day. But on the working end of things, Evans becomes more than an assistant. Chapman lets her run the publication. And she is turning the *Westminster Review* into what Rosemary Ashton in *142 Strand* calls "the best journal of the century."[210] T. H. Huxley has another name for the *Westminster Review*. He calls it "the wicked *Westminster*."[211] Those are words he utters with delight. Later, when he becomes better known, he will confess that he would far rather write for the *Westminster* than for publications like the tony, conservative *Fraser's Magazine for Town and Country*, a twenty-one-year-old publication that pays him real money.[212]

And T. H. Huxley would rather write for the *Westminster Review* for good reason. As Spencer puts it, in 1851, "the Rattlesnake had recently returned; and Mr. Huxley was then waiting until there came the needful grant, enabling him to publish the results of his researches."[213] In other words, Huxley is broke. And Chapman and Evans have rescued him "from poverty and obscurity"[214] and have made him the *Westminster Review*'s scientific reviewer. With pay.

The *Westminster*'s wickedness comes in part from its outrageous politics, "its campaign for the extension of the suffrage [for women's liberation and for women's rights], its support for European movements for national independence 'refugee politics' . . . and its demand for reform in education and central and local government."[215] Then there is one more wicked little twist: the *Westminster Review*'s skeptical, heretical, and sometimes atheistic take on religion. Which means something important about its coverage of science, coverage handled largely by T. H. Huxley. The *Westminster* is challenging creationism and intelligent design—the creationism and intelligent design that Kepler, Galileo, and Newton had believed in—and is pushing a brand-new secular approach: "theories of organic . . . evolution."[216] And the *Westminster* is doing this eight years before Charles Darwin publishes his first book, *The Origin of Species*.[217]

Herbert Spencer is thrown together with Mary Ann Evans at Chapman's soirees often. And he confesses that he finds "Miss Evans" absolutely entrancing. She is "the most admirable woman, mentally, I ever met."[218] Spencer not only thinks that Mary Ann is bright, but his knowledge of the "science" of phrenology—a science that is considered legitimate—tells him that she has a sufficiently large head to handle a brain. As he puts it, during his "frequent" visits to Chapman's "the greatness of her intellect conjoined with her womanly qualities and manner, generally keep me by her side most of the evening."[219] But evenings at Chapman's with Miss Evans are not enough to satisfy Spencer. He grabs at the "opportunities I had for taking her to places of amusement." What were those opportunities? As a staffer at the *Economist*, Spencer is offered "free admissions for two to the theatres and to the Royal Italian Opera."[220] And now that Miss Evans is in the picture, he uses as many of these free admissions as he can get his hands on. What's more, he walks with Mary Ann along the banks of the Thames, talks with her, and even sings with her. Finally he tries to convince her that she can do something that he says she does not think she can handle. She can go beyond translating and editing and take a giant leap into the dark. She can write novels.[221]

Meanwhile, Mary Ann falls madly in love with Spencer and begs him to marry her.[222] But Spencer is not interested. Perhaps because he finds her mind and her handwriting "masculine" and her body a bit too "strongly built."[223] He says point blank, "There were reports that I was in love with her, and that we were about to be married. But neither of these reports was true."[224] Poor Mary Ann. She has been dashed in romance by both John Chapman and Herbert Spencer.

But never fear, there is another romantic candidate waiting in the wings. Or sitting at Chapman's dining table. And he's the man who will do the most for the God Problem. Back in the spring of 1850,[225] Chapman introduced someone new to his soirees. He invited a philosopher, a student of physiology, an adventurer, an actor, and a traveler named George Henry Lewes.[226] Lewes has been born into bohemianism. He popped from the womb in London in 1817, when Europe was still recovering from the wars that stopped Napoleon. His mother had done something scandalous. She'd made a statement on behalf of "free love." She'd given birth to Lewes out of wedlock. Lewes's father was the poet, actor, and writer John Lee Lewes.[227] And Lewes's grandfather was a comic actor. But circumstance had made Lewes's mother even more of a pioneer in single parenthood. Lewes's father died when he was only one. So his mom raised him on her own until Lewes was six. Then she married someone very unbohemian, a retired captain of the Eighteenth Native Infantry Regiment in Bengal. A man with global experience. Lewes was moved from school to school, including schools in Boulogne and Brittany in France, St. Helier in Jersey, a British island off the French coast of Normandy, and Greenwich[228] in South London. So French was a second language to Lewes. And, says science historian Elizabeth Garber, "Paris had become the social and intellectual center for scientific life in Europe."[229]

Like Herbert Spencer, at the age of seventeen Lewes jumped the tracks that led to Oxford and Cambridge. He was an avid self-learner, so he had no question that his education would continue nonstop, with or without school. And he was what one philosopher calls "a renegade" on the track of a "synthesis."[230] The seventeen-year-old Lewes worked as a notary, moved on to work for a merchant who focused on trade with Russia, then he is said to have done a medical stint—he "walked the wards."[231] Those were his day jobs. Meanwhile he was writing.

In 1834, when he was only seventeen, Lewes put together a short story and a poem and sent them out to every review and "eminent man of letters"[232] he could think of. Among these eminences was a critic, essayist, and poet who had been close to some of the greatest masters of poetry in the Western canon—Leigh Hunt. Leigh Hunt had founded an unsuccessful magazine with Lord Byron. He had been a close friend of Percy Bysshe Shelley. And he had introduced Shelley to Keats. On the more practical side, Leigh Hunt had been editing magazines for roughly twenty years—since 1808. And you've probably read Leigh Hunt's poem "Abou Ben Adhem": "Abou Ben Adhem (may his tribe increase!) / Awoke one night from a deep dream of peace."

George Henry Lewes was about to enter a realm with enough intellectual luminaries to burst the walls of a railroad carriage. He was about to enter a social group in which the arts, the sciences, and philosophy—three of the great fiefdoms of metaphor—propelled each other to greater heights. He was also about to meet Herbert Spencer and Mary Ann Evans. And above all he was about to provide a tool with which to confront the problem of how a cosmos without a god creates.

***

It was a hot period for magazines. Leigh Hunt edited the *Monthly Repository*, and when George Henry Lewes was twenty, Hunt published Lewes's contributions. So at a mere twenty years old, Lewes was now a published writer. And with apparent help from Hunt, he lectured on one of his obsessions, philosophy, at a Unitarian chapel, a trendy "free thinking"[233] chapel. Yes, without a university diploma, Lewes gave his take on philosophy in the beating heart of England's intellectual life, the Finsbury district of London.

Then came a book from an unknown twenty-five-year-old author named Charles Dickens. That book was called *The Pickwick Papers*, Dickens's first full-length published work of fiction. Lewes landed the assignment of reviewing *Pickwick* in the *National Magazine and Monthly Critic*.[234] New authors fall in love with those who pay serious attention to their work. So Lewes and Dickens became friends.

Another of the friends Lewes made in London was a neighbor of Leigh Hunt's,[235] the brilliant social commentator Thomas Carlyle, the man who first called economics "the dismal science" and the thinker responsible for the "great man"[236] interpretation of history—the approach to history that says that extraordinary individuals drive the historical process. Or, as Carlyle put it in his *On Heroes and Hero Worship*, "the Great Man was always as lightning out of Heaven; the rest of men waited for him like fuel, and then they too would flame."[237] What, according to Carlyle, allowed one human in a million to ignite fire in the soul of others? A secret weapon: "A great man is ever . . . possessed with an idea."[238] And an idea is a recruitment strategy.

Lewes was not an airhead. He was in deadly earnest about two things: philosophy—the field he'd lectured on—and the rapidly developing field of physiology. But the philosophy of the day was really psychology. Philosophy was an attempt to see what makes minds tick. Especially Scottish philosophy. The two major Scottish philosophers—David Hume and the founder of economics, Adam Smith—had probed the human psyche. Now it seemed as if physiology would provide a missing link, helping to understand that psyche with hard science. That was the project Lewes wanted to undertake: the unification of Scottish philosophy—psychology—with physiology.[239] Then he got distracted. Goethe was another of Lewes's obsessions. Johann Wolfgang von Goethe was more than just "the supreme genius of German literature"[240] and the author of works like *Faust*. Goethe was a towering figure who had loomed over Lewes's years of youth and had died in 1832 when Lewes was a mere fifteen. And Goethe was a philosopher who had dabbled in science. A poet who had dabbled in something very specific: the mystery of form.

Goethe had written an entire book on the way that form changes, the way it progresses. His *Metamorphosis of Plants* had revealed that though plants look very different, they are all variations on the same theme and they all share the same organs. How very much like the embryo observations of Karl Ernst von Baer! Goethe's view, later called "homology," would prove crucial to a theory being upgraded at that very moment in an apartment on Great Marlborough Street in London[241] by the grandson of one of the very first evolutionists, the grandson of the man who had founded the two organizations that had shaped the intellectual milieu of Herbert Spencer's youth—the Lunar Society and the Derby Philosophical Society. The man laboring on Great Marlborough Street over a concept he wouldn't publish for another twenty-two years was the twenty-eight-year-old Charles Darwin.[242] And Charles Darwin had just started a notebook on something he called the "transmutation of species."[243]

But back to the twenty-year-old George Henry Lewes. Lewes was so intense about Goethe that he would someday write a Goethe biography. And it would become his best-known book. But that was in the future. Meanwhile, a leading Goethe biographer in Berlin, the diplomat and intellectual salon leader Karl August Varnhagen von Ense, was a pen pal of Carlyle's. And Carlyle offered to introduce Lewes to von Ense. Lewes jumped at the chance. So in 1837 Lewes took off for Berlin. He was probably pursuing what he called "the spirit of Faust." The spirit of Goethe's *Faust*. Here's how Lewes expressed that spirit: Some of us, he said, refuse to think about the future and work only for today's pleasures. We work for ourselves, not for others. And that damns us. Only those who set aside immediate gratification and work on behalf of our fellow humans are blessed. Wrote Lewes many years later, "The solution of the Faust problem is embodied in his dying speech: the toiling soul, after trying in various directions of individual effort and individual gratification, and finding therein no peace, is finally conducted to the recognition of the vital truth that man lives for man, and that only in as far as he is working for humanity, can his efforts bring permanent happiness."[244] Shades of group selection. Goethe's idea that all men and women must work on behalf of all mankind was one essential thread of political liberalism and political radicalism. And it galvanized Lewes.

However, it's unlikely that Lewes got the sort of enthusiastic response he would have liked when he reached Germany and met Varnhagen. Here's one report on what Varnhagen thought of this twenty-year-old with the professional writing credentials and a bit of philosophy on his resume: "In his diary, Varnhagen made a note of Lewes's 'harsh and often rash judgements,' and, while acknowledging the man's extraordinary versatility, courage and determination, he also insisted, unfairly, on a lack of perseverance in Lewes which prevented him from excelling at anything."[245] In this verdict, Varnhagen would prove to be both right and wrong. None of Lewes's books would stand the test of time. But one of Lewes's words would. That word? Emergence.

BULGING FORTH FROM NOTHING: THE EMERGENCE OF "EMERGENCE"

The concept of emergence began with another celebrity of the mind to whom Thomas Carlyle introduced George Henry Lewes: John Stuart Mill. John Stuart Mill was twenty-nine years old and Lewes was only eighteen when the two met for the first time at Carlyle's house at number 5 Great Cheyne Row in the Chelsea section of London. The month was March of 1835, and it was a dramatic introduction. Lewes told a friend that he "found Mill on the sofa in paroxysms of weeping and sobbing, while Carlyle was trying to comfort him."[246] Why? Carlyle had loaned John Stuart Mill his manuscript of the first volume of his book *The French Revolution*. He couldn't resist. Mill was a huge French Revolution fan. When Mill was a teenager the French Revolution had become his passion. It represented "all my juvenile aspirations."[247] It showed "the principles of democracy" bearing "all before them" like a "champion." Alas, these were the days of open flames: fireplaces, candles, and the occasional oil lamp. Somehow Carlyle's manuscript had gone up in smoke while it was under Mill's care. Burned to a crisp. Pile of ashed. Some suspected the hand of a human—Mill's servant. But one way or the other, the entire body of work had gone kapoof on Mill's watch. And Mill was overwhelmed by remorse.

Despite the trauma, John Stuart Mill took George Henry Lewes on as a protégé. It seems to have been an afternoon of remarkably good cheer all around. Carlyle took the loss of his manuscript with something he apparently didn't display often—good humor. And he managed to reconstruct the missing work. Apparently the extra effort didn't sap *The French Revolution*'s punch. It became the book that made Carlyle's reputation.

But back to the twenty-nine-year-old John Stuart Mill and the eighteen-year-old George Henry Lewes. The age difference explains why Mill, in his letters to another intellectual star of the day, Auguste Comte, in Paris, refers to Lewes over and over again as "my young friend."[248] Mill at the time was utterly obsessed with Comte. So he arranged for Lewes to go to Paris,[249] "the social and intellectual center for scientific life in Europe,"[250] to meet the great man. Why? Because, as Lewes put it, in Auguste Comte "history has had its Newton."[251] Physics had its great man, a man who had put all problems in a brand new light, a man who had fitted all the odds and ends of physics into a new big picture, a big picture that worked—Isaac Newton. And in the opinion of Mill and Lewes, not to mention of Mary Ann Evans,[252] the human sciences had Comte. As Lewes wrote in 1844, Comte had put forth "the fundamental law of human evolution." Yes, that magic word, "evolution." And Comte's "law of evolution . . . is of the same importance to the science of history, as the law of universal attraction was to the science of astronomy."[253] What's more, Comte's "law of evolution" came a full fifteen years before Charles Darwin's *Origin of the Species*.

What was Comte's "Law of Evolution"?[254] Comte had invented something he called "sociology." It had been traditional to regard human societies as perpetually decaying. Crumbling. Falling apart. Ever since man had littered the perfect garden, Eden, with original sin. Comte pointed to Rousseau as one of the primary purveyors of this gloomy doctrine.[255] But Comte had invented a vision of history as a series of steps in the opposite direction from decay, in the opposite direction from entropy. Comte had reperceived history as a series of self-generated steps up. Self-generated steps of "transformation" built, he said, by "invariable natural laws."[256] Self-assembled on a "gradual series of former transformations." Transformations understandable "by simply extending to social phenomena the spirit which governs the treatment of all other natural phenomena."[257] Understandable by simply applying the scientific spirit.

What's more, said Comte, societies are "social organisms . . . analogous to . . . the animal organism with the one difference that in sociology they are more complex."[258] Societies advance in "three stages of progress,"[259] Comte said. Those stages are the "Theological," the "Metaphysical," and the "Positive."[260] Roughly speaking, that's the religious, the philosophical, and the scientific. Societies "evolve" through these stages like "organisms."[261] Or, as Lewes saw it, like embryos. "As in Embryology," Lewes would write about Comte's view of societies, "we record . . . stages of evolution . . . the passage from the simple to the complex—the Inorganic to the Organic."[262] That "passage from the simple to the complex" exists in all living things. And it exists in human societies. To put the cherry on the cake, Comte would lay special stress on a word he'd use one hundred times in just one book, in his *Positive Philosophy*: "progress."

In an 1853 book on Comte's ideas—*Comte's Philosophy of the Sciences*—Lewes would use another key word to describe Comte's concept of social progress. In fact, Lewes would use that word forty-one times. Six years before Darwin's *Origin of Species*. The magic word? You guessed it: evolution.

George Henry Lewes had met John Stuart Mill in 1835, thirteen years before Herbert Spencer got his job at the *Economist*. So how does Herbert Spencer enter Lewes's life? Good question. As you'll recall, Herbert Spencer has date after date with Mary Ann Evans. He takes every opportunity he can get to be with her. But he is not interested in romance. And she is. Meanwhile, George Henry Lewes has shown up at a dinner party, a soiree, at book publisher John Chapman's establishment at 142 on the Strand in 1850. And Herbert Spencer is captivated by Lewes. Not sexually. Intellectually. At the end of the evening, Herbert Spencer and Lewes walk out of Chapman's establishment together. And they talk. And talk and talk and talk.

As you know, Spencer finds that his mind works best when he is walking and talking. So he and Lewes go on walking trips. Long ones. Two-day trips. Four-day trips. Trips deep into the countryside. Local trips. And trips to spots they have to reach by the newfangled railroad train. Like their two-day expedition to Westminster Park in Chester.[263] Or the "ramble" in Kent in which "Gravesend, Maidstone, and Cobham" are, recalls Spencer, "among the places on our route." And these trips produce ideas. On the Kent trip, for example, Lewes brings "with him a volume by Milne-Edwards," a French author of books on zoology, botany, medicine, and geology.[264] Explains Spencer, "In it for the first time I met with the expression—'the physiological division of labour.'" That concept—the physiological division of labor—will play a central role in what Spencer calls his future "course of thought."[265]

But walking with Spencer is not Lewes's contribution to the God Problem. And it is not his contribution to understanding the mystery of big pictures. It is not his contribution to understanding patterns like those spotted by Driesch, patterns that seem to emerge from nowhere and that seem to have an itch for organization all their own. Patterns like the quark, the atom, the nebula, the star, the cell, and the human being. Not to mention the empire, the nation-state, the democracy, and the railroad train. Instead, Lewes and John Stuart Mill have noticed something peculiar in chemistry. What is it?

***

Hydrogen is an element that keeps showing up in this book. That's in part because it is the most abundant element in the cosmos. It's in part because it is one of the three oldest atoms in the cosmos. And it's in part because you and I are descended from hydrogen atoms. You and I have hydrogen in our family tree. We have hydrogen in every cell and nearly every molecule of our body. But hydrogen is a hot new item in 1835 when Lewes starts brainstorming with John Stuart Mill.[266]

How does hydrogen enter the brainstorming sessions of London in the mid-nineteenth century? How does it become a subject of "evening party"[267] conversation at 142 Strand? In 1671, roughly one hundred and forty years before Lewes is born, Robert Boyle finds that if you drop iron filings into an acid solution you get a gas. In 1766, Henry Cavendish discovers that this gas has unique properties. Among other things, it catches fire easily. So Cavendish names the new gas "phlogiston," Greek for easily set on fire.[268] And in 1781, Cavendish also discovers that if you burn phlogiston—hydrogen—you get something totally unlikely. You don't get just a gas. You get a liquid. You get water. Ordinary water. A gas and a bit of fire produce a liquid? How the heck?

In 1783, Antoine Lavoisier in Paris takes things a step further.[269] He does the Cavendish experiment once again and he, too, gets a liquid from, of all things, a flame combined with a gas. He, too, gets water. But Lavoisier is changing the names of the elements. He's using a name change the way that Aristotle did, to jolt "the scientific community by attacking their certitudes about Earth and fire."[270] Lavoisier has noticed that if you put two grams of iron into two grams of acid, you get more than just a radical transformation of a solid into a gas. You get more than just a radical translation from one medium to another. You get two plus two equals four. You get four grams of stuff. Lavoisier has noticed the conservation of matter.[271] And with that observation, he is driving the old phlogiston theory out of chemistry. So he gives phlogiston a new name—"hydrogen," Greek for stuff that produces water.[272] Why? Because the name phlogiston is associated with the old theory of flame that Lavoisier is working to replace. And because Lavoisier is jockeying for position on the stage of attention. He is jockeying to turn his ideas into a recruitment strategy.

Meanwhile, in 1774, in a tiny Wiltshire town known for its natural beauty, Caine, a clergyman named Joseph Priestley, a future member of Erasmus Darwin's Lunar Society, has put mercury into a tube, scorched it with sunlight focused with a lens, and has produced something that mere heat plus mercury should not be able to generate, a gas. Yes, another gas. From a solid. Very strange. Very strange indeed. What's more, Priestley has put a lit candle into the gas and has seen the candle's flame flare dramatically. He's put two mice into the gas and has noticed that the enthused rodents not only jounce around hyperactively, but also outlive the normal mouse lifespan. Then he's tried breathing some of this gas extracted from mercury via heat. And he's liked it. "I fancied that my breast felt peculiarly light and easy for some time afterwards,"[273] he's said with enthusiasm. In fact, the sensation is so terrific that he's speculated breathing it could become a high-priced fad, "a fashionable article in luxury."[274] And he's called this wonder gas "dephlogisticated air"[275]—air without phlogiston.

At the same time, Antoine Lavoisier in Paris is discovering the same new gas, the new gas that made Priestley's chest feel light and that hyperactivated two mice. And since Lavoisier is banishing phlogiston theory, he gives "dephlogisticated air" another name: oxygen.

The names hydrogen and oxygen tell a tale. "Hydrogen" means "water maker." "Hydro" is water and "gen" is maker. And "oxygen" means "acid maker." Lavoisier does not see these two gases as what they seem to you and me. He does not see them as just gases, just airlike things that will always remain airlike. He does not see them as inert and unchanging. He sees them as transformers. He sees them as makers and remakers of other things. He sees them as translators. Yes, translators. And one of the things these two gases make is water. An explosion. And water.

Let's look at this through the eyes of logic. Aristotle's logic. $A = A$, right? And one plus one equals two. Correct? Take hydrogen. It's clear. You can see through it as if it weren't there. You can wave your hand through it and not know the difference. You can fill a balloon with it and watch something strange. That balloon will defy gravity. It will soar to the skies. And you can inhale it, then you can try to talk. Your friends will think you are hilarious. Why? You will sound like Alvin the Chipmunk. Then there's oxygen. It, too, is a gas. Yes, it has some unique properties. Breathe it and, like Joseph Priestley, you will feel remarkably peppy. Put a mouse under a bell jar filled with nothing but hydrogen and it will die. Put another mouse under a bell jar filled with nothing but oxygen, and, as Priestley discovered, it will live. What's more, it will go hyper. But, still, oxygen is just a gas. You can see through it so well that your eyes can't even tell it's there.

Add a gas to a gas and what should you get? More gas, right? After all, one plus one equals two. Gas in, gas out. $A = A$. A gas is a gas is a gas. Ignore the fact that "A is A," says Ayn Rand, and you become the source of "all the secret evil you dread to face."[276]

Let's go back to one plus one equals two. In Newton's science, things are additive. Point a cannon in the direction of the Earth's rotation—east. Fire the cannon. You are brilliant. You've just added an extra 590 miles per hour to the speed of a cannonball that, thanks to the Earth's rotation, is already traveling around the Earth's axis at 1,037.5646 miles per hour. What do you get with your gunpowder's extra boost? A speed of 1,627.5646 miles per hour. Speed in, speed out. Put four pounds of potatoes and three pounds of tomatoes—masses of two different kinds—in a bag, weigh them, and you get seven pounds. But still, seven pounds of nothing but potatoes and tomatoes. Vegetables in, vegetables out.

In Newton's world, things follow the laws of math. The laws of logic. The laws of Aristotle. The laws of one plus one equals two.

But in 1835, when John Stuart Mill and George Henry Lewes first meet, it is known that two gases—hydrogen and oxygen—refuse to follow Newton's laws. And they refuse to follow the rules of Aristotle's logic. Input does not equal output. Two gases in do not equal two gases out. In fact, the two gases equal something radically new. They equal a semisolid. A semisolid with strange qualities. Flabbergasting properties. Unlike its two parent gases, this new something is visible. Unlike its two parent gases, this new stuff does not allow light to pass through it unimpeded. It wiggles, wobbles, and refracts light. Unlike a gas, you can touch it. You can feel it. And unlike a respectable Newtonian solid, a mass, it refuses to just sit there and behave itself. It flows. It seeps into things. It balls up in droplets. It congregates in clouds. It thunders down in storms. It even has the audacity to make the regular patterns of waves. And it has the nerve to make seas and tsunamis. Like the tidal wave Charles Darwin saw unfold before his eyes from the Chilean city of Valdivia at 11:00 a.m. on February 20, 1835, during his voyage on the *Beagle*.

A great wave was seen from the distance of three or four miles, approaching in the middle of the bay with a smooth outline; but along the shore it tore up cottages and trees, as it swept onwards with irresistible force. At the head of the bay it broke in a fearful line of white breakers, which rushed up to a height of 23 vertical feet above the highest springtides. Their force must have been prodigious, for at the Fort a cannon with its carriage, estimated at four tons in weight, was moved 15 feet inwards. A schooner was left in the midst of the ruins, 200 yards from the beach.[277]

Two weeks later, the *Beagle* reached the 285-year-old Chilean city of Concepción and saw what mere water can accomplish. The city was totaled.

> I have not attempted to give any detailed description of the appearance of [the city of] Concepción, for I feel that it is quite impossible to convey the mingled feelings which I experienced. . . . It is a bitter and humiliating thing to see works, which have cost man so much time and labour, overthrown in one minute.[278]

The inhabitants, said Darwin, had enough warning to escape to the hills. But their city was almost erased from the face of the earth. The culprit? Liquid. Water. When it comes to obeying Aristotle, this new stuff has no respect.

Two clear gases refuse to add up. Instead they make a thing with new laws and new forms all its own. Something downright startling. And if John Stuart Mill and George Henry Lewes had been at our café table at the beginning of the universe, they'd have seen just how ridiculous the idea that hydrogen and oxygen can make water really is. They'd have been with you and me at 380,000 ABB (after the big bang) when hydrogen atoms first formed. They'd have hung around with us for another billion years or two. Another billion or two long and extraordinary years. They'd have watched as stars gathered and flared. They'd have seen those stars die and crunch together. And from the star death they'd have seen the very first oxygen atoms mashed together in the dying stars' hearts. They'd have seen that hydrogen was born a mere 380,000 years after the big bang. And they'd have seen that oxygen didn't come on the scene until roughly two billion years later, two billion years crowded with shock and surprise, two billion years in which massive stars gathered space fluff, ignited, burned their candles at both ends, and died. Mill and Lewes would have seen how radically different the birth of hydrogen and oxygen were. And how very far apart in time.

How likely is it that something formed at 380,000 ABB (after the big bang) from a plasma—hydrogen—and something formed at two billion ABB—oxygen—something formed from the agonies of star death, could ever get together? How likely is it that the two could pull off a joint project? If this is a cosmos of six monkeys at six typewriters, how likely is it that the joint product of these two substances would be something this cosmos had never seen before—a liquid? And a liquid with remarkable properties. Unheard of properties. Impossible properties. Water.

Let me repeat this for emphasis: If they make anything at all, hydrogen, oxygen, and flame should make, at most, two hot gases. Gases heated by the flame. But hydrogen gas, oxygen gas, and the merest spark make a huge explosion.[279] And they make water. They make a liquid. That's as radical as the politics discussed at John Chapman's soirees at 142 on the Strand. That's as revolutionary as anything Chapman's European hotheads ever tried to pull off.

In 1843, John Stuart Mill thought that this ability of two things to make more than one plus one equals two was sufficiently peculiar that it deserved a name. The name he gave it? "Heteropathic"[280] causation. A very different kind of causation from hitting one billiard ball with another and predicting where it will go. A very different kind of causation than shooting a cannonball into a parabolic arc and predicting that arc's end point. And a very different kind of causation than the causation that explains how an arc like that of a cannonball keeps a planet circling a sun. But scientists never took "heteropathic causation" seriously. And the name did not stick.

Then Lewes took up the same problem. How do two gases, hydrogen and oxygen, come together and "make" something radically unexpected, something radically new? A supersized surprise? How does an entirely new form of "relation" pop into existence? A new translation? A new defiance of the equal sign? Lewes did not know. But in 1874[281] he came up with two words, one of which flew like a seagull on a riser of air and the other of which died like a sick puppy. He called the pairing of hydrogen and oxygen a "copula"—as in copulation. Despite its pornographic possibilities—or perhaps because of them—that term did not stick. After all, this was the age of Queen Victoria—the sexually panicky Victorian Age.

But George Henry Lewes also called the water that comes from putting hydrogen gas with oxygen gas an "emergent liquid."[282] He wrote, "I propose to call the effect an emergent. It arises out of the combined agencies, but in a form which does not display the agents in action." "The emergent," Lewes explained, "is unlike its components . . . and it cannot be reduced either to their sum or their difference."[283] And the term "emergent" took off. It had legs. It was an effective component of a recruitment strategy.

What's more, Lewes put the problem that emergence poses to science very, very bluntly. "Some day, perhaps," he wrote, "we shall be able to express the unseen process in a mathematical formula; till then we must regard the water as an emergent."[284] In other words, Lewes said that emergence is a challenge to the science that relies on mathematics. It is a challenge to the science of geometry and equations. It is a challenge to the math that men like Bertrand Russell twenty-six years later would feel is logic in disguise. It is a challenge to logic itself. And Lewes was well aware of that challenge. Says Lewes, "Were all effects simple resultants, in the sense here specified, our deductive power would be almost absolute; a mathematical expression would include all phenomena. It is precisely because effects are mostly emergents that Deduction is insecure."[285] Lewes meant that try, try, try as hard as you can, there is no way that current mathematics and current logic can predict the liquid that arises from two gases. No way that math or logic can predict the wiggly, wobbly, splish-splash of a liquid. That limitation of math and of logic was true of Lewes's day. And it is equally true of ours.

What's more, it is a challenge that modern science must face. A challenge that we would begin to face in the late-twentieth century. How? By stepping outside the bounds of math and logic.

Meanwhile, a tremendous number of the phenomenon in the world around us are emergent properties. In fact, since Lewes's day, the number of emergent properties we've discovered is staggering. The big bang is an emergent property. Pressure waves in the plasma at the start of the universe are emergent properties. Quarks, atoms, galaxies, and stars are emergent properties. Leonardo da Vinci and Thomas Young's interference patterns are emergent properties. So are Leonardo and Thomas Young. And so are Isaac Newton's machines. Puzzles, questions, answers, and perceptions are emergent properties. Your atheism at the age of thirteen is an emergent property. The gods inside of us, the gods that you have been hunting since you were thirteen, are emergent properties. And nearly all of the phenomena we can see from our café table at the beginning of the universe, nearly all of the cosmos's supersized surprises, are emergent properties. Says Lewes, "Strictly speaking, the real effect is always an emergent."[286] Right on up to the formation of DNA, cells, life, intelligence, and your next troubled or exuberant thought. Not to mention mine. But few of these were things Lewes knew about.

Nonetheless there were emergent properties galore in George Henry Lewes's nineteenth-century sights. Look, Lewes says, "Who, before experiment, could discern nitric acid in nitrogen and oxygen?"[287] Who could predict that if you add two gases—nitrogen and oxygen—you'd get a vicious liquid, nitric acid? What's more, said Lewes, you can plunge your gold wedding ring into hydrochloric acid and the gold will be unfazed. You can drop your ring into nitric acid, and still, no problem. But mix the two liquids—hydrochloric acid and nitric acid—drop in your wedding ring, and kiss your ring good-bye. Says Lewes, "Who could foresee that gold would be changed into a chloride if plunged into a mixture of two liquids (hydrochloric and nitric acid), in either of which separately it would remain unchanged?"[288]

All of these transformations were what Lewes called emergents. All of them were translations from one medium to another. All of them were what today we call "emergent properties." And the mystery they posed is as baffling now as it was back then. Or nearly as baffling. Thanks to simple rules and axioms, a tentative route to a solution would someday appear. A very tentative route. But that would not happen for another hundred years.

CHARLIE DARWIN SHOWS UP LATE

> *Fragmentary the British mind might be, but in those days it was doing a great deal of work in a very un-English way, building up so many and such vast theories on such narrow foundations as to shock the conservative, and delight the frivolous. The atomic theory; the correlation and conservation of energy; the mechanical theory of the universe; the kinetic theory of gases, and Darwin's Law of Natural Selection.*
>
> —Henry Adams, 1907[289]

In 1839, Charles Darwin, Erasmus Darwin's grandson, publishes his first book, *The Voyage of the* Beagle. But it doesn't seem to say anything new about the gnawing puzzles of the day. The spotlight of attention of the age is about to focus on something that seems to have nothing to do with Darwin's travelogue. Nothing whatsoever. Something called "evolution."

Yes, John Stuart Mill and George Henry Lewes are about to go gaga over a "law of evolution."[290] But it is the "law of evolution" of a Frenchman, Auguste Comte. And in the early 1850s, the folks who dine together at John Chapman's table and who come to Chapman's soirees will hunger for some kind of evolutionary explanation for nearly everything around them. Including an evolutionary explanation for "emergents." That hunger will show itself in 1852 when Herbert Spencer publishes an article in the *Leader* challenging "those who cavalierly reject The Theory of Evolution."[291] It will push to the surface again in 1853 when one of Chapman's authors, Harriet Martineau, translates *The Positive Philosophy of Auguste Comte*[292] and in the second volume alone uses the word "evolution" eighty-eight times.[293] And it will shoulder its way into the conversation again in 1853 when the Scottish chemist and physician Samuel Brown writes an article titled "The Atomic Theory" for Marian Evans and John Chapman's *Westminster Review* and says that the "laws of evolution"[294] prevail in nature and in science. What's going on here? The recruitment strategy of a big picture aching to be is showing itself like the back of a dolphin showing above the surface of a calm sea. An emergent property, an implicit order, is trying to push its way from possibility space into the realm of reality.

But here's the surprise. The word "evolution" does not appear anywhere in Charlie Darwin's *Voyage of the* Beagle. Yet it will appear forty-one times in George Henry Lewes's 1853 book summarizing Auguste Comte, *Comte's Philosophy of the Sciences: Being an Exposition of the Principles of the* Cours de Philosophie Positive *of Auguste Comte*.[295] And when Lewes's book on Comte emerges, it will be another six years before Darwin will publish his *Origin of Species*. It will be another six years before Darwin will benefit from the abilities of Lewes's friend Thomas Henry Huxley to promote a theory of evolution. But as far back as 1844, Lewes has written with longing that "the urgent want of the age is . . . a general doctrine. The general laws of the evolution of society have to be discovered and organized."[296] In other words, evolution is not Charles Darwin's invention. It is a hungry form. It is a new big picture that has gained in power ever since Erasmus Darwin's books in 1794. It is a theory aching to be. It is an emergent property about to pop. It is a recruitment strategy.

Meanwhile Charles Darwin, who has grown sick in 1836[297] and has moved twelve miles from London to a three-story house in the countryside called Down House, is going beyond Comte's evolution of societies. He is covering evolution from the beginning of life[296] to the present. When Darwin finally publishes *The Origin of Species* in 1859, he will at last offer what the evolutionists have starved and lusted for for over twenty years. He will give a clue to emergents in action. He will give a clue to form production. He will lay out not just the "general doctrine" of evolution that Lewes and his tablemates ache for, but he will produce a "mechanism." He will produce the indispensable something that Newton imitators have made essential to science for one hundred and fifty years. Charles Darwin will produce the equivalent to the innards of Newton's windmills. The equivalent to Newton's pulleys and levers. That mechanism will be natural selection. But will natural selection be enough?

Darwin will say that nature acts like a breeder of sheep,[299] pigeons,[300] or strawberries.[301] She gives her prize winners the privilege of sex and reproduction. But she sidelines the lame and the halt. She turns the malformed and the crippled into sexual rejects. So the gorgeous will get to have kids. And the inglorious or the just plain homely will not get that privilege. Nor will those in the wild who just don't get it. Those who can't find a way to make a living in the woods, the meadows, and the mountain slopes won't get the girls. Wild sheep and red grouse who can't find enough food will not get sex. Ever. This will not be "social Darwinism." It will be the real thing. It will be Darwin's mechanism.

Natural selection, nature's pickiness, nature's way of playing favorites, her way of putting her creatures through a game that gives procreational privileges to the winners, that will be Charles Darwin's contribution to a theory that has been around since the days of his grandfather sixty-four years earlier. And the concept of nature's pickiness will give people like

George Henry Lewes, George Eliot, and Herbert Spencer what they are aching for—a secular creation myth.[302] A new story of Genesis. A new big picture. A new secular alternative to religion. In fact, the hunger for a secular substitute for religion is so strong that in 1859, George Henry Lewes and Mary Ann Evans will be among the founders of the "Church of Humanity in Lamb's Conduit Street,"[303] a positivist "church," a secular church in London based on August Comte's ideas.[304] A church with a religion based on Comte's "evolutionary" concepts. Comte's ideas of progress. But Darwin will soon give thinkers like the folks at Chapman's soirees yet another secular story of the origin of life, one that can replace the church and the Bible. Darwin will give these thinkers a worldview with which they can complete their rebellion, their differentiation from mainstream society. Their struggle for a unique place in attention space.

But there will be a big problem with Charles Darwin's theories. And Darwin will know it better than anyone. Nature's pickiness will explain only a part of evolution. It will not explain nature's creativity. It will not explain nature's ability to fashion amazements. It will not explain emergent properties. It will not explain the supersized surprise. Natural selection will not explain the mystery of form production. And Darwin will be very aware of that fact. He will call the appearance of new forms "variation." And he will set the core problem of variation aside. "We are profoundly ignorant," he will say, "of the cause of" even "slight variation."[305] And he will acknowledge that "ignorance" about variation over and over again.[306] But guess what? The puzzle of variation and the problem of emergence are one and the same. And variation and emergence may be one and the same with yet another twin, the implicit properties yanked from axioms. But this will not become clear for another hundred years.

***

Meanwhile, what, pray tell, happens to the beguiling and wonderfully brainy Mary Ann Evans? You and I remember that "Miss Evans" has fallen in love with Herbert Spencer. And much as Spencer is enchanted by her, he is not in love. The masculinity of her mind, he says, gives a certain masculinity to her features. Despite what he calls "the pleasure of her companionship"[307] and the fact that "striking by its power when in repose, her face was remarkably transfigured by a smile,"[308] Spencer is married to his grand synthesis. He is married to his big picture. He is married to pulling all of the sciences and the philosophies together into a single panorama. He is not on the prowl for a woman. He will, in fact, remain a bachelor for the rest of his life.[309] So in 1852 Herbert Spencer introduces Miss Evans to George Henry Lewes.[310] John Chapman, the publisher on the other side of the street from the offices of the *Economist,* the publisher at 142 on the Strand, also does his best to throw Lewes and Miss Evans together. In fact, putting them together is easy. They are both regular guests at John Chapman's soirees. And the relationship takes.

Lewes is ugly as sin. Thomas Carlyle's wife calls him "the ape."[311] But he is a liberated man. An unconventional man. A man who is married, but who has an "open" relationship with his wife.[312] In fact, his wife has had children by other men during the course of the marriage. So Lewes is a man whose marriage gives him the freedom for other liaisons. And he is a man who became deeply unhappy with his marriage almost the moment it began. But he is not into hidden liaisons like those that conventional aristocrats have with their mistresses. He is into open liaisons. Public liaisons. Scandal-making liaisons. Liaisons that make a statement. Liaisons based on love, not law. And Lewes's liaison with Mary Ann Evans will last the rest of his life. As Mary Ann Evans rises to fame, that liaison will become one of the most celebrated scandals— and statements of freedom—of the nineteenth century. What's more, it will appear to be monogamous.[313]

Oh, there's one more thing. Mary Ann Evans will take Herbert Spencer's advice. She will try writing fiction. And she will churn out seven novels, novels riddled with philosophy and shot through with a brand-new thing called psychology, a field Herbert Spencer will name and pioneer. Miss Evans, in fact, will become a celebrity, will grow wealthy, and will become immortal. She and Lewes will make extra scandal by traveling Europe together and by buying a to-die-for summer home—the Heights at Witley—with the profits from her writing.[314] Mary Ann Evans's books will include: *Adam Bede, The Mill on the Floss, Silas Marner,* and *Middlemarch.*

Female authors in these nineteenth-century days, are reputed to write fluff. So to crack into the world of serious novels, novels shot through with serious thought, Mary Ann will write under an assumed name. Her nom de plume? George Eliot.

And guess what? George Eliot's success, too, will be an emergent property.

THE ZYGOTE SNABS HERBERT SPENCER

Meanwhile, in 1851, when he is thirty-one years old and walking, talking, and singing with Miss Evans, Herbert Spencer runs across an idea that will make him one of the biggest big-picture thinkers of all time. It is the idea that will keep Spencer a bachelor married to only one thing, his grand "synthesis." Herbert Spencer will come across von Baer's principle that cells in an embryo start out looking pretty much alike, then get more and more unique to their species. And more and more specialized in their function. Von Baer's principle will change Spencer's thinking. It will become the key to Spencer's grand unification. And to his view of evolution. It will become Herbert Spencer's equivalent to Newton's gravity.

Yes, differentiation and the metaphor of the embryo will enter Herbert Spencer's thinking three years after he comes to the *Economist* and one year after he begins to frequent John Chapman's soirees. Says Spencer, "In 1851, I became acquainted with von Baer's statement that the development of every organism is a change from homogeneity to heterogeneity."[315] And that acquaintance will push Spencer to till the soil in which Charles Darwin will plant a seed.

Once Herbert Spencer is exposed to von Baer's work, the embryologist's influence will show up almost instantly in Spencer's work. It is the grand unifying principle that Spencer has been hunting for. It is another unifying principle to add to what Spencer has taken from George Henry Lewes's explanations of Comte—the principle of evolution, and the principle that evolution constantly churns out something that Spencer calls "progress."[316] So von Baer's principle of differentiation becomes central to Spencer's 1851 first book, *Social Statistics*. The bigger and the more advanced the society, *Social*

Statistics says, the more differentiation, the more specialization. The more "'distinct classes' and 'special occupations.'"[317] Large-scale societies unfold like embryos. They evolve like zygotes in the womb. Spencer publishes *Social Statistics* eight years before the publication of the book in which Charles Darwin premiers his theory of evolution, the *Origin of Species*. But Spencer, like the other habitués of Chapman's get togethers, is already an evolutionary thinker, and he portrays the differentiation of human societies as an evolutionary process. Again, the word evolution has not appeared even once in Darwin's only published book, his *Voyage of the* Beagle. But it appears one hundred times in Spencer's second book, his 1855 *Principles of Psychology*.[318] A book that comes out four years before Darwin's *On the Origin of Species*.

Here's how the combination of evolution and von Baer's differentiation works. Says Spencer, in early societies, everyone did everything—hunting, fishing, and tool and weapon making. But as societies evolved, some men specialized in hunting and fishing and others became full-time tool or weapons makers—full-time spear and fishing hook experts. Way, way down the line, really advanced societies invented machines like railroad engines with hundreds of parts. So in an advanced society, there might be a specialist in Swindon who zeroed in on nothing but hand-making the setscrews for the steam engine, a task so exacting that one real-life machinist of Spencer's day said "it almost made me sick."[319] Meanwhile other specialists assembled the engine, tested it, and ran it. And yet more specialists raised fruits, vegetables, cows, and pigs and sent them into the city via railroad to feed the setscrew specialist. At the same time, even more specialists raised cotton in the American South, carded it and combed it in Manchester, then ran the resulting thread through Manchester's weaving machines to make the setscrew maker's clothes.

The result? Says Spencer, societies are like organisms. And their advance toward higher levels of complexity is like "the development of an embryo or the unfolding of a flower."[320] Yes, societies unfold like flowers or embryos:

> Hence it happens that a tribe of savages may be divided and subdivided with little or no inconvenience to the several sections.[321]

Just as Driesch could break off a branch of a sea squirt[322] and see it become an entire, independent sea squirt, Spencer says that you can divide a primitive tribe, an indigenous tribe, and both halves will become complete tribes able to operate on their own. Why? Because

> each of these contains every element which the whole did—is just as self-sufficing, and quickly assumes the simple organization constituting an independent tribe.[323]

But you can't just arbitrarily cut in two a modern society like the one Spencer lives in, a society with cities that depend on steamships, railroads, and telegraphs that tie together global meshes of trade.

> Hence, on the contrary, it happens, that in a community like our own, no part can be cut off or injured without all parts suffering.[324]

Just as Driesch will not be able to cut the heart out of a rabbit and see that heart become a complete bunny hopping with glee, and just as the poor rabbit will not be able regrow her missing heart, a complex society cannot simply regrow its equivalent of a blood pump. Says Spencer,

> Annihilate the agency employed in distributing commodities, and much of the rest would die before another distributing agency could be developed.[325]

Cut out the supply chain of meat and vegetables to Swindon and you starve the screw maker and his family. As Spencer puts it,

> Suddenly sever the manufacturing portion from the agricultural portion, and the one would expire outright, while the other would long linger in grievous distress.[326]

But this interdependence of specialized parts is not mere theory, says Spencer. It is a blunt fact. Stub a toe and the whole body limps.

This interdependence is daily shown in commercial changes. Let the factory hands be put on short time, and immediately the colonial produce markets of London and Liverpool are depressed.[327]

A society is made up of individuals, yet it works like a massive organism, a single organism.

Thus do we find, not only that the analogy between a society and a living creature is borne out to a degree quite unsuspected by those who commonly draw it, but also that the same definition of life applies to both.[328]

The whole thing works through opposites joined at the hip. Herbert Spencer would have objected strenuously to putting it this way. He found it "impossible to conceive" the idea of opposites that are equally true. How do we know? From 1812 to 1817, Georg Hegel—a teacher at a secondary school in Nuremberg, Germany, who would later become one of his era's most influential philosophers—had written a multivolume book called *The Science of Logic*. In it, Hegel had said that "contradiction is the root of all movement and life." That's a pretty big claim. But Hegel had gone even further. He'd said that "it is only in so far as something has a contradiction within it that it moves, is possessed of instinct and activity."[329] Sounds very much like your "opposites are joined at the hip," doesn't it? Then in 1836 at the University of Kiel an obscure professor of philosophy named Heinrich Moritz Chalybäus had summed up Hegel's approach to contradiction in a series of lectures. And he'd boiled down Hegel's life-giving contradictions to a magic phrase: "thesis, antithesis, and synthesis."[330] What does that mean? When opposites struggle against each other, the appearance of battle is deceptive. Without knowing it, the opposites are working together to give birth to something new. Something larger, something occasionally novel, something occasionally surprising, something that occasionally makes one plus one far greater than two.

Here's a sample of a thesis: you claim that mind is a lonely prisoner in the darkness of the skull. I think about that for a while and though I don't admit it to myself, I have to carve out a separate spot for myself in attention space. I need to make sure you are not the only one getting the spotlight. So I have to say something that makes me unique, something in opposition to what you said. I make a counterclaim, an antithesis. I declare that the mind only exists in the interplay between human beings, in the interplay, for example, between you and me. We wrangle over who is right. Is mind trapped in the cranium, using the brain to create the illusion of an external reality? Or is mind itself external: a product of conversation, competition, collaboration, social structures, and history? We wrangle until we see a brand-new light. Both of us are correct. There is a larger weave, a shared tapestry, a shared kit of mind tools, that somehow arises from the interplay of lonely prisoners of the skull like you and me. Something called *culture* knits itself with the needles of lonely prisoners of the cranium, prisoners seeking each other's company. Mind is both internal *and* external. From our competition we gain a potential new insight into the way culture is built. We even get a glimpse into the way that mind tools may arise from the interplay of individuals seeking a bit of attention. That larger vision is a synthesis. Thesis, antithesis, and synthesis. The positive power of opposites.

In 1837, Chalybäus published the lecture in which he promoted his magic triad of creative opposites—"thesis, antithesis, and synthesis."[331] A student at the University of Berlin who belonged to his university's Hegel Club read Chalybäus's book, grabbed the three magic words of creative competition, and ran with them. Ran with them and in 1847 promoted them as the words of Hegel himself.[332] His promotion campaign was so successful that in the future, most educated men and women would swear that the words "thesis, antithesis, and synthesis" were Hegel's. They were not. The idea merchandiser who gave us this false impression was an occasional guest at John Chapman's establishment at 142 on the Strand. His name was Karl Marx.

But Hegel *had* promoted the positive power of opposites. And Herbert Spencer declared that this was a concept "against which I feel an obstinate prejudice." In fact, once Spencer got wind of Hegel's drift, he refused "to read further any work in which it is displayed."[333] He refused to read any more Hegel. But opposites joined at the hip show up all over Spencer's work. The opposites in this case are differentiation and integration. And that, in fact, was one of Spencer's great contributions: differentiation and integration.

Differentiation, Spencer said, does not occur as a random spray of wildly varied cells. It's not a six-monkeys-at-six-typewriters process. It occurs as part of a larger pattern. A part of a bigger picture. Differentiating cells make new organs—endoderm, ectoderm, mesoderm, neural crests, hearts, toes, brains, and a nose. Differentiation is joined at the hip to its opposite, to what Spencer called "integration."

> This union of many men into one community—this increasing mutual dependence of units which were originally independent—this gradual segregation of citizens into separate bodies with reciprocally-subservient functions—this formation of a whole consisting of unlike parts—this growth of an organism, of which one portion cannot be injured without the rest feeling it—may all be generalized under the law of individuation.[334]

"Individuation." That's differentiation. That's setting oneself apart. But separation is fatal. Unless it goes hand in hand with its opposite—attraction. Integration.

Or, to put it in the terms we've been using, the iteration of simple rules would mean nothing without the emergence of big pictures. Big pictures within which the smaller units fit. The brick would be nothing without the vision of the wall. The wall would be nothing without the vision of the apartment complex at Catalhöyük. Even the number that represents the brick, the barleycorn, the chicken, and the fish would be nothing without the bigger framework in which it fits—arithmetic and a bureaucracy working on behalf of a king. Cells that specialize or people who dive into a tiny wrinkle of interest and make a world of it, people like Herbert Spencer and Mary Ann Evans, commit suicide if they are not part of "a whole consisting of unlike parts." They commit suicide without what Hans Driesch would call "form production." And without something more. Without the emergence of an organismlike bauplan, an invisible blueprint, a big picture into which they fit.

And just as differentiation can be lethal without integration, integration can be dangerous without increasing levels of differentiation. Integration can be poisonous without increasing levels of individuation. Too much togetherness among cells does not produce fingers or toes. It produces a stump. Hence, the development of society, as well as the development of man and the development of life generally, may be described as a tendency to individuate—to become a thing. And rightly interpreted, the manifold forms of progress going on around us are uniformly significant of this tendency.[335]

But, again, opposites are joined at the hip. Individuation only works when it's integrated into a big picture. And integration grows amazing things when individuation gives it new powers.

Everywhere and always there goes on either integration of matter . . . or . . . disintegration of matter . . . the integration of matter . . . is the primary trait of all Evolution.[336]

Few people bother to remember Herbert Spencer. But when they do, they often slam him for his insistence on something totally antientropic—his sense of progress. Progress in the evolution of inanimate matter.[337] Progress in the evolution of simple life forms. And progress in the evolution of man. Spencer, like Driesch, felt the pull of the future beckoning. In the development of human societies and in the development of all of life, Spencer said, "progress . . . is not an accident, it is a necessity."[338] Parts—be they cells or citizens—differentiate. They specialize. But that's not all. Individuals differentiate. Then they cluster and find others who share their oddball interests. And the clusters of oddballs find allies. They find their place in a bigger picture. They form a "whole consisting of unlike parts."[339] That formation of new wholes, new big pictures, is vital to the cosmos.

Meanwhile, Herbert Spencer—as you know—went on to write books about sociology (two of them),[340] psychology, morality, education, biology, and political science. But, he says, none of those books would have existed without the concept of embryological differentiation he pulled from von Baer in 1851. Or, in Spencer's words, "had von Baer never written I should not be doing that which I now am."[341]

Was Herbert Spencer right in trying to draw all the sciences together into one big picture? Was Spencer right about progress? Was he right in his conviction that evolution's secrets lie in the pattern of the embryo?[342]

***

Meanwhile, George Henry Lewes's words "emergent," "emergence," and "emergent properties" would become major terms of discourse. In the 1920s and 1930s, an entire school of "Emergentism" would arise in Britain.[343] Then emergence would take off again in the 1980s when complex systems and self-organization would become hot topics seizing the minds of intellectual leaders at places like New Mexico's Santa Fe Institute.

But from the days of the wildly multidisciplinary George Henry Lewes to today, emergence has been derided as voodoo science. It's been called a word that doesn't belong in the scientific vocabulary. A word "without the conceptual clarity that would have helped real scientific research."[344] In other words, a word that makes no testable predictions and that generates no testable experiments. In science, emergence has often been set aside like the metaphorical systems of art and music. As late as 2011, high-profile string physicist Brian Greene would say with pride, "I believe that a physical system is completely determined by the arrangement of its particles. Tell me how the particles making up the Earth, the Sun, the galaxy, and everything else are arranged, and you've fully articulated reality." And Greene would delight in pointing out that he is not alone. "This reductionist view," he would say, "is common among physicists."[345] It's all about particles and their "arrangement." In Greene's view, the emergence of higher level properties seems irrelevant. And Greene speaks for the scientific mainstream. As a result the puzzle that emergence points to, the mystery of form generation, has often been set aside. But that is changing. It is changing because of something else that would have a profound effect on the answers to the God Problem.

THE EMBRYO GOES COSMIC

After Herbert Spencer and Hans Driesch, the metaphor of embryonic differentiation seemed to disappear from mainstream science. And in the late-twentieth century, as we've seen before, Newton's obsession with devices, gadgets, and machines, his fixation on "mechanisms," came back so strongly that when theories were proposed, it was required that they have a "mechanism." Required absolutely. If you had an idea with lots of evidence but no "mechanism" you were dead in the water. What's more, it was claimed that even something deeply organic, the operation of natural selection in the evolution of life, was a "mechanism." A very strange claim for something with no machinelike characteristics.

But the embryo and one of its most important deep structures, differentiation, was hidden at the very heart of the scientific worldview. Where? In the least likely place—the hardest of the hard sciences,[346] theoretical physics and cosmology. When Georges Lemaître, the highly influential Belgian physicist/priest, first conceived the idea of the big bang in 1932, he called the initial pinprick from which all arose the "Cosmic Egg."[347] And when George Gamow used the lessons from atom-bomb making—from nuclear physics—to take Lemaitre's big bang theory mainstream, he identified what happened after that "cosmic egg" appeared with one key word. Herbert Spencer's word. Hans Driesch's word. The word that came from an unlikely metaphor. The metaphor of the embryo. George Gamow said that in the beginning, there was "differentiation."[348]

What is the validity of applying a metaphor from biology to the pinprick at the beginning of time? What is the validity of applying the metaphor of the embryo to inanimate matter at all? The answer is in the source of metaphor's power, deep structures, Ur patterns. Patterns that repeat at level after level of emergence.

Some metaphors at a high level of emergence capture a pattern that repeats in everything from the big bang to the rise and fall of hemlines in skirts. The interference patterns of two pebbles in a pond, patterns from a highly sophisticated and startlingly recent level of emergence, show up in photons. Patterns from liquids that didn't exist in liquid form until roughly four billion[349] years ago show up in particles 13.73 billion years old. Why? In all probability because the interference patterns of two pebbles in a pond are deep structures. Primal patterns. Patterns this cosmos iterates. Patterns this cosmos repeats. Patterns this cosmos stutters forth in new contexts, new mediums, new forms of matter. Patterns with which this cosmos carves new properties, new processes, new surprises, new things.

Not all patterns are Ur patterns. Not by a long shot. But Georges Lemaître and George Gamow were certain that differentiation appeared in the first flick of this universe.[350]

And that's not the end of it. Herbert Spencer and Hans Driesch's differentiation shows up from the bottom of this cosmos to its top, from the most primitive level to the most complex. Differentiation shows up in the basic patterns that keep one atom separate from another and that keep all the matter in the cosmos from clumping together in one giant undifferentiated ball. Differentiation shows up in the repulsive forces of cosmic inflation, electromagnetism, and even dark energy. Differentiation shows up in patterns of evolution, physics, biology, psychology, and history. Differentiation even shows up in Frank Sulloway's birth-order studies, his battle between brothers and sisters for attention space. Not to mention in Aristotle's attempt to set himself apart.

And differentiation shares something crucial with attraction and repulsion, with ripples in a pond, and with opposites joined at the hip. It is a good candidate. A good candidate for what? For one of the simple starting rules of the cosmos.

***

Meanwhile, in the twenty-first century Hans Driesch's and George Henry Lewes's mysteries remain. Where do new forms come from? What is the form maker? What generates giant leaps like the jump from two gases to a liquid, from two gases to water?

Driesch's and Lewes's challenges call on us to come up with a science that can do the impossible, a science that can predict the next great future shock, the next great leap up the ladder of complexity, the next great act of implication unpacking, the next great cosmic invention, the next inconceivable surprise, the next grand cosmic breakthrough, the next big leap beyond mere life, consciousness, music, science, megacities, and megasocieties. The next great shock that would startle Herbert Spencer, George Henry Lewes, George Eliot, Charles Darwin, Brian Greene, and even you and me.

7

EINSTEIN TURNS AN
AXIOM INSIDE OUT

THE MAN WHO GAVE *STAR TREK* ITS SPACE:
BERNHARD RIEMANN

There are signs that a science of the supersized surprise, a science able to predict emergent properties, is within reach. But to get there we'll have to answer a question. Do axioms and the systems built on them, systems that follow Aristotle and Euclid's formula, systems like geometry, in any way reflect reality?

In their 2010 book *The Grand Design*, Stephen Hawking and Leonard Mlodinow distinguish between two kinds of causality. And two kinds of explanation. Bottom up and top down.[1] Constructing systems from axioms is a bottom-up approach. So is constructing universes from simple rules. These approaches start with bricks and put together palaces.

Metaphor and big pictures, on the other hand, are top down. They start with blueprints and with overarching form. They start with visions of palaces. Then they marshal the bricks to fit. Recruitment strategies are also top down. So are emergent properties. At the other extreme sit Peano's axioms and the city-building termites. They are bottom up.

But does top-down causality also exist? Do big pictures make an impact? Do blueprints marshal bricks? How, for example, does the overall form of the sea squirt discipline the cells within it? There's more. Where do big pictures come from? How do they evolve? Can simple rules produce big pictures? Does the bottom up build its own top down? Or do big pictures come from somewhere else? Is there a severe problem here for an atheist like me? And, since you are an atheist for a day, for you, too? Do big pictures, god forbid, come from a god?

While George Henry Lewes and Herbert Spencer were mixing and mingling with John Stuart Mill and George Eliot on the Strand, another clue to the God Problem was being explored across the English Channel in Europe. In Germany and Russia the influence of the non-Euclidean geometers, the men who changed the parallel axiom, was going great guns. Lobachevsky and Bólyai's books had been out for twenty years.[2] Other mathematicians were chewing on those books' insights. And scientific weirdnesses were showing up. Scientific anomalies. Strange results that defied the going scientific paradigms. Those anomalies would soon become the bricks in a new edifice.

***

When we last left Aristotle's axioms, their evolution had come a long way. First Euclid had shown how you could use axioms to pull together geometric systems. Then Kepler and Galileo had used axioms to establish the rules of modern science. Nearly three hundred years later, Giuseppe Peano had shown that you could reduce an entire number system to axioms. And Bólyai and Lobachevsky had shown that by changing just one axiom, you could generate a new miniverse, a new pocket-sized cosmos.

Which led to a question. A very big one. Do systems based on axioms, on simple rules, have any relationship to the real world? Or is axiom-twiddling merely the self-indulgent play of a bunch of hyperintellectuals doing the things that only nerds would understand?

The answer would lie in the amazing fate of non-Euclidean geometry. And the man who would pave the way for that amazement was a man named Bernhard Riemann.

Bernhard Riemann lived a short but brilliant life. Brilliant and pivotal. He was born in 1826 in Hanover, Germany. He was seventeen years younger than Charles Darwin, nine years younger than George Henry Lewes, and six years younger than Herbert Spencer. When Riemann emerged from the womb and squalled his first cry, János Bólyai and Nikolai Lobachevsky were puzzling out the implications of a geometry in which parallel lines could meet. A geometry of curves and saddlebacks.

Riemann was interested in history and math when he was young. But the first sign that he had a math talent beyond the norm came when he was sixteen years old. The director of the college-prep high school, the gymnasium, that Riemann attended in Hanover, handed Bernhard a book that would be utterly impenetrable to most well-educated adults, not to mention to a teenager. It was a book on number theory. And it was not number theory for dummies. It was a book written by one of the most advanced mathematical pioneers of the era, Adrien-Marie Legendre, member of the French Académie des Sciences and officer of the Légion d'Honneur, who had cracked barriers in forms of math so far into the ozone that only a few math maniacs would be able to follow them—elliptic functions, the prime number theorem, least squares, and the Legendre transformation. Legendre's book was written for his peers, high-level mathematicians. What's more, the book was 859 pages long.

But Riemann found the volume thrilling. He zipped through it in six days, then he handed it back to his school director and gushed, "That was a wonderful book! I have mastered it." And Bernhard Riemann wasn't kidding.

Riemann entered the University of Gottingen in 1846, the year in which Herbert Spencer first supped at John Chapman's table,[3] the year in which Darwin was at Down House "experimenting, observing, and writing,"[4] and two years before the fifty revolutions of 1848. Riemann was twenty. His father was a Lutheran minister. To keep his dad happy, Riemann started off in one prime territory of the God Problem, one isomorphic symbol set with which we humans grasp the mysteries of a slippery reality: theology. But Riemann soon switched to the secular side of deep structures. He moved into math and physics.[5] And when it came time to write his dissertation, Riemann was given a privilege. His dissertation advisor was Carl Friedrich Gauss. Yes, Gauss, the "giant of mathematics." The "colossus"[6] who had influenced both Bólyai and Lobachevsky. The man who claimed that he'd begun an exploration of non-Euclidean geometry decades earlier, but had not written his insights down.

The dissertation Riemann wrote for Gauss touched on an issue vital to the God Problem: the translation of patterns from one medium to another. It included work on "conformal mapping." What's conformal mapping? Mathematically translating a shape from one medium to another. Specifically from one kind of space to another—for example, translating the patterns on the globe in your den to a two-dimensional sheet of paper that you can fold up and carry around to plan a trip around the world.[7]

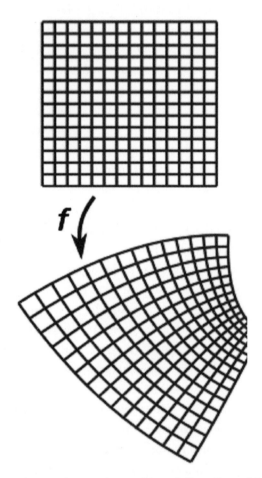

Conformal mapping—a form of translation. The grid stays the same, but the medium it exists in warps and changes. Draw a rabbit on a flat piece of paper. Then roll up the piece of paper. Is the rabbit still the same? *Courtesy of Oleg Alexandrov, Wikimedia Commons.*

But Riemann's really big contribution came two years later in 1854 when he had to write yet another thesis,[8] a thesis that would qualify him to teach at his university, the University of Gottingen. The topic Riemann picked was the epitome of the second law of science: look at things right under your nose as if you've never seen them before, then proceed from there. Riemann presented three topics to his advisor, Gauss. And Gauss told him to work on the one that hit the deepest, "On the Hypotheses which Lie at the Foundation of Geometry." Why did this hit deep? Because Riemann wanted to probe the base of invisible assumptions on which geometry was built. The assumptions that no one else had ever seen.

The result was a paper that would give us *Star Trek* and a massive hunk of modern science fiction. A paper that would give us relativity and string theory. And a paper whose key points would enter even your vocabulary and mine. In his first sentence, Riemann announced that he intended to dig down to something preposterous. "Geometry assumes, as things given [as axioms]," wrote Riemann, ". . . the notion of space."[9] Space, the stuff in front of, under, and above your nose. The emptiness through which you move your feet and your body every time you take a step. Space: the emptiness through which my fingers move as I type this to you on a laptop in my daily haunt, Park Slope Brooklyn's Tea Lounge. Space: something Plato and Euclid took for granted. And Riemann wanted to reexamine this assumption? What hubris.

But Riemann said that space is not geometry's only hidden assumption. Geometry also assumes, declared Riemann, that you can "construct" things in space—circles, triangles, squares, temples, and pyramids. These, said Riemann, are not unquestionable facts. They are "axioms" and "assumptions." And because they haven't been dug out, "the relation of these assumptions remains consequently in darkness."[10] Sorry, leaving things in darkness is not acceptable in science. Said Riemann, we haven't taken a good, hard look at the notions that there *is* space and that we can construct shapes within it, we haven't tested and probed to see how and if these two things—space and our constructions—are true. Riemann was truly looking at things right under his nose as if he'd never seen them before.

What's more, said Riemann, he was about to explore the possibility that more than one kind of space can exist. What does that mean? Isn't the space around us, below us, and above our heads in the starry sky the only kind of space there is? No, said Riemann, not at all. A Babylonian clay tablet, an Egyptian papyrus, a Greek wax tablet, and a piece of paper are examples of one kind of space, a two-dimensional space. They are what Riemann called doubly "extended magnitudes."[11] The cavernous, dark room in which I'm writing this at the Tea Lounge and the room in which you're reading it are three-dimensional spaces. They're what Riemann called "triply extended magnitudes."[12] But Riemann said that it was time to go beyond mere two- and three-dimensional spaces, two- or three-dimensional "magnitudes" or "manifolds."[13] Said Riemann, he intended to explore "the general notion of multiply extended magnitudes,"[14] a field that in his opinion "remained entirely unworked."[15] What in the bejeezus was he nattering about?

Space as we know it, claimed Riemann, is only one animal in a vast zoo of imaginable manifolds. Or, in Riemann's words, "space is only a particular case of a triply extended magnitude."[16] In other words, the space that you and I know is only a three-dimensional manifold. And three-dimensional space, space as we know it, is small potatoes compared to the possible land-scapes of spaces that Riemann planned to probe. Said he, "I have . . . set myself the task of constructing the notion of a multiply extended magnitude out of general notions of magnitude."[17] In other words, Riemann had set himself the task of constructing more dimensions than any previous human had ever conceived.

The notion of space was not the only basic Bernhard Riemann held up to the light and scrutinized like a newborn kitten. He also reexam-ined the very notion of measuring. He looked at continuous spaces, at smooth, unbroken surfaces, versus surfaces divided up into atomlike bits, bits to which he gave a new name, "quanta,"[18] a name that would one day be embedded in the name of a new form of physics, "quantum" physics. And Riemann asked another peculiar question. Is the geometry and math of things that approach the infinitely big the same as the geometry and math of things that approach the infinitely small?[19] Both these questions—whether space is continuous or quantized and whether the math of the infinitely big is the same as the math of the infinitely small—would soon prove crucial tools. Why? Because in science, new questions are sometimes more important than new answers.

***

But "On the Hypotheses which Lie at the Foundation of Geometry" was just a start. Riemann also made significant contributions to the mathematization of two other topics vital to the future of physics—wave equations of light and equations of heat. And on July 30, 1859, when Riemann was thirty-three years old, he took over the chair of mathematics at the University of Gottingen, the chair that Gauss, the colossus of math, had occupied; 1859, the year Riemann ascended to that chair, was the year of publication of Darwin's *Origin of Species*. Three years later, in 1862, Riemann married. Then he caught a cold. A minor thing these days. Not such a minor thing in 1862. The cold turned into tuberculosis. And tuberculosis was deadly. Riemann's doctors sent Bernhard to Italy where they hoped the air and climate would cure him. When he arrived, Riemann made friends with some of Italy's top mathematicians. But the climate did not help. In 1866, with his wife and his three-year-old daughter at his side, Bernhard Riemann died in the village of Selasca, Italy. He was only forty years old. But Riemann had literally reshaped our view of the universe.

Bernhard Riemann had come up with the idea of a geometry that could do more than merely change the axioms of Euclid. He had come up with the idea that you could map out the geometry of universes with a vast change at their base—the number of dimensions into which they extended. You could use geometry and equations to map out what he called "the manifoldness of n-dimensions." Yes, n-dimensions. A term familiar to any sci-fi fan. A term that comes quickly to the lips of any string theory partisan. A term that allows you four dimensions, five dimensions, six dimensions, eleven dimensions, or eleven hundred thousand dimensions. Including the six[20] dimensions and the eleven[21] dimensions of string theory. But "n-dimensions" was a term that had seldom been heard before Riemann.[22] Why? Because before the introduction of the phrase "n-dimensions," the idea of a sixth dimension, an eleventh dimension, and a three hundred thousandth dimension was literally unthinkable.

Really? Yes. There was no vision of these bizarrely layered dimensions in the human mind. And there was no vocabulary with which to describe them. Without mind tools, we cannot think. With n-dimensions, with multiple dimensions, Riemann added a whole new landscape of possibility. In fact, an infinite stack of new landscapes. Riemann also gave science the mathematical tools with which to feel out these unexplored wildernesses. New formulas in differential calculus,[23] modern analytic geometry, differential geometry,[24] and complex function theory.[25] And those new tools would soon find uses beyond Riemann's wildest imaginings.

***

An infinite number of dimensions was not Bernhard Riemann's only major contribution. Riemann also drew a strange line between two types of apparent infinities. He drew a distinction between things that are endless and things that are infinite. Huh? What in tarnation did Riemann mean? Imagine that you are a runner doing laps on a circular track. I'm your coach. I give you a simple instruction: "Stop running when you get to the end of the track." When will you stop running? The answer is never. There is no such thing as an end to a circle. You could continue going around the track from today until eternity. In other words, a circle is endless.

OK, your run around the track would continue infinitely. But does that mean the track is infinite? Not at all. It's small enough so that you can view the whole thing from end to end when you become exhausted and go to sit in the bleachers.

What's the point? Riemann showed how you can have a universe that's endless but not infinite.[26] Endless but limited in size. Sounds remarkably simple, right? Not much of a contribution. But it was a possibility that Pythagoras, Plato, Euclid, Kepler, Galileo, and Newton had never thought of. A possibility that cried out for confirmation in the real world. Was this an endless but finite universe? Was it a universe like a bicycle track? Or was it just plain infinite? That was yet another of the questions Riemann left in his wake. And, once again, in science new questions are sometimes more valuable than new answers.

***

The bottom line? Bernhard Riemann left science hungry. Hungry to see if his curved manifolds and his endless but finite space were real or fantasies. He left science hungry to reread the messages of the planets and the stars, the messages that had fascinated the Babylonians, Kepler, Newton, and Galileo. Hungry to reread those messages through new mind tools, through new lenses. Through the lenses of Riemannian math.

ALBERT EINSTEIN'S PAJAMAS

N-dimensions, six dimensions, eleven dimensions, and three hundred thousand dimensions, what utterly useless stuff, right? And what about endless space versus infinite space? A quibble only a handful of social incompetents could come up with. Only geeks so devoid of social skills that they take refuge in the ridiculous could understand these things. And only geeks could care. Right?

The man who would prove this sort of skepticism wrong was even farther off in the ozone than Bernhard Riemann. Much, much farther. So far from reality that he often walked out of his house in the morning after breakfast on his way to his office at Princeton's Institute for Advanced Study with a minor problem, a problem that only his wife seemed able to solve. She would run to catch up with him after he'd gotten a block or so from the house. Her arms were loaded with clothes. Why clothes? The man who showed that Riemann was for real was so far removed from reality the he often walked out of the house in his bedroom slippers and his pajamas. He forgot to put on his clothes.

The man walking up the street in his pajamas was a brilliant example of Herbert Spencer's human with a mind so specialized that he could only exist in a complex society, a society that would feed, house, and clothe him despite his inability to remember his pants. He was a brilliant example of differentiation and integration. But who was he?

That man was the son of a Jewish electronics startup founder in

Germany, Albert Einstein. A high school dropout. A university graduate so marginal that, as you know, he couldn't get a job in science or math and had to settle for work in a patent office. A lad who at the age of sixteen had imagined what it would be like to run after a wave of light and catch up with it.[27] A lad who had become obsessed with the puzzles left to him by the axiom flippers—by Bólyai, Lobachevsky, and Riemann. A man who worked on the most perplexing problems of physics in his spare time. Worked on them with all his might. Worked on them until, at the age of twenty-six, he had twenty-six papers ready for publication in Europe's leading physics journal. Including four papers that would change the history of science.

***

Albert Einstein was the ultimate outsider. And the ultimate abstract thinker. The ultimate unpacker of implicit properties from axioms. He didn't work in a lab. He didn't use a telescope. He didn't do research. He didn't design experiments. He didn't even have a job as a real scientist. And in a high school essay on what he wanted to do with the rest of his life, he said he wanted to dive into math and physics because of what he called "my disposition for abstract and mathematical thought, and," here comes the kicker, "my lack of imagination and practical ability."[28] The result? Albert Einstein was a full-time thinker. And Albert Einstein had been seduced and kidnapped by a recruitment strategy— the recruitment strategy called a "puzzle." The recruitment strategy otherwise known as a riddle, a mystery, and a problem. And because he was in the fist of a recruitment strategy, Albert Einstein was as far removed from practical reality as any human in the history of the planet. And yet, in another sense, he was the most practical man in all of science. Why?

Albert Einstein put everything he had into one big problem—figuring out the mind of God.[29] Hunting down the "reason," "beauty," and "structure" of what he called a "God, who reveals himself in the lawful harmony of the world."[30] Hunting for God's own geometry. That's why Albert walked out of the house in his pajamas. Every synapse and neuron of his brain was dedicated to really big questions. There was no brainpower left for pants and shoes.

And Albert Einstein came up with the answer to more than just a slew of problems in physics. He produced the answer to a gigantic question left by Bernhard Riemann's work and by twenty-two hundred years of geometry and implication extraction. If you spend over two thousand years, over one hundred generations, and tens of millions of man hours on a multigenerational task, the task of extracting implications from simple rules, the task of unpacking implicit properties from axioms, the task of corollary generation, do you get anything of earthly use? Do you get anything that matches reality? Or are you left with two thousand years' worth of airy abstractions that have nothing to do with anything of substance?

The answer would come from two things: the peculiar behavior of the planet Mercury and the strange displacement of the light from stars in the eclipse of May 29, 1919. In other words, the answer would come from the place where even the Babylonians would have searched for it: from the skies.

***

How did Albert Einstein enter your life? You were ten years old. It was three in the afternoon. The big Tudor house you grew up in was empty. You needed the scissors. Your mom kept just one pair. And she kept them in just one spot—in the drawer of a mahogany chest in the least used room in the house, a small formal dining room. A room that was only occupied on the rare occasions when company came. So you entered the sacred room and slid open the second drawer down of the elaborately carved mahogany chest, the drawer where the scissors were kept. You knew exactly where the scissors would be in that nearly empty drawer—in the very center up at the front. Your mom was very precise about this placement. And you were instantly frustrated. Why? The scissors weren't there. The scissors that always, always were there were nowhere in sight. And the usual spot that held them was nothing but bare and empty wood. Bare and empty wood with a splotch of reddish brown on the yellow boards where the cabinet makers had accidentally splashed a bit of the stain they had used to finish the chest's outside.

So you went on a scissor hunt. First you combed through every room on the first floor—the living room, the kitchen, the narrow breakfast nook where your family ate, the tiny bathroom, and even the hall where the phone was kept on a special table. No luck. So you climbed the stairs and went through every room on the second floor—your parents' bedroom, your room, your brother's room, and the bathroom. Again, no luck. So you hit the attic, with its one guest bedroom and the giant whatever-you-want-it-to-be room with a huge, unused ping-pong table. Again, no sign of the scissors.

By now, you'd been hunting for half an hour. And you were desperate. So you returned to the dining room where the scissors were normally kept, you opened the traditional scissor drawer, and you stared with all your might at the empty spot where the scissors were normally kept. You stared at the naked yellow wood bottom of the drawer in the hope that if you looked hard enough, the scissors would appear from nowhere.

Then you found the scissors. Where? In your left hand. That's where they'd been all along.

That's how you discovered that you were absentminded. And there was only one role model on Earth who validated a ten-year-old's right to such a profound absence of brain cells for down-to-Earth matters: Albert Einstein. So Einstein became a pillar of your life. For the rest of your life Einstein would be there every day, haunting every corner of your cranium.

***

Where in the world did Albert Einstein get his strange ideas?

In popular lore, Einstein is the epitome of genius. He is a solitary individual who plucked a perception-shattering theory from thin air. From the depths and heights of an imagination working in isolation. But that's not true. It is true that Einstein was isolated from the scientific community and was locked out of academia. But thanks to his reading in publications like Europe's leading physics journal, the *Annalen der Physik*, he was in the grip of the most important scientific problems of his day.

Albert Einstein was not just an innovator, he was an integrator. John Chapman the publisher was a brilliant integrator of people at 142 Strand, and Einstein was a brilliant integrator of the ideas and the findings of others.

What's more, Einstein picked and chose the ideas that utterly baffled others. Einstein adopted ugly ducklings.

At the end of the nineteenth century, ugly ducklings, counterintuitive findings, were piling up. Equally important, the math used to try to explain these counterlogical findings looked like arbitrary and jerry-rigged contrivances, mere patches, temporary fixes, ugly Rube Goldberg devices that made no sense. Einstein would give these counterintuitive annoyances meaning. How? He would put them together in a new scheme that would make a whole new kind of sense. He would create a new big picture. A new big picture that would turn patchwork fixes into central pillars and ugly ducklings into swans.

**

As soon as a science has emerged from its initial stages, theoretical advances are no longer achieved merely by a process of arrangement. Guided by empirical data, the investigator rather develops a system of thought which, in general, is built up logically from a small number of fundamental assumptions, the so-called axioms. We call such a system of thought a theory. The theory finds the justification for its existence in the fact that it correlates a large number of single observations, and it is just here that the "truth" of the theory lies.
—**Albert Einstein**[31]

What were the ugly ducklings? What were the loose ends, the puzzling pieces of patchwork, the seven inconvenient and embarrassing threads, for which Albert Einstein would invent a new weave?

Ugly Duckling Number One: In 1629, two hundred and fifty years before Albert Einstein was born, a Dutch Renaissance Man—a founder of Rotterdam's Collegium Mechanicum, Rotterdam's technical college, who doubled as a mathematician, physicist, and head of a candle-making business—toyed with the idea that light might not be instantaneous. It might not shine on the palm of your hand the second it emerges from the sun. But like cannonballs and bullets, light might take time to travel. The thinker who proposed that light might have a speed was Isaac Beeckman, and he designed an experiment to measure the time it takes for a cannon's flash to travel to a mirror on a hill a mile away and to come back again. Alas, Beeckman never tried the experiment. But the idea that light sets out on a journey and takes time to arrive did not die. Nine years later Galileo came up with his own ideas for measuring the speed of light. Then, in 1676, nearly fifty years after Beeckman, a Danish astronomer working at an observatory in Paris, Ole Rømer, estimated the speed of light to be 136,701.662 miles per second. A very good guess. In 1850—twenty-nine years before Einstein's birth—two French physicists, Hippolyte Fizeau and Léon Foucault, devised gadgets with rotating mirrors that measured the speed of light over a distance of twenty miles, hitting the mirrors, then reversing direction and traveling the twenty miles back to its source. Fizeau and Foucault pegged the speed of light to be 185,168.615 miles per second. Even closer. Today we clock the speed of light at 186,282.397 miles per second. But the very idea that light traveled, that it had a speed, was surprising. And it would prove vital to Albert Einstein.

Ugly Duckling Number Two: In 1883, when Einstein was four years old, the Austrian physicist/philosopher/psychobiologist Ernst Mach came up with the peculiar idea of "relativity."[32] Who was Ernst Mach? Mach held the "Chair for the Philosophy of the Inductive Sciences at the University of Vienna."[33] His contributions to physics were so great that the standard measure of the speed of sound is named after him. When you say that a jet does Mach two or Mach three, you are paying tribute to Ernst Mach. Mach also did important work in psychology, helping found the field of psychophysics. So he was aware of the peculiar relationship between physics and perception. What did Einstein pluck from Ernst Mach? Mach upended two axioms—the Newtonian idea of time and the Newtonian idea of space. There was no rigid framework of time and no rigid framework of space, no universal grid containing all of the cosmos, Mach said. Time and space came from the relationship between things, between things like clocks, railroad trains, billiard balls, and stars. Time and space are relative. Mach laid all this out in his 1883 book *The Science of Mechanics*.[34] But it was merely an oddball philosophical concept.[35] Until Einstein.

Ugly Duckling Number Three: From the 1790s to 1866 Carl Friedrich Gauss, János Bólyai, Nikolai Lobachevsky, and Bernhard Riemann laid out their non-Euclidean geometry, the geometry of curved space. The geometry of saddlebacks and hyperbolic surfaces. And in 1854, twenty-five years before Einstein's birth, Riemann gave mathematicians an infinite number of dimensions to play with. What's more, Riemann and Gauss turned their strange geometries into equations. But what in the world did this have to do with the real world? Even Lobachevsky and Bólyai could not find a connection.[36] And Lobachevsky worked very hard at it—poring through the observations made at the Kazan observatory, over which he had become director, for clues that we live in a hyperbolic universe.[37] Then came Einstein.

Ugly Duckling Number Four: In 1861, British physicist James Clerk Maxwell came up with equations for light. As Maxwell saw it, a wave of light is two waves for the price of one. Two forces—electricity and magnetism— do a zigzag dance. Yes, in light, electricity and magnetism do a cross-weave. A braid. A magnetic wave flips up and down. An electric wave flips from side to side. And the two move forward together in a straight line. The resulting dance, the resulting cross-weave, is a wave of light.

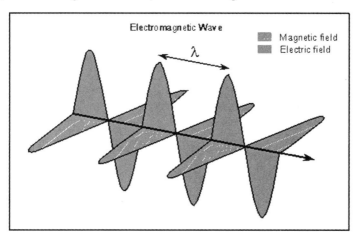

An electromagnetic wave. The electrical field flips up and down. The magnetic field flips from side to side. And both move forward in a straight line. How and why? *Courtesy of Nick Strobel, http://www.astronomynotes.com, © 1998–2011 by Nick Strobel.*

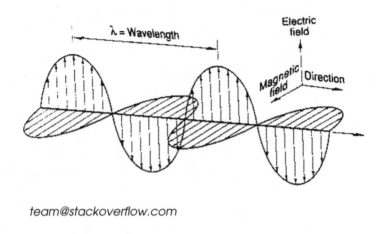

team@stackoverflow.com

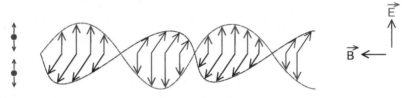

Emmanuel Boutet, Wikimedia Commons

Maxwell proposed this view in his four-part paper "On Physical Lines of Force." Maxwell's braiding of electricity and magnetism and the equations he used to do that braiding would take on a whole new meaning once Einstein toyed with them.

Ugly Duckling Number Five: In 1887, Albert Abraham Michelson and Edward Williams Morley in the inelegant American city of Cleveland, Ohio, set up an experiment with one of the most puzzling results of all. Their laboratory setup was designed to show an extremely logical consequence of the fact that light has a speed. It was designed to reveal the obvious fact that the speed of light seems faster when you're moving toward the source of the light and light's speed seems slower when you're moving away. But that's not precisely how Michelson and Morley saw the problem. There was an extra kink in their understanding. A kink that came from the rock-solid convictions of the scientific community of the day.

In the nineteenth and early-twentieth centuries, space was not the black, cold vacuum that we know today. Physicists were convinced that space was filled with a substance you've heard of, a substance called "the ether." If you were to put yourself in the shoes of a nineteenth-century scientist, you might be convinced of it too. Why? Remember, evidence had been piling up that light was a wave. And a wave has to be a wave in something, right? Or as Archimedes would have put it, you can't have fluxions without something to flux. You can't have ocean waves without an ocean. And without water.

What was the cosmos's equivalent to water? What was the medium in which light made its waves? Ether. The "luminiferous ether."[38] Something that filled the empty space of the cosmos the way that air fills the space between you, me, walls, ceilings, and trees.

OK, if space is filled with ether and if the Earth twirls around the Sun at 67,062 miles per hour, then we have a headwind and a tailwind, a headwind and a tailwind of ether, right? And that headwind and tailwind should influence the speed of light, making light slam into us from ahead and forcing light to catch up to us from behind. To see why, imagine that you and I are in a spaceship traveling toward the sun at 67,062 miles per hour—the speed of Earth's orbit. You're in the cockpit. I'm in an observation bubble in the tail. Sunlight should smash into the forward windshield of your cockpit the way raindrops smash into the windshield of your car when you're speeding down the highway in a storm. And sunlight should drift lazily into the rear window of my tail bubble.

In 1887,[39] Michelson and Morley[40] set up their experiment to show this ether effect. With a grant from Alexander Graham Bell, yes, from the inventor of the telephone, Michelson and Morley put together a device that depended on what *New York Times* science writer George Johnson calls some very "expensive . . . handmade optics."[41] They fixed two mirrors, a lantern, and a telescope to the equivalent of a table in the positions that would be occupied by bridge players. And they used high-precision brass rods precisely one meter long to keep the distances across the table exact.

To visualize the Michelson-Morley experiment, imagine that you are the lantern. Directly across the table from you, in the spot that your partner would take in bridge, there's a mirror. To your left, in the spot where one of your bridge opponents would sit, is another mirror. And to your right, in the spot at the table where another opponent would sit, is a telescope. So it's you and the mirror across from you versus the mirror on your left and the telescope on your right. But the big secret is in the middle of the table. It's a lightly silvered mirror.[42] Sitting at a forty-five-degree angle. Catty corner to you. And catty corner to your fellow bridge players.

Why is the diagonal mirror in the center of the table only lightly silvered? In a sense, it's the dealer. When you, the lantern, shine your light to the mirror on the opposite side of the table, the lightly silvered mirror in the center lets some of your light pass through, but puts up a barrier to the rest of your light and reflects it to the mirror on your left. By the way, that half-silvered mirror in the center of the table has been a favorite gizmo of physicists for nearly a century and a half. Why? Because it's vital to experiments in quantum physics. It takes one beam of light and splits it in two. That's why it's called a beam splitter.

Here's the secret to the Michelson-Morley experiment. You are the light source. You are the lantern. And you are set up so you face in the direction of Earth's movement. Which means that you face in the direction of the ether headwind. The beam you shoot to your partner across the table should be slowed down as it fights the flow of ether. Then it should be sped up again as your partner, the mirror across the table, bounces it back toward you. Meanwhile the beam splitter is taking half of the beam you send out and deflecting it to your opponent, the mirror on your left. And the mirror on the left, in turn, is shooting your light to its partner on your right— the telescope. After your beam is split in two, the beam splitter recombines them and sends them to the telescope on your right. But because one half of the beam has been slowed and sped up again and the other hasn't, the two halves of the beam of light you originally sent out should be out of synch. Very confusing. Right?

Michelson put what should happen in terms of swimmers in a fast-moving river swimming at right angles to each other. Said Michelson, one swimmer swims across the river from one side to the other. The other goes upstream and returns downstream to her starting position. The swimmer stroking and kicking against the direction of the current is "struggling upstream and back, while the other, covering the same distance, just crosses the river and returns." Which swimmer will do the distance the fastest? Says Michelson, "The second swimmer," the swimmer who doesn't have to fight her way upstream against the river's flow, "will always win, if there is any current in the river."[43] Which means the two swimmers will cover the distance in different times. They will be out of synch.

The swimmers represent your two split beams of light. And because the swimming effect will knock your two beams of light out of synch, they should produce Thomas Young's interference patterns. Which is where Michelson and Morley ran into a problem.

The Michelson-Morley experiment. The light beam pointed in the direction of Earth's movement should be slowed down by the ether. It isn't. *Courtesy of Brian Martin, King's Center for Visualization in the Sciences, http://www. kcvs.ca/site/projects/specialRelativity.html (accessed December 29, 2011).*

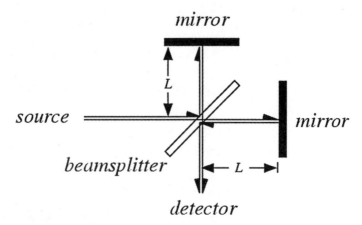

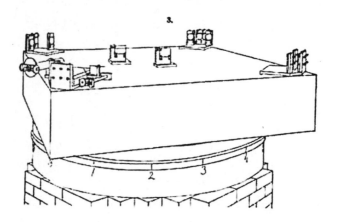

The Michelson-Morley experiment, drawn by Albert Abraham Michelson in 1887. Yes, *the* Michelson (from R. S. Shankland, "The Michelson-Morley Experiment," in *The Encyclopedia of Physics*, 3rd ed., ed. R. M. Besancon (New York: Van Nostrand Reinhold, 1974)).

A big problem: no interference pattern. No matter what direction Michelson and Morley turned their table,[44] the two rays of light were still apparently moving at the same speed. Exactly the same speed. Which meant, god forbid, no ether. And nothing for light to wave in. The result was so unbelievable that Michelson and Morley ran the experiment again and again. Still no interference patterns. The Western world's physicists were baffled. Stumped. Stuck for an explanation. Stuck for eighteen years. Until Einstein.

Ugly Duckling Number Six: In 1900, when Einstein was twenty-one, German physicist Max Planck rolled out a new view of radiant heat.[45] A view that Planck loathed, hated, and despised. A view that he called "an act of desperation."[46] Planck premiered this ugly duckling October 19, 1900,[47] in a meeting of the German Physical Society. At that meeting, Planck presented a mathematical solution to a problem. The earth—the rock and soil beneath your feet and mine—absorbs light from the sun.[48] Then it gives off the energy of that light as infrared radiation. That's called "black body radiation." Why? The fashionable experiment in the physics of 1900 involved two steps. Step one: make a "black body," a hollowed-out block of metal, a thick-walled oven with a small hole. A hole that would be truly black. A hole that would swallow all light. Step two: heat that "black body" to see what kind of electromagnetic energy comes out of the hole when the metal is glowing hot—glowing red, yellow, or white.[49] Classical physics did just fine at handling many of the electromagnetic waves that came from the hole. But there was a problem with ultraviolet light. When you used classical equations to predict how much ultraviolet light the heated "black body" would give off, your equations broke down. Totally. Your classical equations predicted an outpouring of infinite ultraviolet energy. Infinite! More energy than all the suns in the universe combined. Needless to say, this was a tad more energy than had squeezed from the hole of any black body ever tested in the lab. The infinite result was so appalling that it was called "the ultraviolet catastrophe."[50]

Planck was hunting for a math that would predict what really happens when you heat a black body. And he found it. But it was based on an assumption that made Planck shudder. The classical view had it that when electromagnetic radiation comes from matter like earth, soil, and black bodies, the energy that the matter pours forth comes in smooth flows like water pouring from a hose.[51] Planck's new math implied that matter punches out energy in modular packets—in the energy equivalent of bricks. Using a hose, you can fill a swimming pool with one inch of water, 1.1 inches of water, or 1.01 inch. But things are different if you decide to fill a swimming pool with bricks. You can have one layer of bricks, two layers of bricks, or three layers of bricks. But you can't have 1.1 layers or 1.01 layers. Unless you start shaving bricks. To name his nanobricks—his modular units of light—Planck employed a word that Bernhard Riemann[52] had used to denote a fundamental measurable unit. That word? The quantum. Yes, the unit that would later give its name to quantum physics. At first, Planck was extremely uncomfortable with his nanobricks, his quanta. Screamingly uncomfortable. They made sense mathematically. And they fit the facts fantastically well. But to Plank, who didn't even believe in atoms at the time,[53] quanta were nonsense. They were an absurdity. And even the math was hideous. Einstein would show how quanta fit perfectly into a new view of the universe.

Ugly Duckling Number Seven: But that's not the last of the ugly ducklings, the hideous outcasts that didn't seem to fit any big picture in sight. For a really bizarre ball of feathers, swivel your eyes to ugly duckling number seven. In 1904,[54] when Einstein was twenty-five, Dutch theoretical physicist Hendrik Lorentz threw in what Einstein called his "epoch-making theoretical investigations."[55] What did Lorentz's investigations reveal that was so epoch making? What Einstein called "the constancy of the velocity of light in vacuo."[56] And what does that mean? Light whiffles past you at 670,616,629 miles per hour. No matter what. At least if it's in a vacuum. Umm, and what exactly does *that* mean? Something wretchedly and wrenchingly unbelievable. That you and I flatten like silly putty pressed between your hands. We do it every day and we haven't got a clue.

We squoosh? And we don't see it? Lorentz said yes. But why? Pick a convenient vacuum somewhere out in space. Find the best baseball pitcher you know. Ask him to hurl a fastball from a mound in the vacuum. Get out your pocket radar gun and clock the speed of his pitch. Let's say it's eighty miles per hour. Now imagine that you've got a highway in the vacuum. Yes, it's a stretch, but bear with me. Ask your pitcher to stand in the back of a truck. Get a friend to drive the truck past you at one hundred miles per hour. And ask the pitcher to pitch his hardest, to pitch straight forward down the highway as the truck is passing you. When the pitcher pitches from the hundred-mile-per-hour truck bed, clock the ball. Your radar gun should show that the ball is zipping along at one hundred and eighty miles per hour.

That's the one-hundred-miles-per-hour speed of the truck plus the eighty-miles-per-hour fastball zoosh of the pitcher. Now thank the pitcher for his help, hand him a beer, and do another version of the same experiment. But this time not with a baseball. With light.

How? Ask your friend at the wheel of the truck to drive the truck past you at one hundred miles per hour and to turn on his light source—his headlights. The light of the headlights should snick past you at the speed of light plus the speed of the car, right? The light from the headlights should slice past you at 670,616,729 miles per hour. Not true said Lorentz. The light coming from a car—or from a star—that's rushing toward you at one hundred miles per hour hits you at the normal speed of light, at 670,616,629 miles per hour. Even if a car or a star is coming toward you at a hundred million miles per hour, the speed at which its light hits you is *not* the normal speed of light plus a hundred million. It's just 670,616,629 miles per hour. The speed of light is constant, no matter how fast you're moving. No matter how fast the light's source is moving toward you. Or away from you. Just as the Michelson-Morley experiment had shown.

But how does the speed of light stay the same? That's where one of the most unbelievable notions, one of the most peculiar puzzles dangling in the zeitgeist when Einstein came along, entered the picture. It's an implication that Hendrick Lorentz unfolded when he turned the notion that the speed of light is a constant into an assumption, an axiom. In 1904, in a paper published in the *Proceedings of the Royal Netherlands Academy of Arts and Sciences*,[57] Lorentz announced his mathematical formulae for "contractions."[58] What's a Lorentz contraction? It's not something you do in childbirth. It's a peculiar consequence of movement near the speed of light.

Hendrik Lorentz tortured time and matter to keep light speed the same no matter what. Things in motion contract, said Lorentz. Hard and fast things squoomph and squash. In fact, even time is rubbery. The faster you go, the slower time becomes for you.[59] The faster you go, the slower your clock will run.

Here's how the Lorentz contraction works. You stand still on the curb. I jump into a 2011 Cadillac DTS luxury touring sedan and start the engine. The 2011 Cadillac DTS is precisely 17.25 feet long. I floor the gas pedal and hurtle past you at a hundred miles per hour. From your point of view, I contract. My length shortens. I squash. But you don't see it. Silly you. Why does my shrinking elude your gaze? Because the effect is supersmall. Yes, but why? Because I'm traveling much, much more slowly than the speed of light. Now what happens if I can ratchet the Cadillac up to 670,616.29 miles per hour, one hundredth of the speed of light? If you look very closely you will see my length shorten. My car will shrink down to 17.16375 feet in length. That's a decrease of more than an inch. A decrease of 1.035 inches to be a bit more precise. And if I could get the car up to 670,549,567.3371 miles per hour, 0.9999 of the speed of light, you'd really see the difference. My wallowing whale of a car would shrink to less than two and a half feet long. It would shrink to roughly the length of an easy chair. It would still be the same width. Wide enough for three passengers. But my Cadillac would squash down to less than two feet five inches. The closer you get to the speed of light, the more you squoomph down in length. That is a Lorentz contraction.[60] It's a mathematical way to make sense of the Michelson-Morley experiment. We'll explain how in a few pages. But it was a consternation, a curse, and a vexation to Lorentz. Something he called "inventing special hypotheses for each new experimental result." Something Lorentz concluded was "artificial."[61] In other words, something that didn't fit the real universe. Albert Einstein would make sense of this nonsense. He would fit it into a new big picture.

Then Come the Ugly Duckling Stragglers: a fistful of other downright peculiarities that Einstein would work into his weave. There's Maxwell's idea that all forces travel at the speed of light. There's Thomas Young's coining of the word "energy"[62]—a word Sir Isaac Newton only used once in his *Principia*.[63] There's Christian Doppler's idea of the Doppler effect,[64] the idea that waves seem to have a higher frequency when they come from a body rushing toward you and that they seem to have a lower frequency when they come from a body that's rushing away. And there's Hippolyte Fizeau's discovery that light in moving water isn't sped up by moving with the current or slowed down by going against the flow. An observation that seemed to knock the particle concept of light out of the box for good.[65]

But all of these whacky threads would come together in 1905. How?

EINSTEIN GIVES SEVEN UGLY DUCKLINGS A HOME:
THE YEAR OF MIRACLES

The year 1905 was a good year for Albert Einstein. A very good year. Such a good year that later generations of thinkers would refer to it as Einstein's *Annus Mirabilis*, Einstein's year of wonders, Einstein's year of miracles. That year Albert Einstein published four articles in the *Annalen der Physik,* four articles that would change the shape of physics. But in theory, Einstein had no right to be in such a journal. None at all. Why? Albert Einstein was only twenty-six years old, and he was still a graduate student at the Zurich Polytechnic. The *Annalen der Physik* was Germany's leading journal of physics. And Germany was one of the world's leading centers of physics. So there is no way a mere student should have been able to publish in the *Annalen's* pages. But in 1905 Einstein submitted twenty-one reviews[66] of books and journal articles to the *Annalen der Physik's* review journal,[67] *Beiblätter zu den Annalen der Physik, Supplements to the Annals of Physics.* All twenty-one were published.[68] What's more, Einstein had the audacity to submit six papers to the *Annalen der Physik* itself.[69] And four of them were accepted for publication. Yes, four of them. And those four would utterly change the way that physicists see our world.

How did Albert Einstein, a mere whippersnapper with an insignificant "teacher's diploma from the Swiss Federal Polytechnic School in Zurich,"[70] manage to publish four articles in what some feel was the leading journal of physics in Europe?

On paper, Einstein's credentials were pathetic. He'd left high school at the age of fifteen, then at the age of sixteen he had tried to go directly to the equivalent of college, the Zurich Polytechnic. He'd taken an entrance exam designed for eighteen-year-olds, had flunked it, and had been forced go back to high school and finish the Swiss equivalent of a high school diploma. Very humiliating. Five years later, in 1900, when he'd graduated from undergraduate school at the Zurich Polytechnic at the age of twenty-one, he'd been at the bottom of his class. Only his girlfriend and homework-study partner, Mileva Marić, was lower than he was. What's more, Einstein was a bona fide reject. Along with four of his six fellow students, he'd applied for a position as a teaching assistant, a position that would have helped him pay the costs of grad school. The four other student applicants were accepted. Only one was rejected—Albert Einstein.

Einstein then "lived a hand-to-mouth existence while he looked for a post at other universities."[71] But he had no luck. So he turned to a far less ambitious form of work for a would-be physicist—tutoring and teaching in a secondary school.[72] But even the secondary schools he applied to did not want him. The best he could land was a four-month position in what he called "a technical school at Winterthur," Switzerland, subbing for a math professor who was going off to the army for a short stint.[73] Then, by using his meager connections, he nabbed a position coaching just one student, Louis Cohen, at a boarding school in the ancient northern Swiss border town of Schaffhausen. Frankly, he loved teaching. But he was not invited to stay on in Winterhur, and his position in Schaffhausen ended badly.[74] In the end, Einstein settled for a job in the patent office, a job he did not get on the basis of his abilities. A job he got only thanks to the connections of the father of one of his classmates. But even in the patent office, Einstein was the lowest of the low—an entry level patent examiner,[75] a patent examiner third class.[76] So how in the world did Albert Einstein manage to publish his work in what some called the world's top physics journal?

The truth is that Albert Einstein had been publishing in the *Annalen der Physik* ever since he was a first-year graduate student at the age of twenty-one.[77] Despite the fact that publishing in a leading journal in your first year of grad school was a virtual impossibility. In 1900 Einstein had submitted the first of what he'd called his two "worthless beginners' papers."[78] In 1902, when he'd just landed his patent office job, he'd submitted his second. Both of these "worthless" papers were accepted. And both went into print. Then, in 1903, Einstein was allowed to present a paper on the "Theory of Electromagnetic Waves" at a meeting of Bern, Switzerland's, Association of Scientists. Why?

Because Einstein may have been a mediocre student in school. But out of school, he was an unstoppable learner. Like George Henry Lewes and Herbert Spencer, learning was Einstein's sport, his pleasure, and his play. Which is strange. Because Einstein's sister recalls that he was so late in learning to talk that the family was afraid that he was retarded.[79]

However, Einstein was fascinated by electrical and magnetic phenomena. Remember, his father, an engineer, had cofounded an electronics start-up business—J. Einstein & Cie.—making dynamos and "precision electrical measuring equipment,"[80] equipment that worked with something new called direct current. And when Einstein was five, his dad had showed him a compass. Said Einstein, "This experience made a deep and lasting impression on me. Something deeply hidden had to be behind things."[81] The rest of Albert Einstein's life would be a hunt for that "deeply hidden . . . something . . . behind things." A hunt for deep structures. But what tools would Einstein use to find the mysterious "something"?

The answer arrived when Einstein was ten years old.[82] Despite the fact that Einstein was still just a little kid, his Uncle Jacob did something ridiculous. He explained the Pythagorean theorem to this child with the curly hair. And Einstein reciprocated by doing something very strange for a ten-year-old. Something that would have pleased Euclid. He devised a proof.[83] A proof for the theorem. Something most people twice his age would not have been able to achieve. That same year Max Talmud, a Polish medical student who dropped into the Einstein home every Thursday night for a free dinner, not to mention for encouragement and for company, introduced the ten-year-old Einstein to the twenty-volume Popular Books on Natural Science series.[84] At the age of ten, Albert Einstein became a science addict. It's said that he read each book in the Popular Books science series over and over again.[85] But that was not kid Einstein's only heavy reading. Two years later, Talmud gave Einstein Euclid's *Elements*. Euclid's *Elements* had been too tough for a king—Ptolemy—and for over a hundred generations of students. But for the twelve-year-old Einstein, Euclid was mind candy. He called *The Elements* his "holy little geometry book."[86] And in the words of Harvard's Dudley Herschbach, Einstein found "Euclid's axiomatic-deductive method a trustworthy 'road to paradise.'"[87] Yes, "paradise."

Albert Einstein had found his tool to probe the mysterious "something." And he'd been snagged by one of the hooks with which a twenty-three-hundred-year-old recruitment strategy kidnaps, seduces, and recruits. One of the hooks with which a recruitment strategy can entice a human into working out its implicit properties. One of the hooks with which a curious cosmos can snooker a human into exploring her potential.

Like Galileo and János Bólyai, Einstein got an addictive kick out of solving mathematical problems. Remember, little Albert found unfolding implicit patterns from axioms a "road to paradise." So Einstein put himself through the equivalent of a course in elementary geometry, solving a new geometry problem every week, then showing the results on Thursday nights to the med student Max Talmud. Recalled Talmud, "After a short time, a few months, he had worked through the whole book."[88]

But that was just the beginning. When he was twelve, Albert Einstein wanted to skip ahead in math in school. How? By teaching himself during the summer vacation. After all, he had compiled a magnificent track record in self-teaching with Euclid's *Elements*. So his parents bought him textbooks in geometry and algebra. The prepubescent Einstein not only solved the problems in the books, but, once again, tried to prove the theorems behind them. Recalls his sister Maja, "Play and playmates were forgotten. Days on end he sat alone, immersed in the search for a solution, not giving up before he had found it."[89] What Maja didn't understand was that for young Einstein, math *was* play. So from the age of twelve to the age of sixteen, Einstein also taught himself two forms of math that were beyond Max Talmud: analytic geometry and calculus.[90] And his uncle Jacob fed him a steady diet of problems in algebra. Says Talmud, "Soon the flight of his mathematical genius was so high that I could no longer follow."[91]

When kid Einstein was thirteen, Talmud took an intellectual gamble. He introduced Einstein to Kant's *Critique of Pure Reason*. And Einstein awed him. Says Talmud, "At that time he was still a child, only thirteen years old, yet Kant's works, incomprehensible to ordinary mortals, seemed to be clear to him."[92]

By twelve, Einstein's reading of science and math had thrown him into what he called "a positively fanatic orgy of freethinking,"[93] an orgy of agnosticism. One book had hit him particularly hard: Ludwig Büchner's *Force and Matter*,[94] the book that got Büchner fired from his position as a professor of medicine at Tübingen University in the 1850s, the "Bible of Materialism." More specifically, the Bible of "freethinking." When it came time to go through the traditional Jewish rite of passage that marks your thirteenth birthday, a bar mitzvah, Einstein refused. But that wasn't his only rebellion against authority. Coupled to his new religious skepticism was a sense "that youth is intentionally being deceived by the state through lies." Said Einstein, "It was a crushing impression."[95] Albert could do nothing about the manipulations of the state. But he could hate something closer to home: the authoritarian, rote-learning system at his high school. And he did. As a result, Einstein didn't care for his school teachers at the Luitpold-Gymnasium in Munich,[96] and apparently they didn't care for him.[97] He called them drill sergeants. And it's been said that they suggested he leave their school.

When direct current lost out to alternating current as the standard form of electrical transmission, the direct-current electronics start-up of Einstein's father was starved of business. The Einstein family moved from Munich to Italy, where the twenty-year-old Guglielmo Marconi and his professor at the University of Bologna, Augusto Righi, were experimenting on the basics of what would later be called radio.[98] And where Giuseppe Peano was working on a logic-based reformulation of the axioms of geometry.[99] Italy seemed hungry for all things electric, so the family's hope was that Hermann Einstein, Albert's dad, would find a better market for electric devices like his partner, Uncle Jacob's, new amp-meter. And the Einsteins hoped that J. Einstein & Cie. would find less competition from "the big power companies."[100] That's when Albert took advantage of the move to drop out of high school.

The year was 1895, and Albert Einstein was a mere sixteen years old. But during that summer, he penned his first scientific paper, on the "state of ether in [a] magnetic field."[101] A very hot topic in physics and cosmology. The teenage Einstein apparently didn't try to publish it. He merely sent it to his Uncle Caesar.[102] And Einstein performed his first *gedanken* experiment, his first thought experiment. Possibly one of the first ecstatic flights that later led him to describe a scientific insight as "a sudden illumination, almost a rapture."[103] He used his muscles to get at something. He added muscular metaphor to math, science, and philosophy. Einstein imagined what it would be like to, in his words, "run after a light wave" and catch up with it.[104] An imagined experience that would change the course of science.

But that didn't calm the nerves of Einstein's parents about his status as a dropout. Wrote Albert's sister Maja, their father and mother "were very upset over his arbitrary behavior, but he . . . reassured them about his future by assuring them in the most definite terms that he would study by himself until fall in order to prepare for the entrance examination for the Zurich Polytechnic School."[105] Einstein had a superb track record of studying on his own. But the entrance exam apparently covered subjects that Einstein had not bothered to learn. He flunked. Despite good marks in the fields he'd taught himself—math and physics.

The Zurich Polytechnical School insisted that Albert finish his equivalent to a high school education and recommended that he do it at a progressive secondary school in Zurich, the Aarau Cantonal School. Graduating from Aarau, they explained to him, got you into Zurich Polytech automatically. At Aarau, Albert and his teachers got along much better. But he still learned geometry, calculus, and theoretical physics on his own. And later in life, he'd continue learning without the benefit of a school. For example, when Einstein was twenty-three years old, he and two friends would form a reading group that they called the Olympia Academy, a group that dug into Hume, Poincaré . . . and the man who invented the idea of relativity, Ernst Mach.

But in particular, it appears that Einstein read the *Annalen der Physik*. It is likely that he read it from the time he was a teenager. And it is likely that he read it from cover to cover. What clues point in that direction? It appears that the teenage Albert Einstein ate, lived, and breathed the controversies and questions raised in the pages of the *Annalen*. The paper he wrote at sixteen on the state of ether in a magnetic field was perfectly in synch with the *Annalen*'s dialog du jour.[106] And the teenage Einstein knew the work of the *Annalen*'s editor, Paul Drude, backward and forward. That fact must have impressed Drude when he first got a peculiar note from kid Einstein, a note pointing out Drude's "mistakes."[107] Einstein threatened to "make it hot"[108] for Drude by revealing Drude's errors in print. Yet Einstein's attention must have flattered Drude. Here was someone who gave almost infinite attention to the smallest details of Drude's work, work on a difficult and out-of-the-way subject, conduction in metals, work which explained metallic conduction in terms of a new and still-controversial theory, the theory that matter is made up of, brace yourself, atoms. In fact, young Einstein paid Drude's work so much attention that he could debate the fine points in public, and did. Eventually Einstein would publish a total of forty-nine papers in the *Annalen*.[109]

But the four papers Einstein published in the *Annalen* in 1905 were the ones that would put physics on a brand-new path. What were those four papers?

The first, published on June 9, 1905, was "On a Heuristic Point of View Concerning the Production and Transformation of Light,"[110] a paper that flattered Drude by citing him in its very first footnote. And a paper that flattered the man who headed the institute[111] that published the *Annalen der Physik*,[112] Max Planck. But flattery is beside the point.

Remember, Einstein was hooked by ugly ducklings. And he was hooked by a potent multigenerational recruitment strategy. He was hooked by puzzles. "Nature," herself, he said, is "a well-formulated puzzle."[113] And one of the puzzles that had grabbed his attention was the four-hundred-year-old debate over whether light is a wave or a particle, the question argued by Leonardo da Vinci, Isaac Newton, and Thomas Young. But when you knit an old pattern with a new yarn, you often get something new. What new fiber did Einstein pull into the particle–wave debate? One that may have seemed to have no relationship to the question whatsoever. A strand from outside the box. A strand of the sort he'd seen in his father's electrical gadget shop. Put a plate of zinc in a vacuum tube. Hit it with ultraviolet light. What do you get? A flow of, of all things, electricity.[114] Presumably, this was because light knocked new theoretical particles called electrons loose from the atoms that held them and sent those electrons into motion. If you believed in atoms. And if you believed in electrons.

Einstein believed in both.

If light is a wave, said the reasoning of the day, then the more intense the ray of light you shine on the square of metal, the more electrons[115] you should get and the more energetic those electrons should be. In other words, the higher the frequency of the electricity should be. And, in fact, the number of electrons does go up when you up the intensity of the light. But the frequency does not. Why?

Einstein grabbed the idea that energy comes in modular packets from Max Planck. He grabbed the mathematical Band-Aid, the ugly duckling, that Planck loathed. The idea that energy's packets are modular bricks. What does it mean to say that quanta of light are like bricks? Bricks move from my hand to yours without dividing. And you don't crumble them to make a bookcase, you use them as wholes. Planck was convinced that his modular bricks of light, his quanta, were nonsensical monstrosities. Einstein thought they were anything but. In fact, Einstein hinted that quanta are the units of light, light's equivalent to atoms. Or, in Einstein's words, "energy [comes in] quanta that are localized in points in space, move without dividing, and can be absorbed or generated only as a whole."[116] And Einstein treated those quanta as both particles *and* waves.[117] As particles that oscillate like waves. Einstein gave these oscillating bricks the properties of energy and matter simultaneously. In fact, Einstein's oscillating bricks would later be called photons.[118] And Max Planck's loose end would become a thread in Einstein's weave.

Keep in mind that Einstein was still a graduate student. So what was the impact of his proposal about the nature of light? It should have been zilch. But in the words of the Lambeth Palace Library's Hugh Cahill, it "revolutionized the theory of light."[119]

A second puzzle nagging the minds of early-twentieth-century scientists was this: Is matter, too, made up of particles? If we call those particles atoms, do these atoms exist? Many an august figure said that atoms were sheer fantasy. One of those who thought that atoms were horse puckey was Georg Helm, the man who literally wrote the books on mathematical chemistry, electrodynamics, and energy. Another atom disbeliever was Ernst Mach, the man who coined the term "relativity." That's where the paper Einstein published in July 1905 came in—"On the Movement of Small Particles Suspended in Stationary Liquids Required by the Molecular-Kinetic Theory of Heat."[120] Einstein went outside the box to find evidence for atoms. Way outside the box. To the observations of a botanist.[121] A botanist Charles Darwin's wife, at a dinner party in 1839—forty years before Einstein was born—had referred to as "the glory of Britain." That botanist, Robert Brown, had been the naturalist on a voyage of discovery to Australia, had discovered that plant cells have a nucleus, and in 1827 had tried to figure out a key step in a plant's sex life—how pollen manages the act of impregnation. To do it, Brown had trained his microscope on something even smaller than the pollen itself—on the granules, the dandruff, that shows up along with the pollen. And these granules did something very strange when you put them in water. They jittered.[122] They shuddered back and forth as if they were afflicted by palsy. Brown showed that this wasn't just a peculiarity of pollen. Inanimate things like grains of finely ground charcoal, glass, rocks, and metal jittered in water, too. And no one knew why.

Einstein tied this nervous botanical quiver of pollen grains in a liquid to something from a radically different field—thermodynamics. Specifically something the atomists had come up with. The idea that heat might be a result of movement. The movement of atoms. The thirty-three-year-old kinetic theory of heat said that the temperature of anything—from air to a frying pan—was a measure of how fast its atoms were moving.[123] If the atoms of your frying pan moved fast, your frying pan was hot. If the atoms of the frying pan moved slowly, your frying pan was cold. But this was just a hypothesis. An idea. And a controversial one.

What's more, this theory had a minor flaw. Many felt that atoms didn't exist. But what in tarnish could pollen grains have to do with this? Pollen grains in water danced. Einstein said they jiggled and whumped because they were being bumped. Bumped by what? By the moving atoms that the kinetic heat theorists said should be there. Bumped by the very jostle that these theorists said made heat. The jostle of atoms. In other words, Einstein took an oddity from left field and used it as a lens to see the slam and crash of atoms at work. He pulled off a perception shift. He knit together the loose threads of existing scientific thought into a new tapestry, a new picture. He said that Brownian motion came from atoms doing their temperature dance before your very eyes. And in the process he helped validate two theories— the highly controversial atomic theory and the widely accepted thermodynamic theory of heat. Brilliant!

But that wasn't the end of it. Einstein proposed his pollen idea as what Aristotle called a "hypothesis," a guess. And he laid out equations based on that guess. Then he ended his paper with the hope that "a researcher will soon succeed in solving the problem posed here,"[124] the problem of whether the equations were accurate. In 1909 the French physicist Jean Perrin proved that Einstein's math was, indeed, on target. In the process, Perrin helped Einstein drive home the notion that atoms were for real.

So in his first paper, Einstein redefined light. And in his second paper he helped redefine matter. Not bad for a grad student still working on his thesis. What else was up his sleeve?

Paper number three came out two months later, in September 1905. And it took on the puzzle of the Michelson-Morley experiment. The puzzle of the fact that whether a measuring device is rushing away from a source of light or zipping toward the light source, the speed of the light still appears to be the same. The new paper, paper number three, was called "On the Electrodynamics of Moving Bodies."[125] And to solve the Michelson-Morley puzzle, it challenged the most basic assumptions—the most basic axioms—of physics. Not to mention the most basic axioms of geometry and of daily life.

Paper number three challenged our notions of time, space, and the solidity of everyday things. Einstein's thought experiment when he was sixteen had involved running after a beam of light. That fantasy had tapped the power of muscular metaphor, the power of visceral comprehension. Einstein had tried to imagine what things must look and feel like to someone catching up with the beam and running next to it. And he came to a simple conclusion. Everything would look perfectly normal.

Let's put this in terms of one of Einstein's favorite images, a railroad car.[126] A railroad car moving close to the speed of light. As Einstein saw it, everything would look perfectly normal *inside* the railroad car. But the view out the window would be very strange. Why? Because it would be the craziest blur you've ever seen. Everything outside would appear to be flicking past at the speed of light. Just the way that the outside looks as it's flashing past at sixty miles per hour when you're going sixty miles per hour in a train. But the blur out the window of a railroad carriage traveling at the speed of light would be far stranger than what you or I are accustomed to. Why? Because Einstein had a strange notion.[127] What if the speed of light was the fastest you could go in this universe? What if Hendrik Lorentz was right and the speed of light is a constant? What if the speed of light is an absolute limit? A barrier you can't pass? How in the world could the universe enforce this top speed? Einstein's answer was so far outside the box it was ridiculous. It was Lorentz's answer. The answer of the Lorentz contractions.

The cosmos could impose a top speed by treating space and time as if they were something introduced to Europe from South America in

1736[128]—rubber. Here's how it works. I'm a genie in a bottle. You're an ordinary human. You can walk three miles per hour but you wish that you could walk three million miles per hour. How do I, the magic genie, fulfill your wish? I could put rockets on your sneakers. Or I could shrink three million miles down to one mile. I could smoosh space. Then you could walk at your normal pace and cover, guess what? Three million miles. In an hour. I could also fill your wish with another trick. I could slow down time. I could spread time out so that I gave you a million years to cover three million miles. But because I'd make clocks go slow, very, very slow, they'd register the passage of just an hour. Then you could walk at your normal speed and trudge over twelve times the distance to the moon. Assuming you could live that long. And assuming that you could buy snacks along the way.

Now let's take the opposite approach. You've just invented the fastest rocketship in the universe. And you want to break the speed limit. You want to go faster than the speed of light. How can I, the genie in a bottle, stop you? I can cheat. The faster you go and the closer you get to the speed of light, the more I can stretch space out. I can make the distance that you want to travel as long as it takes to keep you from reaching the speed of light. And I can stretch out time. I can make an hour go infinitely slowly. So that it takes you forever to get anywhere.

That, said Einstein, is what the cosmos does. In this universe, no matter how fast you're traveling, everything seems normal. But the closer you get to the speed of light, the more time expands and the more space stretches around you. The more time and space play their rubber tricks to keep you from going faster than the speed of light.

So when I am zooshing past you at the speed of light and waving out the window of my railroad carriage, you look squashed to me and I look squashed to you. And if I hold my pocket watch up to the window so you can see it, it looks to you as if the arms of my watch are moving so slowly it's absurd. Why? Because the cosmos is playing rubber tricks to keep me from exceeding the speed of light.

Einstein called this "the relativity of lengths and times."[129] And it explained why the Michelson-Morley apparatus measured the speed of light as precisely the same whether its beams of lantern light were getting a speed boost by moving in the direction of the Earth's movement or were shunning that speed boost by moving at right angles to the Earth's zoosh through space. The distance in the direction of Earth's movement stretches like rubber to keep the speed of light the same.

So far, Einstein had redefined light, matter, time, and space. And so far he had taken the puzzles of Planck, Brown, and Lorentz and had turned them into pillars of a new view. He had confronted a nagging problem in photoelectricity by using Planck's ugly duckling, the quantum, to show that light was a particle and a wave all at once. He had taken on the problem of whether atoms exist and the puzzle of Brown's jiggling motion and had shown that atoms[130] were the answer to Brown's granule dance. He had confronted the puzzle of the Michelson-Morley experiment and had shown how Hendrik Lorentz's peculiar contractions could explain Michelson and Morley's paradox by keeping the speed of light the same no matter what. Einstein had knit at least three loose ends into the sleeve of a new kind of sweater. He had drawn at least three ugly ducklings together into a new beauty—a new big picture. Not bad. What was next?

The fourth of Einstein's *Annus Mirabilis* papers came out in November 1905, a mere month after paper number three. Called "Does the Inertia of a Body Depend Upon its Energy Content?"[131] this fourth paper went utterly outside the box. It took on all of your assumptions and mine about matter as stuff you can hold in your hand and energy as what you use to throw that matter to me. What did Einstein's fourth paper say? That matter and energy are one. Or, as Einstein put it, "The mass of a body is a measure of its energy content."[132] To take it out of Einstein's language and to put it in the terms we've been using in this book, energy and matter are translations. They are isomorphic. They map onto each other. Because they *are* each other. Matter is energy in disguise. And energy is matter waiting to be. In "Does the Inertia of a Body Depend upon its Energy Content?" Einstein presented the idea at the heart of the most famous equation of the twentieth century, $E = mc^2$.[133] Energy equals matter times the speed of light squared.

But four published papers in five months wasn't enough for Albert Einstein. In the midst of it all, Einstein handed in his thesis at Zurich Polytech. Called "A New Determination of Molecular Dimensions,"[134] it presented a way to calculate the number of molecules in a unit of substance. In other words, like his paper on Brownian motion, Einstein's thesis helped support the newly emerging atomic view of matter. And despite the fact that "A New Determination" was the paper of a mere student, it was packed with practical implications. The result? It "became one of Einstein's most frequently cited papers."[135]

But Einstein's papers of 1905 were just the beginning. They were just the first installment of his theory of relativity. Ten years later,[136] Einstein would decide on a name for that first installment: "the special theory of relativity." Special because it only applied in special cases. It only applied in cases where you didn't take gravity into account. And, as Einstein said, gravity was one thing you could not escape.[137] Ten years later, in 1915, Einstein would publish the second installment, his general theory of relativity. A theory that put gravity into the picture. In the 1905 special theory of relativity, Einstein had turned a speed—the speed of light—into the only rigid measuring rod in the cosmos and had turned time and space to rubber. Now, in the general theory of relativity, Einstein showed how gravity dimples, ripples, curves, rumples, and dents space's rubbery sheet. The general theory of relativity said that the sheet of space and time is "a manifold." And who did Einstein take that manifold and much of its math from? Bernhard Riemann.

Here's how the general theory of relativity says that gravity does its work on the space-time manifold. Let's use an image that's become standard in explaining relativity. Imagine that space is a giant rubber trampoline. When there is nothing on it, it is stretched taut—it is flat. Now take a bowling ball and put it on the trampoline's outstretched rubber sheet. What happens? The bowling ball dimples the sheet. Seriously dimples it. Crouch down and look at the trampoline's rubber sheet from below. What do you see? A neat, symmetrical, curving, funnel-like sag where the bowling ball stretches the rubber. In other words, where the bowling ball hangs. Now stand up again and take a marble. Put the marble on the edge of the rubber sheet and flick it toward the center of the sheet with your finger. If the marble travels anywhere near the bowling ball, what happens? It's caught in the funnel of the bowling ball's dimple, the bowling ball's sag. It's caught in the funnel of the bowling ball's distortion of the sheet. That distortion of the space-time sheet is gravity.

Princeton physicist John Wheeler says that in Einstein's theory of relativity, matter tells space how to bend and space tells matter how to move.[138] The tool that matter uses to bend space is gravity. The tool that space uses to give matter its traveling instructions is also gravity. In other words, gravity is a language. It's the common language with which matter and space communicate. It's a language communicated by the curves of space. And the way that gravity curves space and gives instructions to matter is described by the math of Bernhard Riemann[139] and of Riemann's thesis advisor Carl Friedrich Gauss.[140]

Matter translates into energy. Energy can be translated into matter. Space's curves are a language with which glumps of matter talk to each other. How very isomorphic-symbol-settish.

***

Albert Einstein was a loner who was not alone. Like you when you were a kid, he lived in a tribe, many of whose members were dead. But that tribe's members nourished him. They excited him. They motivated him. They gave him the raw material with which he worked. They gave him the old ideas he could translate into a new medium. And he knew it. From 1905 to 1915, Albert Einstein made no bones about the fact that he was knitting together the ideas of others. In fact, he gloried in it. Gauss's and Riemann's names pop up thirty times in an anthology of Albert Einstein's work pieced together by über physicist Stephen Hawking.[141] Hendrik Lorentz's name comes up sixty-three times. James Clerk Maxwell's name appears sixty times. Ernst Mach's name pops up twelve times. And Max Planck is credited fifteen times. Einstein was piecing together implicit properties no one else had the vision, the off-kilter imagination, to see. And he was knitting them together in something crucial—a new big picture. A new tapestry.

EINSTEIN'S SECRET WEAPON:
ARISTOTLE'S INVENTION

Do axioms have anything to do with Einstein's spate of creativity? They have everything to do with it. And understanding Einstein's axiom flip is the key to understanding the theory of relativity.

In writing to his friend Conrad Habicht, Einstein was self-conscious about the number of questions his four papers left unsolved. His ideas were "not fully worked out," he said. But in 1905, his miracle year, the twenty-six-year-old patent examiner third class did know one thing. His new work, he said to Habicht, was "revolutionary."[142] Why revolutionary? Because Einstein was like Riemann. He was on a prowl for assumptions. On a prowl for axioms. For axioms that mislead. For axioms that blind us. Einstein may have been sidelined in a patent office. But he was the very incarnation of the second law of science—look at things right under your nose as if you've never seen them before, then proceed from there.

In his "Autobiographical Notes," Einstein gives a brief sketch of his life-long struggle with axioms. "At the age of twelve," he writes, "I experience[d] a . . . wonder in a little book dealing with Euclidean plane geometry."[143] That book, as you and I know, was Euclid's *Elements*. At that point, Einstein says, the fact that axioms "had to be accepted as unproved did not disturb me."[144] However, later he noticed how modern science in its early days was forced to accept "Newton's law of force as an axiom."[145] That apparently did not sit well with Einstein.

Then came the movement at the end of the nineteenth century, when Einstein was a kid, to reduce all math and logic to axioms, the movement of which Giuseppe Peano was a part. Einstein was disturbed by the way that some of the axiomatizers tried to make math a pure thought process with no relationship to reality. There is no such thing, Einstein says, as math without the real world. "Mathematics generally," he writes, "and particularly geometry, owes its existence to the need which was felt of learning something about the relations of real things to one another. The very word geometry, which, of course, means Earth-measuring, proves this."[146] Those are Einstein's words. Even non-Euclidean geometry, he says, is not just a thought exercise, an exercise in logical deduction. It's a hypothesis about the real world. Non-Euclidean geometry leads to a simple question, Einstein insists. Non-Euclidean geometry, geometry that flips the parallel axiom on its head, slams you into "the question," Einstein explains, of "whether the practical geometry of the universe is Euclidean or not."[147] A question Albert Einstein would answer with his work.

What would Einstein's conclusion be? The universe is non-Euclidean. Gauss, Bólyai, Lobachevsky, and Riemann were onto something basic in the cosmos. Not something absurdly abstract. Something absurdly real.

Again, do axioms have anything to do with Einstein's work? At heart, Einstein says, his work is all about overturning an axiom. Yes, just one axiom. His work, he says, overturns what he calls "the axiom of the absolute character of time."[148] In fact, overturning that axiom was the key to creating a new system of thought. "Clearly," Einstein writes, "to recognize this axiom and its arbitrary character really implies already the solution of the problem."[149]

In science, questions are sometimes more important than answers. In a question is the call of a new form aching to be. And that is the value of axiom flipping. Spot an assumption, yank it into the open and question it, and you are up and running. State a problem, and you are halfway to a new solution. Albert Einstein is so intent on the importance of axiom flipping that he advises you and me to dig our assumptions out of the darkness and bring them to the light whenever we can. He advises that we, too, become axiom flippers. "Concepts which have proved useful for ordinary things," he writes, "easily assume so great an authority over us, that we forget their terrestrial origin and accept them as unalterable facts." Our assumptions become invisible to us. We think that they are unchangeable realities. And in science, says Einstein, our assumptions "then become labelled as 'conceptual necessities,' a priori situations, etc." They become labeled as basics we should not contest.

But taking things for granted can stop us dead in our tracks. Says Einstein, "The road of scientific progress is frequently blocked for long periods by such errors." And progress—the move forward and upward that Herbert Spencer was keen on—is a scientific necessity. A personal necessity. So digging out assumptions, bringing them to the light, and questioning them is crucial to science. And it is crucial to your life and mine. Hauling assumptions out of the darkness by any means necessary. "It is therefore not just an idle game," Einstein writes, "to exercise our ability to analyse familiar concepts, and to demonstrate the conditions on which their justification and usefulness depend." Take a good, hard look at your axioms, says Einstein. Especially the ones it's hardest to see. When you drag an assumption from its hiding place into the spotlight, you may kick start a vital scientific process. "In this way," says Einstein, your assumptions "are deprived of their excessive authority." What's more, if your assumptions don't fit the facts, you can change them. Or, as Einstein puts it, when you hold assumptions up to the light, "concepts which cannot be shown to be valid are removed. Those which had not been coordinated with the accepted order of things with sufficient care are corrected." Question your assumptions, and you might even "produce" what Einstein calls "a new system."[150] A new big picture. And Einstein should know. Producing a new system is precisely what he did. But how?

With one giant axiom flip. The new axiom? That the only constant in the universe is the speed of light. What in the world does that mean? Einstein spoke frequently of measuring rods. Measuring rods show up thirty-seven times in Stephen Hawking's anthology of Einstein's work, *A Stubbornly Persistent Illusion.* The speed of light, Einstein said, is a measuring rod. A measuring rod like the Nippur Ell in Babylon. In fact, the speed of light is the only unchanging measuring rod in the universe. The only measuring rod that doesn't shrink, that doesn't contract, that doesn't squash like bubblegum under a cinema seat. The speed of light is strict, stern, and unyielding. Everything else in the cosmos goes along to get along. You and I meekly shrink and slow our clocks if that's what it takes to keep the speed of light unchanged. From that not-so-simple axiom shift all else pours forth.

From that axiom flip comes the notion that everything else in this cosmos is flexible, bendable, and rubbery. From that axiom flip comes the idea that the rubbery stuff includes time, space, and matter. From that axiom flip comes the idea that the rubbery stuff of the cosmos includes you and me. Why does this universe treat you and me like silly putty? Like wet clay? To make sure that we don't get past the one absolute limit. To make sure that no matter how fast we move, no matter how fast we spin on this rotating planet, no matter how fast our planet swivels us around the sun, no matter how fast our solar system races around the galactic core, and no matter how fast the galaxy moves on its race toward the edges of the cosmos, nothing challenges one single rigid measuring rod: the speed of light.

***

Albert Einstein's life and work was an answer to a question. A basic question of the God Problem. Does abstract thinking, the abstract thinking of reason and math, the abstract thinking that extracts implicit properties from axioms, the abstract thinking begun by Aristotle and Euclid, the abstract thinking of corollary generation, have anything to do with reality? If deep structures, Ur patterns, exist, does abstract thinking based on axioms help us get at them? Is abstract thinking based on axioms divorced from the real world? Is it simply a sandbox for socially incompetent geeks? Geeks like the ten-year-old you with the scissors in your left hand? Or is it a tool that mirrors the real world, a tool that in some mysterious way captures a hidden essence? That captures what Einstein called "a deeply hidden ... something?"

Does axiom-based math help you get a grip on real-world facts? And if so, why? Albert Einstein used the highly abstract math of the nineteenth century's non-Euclidean geometers to arrive at the theory of relativity. He used a math based on twenty-three hundred years of unpacking implicit properties from axioms. But even Einstein recognized that this math can be tossed aside as a mere "product of human thought which is independent of experience"[151]—in other words, as mere mind fluff, the stuff that only a handful of dedicated superbrains can understand. Superbrains so lost in thought that they are radically disconnected from reality.

No matter what the average jock and nerd basher thinks, math is profoundly practical, says Einstein. Remember his pronouncement that "the very word geometry, which, of course, means Earth-measuring, proves this."[152] But was Einstein right about the practical implications of incomprehensible math? Or, to put it differently, can starting with a handful of magic beans, axioms, and working for twenty-two hundred years, working by logic alone, can this airy process help you x-ray reality? Can it help you see behind reality's face to something more basic? Something vaguely like Plato's "Ideas?" Something vaguely like Giuseppe Peano's and Bertrand Russell's "primitives"? Something vaguely like your Ur patterns? Can axiom noodling have anything to do with the real world? And if it can, why?

One answer would come from the fate of the theory of relativity. And from predictions.

THE ADVENTURES OF EINSTEIN'S PREDICTIONS

> *How can it be that mathematics, being after all a product*
> *of human thought which is independent of experience, is so*
> *admirably appropriate to the objects of reality?*
> —Albert Einstein, "Geometry and Experience,"
> an expanded form of an address to the
> Prussian Academy of Sciences in Berlin, January 27, 1921[153]

Einstein's prediction number one? The speed of light is a constant. Remember the Michelson-Morley experiment? The one that showed that when light was zipping along at, guess what, the speed of light, it refused to act like raindrops hitting your windshield or drifting into your rear window? It refused to act like every other sensible substance, object, or moving thing in the cosmos. No matter how fast you moved toward it or fled from it, the speed of light stayed the same. Like the moon following you as you hike at night.

Remember how puzzled the scientific world was by this peculiar finding? For eighteen long years? Then came Einstein's special theory of relativity in 1905. The theory of relativity didn't present a formula to explain the constancy of the speed of light. It used the unchangeability of the speed of light as an axiom. And that axiom "solved" the Michelson-Morley problem. But only if the rest of the theory of relativity proved to be right. Which is where Einstein's predictions came in.

Einsteinian prediction number two centered around a tiny twist that Isaac Newton's math could not account for. A tiny rotation in an ellipse. A rotation in the ellipse of Mercury's orbit.[154] "The precession of the perihelion of the orbit of Mercury."[155] A precession in an orbit? What in the world does that mean? Mercury's orbit is like the orbit of every planet—roughly egg shaped. And that egg, the egg of Mercury's orbit, rotates ever so slowly around the Sun. In other words, the point of that egg turns a 360-degree circle around the Sun like an hour hand slowly creeping around the pivot at the center of a clock. Creeping completely around the Sun roughly every 250,000 years.[156]

Newton's math predicted this swivel of the egg. And the predictions of Newton's math were ferociously close. They landed almost exactly on what generations of astronomers had observed. Almost. They were close, but not close enough. In 1846, way back in the days when Herbert Spencer was still in his "nomadic period,"[157] torn between railroad ventures, inventing things like a flying machine,[158] devising a paper clip,[159] and trying to find a job as a writer, and when Mary Ann Evans was still in Coventry and her translation of Strauss's scandalously secular *The Life of Jesus*[160] was just hitting the bookstores, the ambitious Parisian astronomer Urbain Le Verrier[161] had fixated on a tiny wobble in the orbit of a newly discovered planet, Uranus. By dissecting that wobble mathematically, Le Verrier had predicted the existence of yet another new planet.[162] Le Verrier had used standard Newtonian math to make his prediction. And Le Verrier's math proved to be on target. Two German astronomers followed the predictions made by Le Verrier's calculations and found, guess what? Neptune. The farthest planet from the Sun.

So orbital wobbles might be the clue to the existence of yet more planets. And if discovering one planet gives you a permanent place on the stage of attention, a permanent place in history, presumably discovering two planets could give you twice as much fame. So Le Verrier went on a wobble hunt.[163] And he pounced on the peculiarities of Mercury, discovering that the slow turning of the egg of Mercury's orbit, the precession of Mercury's perihelion, defied Newton's predictions by 38.3 seconds of arc[164] per century. So in 1859 Urbain Le Verrier did the math on Mercury's wobble and predicted yet another new planet, a planet he called Vulcan. But by the 1900s, when

Einstein was noodling with his formulae, no planet Vulcan had appeared. What's worse, the observed error in the wobble of Mercury's orbit had gone up to 42.98 seconds per century.[165] And that error in Mercury's orbit was unaccounted for. That error in Mercury's orbit was an ugly duckling.

But this particular ugly duckling had become a scientific challenge. A recruitment strategy. A competitive puzzle whose solution Einstein counted on to help him establish his new theory of relativity. So Albert the Extraordinary began work on the riddle of Mercury in 1907,[166] two years after his miracle year and the publication of his theory of general relativity. He was still working in the patent office, but he was intent on beating far more established scientists to the punch, beating others to the explanation of the 42.98 second per century anomaly. And intent on beating them by using his new theory, relativity. For eight years Einstein tried one set of equations after another. In 1913[167] he came up with what he thought was a solution. It was not. His elaborate equations predicted a deviation from Newton's math of only seventeen seconds of arc per century.[168] The real figure was 42.98 seconds of arc. Einstein's predictions were a failure. So he went back to work, trying new equations. And when those didn't work, yet more new equations. Over and over again. Finally he found a set of equations that worked.

They were damnably difficult equations. Equations with ten variables. Equations with forty variables.[169] Equations based on Einstein's new theory of a rubberized universe. His theory of a rubberized sheet of space in which massive bodies made funnels, bends, and dents. The funnels, bends, and dents of gravity. The equations in Einstein's tool kit were derived from non-Euclidean geometry,[170] the non-Euclidean geometry that described space's rubbery potholes. They were equations based on the work of Bólyai, Lobachevsky, Gauss, and Riemann. And they predicted a difference of 43 seconds of arc per century.[171] As Einstein put it triumphantly, 42.98 seconds of arc, the real figure, "does not differ sensibly from" relativity's figure of "43 seconds of arc per century."[172]

The implication? That the math of Einstein's theory of relativity, the abstract math of the nineteenth century's non-Euclidean geometers, the math based on unpacking the meaning of an axiom flip, wasn't just ivory tower fluff. You could start with simple rules—with a handful of axioms—

and you could use logical deduction to build (or find) a system implicit in those rules. You could use an axiom shift to build a picture of the universe.[173] And that picture could match reality.

However, it takes more than one good guess to convince the scientific community of the validity of a new theory, especially a theory as peculiar as Einstein's. The explanation of the Michelson-Morley experiment was validation number one. The explanation of the precession, the peculiarity of Mercury's orbit, was validation number two. But what was validation number three?

In 1907, in what he calls "a memoir,"[174] Albert Einstein predicted "that rays of light, passing close to the sun, are deflected by its gravitational field."[175] Einstein predicted that the gravity of the sun would bend a ray of light. Gravity? Bend light? Surely this was ridiculous. Gravity tugs at hard stuff. Bowling balls, marbles, and railroad cars. But light is not hard stuff. It is not stuff you can touch or hold in your hand. It is not stuff you can weigh on a scale. In fact, it is not "stuff" at all. But the notion that gravity can yank and tug on "a ray of light," said Einstein, was a testable proposition, something you could go out and prove. All you needed was a good eclipse.

Where did Albert Einstein's peculiar idea that light would be bent by the sun come from? After all, even Leonardo da Vinci had known that "the lines of radiant light are straight lines."[176] The notion of bending light came from Einstein's idea that gravity rubberizes space. Here's how it works. Let's head back to the trampoline with the rubber sheet. The one we left with a bowling ball dangling in the middle. A bowling ball denting the smoothness of the rubber sheet, punching a funnel-shaped V into it, a funnel dangling toward the ground. Imagine that the bowling ball is the sun. Now put a marble on the edge of the sheet. You're about to shoot the marble. Again. But first aim carefully. Aim so that the marble goes close to the bowling ball but keeps on going past it. What happens to the marble as it scoots past the bowling ball? Its straight-line trajectory is curved as it's caught by the funnel's curve. Your well-aimed marble escapes the funnel's dip and continues on its path. But its path is bent. The same thing happens to a ray of light from a star when it passes close to the sun on its way to a telescope or to your eye. Or so said Albert Einstein.

Which means that if Einstein was right, when light comes from a star, a star whose position in the sky has been tracked by astronomers ever since the days of the Babylonians and of Tycho Brahe, a star whose precise position we know, that position should look shifted. Shifted away from its normal coordinates.

But this isn't easy to check out. Why? There's a problem with starlight passing close to the sun. We can't see it. Starlight only scoots past the sun's rim into our eyes during the day. And during the day, the sun's bright light makes the star's faint light impossible to see. Even with a telescope and photographic plates. Which is where an eclipse comes in. In an eclipse, the moon blacks out the sun and you can see around the sun's edges. For a few seconds you can actually see the stars. In the middle of the day. Including the stars close to the sun's rim. The stars whose light, if Einstein is right, skedaddles past the sun the way the marble you shot skimmed past the bowling ball.

In 1916, two men worked out the precise math of that shift in sun-skimming starlight: Einstein and another German physics prodigy, one who had mastered celestial mechanics at the age of sixteen, Karl Schwarzschild. Now all Einstein and Schwarzschild needed was an eclipse. And they needed the sort of social magnetism acquired by a very high termite pile. Why? Checking the math would take a big budget and a willing team of astronomical observers. Einstein and Schwarzschild lucked out. Arthur Eddington, the director of Cambridge's observatory[177] and the secretary of the Royal Astronomical Society,[178] was one of the towering scientists of his age, a man who would become a legend, a man who would gain fame as what the title of one of his biographies would later call the most distinguished astrophysicist of his time.[179] When Einstein's *Annus Mirabilis* papers had come out in 1905, Eddington had just gotten his master of arts at Cambridge and had gone to work on thermionic emission at Cambridge's Cavendish Lab. Einstein's papers did not interest him.[180] Five years later, in 1910, his colleague,[181] Ernest Rutherford, the man the *Encyclopedia Britannica* calls the "father of nuclear physics," would say that "no Anglo-Saxon can understand" this peculiar German science—Einstein's science. And another colleague, Wilhelm Wien, would answer Rutherford with a quip that Anglo-Saxons "have too much sense."[182] Then in 1915 Einstein came out with his theory of rubberized space and time, his theory of general relativity. And that utterly turned Eddington around. It made Arthur Eddington a passionate Einsteinian.

What's more, there was a problem in the English scientific community.[183]

World War I was raging, pitting, of all people, the Germans—the masters of physics—against the English and the French. A major English scientist—H. G. J. Moseley, the man who had come up with the idea of atomic numbers[184]—had been killed in the Battle of Gallipoli—Britain's scandalously bloody but failed attempt to capture Constantinople. The English scientific community felt that its progress depended on a handful of brilliant minds, irreplaceable minds. It felt it could not afford to lose another one of these fountains of light. And one of these fountains of light and insight was Arthur Eddington. What's more, Eddington was eligible for the draft. But if the scientific powers that be—men like the Astronomer Royal Frank Watson Dyson[185]—could put Eddington to work on some indispensable project, they could get him out of conscription. They could help him dodge the draft. What project could they find for him? Einstein had made a prediction about the bending of light.[186] And there was something very convenient coming up in only two years—an eclipse. An eclipse that would provide an opportunity to see if the sun's gravity did, indeed, bend the light from a nice, bright, very well-studied group of stars—the Hyades. And that eclipse would occur at shortly before one thirty in the afternoon on May 29, 1919.

So Arthur Eddington was drafted to do something that would keep him away from bullets, artillery shells, and mustard gas. He was drafted to see if Einstein's and Schwarzschild's predictions were accurate. Not an easy task when all the instrument makers and equipment suppliers in England are working on the war effort and don't have spare time to make precision apparatus for curious scientists. But World War I ended on November 11, 1918. And in 1919, Eddington and his expedition went to the African island of Principe,[187] where the viewing should have been best. What's more, another expedition mounted by the British Royal Society's Joint Permanent Eclipse Committee[188] went to Sobral in Brazil to check Einstein's predictions out.

Eddington ran into a problem on Principe. The day of the eclipse was cloudy. In fact, it was punctuated by a storm. But the clouds parted for a minute or two and allowed Eddington and his team to get sixteen photographs.[189] Just sixteen! And in Eddington's opinion, those photos validated the Einstein-Schwarzschild predictions.[190] Meanwhile, on the other side of the globe, the Brazilian expedition had a cloudless day. And when it returned to England, its photos seemed to prove the old Newtonian equations correct. But Eddington pointed out that the heat of the sun on the mirror in the Brazilian expedition's main telescope may have warped the mirror's surface and shifted the apparent position of the Hyades. Eddington urged the Brazilian team to check the seven photos from their secondary telescope, a telescope with a four-inch lens.[191] Those photos seemed to confirm Einstein.[192]

With the war over, the world was seriously shaken. The old assumptions of the prewar days no longer seemed to apply to a world in which two hundred thousand men could be killed in a single battle. Just as in 1859 the world had been hungry for a secular story of genesis, the world of 1919 was ravenous for a new big picture. Or, as Ernest Rutherford said, "the total destruction of the Edwardian social order was seen to have been followed by a new world."[193] That insecure world was looking for new certainties. New certainties in which, as Rutherford said, you could "have the triumphal confirmation, by British astronomers in Brazil and West Africa, of an exotic prediction by a German physicist." A new world in which old enemies could live, one hoped, in peace. The theory of relativity seemed to provide a new framework. In fact, it provided a warped, weird framework in which even rival cultures could be seen as live-and-let-live affairs, in which even rival cultures could be seen as relative.

What's more, Einstein's ideas had focused a spotlight on the previously inexplicable work of a whole mess of established scientists—atomists like the Swedish Nobel Prize–winning physical chemist Svante Arrhenius,[194] men of enormous power in the science community like Max Planck,[195] who served as president of the German Physical Society from 1905 to 1909, and high-placed figures with views that at first seemed outlandish like Ernst Mach and Hendrik Lorentz. Not to mention Albert Michelson and Edward Morley. And these people stood to benefit enormously if Einstein's theory was proved correct. So a massive phalanx in the scientific community was willing to promote Einstein with all its might. For example, when the *Scientific American* offered a $5,000 prize "to the writer who shall best explain Einstein's 'relativity' conceptions to the reading public,"[196] Hendrik Lorentz answered the challenge with an entire book, *The Einstein Theory of Relativity*.[197] And Eddington wrote five books on relativity. Five.[198] The termites were putting new bricks on the pile. And turning it into a pillar.

The result? The confirmation of Einstein's theory made headlines. Worldwide. For example, on November 7, 1919, the *London Times* ran one of the most impressive headlines in the history of science: "Revolution in Science—New Theory of the Universe—Newtonian Ideas Overthrown."[199] And the confirmation of the eclipse of 1919 made Einstein what *Time* magazine on December 31, 1999, called "the Man of the Century."[200] It put Albert Einstein in the very center of attention space. It made Einstein a celebrity.

Admittedly, the confirmations of 1919 were a good deal more cloudy—literally—than the headlines implied. But the Einstein and Schwarzschild predictions of rays of light bent by gravity have proven to be on target over and over again for more than ninety years since.

What does Albert Einstein's accuracy mean? What does it mean for the God Problem? It means that math unpacked from axioms, unpacked in a twenty-three-hundred-year process, a process of implication extraction, a process of corollary generation, matches the real world. What's more, it means that math derived from flipping just one assumption can produce a superstar. And what is an assumption? An axiom. A simple rule.

***

But the explanation of the Michelson-Morley experiment, the explanation of Mercury's orbit, and the prediction of the bending of light were just the beginning. Einstein's theory had yet more implications . . . and more predictions . . . up its sleeve. The next was a prediction that came to be known as the "third crucial test of relativity."[201] It was called the "gravitational red shift."[202] Here's how it worked. By 1911, Albert Einstein had figured out that gravity is like acceleration.[203] To understand how, think of yourself in a Porsche. You've gone to Hanover, Germany, to meet with the members of a rock band, the Scorpions. The Scorpions' European manager, Olaf Schroeter, is very proud of his Porsche. So he takes you down a country road that feeds into the autobahn. He turns into one of the autobahn's feed loops, hits the merge lane of the six-lane highway, waits for a break in the traffic, then shows you what acceleration is all about. He smashes the gas pedal down as far as it will go. The Porsche's speed-jolt is beyond that of what you've experienced in any other car. It plasters your back against the seat. It snaps your head back. It flattens the contents of your abdomen against your backbone. It is a thrill. But Einstein said that acceleration is more than just a form of entertainment. It is an equivalent of gravity. Both acceleration and gravity plaster you against something. In gravity's case, you are not plastered to a bucket seat. You are plastered to the ground. And you fight that plaster effect every morning when you wake up, put your feet on the floor, and defy the laws of gravity by standing.

The idea that gravity and acceleration are in some way the same is what Einstein calls "the equivalence principle."[204] Here's how Einstein's reasoning goes: "It is impossible to discover by experiment whether a given system of coordinates is accelerated, or whether . . . the observed effects are due to a gravitational field."[205] What in the world does Einstein mean? Imagine being in solitary confinement in a windowless room in a spaceship. If something plasters you to the floor, you have no way of knowing whether the force smooshing you is gravity or acceleration. You have no way of knowing whether your spaceship has landed on a hefty planet or your prison's rocket engines are doing a Porsche on you. So, brace yourself, gravity is the equivalent of speed. That's the "equivalence principle." Gravity and acceleration are equivalent. The "equivalence principle" is translation from one medium to another run amuck. It's the peculiar process of $A = A$, the peculiar process of "equation" gone hog wild. But is it right? Does it fit the real world? Does it work?

Here's where things get even trickier. Remember, in 1905,[206] Einstein figured out that speed should slow clocks. The closer you get to the speed of light, the more your clock slows down. The closer you get to light speed, the longer an hour stretches out. It's all a part of nature's plot to keep you from passing the speed-of-light speed limit. And, brace yourself for a stretch, since gravity is the equivalent of speed, gravity, too, should slow clocks. Yikes. Yes, gravity and acceleration are the same. So gravity should slow clocks? Just like speed does. A very strange turn of thought. And hard to believe. Very hard.

But, once more with feeling, is it true? Or, to put it in more scientific terms, does the notion that gravity slows clocks make any testable predictions? Yes. Here's how. One of the most basic ways of keeping time is feeling your pulse. Your pulse pounds away at roughly one beat per second. Legend says that Galileo used the timekeeper of his pulse in 1581 when he watched chandeliers swing in the Cathedral of Pisa during a church service and figured out the basic principles of pendulums.[207] Principles that would later lead to the invention of mechanical clocks. The clock—the device that powered Galileo's pulse and that powers yours and mine—is the heart. The chambers of the heart bunch like a fist, then relax again. And they do it rhythmically. Squeeze, relax, squeeze, relax. In other words, your heart is an oscillator. Like the crystal oscillators we use in quartz crystal clocks,[208] cesium clocks, and atomic clocks. What else is an oscillator with a dependable pulse, an oscillator with a dependable frequency? Hang on to your socks. Light.

Light is a clock? You've got to be kidding. Not at all. It may be strange to think of it this way, but green light pulses at 590 trillion beats per second.[209] Yellow light is slower. It pulses at 540 trillion beats per second. And red light is even slower. It slogs along at a mere 440 trillion beats per second. Now here's the trick. If gravity slows down clocks and oscillators, it has to slow down light. Specifically, if Einstein is right, gravity has to slow light's clock. Light's clock is its beat, its pulse, its oscillation. What happens if you slow light's pulse down? It changes color. It gets redder. Or at least if Einstein was right, that's what light tugged by gravity should do—turn a tad reddish. Bizarre, right?

But the reddening of light by gravity was Einstein's prediction number three. And it wasn't just a wild guess. It came straight out of Einstein's math. The math of the theory of relativity. Now for the big question. Does gravity really slow clocks and oscillators down? Does it really make light a squint redder? Is there really a "gravitational red shift?"[210]

At first the news was bad. No one could prove the prediction of the gravitational red shift. No one could prove it in the 1920s. No one could prove it in the 1930s. And no one could prove it in the 1940s. Could Einstein have been wrong? Could pulling implications from axioms, pulling math from a handful of starting rules, prove wrong? Were Einstein's assumptions, his simple starting rules, his notion that time, space, and matter are rubbery, bendable, and stretchable, and his axiom that only the speed of light is a rigid measuring rod, were these wacky ideas wrong? Not to mention Einstein's equivalence principle. His idea that acceleration equals gravity.

In 1960 two Harvard physicists, Robert V. Pound and Glen A. Rebka Jr., decided to try the equivalent of a prank. A trick they planned to pull off in the seventy-four-foot-high Jefferson Tower of Harvard's physics lab, a tower built in 1884 on its own foundation, isolated from the vibrations of classrooms and street traffic and built to minimize even ferromagnetic interference, a tower built specifically, as Harvard's Physics Department puts it, "to support delicate measuring instruments."[211] Pound and Rebka measured the wavelength of light trying to fight against gravity[212] in the Jefferson Tower's eight-floor[213] elevator shaft.[214] Would the pulse of light going up the elevator shaft be slowed down? Would light's clock, its throb, be retarded? Would it be lethargized and leadened? By gravity? And would that slowdown turn the light just the slightest tad red?

One description of the results comes from science writer Marianne Dyson. The light that the Harvard physicists tested was "a beam of high energy gamma rays."[215] Says Dyson, "The redshift predicted by the GTR [general theory of relativity] for the 74-foot tower was only two parts in a thousand trillion." Not an easy thing to compute, much less to measure. But, says Dyson, "the gravitational redshift detected came within 10 percent of the computed value." Chalk up another victory for Einstein. And another victory for math based on geometry and on an axiom flip. Another victory for math based on simple rules. Another victory for corollary generation.

That was Einstein's victory number four. Triumph number one had been the explanation of the Michelson-Morley experiment. Triumph two had been the explanation of the peculiar wobble in the orbit of Mercury. Triumph three had been the prediction that the gravity of the sun bends starlight. And triumph four had been the prediction that gravity slows light's pulse—the prediction of the gravitational red shift.

Then came prediction number five. This prediction didn't come from Einstein himself. If you set forth a framework based on simple rules, others can build on it. Others can extract its implications, its implicit properties. They can build on it the way that Euclid built on the framework of axioms, definitions, and proofs set out by Aristotle. And the way the non-Euclideans built on—and changed—the framework constructed by Euclid. What's more, if you set out a system that's sufficiently compelling, it will attract others the way that the height of a pile of fecal bricks attracts termites to build a wall. Your new framework will become a recruitment pattern, a self-propelled recruitment strategy, a culture wave. Einstein, like Plato, Aristotle, and Euclid, is one of those few who kicked a recruitment strategy into motion. A really big one.

By 1920, the year after Arthur Eddington's expedition to Principe to view the eclipse that would prove Einstein right or wrong, Eddington, the man formerly indifferent to relativity, was a convert. Einstein's theory of relativity had become famous as one of the most difficult-to-understand ideas ever presented to the human mind. And that reputation gave relativity recruitment power. After the November 6, 1919, meeting of the Royal Society, theoretical physicist Ludwig Silberstein, who had just authored a book on relativity, walked up to Eddington and said, "Professor Eddington, you must be one of the three persons in the world who understands general relativity." When Eddington did not reply, Silberstein said, "Don't be modest, Eddington." To which Eddington answered, "On the contrary. I'm trying to think of who the third one might be."[216] Which led to the legend that only three people on the planet understood the theory of relativity.

Remember, Arthur Eddington wrote a total of five books trying to explain the theory of relativity to the masses. Not to mention to his fellow scientists. That's a huge investment of time, reputation, and life force. But Eddington went even further. In his 1920 book *Space, Time, and Gravitation: An Outline of the General Relativity Theory*,[217] Eddington extracted yet another prediction, prediction number five, from Albert Einstein's math. It was called "gravitational lensing."[218]

A lens magnifies the words on the page in front of your nose by bending rays of light coming from the page. But only at a precise distance. Hold the lens too close or too far from the page and it distorts. Sometimes it even splits up the image of the word you're looking at and gives you more images than one. Eddington's eclipse had proved that gravitational bodies like suns bend light. So, said Eddington, according to Einstein's principles, a sun should act like a whompingly big lens. When light from a very distant star passes around the edges of another star on its way to your eye, the near star's gravitational curve should bend the light of the star behind it and serve up a distorted image of that star. In fact, said Eddington, when one star is directly behind another star, the light coming around one side of the blocking star should produce one image, and the light passing around the obstructive star's other side should produce yet another image. Yes, the light of a star completely hidden behind another star should reach your eye despite the obstacle. But it should reach your eye as multiple images.[219] In 1936, Einstein came up with the math for Eddington's prediction.

But ripening the concept of gravitational lensing was a group effort. A multinational and multigenerational effort.[220] A termite-tower effort. In 1937, Fritz Zwicky—a Swiss astronomer who had migrated to the California Institute of Technology—figured that if a star had enough gravity to bend light, an entire "extragalactic nebula" would have even more lensing power. Today we call "extragalactic nebulae" galaxies. But Zwicky's galaxy prediction would not prove out until 1979, when a multinational team of astronomers—two Brits and an American—using the 2.1-meter telescope at the Kitt Peak Observatory in Arizona, discovered two images of the high redshift quasar Q0957+561 separated by 6.1 arc seconds. Two images of a quasar eight billion light-years away. How very Eddington. The team hypothesized that the double image was the product of just the sort of lens that Zwicky, Eddington, and Einstein had foreseen, an "extragalactic nebula," a galaxy. And a year later an American astronomer using a telescope at the University of Hawaii found the guilty galaxy, the gravitational lens, the distorting light bender, at a distance of 3.75 billion light-years. But the validation of this Einsteinian prediction, gravitational lensing, didn't just come once. It came over and over again. How? Gravitational lensing is in constant practical use today. It has become a standard tool of astronomy. That's the most impressive confirmation you can get.

Prediction number six came from Karl Schwarzschild, the former physics prodigy, who continued laboring mightily to extract new implications from Einstein's math. After all, being able to handle Einstein's mathematics even in the slightest degree put you front and center on the stage of attention. It marked you off as a genius. Another sign of a recruitment strategy at work. In 1914, when World War I broke out, Karl Schwarzschild volunteered to fight for his country, Germany. He was sent to Russia[221] to use his mathematical skills to make computations about moving bodies—computations used to aim artillery shells at Russian targets.[222] The same sort of task that another math whiz, János Bólyai, had trained for years earlier. Grisly. But in his spare time, Schwarzschild continued to work out the implications of Einstein's equations. Including the implications for moving bodies, moving bodies that shared the properties of artillery shells and that also shared the properties of far bigger bodies, gravitational bodies. And Schwarzschild sent his work to Einstein, who said, "I had not expected that one could formulate the exact solution of the problem in such a simple way."[223] One of the implications that Schwarzschild unpacked from Einstein's math was downright weird. In 1916, Schwarzschild made a calculation about gravity balls. Really, really big gravitational bodies.

Gravity balls in this cosmos are hungry. Gravitational bodies compete to snag matter and to swallow it, bulking themselves up in the process. However, this big picture of an evolving cosmos wasn't available to Schwarzschild and Einstein in 1916. That's one reason Schwarzschild was certain that his extrapolations from Einstein's equations predicted something utterly unreal.

What did Schwarzschild come up with? As Saint Andrews University's School of Mathematics and Statistics online history of math puts it, Schwarzschild's calculations concluded "that bodies of sufficiently large mass would have an escape velocity exceeding the speed of light and so could not be seen."[224] What does that mean? A ball of ginormous gravitational power would do more than just lengthen the waves of light struggling to escape it. It would do more than merely gentle light and produce a gravitational red shift. A truly humongous gravity ball would swallow the light trying to shoot from it. It would make it impossible for light to escape. It would make it impossible for light to go beyond the spherical boundary that came to be called a "Schwarzschild radius." Gravitational bodies of this sort, gravitational bodies so extreme that they would imprison light, would come to be called black holes.

But Schwarzschild was convinced that his "theoretical solution is physically meaningless."[225] In other words, a black hole cannot exist. It is a sheer figment of mathematics. It's an implicit property of Einstein's axioms with no chance of making it into reality. It's an ugly duckling. Today we've detected black holes all over the cosmos. In fact, black holes seem to sit at the core of nearly every galaxy.[226] And black holes also seem to play a vital role in the cosmos's own mathlike process—in the way the cosmos unfolds the implications of her starting axioms, in the way the universe unpacks her simple starting rules. That process of axiom unpacking—that process of corollary generation—is cosmic evolution. And black holes, we now believe, contribute to the cosmos's evolutionary process.

The black hole was Einstein's victory number six. Validation number six for the theory of relativity. And for the theory of relativity's axiom-based math. But that victory did not arrive until 1972,[227] seventeen years after Einstein's death. Despite Einstein's absence, the termites had continued to add to his towering pile.

Prediction number seven from Einstein's theory helped end World War II. It came from $E = mc^2$. What does $E = mc^2$ mean? That energy and matter are different versions of the same thing. Different translations. Different transformations. $E = mc^2$ means that just as Giuseppe Peano could translate geometry into equations and logic into mathlike symbols, energy can be converted to matter and matter can be converted to energy. But the equality is very unequal. From a tiny amount of matter, you can get a huge amount of energy. And from a huge amount of energy, you can get only a tiny amount of matter. To see how, look at the formula. Take matter and multiply it by a very big number, the speed of light squared, 34,596,000,000 miles per second. Yes, over thirty-four billion miles per second. That gives you the amount of energy in your glunk of matter. Or, to put it differently, it takes a lot of energy to make matter. But it takes very little matter to make energy.

The formula is bizarre. All of it. From the idea that matter equals energy to the size and seemingly arbitrary nature of the numbers. But the most arbitrary number in the mix is the speed of light. Or is it arbitrary? Remember Einstein's one big axiom flip—that the speed of light is the most unchangeable thing in the cosmos. The speed of light is the cosmos's standard measuring rod. Everything else shrinks and stretches to fit it. Including you and me. If that's true, then maybe putting the speed of light into an equation along with matter and energy is not so daft. But how do you prove it? How do you show that this airy and frankly lunatic thinking isn't just a grand geek fantasy? With a prediction.

In July 1939, Europe was on the brink of war with Germany. Again. On the brink of the Second World War. An iteration in a new medium of World War I. Over a year earlier, one hundred thousand of Adolf Hitler's soldiers[228] had marched into Austria and taken over. Then Hitler's troops had grabbed Czechoslovakia. And it was obvious that Hitler wanted more. Much more. Germany's reigning ideology, its new religion, was Nazism. Nazism was a powerful recruitment strategy. It grabbed the lowest levels of the animal brain. How? By blaming all the world's problems on a people too small and helpless to fight back—the Jews. A big-picture idea with enormous appeal. Ultimately the Nazi worldview would lead to the death of six million Jews in concentration camps. But Jews were at the heart of the new physics, and they were not enthusiastic about being exterminated. So Leó Szilárd, a Hungarian Jewish physicist[229] who had fled to America, wrote a letter to President Franklin Roosevelt urging him to explore the possibilities of a weapon based on $E = mc^2$. If $E = mc^2$ was right, the weapon would work. If $E = mc^2$ was wrong, it would be a dud. A very expensive dud. But Szilárd did not feel that he was well enough known to get Roosevelt's attention. And he felt that the crisis was urgent. The Germans who had once been Albert Einstein's colleagues, the physicists at the Kaiser Wilhelm Institute for Physics in Berlin, were closing in on the atom bomb's secret fast. Einstein was vacationing in a gray-shingled cabin in the tiny artist colony of Peconic, over a hundred miles away from New York City on Long Island's northern tip. Szilárd couldn't drive. So he recruited a young physicist from Columbia University who owned a 1935 Plymouth, Edward Teller, and the two jumped into Teller's car and drove from Manhattan out to the wilds of Long Island. When Szilárd arrived, he urged Einstein to sign the letter to Roosevelt. Einstein did some rewriting, then added his signature.[230]

The letter languished in a White House in-box for close to three months, but after Adolf Hitler attacked Poland on September 1, 1939, and started World War II, Einstein's name did, indeed, get attention at the White House. Fame is a recruitment device. A place at center stage in attention space has the power to seduce and kidnap. President Franklin Roosevelt approved a series of development projects that evolved into the Manhattan Project, one of the most expensive weapons projects in history.[231] From the Manhattan Project came the atomic bombs, "Little Boy"[232] and "Fat Man."[233] By the time these bombs were ready in 1945, Hitler had been defeated.[234] But a war was still raging in the Pacific with Hitler's allies, the Japanese. So Little Boy and Fat Man were dropped on Hiroshima and Nagasaki. And they did what Einstein's equation said they would. They translated small amounts of matter—two pounds of 70-percent-enriched uranium U-235— to the energy that flattened two cities and killed between 150,000 and 246,000 people. They translated two pounds of uranium[235] into the explosive force of twenty-five million pounds of TNT. Yes, Little Boy and Fat Man translated just two pounds of uranium into what six million American propaganda leaflets dropped on forty-seven Japanese cities said was "the equivalent in explosive power to what 2,000 of our giant B-29s can carry on a single mission."[236] Two pounds of uranium equal 2,000 B-29s with their bellies full of bombs. That is an amazing act of equation. An astonishing act of translation. The propaganda leaflets, by the way, begged the Japanese people to "petition the Emperor to end the war."[237]

Little Boy, Fat Man, and the nuclear arsenals they spawned proved the predictions of $E = mc^2$. They also saved what former President Herbert Hoover in a memo to President Truman's secretary of war estimated at "500,000 to 1,000,000 lives."[238] The "500,000 to 1,000,000" Japanese and American lives that would have been wasted if America had been forced to invade Japan in order to persuade the Japanese Emperor to surrender. However that claim is controversial. What is not controversial is the two mushroom clouds that came from $E = mc^2$.

And that was not the end of Einstein's victories. That was not the last confirmation of Einstein's belief that abstract math has the power to suss out "deeply hidden" properties of the real world. Forty-three years after Einstein's death came victory number eight. The victory of yet another implicit property of Einstein's math, an implicit property of Einstein's axiom flip. But this was not an implication that Einstein believed in. In fact, he thought it was a mistake. He told George Gamow[239] that it was his biggest blunder. It had to do with non-Euclidean geometry.

***

The non-Euclidean geometry that Einstein used to feel out the shape of the cosmos mapped out two different kinds of curved surfaces: spheres and saddlebacks.[240] But what do the curves of these two shapes—spheres or saddlebacks—really mean? In the general theory of relativity, curves in the sheet of space and time—curves in the space-time manifold—are like the deep-welled funnels that bowling balls punch into the sheet of a rubber trampoline. They relate to gravity. And to gravity's traffic instructions. Remember "matter tells space how to bend; and space tells matter how to move." Curves are space's way of telling matter how—and where—to go. And what tells space how to curve? Matter. Gravity.

If the universe's space-time manifold is spherical, things will turn out rather badly. The universe will first expand, then it will contract. Its gravity will yank it together into what is today called "the big crunch."[241] The cosmos will end in a painfully clotted ball of galaxies that just can't resist each other's attraction. And that ball of crushed galaxies will be shrunk by its own gravity down to a pinprick, a singularity, a singularity like the one that gave us our big bang.[242] On the other hand, if the cosmos's space-time manifold is saddlebacked, things will fly apart. Forever. Galaxies will eventually speed so far apart that they can no longer reach each other with their light. Things will go dark and lonely. You in galaxy NGC 3115 will not be able to wave and say hello to me in the Milky Way even by radio or TV signals that travel at the speed of light. The cosmos will end in a "big chill." Only in a Euclidean universe, a flat universe, will things stay the same. But

Einstein's math didn't allow for a flat universe. It implied that the universe was either spherical or saddlebacked. There was no middle ground. The cosmos was doomed to either fly apart or collapse.

But in 1917,[243] when Einstein was scratching his curly head over this problem, everyone with any sense in science knew with absolute certainty that the universe was stable. It was not rushing apart. And it was not falling in upon itself. Edwin Hubble's discovery that the cosmos was expanding wouldn't hit the scientific community for another twelve years.

How could Einstein do what Marduk, the upstart Mesopotamian god, had done when he ripped the mammoth mussel-shell of the saltwater monster Tiamut apart and turned her curved upper shell into the flat roof of the sky? How could Einstein get his math to describe a flat universe, a nice, calm, stable universe? Tiamut had inserted a brace. He'd "fixed the crossbar."[244] Einstein inserted his own crossbar. A brace to hold the universe in place. A brace to make the geometry of the space-time manifold stay flat. That brace was a mystery force. A repulsive force that kept the universe from caving in on itself. From crunching into a dense apocalypse, undone by its own gravity. Albert the Frizzy, Einstein the Great, called this artificial force, this cross brace, the "cosmological constant."[245]

The cosmological constant fit the implications of Einstein's axioms and of the math that had spilled forth from them. It fit the slippery flip between two alternative forms of curves that had spilled as an implicit property from assumptions—non-Euclidean assumptions. But it didn't fit the fact of a stable universe. Which meant that it was a blot on corollary generation. It was a patchwork fix. Like the patchwork fix that had irked Planck—the quantum. It was an extremely ugly duckling. Or so it seemed. The result? Einstein hated the cosmological constant.

That's why he called it his "biggest blunder." A miserable mistake. Little did he suspect that sixty-nine years later astronomers would be shocked by a discovery that would defy their theories and their intuitive sense of the cosmos. A discovery that would challenge the hell out of the big picture of the day. In 1998 an international team of astronomers was using telescopes in Chile, Arizona, and Hawaii, then checking its results by using the Hubble Space Telescope. The team was studying a special class of novas, exploding stars called "standard candles," Type 1a supernovas.[246] And there was something peculiar about their data. The light from some supernovas was dimmer than it should be. As if the supernovas were farther away. And as if they were gaining speed. Then one Berkeley astronomer on the team, Adam Riess, realized why. Roughly seven billion years after the big bang, the cosmos's expansion had begun to speed up. As the media coverage of 1998 put it, the cosmos had begun to accelerate away from itself.[247]

And astronomers, cosmologists, and theoretical physicists had no idea of why. Only two concepts helped them get a handle on this inexplicable acceleration, this baffling hurry-up in the speed at which galaxies put space between themselves and other star communities. Concept number one was a mystery idea, a patchwork fix, an arbitrary prop, a prop they called "dark energy." A prop for which they had no explanation. And concept number two was Einstein's blunder, Einstein's ugly duckling, Einstein's mathematical crossbar, his jerry-rigged repulsive force— the cosmological constant.

The cosmological constant wasn't a fantasy. It was apparently on target. It showed up not just on paper but in the hardest of all hard and fast realities. The heavens, the skies, the cosmos.

Chalk up victory number eight for the implications of Einstein's strange geometries, victory number eight for the implications of Gauss and Riemann's bizarrely abstract math. Chalk up victory number eight for logical deductions extracted from axioms. Chalk up victory number eight for implicit properties. And chalk up victory number eight for the power of mere symbols, the power of scratch marks. In other words, chalk up victory number eight for isomorphic symbol sets. Victory number eight for the power of translation from one medium to another.

And there would by many more of these Einsteinian victories.

***

What's the point? What does Einstein's story reveal about the God Problem, the problem of how the cosmos creates? It's all about axioms, iteration, and simple rules. Ur patterns. Not to mention recruitment strategies. And it's all about something else, big pictures. What in the world do big pictures have to do with simple rules? They reweave old threads in new ways. In fact, they turn old patterns, old disconnected iterations, into threads of a new tapestry. They make a new sense of old things.

Which leaves the question of where in the name of Planck's constant do big pictures come from? Do axioms build their own big pictures? Do simple rules have big pictures implicit in them from the beginning? Or do big pictures come from someplace far beyond the explanation space of this book? Do they come, god forbid, from an intelligent designer? Do they come from a god? Hold on to your running shoes and we'll come across a few radically new hints to this puzzle. Very strange hints indeed.

***

It has been said many a time that Einstein is overrated. He isn't as original as he's made out to be. Someone else came up with relativity. Someone else came up with the equations. Someone else came up with the speed of light as a constant. Someone else came up with things scrunching as they moved. And all of that is true. But you don't look at a new invention like the world's very first sweater, name the people who made the yarn, and claim that the sweater isn't an achievement. You don't claim that the first sweater in history was really invented by the Coptic Christians in Egypt who invented knitting in roughly 200 CE. The fact is that for the next fourteen hundred years, there was no such thing as a sweater. And you don't claim that the sweater was really conceived by the twisters of the first yarn in the 1400s. Despite the existence of knitting and of yarn, we still had two hundred chilly years to go before the first sweater would be conceived in the 1600s.[248] The sweater is an accomplishment on its own, a radical upgrade from a mere ball of yarn, no matter who plucked the wool and who twisted it into strands. The latest—and newest—iteration counts. The iteration in a new context. The iteration with a new big picture, with a new unifying concept, with a new grand design.

Yes, Einstein was an iterator, an idea repeater. He repeated the old processes of geometry and inductive reasoning in a new context. But many other scientists had repeated old concepts in a new context. What made Einstein unique? He sutured together a new big picture, a new big picture that he called relativity. A new big picture derived from the flip of just one primary axiom. An axiom we didn't even know we had.

***

Which leaves yet one more question. Einstein used math and muscular comprehension to unravel the mysteries of the cosmos. But to what extent were math and muscular comprehension using him? To what extent was the math of axioms using Albert Einstein to advance its interests? To what extent was the math of axioms using Albert Einstein to unfold its implications, its corollaries? To what extent was a recruitment strategy using Albert Einstein to upgrade itself? And to what extent was an impatient cosmos using Albert Einstein to feel out her next step away from entropy? Her next step up?

8

THE AMAZING
REPETITION MACHINE

FORGET INFORMATION:
OR HOW CLAUDE SHANNON GOT IT WRONG

*Theories permit consciousness to jump over its own shadow,
to leave behind the given, to represent the transcendent, yet,
as is self-evident, only in symbols.*
—Hermann Weyl, mathematician, logician,
and teacher of Claude Shannon[1]

Einstein's theory of relativity is about, guess what? Relationships. In Einstein's words, it is about "the relationships of real things to one another." In its own strange way, relativity is a theory about how things beckon each other. How they speak to each other. And how they utterly change each other. When two things are moving close to the speed of light relative to each other and they look at each other, they see each other as squashed and running in slow motion. When space is bent it "speaks" to matter. It gives matter traveling instructions. And matter talks back to space, telling it how to bend. Einstein's theory of relativity was about language and translation from one medium to another.

But relativity was one of the last of the great theories to arise before the appearance of a tool that would utterly change the way we deal with axioms, a new tool that would utterly change the way we work with simple rules, implicit properties, and with George Henry Lewes's emergence. That new tool would also change the way we relate to each other. And to the world around us. That tool would be the computer.

One of those who helped bring us the computer made a big mistake. A mistake that influences the way that you and I think—or misthink—today. That mistake? He failed to see the essence of relationships, the essence of sociality. He misled us about relationships' central carrier—communication. Not to mention translation from one medium to another. How? He misled us about the nature of information.

Or, to put it differently: Forget information. It's all about meaning.

***

In 1948, when you were five years old, Claude Shannon,[2] a skinny, remarkably good-looking thirty-two-year-old, a man who could not quite silence a room with his looks, but a man with cheekbones a model would die for and with a smile that promised both mischief and warmth,[3] was working in a cubbyhole in a huge, warehouselike twelve-story, thirteen-building complex[4] at the farthest edge of a very unlikely place, New York's Greenwich Village, close to the Hudson River. That behemoth of a building in the capital of bohemianism belonged to Bell Telephone.[5] What was Shannon up to? Aside from inventing a motorized pogo stick and riding his unicycle at night in the hallways?[6] He was trying to solve a problem for his employer, Bell Labs.[7]

Bell Labs was the research arm of AT&T and its Bell System, an interlinked pair of companies that had sprung from the original Bell Telephone Company founded by Alexander Graham Bell, the inventor of the telephone, in 1877. AT&T and the Bell System's monopoly on phone service in the United States during most of the twentieth century was so all-encompassing and so benevolently dictatorial that the twinned companies were referred to as "Ma Bell." What was Ma Bell's problem? She had wired the United States with sturdy copper electrical cable. A lot of it. Reports James Gleick in his book *The Information*:

> By 1948 more than 125 million conversations passed daily through the Bell System's 138 million miles of cable and 31 million telephone sets.[8]

And the more phone calls Ma Bell could squeeze through those 138 million miles of copper wires, the more money she could make. The more money Ma Bell could make without an expensive investment in more blue-hard-hatted cabling crews, more blue 1948 Ford F-1 two-door trucks, more telephone poles, more land right-of-ways, and more copper cable.

AT&T and the Bell System were smart. Very smart. Their basic science arm, AT&T Bell Telephone Laboratories, was one of the most admired scientific research facilities in the world. In the early 1940s Bell Labs had developed a usable version of a technology that had obsessed young Albert Einstein in 1905—the photovoltaic cell. At roughly the same time, Bell Labs had also developed the coding techniques that had helped the Allies—our side—win World War II. And in 1947, two years after World War II ended, a trio of Bell Labs employees had invented the transistor, for which two of Bell Lab's researchers would win a Nobel Prize. In fact, one of those Bell Labs researchers—John Bardeen—would win two Nobel Prizes. Then, seventeen years later, in 1965, two more Bell Labs researchers would discover the cosmic background radiation predicted by big bang theory. They would discover the leftover radiation from the big bang while trying to winkle out the source of microwave interference in a giant horn antenna at the Bell Labs campus in Holmdel, New Jersey.[9] And these discoverers of the cosmic background radiation, too, would win a Nobel Prize. But that was a quarter of a century in the future.

Back to the 1940s. Bell Labs hired superscientists. So when Ma Bell wanted to figure out how to squeeze the greatest number of phone calls into the smallest amount of wiring, she hired, of all things, a mathematician. And not just any mathematician.

Claude Shannon had been born in the tiny town of Petoskey, Michigan, in 1916, one year after Albert Einstein had published his general theory of relativity. And little Claude had grown up with his probate judge father and his high school principal mother in nearby Gaylord.[10] One of Claude Shannon's hobbies had been a form of sending and receiving: transporting objects in a precise order from one hand to another—juggling. Claude had also loved two forms of play that involved isomorphic symbol sets and translation—games and codes. And he'd built a handmade telegraph system.

Despite these frivolous hobbies—or perhaps with their help—Shannon had gotten his undergraduate degree at the University of Michigan. Then he had moved to the big time for grad school, MIT.

In his first year at MIT, Shannon had been mentored by President Franklin Roosevelt's future "science czar" and future vice president of MIT, Vannevar Bush,[11] an MIT faculty member who way back in 1922 had combined science and next-tech to found the American Appliance Company,[12] one of the first manufacturers of electronic tubes. Three years later, the American Appliance Company had been renamed Raytheon.[13] Shannon had been *the* student tending Vannevar Bush's mechanical dream machine, a one-hundred-ton iron monstrosity that used gears and an occasional control switch to solve differential equations. And not just any differential equations. Differential equations with up to eighteen variables. This precomputer contraption knew nothing of binary codes or bits and bytes. Yet one headline of the 1930s dubbed it as something impossible: a "thinking machine."[14]

But it wasn't Bush who would help make a computer revolution. It was Claude Shannon. And Shannon would do it with his 1940 master's thesis.[15] How?

Back in the late-nineteenth century, just a few decades before Claude Shannon was born, people like Bertrand Russell had suspected that logic was math in disguise and that math was just logic wearing a different costume. As you and I already know, the late-nineteenth century was an era of stripping things of their costumes in the hope of finding that they were all the same naked body underneath. It was an era of boiling things down. It was the age in which Giuseppe Peano boiled the natural number system down to five axioms. And it was the era in which an Englishman named George Boole managed to boil down all of logic to a tiny number of symbol strings[16] that looked like equations. The language of those simple equations was called Boolean algebra.

You may have seen Boolean algebra if you've noodled with the advanced search functions on search engines like Google. It's the algebra of "and-or" and "if-then" statements. What are if-then, and and-or statements? *If* you slither into your little black dress, *and if* you go to the Harvard Club, *and if* you snag the interest of the man of your dreams, *and if* you haul him home, *and if* you disregard birth control, *and if* one of your ova chooses (yes, eggs choose) to open its membrane gates to one of his sperm, *then* you will be stuck paying college tuition in nineteen years. That's an if-then statement. Complete with five "ands." Here's another if-then statement. *If* all purple snakes are poisonous *and if* the snake curling around your ankle to get some sleep while you sit on your veranda in shorts and sandals sipping a mint julep is purple, *then* the snake you are wearing as an anklet has a medically disturbing bite. Or, as Aristotle put it, *if* all men are mortal *and if* Socrates is a man *then* Socrates is mortal. Boole boiled this down to what was called "symbolic logic."

But, says Bertrand Russell, to whom symbolic logic was vital, it was Giuseppe Peano, our old friend Giuseppe Peano, who would really drive symbolic logic home. Explains Russell, "Since the publication of Boole's *Laws of Thought* (1854), the subject [of symbolic logic] has been pursued with a certain vigour, and has attained to a very considerable technical development. Nevertheless, the subject achieved almost nothing of utility either to philosophy or to other branches of mathematics, until it was transformed by the new methods of Professor Peano."[17] But it was Boole's name that stuck.

No matter who got the credit, symbolic logic would bust loose in ways that even Bertrand Russell never imagined. Symbolic logic would penetrate every nook and cranny of your life and mine. And this explosion would take place because of Claude Shannon. What would be Shannon's contribution?

In his 1940 MIT master's thesis, Claude Shannon the juggler took Boole's symbolic logic—his Boolean algebra—and translated it into a new medium. He built a new isomorphic symbol set. And a very strange one at that. One very different from traditional scratch marks on clay, papyrus, wax, or paper. Or from the syllables tumbling from your tongue and mine. And far, far different from Vannevar Bush's gears. Something far, far simpler.

Shannon showed how you could represent Boolean algebra with, brace yourself, a series of electrical switches. Yes, electrical switches like the wall switches for your bedroom light. A string of electrical switches in which the switches that were on represented yeses and the electrical switches that were off represented nos. A series in which switches that were on represented true and switches that were off represented false. A series in which turning your bedroom light on can represent an ummm hummm and turning it off can represent a nope. Shannon showed how you could use these electrical switches to represent "Did you remember to put on your little black dress?" If you remembered to slither into that night-dark bit of eye-catching silk, turn the switch for little black dress on. Turn your bedroom switch on. When you went to the Harvard Club on New York's West 44th Street just off Fifth Avenue to look for a man with glamour and money, did you find a man worth taking home? Not a chance. OK, turn the switch for "the man of your dreams" off. Turn your living room switch off. Did you get pregnant? Let's ask the machine. Shannon showed how you could wire your electrical switches so that they would figure out the conclusion, the logical conclusion—"no." If you made the mistake of turning your household wiring over to Shannon, he could hook things up so that your kitchen light would tell you "no." How? By turning itself off.

Sounds silly, right? But in fact Claude Shannon was inventing a new variation on the clay hand tablet of the Mesopotamians. A new variation that would give birth to a new world of isomorphic symbol sets, isomorphic symbol sets that would change the way we extract implications from axioms. Isomorphic symbol sets that would make the nineteenth century's non-Euclidean axiom flip look primitive.

The ons and offs in Shannon's thesis did more than just work out George Boole's symbolic logic. They handled yet another symbol set. The symbol set of math. If you wanted to flip from logic to arithmetic, when a switch was on, it represented a one. And when it was off, it represented a zero. With ones and zeroes you could represent any mathematical function you wanted. As long as you used a binary number system—a system with only two numbers, one and zero. (A system pioneered by Gottfried Leibniz 247 years earlier.[18]) Talk about translation from one medium to another! This was isomorphic symbol sets gone berserk.

Iteration of something old in a new medium frequently produces something new. Something unexpected, something surprising, something with the quality of cosmic creativity shock, cosmic shape shock. Claude Shannon's translation of symbols on paper to switches in an electrical circuit paved the way for the computer. Every time you type a sentence into an e-mail, every time you hit the send button, and every time you tweet or twiddle with Facebook® you owe a debt of gratitude to Claude Shannon's master's thesis. So do I. And I live on the computer. So I owe Shannon a debt that's huge. Nonetheless, there is one simple fact. Claude Shannon opened a new frontier. A new frontier for the human mind. And Shannon made a mistake. A big one.

Legendary physicist David Bohm points out a crucial trap in science. He warns that you make a huge mistake when you get the math right and the metaphor wrong. And when it came to Shannon's biggest theoretical contribution, he got something very wrong indeed.

When Claude Shannon finished his thesis and graduated in 1940[19] he went from grad school at MIT to Princeton's Institute for Advanced Study as a National Research Fellow and apparently never bumped into the man around whom much of the Institute had been built, Albert Einstein.[20] He never bumped into the man who pleaded with us to find our hidden assumptions and bring them to the light. Which is too bad. That plea would have stood Shannon in good stead. Then, in 1941,[21] Shannon landed at Bell Labs.

It was at Bell Labs in 1948 that, in his attempt to solve the problem of how many phone calls you could squeeze down the pipeline of a copper wire, Shannon came up with a formula.[22] Steady yourself for tough medicine:

$$H = -\sum p(i)\log_2 p(i)$$

What in the world does that argle-bargle mean? Richard W. Dillman, former chair of the communications department at a small, exclusive school in Maryland, McDaniel College, put it better than the Ivy Leaguers: "Claude Shannon's famous formula provides a way to compare one code against the other to find out which can send the most messages with the smallest number of symbols."[23] Just what Ma Bell and her 138 million miles of copper cable needed. Fifty-one years down the line, in 1989, Shannon's work would lead to a milestone in data compression—the technique that generates every MP3 file you've ever listened to.[24] So far, so good. But then came the problem.

Shannon had to name the factor his equation described. He had to figure out what to call the big *H* at the formula's beginning. The big *H* that the whole formula hinged on. Claude Shannon had to name what he'd identified. That name would determine the metaphorical interpretation, the common interpretation, of his theory for as long as that theory lasted. And theories whose math is right, but whose metaphor is wrong, can be dangerous. Princeton Institute for Advanced Study mathematics professor and legendary Hungarian-born Jewish mathematician John von Neumann recommended that Shannon label the big *H* with the word for something that we've fingered in this book as a toxic concept—entropy. Why did von Neumann suggest that Shannon call *H* entropy? Because entropy is based on a bit of statistical reasoning. Here's how that reasoning goes.

The odds of a highly structured cosmos in which you have eyes, a brain, and language, a cosmos in which you can read this sentence, are zillions to one. There are only a tiny number of unique paths that get you to this state. A tiny number of unique paths that lead to a pile of atoms assembled into one hundred trillion cells that breathe, speak English, know how to turn the pages of a book, have your street address, your credit card number, your name, and your Internet passwords. But a small number of paths that lead to you is an overstatement. Let's be blunt. In reality, the number of paths that can lead to you and me in the here and now communicating via this sentence may be as small as one.

On the other hand, says entropy and its math, there are quintillions upon quintillions of paths that could lead to an utter chaos, a soup of atoms without planets, without clouds in the sky, without clumps of dirt, and without cars whose engines you can start by hitting a button on your key ring. Hence everything must tend toward chaos. Everything must tend toward particle soup. Why? Because the chaos of a particle soup is the most probable state. There are quintillions of ways to achieve it. And there are hardly any paths that lead to you and me. If you carry this reasoning to its extreme you come to an interesting logical conclusion. A conclusion that's rock solid and irrefutable. You and I do not exist.

Probability rules, say the entropists. More specifically, all power goes to the *equations* of probability theory. Which is why you and I do not exist. The odds are against us. At least in theory. In reality, universes with complex form seem to be far more probable than universes of soup. But that is something that the entropists deny. And it is something that—surprise, surprise—a universe based on simple rules, a universe yanked from axioms, implies. However, that is a subject for another time.

Whatever its flaws, it turns out that the math behind this sort of probabilistic reasoning—the math behind the equations of entropy—is very helpful in understanding the electrical impulses that carry telephone calls down wires. It's useful in compressing the greatest number of messages into the smallest amount of cable space. Not to mention useful in blocking the static that can interfere with those messages. Why? There are zillions of paths to disorder in an electrical cable.[25] There are zillions of paths to crackle, static, and hiss. But there are very few paths that lead to the message "I met absolutely no one interesting at the Harvard Club last night. Do you think I should change my lip gloss?" Each message is unique. Just as you and your passwords are unique. So the math that describes the probabilities of entropy versus the likelihood of the extremely slim path that led to you also applies to oodles of forms of noise in an electrical wire versus messages that are one of a kind.[26]

Hence Shannon's formula is almost precisely the same as the formula for entropy. That's why John Von Neumann thought that entropy seemed like a logical name. But no, the word entropy—and almost the same formula—already existed. What's more, Shannon was out to fry bigger fish.

Shannon had worked his equation out to help increase what Oxford University's Vlatko Vedral calls "channel capacity."[27] Shannon had produced his equation to solve a problem in the communications business. So he named his *H* for something that sounded like it relates to communication. Something with application to a lot more than just signals in a cable. "Information."

The result? When Shannon wrote a two-part article that appeared in the July and October 1948 issues of the *Bell System Technical Journal* on his formula and on his formula's implications, he called it "A Mathematical Theory of Communication."[28] And in the 1949 book version of his article, he presented something startlingly new, something that made his book a scientific hit overnight. He called his math "information theory." But beware. Do not get your math right and your metaphor wrong.

What was the problem? What was the big mistake? Claude Shannon saw communication as a form of juggling. "The fundamental problem of communication," he wrote, "is reproducing at one point either exactly or approximately the message selected at another point."[29] With the limitations of that point of view—the very severe limitations—Claude Shannon sent the world of science on a wild goose chase. A goose chase that has gone on from 1948 until today. Why?

Here's a clue. As one book on the basics of Claude Shannon's information theory puts it, "for Shannon, the messages 'CONSTANTINOPLE' and 'JFUEJSHUHESEF[J]' were identical from a communications perspective."[30] How could that possibly be? If I whisper Constantinople in your ear you imagine an exotic city that once had a fabulous empire. A city that legend says paved its streets with gold. If I whisper JFUEJSHUHESEFJ, you wonder why I am gargling in your ear. However, the book *Information Science 101* explains that from a Shannon information theory point of view, both CONSTANTINOPLE and JFUEJSHUHESEFJ "were each fourteen-character messages." And the information theory task for each is the same. To juggle the fourteen characters in the correct order. And to keep them intact as you toss them from hand to hand. Or, to put it in Bell Labs terms, the challenge is to transmit them accurately. Hence, from an information theory point of view, the messages are the same. They are identical.

That's the Bell Telephone point of view. What you say into your phone receiver is up to you. Our job is to get whatever it is to whoever you are talking to. Content is not our business. We are in the transport trade. And Shannon's formula dealt with transport only. But many ordinary people in the street might think that information means more than transport. It means content.

But that is just a tiny fly in the copper cable, right? A minor issue. In fact, it is not as minor as it might seem. As Shannon's information theory conceived things, handling communication and its central ingredient, information, was a bit like juggling fortune cookies. In the case of JFUEJSHUHESEFJ and CONSTANTINOPLE, that would be fourteen fortune cookies. And from an information theory point of view, your job as a juggler is to get all fourteen fortune cookies from your right hand to your left hand in one piece. In the right order. But here's the key. Your job, from an information point of view, is not to read the messages.

Was information theory overlooking something? For example, the whole point of fortune cookies? And the whole point of information? Reading the message? Getting across an idea?

Shannon had mangled a word. James Gleick says he "hijacked" it.[31] According to the ultimate source on the English language, the twenty-volume *Oxford English Dictionary*, the word "information" means, and I quote, the "communication of instructive knowledge." Information, says the *OED*, is the "communication of the knowledge or 'news' of some fact or occurrence." In other words, information is not the mere act of tossing a fortune cookie from one hand to the other. Information is not information until you open the fortune cookie and read it.

To repeat, information is the act of getting across a message. It is of little value for you to smuggle out a fortune cookie with a cry for rescue like "Help, I am being held prisoner in a Chinese fortune cookie factory," if some bozo mathematician from Michigan uses the fortune cookie for juggling but never opens it. The whole point of the fortune cookie with your urgent plea for help is to get someone to read it and to respond. Preferably with a SWAT team. You are sending out a stimulus and you are desperate for a response. That is communication. And information, says the *Oxford English Dictionary*, is communication.

Again, Shannon's definition of information was missing something. Warren Weaver, director of natural sciences for the Rockefeller Foundation, was Shannon's coconspirator in error. Weaver wrote a *Scientific American* article in July 1949 trumpeting the world-changing nature of Shannon's information theory.[32] Weaver's essay and Shannon's two-part article on information theory were then combined into a book, the book that put Shannon's information theory on the map, Shannon and Weaver's *A Mathematical Theory of Communication*. The missing ingredient was what Shannon and Weaver called "meaning."

In information theory, the word information has nothing to do with the message you are trying to get across, says Weaver.[33] Weaver tells us point blank in the book he coauthored with Shannon that "the word *information*, in this theory, is used in a special sense," a special engineering sense. Continues Weaver, it "must not be confused with its ordinary usage."[34] And Weaver warns the world that "in particular, information must not be confused with meaning." But is information without meaning really information? Is the mere transport of information really communication? If you are awaiting release from mopping floors and memorizing the works of Mao and Confucius in an oriental cookie-baking operation, has your fortune cookie crying out for help done its job? Has it completed its appointed task if it is delivered to the police department intact but no one opens and reads it?

The separation of meaning from information did not sit well with some of the best minds of Shannon's time. At New York's Beekman Hotel on March 22, 1950, there took place one of a series of conferences of super-brains funded by the Josiah Macy Jr. Foundation—conferences on cyber-netics. At those conferences, Shannon laid out his ideas. And the aristocrats of intellect who gathered to hear him, the superbrains who sizzled with excitement at the idea that information could at last be translated into math, that human thought could at last be translated into hard science, included math legend John von Neumann, anthropology celebrity Margaret Mead, Mead's husband anthropologist Gregory Bateson, and a select smattering of others from psychology, brain physiology, physics, electrical engineering, and more. But there was a problem. Reports James Gleick, "Margaret Mead and others, felt uncomfortable with the notion of information without meaning."[35] The Viennese physicist Heinz von Foerster was more than uncomfortable. He said, "I wanted to call the whole of what they called information theory signal theory." Why? "Because information was not yet there. There were 'beep beeps' but that was all."[36] Von Foerster was on to something.

In Gleick's words, "Hard as Shannon tried to keep his listeners focused on his pure, meaning-free definition of information, this was a group that would not steer clear of semantic entanglements."[37] Separating meaning from information may have seemed logical to Shannon. But it did not make sense to these very smart people.

Shannon's mistake would count. If his math was right but his metaphor was wrong, his error would have enormous consequences. Why? Shannon's infor-mation theory would turn the use of the word "information" into a scientific fad. By March of 2011, Amazon.com® would list 47,079 books with the word "information" in their titles. A few were books that had nothing to do with Shannon—for example books of information about how to make millions by training your dog's fleas as entertainers and by starting your own flea circus. OK, no books on training fleas. I made that up. But you get the general idea. Here's the point: the vast majority of these books were Shannon derived. One title that captured the enormous ambition of the information theory enthusiasts in 2011 was Charles Seife's *Decoding the Universe: How the New Science of Information Is Explaining Everything in the Cosmos, from Our Brains to Black Holes.* Yes, you heard it right. Information theory claimed to explain everything from brains to black holes. Information theory claimed to explain everything from the pile of neurons with which Pythagoras did his pondering to Einstein and Schwarzschild's heavenly bodies from which light could not escape.

Physics was just one of the fields that Shannon's work touched, but it was a good example. Physics book after physics book interpreted the entire cosmos in terms of information, books like Seth Lloyd's *Programming the Universe: A Quantum Computer Scientist Takes On the Cosmos,* Vlatko Vedral's *Decoding Reality: The Universe as Quantum Information,* or Paul Davies and Niels Henrik Gregersen's *Information and the Nature of Reality: From Physics to Metaphysics.*

Then there were the new "information sciences." In 1958 the *Harvard Business Review* named a new discipline and a new career slot after Shannon's "information." The Harvard folks called this hot new way to make a living IT, "information technology." By 2009, IT was a $763 billion business,[38] a nearly trillion-dollar industry.

Information science spread so far that by 2011, *Wikipedia*—the people's data source—listed twelve subject areas and seventeen other "topics" (from bibliometrics to user-centered design) into which information science had seeped. Yet *Wikipedia* missed a massive flood of other "information" specialties: from information architecture, business management information systems, healthcare information systems, and accounting information systems, to information ethics, quantum information, information marketing, and even "information as medicine."[39] Yes, Claude Shannon's information as a form of medicine. Shades of Pythagoras! And all of these had books dedicated to their practice.

But one book, *Reliability Criteria in Information Theory and in Statistical Hypothesis Testing,* says that's not all. The authors gush that "the sensational aftermath of Shannon's"[40] work also rocked mathematics, statistics, cryptology, economics, biology, and linguistics. In the subtitle of his 2010 book *The Master Switch,* Tim Wu even told us that our lives in the twenty-first century were being swayed by "the rise and fall" of massive "information empires."[41] And the cosmos of the big bang became the informational universe. No wonder the 1990s and the early twenty-first century were called the information age. Blame it all on Claude Shannon.

THE CASE OF THE CONVERSATIONAL COSMOS

What does the quibble over "information" versus "meaning" have to do with the God Problem? What does Claude Shannon's information error have to do with the simple rules that may have started the cosmos? A few more questions. What does Claude Shannon's mistake have to do with the hypothesis that simple axioms, basic algorithms, and corollary generation were the source of the bricks of the cosmos? Not to mention the universe's mortar, its rules for bricklaying, and perhaps even the universe's architecture?

A great deal more than you might think. Why? Because the information theorists are right about one thing: at bottom this is an informational universe. It is a conversational cosmos. This is a cosmos of constant communication. A gossiping, whispering, and shouting cosmos. A cosmos in which it's not enough to shift a fortune cookie from your right hand to your left hand. A cosmos in which opening the fortune cookie and reading the message is the meat of the matter. Or, to put it in Claude Shannon terms, this is a cosmos in which meaning means everything.

Meaning? Surely this is lunacy. Surely this is anthropomorphism on a binge. Surely there is no such thing as meaning until more than thirteen billion years into the evolutionary process when the cosmos coughs out humans, humans with curiosity, suspicions, and IQs. Humans who can talk on telephones and read.

But restricting communication and meaning to humans is a big mistake.

Meaning has been here since the first flick of the cosmos. Yes, we've had communication since the cosmos first twitched. And it's been communication in which meaning has meant everything. How do we know?

Let's go back to our café table at the beginning of the universe. In the beginning there was nothing but an unfurling sheet of space-time, a rushing manifold of speed. And that sheet of naked speed, that lickety-split, sprinting sprawl of naked energy, precipitated over 10^{87} particles, particles you know well by now—the six forms of quarks,[42] six forms of leptons,[43] and bosons like photons.[44] We will skip over what that sheet of speed "communicated" to its offspring, the quarks and leptons. We will skip over the fact that somehow that sheet "informed" these tiny particles in a manner that the *Oxford English Dictionary* would have approved of—a manner that appears in a now-obsolete meaning of the word "information," a meaning that was in use from 1387 to 1813: "The action of informing . . . formation or moulding of the mind or character, training, instruction, teaching; communication of instructive knowledge." We will forget about the etiquette book of social instructions with which the cosmos endowed her daughters, the first particles—instructions on whom to join and whom to flee. Instructions on attraction and repulsion. We will forget the way the cosmos "informed" particles with social rules. We will forget the fact that this is communication.

Instead, we will go directly to what quarks did when they met. And meet they did. With 10^{87} quarks jouncing around, the numbers of permutations and combinations was way up there in figures with more than a hundred zeros. And what did those quarks do when they met? They checked each other out. Whoa. Checked each other out? That's a big claim. The beginning of the universe was not exactly a pickup joint. It was not a sleazy rendezvous for quick hookups.

Actually, that's exactly what it was. But for the proof, let's make a quick visit to the leading psychologist of the 1950s, an ultraserious scientist who confesses that in his youth he dedicated himself to becoming a poet and writer, but "I had failed as a writer, because I had nothing important to say."[45] His name? B. F. Skinner. Burrhus Frederic Skinner. B. F. Skinner did not understand the human psyche. And he made no bones about it. Very strange for a psychologist. But Skinner had a greater impact on mid-twentieth-century psychology than any thinker since Sigmund Freud. Why?

The mind, B. F. Skinner said, was an "explanatory fiction."[46] His critics said that Skinner saw the mind as a "black box."[47] Skinner's vision turned your mind and mine into sealed containers that no scientific equipment allows researchers to peer into. In Skinner's day there were electroencephalographs with electrical contacts on your head attached to a bunch of pens that squiggled on a piece of paper and charted your brain rhythms.[48] And in the final decades of Skinner's life, PET scans and MRI[49] machines came along to show perfect strangers hot spots of activity in your brain. But the real heavy-duty brain activity revealer, fMRI, did not appear until the year after Skinner's death.[50] However, even if you use the most advanced fMRI machines on someone you'd like to work up the gumption to date, you can't tell what she's thinking. You can't glimpse the words going through her mind, the emotions rolling like giant tumbleweeds through her cerebral corridors, and the visions dancing in her head. More important, you can't see what she's thinking about you. So what can you see? What clues to psychology could you see in Skinner's day? And what clues to the hidden workings of the psyche can you see today?

Skinner came up with two magic words: "stimulus" and "response."[51] Those were things you could eyeball. You could see input and output. But input and output were not Skinner's words. Stimulus and response were. You could only see one thing, said Skinner. You could see what stimulus and response amounted to. You could only see behavior. So the form of psychology that Skinner put on the map was called "behaviorism." And it was so successful in policing and intimidating mainstream psychologists that the word "psyche" was banished in the 1950s and 1960s. From *psych*ology. From the science of the psyche. Why? The psyche was too wishy-washy. It was too squiffy and soft. It implied stuff going on inside the brain, squishy things like emotions. And, Skinner emphasized, you cannot see emotions. You can see grimaces. You can see tears. You can hear screams. But those are behaviors. Those are responses. Emotions do not exist. Why? Because you cannot see them.

Yes, B. F. Skinner went a bit overboard. In the end he denied that there was a mind at all.[52] Why? Because you can't see my mind. All you can see is my face. Or my typeface. All you can do is listen to me talk. All you can do is read what

I write. All you can do is imagine me pounding on a table. All you can see is my behavior. You cannot see my mind. So my mind does not exist. To repeat, all psychology, according to the pope of mid-twentieth-century psychology B. F. Skinner, comes down to what's visible. All psychology comes down to what Skinner called "behavior analysis."[53] All psychology comes down to stimulus and response.

But stimulus and response, not to mention behavior, have nothing to do with the first flutter of the cosmos, right? There was no psyche, no mind, no feeling in the cosmos's first flick. Correct. Though many spiritually oriented folks and even a few scientists believe that the universe began with consciousness, I think that is extremely unlikely. Consciousness is an animal and a human thing. It is not a thing of protons and stones.

But it's very different for stimulus and response. Stimulus and response are not just human. Not at all. Stimulus and response are at the very core of the cosmos. Let's get back to that moment at our café table at the beginning of the universe when, in the first nanotwist of the big bang, quarks precipitated out of the whooshing time-space manifold. Those quarks were social. And they communicated. What's more, they did not communicate with Shannon's raw information. They communicated with Shannon's missing ingredient—meaning. How do we know? Stimulus and response.

No quark is an island. No quark can live on its own. A quark must gang up with other quarks. Instantly. And each quark comes with that inner rule book of attraction and repulsion I keep jabbering about. Each quark comes with an etiquette book built into it that tells it who to rush toward and embrace. Not to mention which other quarks to dodge, to escape, and to flee. So how do quarks gang up in groups of three? By reading each other's meaning. Not each other's Shannonish information. Each other's meaning.

Another whompingly big and unlikely claim, right? What in the world indicates that quarks register meaning? It's simple. Watch the way quarks act. Stimulus and response. You can see how quarks interpret information by watching their behavior. By watching to see if they run to meet each other or rush away. At least you could see this if we found a way to watch quarks. The fact is that we haven't. And theory says we never will.[54]

But if current theory about quarks is right, quarks are all about behavior.

Behavior, in turn, is all about stimulus and response. And the response a quark makes depends on its interpretation of information. It depends on the quark's reading of another quark's fortune cookie. If you and I are up quarks of precisely the same kind, we turn our backs on each other and rush away.[55] But if you and I are different in just the right way, we whoomph together and hold on tight. Meanwhile we attract one more quark of precisely the right kind. How? By using our tool of communication. Our tool of seduction, recruitment, and kidnap—the strong force.[56] And the strong force—one of the four forces of the cosmos—is a form of what Shannon calls information. It conveys a message.

The result of this instant dating? The result of this exchange of information? The result of interpretation and meaning? The result of this stimulus and response? The result of this self-assembly? The result of this fortune cookie reading? Trios. Two up quarks and one down quark are a proton. And two down quarks and one up quark are a neutron.

Again, all of this attraction, repulsion, flirting, and fleeing is done courtesy of the strong force, one of the four fundamental forces of the cosmos. What is a force? It moves things. It is associated with what Newton called "action at a distance." What is the mover, the propulsion mechanism, the means of transport that shuttles things around? Newton did not know. He had to leave the question dangling. Since Newton's day we've mapped the four forces. But we still haven't explained how they work. We still don't know how "attraction at a distance" does its thing. Yet we do know one thing. Objects in this cosmos somehow communicate with each other. They do it using the strong force, the weak force, the electromagnetic force, and gravity. They do it by curving space. They read each other's signals. And they move according to the social rules built into them. They respond to what they read. They obey what Galileo called "the terms and the laws imposed upon"[57] them. They do it by either rushing together and hugging or by running away.

The signal, whatever it may be, is a stimulus. And the movement toward or away from each other is a response. The instant skitter toward or away from each other is translation of a signal into another language—the language of travel, the language of getting a move on. So elementary particles at the first flick of the cosmos showed the signs that B. F. Skinner associated with psychology. They showed behavior.

Does that mean particles have a psyche? Does it mean that they brood, stew, have crushes, and rejoice? Not by a long shot. But it does mean that particles are under the sway of a deep structure, a primordial pattern, perhaps even an Ur pattern. And it does mean that the pattern of attraction and repulsion will do something strange as this cosmos unfolds. As the cosmos evolves, attraction and repulsion will show up among protons and electrons, atoms, dust clouds, galaxies, stars, planets, molecules, cells, bacterial colonies, sexual creatures, and mating strategies. Attraction and repulsion will show up in the loves and hates of human beings. Attraction and repulsion will reappear in everything from families, tribes, wars, and nations to religion, art, philosophy, and science. In fact, University of Calgary evolutionary biologist Valerius Geist, author of the landmark book *Life Strategies, Human Evolution, Environmental Design,* will eventually conclude that every act of communication between bacteria, plants, animals, or humans boils down to attraction cues and repulsion cues. That's right: attraction and repulsion.[58] Every act of communication, no matter how primitive or complex.

Attraction and repulsion will show up on level after level of emergence. Every time it appears, it will be something very old becoming something very new. Something old becoming something very new by its translation into a new medium. Something old becoming something very new via the change of its place in a big picture.

And at bottom is a simple fact. Attraction and repulsion are what loop quantum gravity master Lee Smolin calls "relational."[59] Attraction and repulsion are the movers and the shakers that quark the social cosmos. Attraction and repulsion are the choreographers of the big-bang tango.

***

The tango is a dance in which a gorgeous woman flees a man, teases him, and comes together with him, but just enough to tease him once again. Then she runs away all over again. A tango is based on rejection and seduction. A tango is based on attraction and repulsion. A tango is based on the patterns of courting and mating, the patterns of romance. Intricate and often painful patterns. Patterns of stimulus and response. Patterns of information and meaning. But at heart the tango is a repetition of the processes that made the protons of which the dancers are made. It is a repetition of a 13.7-billion-year-old pattern. Stimulus and response. Attraction and repulsion. Information and meaning.

The bottom line? The nitty-gritty? The message in this particular fortune cookie? This is a communicative cosmos. Electrons communicate with protons via the electromagnetic force. Gas wisps communicate with each other via gravity. So do stars, planets, and galaxies. And the macromolecules in the center of your cells and mine use millions of electromagnetic pluses and minuses, millions of nodes of attraction and repulsion, to carry out the complex communication between molecules that created life nearly four billion years ago. And that sustains life from second to second within you and me today.

Even the curves and rumples in Einstein's cosmos are communication in action, conversations using the language of non-Euclidean geometry. They are patterns of attraction and repulsion, of stimulus and response. The very shape of the universe is semiotic and linguistic. Space tells matter how to move and matter tells space how to bend. Note the word "tells." If no one opens the fortune cookie, you are not able to "tell" a single thing. In "telling," meaning means everything. And meaning amounts to one simple thing: response. If one quark responds to another, it has opened the fortune cookie. It has read what Claude Shannon's cowriter, Warren Weaver, calls that quark's "meaning."

The conversational nature of the cosmos may be why archphysicist John Archibald Wheeler, a man who collaborated with Einstein at Princeton and who taught physics legend Richard Feynman, says that this is a "participatory universe."[60] It may even be why Wheeler sees that at its heart this is a cosmos of signal exchange. A cosmos of communication. Says Wheeler, "The universe . . . is built upon query . . . and reply."[61] The result? "All things physical are information-theoretic in origin."[62] Or, to repeat the way loop quantum gravity master Lee Smolin puts it, all things physical are "relational."[63]

Claude Shannon gave us an enormous gift when he translated math and logic into on and off switches. He gave us a massive present when he turned an array of switches into the new clay hand tablet of the twentieth century. He gave us a boon and a bounty when he gave us the computer. He gave us a gift that would change the way we work out the implications of axioms. He gave us a tool that would promise to turn metaphors from the mere word images of Herbert Spencer to precise predictors like the equations of Einstein. He gave us a device that would change our ways of fathoming Einstein's mysterious "something" utterly. But he misled us with his information theory. Why? Because this is not a cosmos of unread fortune cookies. It is a cosmos of meaning.

HOW GOSSIP GROWS THE UNIVERSE

In 1998, one of your favorite brainstorming partners, Eshel ben-Jacob, said something crucial in a telephone call between New York and Tel Aviv. At the time, Eshel was the head of the department of condensed matter physics at the University of Tel Aviv, head of the Israel Physical Society—the Israeli national society of physicists—and the founder of the online physics magazine *PhysicaPlus*. The questions roused in Eshel by his primary field, condensed matter physics, had led him far beyond physics. They had led him to become one of the most exciting researchers on the planet. Eshel had done breakthrough work on the group behavior and the emergent properties of two very similar self-assembling complexities: bacterial colonies and neurons, the communities of cells that colonize your gut and the communities of cells that make up your brain. In fact, as you know, Eshel's work on bacterial colonies had made the cover of *Scientific American* in October 1998.

What do bacteria and neurons have in common? Among other things, they are supremely "relational," supremely social. They work in massive groups, groups of billions or trillions. They self-organize into big-picture patterns—the big-picture patterns of highly organized colonies glued to their environment of choice. Bacteria, for example, self-organize in the gorgeous, big-picture forms that illustrated Eshel's work on the cover of *Scientific American*. And bacteria and neurons are manic communicators.

What's more, like quarks, they communicate with the language of attraction and repulsion. They, too, quark in the social cosmos. They, too, do the big-bang tango.

A colony of *Paenibacillus vortex* bacteria on the hunt for food fans out in a fractal pattern. Why? *Courtesy of Eshel ben-Jacob, Tel Aviv University, and the Center for Theoretical Biological Physics at the University of California, San Diego.*

But back to your phone call. Said Eshel, define information and you can crack the secrets of the universe. OK, so you thought about that problem for a few days. At first it stumped you. Then you came back to Eshel with a definition—information is anything that a receiver can decode. Information is anything a receiver can translate. Information is anything that a receiver can understand. Information, in short, is in the eyes of the beholder.

What does that mean? Information is not information until it has been interpreted, until it has been understood. It is not simply the signal going down the copper cable. It is the conversation you have when you pick up the phone. Information includes opening the fortune cookie.

When you brainstormed with Eshel back in 1998, you knew Claude Shannon's formula, but you were unaware of Shannon's peculiar distinction between information and meaning. Your definition included them both. So let's alter what you said back then to fit the Shannon vocabulary. Let's ignore the fact that there is no such thing as information without meaning. And let's focus on meaning alone.

If meaning is anything that a receiver can understand, if meaning is any-thing that an entity can interpret, if meaning is in the eye of the beholder, then how do you know when a thing or a person "understands" something? Follow the B. F. Skinner rule. Watch his or her behavior. Watch for the signs of stimulus and response. Watch to see if the receiver does something in response to the stimulus. Watch to see if the receiver moves. Quarks exchange meaning with stimulus and response. So do gas wisps competing to swallow each other. And so do would-be planets using their gravity to snag and can-nibalize comets and space debris. How do we know the receivers get the meaning? All of them respond to the signals they receive. They move. They move toward each other. Or away.

And that movement is response to a stimulus. That movement shows that quarks, protons, electrons, and gravity balls in some primitive and utterly non-conscious way, interpret each other. They get the message. They "understand" each other. They translate each other's signal into action. In other words, movement inspired by another object is the undeniable mark of something we think is uniquely human. It is the undeniable mark of meaning.

**

There are several strange corollaries to the proposition that information is in the eye of the beholder, the idea that information is anything a receiver or a translator can decode. Corollary one is this—information is anything you can *turn* into a fortune cookie. Anything in which you can read a message. Even if no one or no thing "sent" that message. A fossil ceases to be a deaf and dumb piece of stone in 1806[64] when you develop paleontology and can "read" its "message." It ceases to be just a lump when you "find" its "meaning." Yet no one has sent a message. No pterodactyl packed its bones into limestone to send you a signal. But once you can find a signal, a fossil "contains" information.

So information is not necessarily two-way communication. Information can go one way. What turns it into information? Translation. Interpretation. In other words, the key to making something neutral into information is Shannon's missing ingredient: meaning. And what is meaning? Movement.

The movement of a quark, the movement of a mote of space dust, the movement of a tongue, the movement of a pen, the movement of a hand on a keyboard, or the movement of Robert Darwin's block of stone with fossilized plesiosaur bones to the Royal Society.[65]

Which leaves a question. Is anything really neutral? Is everything a meaning waiting to be invented? Waiting to be understood?

But there are more corollaries to the idea that information is anything that a translator can decode. There are more truly peculiar implications to the simple idea that information is any signal that can be turned into a response.

***

Here's peculiar corollary number two. If meaning is anything that a translator can understand, anything that a translator can interpret, anything that a translator can decode, then the amount of meaning in this cosmos is constantly increasing. Meaning defies the law of entropy, the second law of thermodynamics. Meaning does not ebb away. It is not erased by disorder. It is on the rise. It is constantly piling up. And its pile is reaching toward the heavens. Not to mention pouring from the skies.

Let's take a simple example—starlight. This planet, Mother Earth, pulled itself together from random pebbles, iceballs, and supersized gravity balls 4.5 billion years ago. For the first billion years of Earth's existence, streams of photons from emitters far, far away, rays of light from distant stars, rays of light that looked like pinpricks in the black of the night sky, hit the surface of this Earth's stone and water, its land and seas. And those beams of light found no takers. They found no receivers, no interpreters, no translators. Planet Earth's stone and water were indifferent to the existence of light from stars. They were literally not moved by starlight. The result? Starlight had no meaning.

Were these trickles of light from stars information yet? No. Not by the standard of "information is anything decoded by a receiver." And not by the standards of Claude Shannon's "meaning." But things would not stay that way forever.

Roughly 3.85 billion years ago, life assembled in the shallows and in the depths of the seas. And roughly 350,000 years into life's existence, cells of life stuff first registered the existence of light. The life forms that pulled off this trick were cyanobacteria. Cyanobacteria were single-celled creatures that live in societies of trillions. And cyanobacteria did more than merely register light's presence or absence. They acted on what they "saw." They used light as a power source. They used light to manufacture food. And they used light to make copies of themselves. They used light to multiply. They used light to conquer the newborn Earth's rivers, lakes, and seas.[66] How? They invented photosynthesis. They invented an industrial process, a process of manic mass production, that turned light into polypeptides, sugars, hydrocarbons, and proteins. A process of translation. Translation from one medium to another. A process of motion. Electron-and-atom motion. Highly orchestrated motion. An extraordinarily sophisticated response to a stimulus.

Back to our question. Was light information yet? Yes. Translators were decoding it. Translators were interpreting it. Translators were transforming it into energy conveyors like ATP (adenosine triphosphate)[67] and social signaling molecules like N-acyl-homoserine lactones and cyclic oligopeptides.[68] Turning light into a new language. A language of chemical sentences. What's more, translators were grabbing hold of light as a stimulus. And they were responding to it with action. With metabolism. With movement. With migration to new territories. Was light information yet? You bet. Why? Because translators had invented a meaning. A meaning for the light of the sun.

OK, that was true of sunlight. But what about starlight? Sorry. It was too weak to register. It still had no translators. No interpreters. So was starlight information yet? No.

Was starlight destined to be an informational orphan forever? Was it condemned to go unto eternity without meaning? Or, to put it differently, would starlight's lack of eager translators ever change?

Over three billion years later, there were light translators all over this planet. Not just in the sea. They had also conquered the land. They were plants. And their ability to coat the planet with light translators—with the solar panels we call leaves—was astonishing. Did this spread of plants, this astonishing increase in the number of translators, increase the amount of meaning "in" sunlight? Had rainforests and ocean kelp increased the number of implicit properties that the cosmos extracts from sunlight? Had they increased the translation of light from one medium to another? Or, to put it differently, had coating the land and lining the seas with photosynthesizers increased the amount of Shannon's style of meaning? Had it increased the raw total of response to the stimulus of sunlight? Again, the answer is yes. Absolutely.

But what about starlight? Still no takers. So was starlight information yet? Not so far as we know.

Let's skip ahead another 999 million years or so. Let's fast forward to humans. Roughly thirty-six thousand years ago,[69] humans invented a simple isomorphic symbol set, a system of notation. And they carved their notes in mammoth, baboon, and eagle bones.[70] What did they keep notes about? What did the symbols try to capture? What did they try to translate? To what were they isomorphic? The phases of the moon.[71] The repetition roughly every thirty days of a cycle that sees the moon transform from a fingernail-like sliver, a thin crescent, to a fat and full circle of light. These early *Homo sapiens* apparently used their carved bones and tusks to keep track of something that they were in the process of inventing, the concept of time. So moonlight now had translators and interpreters. Was moonlight information yet? You bet. Moonlight had meaning extractors. It had creatures that responded to its changes. It had stimulus, response, and meaning. Did that make it information? I leave the answer up to you.

But what about starlight? It appears that we humans didn't make sense of the random spray of stars in the black of night until well after the invention of agriculture ten thousand years ago. Then, in roughly 4000 BCE, the Babylonians got into the act and pioneered star-based mythology, star-based astronomy, and astrology. Two thousand years later the inhabitants of Britain and Scotland built hundreds of groupings of massive boulders like Stonehenge and apparently used those boulder circles to translate alignments of the sun, the moon, and the stars into a language whose letters were fashioned from stone.[72] And across the Atlantic Ocean, the Aztecs, Incas, and Mayans, too, translated the connect-the-dots of the stars into stone, into ritual, and into the synchronized behavior of citizens far and wide.[73]

Which brings us back to the basic question. The amount of sunlight has gone up 26 percent since life first evolved.[74] And old stars have died and new ones have been born in the night sky. Is that what has jacked up the amount of information on this earthly ball? Not a bit. But has the information content on this planet grown? Has the meaning increased? Have the number and variety of responses to light's stimulus gone up? Have the number of breakthroughs that light inspired soared? Have the number of inventions that light triggered climbed? You bet.

So in the days of the henge makers, was the cosmos following the second law of thermodynamics? Was the universe demonstrating entropy? Was information sliding down a slippery slope to disorder? Not one bit. Claude Shannon's style of information may or may not have been on the increase. But meaning was rocketing.

Then, in the land between the two rivers, in Mesopotamia, came tribes, city-states, and empires. With full-time star priests, full-time scribes who thought that they could read the secrets of the universe and the secrets of their politicians' futures in the stars. For one hundred generations—for roughly two thousand years[75]—these astronomers and astrologers watched the stars for the kings of Mesopotamia, the kings of the thirty-one cities of the Land of the Lords of Brightness. For one hundred generations the professional star translators made meticulous observations, translated what they saw into the symbol set of cuneiform, recorded those cuneiform translations on clay hand tablets, and deposited the tablets in libraries of as many as twenty thousand clay tablets[76] each in the palaces of kings. Today there are over 1.5 million cuneiform tablets in museums around the world.[77] Needless to say, not all of them concern astronomy. But all are translations of experience into isomorphic symbol sets.

How very much like cyanobacteria translating sunlight into a language of biochemicals. How very much like leaves translating sunlight into panels, sheets, threads, and stems of cells.

The Mesopotamian priestly tablets recorded the movements of the constellations and the stars. But that wasn't all. The Mesopotamian scribe priests built one layer of symbol set upon another. The scribe priests invented three new symbol sets—written language, mathematical procedures, and charts. Why? To understand the "messages" of starlight. And they used those "messages" to read the minds of the gods. What's more, they advised that rulers act according to the stars' "messages."

Had the amount of starlight making it to the surface of Earth gone up? Not a single iota. But had the amount of information shot up? Had the number of meanings and the number of creatures paying attention to those meanings skyrocketed? Had *responses* to the tiny bits of light from the stars been fruitful and multiplied? Even in Claude Shannon's crippled terminology, the amount of meaning had soared.

Meanwhile, Babylon's star priests were just starting starlight's informational odyssey. Today there are hundreds of thousands of professional and amateur telescopes pointing at the heavens, and all of them are trying to find yet more meanings in starlight. We've used our telescopes to see that some dots in the black heavens of night, dots that we originally thought were stars, are sky-swirls, tiny spirals in the sky. We've had the "Great Debate" of April 26, 1920, between Heber Curtis and Harlow Shapley at the National Academy of Sciences in Washington, D.C.,[78] a debate over whether those sky twirls are mere spirals of gas inside our Milky Way, inside our star cluster, or whether they are swirls of something far more substantial than gas, whether they are swirls of stars. We've had the great debate over whether those swirls are inside our star cluster, our "globular cluster," or outside of it. We've had the debate over whether our globular star cluster is a spiral like those strange spiral wisps. We've had the debate about whether our globular cluster is a tiny thirty thousand light-years across or a giant three hundred thousand. We've had the great debate between Curtis and Shapley over whether this is a nice, cozy universe that includes only our star cluster or whether the cosmos is an unimaginably vast space in which "island universes" like ours, things called "galaxies," exist at great distances from each other, huge, lonely, unimaginable distances. We've seen a winner to that debate—the argument for many galaxies spread over unimaginable distances.

We've used lenses and mirrors to magnify starlight. We've used drawings on paper and images on glass photographic plates and on cellulose film to capture the images of stars and to record their positions. We've turned that data into electron flows, into Claude Shannon's pluses and minuses, ons and offs, ones and zeros, into binary numbers and into Shannon's brilliant language of electronic circuits—the language of computers. We've stored these translations of starlight on magnetic film and hard drives.

And we've used starlight, the streams of photons from the stars, to theorize about the origins of the universe and about the universe's future. Our libraries of scholarly articles and popular books about starlight interpretation, starlight translation, have grown huge. So have the numbers of cosmologists, astrophysicists, and astronomers who've dedicated their lives to interpreting that trickle of light from the stars. What's more, we owe colossal achievements like Newton's physics, Einstein's relativity, and NASA's space explorations to starlight. Has the amount of starlight falling on this planet at night increased? Not a sliver. Not a scratch. So what has gone up? The quantity of interpretation. The quantity of translation. The quantity of response to a stimulus. The quantity of action. The quantity of repetition in a new context. The quantity of raw glass, iron, steel, and money dedicated to starlight. And most important, the quantity of meaning.

What does this radical increase mean for the quantity of information "in" starlight? What does it mean for the total amount of information and meaning on this third gravity ball from the sun? And what does it mean for the total amount of information—the total amount of meaning—in the cosmos?

If information is anything a receiver can interpret, anything a translator can translate, has the amount of "information" gone up? Or is this merely an explosion of "meaning"? It's a semantic quibble. A quibble you can decide better than I can. But something has been on the increase. Something has shot up dramatically. Something complex. Something extremely social. Something profoundly conversational. Something that utterly defies the pessimistic predictions of entropy. And something that seriously challenges an information theory without meaning.

THE MAGIC ONION OF MEANING

Corollary number one of the notion that meaning is anything that a receiver can interpret is that information and meaning can be a one-way process. A process with no sender. Corollary number two of the notion that information is anything that a translator can interpret is that the amount of information and meaning in this cosmos is on the rise.

What's corollary number three? Your meaning—the meaning that you have whether you are a quark, a quadruped, or a quantum physicist—comes from the number of big pictures into which you can fit. Your meaning comes from the number of schema, the number of frameworks, the number of emergent properties to which you can prove useful. If three quarks join together to make a proton, they have meaning. If you are a quark, you have interpreted the call of two others and have ganged together with them. Your role in a threesome is one layer of your meaning. But stay tuned—you are about to acquire meanings you never suspected, meanings you never knew.

From the threesome of which you are a part comes a new big picture, a new emergent property—the proton. If you come from quarkland, if you come from the flick of cosmic time in which only quarks existed, the proton is a new and startling sort of entity—a shockingly new sort of identity. But the peculiarities of being a part of a proton are not the end of your participation in the strange. Next the proton of which you are a part participates in the massive dance of pressure waves, in the musical throbs, pulsations, and oscillations that ring through the cosmos like a gong. Now you have yet another layer of meaning. You are a part of something else far, far bigger than yourself. For an instant, you are part of a wave. Then you are part of a trough. Then you are part of the next wave. You are now a part of the music of the cosmos. On top of your meaning as part of a proton. Good work!

Let's skip over the additional meaning you acquire when you join up with an electron to form a hydrogen atom 380,000 years after the big bang. Let's skip over the meanings you pile up like new skins of an onion when you become a part of a wisp of gas, when that wisp of gas becomes a part of a swirl that turns into a galaxy, and when you are stripped of your electron and clump together with a multitude of others to form a star. Let's skip over the next layer of meaning you get when your star is in its death throes and when you are crunched together with other naked atomic nuclei to make a radically new proton-neutron-electron team—carbon.[79] And let's skip over the even higher level of meaning you acquire when you participate in making biomolecules, carbon-based molecules, way out there in the bleak clouds of cold interstellar dust. Not to mention the extraordinarily complex new meanings you acquire when you participate in cells and DNA.

You are acquiring what's called a "nested hierarchy"[80] of meanings. And now that you're a part of the life process, you change meanings constantly. Let's dial you forward to your life in the twenty-first century as part of a hair on a sheep in Australia. Remember, you are still a quark. A quark in a proton in an atom of carbon in a molecule of keratin in a tangle of proteins that makes a thread of wool that keeps a sheep warm, a sheep that lives in a flock and that will someday mate to have a kid. Your role in the sheep gives you meanings far beyond just participation in a proton and in a carbon atom. You are a part of the property of a sheep man in Australia. A sheep man who is counting on you to feed his family. When spring[81] comes, his hired hands shear you from the sheep and send you to China to be spun into yarn.[82] So now you've had meaning to more than just the life of the sheep and of the sheep man. You've acquired meaning in the life of the mill owner and the mill hands in China. And you've acquired meaning in a network of global commerce.

You are piling up new memberships, new affiliations to new groups, new roles in new processes, new affiliations in new skeins of emergent property. You are piling up citizenships in new layers of the onion of meaning. But why in the world do these new affiliations equal levels of meaning? Stimulus and response.

Each new collective identity is capable of kidnapping, seducing, and recruiting. Each new collective identity is a recruitment strategy. Potential stars compete with other gravity balls to see who can move whom, who can swallow whom. Galaxies compete to see who can swallow whom. And galactic clusters kidnap, seduce, and recruit entire galaxies into galactic herds and flocks. What's more, wool tempts sheepherders in Australia. Sheepherders tempt mill executives in China. And you, the quark in the keratin of a strand of wool, respond to each layer of emergent property.

Every level of emergent property is a kidnapper, seducer, and recruiter. And every level of emergent property is seduced, kidnapped, and recruited. It's a two-way process. You are among the seduced. And you are among the seducers.

Back to your fate as keratin in a hair unceremoniously snipped from the back of a sheep. You are sheared and shipped to China to be knit into yarn. As a participant in a ball of yarn, you are shipped to North America and trucked to Milwaukee. You are put on sale in a yarn shop and are purchased by a lawyer who likes to work off her stress by knitting. She knits you into a sweater for her seven-year-old. You take your place in the seven-year-old's closet as a part of the blue-jeans outfit he will wear for the first time Thursday. When the seven-year-old gets to school, two kids make fun of him for the new sweater and for being a mama's boy. And three kids compliment him.

So where's the meaning? At every stage a new emergent property makes a big difference in your destiny. It makes a big difference in how, where, and when you will be transported. And it makes a big difference in why. Every level of emergent property is responsible for what we might call your fate. Every layer of emergent property is a stimulus and it produces a response. It influences your meaning.

If the seven-year-old obsesses on the ribbing he took for wearing you, he may keep you in his closet and never wear you again. If he focuses on the compliments, he will wear you as often as he can until he finally outgrows you. The hundred-billion-neuron web of his brain will measure his place in a social web, and that measurement will affect your destiny.

What is the source of all these layers of intersecting meaning? Meanings nestled inside of each other like Kepler's boxes and balls. Emergent properties crop up in part because this cosmos is profoundly social. Emergent properties crop up as forms of group behavior. Like the group behavior of those hundred billion neurons in your brain. Like the group behavior that turns you and me into members of families, subcultures, political parties, and civilizations, not to mention participants in the 2.5-million-year-old group project of technology and ideas, the 2.5-million-year-old group project of human culture.

The properties that emerge from massive sociality keep the number of meanings in this cosmos piling up like the layers of fossil rock beneath our feet. Emergent properties determine whether you, as a quark in a proton of hydrogen, will be isolated in the space between the galaxies or become part of the swirl of plasma in a star. Emergent properties determine whether you, as an electron in a leaf, will participate in the cellulose that makes the panel of green solid or will help translate sunlight into an energy-transport molecule of ATP. Emergent properties determine whether you, as a molecule of keratin in a sweater, will stay in a closet or will see the light. Emergent properties keep meanings growing like skins of the onion. Growing like new layers of cerebral cortex. Growing new layers of meaning.

***

What is the source of George Henry Lewes's emergent properties? What is the source of the sloshing and soaking that emerge as properties of two gases—hydrogen and oxygen—and a bit of flame? What is the source of the astonishments that arise from a bunch of isolated water molecules gathered in a ripple tank, a pond, or an ocean? And what is the source of the big pictures that knit together keratin proteins, sweaters, moms, lawyers, and the pleasures and pains of compliments and disapproval?

Emergent properties and big pictures are among the biggest puzzles of the God Problem. They are puzzles beyond the reach of Claude Shannon in 1948. But they are puzzles that Claude Shannon's legacy—the computer— would bring almost within our grasp two decades down the line. Almost but not quite. How? For the answer, it's time for a side trip away from computers, a side trip to London and to the television set of David Bohm.

DOING THE GLYCERIN TWIST: DAVID BOHM

In the 1960s, while he was teaching[83] at the University of London's research-oriented Birkbeck College,[84] Philadelphia-born physicist David Bohm came up with an idea that looked like it would solve the God Problem. An idea that looked like it might solve the primary puzzle of corollary generation, the riddle of how ornately strange outcomes can nest invisibly in a handful of axioms. Bohm called his concept "implicate" order. The word "implicate" was an antique variation of the more common word "implicit." What do the words "implicate" and "implicit" mean? They come from the Latin "implicare"—to fold or to twist. The *Oxford English Dictionary* puts the meaning of "implicate" like this: "Intertwined, twisted together; also, wrapped up with, entangled or involved in." Add to that one of the *Oxford English Dictionary*'s definitions of "implicit"—"virtually or potentially contained in"—and that gives you a sense of the meaning. The implicate is something lurking, something unspoken, something unseen, something that can be deduced by logic or by hunch. Something that's not there but is. If only you can get at it.

When "implicit" refers to language, it means that the sentence you just uttered has a fistful of hidden meanings. Your words have a grab bag of silent references, wordless ties and tangles, tucked up, twisted, and folded into them. Meanings that you can unfold if you take the time.

When you tell me, "There's a banana in your soup," your six words bristle with implicit meanings. They imply the existence of a tree that produces long, curved, yellow or green fruits with a sweet, pulpy, crescent-shaped core that you can get at by peeling the skin. They hint at the chain of agriculture and commerce that brings bananas from plantations in Honduras to North America.[85] They suggest the way that your taste buds and mine delight or dislike, and the way that our digestive processes turn bananas into fuel for our system. And they hint at delicacies like a banana split. "There's a banana in your soup" also hints at a kitchen, a stove, a pot, a cook, broth, and a source of the electricity or gas that fuels the flame. On top of that, your six naked words imply that bananas don't normally belong in soup. They imply that you're surprised. Or that you're pulling my leg.

Why? because your six words are not really naked. They are uttered in a context. They are uttered in a nest of meanings. A nested hierarchy. An onion of meanings.

Steven Levy explains that in its early years, Google was stumped trying to find the right nest of meanings when you and I use the word "dog." Do we mean a pooch or a skinny sausage in a long roll? Says Levy, "The problem was fixed by a breakthrough late in 2002 that utilized Ludwig Wittgenstein's theories on how words are defined by context. As Google crawled and archived billions of documents and web pages, it analyzed which words were close to each other. 'Hot dog' would be found in searches that also contained 'bread' and 'mustard' and 'baseball games'—not 'puppies with roasting fur.'"[86]

Implicit meanings are all over the place. The sentence "Let's not discuss it anymore" is riddled with implicit meanings. You know it's a phrase used to stop a squabble. So if I use it, it implies that you and I have been sparring and scrapping. It implies harsh feelings. It implies impatience. It also implies that something called "discussion" exists. Discussion implies creatures who can handle speech. Since parrots, prairie dogs, and patas monkeys can handle some form of language but can't whiffle through the give and take of complex conversation, that implies human beings. "Let's not discuss it anymore" also implies the existence of time. More specifically, the time it takes for a give and take to become heated. Not to mention the future time implied by "anymore." Finally, "Let's not discuss it anymore" implies free will. It implies that if we set our minds to it, we could stop verbally slapping and whacking each other. Yet another onion of multiple meanings.

But there's more. "Let's not discuss it anymore" implies that we have enough air to breathe, or we couldn't get the words out. It implies that we have lungs, a brain, and a tongue. And it implies the 13.73 billion years of cosmic evolution that's created tongues and lungs. That's a lot of meaning to fit invisibly into just five words. But here's the key. A long history has stuffed these five words with meanings. A history that includes things like the big bang, the evolution of multicellular beings, and the success of English-speaking peoples in spreading their language across continents. A lot is packed into "Let's not discuss it anymore" because the sentence has a rap sheet, a pedigree, a past.

That's also the problem with David Bohm's concept of implicate order. Why? Like Newton's gadget-making God and Leonardo's light as a wave, Bohm's implicate order is based on a central metaphor.

Here's the story. David Bohm was a grad student of physicist extraordinaire J. Robert Oppenheimer,[87] the team leader who would later be responsible for the atomic bomb. The bomb whose success would prove Albert Einstein right. Bohm's father had wanted him to go into the family furniture business in Philadelphia, where young David had grown up. But Bohm had refused to be practical and had insisted on becoming a physicist. So Bohm was in California studying at Berkeley during World War II, going for his doctorate.[88] Then Oppenheimer was asked to organize the Manhattan Project, the crash program that worked madly to produce an atomic bomb before the Germans could create one. Oppenheimer, it is said, wanted Bohm in on the effort.[89] But Bohm had joined the Communist Party for nine months in 1942. He'd found the meetings boring, but the philosophy exciting.[90] So the army[91] general with the final word on the bomb project, Leslie Groves,[92] said no. Absolutely not. No Bohm allowed anywhere near the bomb project. Meanwhile, Bohm worked on his own and developed calculations on the scatter produced by collisions of elementary particles, calculations that looked like they'd come in handy for developing guess what? The bomb. Bohm did this for his grad thesis. But the government grabbed his equations and classified them, then banned Bohm from writing about them. Why? Because Bohm was a campus radical. He didn't have security clearance. Far from it. In fact, he was considered a suspicious character. Yes, Bohm was forbidden from writing about his very own equations.

Since Bohm had developed his equations to complete his doctoral requirements, this meant he was forbidden by law to complete the requirements for his degree. Fortunately, Oppenheimer came to Bohm's rescue. He wrote Berkeley a letter "certifying that his student had nevertheless met the requirements for a thesis."[93] Bohm got his degree. No thanks to the weirdness of top secrecy.

That was 1943, the year that you were born. Then Bohm moved to Princeton and worked with Albert Einstein. Things were looking up. Until the spring of 1949, when the House Un-American Activities Committee, which had been hunting for Communists in government since 1946, reached David Bohm. The committee had "launched a major investigation of atomic spying at Berkeley's Rad [Radiation] Lab."[94] In the process, it closed in on J. Robert Oppenheimer and his students, subpoenaing four of those students to testify. Bohm was among them. At the time, Bohm was teaching at Princeton, Albert Einstein territory. And no less a figure than Einstein himself advised Bohm not to testify. Remember, back home in Europe, Einstein had hated the high-hatted nature of government authorities. He had felt that "youth is intentionally being deceived by the state through lies."[95]

So Bohm went before the House Un-American Activities Committee twice, and pleaded the Fifth Amendment, his Constitutional right not to incriminate himself. He also cited the First Amendment's freedom of speech and assembly.[96] The committee didn't take this kindly. Bohm was arrested on December 4, 1950,[97] for refusing to spill the beans. That persecution forced him to flee his native country, America. During his years as a political refugee, Bohm became a professor of physics in many unlikely places: first Brazil, then Israel, and finally the University of London's Birkbeck College. So in the roaring sixties, in the era of hippies, the Beatles, the Rolling Stones, LSD, the mods and the rockers, paisley fabrics, and fashions from Kings Road, David Bohm was living and teaching in England. One evening he saw something on BBC-TV that held him for the rest of his life.[98]

Above, the equipment for David Bohm's glycerine experiment. Below, how you use the equipment. *Courtesy of Physics Department, University of Illinois at Urbana-Champaign, "Shear Demo—Ink In Cylinder (Viscosity)," http://demo.physics.uiuc.edu/LectDemo/scripts/demo_descript.idc?DemoID=805 (accessed January 3, 2012).*

Illustration by Kevin Shluker, from Lee Nichol, ed, The Essential David Bohm *(London: Routledge, 2003), p. 88.*

Courtesy of Jaap Bak, http://www

To get a grip on what Bohm saw on his TV screen, imagine this little kitchen experiment. Take a pitcher. Put a tall drinking glass inside of it. Right in the center. That leaves a gap, a space, a canyon, a ravine, an empty circular cleft between the outside walls of your drinking glass and the inner walls of your pitcher. Now pack Vaseline®, petroleum jelly from the drugstore, into that circular space between the outer wall of the drinking glass and the inner wall of the pitcher. Then take an eyedropper and drip a drop of ink onto the surface of the Vaseline. Sit back and admire what you've done. And look carefully. The drop of ink makes a well-defined circle. Right? It appears as a tiny splotch of blackness on the greasy tan of the Vaseline.

Now hold on to the handle of the pitcher so the pitcher doesn't move a bit. Keep the pitcher still, and very slowly turn the glass at the pitcher's center. Turn it slowly like the blades of a blender. As you rotate the glass inside the pitcher, you'll move the Vaseline. And the drop of ink will stretch out like a thread.[99] Then the ink drop will smear and blur. It will make a long smudge that looks like the tail of a comet. And slowly it will turn from black to gray. Turn the glass far enough, and the ink drop will fade into the Vaseline. It will disappear entirely. In fact, if you turn the glass far enough, you'll see no clue that the ink drop ever existed.

Now for the clincher, the pièce de résistance, the part of the exercise that grabbed David Bohm by the frontal lobes and would not let go. You now have what looks like blank Vaseline, right? You have what looks like utter emptiness. Slowly turn the glass in the center of your pitcher back to its original position. Turn it back to its starting point. In the process, you'll move the Vaseline back to its starting point, too. And guess what will happen? The ink drop will ever so slowly reappear. Seemingly from the emptiness. First you'll see a mist of darkness in the Vaseline. Then you'll see a cometlike smear. A thread of blackness. And bit by bit the thread will shrink and firm up. It will self-assemble as the ink drop you started with. It will come together as the sharply defined black dot you originally deposited.

Your kitchen apparatus is a simple version of the apparatus that Bohm saw on BBC-TV. But the BBC's equipment was a bit more sophisticated looking than yours. It involved a custom-made setup in which one skinny laboratory glass cylinder was placed inside a much fatter cylinder of glass. The skinny glass cylinder was centered within the fat one like an axle centered in a wheel. And in the BBC demonstration that Bohm watched, the material packed between the two concentric cylinders of glass was glycerin. A demonstrator squeezed a drop of ink onto the surface of the glycerin. And as the BBC demonstrator turned the central cylinder, Bohm watched the drop of ink disappear. Then he watched as the inner cylinder was turned back to its original position. What happened? The ink drop slowly reappeared as if coming together from the emptiness. As if forming itself from elementary chaos. As if coming together from naked glycerin.

Said Bohm, "This immediately struck me as very relevant to the question of order, since, when the ink drop was spread out, it still had a 'hidden' (i.e. non-manifest) order that was revealed when it was reconstituted."[100] In other words, there was an ink drop hidden in the seeming emptiness of the glycerin. There was what Bohm would call an "implicate order."

Later, Bohm apparently tried the experiment himself. He discovered that if you put five drops of ink on the glycerin instead of just one, the five drops will disappear as you turn the central cylinder. Then the five drops will reappear again when you twist the central cylinder back to its starting position. And if you lay out the drops on the glycerin in a pattern—say a stick figure of a human—you can twist the central cylinder and make the stick figure disappear. Then you can turn the cylinder back to its starting point and watch the stick figure seemingly self-assemble from the nothingness.

What's more, Bohm became enthusiastic about yet another approach. This one is hard to describe, so bear with me. Hold the handle of the outer pitcher tight so the pitcher doesn't move. Put an ink drop on the glycerin, turn the inner cylinder a few degrees, then, move your dropper a tad to the right, lay down another drop, turn the inner cylinder again, move the dropper a tad farther to the right, drop another drop, then turn the inner cylinder, move your hand, and drop again and again. You've just laid down a line of dots. Now stop squeezing out drops of ink. If you turn the center cylinder far enough, all of your ink drops disappear. You now have a nothingness in your glycerin. Now do the turning in reverse. Slowly rotate the center cylinder back to its starting position. Your ink drops will reappear one at a time. First the first drop you deposited will reappear. Then it will disappear and drop two will appear. Then drop two will melt away and drop three will pop into view. Then drop four. And each drop will be just a bit farther to your left. You've created the equivalent of a mini-movie. It will look as if a single drop is moving, as if it's skipping across the glycerin. Says Bohm, this provides "a way of understanding discontinuous 'jumps' of the electron from one quantum state to another."[101] That's a big leap. A very big stretch.

Then Bohm took his leap a step further. He guessed that "perhaps the movement of enfoldment and unfoldment is universal."[102] Perhaps there is continual oscillation between enfoldment and unfoldment in the entire universe. How did Bohm fit the big bang and the history of the cosmos into this? Bohm saw the big bang as just "a little ripple . . . in the immense ocean of cosmic energy."[103] Just another drop emerging from the nothingness of the glycerin. A drop that was hidden but implicit all along. A drop that lay invisibly in the emptiness the way that a drop of ink lies invisibly in your seemingly empty Vaseline.

With your glass inside of a pitcher and your Vaseline, you, too, have just watched something materialize from nothing. Or have you? You've just watched an invisible but very real implicit possibility emerge as an explicit reality. You've just seen a plain, normal-looking goo—Vaseline—patch together an ink drop seemingly from chaos and emptiness. That's the metaphor that made it from a BBC-TV studio into Bohm's mind in the 1960s and became the basis for his "implicate order"—an order hidden in the nothingness. An order aching to reveal itself. An order aching to translate itself into a hard and fast reality.

Bohm saw the glycerin, ink, and glass experiment as a metaphor for a self-assembling universe, a universe that seems to emerge from nothing. A universe that begins with less than nothing and disgorges a zoo of hitherto unseen forms—quarks, atoms, stars, galaxies, physicists, and information theories. To Bohm, it seemed that a vast menagerie of somethings lay implicit in the chaos at the moment of the big bang the way that the ink drop lay invisibly in your Vaseline.[104] But to Bohm, there was no chaos. There was a cosmic equivalent to the glycerin in the BBC's glass container. Bohm wrote in his 1980 Book *Wholeness and the Implicate Order* that "what we call empty space contains an immense background of energy, and that matter as we know it is a small, 'quantized' wavelike excitation on top of this background, rather like a tiny ripple on a vast sea."[105] Space, he said, is "full not empty."[106] Full of what? Implicate order.

Meanwhile, Bohm pulled off a tour de force. With encouragement from Albert Einstein, he created a reformulation of the mathematics of quantum physics.[107] And his new mathematical approach seemed to be as effective at making predictions as the standard math of mainstream quantum physics. For example, it predicted[108] the puzzling Aharonov-Bohm Effect, in which electrons going through two slits are wrenchingly influenced by a magnetic field,[109] a magnetic field that, in Bohm's words, should not be able to "touch them."[110] But Bohm's concept of "implicate order" lingered at the edge of the physics community. Says Indian philosophy of science professor Mathew Chandrankunnel, "From its inception, Bohmian mechanics was deliberately ignored, overlooked and generally rejected by the scientific community."[111] When J. Robert Oppenheimer, Bohm's former teacher, was asked how respectable physicists viewed Bohm's reformulation, he answered, "'We consider it juvenile deviationism' and 'we do not waste our time' by reading it."[112]

Strangely, Bohm had his greatest impact on the New Age movement. In 1985, he cowrote a book titled *The Ending of Time* with legendary Indian "World Teacher" Jiddu Krishnamurti,[113] and his dialogues with the Indian mystic were collected in two more books.[114] Bohm's concept of implicate order served as a seemingly scientific platform for the breed of wishful thinking summed up in the 2004 film *What the Bleep Do We Know?*[115] and for mysticism.

There was, in fact, a severe limit to Bohm's metaphor. A mistake. Bohm's error was the equivalent of running a video of a breaking wine glass backward, then claiming you'd just shown a video of how the glass was made. The folks at the glass factory might disagree. In other words, the appearance of the ink drop was not the production of form from nothing. Not at all. It was the result of resurrecting a past.

But Bohm had another key truth up his sleeve. One that you and I have used. He made a crucial point few seemed to listen to. A point based on the importance to science of central metaphors. He said that science can go wrong when its math is correct but when the metaphor it uses to interpret that math is wrong.[116]

Which leads to the real question: was Bohm's central metaphor of the glass and glycerin a correct interpretation of the world around us? Or was it the sort of mistaken explanatory device that David Bohm himself warned against: a misleading central metaphor?

***

The concept of implicate order is useful for probing the creativity of axioms, the creativity of simple rules. For when Leonardo, Galileo, Einstein, Claude Shannon, or you make a creative leap, there's a big question. To what extent are you pulling a corollary from the axioms? A corollary that is aching to be? A corollary that is kidnapping, seducing, and recruiting you? A corollary that's a recruitment strategy? And to what extent are you inventing something new?

But the hidden presence of the past is the Achilles heel, the fly in the glycerin, the giant weakness in Bohm's central metaphor for implicate order. It is also the flaw in a metaphor that Immanuel Kant and many others have used to describe the way a universe springs from nothing. Kant used the metaphor of the seed. He declared that "an infinitely small part of [the universe] has the seed of future worlds in itself."[117] And the seed metaphor has hung in there. One hundred and seventy-seven years after Kant, Georges Lemaitre—the physicist/priest who helped start big bang theory—kicked off his hypothesis on the origin of energy and matter with two phrases: "the cosmic egg" and "the cosmic seed."[118] What's wrong with using a seed as a metaphor with which to probe the creativity of the cosmos? What's wrong with using it to solve the God Problem? The seed is like David Bohm's ink drop. It has a past packed within it. It drags its history around like an army hauling around its baggage train. Specifically, it has the history of its evolution knotted, tied, and folded into a single very long and ropelike molecule—its genome. A molecule that if stretched out and untangled would be three feet four inches long.[119]

Imagine that you are a seed. The plant you are itching to manufacture does not spring from nothing. Your genome is your memory. And that genomic memory carries the lessons that your forebears learned during nearly four billion years of evolutionary history. Your genome is packed with lessons that your ancestors learned about how to use your string of nucleotides, your string of DNA, to make yet more DNA. It is packed with lessons from the past on how to construct a cell and how to use that cell to make more cells. In its base pairs and nucleotides, your genome records the secrets of how to manufacture hard cellulose and flexible proteins, lessons on how to make stems, leaves, and greenery. Your genome records your forebears' techniques for turning sunshine and carbon dioxide into sugars.[120] It records how your ancestors managed to pack that sugar away as starch, storing it up for sunless days. In its 20,000 to 40,000[121] genes, your genome records the tactics with which your ancestors outwitted competitors and escaped the onslaughts of predators.

Your genetic code is packed with lessons on how to fight for light in a crowded environment. Yes, you carry a legacy of lessons on strategy. You may be prepped by your genes to put out broad leaves that hog the sunlight. In other words, you may be genetically primed to be a light monopolizer. A Bill Gates blotting up all the sunshine. Or you may be genetically armed for guerrilla warfare. Your genes may code you to put out long, spearlike leaves that poke through the gaps in the roof of leaves spread by light monopolizers. You may be equipped to assemble leaves that stab their way upward to the sun, piercing the spaces between the leaves of your competitors. Or you may be genetically primed for yet another tactic. You may put out long, powerful stems that stretch horizontally to find the sun beyond the edges of the monopolists' broad ceiling of leaves. Or you may be genetically tweaked to be a nonconformist. You may carry an outside-the-box way to gather light despite the thick roof of leaves your competitors have erected, despite the leaves of competing plants that snarf up sunlight and cast you in shade. You may have genetic instructions for black and reddish leaves that snag the wavelengths of light that the green plants overlook. No matter which strategy is built into your genome, you, the seed, have the genetic equivalent of an instruction manual for survival and, better yet, for exuberant victory. Your genomic how-to manual comes from roughly a trillion generations of experience. You are prepacked with nearly four billion years of creative breakthroughs.

So you, a seed, are even more preloaded with how-tos from your history than Bohm's glycerin. You may be a mere pip, but you are jam-packed with recruitment strategies. With ways to pull things together and give them a new and bigger identity. You are packed with communications tools based on the onion layers of what Claude Shannon called "meaning."

But none of this preloading is true of cosmic creativity. Why? In this book, we've assumed up until now that the big bang had no past. However, there is a small army of physicists like loop quantum gravity specialist Martin Bojowald who've been promoting the notion that this is a cyclic cosmos, a cosmos that big bangs into existence, dies, and big bangs again. Here's the problem. Even if this is a cyclic cosmos, the question remains of how that cycle came to be. The question remains of how the complexities implicit in that cycle self-assembled from nothing. The problem of the cosmos's creativity continues to stare us in the face.

The metaphor of the glycerin and the metaphor of the seed translate a past into a hidden code, then reassemble it. They sidestep the God Problem. But there *are* metaphors that don't cheat. Metaphors that don't carry a past stuffed within them like cheese in a ravioli. These are metaphors that *do* seem to make something from nothing. Metaphors that *do* hint at the secret of how termites picking up their own excreta and putting it in the neatest pile around create an architectural astonishment.

The metaphors with a radically new explanation for form production would appear when Claude Shannon's computer would begin to do its thing.

BENOÎT MANDELBROT ZIGS AND ZAGS

So this is a social cosmos. It is a communicating cosmos. It is a conversational cosmos. It is an informational cosmos. It is a cosmos of meaning. And it is a cosmos of form production and emergent properties. But what does that have to do with the story of axioms? What does it have to do with simple rules? What does it have to do with corollary generator theory? And what does it have to do with the mystery of how a godless cosmos constructs itself?

Over a hundred years of scientific experiment and observation proved that Albert Einstein's axiom shift got at something very basic in the cosmos. Over a hundred years of experiment proved that the abstract, ivory-tower math of axiom flippers and of implication extractors can uncover the secrets of something very real, the cosmos. The eight validations of Einstein's predictions hinted that the math of axioms and logic can actually uncover what Einstein called "deeply hidden" secrets. Secrets that may be basic patterns, deep structures, patterns that repeat at level after level of the cosmos. Ur patterns. The basic patterns that allow math and metaphor to work.

Now the question is whether the same kind of validation will spill forth for another scientific technique based on simple rules, another scientific technique based on extracting implicate properties from axioms, another scientific approach based on flipping as many axioms as it takes to get a system that matches the cosmos. A scientific system that gives a hint of what big pictures may be. This new system throws equations aside, discards the six-thousand-year structure that mathematicians have built the way that termites build a hive with walls, arches, ventilation shafts, chambers, chimneys, and towers. The new system substitutes something else for equal signs, for squaring, for Greek letters, and for x's and y's. It substitutes a new technology, a technology that the Babylonians, Aristotle, Euclid, Kepler, and Einstein did not have. And it substitutes a new symbol set. A new metaphor. A new sort of translation. A new kind of scratch mark. A scratch mark in a medium that's radically different from a clay hand tablet, a roll of papyrus, a wax tablet, or a sheet of paper. A scratch mark in an electron flow.

The new replacement for the clay hand tablet is the computer. And the man who would pioneer the computer's use to explore the mysteries of form production, the puzzles of the big picture, the riddles of meaning, and the challenges of the God Problem was Benoît Mandelbrot. Who was Benoît Mandelbrot? And how did he use the computer to redefine the relationship between axioms, simple rules, and cosmic creativity?

Mandelbrot's story begins six years before he was born. It begins in 1918, when Albert Einstein's relativity was taking over the world of physics and when Hans Driesch was unsuccessfully promoting his embryo meta-phor to his fellow scientists. Just as scientific thinkers refused to confront the challenge of the embryo, mathematicians had tossed a small set of oddities into the trash. A handful of ugly ducklings.

Math was obsessed with smooth curves and smooth sheets. Albert Einstein, for example, had come out with a theory that explained the cosmos in terms of rubbery sheets of space and time. Rubbery sheets as smooth as smooth as smooth can be. But in 1918 in France, Gaston Julia[122] had discov-ered an odd set of patterns that were the very opposite of smooth. These patterns were jagged and bumpy—so jagged that their contours couldn't be measured. They were even more jagged than the zigzag patterns of the Babylonians. They looked something like the coast of England. A coast-line with big indentations, small indentations, and microscopic indenta-tions. Measure those indentations with a big measuring rod and you get one number. Measure them with a smaller measuring rod and you are able to fit that measuring device into more of the indentations of the crevasses, crags, and outcrops. So the measure you get of the coastline shoots up. Try using a microscopic measuring rod to measure the boundaries of these zigzag pat-terns, and you run into a size problem. The zigzags of the coast's indenta-tions continue right down to the microscopic level. With your super-tiny measuring rod, you're able to measure the microjags and indentations of even more ragged outcrops and inlets. You're able to measure even the microscopic indentations of sand and stone. So the length you get from your measurement soars even higher. In theory, if you were to use an infinitesi-mally small ruler, the length you'd get would be . . . infinite.

Sorry, this will not do. In math, infinities bollox things up. Divide a simple number like one by infinity and you no longer get numbers. You get nonsense. So mathematicians labeled these jagged objects "monstrosities" and said they did not belong in mathematics. Yes, mathematicians banished a reality. In essence, they said that zigzags were above their pay grade. But their way of saying it was a bit more peculiar. They basically said that since it screwed up their math, jaggedness did not exist. Lumps, bumps, and ser-rations were out. Then came Benoît Mandelbrot.

Benoît Mandelbrot was born in Warsaw, Poland, to a Jewish family at a time when being Jewish in Poland was about to become impossible—1924. You are Jewish for a day, so you can relate. Benoît's father was a mere clothing merchant. But two of his uncles were in a realm high above clothing. They were mathematicians. When Benoît was nine, a strange little man with a Charlie Chaplin mustache was elected premier of Poland's next door neighbor, Germany. The little man with the mustache, a guy who shouted his speeches with all his might, told his listeners that Jews were vermin, they were a plague that had sickened Germany. Most Jews knew that a bizarre ranter like this could never have a real impact on the country of Mozart, Beethoven, Hegel, Kant, and Goethe. This laughable man who shouted his speeches could never pull the wool over the eyes of the most culturally sophisticated people in the world. So most Jews stayed where they were and waited for Germany to regain its sanity. Benoît's parents had a different opinion. Adolph Hitler, they felt, was a threat.

So the family moved to France . . . then moved around inside France, dodging the menace of Hitler's extermination plan for Jews. This broke up Benoît's education. Which means that Mandelbrot, like Herbert Spencer, George Henry Lewes, and Albert Einstein, was free to teach himself. One of Mandelbrot's mathematician uncles tried to fill in the gaps. Among other things, he told Benoît about the 1918 paper by Gaston Julia, the father of the craggy monstrosities that most mathematicians would not touch with a ten-foot slide rule.[123] Benoît read the despised paper, and it determined the shape of the rest of his career. It acted as a form producer for Mandelbrot's budding intellect. And "budding" would become a key to Mandelbrot's discoveries.

When he hit the age of twenty-six, Benoît Mandelbrot was irked by his uncle Szolem. Why? His uncle was a cofounder[124] of a movement that Mandelbrot says "worshipped abstraction and math for math's sake."[125] That movement was led by a secret society of French mathematicians who wrote joint books under the pen name of a single, made-up mathematician, the fictitious Nicolas Bourbaki. You heard it right, a secret society of mathematicians. And Benoît's uncle had been one of the founding members. The Bourbaki group's secrecy was a tip-off. The gang was determined to make math obscure. Says Mandelbrot, the doctrine established by this secret society "scorned pragmatism, applications, or math as a tool for science."[126] To make matters worse, the Bourbaki group's proudly super-abstract approach, says Mandelbrot, was "dogma"[127] in France. But that's not all. Mandelbrot's uncle Szolem was also an admirer of G. H. Hardy, a Cambridge mathematician who had seen the ravages of World War I—the first war to use products of science like mustard gas—and didn't want those atrocities repeated. (One of Hardy's friends, by the way, was Bertrand Russell, who had been jailed in World War I for his pacifism.[128] Russell crops up everywhere.) G. H. Hardy felt that mathematicians should keep their discoveries away from politicians, industrialists, and engineers. He apparently feared that any math that landed in the hands of the public would be turned into weapons. Explains Mandelbrot, "Hardy was an outspoken pacifist who recoiled from the practical uses of . . . mathematics." Hardy's "ideal," adds Mandelbrot, was "pure mathematics. . . . For him, good mathematics could have no bad application—for the simple reason that it could have no application of any sort."[129] In fact Hardy bragged that "I have never done anything 'useful.'" The result? In 1940 a Nobel Prize–winning chemist reviewed one of Hardy's books for *Nature* and concluded that Hardy's preoccupations were so carefully removed from reality that "from such cloistral clowning the world sickens."[130]

What technique did G. H. Hardy, the Bourbaki group, and Mandelbrot's uncle Szolem use to hide their math? Most math is a translation of things that you can represent in pictures. But pictures are easy to understand. So these "cloistrally clowning" mathematicians banished pictures. Utterly.[131] Instead they substituted an isomorphic symbol set, one so difficult that it hid their meanings. What was that isomorphic symbol set? Equations.[132] Benoît Mandelbrot, however, had a mathematical curse. Or was it a blessing? He "often preferred to draw pictures of data rather than write equations."[133] So Mandelbrot was upset by his uncle's obscurantism, his uncle's insistence that mathematicians speak only in a language no layman could understand— the language of equations. And Benoît hated the Julia paper his uncle had praised as "a masterpiece."[134]

But there's a strange twist to hatred. What you hate the most is often what you pay the most attention to. And attention is the suction pump of information. Attention is an engine of group IQ. Those who hate a concept, a nation, a people, or a race often know far more about what they despise than folks who never heard of the hated thing or who simply never felt it was worth a second thought.

When World War II was over, Benoît Mandelbrot finished his fractured education at l'École Polytechnique in France, then he landed a rather amazing job in New York State's Yorktown Heights at IBM as a research fellow. Meaning that Mandelbrot was paid a good salary to think about anything that pleased him.

What did he think about? Something that was right under his nose and under the nose of everyone around him in the mathematical community. That something? The mathematical monstrosities, the forbidden mathematical grotesques that others had discarded and loathed. Specifically, the hideous forms of Gaston Julia, forms that even he, Benoît Mandelbrot, had hated when his uncle had first tried to introduce them to him. The zigging, zagging, outcropping, and inletting forms that led to infinity.

In 1976, Benoît Mandelbrot gave these mathematical elephant men a name—fractals. And fractals became one of the most important mathematical discoveries of the twentieth century.

9

IT'S FROM BITS:
THE TWO-BIT TARANTELLA

HOW MATH LOST ITS PICTURES . . .
AND HOW IT GOT THEM BACK AGAIN

The product of Claude Shannon's work, the computer, would be the tool that would allow Benoît Mandelbrot to develop a math that would hop, skip, and jump beyond the Bohm Cheat. The computer would allow Benoît Mandelbrot to develop fractals.

But why would the computer open the way to a brand-new form of math? For six thousand years, math had depended on repetition. Yes, repetition. Remember how you, a Babylonian priest, invented arithmetic? I brought you a load of barleycorns. You invented markings on clay to keep track of what I brought you. And you sat down for fifteen hours to count out the barleycorns in my load. Then you wrote the figure down with a reed in clay. When I went for a second load, you got tired of counting every grain of barley. You standardized the load. You took the 10,800 acts of counting and compacted them into one symbol, the load, the talent, the gu. Then you "heaped" the loads. You added them. Finally even that tired you. Let's face it. Counting thousands of loads of barley was tedious. So you compacted the load counting into a multiplication table. You worked out ways to nest one layer of iterations in another. You compacted the tediously repeated process of counting in a shortcut. Then you compacted the tedious repetitions of your shortcut in yet another shortcut—your multiplication table.

But at bottom, it all came down to counting barleycorns. It all came down to counting simple, modular things. Over and over and over again. Repeating was the heart of math.

If you look at the procedures that the Babylonian and Egyptian mathematicians try to teach to kids in their clay and papyrus math books, you'll be horrified. Babylonian calculations of the amount of copper it would take to shield a city's walls are done step by painful step. Even if it takes hundreds of these tiny steps. And the growth of math as a science has also depended on millions upon millions of these calculations, these tiny steps. Who does all the step taking? The mathematicians who enter math's puzzle contests, math's competitions for glory and fame. Which means that in six thousand years of math the total number of computations—the total number of tiny repetitions—that it has taken to go from Mesopotamian arithmetic to Einstein is in the hundreds of billions.

But the computer is the ultimate repeater. The ultimate iterator. It can do in one second more calculations, more iterations, more tiny steps, than all of the mathematicians in history.[1] It can do in a second more than the calculations that men like Gauss were able to carry out in a lifetime. It can take manic mass production to the nth degree. What's more, it can unfold implicate properties in ways that David Bohm's ink drops on glycerin never could.

The computer can evade the David Bohm Cheat. How? David Bohm's ink drops were made, then hidden, then brought back to their original form. They were not formed from nothing. They were not surprises to their maker. They were not things this universe had never seen before. But that's not true of form production in the computer. The computer can unfold the implicit properties of axioms. And it can unfold them without having the answer built in. It can unfold a vision of a future without having that future tucked into it in advance. It can even unfold new big pictures. New tapestries woven from old threads. Tapestries that are utterly novel and unexpected. Tapestries that eerily ape the supersized surprise.

And there's more. Aristotle was half right when he banned metaphor from science. Why? In the days of Herbert Spencer, metaphors often failed to cut it in the realm of prediction. When Spencer died in 1903, his concepts of differentiation, integration, and social organism could not make the kind of exact and testable predictions that Einstein's math would kick off a mere two years later in 1905. In the days of Galileo, Newton, and Einstein, metaphors worked best when they pulled equations together with a big picture, the way that Newton's cannonball cosmos pulled together the math of falling bodies with the big picture of planets swinging in circles around the sun. Other metaphors worked when they were generated in a laboratory, generated like Thomas Young's interference patterns in a ripple tank. Generated in a way that was precisely reproducible and subject to detailed study. On the other hand, when Spencer set out to unify all the knowledge that he could understand, his embryo-based metaphor wasn't mathematizable. And it couldn't be summed up in a laboratory simulation. It couldn't be used to make predictions. So Darwin, Huxley, and Einstein were remembered. And Spencer was forgotten.

But starting in the 1960s with Benoît Mandelbrot, the computer would be able to yank pictures and calculations together in radical new ways. The computer would give metaphor's core—visions, things you can picture—predictive powers. The computer would give pictures and metaphors predictive powers that wouldn't need equations. And the computer would produce predictive powers that wouldn't rely on laboratory simulations in tanks of liquid. Why? Because the computer would create its own simulations. And it would perform those simulations using something that you can reproduce. Simulations you can reproduce even more precisely than the demonstrations in Thomas Young's ripple tanks.

How did Mandelbrot pull all these implicate amazements from a mere office device? Remember, Benoît Mandelbrot was a professor at the University of Lille in 1958, when he got a peculiar offer from a business machine company founded in 1911 in New York City that made punch card tabulators and other counting machines.[2] That company offered to bring the thirty-four-year-old Mandelbrot from France to New York's tony suburb of Yorktown Heights. To do what? To be a brain for hire. A brain exploring the furthest potential of a new kind of machine that the company was manufacturing. A machine that the company was continuously improving. That new machine was the computer. And the company making the offer was the

International Business Machine Company, IBM, the company that would dominate computer development and production from 1960 to 1990.

The computer turned out to be a strange machine. It was not smart in the human sense. It did not have creativity. One motto described its limitations as "garbage in, garbage out." It could only work out the implications of what it was fed. It could only work out the "implicate properties" of the assumptions hidden in the hardware and software that its programmers and engineers had pumped into it. It could only go as far as its hidden assumptions. But, boy, could it work out those implications. Why? The year when Mandelbrot joined IBM—1958—was also the year of the first integrated circuit. And it was one year before the replacement of fist-sized vacuum tubes in computers with dime-sized transistors. Yet the computers of 1958 could repeat simple rules like a nuclear blizzard. They could repeat simple rules as many as forty-two thousand times per second.[3] Over 362 million times per day. Over ten billion times per month. When it came to spinning out the implications of simple rules, the computers of 1958 could outdo Euclid, Kepler, Gauss, Bólyai, and Lobachevsky combined. And they could do it in less than four minutes.

Then there's another twist. The computer is smarter than we are, says Pavel Kurakin of the Keldysh Institute of Applied Mathematics of the Russian Academy of Sciences in Moscow. The computer, says Kurakin, is both smarter than we are . . . and dumber.[4] And he's right. Why? Because a computer has a hard time understanding an equal sign. It has a hard time with Aristotle's identities. It has a hard time with equations. And that handicap is the computer's advantage. Why? Because the computer "thinks" with a different kind of logic than your standard equation-juggling mathematician. Instead of working with "this equals that," it works with "and" and "or." It works with "if-then" statements. *If* you are reading this, *then* you have eyes. *If* you put a tomato seed in the ground and water it just right, *then* you will get a tomato plant. *If* you put an apple in a blender and turn on the switch, *then* you will get apple sauce. Those are all if-then statements.

And guess what? Reality often ignores *equals* and goes with *if-then*. It often works with "if *x* and *y* happen, then *z* will occur." Even if *z* is radically different from just *x* and *y*. Even if what you get out of putting two apples in the ground and watering them is often more than just two apples. Even if you don't get one plus one equals two. Even if you get two apple *trees*. And *if* you are in estrus, *if* you have poured your perfect, gym-toned and beach-tanned body into your little black dress, *if* you have made yourself up to be the sexiest thing on the planet Earth, *if* you have gone to the most prestigious club you can get into, *if* you have met the man of your dreams, *if* you have gone home with him that night and thrown caution to the winds, *if* you have ignored birth control, and *if* your egg and his sperm do just the right thing, you will get far more than one small cell with a tail invading one big round cell. You will get a swelling in your belly. A swelling that will puff up to 250 million cells. A swelling that will keep you busy mothering for the next twenty years. This, too, is an if-then proposition. It is not a mere one plus one equals two. If-then statements fit a world that has sequences in time. Sequences of causality. Sequences of one plus one equals something shocking, something way off the number line. If-then statements also fit the strange ways of transformation. The strange ways of emergent properties. The strange ways in which the cosmos creates.

And a computer can also do what Thomas Young and Giuseppe Peano were obsessed with, translation. A computer can speak many languages. It can translate to many isomorphic symbol sets. Like the Rosetta Stone, the computer is a translator. It can translate numbers, words, and letters on a screen into the language of the binary number system, the language of electrical impulses, and the language of an increasing number of computer programs. And it can translate that language of offs and ons, the language of electron flows, into the language of printed text and even into the language of speech. Despite its difficulties, the computer can even translate into or out of equations. But most important, the computer can translate equations and programs into a visual language. And it can do what a four-year-old child can do. It can draw and color. It can make pictures. It can churn out graphics so simple and brilliant that even you and I can understand them. Graphics so spectacular that we can love them. The computer can turn mathematics into poster art.

Why are pictures such a big deal? Pictures reveal the meaning of relationships instantly. They reveal why the parts relate to the whole, why the pieces relate to the big, well, ummm, the big picture. Let's bounce back to a fact we stepped over earlier. During most of its six thousand years of development, math was done with pictures. In 300 BCE, Euclid did math by drawing with a compass made of string[5] and with a straight edge. He used pictures. In 1619, Johannes Kepler did math by drawing as many as forty trianglelike lines within a circle. And he made drawings. Detailed, gorgeous illustrations. Kepler did math by drawing pictures. In 1637 even René Descartes used drawings in his *Discourse on Method*, the book in which he translated geometry into a radically new language, the language of algebra.[6] What's more, Descartes—a man who may have done more than any before him to banish visuals—left us the seeds of another picture-based system, the use of grids, grids with an x-axis and a y-axis. Cartesian grids. The grids that you and I learned in first-year algebra. Descartes left a legacy of pictures. And pictures reveal the meaning of a network of relationships.

But in the late-nineteenth and early-twentieth centuries, mathematicians like G. H. Hardy and the Bourbaki group abandoned pictures. They hid their math by using the magic of isomorphic symbol sets. They banished pictures and used a language that held the same meanings but was nearly impossible for normal mortals like you and me to understand. That different language, that isomorphic symbol set, was a weave of something that even Kepler and Galileo did not have. The magic hiding device? The equation.

You and I already know that Benoît Mandelbrot's uncle, the prestigious Parisian mathematician Szolem Mandelbrot, was one of those who hid his work in equations. Recalls Benoît, "I would often stop by his office" in Paris's Collège de France "at the end of the day for a chat; it often turned to debate."[7] Why? Because the younger Mandelbrot refused to follow his uncle's example. In fact, the twenty-six-year-old Benoît broke out, budded, and rebelled. Rebellion is the very word he fixes on when he tells you that abstraction was the "reason why I ultimately left Paris for IBM. I was a young rebel, much to my uncle's consternation."[8] How did Mandelbrot turn against his uncle's role modeling? How did he differentiate himself? How did he strike out for his own position in attention space? He did the unthinkable. He returned math to simplicity. He returned math to pictures. But Benoît Mandelbrot was able to give pictures back to math because of his new tool. A tool his uncle never had.

FUSE AND FIZZ, THOU SHALT BUD:
FRACTALS AND THE BOUNCE FROM BOOM TO BUST

> *Science is possible because the world seems very complex but is actually governed by a small set of laws.*
>
> —**Gregory Chaitin**[9]

The secret of simple rules—the secret of extracting the ornate from axioms—busts loose and does whole new things in Benoît Mandelbrot's fractals.

In fractals, you follow a simple rule. That gives you a result. Then you repeat the simple rule once again on the result. Like heaping a fecal brick on a pile. Then heaping the pile on another pile. Then heaping that pile on yet another pile. "And," in the words of Dr. Seuss, "so forth and upward and onward, gee whizz!"[10] In fact, you do this over and over again as many billions of times as your access to the computer and your patience allows. This is what computers specialize in: faithful, high-speed repetition. But, as you know, there's more. A computer can turn this process into visuals, visuals it can show on your monitor or printout. And you've almost certainly seen the product of Mandelbrot's fractals—pictures so stunning that they became a fad in the 1980s and 1990s, when they were used to decorate calendars, stationary, wrapping paper, and even kitchen aprons. Fractals produce pictures that explode. Pictures that erupt with bulging, budding circles forming swirls, curls, spindles, spires, straight lines, rosettes, florets, blossoms, and blazes of tracery. Pictures that appear to bloom with something stunning and stunningly God Problem-ish: creativity.

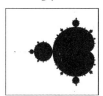

The underlying pattern of the Mandelbrot set. The basic rule? Huddle tight in a circle, then bud. Bust out. Rebel. Every pattern that emerges is a repetition of this pattern in disguise. *Courtesy of David Dewey, "Introduction to the Mandelbrot Set," http://ddewey.net/mandelbrot/.*

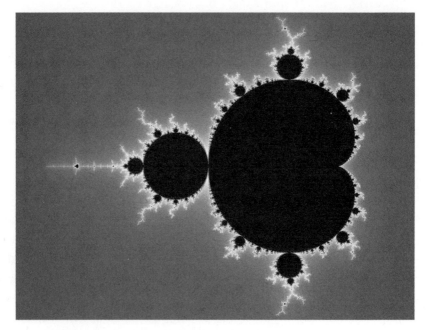

Benoit Mandelbrot's fractal starts to get ornate. *Courtesy of Wolfgang Beyer, Wikimedia Commons.*

The superstar of fractal patterns, the best known and most widely seen, is the Mandelbrot set. I hate to go incomprehensible on you, so please grit your teeth for a second. A Mandelbrot set is based on an equation like $Z = Z^2 + C$. What does $Z = Z^2 + C$ mean in English? It's a basic rule repeated over and over upon itself like the rules of the ripple, the rules of the termite, and, yes, the rules of the mathematicians in Babylon working out the problem of how much food and water it will take to feed the army of workers who will sweat and toil to build city walls sixty feet high and sixty feet wide. In English, $Z = Z^2 + C$ means gather together around a common core. Make a circle. Then bud out. Rebel. Separate.

The rule of the Mandelbrot set is very much like Frank Sulloway's rule for rebellion, the rule that often dictates how the second baby in a family will carve out a niche in attention space. The Mandelbrot rule is very much like what Aristotle did when he set himself up in opposition to Heraclitus. The Mandelbrot rule is very much like what Galileo did when he dove into geometry against his father's orders. The Mandelbrot rule is very much like what the non-Euclideans did when they rebelled against the parallel axiom. And the Mandelbrot rule is very much like what Einstein did when he rebelled against his teachers and learned by teaching himself. In fact, the Mandelbrot rule is very much like what Benoît Mandelbrot did when he rebelled against his uncle.

First you rebel. You hive off. You set yourself apart. You differentiate. Then what? You congregate around a common core again. A new common core, a rebel common core. A core of outriders. You integrate. And then? What's the next step? The same step you began with. Bud. Separate. Rebel once more. Rebel against your fellow rebels. Break out again. Two rules. Clump, then break out. Fuse, then fizz. Hug tight, then separate. Or, to repeat the magic words from von Baer, Driesch, and Herbert Spencer, integrate then differentiate. Then integrate and once again differentiate. Old rules. Very old rules. The rules of attraction and repulsion. Repeated in a new form. And in a new medium. Repeated with a persistence that only a computer can muster. Repeated octillions of times. Or more.

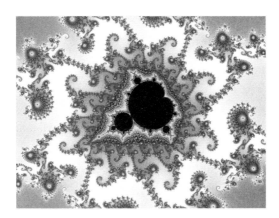

Mandelbrot sets explode with intricacy. Thanks to repetition, thanks to iteration. *Courtesy of Wolfgang Beyer, Wikimedia Commons.*

A close-up of the Mandelbrot set. *Courtesy of Wolfgang Beyer, Wikimedia Commons.*

But zoom in on the extravagant shapes made by fractals and you discover that no matter how flamboyant the patterns, they are all composed of the same thing, the rule that you began with—circles with circular buds blistering from their outer edges. Circular buds with yet more circular buds on their peripheries. The ornate complexity you see in pictures of fractals is the product of simple rules followed over and over again, simple rules repeated within the changing context that they themselves make. Repeated within a new medium that the rules themselves have brought to be.

The rule of the Mandelbrot set is a starting assumption, an axiom. And like a geometry unfolding from Euclid's axioms or a mathematics unfolding from Peano's axioms, every new surprise is implicit in the simple rule that started it all, every new twist and twirl lies dormant in the simple formula of $Z = Z^2 + C$, dormant from the beginning. Every new curlicue and line is implicit in the simple rule of gather together then separate, cluster then rebel. In some strange way, ornate and showy twists, turns, corkscrews, lines, and shapes are hiding in that simple formula from the very start. A complex form is lurking unseen as a mere potential in a variation of the most ancient and oft-repeated rule of the cosmos—attraction and repulsion. But how?

No matter what the answer, this implicit form does not rely on the David Bohm Cheat. Nor does it rely on the cheating of Immanuel Kant's seed. The curlicues and twirls, the straight lines and explosions are not built-in in advance!

How can complexity lurk in simplicity? How can the ornate and the outrageous hide invisibly in rules so simple that a child, a quark, an atom, a ripple, a baboon, or an economy can follow them? And what in the world does this have to do with everyday life—with oscillating moods and their role in the search engine of society, the search engine of the cosmos? Not to mention cosmic creativity?

Those are hard questions to answer. But fractals do make one thing very clear. They overcome the Bohm Cheat. They don't resurrect a hidden past. They burst with genuine surprise.

But does the Mandelbrot set help us with the God Problem? What, exactly, is that problem again?

> How does a godless cosmos create itself? How has the cosmos created stars, planets, galaxies, cells, DNA, muscles, neurons, rotary motors for flagella, flicking tongues for toads, and self-defenses for tobacco plants? How has the cosmos created minds, cultures, and you and me? How has the cosmos built us from the big bang's simple seeds?

Does the Mandelbrot set help us solve the God Problem? In the six thousand years of thinking we've covered, from the Mesopotamians and the twelve-knot rope of the Egyptians to the fluttering switches of Claude Shannon, the Mandelbrot set is one of the first metaphors, one of the first mathematical systems, that does something genuinely God Problemish. Without human intervention, without preplanning from a ziggurat-or-pyramid-planning architect, without a visionary big-picture synthesizer like Albert Einstein, it does something impossible, maniacal, and astonishing. What? It produces a wild proliferation of forms from the simplest of beginnings. It starts with an equivalent to Peano's axioms. It starts from a simple rule, a simple equation. An equation with no future built in. It does not hide an ink drop in the glycerin. It starts with almost nothing. Then it runs its system forward and spills forth forms we didn't have a clue were lurking within it.

Mandelbrot's set is one of the first really big hints to the puzzle that you and I have been hunting down, the puzzle of a cosmos of future shock, a cosmos of the supersized surprise.

***

Which leads to the same question we saw with non-Euclidean geometry and with Einstein's math. Are fractals merely creatures of math and fantasy? Are fractals mere figments of a computer's imagination? Or do they capture something at work in the real world?

***

Fractal patterns are real as real can be. Fractals show up in coastlines, their point of origin. But fractals also appear in clusters of galaxies, in chromosomes, in DNA, in broccoli, in cabbages, and in trees. Fractals even show up in human sexual behavior. Not to mention in the tango. What's more, the rules of the Mandelbrot set make the sort of shapes that Euclid dealt with. The sort of shapes that Leonardo and Thomas Young found in water. Circles. But circles that interact to create brand new skeins of relationship. Circles that create brand new shapes.

Then there are even higher-level fractal relations to reality. The fractal variation on attraction and repulsion is similar to something that primatologists in the 1970s called the "fission-fusion search strategy."[11] A strategy you mapped out in another book, your 2009 *Genius of the Beast: A Radical Re-Vision of Capitalism.*[12] A strategy that underlies the most basic cycle of economies—the cycle from boom to bust and back again. How? Let me give you a quick summary of the fission-fusion strategy.

Baboons in South Africa and along East Africa's Zambezi River use the fission-fusion strategy to find food.[13] They spread out across the countryside during the day, looking for old and new sources of nourishment. Then they get together at night, sleep near each other, and in the morning their dominant males use body language to compare notes. Each male argues for a different destination for the day's foraging. Then the baboons spread out again and explore. Stretch out, explore, then come together and consolidate your information, that's the fission-fusion strategy. The fission-fusion strategy is a search strategy. A way of finding new things.

Humans unknowingly follow the fission-fusion strategy, too. We have recessions roughly every 4.75 years.[14] And we have great depressions roughly once every sixty-seven years, roughly once in a generation. Why? Like baboons, we become exuberant about new possibilities. That exuberance gets us to explore new nooks and crannies of opportunity. Exuberance prods us to spread out in complexity specialist Stuart Kauffman's "possibility space." Exuberance gets us to speculate.

The result is a boom. Complete with a speculative bubble. And what do speculative bubbles accomplish? They explore the frontiers of the implicit, the frontiers of emergent properties. Speculative bubbles explore the boundaries of the absurd and the impossible. And they yank the impossible into reality. The speculative bubbles of the early-nineteenth century in the United States, for example, were over western land, land in the distant territories of Kentucky, Tennessee, West Virginia, and the western Carolinas. What do booms like the western land bubble do to you and me? During each boom, land in the nothingness looks like it will make you rich. And during each crash, you wake up from your frenzy. You see with clarity that your enthusiasm for western land has been a wild mistake, a disastrous error, an irrational exuberance that is going to send you to the poorhouse. So you try to sell your western land. But everyone in sight is as panicked as you are. Which means there are very few takers for your acres. And those acres plunge in price. Making you a pauper on paper.

When are you right? When you fantasize riches? Or when you imagine destitution? Are you on target when you are sure that western land will find a thousand new uses? Or have you sobered up to the truth when you realize that western land will never be worth a cent? To put it differently, did betting on western land pay off in the 1790s or in 1810? You bet. Western land that once seemed overpriced at twelve-and-a-half cents per acre[15] sells today for between $505,972[16] and $127 million[17] per acre. The speculators and the bubble makers were right. And the skeptics were wrong. But underneath your frenzies and your fears are the rules of the Mandelbrot fractal: huddle together in fear, then rebel, bust out, explore. Then huddle tight in a state of insecurity again. When the Mandelbrot rules are translated into the social medium of living things—from bacteria to human beings—they are transformed into the template for a search strategy.

Which means that you are right when you speculate. But you are also right when you are terrified that you've thrown your money away. Prices of western land will soar and crash many a time. Western land will switch from the power of attraction to the power of repulsion over and over again. Western land will do a Mandelbrot. And you will have to hold on tight to ride the long-term curve. The curve of what Herbert Spencer called "progress." The curve that has defied the law of entropy for 13.73 billion years. The curve of cosmic creativity. The curve up.

What did you, a mere termite in the corridors of investment, accomplish when you purchased western land? You put your fecal brick, your speck of savings, into a pile that pushed into the West. You were part of a search engine of possibility space. A search engine that transformed plains of wild grass in which the buffalo roamed into the seas of waving grain that would soon save Europe and Russia from famine. You were part of a search engine that found and dug the Michigan iron mines that would soon turn America into a major industrial power. You were part of a search engine that would soon turn California from a land that experts said was poisonous and filled with nothing but scorpions and rattlesnakes into Silicon Valley and Hollywood. You were part of the search engine that would soon spread the ideas of freedom of speech and assembly worldwide.

Here's how effectively that search engine worked. Nearly two hundred years ago, in 1824, there was a wide spot in an Indian walking trail on the southern shore of a massive lake way, way out in the wildness of the American West. In essence, this minor expansion of a walking path was nothing but a greasy patch between the woods and the shore. But it had a name—the Menominee Indian word for a wild leek. And it had a few European settlers, folks capable of living far beyond the bounds of civilization. Nine of them.[18] One of the new residents, James Galloway, had left another frontier province, Ohio, to escape the ague—an aching sickness of the day. By 1833, Galloway and his fellow settlers had been joined by others. Three hundred and fifty others. Enough residents to make this trail stop in the wilderness a town. A very small town. Then came the speculators. And the wild enthusiasms. The irrational exuberances. The fantasies, the get-rich-quick dreams. The hot new technologies of the 1830s were tools of transport—the canal and Herbert Spencer's favorite, the railroad. But canals and railroads were expensive. It could cost over six million dollars to lay down one hundred miles of track. That's over $157 million in 2010 dollars.[19]

Expense or not, the speculators had two schemes. The town in the wilderness, the town named after a wild leek, was on the southern shore of one of the Great Lakes. And it was ninety-six miles from the tributary system of the longest river in North America—the Mississippi. From 1810 to 1836, wild dreamers in the government of the new territory of Illinois were joined by wild-dream promoters in the growing territory's budding newspapers and by wild fantasizers who held public meetings and made demands. Demands for expensive new forms of transportation. These passionate believers painted extravagant pictures of a government-built canal that would connect the Great Lakes to the Mississippi.[20] That canal would be close to the greasy spot on an Indian trail. The town with 350 citizens. In other words, it would open the way to nowhere. In 1836 another group of speculators sold feverish visions of a railroad to the almost nonexistent town that had grown up in the middle of nowhere. And that was the key weakness in the scheme—the middle of nowhere. The lands around the western Great Lakes were not a location. They were not a node in a network of relationships. They were not a dense patch of paint in a big picture. They were an empty space. There was nothing there but a handful of Indian tribes and a fly speck of European settlers. The whole scheme was clearly a scam.

But the money was raised and the canal and the railroad were built. The rail line opened in 1848. So did the canal. The result? By 1858 the feeble town on an Indian path in the wilderness had 91,000 inhabitants. It went from 350 settlers to close to 100,000 in a mere twenty-five years. And by 2010 that figure had reached 2,695,598—more than two and a half million.

The wild leak after which the Indians had named this two-man-wide spot on a foot path was called the shikaakwa. And the town that couldn't possibly pay off as an investment was Chicago. Why did Chicago become so big so fast? Why did it go from a nothing to a something? Why did it go from a fantasy to a radical new reality? Why did it become a node in a many-layered onion of meanings? Or, to put it differently, why were the fantasies of the speculators on target? And why had the previous bubbles in Western land also hit the bull's-eye?[21] Slowly the old wilderness far beyond civilization was settled by farmers. The federal government of 1860 was controlled by a brand-new political party, the Republican Party. A party just five years old. The Republicans under their president, Abraham Lincoln, worked hard to increase the number of voters who would go Republican in future elections. One way to do it was bribery. Give away land to people who would settle and farm it. Charge a trifling ten dollars for 160 acres. Extend this astonishing deal to anyone who had filed papers for citizenship and who would commit to stay on the land for five years and improve it.[22] Give away over 2.4 million acres of land.[23] Land taken from the Indians. Thanks to settlement, those crazy lands in the wild, wild West slowly gained a new meaning, a new place in a meshwork of relationships. A new place in many overlapping big pictures. Those meanings were encapsulated in a new name: the Midwest.

The new farmers of the Midwest raised grain. Lots of it. They raised what the 1893 song "America the Beautiful" called "amber waves of grain." And those seas of waving grain changed the texture of, brace yourself, European life. Yes, they changed life in Europe, an ocean away. Why? When Europe went into economic depressions, those depressions were often accompanied by famines. So in a depression, you didn't just lose your house. You lost your life. You starved to death.[24] In 1891, the Russian wheat crop failed.[25] The Russian and European poor were threatened with starvation. What did the Europeans do? They purchased grain from the new farmers of the American Midwest. They literally shipped gold from Europe to the United States to pay for it. And for one of the first times in a famine, Europeans did not starve.

How did that grain from Western lands get to the Europeans? Via a new network of relationships. Via the Great Lakes. Via the canal that connected Lake Michigan and the Mississippi. Via another wild boondoggle. Another canal to nowhere—the Erie Canal in New York State. A canal that had cost eight and a half million dollars to build[26]—over 161 million dollars at 2010 values. A canal that had connected the miniscule and meaningless settlement of Buffalo, New York, at the eastern end of the Great Lakes, to New York City in 1825. A canal that had connected the Great Lakes to the body of water for which New York is a port—the Atlantic Ocean. What's on the other side of the Atlantic Ocean? Europe.

Chicago became the central point for bringing the wheat, the iron ore, and the meat of the Midwest to the world. Via its railroad to a footpath and via two canals to nowhere. All because of the fission-fusion search strategy. All because of the search strategy of spread out and explore, then crunch down and consolidate. The search strategy that makes bubbles, booms, and crashes. The search strategy that brings radical new things from nothingness to existence. All because of a primary recruitment strategy of the cosmos. A recruitment strategy based on the simple rules of attraction and repulsion. A recruitment strategy, in Herbert Spencer's words, based on the rules of differentiation and integration. A recruitment strategy based on oscillation, the wobble back and forth between opposites. Based on the fact that opposites are joined at the hip.

A recruitment strategy that is aped, mirrored, simulated, and metaphored by the Mandelbrot set.

Do the Mandelbrot set and its pretty pictures have anything to do with how you earn and eat your daily bread? Do fractals have anything to do with how the cosmos creates? You bet.

***

It all comes down to simple rules. It all comes down to axioms. Fission and fusion are attraction and repulsion in disguise. They are among the oldest patterns of the cosmos. They are good candidates for the cosmos's starting rules. And they are rules of sociality. They are rules of communication. They are rules of information. They are rules of meaning.

THE SORCERY OF SIMPLE RULES

> *Big whirls have little whirls that feed on their velocity,*
> *and little whirls have lesser whirls and so on to viscosity.*[27]
> —Lewis Fry Richardson, mathematician,
> weather-prediction pioneer,
> mathematical-war-prediction pioneer,
> mathematical analyzer of coastline measurement,
> and pioneer of fractal mathematics

As you predicted at our café table at the beginning of the universe 13.73 billion years ago, the big bang whomped forth from an infinitesimal pinprick of space. Then the cosmos added space, time, and motion to yet more space, time, and motion and got far more than just more space, time, and motion. The cosmic act of addition made quarks. Space, time, and motion added to themselves became matter. But how?

Here's a clue from Benoît Mandelbrot. The repetition of an old pattern in a new medium can make something breathtakingly new. In math and in computer programming, it all comes down to "iteration." And here's the secret. The secret to why one *A* does not equal another. The repetition of an old pattern changes the nature of the cosmos. Stuttering forth the same old thing in a new time and place changes the very nature of the medium in which the next iteration—the next repetition—takes place.

Remember Leonardo da Vinci's two stones in a pond? When only one stone hit the pond, it kicked a simple rule into operation. It made waves. More specifically, it made waves that corduroyed the surface of the water into rings, circles that resembled the rings around the bull's-eye of a target, rings in motion, rings that moved steadily outward. Leonardo had summoned the simple rule that makes ripples. A simple rule that translates the stone's movement into circles. An amazing act of transformation.

But what happened when Leonardo dropped two pebbles at the same time, two pebbles two feet apart? Leonardo saw only one thing—that the two sets of ripples retained their identities when they met and crossed. But you know that more happened. Why? You and I are privy to the work of

Thomas Young. And Thomas Young noticed more in intersecting ripples than just the mighty feat of retaining identity. Thomas Young noticed an act of cosmic creativity. Yes, just as Leonardo had seen, each splash point sent out a concentric ring of waves. Each splash followed the simple rule of the ripple, the simple pattern of a target's rings in motion. But when the two rings of ripples met, the simple turned complex.

Where the two rings of ripples intersected, they made a crazy plaid. A pseudo-Scottish tartan. A moiré. A geometric gingham. An argyle. Something you'd think mere circles could never make.

An interference pattern. © 2011 Stephen Wolfram, LLC, http://www.wolframscience.com.

That was just the tiniest hint of the magic of simple rules. It was just a very small clue to the wizardry that happens when simple rules socialize. It was just a whisper of the sorcery and the circus of forms that emerge when things made by the same simple rules interact.

Mandelbrot-like iterations working simultaneously can produce unexpected surprises even in the simplest of natural things. And guess what? This is a universe of more than just occasional simultaneity. It is a universe of supersimultaneity. A universe of supersynchrony.

Imagine what would happen if you dropped ten pebbles into the still pool. What would happen if you repeated the same simple ripple pattern in a trillion different places and let those patterns intersect. What would happen if you repeated the same simple rules in roughly 10^{81} different locations. What sort of tartans, plaids, and weaves would you get?

That, in essence, is what the cosmos did in the first 10^{-9} second of the big bang. The universe did a Leonardo. The universe did a Mandelbrot.

THE JAPANESE SWORD MAKER
AND THE ALCHEMY OF ITERATION

There is a secret at the center of Leonardo's, Gaston Julia's,[28] and Benoît Mandelbrot's work. It's iteration. Repetition. Repetition of an old rule in a new context. Repetition in a relational context. Repetition in a social context. Repetition in the social context that the rule itself has made.

Manic repetition in a social context has the ability to make one plus one equal something very different from two. Manic repetition has the ability to summon forth invisible phantoms. The ability to call forth the new. The startling. The seemingly impossible. Manic repetition in a social context has the ability to pull stunning new implicit properties, new recruitment strategies, new corollaries, from nonexistence into being. Manic repetition in a social context has the ability to conjure emergent properties. Manic repetition has the power to summon the unseen spirits of Hans Driesch's "form." In other words, manic repetition in a social context has the sort of force that termites tap to build their walls and their towers. Manic repetition in a social context taps the power that pulses at the heart of cosmic creativity.

***

A sword maker in medieval Japan or in medieval Toledo in 900 CE was capable of creative miracles. Old weapons like the eighth- and ninth-century Viking iron sword were heavy as hell—four pounds or more.[29] Lifting them above your head took both your arms. And lifting the sword above your head did something even worse. It opened your belly, chest, and neck to the daggers of your enemies. On top of that, your sword blade was stiff, breakable, and only capable of holding a clunky cutting edge.[30] All it could do was a clumsy sort of cleaving. "Cutting heads to pieces,"[31] as the tales of seventh-century Muslim battles put it. Cutting off arms and legs. But at the cost of making you, the swordsman, lumbering, slow, and vulnerable.

But what would happen in 900 CE if you traded in your iron longsword[32] for an incredibly expensive, next-tech import from Toledo, Damascus, or Japan? What would happen if you entered battle against an army of long-swordsmen carrying a sword that was superlight and superflexible? A twenty-four-ounce sword[33] with a skinny blade, a blade whose tip could be honed to a slickly piercing point and whose edges could be made so razor sharp that you could toss a silk handkerchief into the air and slice it to ribbons before it hit the ground?[34] While your athletic enemy was straining his massive biceps to heave his sword above his head, you could spear him straight through to the heart, stop him dead in his tracks, withdraw your superskinny blade in a snick, and move on to skewer another lumbering longsword-wielding goliath through the gizzard while he tried to hoist his sword in midair to clunk you in half.

But were such miracle blades, were such David and Goliath blades, makeable? And if so, how? By repeating a simple rule over and over again. By using the fact that A does not equal A when you move it to a new location. By using the rules of context and meaning, the rules of repetition of an old pattern in a new medium, a new relational medium. The repetition of an old pattern in a new social medium. By using the rules that make each of the two "A's" in the name "Shakespeare" very different in sound and meaning. In other words, by using the power of one plus one can equal something way off the number line.

It's 700 CE[35] in Japan's Yamato, the territory near the city of Sakurai, and you are the legendary swordsmith Amakuni. When the emperor returns from battles with his troops and passes your shop, he usually nods appreciatively in your direction. The recognition gives you a thrill. But not today. The emperor and his troops pass you by as if you do not exist. Why? You look carefully at the warriors filing past and notice something shameful. Half of them have broken swords. Your eyes fill with tears. So you beg the soldiers for their broken blades. You examine them thoroughly. And you come to these conclusions:

(1) The warriors have been hacking at hard stuff—bones, stones, and armor.

(2) Your swords have not been made to stand up to such abuse. And

(3) "If they are going to use our swords for such slashing, I will make one which will not break."[36]

So you set out to achieve the impossible—a superlight, sharper-than-a-razor ribbon of metal. A ribbon so flexible that it will not break. And so hard that it will keep the world's most impossible edge.

Here's the secret to your miracle blade. You lock yourself in your forge "and pray to the Shinto gods for seven days."[37] You fast and abstain from sex. Which probably accomplishes very little. Then you hunt down iron, the very same material that swordsmiths in Europe are using to fashion Viking longswords. The very stuff that you used to make the swords that shattered. You go to the ocean beaches and riverbeds and collect "black sand"—fine grains of iron ore. And with equal care you collect pine[38] wood. Then you burn the pine, depriving the flame of air, and turn a pollutant produced by your fire into a resource. You powder the blackened and charred pellets of wood that your fire leaves behind. You mix your carefully made charcoal powder with a nearly equal amount of your "black sand," your grains of iron ore. Why? To tweak your iron's carbon content. Then comes the real secret: iteration. Repetition. Repetition in a new social medium. You upscale the magic that allowed two intersecting rings of circles in water to make a plaid. You harness the power of repetition in a new relational context to bring forth new properties.

And, strange as it seems, the new context is one that you make not by changing your raw materials but by changing the relationships *within* the raw materials—the relationships of the raw materials to themselves. Here's how you do it. First you dig into the massive mix of sandy iron ore and charcoal you've made and toss shovelfuls into your blast furnace every half hour, day and night, twenty-four hours a day for three or four days while your son pumps your bellows ferociously. You repeat this process roughly 192 times and shovel a total of twenty-six tons of raw ore and charcoal into your furnace during those days and nights. That's repetition number one. That's your start at creating a new social context, a new set of relationships for iron atoms. Then you break down the walls of your furnace and extract a craggy, uneven block of metal roughly two and a half feet wide by two and a half feet high. You look that block over very carefully and take from it the highest quality scraps and bits, the scraps with the best mix of carbon and iron. You heat those bits and scraps, pound them on a square slab of steel anchored in the floor—a very un-Western anvil—and heat them again, turning flakes and nuggets into solid bricks. But your solo hammering is not enough. Your son wields carefully graduated hammers with springy handles and pitches in. The number of repeated hammer blows is in the tens of thousands. That's repetition to create a new social relationship between iron and carbon atoms number two.

Meanwhile, you keep your forge, your sword-making room, very dark. Why? So you can tell the precise heat of your metals by seeing the glow of white, blue, or red. Like Max Planck and his black bodies. You heat a five- or six-pound brick of your carbon-charged iron until it is white hot—thirteen hundred degrees. Then you hammer it out to twice its length. Now you use the secret of iteration once again. The secret of repeating something old in a new social context. You hammer a cut mark at the halfway point of your elongated brick and you fold the brick over upon itself until you get another stubby brick. You hammer that brick out to twice its length again.[39] Then you fold the brick of iron over on itself once more as if you were folding a piece of cardboard—a very thick piece of cardboard. And you hammer the folded brick out again.[40]

You repeat the pattern of pounding, elongating, and folding for thirty days to three months. You repeat it so many times that one Japanese sword aficionado, Stanford D. Carman, says your "blade . . . could have as many as 32,768 separate layers of high carbon steel for the cutting edge."[41] That's a radically new kind of social context. A social context that this cosmos has never seen.

You end up with two bricks of the most exquisite steel that's come from this process. One of those bricks began as bits of iron that picked up a high carbon content as you forged them in your furnace. The other began as bits that your trained eye told you had picked up a much lower carbon content in the furnace's fires. Finally, you hammer your low-carbon brick down to make it slender and flat and you pound it, red hot, into the molten side of your high-carbon brick as if you were slipping a credit card into its case.[42] Your high-carbon brick on the outside will eventually carry a sharp edge. And your low-carbon core will make your sword flexible. You have fashioned a very elaborate new kind of social context indeed.

All this pounding and folding sounds useless, right? A foolish waste of time. Not to mention a miserable job. Let's look at it with logic: One plus one equals two. No matter how many times you pound an iron and charcoal mix, all you'll get is iron and charcoal. Right? Iron and charcoal in, iron and charcoal out. $A = A$. But in the spring, the emperor leads his troops to war once again. Troops equipped with the radically reinvented swords you've made during the winter. And when the war is over and the soldiers march past your shop, you look carefully at the waist sash of each one, trying to count the number of swords broken this time around. To your surprise, there are precisely . . . none! And when the emperor passes you he pauses to acknowledge you and to give you the ultimate compliment: "You are an expert sword maker."[43] Ahhh, attention, the oxygen of the human soul.

Eventually warriors thousands of miles away hear of your work and regard you as a wizard. Why? By adding one plus one over and over again, by adding A's together in a new social context, by pounding A's into a new webwork of relationships, a webwork of new meanings, you convince the atoms of iron and carbon to yield an impossibility. You coax the atoms of iron and carbon to haul an implicit pattern from the airy realm of possibility space. You coax those atoms into yielding a new reality.

What is that reality? It's a new kind of sociality. A new kind of community. A new kind of architecture. A new kind of form production.

Let's go back to our café table at the beginning of the universe. The year is 380,000 ABB, after the big bang. Remember how protons and electrons slowed down after the era of crash, bash, collide, and ricochet—after the era of the plasma—was over? Remember how naked protons and electrons joined up and discovered a handful of hidden properties, new properties that seemed implicit in their very nature? Remember how they discovered the bizarre emergent properties we call an "atom?" Remember how they discovered the unsettlingly new emergent properties we call hydrogen, helium, and lithium?

But there was something more. A strange mystery. A mystery very much like the ripples spaced neatly apart when Leonardo tossed his stone. The protons and electrons mated and "discovered" the patterns of electron shells. They discovered what seemed to be a pattern of invisible spheres at precisely fixed distances around the proton. They "discovered" shells that danced a ring-around-the-rosy around the proton like ripples that held still. Shells like the sphere within a sphere within a sphere on which Pythagoras and Kepler felt the planets were carried.

Electrons could orbit on one of those shells. But when electrons were motivated to travel to a higher or lower shell, they did not move smoothly from one shell to another. They did not trek through the empty space between shells. They disappeared from one shell and instantly appeared in the other.[44] Like deciding to go from Boston to Washington, disappearing from your room overlooking Copley Plaza, and reappearing in front of the Capitol dome in an instant without ever traveling through the space in between. What's more, like quarks, protons, and electrons, shells came complete with rules. Social rules. Shell one around a proton would only hold two electrons. Shell two would only hold eight. And shell three would only hold eighteen.

Electron shells are elegant. But they are all alike wherever they appear in the cosmos. They all follow the same rules. And they appear whenever you put an electron and a proton together. Electron shells are implicit properties hidden within proton-electron pairing. But where the hell do these implicit properties come from? Not to mention how and why? How can this delicate nesting of spherical shells around a proton exist unseen? Why can it be summoned like a genie? What can explain this Harry Potteresque wizardry of form production?

Electron shells are like corollaries hidden in an axiom. Electron shells are not invented. They are found. Found and coaxed into the open. They are implicit. They are emergent properties. But what explains emergent properties?

The same sort of revelation of implicit pattern happens in the iteration of your repeatedly hammered metal. What is the pattern implicit in iron and carbon when they are repeated over and over upon themselves? When they are repeated tens of thousands of times in just the right way? Repeated in a radically new social context? The new pattern is a crystal structure. A crystal structure of lines that you can see on the blade with your naked eye. Even the molecules of that crystal have a new structure—a shoebox structure. A squared-off Lego®-like new molecular architecture. A new social structure. A new rulebook of manners and courtesy. A new big picture. And guess what? At heart this radically new square dance is really just the stuff you started with—iron and carbon.

But the new structure of relationships changes everything. A new structure of relationships, a new architecture and a new shape, has the power to produce surprise and shock. It has the power to transform. Why? Location, location, location. Like the "context" that Wittgenstein says gives meaning.[45] Like the locations generated by a new sentence of Shakespeare. A new Shakespearian sentence that uses the same old twenty-six letters of the alphabet tossed around by Will Shakespeare's competitors, Thomas Kidd and Christopher Marlowe. But a Shakespearian sentence that bursts with new meanings.

Iron and carbon atoms joined in a shoebox molecule and a plethora of those shoebox molecules gathered in a crystal pattern aren't just iron and carbon anymore. Thanks to a new pattern of relationships the atomic shoebox and crystal spicules have radically new properties, emergent properties so radical that this rectangular mesh of carbon and iron has a different name entirely. It's called steel.

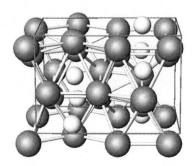

The crystal structure of one form of steel—cementite. *Courtesy of T. Ohba, Ohba's Laboratory martensite webpages, Shimane University, Japan, http://www .geocities.jp/ohba_lab_ob_page/Structure/Cementite .JPG (accessed December 31, 2011).*

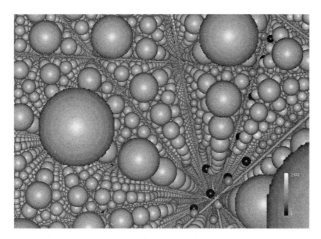

After steel has been pounded and folded thousands of times, its atomic structure becomes astonishingly intricate. *Courtesy of Culham Centre for Fusion Energy.*

Which leads to a question. Is a human a tool that iron molecules use to reinvent themselves? Is a human a molecule's way of making new molecules? More to the point, is a human a tool with which the cosmos summons a molecular structure from the realm of the implicate into the hard and fast of reality? Is a human a tool with which the cosmos feels out her potential? Is a human a tool that the cosmos uses to create?

GAMING YOUR WAY TO FAME:
JOHN CONWAY ENTERS THE SCENE

Where the hell does the shoebox molecule that makes steel come from? How does mere repetition summon it from the nothingness? Where do electron shells come from? Are these things all corollaries of the axioms of the cosmos? Are they all implicit properties? Or are the ideas of corollaries and implicit properties copouts? Are they missing the essence of the mystery that Driesch called "form production"?

Are we missing a metaphor, a key concept, the way that the Babylonians and the Egyptians were missing the circle and the sphere? Remember, the

Babylonians *did* have the circle. They used a compass and drew it. They decorated squares of clay with it. They had it in their art, but not in their tool kit of ideas. They had it right under their noses. But they didn't have it in their minds. Is the key idea that would help us comprehend the mystery of the shoebox steel molecule right under our noses, too?

When Benoît Mandelbrot moved to IBM in 1958 and broke open the piñata of the computer, he gave us at least one crucial new metaphor for form production: fractals. And when he introduced the concept of fractals in 1975,[46] he answered a question. Can intricate forms come from axioms? Can ornate amazements come from simple rules? Mandelbrot's fractals delivered the answer: an emphatic yes. His fractals showed how a glorious garden of forms can come from a rule so simple that it can be summarized in six scratch marks on paper or on a computer screen: $Z = Z^2 + C$. Mandelbrot produced a system that gushed a cornucopia of emergent properties, emergent properties of the sort that John Stewart Mill and George Henry Lewes had goggled over. More important, Mandelbrot produced the germ of a system that might someday be able to test the generalizations of a George Herbert Spencer. He produced a replicable metaphor. A computable metaphor. A metaphor based on an implication-extraction process so solid that it might even someday be able to produce the kinds of predictions that made Einstein great.

And what was at the heart of Mandelbrot's metaphor? Herbert Spencer's differentiation and integration. Attraction and repulsion.

But that was just the beginning of showing the form production that's implicit in simple rules. The next step would come from an unkempt English mathematician and backgammon fanatic named John Conway.

***

In 1970, Fred Hoyle was puzzling out what sort of building to construct for a new institute he was founding, Cambridge's Institute of Theoretical Astronomy.[47] Benoît Mandelbrot was finding fractal patterns in Brownian motion, in the changes in the rise and fall of the Nile, and in the ups and downs in the price of cotton.[48] George Gamow, alas, had been dead for two years. And you were on a strange voyage of the *Beagle* into mass behavior and the creative process, a voyage that would lead you to work with Michael Jackson, Bob Marley, and Prince.

And 1970 was the year when John Conway unveiled a game that deliberately apes your emotions and mine—The Game of Life. A game that, like Benoît Mandelbrot's fractals, would show promise of yet more answers to the puzzles of form production. Who was John Conway? Conway was a bearded and disreputably rumpled-looking[49] mathematician from Cambridge University who would become a fellow of the Royal Society in 1981 and who five years later would migrate to a high-prestige professorship at Princeton. Mathematical author Michael John Bradley says that Conway "introduced new ideas into the mathematical analysis of games, the theory of numbers, and the classification of finite groups."[50] But none of these were Conway's greatest and most famous achievements. His greatest achievement was his demonstration of amazements that could emerge from simple rules.

John Conway was born in 1937 in Liverpool. His father was a chemistry teacher who taught a few local wannabe musicians. Those musical hopefuls would later form a band called the Beatles.[51] Says fellow mathematician Marcus Du Sautoy, who has known Conway since 1985, "It's as though John Conway's brain is hard-wired for mathematics.... His mother discovered him at the age of four reciting increasingly higher powers of 2 to himself."[52] When Conway was only two, World War II broke out. And when he was six, the war ended. But Britain was in dire straits. It had been impoverished by the war. And, worse, its cities had been bombed. The basics of life, things like food and gasoline, were rationed. There were no luxuries. The only special treats were those of the mind. And Conway took full advantage of these. He was a star pupil from the time he first entered school. And, says his biography from St. Andrews University's History of Mathematics, "when he went to be interviewed at age eleven before entering secondary school he was asked what he wanted to be when he grew up and he replied that he wanted to be a mathematician at Cambridge."[53] John Conway got his wish. He earned his doctorate at Cambridge in 1964, just as his dad's students, the Fab Four, John, Paul, George, and Ringo, were breaking big time on the record charts. Then he became a Cambridge lecturer.

But music was not what pumped John Conway's passions. At Cambridge,

Conway became a puppet of another kind of recruitment strategy. A recruitment strategy that demands endless iteration. Endless iteration within a framework of simple rules. Conway became an obsessive backgammon player. Yes, John Conway was caught up in a recruitment pattern called the game.

What's a game? A repetition of simple rules to achieve one of two well-defined outcomes. To beat your opponent and to win by outsmarting, outfoxing, and outlucking her. Or to lose. But the rewards and punishments of games are not just human artificialities. They are built into our biology. Win a game and you get more than just two minutes of praise, envy, and attention. If you win, your biology rewards you. It perks you up and tunes your immune system to high.[54] It gives you a dopamine rush,[55] a testosterone boost,[56] and an endorphin[57] lift. Lose too often and your biology goes into a slump. Your mind gets dazed and foggy and your immune system dials down a notch or two. You are slowed by stress hormones, glucocorticoids. And that's not all. Win and you become more attractive to others. Lose and you lose your popularity. So winning or losing is a bigger deal than most game critics think.

Why did evolution build our zest for games into our biology? Could it be because games are isomorphic symbol sets? Could it be because games map our daily reality? But in a nice, confined, easy-to-understand way? A way that gives us an easy path to a quick reward? A path that makes us think and sometimes even makes us innovate? Could it be because games are calisthenics for our pattern-recognition abilities? Could it be because games motivate us to feel out the patterns that we think will emerge one move or seven moves down the line? Implicit patterns? Could it be because games test our guesses in a simulated real world? Could it be because games test the symbol sets of the mind in a competition outside the fortress of the cranium? And could it be because games are something crucial to human survival: prediction practice?

John Conway's obsession with games was so great that even he was disturbed by it. Said Conway, "I used to feel guilty in Cambridge that I spent all day playing games, while I was supposed to be doing mathematics."[58] And that presented a career problem. Who would want to promote an academic who spent his workday playing backgammon? So how in the world would a game make John Conway famous? And how in the world would a game provide a clue to the mystery left by Hans Driesch, the mystery of form production?

AXIOMS IN SILICON: CONWAY'S GAME OF LIFE

In 1970 John Conway unveiled a game so perception altering that legendary mathematician Martin Gardner, the creator of the *Scientific American*'s Mathematical Games section, a section you grew up reading obsessively, would say, "The game made Conway instantly famous."[59]

How does John Conway's Game of Life work? Imagine a chessboard in which every panel, every square, is translucent. Every square is electrified and has a built-in LED. So each square can be either on or off. Each square can be dark or light. Each square can either live or die. You are a square on this chessboard. How do you determine whether you are on or off, whether you are dark or light? How do the laws of nature in this miniverse determine whether you are dead or alive? It all comes down to simple rules. Simple rules of relationship. Simple rules of sociality.

If you are all alone, you die. The light in your core is turned off. If you have company, you light up. You are alive. If you are overcrowded, it's death again. Your light goes out. You are dark as dark can be.

To be more specific, companionship warms your heart and sparks your LED. If you have three neighbors who are lit, you spring to life. You, too, light up. If you have at least two neighbors who are lit, you still cling to life. You stay lit. You survive. But if you have only one neighbor, or, even worse, none, it's curtains for you. Loneliness does you in. You die. You go dark. And the opposite is true. You can be killed by kindness. Killed by too much company. If you have four lit neighbors or more, if you are surrounded by four, five, or eight lit squares, all the oxygen is sucked out of the room. You die of overcrowding. The competition kills you. You switch off and go dark. Very realistic, isn't it?

Those are the rules, the commandments, the algorithms, the axioms. Three simple rules plus iteration. A lot of iteration. That is the essence of the Game of Life.

But the real secret to the game of life is Claude Shannon's gift, the computer. The Game of Life is played in a computer's bowels. And thanks to the computer, in the Game of Life, the chessboard is not just eight by eight panels in size. It's hundreds or thousands of panels in size. It's as many panels as your computer screen can show you. And more. In theory, the Game of Life's chessboard is infinite. And so is the number of iterations that the computer can crank out. In one minute, the Game of Life can go through a trillion[60] iterations thanks to the scribe that works at superspeed, the scribe that never gets tired, the scribe that never takes Egyptian beer breaks, the scribe that never needs new man loads of clay or barleycorns, the scribe that writes in electrical switches.

But can simple rules and chessboard squares produce anything more than a random scatter of on or off squares? Can simple rules in a game based on crude sociality give a clue to the reason a shoebox molecule arises from the manic iteration of hammering on the swordmaker's forge? Can the Game of Life give any clues to the puzzle of the big picture and the riddle of the supersized surprise? You be the judge. You are a square on the Game of Life's chessboard. The rules you follow are what researchers in the area of cellular automata call "local." The only thing you know is what the neighbors on your four sides and on your four corners are doing. The only thing you can tell is whether the eight neighbors scrunched up against you are lit or dark, dead or alive. You have no idea of what is going on in the great beyond. You don't know what is happening three, four, twenty, or two hundred squares away.

Yet large-scale patterns crop up on the game board. Big pictures. Literally. Things that look like stealth bombers, V's of dark squares. They're called "gliders." Why? Because they fly across the board from one end to another.

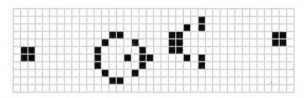

Gliders in the Game of Life. Shapes that arise from nearly nothing. *Courtesy of Bryan Burgers, Wikimedia Commons.*

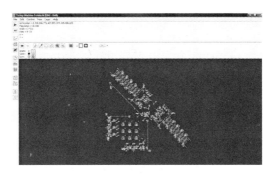

Game of life. "The 6,366,548,773,467,669,985,195,496,000th
(6 octillionth) generation of a very complicated Game of
Life pattern computed in less than 30 seconds on an Intel
Duo 2GHz CPU using Golly in Hashlife mode" ("Game of
Life," *Wikipedia*, http://en.wikipedia.org/wiki/Conway's_
Game_of_Life#Origins (accessed November 17, 2011)).
Courtesy of Simpsons contributor, Wikimedia Commons.

Then there are oscillators, spaceships, pulsars, blinkers, toads, methuselahs, diehards, acorns, guns, and puffer trains. What are these strange forms, these flying wedges, these skimmers, speeders, sliders, and fliers? No thing. Nothing. Nothing and something all at once.

Imagine you are a square in the middle of the chessboard. Three of your neighbors light up. Ahhh, it's showtime. You've been dark, but now you have company. You light up. Isn't life grand? But the grandness doesn't last long. The neighbor on your right dies. She goes out. Damn, things are getting lonely. But with two neighbors—the one above you and the one on your left—you can still hang in there, you can cling to life. On the next turn in the game, the next iteration of the rules, even those two neighbors disappear. They go dark. You are on your own and can no longer survive. You go dark, too. You die. But guess what? While you were lit up and alive, you were a part of a larger pattern, a pattern too big for you to see. A roughly triangular pattern six squares in size, a glider. And you have winked out, but the pattern you were a part of has not died. It is still inching across the screen turn by turn by turn. And it is a nothing. Why? Because in the beginning it was made up of you and of five of your neighbors. But now that it's moved on, it's made up of six entirely different squares. It's not made up of a permanent team of things. It takes advantage of new things, new squares, to sustain itself with every move.

None of its participants "know" what they are creating. Yet the creation retains its identity. Even though in theory it does not exist. With every four turns, it discards the squares it was made of. It leaves them behind. The glider is not a specific set of squares. It's not the sum of the things that make it up. It's not the sum of its parts. It is a pattern. A pattern with a "life" all its own. A pattern with an apparent hunger for survival. A pattern able to pull together new participants over and over again. A pattern able to sustain itself. A pattern very much like a wave in the Atlantic or in Leonardo's pond. It is a recruitment strategy.

Your life as a square in the Game of Life is fleeting. It's an on-again, off-again proposition. But, like a termite putting fecal bricks on a pile, you have briefly been a part of something bigger than you are, something too big for you to see. In this case, a flying wedge. And now that you are off, you are a part of the empty space that helps highlight the wedge's identity. What's more, even in death you are a part of the empty space through which other wedges might fly. Does this sound to you vaguely like meaning?

But what the heck is that flying wedge if it is something new with every turn? What the heck is it, if it is not a sum of a permanent team of things? What is it if it's not simply one plus one equals two and six squares equals six squares and nothing more? A flying wedge, a glider, in the Game of Life, has the same problem that Theseus's ship had. Remember how every few days one of the boards in Theseus's ship wore out and had to be replaced by another? By the time Theseus's ship had been traveling for a few months, there were no original boards left in the ship. What's more, Theseus's crew had used the discarded boards to build another ship. A ship that looked exactly like Theseus's ship. So when the pair of vessels pulled into a harbor, which was Theseus's ship? Was it the old ship with not a single old board left? Or was it the new ship made from the discarded pieces of Theseus's ship?

What is this ghostly flit called a flying wedge? It's a way of organizing things. A social structure. An onion skin of meaning. It's a form, an emergent property, that employs an ever-changing membership of squares to retain its oneness and its shape. To retain its identity. It recruits the way that genomes recruit the hundred million cells of your body, the same way that plants recruit pollinators—bees—and the same way that an apple recruits the transport mechanism of an animal's gut to spread around its seeds. Again, the flying wedge is a recruitment strategy.

The really hard part to understand is how and why a glider arises on the game board and retains its identity. The answer is that the glider is an implicit property. It's the real deal of what Bohm called an "implicate property." It's implicit in the rules of the Game of Life. Those three extremely simple rules of sociality, cozy companionship, overcrowding, and survival. Rules of relationship. The glider is also implicit in something else—the medium in which it exists, the chessboard. The computerized chessboard. It's implicit in the way the rules interact with a pattern of lit squares that you lay out on the game board before you hit the start button. And it's implicit in the starting pattern you lay out before you let your computer churn out its iterations. The glider is implicit in a tiny number of axioms. In a tiny number of magic beans.

Does the Game of Life apply to anything real? Or is it just a computer hobbyist's whimsy? Says *Wikipedia*—today's summary of our collective knowledge—the Game of Life has been used by "computer scientists, physicists, biologists, economists, mathematicians, philosophers, generative scientists . . . to convey the somewhat counter-intuitive notion that 'design' and 'organization' can spontaneously emerge in the absence of a designer." And, to return to the words of legendary mathematician Martin Gardner, "The game [of Life] . . . opened up a whole new field of mathematical research, the field of cellular automata. . . . Because of Life's analogies with the rise, fall, and alterations of a society of living organisms, it belongs to a growing class of what are called 'simulation games' (games that resemble real life processes)."[61]

The Game of Life is yet another form of translation into a new medium. It is yet another form of isomorphic symbol set. It is yet another form of metaphor. But unlike metaphor in George Herbert Spencer's day, this is metaphor with the potential to predict like Einstein's crucial tool, the equation.

***

Just how far can you go in understanding emergent properties, the evolution of big pictures, and the wham of supersized surprises with the iteration of simple rules? Can you go beyond mere sliders and gliders. Can you build an entire cosmos from simple rules? A man named Stephen Wolfram is convinced that you can. In fact, he's certain that a variation on John Conway's computer game can even solve such basic scientific mysteries as the unification of quantum physics and relativity, one of the key puzzles—and recruitment strategies—of twentieth- and early-twenty-first century physics.

GOOD-BYE TO EQUATIONS: STEPHEN WOLFRAM'S NEW KIND OF SCIENCE

It takes a lot of stabbing around to find implicate properties. It took twenty-two hundred years of groping to figure out that a simple flip of Euclid's parallel axiom could produce a picture of an entirely different universe. It took a doctor in Germany in 1909, the Nobel Prize winner Paul Ehrlich, 606 tries to invent—or to find—the molecule for the first antibiotic—Salvarsan—the drug that nearly eliminated syphilis.[62] It took Thomas Alva Edison what he called "3,000 different theories"[63] and the experiments those theories engendered to find a material that would last long enough under high heat to be a filament for a lightbulb. And it took 358 years and over thirteen million people-hours of work to come up with a solution for Fermat's last theorem. But from the 1960s onward, the computer would make this sort of stabbing and probing considerably easier. Almost infinitely easier. Why? Because of the computer's power to repeat, repeat, repeat. Because of the computer's ability to iterate. But the computer would also make stabbing and probing easier because of its ability to unfold implicate properties. Because of its ability to pull implications from axioms. And because of the computer's ability to take a handful of axioms and use them as a foundation on which to build what physicists like Freeman Dyson call a toy universe.[64]

One man would take on the challenge of modeling toy universes with the greatest persistence. One man would work the hardest to establish a variation on Conway's cellular automata as a new metaphor with which to probe the creativity of a godless cosmos. And that man's name is Stephen Wolfram.

Stephen Wolfram started with advantages and built on them magnificently. He had brainy parents. His father was an author—the writer who would give us the 1967 novel *Into A Neutral Country* and the 1969 *Root and Branch*. His mother was a professor of philosophy at Oxford.[65] His parents shared something in common with Benoît Mandelbrot's father and mother. Wolfram's parents were Jews who in 1933 had fled Germany to escape Adolph Hitler's program to exterminate Jews.

Like John Conway, Hugo and Sybil Wolfram's son Stephen was a born mathematician and scientist. But he was a scientist with an advantage that even John Conway didn't have when he was a child: the computer. Wolfram was born in London. Then, when he was twelve, he won a scholarship to England's snootiest boarding school, Eton.[66] As a kid, Wolfram was called the "Young Einstein."[67] When he was eleven, he was transfixed by HAL, the smooth-talking, ultrabrainy, emotion-riddled computer in the Stanley Kubrick movie *2001: A Space Odyssey*. Eleven-year-old Stephen went to see the film over and over again. "It was all so majestic and so alive,"[68] he recalls. But that was just the beginning. Wolfram explains that "I became a card-carrying physicist when I was a teenager."[69] And he's not exaggerating. Says one of Wolfram's bios, "At 14, he wrote his first book on particle physics. At 17, the scientific journal *Nuclear Physics* published a paper he'd written. At 18, he wrote a widely acclaimed paper on heavy quark production."[70] Wolfram also became the youngest person[71] to win a MacArthur Genius Award.

More than just Hal, the computer in *2001*, smashed its way onto the scene when Wolfram was eleven. Conway's Game of Life went public in the pages of the *Scientific American*. That was it. Says another of Wolfram's bios, cellular automata became Wolfram's obsession.[72]

Wolfram finally managed to get his hands on a real-life computer when he was fourteen. That's a near miracle. Computers were hideously expensive, hideously huge, and hideously scarce in 1973, when Wolfram began working with them. The IBM personal computer that would put computers in nearly every home would not be introduced for another ten years. And it would not go mainstream for another twenty.

When Wolfram was twenty-one, he became one of the youngest faculty members at the California Institute of Technology. By that time, Wolfram had lived with computers for 39 percent of his life. Professors on a prestige faculty have to publish or perish. What did Wolfram choose to write about? Computers. Or, more specifically, cellular automata. The kind of computer games that John Conway had introduced with the Game of Life. And Wolfram wrote about cellular automata in article after article.[73] Says one of his bios, he "singlehandedly" revived interest in these squares that flash on or off by following simple rules. Squares that form larger patterns, patterns with a seeming life of their own.

To study cellular automata further, Wolfram created a program "that could juggle high-level algebra, advanced formulas, and graphics."[74] And he founded a journal in which to publish work on "systems with simple components but complex overall behavior,"[75] *Complex Systems.* Then, in 1988, Wolfram ditched teaching, started his own company, Wolfram Research, and put the program for high-level algebra, advanced formulas, and graphics that he'd developed on the market. It became one of the most widely used mathematical programs in science. And it "made Wolfram a millionaire."[76] Its name? *Mathematica.* Which is ironic. Because Stephen Wolfram was about to rebel against math itself.

Why was Stephen Wolfram so fixated on cellular automata? Why bother with self-playing games on a giant checkerboard? Why not use equations? After all, Wolfram was masterful at handling the complex mathematics of his era. In fact, when he was twenty, Wolfram had created what his website calls "the first modern computer algebra system, called SMP." But, says Wolfram, "there is some kind of secret ingredient that nature is adding to make stuff complex," some kind of secret ingredient "that we don't know from a scientific point of view."[77] An ingredient like Einstein's "deeply hidden" "something." In fact, in Wolfram's opinion, science was blind to many of the most important mysteries of the real world. For example, science seemed good at handling physics, but Wolfram pointed out that it wasn't able to achieve a major goal it had been lusting after for nearly three hundred years, "an ultimate theory of the universe."[78] Worse, Wolfram pointed out that science was a flop in turning "the biological and social sciences" into principles "we can calculate."[79] Why?

There was a culprit. A villain. A stumbling block. That obstacle was a tool of enormous power. And a tool with equally enormous limitations. The name of that tool of both light and blindness? The equation.

There's an old saying attributed to psychologist Abraham Maslow: "When all you have is a hammer, everything looks like a nail."[80] The nails of science for three hundred years had been equations.[81] And, said Wolfram, in a statement that most scientists would have found outrageous, a statement that threatened to overturn the scientific applecart entirely, "It's our reliance on mathematical equations and traditional mathematics that have made us miss what's going on."[82] Equations were not the solution, said Wolfram. They were the problem. Explained Wolfram, "It's often imagined that mathematics somehow covers all arbitrary abstract systems. But that's simply not true."[83] What did Wolfram mean by abstract systems? Though he would not have phrased it in these terms, he meant isomorphic symbol sets. He meant metaphors. He meant the very symbol sets we use to understand stars, strings, and statisticians. He meant the symbol sets that grasp the quark but fail to understand the embryo.

In the end, it all comes down to axioms. Says Wolfram, "When one starts investigating the whole computational universe" it turns out there are tons of "possible axiom systems that might be used to define mathematics."[84] And, like the shift of just one axiom in non-Euclidean math, each "axiom system" produces what Wolfram calls another "possible mathematics," another "alternative mathematics,"[85] a whole new mathematical universe. Says Wolfram, if you explore all the possible axioms, you'll find "lots and lots of axiom systems that seem just as rich as anything in our standard mathematics. But they're different."[86]

And that cornucopia of axiom systems reveals something that is holding modern science back—the limited scope of traditional math. Modern science's math, says Wolfram, is just one among hundreds of thousands of possible symbol sets. Or more. Explains Wolfram, "It's just a particular formal system that arose historically from the arithmetic and geometry of ancient Babylon. And that happens to have grown into one of the great cultural artifacts of our civilization."[87] What's the result of worshiping just one form of math among hundreds of thousands? What's the result of treating that form of math as the only tool with which to comprehend the universe? Implies Wolfram, our math acts like blinders on a horse—panels fitted to a horse's head that block out what's on the left and right and allow the horse to see just one thing—the course straight ahead. And if that course leads to a cliff, the horse is in trouble. Like blinders, the math of equations limits our vision.

We tend only to ask questions that we know we can answer with the mathematical tools we have at hand. And that cripples us. Says Wolfram, "The questions that get asked in a sense always tend to keep to the region of computational reducibility."[88] We only ask the questions we can answer with equations. "Natural science," Wolfram adds, "has been limited too—in effect to just those kinds of phenomena that can successfully be captured by traditional mathematics!"[89] What's worse, there are vast flocks of "questions" that simply "would not fit into the existing cultural framework of mathematics."[90] The hammer of our math limits our questions to riddles we can answer with nails.

The math of equations has become the kind of unquestioned axiom that Einstein warned can blind us. It's the kind of unspoken assumption that Einstein warned us to hold up to the light so we can see it clearly. And so we can question it.

What's more, in Stephen Wolfram's opinion, we have hit the wall. Says Wolfram, "I actually suspect that we're fairly close to the edge of what's possible in mathematics. . . . My intuition is that the limits to mathematical knowledge are close at hand."[91] Adds Wolfram, "Indeed this is precisely why—to use the title of my book—one needs a new kind of science."[92]

Does Wolfram really have another science in mind? One based on a tool that he thinks can do more than equations to explain everything from nebulae to nose rings? Not to mention the ultimate challenge, embryos? Of course he does. The tool he grew up with. The tool that gave us John Conway's Game of Life. Cellular automata. Said Wolfram in 1998, "If, instead of using mathematical questions, one thinks about things in terms of simple computer programs, then one can quite quickly see what's going on."[93] By what's going on, Wolfram means the "secret ingredient" of complexity. And Wolfram has a very specific plan in mind for exploring these "simple computer programs" that uncover the world's secret ingredients. What is it? Model as many simple programs in the computer as your time, your patience, and your access to computers will allow. Model every simple system conceivable. Or, as Wolfram puts it, "Look at all possible simple computational systems, say all possible small programs of a certain form."[94] Check out the whole "computational universe and see what's there."[95]

An ambitious program. Something Euclid, Gauss, and Einstein did not have the tools to achieve. Run a zillion simple programs in the computer and see what they cough out. See what implications are hidden in their handful of givens, their handful of simple rules, their handful of axioms. It took the scientific community twenty-two hundred years to flip just one axiom—the parallel postulate. Now Wolfram wanted to try out new axioms by the billions.[96] Sounds impossible, right? But, said Wolfram, "This is something I have spent a great deal of time doing."[97] By a great deal of time, Wolfram meant twenty-four years. And that was way back in 2007. The effort appeared to pay off. Continues this greatest of all axiom testers, "The big discovery I made in the early 1980s is that there are some very simple computer programs that can do very complex things—things that are just like the things we see in nature."[98]

Which brings us back to the secret ingredient of the natural world. The secret ingredient of complexity that Wolfram thought was beyond the grasp of equations. In 1998 Wolfram explained that "for the past fifteen years I've been working to try to find that ingredient."[99]

Here's how Wolfram methodically pawed through "the computational universe" to "see what's there."[100] He simplified John Conway's checkerboard. He reduced the checkerboard squares to segments of a two-dimensional line. Segments that took up far less space on a computer monitor. Segments that could be dark or light, on or off, dead or alive. So if you were one segment on the line, you'd look like a piece of thread a half inch long. Other segments of string exactly like you would be your neighbors on your row, neighbors on your left and right. And you would be programmed so you could be off or on, dark or light, black or white. But the next iteration would take place in a string below yours like another thread in a weave of cloth. The next iteration would take place on your chest. On the next row down the line.

Like Conway, Wolfram gave you local rules, very simple rules. And Wolfram unfolded the implications of those rules with the first row in his compacted checkerboard. Each segment of thread in that first row had to determine whether it should live or die depending on the rules Wolfram fed it. That included you, if you were in the starting row.

Then row number two came to life. And each line segment in row two "looked"[101] back at the ancestors directly behind it in row one, followed the simple rules, and figured out whether it should be on or off, dead or alive. In other words, row number two ran the rules of the system on the stimulus it "received" from row number one. It used the rules to interpret, translate, and spell out the implications—the "meanings"—of row number one. Next, the cells in row number three came to life, looked back over their shoulders at their ancestors, the ancestors they touched directly, and determined whether they should be on or off, dead or alive. In other words, in Wolfram's cellular automata, rules were repeated upon themselves. They were repeated on the environment they themselves had made.

As row after row unfolded, the simple rule changed the nature of the context in which it was repeated. In the process, it generated massive new patterns. New patterns like John Conway's sliders and gliders. New big pictures. Astonishing recruitment patterns. Patterns that appear to come from nowhere. Patterns with a stubborn persistence. Patterns with a ferocious ability to retain their identity. Patterns far larger than any of their cellular participants could see. Patterns that repeated. And patterns that sometimes evolved.[102]

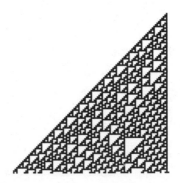

Stephen Wolfram's rule 110 at 100 steps. © 2011 Stephen Wolfram, LLC, http://www.wolframscience.com.

Wolfram's rule 150 at 1,000 steps into the process of form generation. © 2011 Stephen Wolfram, LLC, http://www. wolframscience.com.

Those patterns were implicit in the starting axioms, in the simple rules. And those patterns were implicit in a key tool—the computer.

***

John Conway had focused primarily on just one set of founding axioms, one handful of simple rules. But Stephen Wolfram worked with hundreds of millions of them. Wolfram allowed his cellular automata to run for a cumulative total of roughly a billion billion generations. And, again, he tried out what Cambridge integrative biologist Dennis Bray estimates to be a billion different rules.[103] In the beginning, Wolfram did this for only eighteen years straight, from 1983 to 2001.[104] Then he took time off to write a book about what he'd discovered. How did Stephen Wolfram's grand plan work out?

What did Wolfram find? Tons of simple rules that produced nothing of interest.[105] And some simple rules that produced amazements. Some rules that produced order. Order peppered with astonishing complexity.[106] Peppered with ornate forms. And peppered with something even more important than ornate complexity. Peppered with patterns that sometimes switched from brilliant structure to astonishing chaos.[107] Not the chaos studied in "chaos theory." The chaos of chaos theorists has deep structures you can easily see in a computer graphic. But Wolfram's chaos was an utter churn of confusion. A distressing blast of noise and randomness. A blast in which nothing made sense.

Why is chaos astonishing? Remember, each miniverse, each toy universe that Wolfram generated, was based on simple rules. Staggeringly simple rules. Rules that generated what Wolfram called "the simplest possible underlying models."[108] But imagine once again that you are a cell in one of these miniverses. You are a cell one hundred thousand iterations, one hundred thousand generations, one hundred thousand lines into this toy universe's existence. And imagine that you are a bit more than just the ordinary cell. You are a scientist. You look around you. What do you see? Utter chaos. Incomprehensible jumble. What conclusion do you come to? That your universe is unexplainable. You come to the conclusion that there is no way that your universe can be based on simple rules. There is no way it can be based on deep structures. There is no way it can be built upon mere axioms. And you conclude that there is very little hope for understanding it. You'd say that you live in a cosmos of "irreducible complexity,"[109] to use the arch intelligent design advocate Michael Behe's phrase. A cosmos of "complete disorder" and "apparent randomness," to quote Wolfram Research's Hector Zenil.[110] But you'd be wrong. You *do* live in a cosmos built upon simple rules. But the creative power of that cosmos has produced an apparent randomness that's pulling the wool over your eyes. Simple rules can produce wonders of order. And they are so good at producing complexity that they can even generate what looks like the ultimate form of disorder, a storm of nonsense—chaos.

Which means that behind every nonsense, there may be a sense that's astonishingly simple. Behind every chaos, there may be simple rules.

***

After running hundreds of millions of these miniverses for roughly a billion billion generations, what other conclusions did Stephen Wolfram come to? Once again, that equations were too narrow a tool. That equation-based math was what Wolfram called "one of the biggest shortcomings of present-day science and technology."[111] But Wolfram went beyond that Mandelbrot-like rebellion against traditional math. He also concluded that cellular automata based on simple rules, cellular automata unfolded from simple axioms, could ape the behavior of everything from the actions of elementary particles and the flow of liquids in Heraclitus's eddies and whirlpools to the behavior of human beings. He concluded that cellular automata could take you beyond equations and could allow you to use your computer "to find by simulation what a system will do."[112] Just about any system.

In fact, Wolfram felt that his rules didn't need computers to run. They ran in the natural world. He explained, "Lots of systems we find all over the place in nature can act as universal computers."[113] What did Wolfram mean? He gave the example of the whorl of water in a stream. That whorl, he said, was a computation in action. Explained Wolfram, "The system starts off in some state—that's the input—then does its thing for a while, then ends up in some final state, which corresponds to the output." Input followed by output, said Wolfram, was "a computation." Or, as Wolfram explained it, "When a fluid flows around an obstacle, let's say, it's effectively doing a computation about what its flow pattern should be." And Wolfram exalted the whorl's computation to a very high level. He declared that "all our big fancy computers—and our brains for that matter—really aren't capable of computations that are any more sophisticated than a piece of fluid."[114] The bottom line? Cellular automata running simple rules can do things that are far beyond Aristotle. They can crack the mysteries of Heraclitus's river, the one you can never put your foot into twice.

To repeat, in Wolfram's view, things in the real world, in the natural world, are based on simple rules. And they work by running those rules the way that cellular automata do.

But fluids were just the start. Wolfram was up to something far, far bigger: grappling with a scientific challenge on a par with the embryo—explaining consciousness and human thought. Using his game-board-like iteration of simple rules. In fact, he said, simple rules are the key to "the high-level aspects of thinking identified by cognitive scientists or psychologists." Other approaches to the mysteries of thought, said Wolfram, are "not going to go anywhere." Why? "Thinking is, I'm pretty sure, a much lower-level process. All those cognitive things are just icing on the cake—not fundamental at all."

So what is "fundamental"? It all goes back to the metaphor of the whirlpool, and to simple rules. Explains Wolfram, "It's like in a fluid: there are vortices that one sees. But these vortices are not fundamental. They are a complicated consequence of the microscopic motions of zillions of little molecules. And the point is that the rules for how the vortices work are fairly complicated—and hard to find for sure. But the rules for the molecules are fairly simple. And I'm guessing that it's the same way with the underlying processes of thinking."[115]

Under the complexities of consciousness are simple rules. Axioms.

Wolfram was sure that in addition to understanding consciousness and the mind, you could use his computer cellular automata to tackle what he called "hard problems"[116] in artificial intelligence, problems "like scene recognition,"[117] problems like pattern recognition, problems like how the mind solves problems with deep structures and metaphors. And to repeat the really big challenge, the one baffling the science of his time, Wolfram concluded that you could even use cellular automata to solve seemingly impossible problems like how to reconcile quantum physics with relativity.

In 2002, Stephen Wolfram issued a call for an entirely new kind of science based on the use of the computer to spell out the implications of simple rules, the implications of axioms. And in 2002, he used the millions he'd made from writing his scientific calculating program, Mathematica, to self-publish a book. A book even longer than Ayn Rand's 1,168-page *Atlas Shrugged*. A book that came in at a walloping 1,197 pages. That book was called, as you'd expect, *A New Kind of Science*. A new kind of science that tossed the tools of the old science away.

Wolfram was not timid. But he knew that to change the scientific method, to change perceptions, you have to change not just the perceptions of individuals. You have to change the collective perception of the scientific community. Which means that you have to do more than publish. You have to seduce, kidnap, and recruit. You have to promote. So Wolfram created a public relations staff within his deep-pockets Mathematica-selling company, Wolfram Research. That PR team made *A New Kind of Science* one of the most talked about books in the scientific community for roughly two years.

And Wolfram went further. He did things that most scientists with lesser funding would have found impossible. He toured the country at his own expense doing interviews and holding small parties for people of influence to bring them on board with his new kind of science. He sponsored scientific conferences in which those who wrote papers on his new kind of science could present their results. And he offered a $25,000 prize to anyone who could prove or disprove the idea that a "2-state 3-color"[118] rule-based system was, in fact, a universal Turing machine, a device that could ape the computational processes of any kind of computer, not to mention a device that could ape what Wolfram saw as the "computational process" underlying everything from black holes and whorls in a river to the life of a dandelion and your delight in a puppy.

In the years since his *New Kind of Science* Wolfram has become even more intellectually ambitious. He confessed in 2007 that he has a hobby: "universe hunting."[119] Trying to find the handful of simple rules that crank out our universe. And more. Hunting to find the simple rules that generate the range of all possible universes. With ours as just one among many. This, says Wolfram, is "a very technology-intensive business."[120] It means not only having the computer power it takes to run millions of possible rules billions of times, but inventing programs that can go through the results and pick out the promising candidates.

For example, way back in the distant days of the 1990s, Wolfram was trying to generate something almost as challenging as entire universes. He was trying to produce simple-rule-based cellular automata that would generate not just the mathematical systems that we know and use, but *all* mathematical systems. All the math systems that could ever be. Wolfram explains, "When I searched, for example, for Boolean algebra (logic), I did indeed find a tiny axiom system for it."[121] But finding that axiom system wasn't easy. Remembers Wolfram, "It turned out to be about the 50,000th axiom system in the enumeration I used."[122] Then came a problem: "Proving that it was correct." And "proving that it was correct," Wolfram says, "took all sorts of fancy automated-theorem-proving technology."[123] Technology that used tens of thousands of central processing units, the equivalent of tens of thousands of personal computers.

But by 2007, Wolfram was hunting bigger game. Or, as he puts it, "OK, so if there's a simple rule for the universe, what might it actually be like?"[124] How do you figure that out? Explains Wolfram, "One starts one's candidate universe off. And it grows to millions or billions of nodes."[125] Then what? You have to see if the universe generates anything that looks like time, space, particles, quantum physics, and universe hunters who use computers instead of telescopes and microscopes. Does Wolfram have what he calls "candidate universes" yet? Says he, "The answer is yes."[126] And what, pray tell, may the candidate cosmoses be like? What may their starting rules be?

The leading candidates, says Wolfram, are "small networks."[127] Networks that work according to what Wolfram calls "causal invariant rules."[128] And what are "causal invariant rules"?[129] Explains Wolfram, they are "rules which have the property that whatever order they're applied in, they always give the same causal network."[130] And what makes Wolfram feel that these may be the rules of the really big enchilada, the tossed salad to beat all tossed salads, the universe? For one thing, causal invariant rules seem to cough out time and space. But not just any time and space. They "imply the particular relation of space and time that is special relativity."[131] Yes, "small networks" based on "causal invariant rules" spit out Albert Einstein's special relativity. Einstein's 1905 theory. Holy moly!

And there's more. Let's go back to the fact that one of the biggest puzzles confronting physicists today is the seemingly impossible project of unifying Einstein's relativity with the weird unpredictability of Schrödinger's cat and of Heisenberg's uncertainty principle, uniting relativity with the weird unpredictability of quantum theory. Wolfram seems to have pulled both rabbits—relativity and quantum physics—from the same hat. Which means he's found a way to unify relativity with quantum physics. He's done it with his "small networks" using "causal invariant rules." Says Wolfram with glee, "In a network" of this sort "one doesn't just have something like local 3D space, it looks as if one automatically starts to get a lot of the core phenomena of quantum mechanics."[132] Yes, says Wolfram, you get the probabilistic unpredictability of quantum mechanics "even from what's in effect a deterministic underlying model."[133] You get relativity and quantum mechanics from the same set of simple rules. Not bad. Not bad at all.

What's more, Wolfram is confident that "our whole universe and its complete history could be generated just by starting with some particular small network, then applying definite rules."[134] But one universe is not enough to satisfy Wolfram. He feels he is on the track of simple rules that can spill forth every universe that could ever be. Every conceivable and every inconceivable cosmos. "I certainly think it'll be an interesting—almost metaphysical—moment," says Wolfram, "if we finally have a simple rule which we can tell is our universe. And we'll be able to know that our particular universe is number such-and-such in the enumeration of all possible universes."[135] Declares Wolfram, "It's a sort of Copernican moment,"[136] one of those moments in which we realize that we humans are not the center of all things. And that our universe is just one individual in a cosmic crowd, a crowd of universes.

What is the one thimbleful of simple rules that will crack open the coconut of the cosmos? Says Wolfram, "I don't know yet."[137] But he's on the case. "Universe hunting," he concludes with delight, "is a good hobby."[138]

***

There's a power to Wolfram's work that even he didn't see. Says Wolfram, "Over and over again I've found these systems doing things that I was sure wouldn't be possible—because I couldn't imagine how they'd do them."[139] And that is the mark of a crucial achievement. It is a mark of a system that cuts free from the Bohm Cheat. Wolfram's surprise was an indication of the fact that at last he and John Conway had devised a simulation that starts with axioms, that starts with simple rules, then spills forth things that no human can predict. A simulation that disgorges form production. A simulation that, like Mandelbrot's, spills forth shape shock—emergent properties. And that does all this without the sneaky tricks of Bohm's ink drop or Kant's seed.

The bottom line? With his cellular automata, Wolfram has developed a new metaphor with which to confront the God Problem, the problem of how the cosmos creates.

***

Oh, and one more thing. Conway and Wolfram have devised a simulation that, like Thomas Young's, is repeatable. They have done something the scientific community demands. They have made their work replicable by others. In the process, they have devised a new way of capturing deep structures and their consequences. They have upgraded the precision of metaphor.

10

WHAT ARE THE RULES OF THE UNIVERSE?

THE CASE OF THE OBSESSIVE-COMPULSIVE COSMOS

Termite architecture, the Game of Life, and Stephen Wolfram's cellular automata are all based on simple rules. If this is a cosmos that follows the termite and cellular automata pattern, the universe, too, may have started with a handful of magic beans. A handful of axioms. A handful of simple rules. But what, pray tell, might those simple rules have been? What are the simple rules of cosmic creativity? The clues are in a scientific sin.

Back to metaphors and to Aristotle's claim in his *Posterior Analytics*[1] that metaphors are "unscientific." Granted, you've made a case for metaphor based on Ur patterns, Bloom. A case based on simple patterns upon which the cosmos may, perhaps, be built. A case based on the sort of simple patterns at the foundation of John Conway's Game of Life and Stephen Wolfram's new kind of science. And based on the axioms beneath traditional geometry and non-Euclidean geometry. Not to mention the five axioms of Peano's postulates and the flipped axiom of time in the work of Einstein. But let's get down to brass tacks. There is an Achilles' heel to metaphor. And there is an Achilles' heel to the writing style you are using in this book. It's anthropomorphism.

But is anthropomorphism always a sin? Or are those who despise anthropomorphism guilty of yet another crime—anthropo*centrism*?

Let's pin this book to the board like a butterfly and dissect its ideas.

You've claimed that photons—wavelike particles of light—are recruitment strategies that hang tight. They are insubstantial forms that insist on maintaining their identity. Vast herds of photons, you've said, have shot across the cosmos at 670,616,629 miles per hour, holding on to their pattern, staying true to their oscillating dance step, for over thirteen billion years. Photons, you've claimed, are recruitment strategies that iterate with insane persistence. That's where you toss in something utterly inappropriate. Cute but unscientific. That's where you toss in anthropomorphism. Right?

Persistence? In a photon? Get off it. You're clearly reading human qualities into the inanimate world. But is there justification for it? Yes. We humans have the ability to persist. We may think that it's unique to beings with consciousness. But it is not. We didn't invent persistence. It was here long before us. It was here from the beginning, from the big bang.

There's good reason for calling this a driven, motivated cosmos. A persistent cosmos. This is a cosmos that keeps pushing forward, no matter what. This is a cosmos that's kept up that push for 13.73 billion years. It's a cosmos that's kept up that push for 4.3298928×10^{17} seconds. A number way up there in the hundreds of quadrillions. This is a cosmos that has shown a primitive precursor of will. A primitive precursor of stubbornness. Are photons really persistent? Or is that an idiotic metaphor? And, what's worse, is it an idiotic reading of a human quality into a mere thing? Let's answer that question with two more. How many times does a photon flick back and forth? How many times does a photon repeat its pattern of moving from one end of its arc to another? Remember, a photon of yellow light corkscrews from one extreme of its amplitude to the other 540 trillion times a second.[2] It undergoes more back and forths in one second, just one second, than all the booms and crashes humanity has endured in the 2.5 million years since we first fashioned stones into tools. And one second is just a tiny part of a yellow photon's lifetime. We've detected photons that have been traveling from one end of the universe to the other for over thirteen billion years.[3] And those photons have been doing their crazy wobble all the way. They've repeated that wobble 2.333×10^{30} times. Roughly 233 billion billion billion times. That's iteration. That's persistence beyond belief. No, you are not exaggerating or anthropomorphizing when you say that a photon is persistent.

In fact, there is something presumptuous about the notion that anthropomorphism is always wrong. There is something arrogant about the conviction that all anthropomorphism is a criminal offense against sanity and reason. For example, we humans believe that we invented free will. But renowned Princeton Institute for Advanced Study physicist Freeman Dyson disagrees.[4] So do the Santa Fe Institute's arch complexity theorist Stuart Kauffman[5] and the Game of Life's father, master mathematician John Conway.[6] Dyson says, "There is a certain kind of freedom that atoms have to jump around, and they seem to choose entirely on their own without any input from the outside, so in a certain sense atoms have free will."[7] What? Is he kidding? Or is he just stooping to sloppy wording in order to communicate with the great unwashed? Apparently not. Stuart Kauffman cites with approval a quote that calls "the free decisions of particles and humans . . . free will."[8] And he does it in an essay so complex that only those with an extraordinary range of scientific knowledge and a stratospheric vocabulary are likely to understand it: "Five Problems in the Philosophy of Mind"—an essay that appears on one of the most prominent websites for advanced physicists and mathematicians, arXiv.org. Yes, Kauffman repeats Dyson's heresy. He throws his weight behind the claim that elementary particles have volition. That they have free will.

Where did Kauffman get the quote labeling "the free decisions of particles and humans . . . free will"? From the Game of Life's John Conway and from Conway's fellow Princeton mathematician Simon Kochen. In 2006, Conway and Kochen set out what they boldly called "the free will theorem." In its opening lines they asked an old question: "Do we really have free will, or, as a few determined folk maintain, is it all an illusion?" And they gave an outrageous answer, "We don't know, but will prove in this paper that if indeed there exist any experimenters with a modicum of free will, then elementary particles must have their own share of this valuable commodity."[9] In other words, Kauffman, Dyson, Kochen, and Conway are telling you and me that if we have free will, then electrons, photons, and atoms have free will too. What appalling anthropomorphism. Or is it?

If you rerun Thomas Young's two-slit experiment, a photon shooting from your light source has to "decide" which slit to go through. Should it go through the left slit or the right? Writes Reinhold Blümel, professor of physics at Wesleyan University, "a photon . . . has to 'make up its mind.'"[10] Blümel puts "make up its mind" in quotes because he is using a figure of speech, not a scientific description. He is not implying that photons can think. He is not suggesting that photons have minds. He is using a metaphor. But when metaphors work, it is often because they capture Ur patterns, patterns repeated on many levels of emergence. It is often because they capture deep structures of the cosmos. Structures as deeply embedded as axioms. Why deeply embedded? Because they are often structures that have been here from the beginning. Structures on which everything around us has been built. Structures the cosmos has repeated in new mediums, iterating them the way the swordmaker flattens and folds his iron. Repeating old rules in a way that makes something very old into something very new.

The Ur pattern Blümel refers to here is the photon's "selection" of a choice. "Selection of a choice"? Isn't that unacceptable anthropomorphism? Isn't that a mindless reading of our own peculiar emotional experience into emotionless matter? No, it is *not* mere anthropomorphism. At least according to Dyson, Kauffman, Kochen, and Conway—extraordinarily credible scientists all. They tell you bluntly in their interviews and in their writings that the choice the photon makes is a primitive precursor of what we call "will."

Photons are not the only particles with choices. If a particle is an electron, it can spin in one of two different directions. It can spin up or down. And if a particle is a neutron, it can flip through two choices. It can huddle with a proton and retain its identity or it can give up, stay solo, and decay.[11] The photon, the electron, and the neutron exist in either-or states. Either-or states described by the "waveform" of Schrödinger's equation. According to quantum theory, these particles maintain opposite states simultaneously. But eventually, when they make contact with something that takes their measure, when they make contact with something in their environment,[12] something that "observes" them,[13] something that interprets them as a stimulus and makes a response, something that extracts a "meaning" from them,[14] they are forced to "pick" one option and discard the other.[15] Dropping from several states to just one is called quantum decoherence. And quantum decoherence is the very phenomenon that Dyson, Kauffman,

Kochen, and Conway all zero in on when they tell you that your oldest ancestors and mine, particles and atoms, have free will.

The implication of Kauffman, Dyson, Kochen, and Conway's argument is devastating. Devastating to the notion that anthropomorphism is a scientific sin. If elementary particles have free will, then will, volition, and decision making began in the first tiny nanosliver of a second that gave birth to particles. Free will began in the first flick of the big bang. How? Remember how, in the beginning, in the universe's first 10^{-35} seconds,[16] this cosmos went from a nothing to a hugeness at a speed that defies belief? That starting burst of superspeed is called inflation. Physicists like Ignazio Licata and Ammar Sakaji, editor-in-chief and coeditor of the *Electronic Journal of Theoretical Physics*,[17] not to mention Urawa University's Kohsuke Yagi, the University of Tokyo's Tetsuo Hatsuda, and the University of Tsukuba's Yasuo Miake, coauthors of *Quark-Gluon Plasma*, are among the many theoretical physicists and cosmologists who are certain that this embryonic cosmos was in several states simultaneously. Yagi, Hatsuda, and Miake spell out chains of reasoning based on quantum mechanics and information theory to prove that the entire cosmos had to make a choice. It had to decohere. That primal "decision" gave us "a classical universe"—the universe you and I imagine when we picture the plasma soup and the bump-em car smash of ricocheting protons that followed the inflationary burst. That was the first Big Choice. And a tower of choices rose from there. Rose until decision-making protons, neutrons, and electrons gathered together as you and me.

We humans have made free will far more elaborate. Far more ornate and gussied up than it was in the primitive first seconds of the big bang. We've brought the hundred billion cells of our brains into the picture. And we've hauled in consciousness. Not to mention the complications of culture. And ego. But in the end, when we are torn between opening our umbrella in the rain or taking the chance that the moisture in the air will simply be a mist, when we try to keep ourselves from eating that raisin brownie in the kitchen, when we wonder whether we can get away with touching the hand of the person we are dating for the first time, when we use our will, it all comes down to decisions. To choose to go left instead of right.

In other words, Dyson, Kauffman, Kochen, and Conway's arguments imply that we did not invent free will. It was passed down to us. We inherited it. From what ancestors? From our great, great, great forefathers and foremothers: neutrons, protons, electrons, and photons. From particles like the protons that keep you from poking the index finger of your right hand straight through your left palm. Talking about free will in particles, according to Dyson, Kauffman, Kochen, and Conway, is not anthropomorphism. It is scientific accuracy. And it is scientific humility. It gives proper credit to the particles whose summed decisions made us what we are today.

***

But will is not the only primitive pattern that we inherited from the particles and atoms that came before us and from the particles and atoms that we are made of. We also think we invented competition. We did not. Competition is not a product of patriarchal societies bent on evil. And it is not a product of agriculture, industrialism, or capitalism. It is in the deep structure of the cosmos. Like free will, competition appears to be a primal recruitment strategy, a primal building strategy, and a primal way of knitting together new networks of relationships. New onionskins of meaning.

It's time to go back to our café table at the beginning of the universe. Electrons and protons mated and formed atoms 380,000 years after the big bang. And that's when the conflict began. It was the era of the Great Gravity Crusades. Atoms clustered and competed. Competed for what? To kidnap, seduce, and recruit yet more atoms. Those atom clumps that grew the fastest grabbed and swallowed atom masses that grew more slowly. The big ate the small in what, as you probably remember, astrophysicists and astronomers call cannibalism. The biggest winners became galaxies. The smaller winners became stars. The winners in the number three slot became planets. And the runners up became moons. Those Great Gravity Crusades continue today. As I type this and as you read it, galaxies are gathering in clusters, and the biggest clusters are eating their smaller brethren to bulk up and become superclusters. Yes, galaxies are competing. Competing to commandeer matter. Competing to literally make a dent in space. Is it wrong to call this competition? Are the astronomers and astrophysicists wrong in anthropomorphizing?

We also think we invented war. We did not. Like protons and photons, colonies of bacteria are among our ancestors. And they began making war nearly four billion years ago. Their armies were eleven million times the size of Napoleon's mass conscription forces. And their weapons were weapons of mass destruction. Chemical weapons. Weapons of utter extermination. These microbial weapons are the molecular harpoons we would steal from microorganisms in the 1940s and put to work as "antibiotics."

We also think that we invented dominance hierarchies, pecking orders. We did not. Dominance, too, appeared on the scene shortly after the big bang. In the first seconds of this explosively expanding cosmos, when the forces of compression jammed two protons together, the meeting was not so cordial. In fact, the struggle for dominance began. One proton—the winner—retained its identity. The other proton lost. It submitted and decayed. It lost its identity and dissolved into a neutron and a positron.[18] A neutron that hung around as a subordinate to the proton it had been jammed into. The result was a deuteron, the one-proton-plus-one-neutron nucleus of a deuterium atom.

Let's look at this story of protons critically. I've used a batch of human terms to describe a proton mashup. Is there even the slightest bit of justification for this? Let's answer that with another question. In animal and human hierarchies, how can you tell who is on top and who is not? The top crayfish, lobster, lizard, chicken, dog, or chimpanzee gets certain privileges. He or she (yes, there are dominant females) gets influence and power. And the top dog, lobster, lizard, or chimp commands attention. Lots of it. Does anything like that happen when two protons pair during a post-big-bang mashup? You bet. The proton that retains its identity hangs on to its ability to seduce and recruit electrons. It holds on to its electrical charge, to its force of attraction. Meanwhile, the submissive neutron gives up that privilege. It becomes "electrically neutral."[19] It has no ability to attract an electron. It has no influence.

Dominance hierarchies show up once again 380,000 years after the big bang when the first atoms form.

Dominance? Really? Yes. It all begins with a primitive precursor of love. Up until now, electrons and protons were like bump-em cars in a superhot plasma, a soup in which particles slammed into each other at unbelievable speeds, then bounced away, only to ricochet off yet another particle. Up until now the slam, smash, crash, and ricochet were nonstop. But, as you know, at 380,000 ABB (after the big bang), the plasma cooled down. Which means that particles slowed down. And once the particles of the early plasma slowed, you remember what happened. Electrons discovered something strange. They were attracted to very unlikely mates. They were attracted to particles 1,837 times their size.[20] And those humongous particles found that they, too, were attracted. To what? To the tiny particles that swooned over them, to electrons. This match was so unlikely it was absurd. But it turned out that the "needs" of the proton fit the "desires" of the electron perfectly. With absolute precision. Could this match have been the primitive pattern upon which human love would someday be built?

Then came the pecking order. Once a proton and an electron joined, hierarchy took over. The proton was dominant. The electron was subordinate. Whoa. Let's not substitute poetry for science. Let's not anthropomorphize. What in the world is the evidence that anything akin to dominance and subordination, anything akin to the pecking order of puppies and people, was going on here?

Princeton University's "lexical database," WordNet, defines dominance as "the state that exists when one person or group has power over another."[21] And it gives the word "control" as a synonym for dominance. In the proton and electron relationship, what do power and control mean? The electron circles the proton. Not the other way around. And the proton has most of the mass. Mass is power. The electron is forced to travel wherever the proton travels. What's more, the proton determines the centerpoint of the electron's orbit. This is power and influence. And it's all in the hands of the proton.

But the electron, too, has its privileges. It determines which other atoms the proton-neutron duo will join in a chemical reaction. The proton handles the form of movements produced by bulk. The proton handles the job of traveling. And the electron takes care of social chores. Does this sound familiar? A bit like male-female partnerships among human beings? And if it does, to what extent do our male-female duos repeat the patterns native to the atoms of which we are made?

Dominance hierarchies continued to show up in the era of the Great

Gravity Crusades, the crusades that have gone on from 380,000 years after the big bang to today. How? Evolutionary biology thinker Michael Waller coined a phrase that goes like this: "Dominate, subordinate, or die."[22] It's a harsh dictum. And it may overstate evolution's imperatives. But, in fact, Waller's principle seems hyperactive in the world of competing gravity balls. If you were a giant ball of atoms, a gravity glump, roughly a billion years[23] after the big bang when star formation began, there was one way you could avoid being swallowed by a star racing toward obesity. A star with enormous gravitational power. A star with the power to suck you in. What was your path to survival? What was your last-gasp chance to retain your identity? You compromised. You subordinated. You became an obsequious courtier. You settled into an orbit around the star, constantly bowing to that star's gravity. You became a planet. But as a planet, you, too, were competitive. You, too, were hungry. And your compromise with a star gave you a privilege. The privilege of swallowing smaller gravity balls. Gravity balls called planetesimals. If you were greedily reaching out to grab a planetesimal with your gravity, there was one way the gravity clump that you'd caught could avoid being swallowed. You, a planet, had subordinated to a sun, to a star. And the planetesimal, too, could subordinate. It could submit subserviently to your gravitational force. It could circle around you in an orbit that provided benefits to both of you. It could become a moon.

Admittedly, I've used anthropomorphism galore in describing all of this. And admittedly, all of this is an extraordinarily primitive precursor of the pecking orders among lobsters, lizards, and humans. Extremely primitive. But it is real. And there is more than an even chance that we humans have free will, competition, dominance hierarchies, love, and war because we inherited them from the cosmos that gave us birth. There is more than an even chance that we have free will, competition, dominance hierarchies, love, and war because these things were basic patterns that shaped the behavior of the earliest particles, atoms, and colonies of cells. There is also more than an even chance that we have these nasty—and sometimes brilliantly creative—characteristics because they are deep structures, Ur patterns. Because they are patterns that repeat over and over again in each new medium that the cosmos generates, from the massive slowdown of particle ricochets 380,000 years after the big bang through the evolution of the first cell to the evolution of your mind and mine. There is more than an even chance that we have free will, competition, dominance hierarchies, love, and war because they are patterns like the basic rules of the steelmaker and of Benoît Mandelbrot's fractal set. Rules that, when repeated in a new medium, make radically new things. Rules that have been repeated trillions of trillions of times to fashion new mediums, new contexts, new realities. Rules that have been repeated with unstoppable persistence. Rules that have knit a universe.

***

There is also a good chance that we have free will, competition, dominance hierarchies, love, and war because they are among the earliest outgrowths of attraction and repulsion, among the first manifestations of differentiation and integration. There is a good chance that we have free will, competition, dominance hierarchies, love, and war because they are outgrowths of the starting rules of the universe. Or, to put it differently, there is a good chance that we have free will, competition, dominance hierarchies, love, and war because they are among the earliest iterations of the axioms that big banged this cosmos.

TIME, THE GREAT TRANSLATOR: AN INFORMATION THEORY OF TIME

Once you have a set of simple rules, you have to extract their implications. In geometry, twenty-three hundred years of geometers have done the extraction, working out one proof after another. In a math class at Reed College, you and eleven other students spent two semesters extracting the implications from Peano's axioms. In Benoît Mandelbrot's fractals, John Conway's Game of Life, and Steven Wolfram's cellular automata, a computer extracts the implications. What or who is the implication extractor, the implication unpacker, in this peculiar cosmos of ours? Time.

Time as an implication unpacker? Surely that can't be true. I mean, let's face facts. Mainstream physicists like Caltech's Sean Carroll, author of one of the most definitive popular books on time in the early twenty-first century, *From Eternity to Here: The Quest for the Ultimate Theory of Time*, are absolutely certain that time must be defined in terms of entropy. And implication extraction is not compatible with entropy.

Implication unpacking builds things up. It yanks the complex from the simple. Just look at the history of geometry from Euclid's *Elements* to Einstein. Geometry started simple and it became so intricate that it could predict the way light would behave while shooting up an elevator shaft at Harvard. Or take a look at two other examples of implication extractors: the Game of Life and Wolfram's cellular automata. By yanking implications from simple rules, these two simulate mini-cosmoses. They make wonders from nearly nothing.

And that is not the way entropy works. Entropy tears things down. Entropy pulls things apart. Entropy scatters things. So time cannot be implication unpacking. Not at all.

Just how stubbornly do mainstream physicists cleave to the belief that time and entropy are Siamese twins? In *From Eternity to Here*, Sean Carroll refers to the second law of thermodynamics—the law of entropy—seventy-six times. And he refers to the second law's beloved product, entropy, one hundred times. Carroll is very blunt about physics' love affair with entropy—and his. He says point blank that "the Second Law is arguably the most dependable law in all of physics." And he devotes a full chapter to what the title of that chapter calls "Nature's Most Dependable Law."

To drive home his message, Carroll heads that chapter with a quote from a man we know well, Einstein's explainer and the man behind the eclipse experiment of 1919, the experiment that put Albert Einstein into headlines worldwide: Arthur Eddington. Eddington's quote?

If someone points out to you that your pet theory of the universe is in disagreement with Maxwell's equations [the laws of electricity and magnetism]—then so much the worse for Maxwell's equations. If it is found to be contradicted by observation—well, these experimentalists do bungle things sometimes. But if your theory is found to be against the Second Law of Thermodynamics I can give you no hope; there is nothing for it but to collapse in deepest humiliation.[24]

Is Eddington right? Is it time to collapse in deepest humiliation? Vladislav Čápek of Charles University in Prague and Daniel Peter Sheehan of the University of San Diego dare to disagree with Eddington. Yes, they use Eddington's quote too. But in their book *Challenges to the Second Law of Thermodynamics: Theory and Experiment* they point out that "there is no general theoretic proof" for the second law.[25] No general theoretical proof that all things tend to disorder, to entropy. No theoretical proof at all. Čápek and Sheehan emphasize that they are believers in the second law of thermodynamics. Deep believers. In essence, they plead with the reader not to view them as heretics. But they explain that "for more than a century" the concepts of entropy and the second law have been "beyond the pale of legitimate scientific inquiry" in large part because of "peer pressure against such inquiry." Nonetheless Čápek and Sheehan admit that the second law is an antique, a "remnant of nineteenth century physics, whose foundations were admittedly suspect." And an end may be in sight. As Čápek and Sheehan report, "There grew around the second law a nearly unpenetrable mystique," but that mystique "now is being pierced."[26]

Entropy is not the only tool with which to understand time. One alternative is a conversational model of time, something you first published an article about in 2005. But you were not alone in producing this strange new view, the "conversational model" of time. And how you acquired your partner in turning time into communication and meaning is a tale that leads to Moscow.

✳✳✳

The year is 2002. You've been questioning the validity of entropy since the 1970s. However, entropy, much to your chagrin, remains stubbornly mainstream. So does the more-than-hundred-year-old habit of defining time in entropic terms. Then an e-mail friend of yours in the evolutionary biology community, David Livingstone Smith, cofounder of the New England Institute for Cognitive Science and Evolutionary Studies, catches wind of your theoretical physics drift and introduces you to a mathematician and physicist in the Vatican of American science, the National Science Foundation. That mathematician and physicist is Paul Werbos, the NSF's program director for control, networks, and computational intelligence. Paul is a man in his fifties with a pleasant round face and a love of conversation over beer. What's more, he has been able to visualize the operations of complex equations in his head since he was six. Yes, six. He makes you feel small by comparison. After all, you didn't get into science until you were ten.

When Paul Werbos sees that you are taking a strange turn of thought, he introduces you online to someone he thinks you'll appreciate, Pavel Kurakin of the Keldysh Institute of Applied Mathematics of the Russian Academy of Sciences in Moscow. These are the days before Skype™ and Facebook®, but 2:00 a.m. e-mail exchanges suit Paul, Pavel, and you just fine.

Pavel has a very strange theory of time. He calls it the *hidden time theory*. Here's how it goes: Imagine time as a stairway. Every stair is separated from the one below it by a riser, the vertical separator between one step and the step above it. Imagine that vertical separator between steps as what *Wikipedia* describes when defining a riser—"the near-vertical element . . . forming the space between a step and the next."[27] What's in that vertical space? It certainly isn't time. Time exists only on the steps. Time exists only on the flat plane of the stair above and the equally horizontal plane of the stair below. So what's in the riser? No time. Timelessness. A space utterly without clocks, without deadlines, without hurry up and rush, and without urgency. In a sense, it's a space with all the time in the world.

So you and Pavel have over a hundred discussions of what could possibly happen in that timelessness, in that infinity of nontime between the steps of time's staircase. You pull in experts on computer science and network communications. Experts like Nova Spivack, who made the front page of the *New York Times* for his expertise in semantic webs. Experts like computer scientist Joel Isaacson. And your intuition is telling you something. You propose to Pavel that the cosmos is social. And that the cosmos is conversational, gossipy, and communicative. What's more, you propose that the next stairstep in line looks back at the stairstep before it, allows the elements on that stairstep—the usual suspects: quarks, atoms, stars, galaxies, molecules, cells, plants, animals, neurons, and human beings—to compete for attention, then makes a decision about how to interpret those elements and their interaction. When it makes up its mind, the stairstep moves everything forward one turn and produces the present. Then the pattern of the present is locked in place and becomes the past. Meanwhile, the next stairstep in line has to look over the present and ponder it in the timelessness, in the non-time between the stairsteps. Then it has to come up with alternative translations, alternative interpretations, and make up its mind.

Which leads to a puzzle. How in the world does time do it? How does it make up its mind? What rules does it use to interpret the past? There are roughly 10^{87} particles in this cosmos. And they make up all kinds of emergent forms—from neon atoms forged in the hearts of burning stars to dancers on ecstasy in modern dens of iniquity. This is a cosmos in which crowds count. A cosmos in which trios can be quarks, in which atom clumps can group in greedy, competitive gangs, in which bacteria can mass in colonies of trillions, and in which even birds can have families and flocks. It is a cosmos of mass behavior. So you look for a system of mass behavior to suggest how a cosmos of mobs and crowds may make up its mind.

And you come up with your favorite mass behavers, bees. Bees have a problem.[28] A life-and-death problem. And it's a problem with time. More specifically, a problem with a time limit. And a problem with decisions. There are roughly twenty thousand bees in each hive. And they have to act as a group brain, a collective intelligence. Why? The hive has only six weeks in which to gather enough pollen and nectar to make forty pounds of honey, the honey it will need to get it through the winter. If it makes the wrong decisions, the hive will not reach that figure. And failure to produce the quota is deadly. If the hive fails to manufacture the minimum cache of honey within its time limit—the six weeks of spring when pollen is abundant— then sometime roughly six months later, in the snow and ice of winter, the hive will run out of food. And the entire colony—all twenty thousand bees—will die.

How do bees solve the problem? How do they make up their mind time after time after time? And how do they arrive at the best decisions available? In the words of bee researchers, how do they arrive at the "optimal decisions"?[29] With a fine-tuned balance between fission and fusion, between differentiation and integration, between explorers and consolidators, between searchers and workers. Between speculation and sticking with a sure thing. And with, of all things, a fine-tuned balance between labor and entertainment. Between muscle work and communication, between toil and discouragement. Between sweat and information exchange. Between purposelessness and meaning. Yes, Claude Shannon's orphan term, "meaning."

Ninety-five percent of the bees are hard workers. The young ones, the adolescents and young adults, stay indoors and do housework. They take care of the queen, feed the babies, the pupae, store incoming foodstuff, repair the honeycombs, and keep the place clean and neat, literally. As they grow older, they graduate. They become outside workers, gatherers. They fly out time after time, day after day, to mine patches of linden flowers, sumac, goldenrod, red clover, hyacinths, crocuses, sunflowers, and raspberry bushes. They bring back the pollen, the nectar, and the water of which honey, the hive's daily bread, is made. Remember, they are up against a killer deadline.

But something doesn't make sense. Roughly 5 percent of the bees seem to be infuriating time wasters. This irresponsible minority is a bunch of good-for-nothing Bohemian wanderers who go out on pointless, solitary rambles, indulging themselves to the nth degree. Sounds like Herbert Spencer and George Henry Lewes on one of their four-day walks, doesn't it? Thank god there are conformists who stick with the group and do what others do. Those conformists carry the burden of food gathering. Their slavish imitation of their sisters is a remarkably efficient device for strip-mining the nectar and pollen in a hot flower patch. But if you are one of these dutiful worker bees, you have a problem. What do you do when the pollen and nectar run out? What do you do when you've plundered your accustomed flower patch to its very last pollen grain?

Frankly, you get depressed. You go out to the familiar patch over and over again. You have a hard time believing that it's not panning out. You have a hard time believing that the factory is closed and that you are out of a job. You return home with the pollen-carrying hairs on your back legs empty.

Attention is the oxygen of the human soul. And it's also the transmission device that drives the mind of a hive. When you arrived in the days of plenty with your pollen-carrying hairs bulging, you were the hit of the hive. You were the bee's knees. Unloader bees rushed over to you, felt you all over, stripped you of your cargo, and excited you so much that your body temperature rose. But now when you come home empty, no one pays attention to you. No one at all. Eventually you get the message. You stop going back to the empty patch. Again, you get depressed. How do we know? Your temperature goes down. And you literally crawl into the hive ignominiously and are forced to beg for food. Cornell's Thomas Seeley, the key researcher on this form of bee behavior, calls you an "unemployed" bee.[30]

How do you cope with your misery? This is where the Bohemian time wasters come in. Why? Because with their seemingly arbitrary curiosities, they are explorers. They are the eyes and antennae of the colony. While you've been going back and forth to the flower patch that you felt would occupy you for the rest of your life, anywhere from five to ten of the Bohemians have found new flower patches and are at this very minute dancing their discoveries.

Let's drill down to something you'd think would be irrelevant—your feelings, your emotions. And your hunger for attention. You are in desperate need of two things: excitement and meaning. In this case meaning means more than it does in Claude Shannon's vocabulary. Meaning is a sense of direction. A sense of where to go next. And meaning is a sense that if you follow that next direction, if you aim at that next goal, you will be rewarded. Meaning is the sense that when you return home from a pollen flight, the unloaders will give you the kind of attention that you used to get when you landed with full pollen hairs at the loading dock just inside the hive. Or, to put it in human terms, meaning is a sense that you are contributing to something higher than yourself. Which is exactly what every bee does every day. Especially when she delivers the goods—pollen, nectar, and water.

As for excitement, that seems a strange word to apply to bees. It's not. When a bee is excited, her temperature goes up. When she is depressed, her temperature goes down. It's as simple as that. Stimulus and response. And as you'll see in a second, emotions are an information engine. They are vital to the next big decision of the hive.

Back to you, the unemployed bee, the bee who no longer gets attention, the bee who has to beg (yes, bees beg, they humble themselves and crouch close to the ground) for food. Back to you, the bee on welfare. You are depressed. You need entertainment. You need excitement. You need something that will raise your temperature again. And you can find it. Why? Roughly five of those damned bohemian bees have found flower patches that they think are hot. Flower patches that excite them. And they've come back home, have used the unloading dock just inside the hive as a stage, and are dancing their discoveries. They are dancing a figure eight that gives instructions on how to get to the patch that they are advertising. And a figure eight that also gets across how excited—or tepid—they are. How do these explorer bees flash their excitement? With the power and the length of their dance. Mildly excited explorer bees may dance for less than a minute. Wildly excited explorer bees may dance for as long as half an hour.[31]

You and your fellow unemployed sisters literally have nothing better to do. So you crowd around the dancers. Why? Because they excite you. Or, to put it in human terms, they entertain you. They lift your spirits. Those who dance for half an hour fire your enthusiasm more than those lukewarm bees who dance only a minute or two. So you and your sisters crowd around the most excited dancer. And if her wild boogie-woogie, her buzzing, abdomen-waggling figure eight excites you sufficiently, if her dance lifts you out of your lethargy, you may fly out, follow her instructions, and check out the flower patch that she is promoting. If that patch of blossoms excites you, too, you will come back to the hive and dance out your exuberance. You will become a backup dancer. A confirmation conveyor.

The hive is up against a crucial choice. It may invest ten thousand bee miles of travel into the next flower patch to which it sends its conformists. If it picks the wrong flower patch, it won't outpace the cold of mother nature when winter comes. It will lose the bee-and-honey race. How does the hive handle its prediction problem? Out of many possibilities, how does it pick just one? The dancing bee, the bohemian bee, the explorer bee who excites the greatest number of backup dancers wins. And once this American Idol contest with six legs and yellow and black stripes is over, you go out with all of your sisters to mine the new hive of the day. You go out with oomph and eagerness. You no longer show the sluggishness you did when you were getting the message that your old flower patch had no more to give. And you go out with the certainty that when you return home, you will get attention. Lots of it. The unloader bees will treat you like a rock star once again.

Unemployment, depression, and a midwinter death are the sticks. Then there is the carrot. The same carrot that motivated Aristotle. Attention. Not to mention sex and procreation. If your hive pulls in a surplus of honey it will be in a position to reproduce. It will be in a position to feed a lot of kids, raise them to maturity, then hive off, to split in two, and to send out a daughter colony. Or more than one.[32] And even better, when the time of the year comes for a sexual tryst, your hive will be able to send out more adolescent queens and males than its neighbors and will stand a good chance of spreading its genes in yet more brand-new colonies. That, for bees, is the supreme act of interpretation, translation, and meaning. The supreme act of prediction practice. That, for bees, is victory.

What on this peculiar planet of bacteria and baseball bats does this have to do with cracks between the stairsteps of time? What does it have to do with time as the ultimate meaning maker, the ultimate interpreter and translator?

The crack between the steps of time is a crack of timelessness. And in that timelessness, in that riser before the next step, the stairstep of the future has all the time in the world to look over the present and to make up its mind. It has all the time in the world to look over the implications of the moment that came before it. It has all the time in the world to see if there is just one possible implication, one next move, or many. And it has all the time in the world to check the positions of the 10^{87} particles in the cosmos. It has all the time in the world to check out all of the emergent properties in which those particles participate, from clouds of interstellar dust congealing as future stars to humans scrolling through Monster.com® for new careers. It has all the time in the world to check out umpteen zillion onionskins of meaning.

But if there is more than just one possible future, how does the next stairstep of time called the future decide? How does it make up its mind? The bees may offer a clue.

Or at least that's what Pavel Kurakin thought. You did too. And Pavel and you were not alone. Pavel's mentor, George Malinetskii, one of three coordinators of the Russian Academy of Sciences' program on "System Analysis and Mathematical Modeling of World Dynamics,"[33] was impressed with your bees. So impressed that he became the lead author on the paper that you and Pavel decided to write on the stairsteps of time and the way that beehives make up their minds, "Conversation (Dialogue) Model of Quantum Transitions." Pavel wrote his part. You wrote the section on bees. George did his thing. And you suggested other mass decision-making processes—for example, how centrioles in cells "make up their minds" about which tubular extrusions to keep and which to discard; how neurons in an infant "make up their minds" about whether to live or die, and more. And the paper that you and Pavel pulled together with George Malinetskii—"Conversation (Dialogue) Model Of Quantum Transitions"—was accepted for publication in ArXiv.org, the preprint archive originally hosted by Los Alamos National Labs for papers in advanced mathematics and physics.[34]

But here's the shocker. Pavel Kurakin's hidden time model treats time as a form of communication. It treats time as a form of information extraction. It treats time as a form of translation. In fact, time is the ultimate extractor of implicate properties. Or, to use Claude Shannon's word, time is the ultimate extractor of meaning.

What in the world does that, well, ummm, mean? First off, Pavel Kurakin is not alone in regarding time as something like a flight of stairs. In the eyes of most modern physicists, time is not continuous. Time is not like a children's slide. It is not an unending ribbon along which we slip imperceptibly from one second to the next with no spaces in between. Time is like a staircase. You have to take it one step at a time. And each step is the same distance apart. Imagine time as the elevator in a skyscraper that extends to the heavens and beyond. You can stop on the fourth floor, the fourteenth, or the hundred-and-fourteenth, but you can't stop on the 14.756th floor. You can't stop in between. To toss in yet one more image, time is not like a hanging rope up which you can shimmy to a tree house. It is like a ladder. You climb a ladder one rung at a time. And each rung is separated from the rung before it by precisely the same distance.

The stairsteps, floors, or rungs of time are in all probability spaced precisely one Planck unit apart from each other. What's one Planck unit? It's the time it takes a beam of light to traverse one Planck unit of distance. A Planck unit is 10^{-43} of a second. Which means that there are 10^{43} Planck units of time in every second of your life and mine. That's ten with forty-three zeros after it. Meaning that time can do something astonishingly iterative. It can repeat its process of implication extraction ten with forty-three zeros after it times per second.

To use yet more metaphors, time is sliced up the way that an animated movie is sliced in frames. Like Disney's film in which Bambi's next move unfolds one animation cell at a time. Except each frame of time is self-assembling. Each frame draws itself. Each frame looks back at its predecessor, then inches the action along. Without animators, directors, or cameramen. Each frame interprets the action of the frame that came before. Each frame sketches itself by unpacking the implications of the frame that gave it birth. Or, more precisely, time is like a line in Stephen Wolfram's cellular automata "deciding" its configuration based on "reading" the line before. Making a decision based on reading the previous line's stimulus and producing a response. A response based on simple rules.

Yes, it bears repeating. Time is a process of communication, information, translation, and of what Claude Shannon calls "meaning." Time really is like a student at Reed College doing her math homework, unpacking the possibilities from a handful of starting axioms. Unpacking implicate properties one at a time.

***

But that was not the end of it. In 2006, the Russians put together an international conference on quantum physics in Moscow, Quantum Informatics 2006. One of the conference's organizers, Dr. Yuri Ozhigov,[35] the chair of quantum informatics at the Faculty of Computational Mathematics and Cybernetics of Moscow State University, had been impressed by your paper and had invited you and Pavel to speak. So you flew to Moscow and met Pavel, who was tall, balding, a tiny bit awkward, youthful, and newly married. And you met Dr. Ozhigov, who was short, round, and impatient. Impatient that you were trying to use a credit card to pay for your lodging in the 1960s-architecture, red-brick cross between a dormitory and a motel twenty-four miles outside of Moscow where the conference took place.

But you, indeed, did speak. You told thirty assembled quantum physicists in a session organized by your newfound nemesis, Dr. Yuri Ozhigov, why everything they knew about quantum physics, everything they knew about Schrödinger's equation, is wrong. Your argument? Quantum physics says that until a particle is measured, it is in several states simultaneously. But, you said, no particle is an island. There is no such thing as an unmeasured particle. Particles are not solitary, they are not loners. Particles do not wander around on their own. They travel in packs, in mobs, in armies, and in gangs. So does virtually everything in this universe.

To understand the cosmos, you have to understand group behavior. Mass behavior. And the mass behavior of bees is just a suggestive start. More to the point, every particle in the cosmos influences others and is influenced by them. Nonstop. It's stimulus and response. No particle goes unmeasured. At least one fundamental assumption of quantum physics is wrong.

You thought you would be thrown out of the conference. Instead, thirty theoretical physicists heard you out. Then they beamed like proud uncles. And you couldn't figure out why. Were they just humoring you? Were they entertained by the ignorance of an odd-looking American? Surely they did not agree with you. Or did they?

Five years later, in 2011, you received an e-mail from Pavel informing you that Dr. Ozhigov had just written a book and suggesting that you read it. The name of the book? *Constructive Physics.*[36] So you downloaded Yuri Ozhigov's book from arXiv.org to your Kindle and read it. In it, Dr. Ozhigov suggested going beyond equations. Including the most revered equation of all, Schrödinger's equation. In fact, Dr. Ozhigov suggested abandoning traditional math altogether and doing a Wolfram, going entirely into computer models, diving into visual simulations. And beneath the new models of quantum physics, said Ozhigov, would be an escape from the fiction that particles flit about on their own, the fiction that particles manage to go without observers. In place of solitary particles, Ozhigov proposed focusing on "collective behavior." In place of individual behavior, Ozhigov proposed using mass behavior. The behavior of crowds, mobs, and cliques.

Cited in Ozhigov's book was your article with Pavel and George Malinetskii. You were impressed by the daring of the book's arguments. After all, it proposed a radical revolution. So you wrote an e-mail to Dr. Ozhigov praising what he'd accomplished with *Constructive Physics*. You began it by saying, "I don't know if you remember me, but . . . " After all, it had been five years, and it seemed very unlikely that anyone in that Moscow theoretical physics crew had taken you seriously. Dr. Ozhigov responded within two hours. His words? "Of course I remember you. Didn't you read the first half of the book?"[37]

What was in the first half of Ozhigov's book? Nearly every crazy notion with which you had pelted those thirty quantum physicists in Moscow, nearly every heretical idea. Every one of the heresies you'd articulated was now a basic. A basic to an entirely new way of doing quantum physics. Perhaps a new way of doing all of physics. At least if it succeeds. Quantum physics is a game of mass behavior, and the groups that promote new ideas are often like the explorer bees who lose the competition and whose glad tidings are attended to briefly, then forgotten. Most new ideas ebb and disappear.

The bottom line? Quantum physics is based on the idea that you can be alone. It is based on particles in isolation that only make up their minds when they finally make a connection. And the second law of thermodynamics is even worse. It says that patterns of relationship ebb and disappear, leaving particles in a random soup. But this is a conversational cosmos. It is a cosmos of crowds and communication. It is a cosmos that grows big pictures and onion layers of social structure. Even time is communicative. Time interprets, translates, and extracts implications. Time opens fortune cookies. Every flick of time is an act of meaning.

***

In a universe of time, the complexity of relationships is always on the increase. Thanks to webs of meaning and thanks to implicate properties, this is not a cosmos stepping down to chaos. This is a universe on a constant upward climb.

WRAP YOURSELF IN STRING:
ITERATION AND EMERGENT PROPERTIES

The loop is a remarkably useful metaphor with which to tie the God Problem together. Remarkably useful for explaining the transformative power of communication, translation, and relationships. Why? The greatest amazement in this cosmos is its creativity. And one clue to that creativity is in your knitting.

New weaves in old strings produce new surprises. Think about it. You can buy a ball of yarn and stretch it from the front of your house to the house across the street like a clothesline. Or you can knit a sweater from that very same long, serial line, a line that is nothing but the very same thing inch after inch after inch. But by repeating the string of yarn over and over upon itself, by using a simple iterated rule, a knitting stitch, you can produce something radically new—a collar, a sleeve, a glove, a blanket, or a hat. The trick is the big picture. The trick is in two things: the vision of the stitch, and the vision of a blanket, a hat, a glove, or a sweater.

String was invented roughly eighteen thousand years before Pythagoras arrived on the scene.[38] It was the technology that made the compass possible. It was the technology that the Babylonians, Pythagoras, and Euclid used to make circles. If you'd lived back in the days of Euclid and I'd told you that the string from your compass could keep you warm, you would have said I was crazy. If I'd told you that there was a magic way to wrap string around you, a way that would hold the shape of your torso and your arms when you took the string off, you would have said I was gibbering nonsense. After all, string is string is string. Wrap string around you and you simply turn yourself into a giant spool. Unwrap the string to take it off and you have an appalling tangle on the floor.

But invent a simple new rule, a stitch, and repeat that rule over and over upon itself fifteen hundred times, repeat it with maniacal persistence, and you get an amazing new process of transformation. An amazing new form of translation from one medium to another. You get knitting. Go a step further. Invent the sweater. Whammo, you've invented something that plugs into human needs the way that the dance of a winning explorer bee plugs into the needs of the unemployed and into the needs of the entire hive.

Looping, hammering, weaving, and stringing old things together using new simple rules produces the unexpected, the shocking, or the strange. Repeat the brick and you can get enough apartments to house sixty thousand people. Repeat the scratch mark in clay and you can get Mesopotamian mythology, astronomy, and astrology. Repeat the twenty-six letters of the Western alphabet and you can get Shakespeare. The trick is a big picture. A big picture that plugs into onionskins of need the way that the message of a winning explorer bee plugs into the needs of the hive.

**

Uncovering the power of axioms began with the Mesopotamians who invented math six thousand years ago. The Mesopotamians who invented the simple rule of solving problems tiny step by tiny step. And the Mesopotamians who based their mathematical system on simple modular units—the brick and the barleycorn. The hunt for the power of axioms gathered momentum in Greece when Aristotle invented and promoted a procedure that laid out definitions, axioms, propositions, and proofs and when Aristotle named that technique "science." The hunt for the power of axioms crystalized as a recruitment strategy, a template with social magnetism, in Alexandria when Euclid showed how to use the axiom in his *Elements*. The hunt for the power of axioms plowed ahead in Europe in the works of Galileo, Kepler, and Newton. The hunt for the power of axioms spread into political philosophy in England and North America with Hobbes and the Founding Fathers. The hunt for the power of axioms showed the possibility of scoping out entire universes in Germany, Hungary, and Russia with the non-Euclideans of the nineteenth century, Gauss, Bólyai, Lobachevsky, and Riemann. The hunt for the power of axioms came to a point in Italy when Giuseppe Peano reduced the entire natural number system to five axioms. And the hunt for the power of axioms exploded in Switzerland in the theories of Einstein, theories based on what Einstein claimed was the change of just one axiom, the axiom of time.

The axiom underlay the logic with which Kepler, Galileo, and Newton were certain that God had thought out the world. God, they felt, had used reason. And reason was based on axioms. But could a cosmos really be based on unfolding implications from axioms? Could a universe really be created by unfolding corollaries from simple rules?

It's back to the question we began with. If there is no god, how does the cosmos create? How does it fashion itself? How does it build itself up from a big bang to brains? Does the cosmos start with simple rules and extract their implications? Does it do what Euclid, Kepler, Galileo, and Newton did? Does it start with axioms and work its way up? Or does it contain both rules and a big picture, a grand vision of its future forms? Could corollary generator theory really help explain how a godless universe pulls off acts of genesis?

Here's a translation of the same question in a different form. Does a twenty-three-hundred-year process of human reasoning based on axioms reflect reality? Do generations of abstract, airy, inductive thinking have any relationship to the floor you walk on, the ceiling above your head, the solidity of your fingertips, and the stars you see overhead when you step out at night to walk the dog? Or is axiomatic reasoning merely a sandbox for socially clumsy humans with oversized brains? Is axiomatic reasoning merely an indulgence, a playground for geeks? Is there any way to know? Yes, there is. And Einstein found it. Generate predictions, then see if they match the real world. Einstein generated eight of those predictions. Eight predictions based on building from axioms. And every one of those predictions turned out to be on the money. Every one of those eight predictions was spot on.

But there's a problem. Twenty-two hundred years before Einstein, Euclid had cheated. He hadn't really extracted implications from his axioms. He'd had hunches about what might be possible. Hunches left to him by the geometers who had come before him. Then in his proofs he had worked his way backward to prove that these hunches were consistent with his axioms, that they were in tune with his assumptions. He'd started with the final product and had worked in reverse. And twenty-two hundred years later in Italy, Giuseppe Peano had worked backward from a six-thousand-year-old mathematical system to what he felt were its starting seeds. Peano had worked backward from the complex to the simple in order to derive his five postulates, his five axioms.

Then there's what David Bohm did in England in the 1960s. Bohm didn't show a system unfolding from nothing. He didn't show that a simple system could evolve into ornate complexity. He showed that you could hide complexity in what looks like nothing, then bring it back again. He showed that you could hide an ink drop in what looked like blank glycerin, then you could bring it back to its original form. But this was a cheat. A cheat if you want to answer the question of how the cosmos creates. A cheat if you want to answer the question of how the cosmos creates from scratch.

Is there a system that doesn't cheat? Is there a system that can tackle Hans Driesch's mystery, the puzzle of form production? Is there a system that can lunge forward from almost nothing and produce the supersized surprise?

Yes. At MIT in 1940, Claude Shannon translated logic and math into the ons and offs of electrical switches. Then came the child of Shannon's translation, the computer. And by the 1960s, Benoît Mandelbrot at an IBM office in Yorktown Heights, New York, showed that you could, indeed, unfold astonishments from just one simple rule. Astonishments that didn't cheat. Astonishments whose outlines were not packed into the starting rules in advance by their creator. Astonishments that stunned even the man who had let the simple rules loose, Benoît Mandelbrot. Next came John Conway in Cambridge in 1971 with his Game of Life. He showed how a system of simple rules could generate sliders and gliders, recruitment patterns, patterns that, like the waves of the sea, had a stubborn identity, an identity that hung in there even though the slider or glider was no thing, even though the slider or the glider yanked together one cluster of squares as its constituents, then abandoned them and yanked the next into its form.

And Stephen Wolfram at the headquarters of his company in Champaign, Illinois, in the 1990s went even further. He showed that you could generate axioms by the millions and that you could use your computer to derive the implications from each. Some axioms gave you nothing. And some axioms gave you elaborate pattern. Elaborate form creation. Including forms reminiscent of the shoebox molecule of steel. What's more, the power of unfolding the implicit properties of axioms proved so great that Wolfram said it was time to throw away equations. His peculiar brand of axiom systems, his cellular automata, he said, would eventually be able to explain everything from quarks to quibbles.

Mandelbrot, Conway, and Wolfram showed that you could, indeed, produce intricate astonishments by letting axioms and simple rules do their thing. Mandelbrot, Conway, and Wolfram showed that simple rules could generate new big pictures, big pictures that changed the meanings of everything within them. But would the systems of simple rules, the systems of axioms, ever be able to take on the challenges left by von Baer and Driesch? Would axiom systems ever be able to explain the unfolding of the embryo? And what about the challenges left by John Stuart Mill and George Henry Lewes? What about the challenge of emergent properties? What about the challenge of explaining why one plus one does not equal two when you add oxygen to hydrogen. What about the challenge of explaining how combining two gases makes a liquid with shocking properties? What about the challenge of explaining how combining two gases makes a drop of water?

Would the new tool of science and reasoning, the computer, go even further? Would it improve the predictive power of what Herbert Spencer worked with, metaphor? Organic metaphor? Metaphor based on the patterns of living things? Would simulations in the computer make it possible to pull predictions from the sort of simple, overarching patterns that Spencer was after—simple patterns like differentiation and integration? Would simulations in the computer translate metaphors from mere word pictures into patterns from which you could extrapolate future outcomes? Patterns whose implications you could map with a precision as great as the exactitude produced by equations?

And does the notion that this is a universe built on simple rules solve any problems in science? Does the axiom connect with reality?

***

Yes, it does. Corollary generator theory helps explain two peculiar aspects of this cosmos we live in—supersimultaneity and the Xerox Effect. What are supersimultaneity and the Xerox Effect? When you and I sat at our café table at the beginning of the universe, the big bang sneezed forth a handkerchief of space and time, a handkerchief that zooshed to massive size at a speed beyond belief. Then you had a ridiculous notion—you uttered strange words: "matter," "things," and "particles." You predicted particles made of time, space, and speed. Nanonuggets made of space, time, and energy. Give me a break. Things made of motion? Plus space and time? The notion, you recall, was ridiculous. And I told you so. Then, suddenly, whammo, a hailstorm of particles, the very first "things." And you were so right that it was ridiculous.

But here's the peculiar part. If this were a cosmos of six monkeys at six typewriters, those "things," those particles, would have come in a zillion different shapes and sizes. Not to mention a zillion colors and textures. And a zillion smells and tastes. But they did not. No way. Particles popped forth in only fifty-seven species.[39] Separate species. With roughly 10^{86} copies of each. Identical copies. That's the Xerox Effect—a gaggle of identical things whooping into being. Then there's supersynchrony and supersimultaneity. The zillion copies of these fifty-seven species of particles spooshed from the sheet of space, time, and speed at precisely the same instant. They didn't copy each other. They had the same form because of something else. But what was that something else?

Could the answer be axioms and simple rules? Could these particles have been so rigidly and perfectly identical because they were all the children of axioms, because they were all implications extracted from the same simple rules? Could they have spatted from time and space with such supersame-ness and supersynchrony because this plethora of particles was one of those simple rules' first implications, one of those simple rules' first corollaries? Could the high-precision sameness exist because the particles were all corollaries of the same basic assumptions? And could it be that you get a zillion copies of identical things when the cosmos has only gotten up to a primitive step in her axiom unpacking, in her Planck-step-by-Planck-step process of implica-tion extracting? Her Planck-step-by-Planck-step process of time's basic task: extracting meaning? And could it be that an early act of implication unfolding only generates a handful of forms? Could it be that an early act of implication extraction only generates a handful of what George Henry Lewes called emer-gent properties? Could it be that if you are time, if you are the cosmic implica-tion unpacker, in move number one or two of the game, in homework assignment number one or two, there are very few things the rules allow you to do?

Try making your first move on a chessboard, a board constrained by simple rules. How many moves can you make? Can you zoom anywhere on the board? Can you create your own new pieces? Can you move 12,500 miles around the earth and place a pawn in China? Or can you move a knight to an orbit in outer space? No, you are chained by the rules of the game. All you can move is one out of eight pawns and two knights. And you can only move them the tiniest squeak down the board. Take the first move in a universe of simple rules, a universe unfolded from axioms, and what can you do? Manic mass production. A zillion particles, 10^{87} of them. But particles as constrained, as yoked, as chained, and as limited as your first move of a pawn or a knight. Only fifty-seven different forms of particles. But nearly 10^{86} copies of each. Precisely identical copies. Manic mass production and supersynchrony.

As the game of chess continues, your choices open up. The number of moves you have to choose from rises. In fact, the number of possible moves rises so high that it can sometimes utterly addle your brain. Does anything like that loosening up happen in the real world? Yes. Four hundred thousand years after the big bang, when gravity begins to pull together wisps of gas and dust, the sizes of those smudges and smirks vary far more than the sizes of the particles at the beginning of the cosmos. And these gravity glumps no longer have a precise circular form. They are ragged, wispy, and lumpy. Then a hundred thousand to a billion years later,[40] when those gravity balls gang up in galaxies and stars, the timing is more ragged, and so is the shape.

One galaxy might clomp together at one billion ABB (after the big bang). Another might form five billion years later at six billion ABB. One galaxy might look like a lumpy potato. Another might have elegant spiral arms. The same with stars. Some may be born early. Some may be born late. And the number of forms and sizes is substantial, from small stars to Gargantuas. Then there's the variation from brown dwarfs to bright yellow and sallow red, from neutron stars to supernovas. Quite a range, right? The six monkeys would approve. Or would they? All the stars seem remarkably different. And yet, at heart, they are all the same—big spheres compacted and kindled by gravity.

Yes, there is manic mass production. Yes, the number of stars is in the sextillions.[41] Of all different sizes and shapes. But that isn't entirely true. The stars in the universe only vary in size by a factor of five hundred. No star is so big that it hogs up half the universe. And no star is so small that it can fit in your pocket. Then there's that shape, the sphere. It's cookie-cuttered into stars from the universe's guzzle to the universe's zatch. That's the Xerox Effect. The same thing happening all over the place. The same thing without copying. Yet aping each other's pattern for reasons that have nothing to do with monkey see, monkey do.

What could account for this incredible sameness? What could account for the Xerox Effect? Simple rules. Axioms unfolding their implicate properties. Unfolding the very same rules all over the place. All at the same time. You, a Reed College student doing your homework, help explain the Xerox Effect. How? It's a month into the class. You reach the stage where a new corollary pops into sight. A corollary more complex than the ones you extracted last week. A corollary that dictates a new shape, from a proton to a planet to a protein. A corollary that dictates, allows, or sneezes forth a new recruitment strategy. But a corollary that's limited in its wiggle room. A corollary that only gives birth to a few new emergent properties. Astonishing emergent properties. Jaw-dropping emergent properties. But emergent properties operating within rigid constraints. Emergent properties that can do their thing, that can dance their brand-new dance, pretty much at the same time and pretty much all over the place.

Imagine a hundred trillion students doing their homework in whatever corner or crease of the cosmos they can find, from the fourth planet of the red dwarf star Gliese 876, fifteen light-years from where you are sitting now, to a desk deep in the stacks of the Reed College library in Portland, Oregon. You are all working from the same 165 words, the same simple rules, the same axioms, at the same time. Early in the class, you all yanked the same corollary from your axioms pretty much simultaneously. Later in the class, some of you found one corollary while others found yet another. But the number of corollaries you found was strictly limited by the axioms. You all hauled the same form—from a quark to a lithium atom to a galaxy and a star—from your axioms pretty much at once.

Even when you get ten billion years into your homework, the possibilities that you can yank from your axioms and from their ten billion years of corollaries will be yoked and chained, rigidly constrained. Take one corollary that the cosmos coughed out at roughly the ten-billion-year mark: life. All the life forms we know show the marks of the Xerox Effect. All use cells. And all use DNA. Even viruses. Viruses are so simple that they don't have cells. But they are cell-and-DNA dependent. They are a recruitment strategy that's evolved the ploy of the pirate, the ploy of hijacking the DNA and cells of others. Then using those captured cells and DNA to produce copies of themselves. So the number of forms of life on this planet is far more limited than we like to think. All are drawn from the implicate properties of what cells and DNA can achieve. And among those implicate forms and processes are you and me.

Again, why such sameness underlying what looks like rich and rollicking diversity? The simple rules. The axioms. We are all children of the big bang. We are all children of the same starting algorithms, the same deep structures, the same Ur patterns, the same handful of cosmic commandments. We are all children of attraction and repulsion and their spinoffs, differentiation and integration—children of opposites joined at the hip. We are all children of a cosmos of enormous cruelty and of staggering wonders, children of a universe that in the long run always steps up, not down.

We are all children of simple rules generating new big pictures and we are all children of new big pictures coaxing new implications from the simple rules that gave them birth. We are all emergent properties run amuck. But run amuck within a narrow range of possibilities. We are all children of the magic beans. We are all children of the axioms at the start of the cosmos.

BAKING THE BIG BAGEL:
HOW TO START AND END A UNIVERSE

One last story, then I'll let you be. A story about pulling implications from simple rules. From simple assumptions. About discovering that those implications make a prediction. And about a prediction that comes true.

It's not a story about much. It's just a tale that explains the beginning, middle, and end of the cosmos.

You are twelve years old. You've been in science one way or another since you were ten. One day in school one of your female classmates swivels her eyes toward you and makes eye contact. You are shocked. You haven't realized it until now, but your fellow students do not normally look at you. And today your female costudent is about to do something else abnormal. She is going to talk to you. What in the world could drive her to such lengths?

"I told my mother," she says, "that you understand the theory of relativity." The year is 1955, and in those days it is said that only seven people on the planet understand the theory of relativity. The number is up from the three of Eddington's day. You are committed to absolute honesty, to the first rule of science, the truth at any price including the price of your life. But on this one, you keep your mouth shut. The only thing you have going for you at the age of twelve is your science and your reputation for having a brain. So you do not blurt out the simple fact that you do not know the theory of relativity.

Instead, when school lets out, you ride your bicycle straight to the green and leafy Buffalo street that holds your local library. The librarians know you better than your mother does. So you park your bike outside, go in, and ask for everything the library has on the theory of relativity. The librarians rummage through the card catalog and give you two hardcover books. One is by Albert Einstein and two collaborators. It is big and fat. The other is by Einstein alone. It is skinny with a blue cover. You take the books home, hole up in your beige second-story bedroom overlooking the trees of Delaware Park, and read the big fat book first. There is very little you can understand. Each page has roughly twenty words of English and a flood of equations. But you stick with it for four hours. You've discovered that sometimes if you read something you don't understand straight through, you end up understanding more than you thought you would.

Then comes eight o'clock, just two hours before bedtime, and you are only sixty pages into the book. You have a mere two hours left in which to understand the theory of relativity or face humiliation the next day at school. So you abandon the fat book and turn to the skinny one, the one written by Einstein on his own. In his introduction to his book, it feels as if Einstein is reaching out through the pages and grabbing you by the collar. It feels as if

Einstein has written this introduction specifically to you. In essence, Uncle Albert says that to be a genius, it is not enough to come up with a theory only seven men in the world can understand. To be a genius, you have to be able to write that theory so simply and clearly that anyone with a reasonable degree of intelligence and a high school education can understand it. In other words, Einstein tells you that to be a scientific thinker, you have to have more than your knowledge of science. You have to become a writer.

Fine. A superb lesson. But you still have a problem. By 10:00 p.m., you still do not understand the theory of relativity. At least you do not think you understand it. Many years later it will turn out that you do. You do understand the theory. But you don't believe it. Without the context, without the six-thousand-year story of the evolution of the axiom, it feels to you as if what you understand must be wrong. All wrong.

Flip forward four years. You are now far older and more sophisticated. You now know far more about science. Why? You are sixteen. You've been reading two books a day since you were ten. Mostly science fiction and honest-to-god science. And you are working during your summer vacation as a lab assistant at the world's first cancer research facility, the Roswell Park Memorial Cancer Institute,[42] in, of all places, your hometown, Buffalo. You've been smuggled in by your best friend's father, the head of the biochemistry department, Dr. David Pressman. Pressman was a student of Nobel Prize–winner Linus Pauling, and he is a pioneer in research on the immune system. You are illegal at the cancer research institute. There is a student summer program, but it's for nineteen-year-olds. You are three years too young.

What's more, you are a terrible lab assistant. You are OK with the photospectrometer and the scintillation counter. You do a fine job of injecting noxious things into the veins in the ears of poor, innocent rabbits. But washing test tubes with acetone is not your forte. Thank God that you are reasonably good at something else. Brainstorming.

You have been given a minder, a scientist over your head, an adult to make sure that you do not destroy too much lab equipment. His name is Phil Fish. He is a biochemist. He is a short and chunky native of Boston who feels that by going to Buffalo, he has planted himself beyond the pale of civilization, in the wild wild West. When you first meet him, he shows you his desk. Piled on it are six heaps of books. Six heaps. Roughly forty-eight books. And they are in German. Every single one of them. Dr. Fish has spent years reading the books on the piles on the right. And he feels that he has another three years to go before he finishes reading the piles on the left. Why is he doing all this Teutonic cramming? To work out a way to synthesize one molecule. Just one. Making that molecule will be the only raison d'être of Phil Fish's career for over five years. This, you decide, is not the kind of scientist you want to be. You do not want to be a gopher tunneling a hole so deep that you can no longer see. You want to be an eagle flying over the landscape, seeing the panorama. And piecing together the big picture.

One of the nineteen-year-old students in the Roswell Park summer program is someone you've known in the past. When you were twelve, he was the kid you conspired with for a full summer to conceive a game-playing electronic machine. A precomputer that won several local science fair prizes. Every day at lunch you, Phil Fish, your former game-playing-machine partner, and another nineteen-year-old who is a brilliant cellist with a mind for science get together and talk. And you have a soaring, roaring time. You fly over the face of all the sciences and combine them with everything else you know, including the arts and history. Washing test tubes you are in hell. But synthesizing knowledge, you are in heaven. Herbert Spencer would have approved. So would Albert Einstein.

The lunch discussions are so exciting that two or three times a week you continue them after the cancer lab closes at 5:00 p.m. All four of you—including Phil Fish—drive out to the big three-story house of the cellist's parents in Clarence, NY, and keep jabbering in the living room until 2:00 a.m. What are you jabbering about? Among other things, you are in pursuit of a mystery.

In 1927, when he was twenty-five years old, Paul Dirac[43] was a fellow of St. John's college, Cambridge. Dirac was the son of a French language teacher from Switzerland and a British librarian. A librarian whose dad had been a ship's captain.

With his pointed chin, his high forehead, his near-Mohawk-like shock of hair, and his intense eyes, Paul Dirac looked as if he was flying through a life. But he was doing it quietly. So quietly that if he spoke two sentences during a dinner party, it was counted as a night of stunning loquacity. For example, there was the dinner party where Dirac was seated next to another bright man known for his silence, the celebrated novelist E. M. Forster. It is said that Dirac and Forster both sat in utter wordlessness through the soup course. Then, just before the main course arrived, Dirac became chatty. He turned to Forster, whose works he had read, and asked, "What happened in the cave?" He was referring to a cave that had appeared in a crucial scene in Forster's book *A Passage to India*. And those six syllables were Dirac's only words. Forster said nothing. But he had been listening. He was just thinking the question through. Both Forster and Dirac remained in silence through the main course. They maintained their silence until the dessert arrived. Then Forster turned to Dirac with an answer: "I do not know." No wonder one of London's newspapers said Dirac was "shy as a gazelle, and modest as a Victorian maid."[44]

But E. M. Forster's cave was not Dirac's biggest mystery. Dirac was dissatisfied with the existing equations for the peculiar movements of the electron. So he combined Einstein's relativity and a new piece of math—the math that described an electron's quantum leaps inside the atom. The math that described how an electron skips from one quantum shell to another without traveling through the space between.[45] When Dirac put the two forms of math together he got a wild hybrid. Among other things, it was a new description of the movement and the spin of the electron. It was a description, a formula, that matched the experimental evidence brilliantly. But Dirac's equation had a bizarre implicit property. It predicted an impossible symmetry. It predicted opposites joined at the hip. Specifically, it predicted a particle that would be a symmetrical counterpart to the electron. It predicted a "positron."

The electron has a negative charge. Dirac's fanciful positron, on the other hand, would be the spitting image of the electron, but it would have a positive charge. But that's not the freaky part. The positron would not be normal matter. It would be something few had ever imagined before: antimatter.

Surely antimatter was fluff and science fiction, a joke. Even Dirac thought it was a glitch in his math, an unpleasant error, an ugly duckling.

But in 1932, four years after Dirac derived his equation, a twenty-seven-year-old American physicist, Caltech's Carl Anderson, saw a peculiar particle streaking through his cloud chamber.[46] That particle fit the predictions made by Dirac's formulae. Dirac's mathematical glitch, the positron, turned out to be real. Dirac's implication derived from new rules was not a wild-assed fiction. And its discovery won Carl Anderson a Nobel Prize.

Antimatter was not a fantasy?! Very strange. The world of the abstract mind, the world of thinking based on axioms, the world of thinking based on finding implicit properties, was matching the real world just as it had when Einstein had put non-Euclidean math together with his eight ugly ducklings from the world of real facts. What was going on here?

***

In 1957, two years before you frantically spout ideas at your lunch table in the cafeteria of the Roswell Park Institute, a new theory—CPT (which stands for charge, parity, and time reversal)[47]—makes a bizarre prediction: "For every particle that exists in nature there is a corresponding antiparticle."[48] There is an entire zoo of antimatter. A carnival, a cavalcade, and a menagerie of antiparticles. And that's where the great mystery you try to solve in the cafeteria of the Roswell Park Institute in 1959 comes in. The spanking-new math of CPT says that matter and antimatter are born together and born in equal amounts. So there should be an equal amount of matter and antimatter in this universe. But there isn't. There is, in fact, a lot of matter. And there is very little antimatter.

So where has all the antimatter gone? The problem is unsolved in the year of your brainstorms—1959. It's still unsolved today. But in 1959, you come up with a solution.

It takes you two months of bouncing ideas off of your friends, but by the end of the summer, you have a theory of the beginning, middle, and end of the universe. You call it the Big Bagel. The Bloom toroidal model Here's how it works.

You imagine that the cosmos is a torus. What's a torus? Topology is a mathematical study that deals with the ways you can twist, bend, and stretch things without tearing their surfaces.[49] Things like the surface on which a cosmos might ride. And in topology, a torus is a doughnut. Or, because you are Jewish, a bagel.

Imagine a bagel with a very tiny hole. You've seen them. One of those tightly puckered, anally retentive holes. In the beginning is the big bang. The big bang explodes from the bagel's infinitesimally tiny hole. And the big bang gives birth to two universes: universe number one gushes upward from the tiny hole and climbs toward the top of the bagel. And universe number two simultaneously bursts forth down below and spreads on the bagel's bottom. The universe that's climbing toward the bagel's top is the universe of matter. The universe spreading on the bagel's bottom is the universe of antimatter.

So the universe gives birth to equal amounts of matter and antimatter. But each is on a different surface.

Now for the implications of the bagel's shape. A bagel is a bendy and curvaceous baked good. And bends are the name of the game in Einstein's general theory of relativity—his theory of gravity. Space tells matter how to move and matter tells space how to bend. Right? So the bagel's curves tell matter where to travel and how fast to go. The climb from the hole of the bagel toward its upper surface is steep.[50] That means that matter moves extremely fast, fleeing from its birth spot. As you know, today that rapid expansion is called "inflation."[51] Then the curve of the bagel levels off. Which means that matter's outward rush slows down. But what happens once matter goes over the bagel's hump? What happens once matter passes the highest point on the bagel's upper curve? Big bagel theory says that matter begins to gain speed again. It begins to rush. It slides down the bagel's steep outer curve toward the bagel's outer edge.

Why? Gravity.

The same thing that's going on on the bagel's top happens on the bagel's bottom. But it's happening with antimatter. Antimatter rushes from the bagel's hole down the steep well on the underside, levels out on the very bottom, passes the underhump, then begins to rush upward again toward the outer edge.

Yes, once they pass the bagel's hump, the matter and antimatter universe pick up speed and rush toward each other's embrace. From a position in just one of these universes, it looks as if matter that goes over the bagel's hump is "accelerating away from itself," picking up speed in a frantic effort to flee from its fellow matter. But what makes matter flee? What makes it rush away? An irony. The speed rush that looks like repulsion isn't. Instead, it's a force of attraction. Gravity.

Opposites are joined at the hip.

Gravity is a language, the language that the matter universe on top of the bagel shares with the antimatter universe on the bottom. Gravity is a form of communication, a form of stimulus and response with which the two universes call to each other. Gravity is a common whisper with which they beckon and seduce. And once the two universes run out of the energy that has shot them away from each other, they "sense" each other's call. They slowly begin to fall into each other's arms. They slowly begin to succumb to the pull of each other's gravity.

The bulges, humps, and slopes of the bagel are the shape of a gravitational field. The gravitational curves of the bagel tell the two universes how to separate at the bagel's hole. And they tell the two universes how to rejoin at the bagel's edge.

So how does the universe end? Matter and antimatter meet on the bagel's outer rim. And they annihilate. But there is a topological trick. A trick based on the notion in topology of the Klein bottle. What's a Klein bottle? It's a bottle whose neck is stretched as if it were melted and reworked by a glass blower. Reworked so that the neck loops downward, reenters the bottle, and becomes the bottle's bottom. Reworked so that the neck loops down and pierces the bottle's side.

Topology's Klein bottle. The bottle with the neck that goes into another dimension. *Courtesy of Thảo luận Thành viên: Tttrung, Wikimedia Commons.*

Very hard to describe in words. But here's the trick. The Klein bottle's neck loops down and goes through its side. The neck pushes through the side of the bottle like a red-hot poker. And yet it never slices, pokes, or punctures the side it passes· through. It leaves that side untouched, unstabbed, and intact. Huh? How do you punch through something without harming it? How do you slice through a sheet without cutting it? You go into another dimension. You go into one of the many extra dimensions left to us by Bernhard Riemann. And this is not science fiction. It is standard topology.

Big bagel theory has the same sort of trick. When matter and antimatter meet at the other edge of the bagel they annihilate. They turn to raw energy. And they do a dimensional flip. The outer edge of the bagel becomes the bagel's hole. The hole from which a new big bang emerges.

That's it. Big bagel theory. A doughnut theory of the universe. So simple, yet it took you an entire summer. Sometimes you can be very slow.

What happens to big bagel theory? Nothing. You abandon it. It is so simple that you are sure that it is comic book science. Kid stuff. Then, in 1997, when you are e-mailing and telephoning with University of Tel Aviv department of physics head Eshel ben Jacob, you have a strange notion. An intuitive hunch. This is a universe one of whose deep structures is symmetry. This is a universe in which opposites are joined at the hip. That is one of the intuitive reasons you came up with big bagel theory forty years earlier: to fill out a symmetry. Now another symmetry is tugging at you. Just as the electromagnetic force has two opposite and equal faces—attraction and repulsion—you feel that gravity has to have a repulsive side. And you tell Eshel, for Lord knows what reason, that we are about to discover it. The negative side of gravity. The repulsive side of gravity.

A few months later, an announcement comes from the astronomical community. By tracking the redshift of "standard candles," Type 1a super-novas,[52] astronomers have arrived at a strange conclusion. Galaxies are accelerating.[53] They are gaining speed. They are rushing faster and faster away from each other. The scientific community is stumped. Where does the energy for this acceleration come from? What is the source of the thrust for this increase in speed? And what does this speedup mean for the ultimate fate of the cosmos?

A few months later the astronomical community comes up with another finding. The acceleration started roughly 7.7 billion years into the cosmos's existence, 7.7 billion years ABB, seven billion seven hundred million years after the big bang.[54]

And suddenly the big bagel theory looks viable. Not just viable, necessary. Why? Scientists are stumped about the source of the energy powering the acceleration. They are stumped about the power provider, the provider of the push. They are so desperate that they revive Einstein's idea of a cosmological constant, an idea related to the curve of the universe. The idea that you recall Einstein slammed as his biggest blunder. But the cosmological constant does not explain the mysterious power source. It doesn't explain the acceleration generator. It merely describes what we've just discovered.[55] It translates the finding of acceleration into equations. But it offers not a whit of explanation. So the stumped cosmologists come up with a name for the mystery power source, the unexplained force responsible for the cosmic speedup: dark energy. But this is of no more use than the cosmological constant. Why? In reality physicists are reduced to guessing games about what dark energy might be.

But big bagel theory has an explanation for dark energy. What is it? Gravity. The gravitational pull that summons the matter universe on top of the bagel to rush toward the embrace of the antimatter universe on the bagel's bottom.

The bagel's hump is crucial in all of this. Once they go over the bagel's hump, says big bagel theory, galaxies on the top of the bagel seem to flee from each other. The galaxies on our surface of the bagel—the upper side—speed up, putting distance between themselves and their fellow galaxies. Where is that acceleration hump? Where is the curve that flicks matter into a mad rush to escape the galactic herd? The evidence indicates that it's at the 7.7-billion-year mark, the mark, astronomers have discovered, at which the universe begins what they call "accelerating away from itself." What does that imply for the cosmos? Its end may not be hundreds of trillions of years away, as many cosmologists think. Its end may be a mere billion years or so away.

And what does that mean for us human beings? It is our obligation to defeat this annihilation by squeezing all that we are, all that we value, through the annihilation at the bagel's edge, through the anally tiny hole at the next universe's center, and into the universe to come. It is our task to come through the next annihilation rejoicing. Intact and giddy with the power of our feat.

And what is dark energy again? It's the gravity of the antimatter universe. The gravity of the matter universe and the antimatter universe rushing toward each other. Rushing toward annihilation in each other's embrace. Annihilation and rebirth.

Which means that Fred Hoyle and David Bohm may be right about one thing. Universes may oscillate like a photon. Pulsing from birth to death and back again. Repeating fundamental deep structures, simple rules, Ur patterns. Repeating the patterns of opposites joined at the hip. Repeating the patterns of attraction and repulsion. Repeating the patterns of Pythagoras and of Herbert Spencer—differentiation and integration. Repeating the patterns of massive big-picture integration. Integration that opens fortune cookies and redefines meaning over and over again.

***

Is there support for the big bagel model? In 1984 at the Landau Institute in Moscow, Dr. Alexei Starobinski studied the data available at that point on the cosmic microwave background radiation and concluded, in the words of the *New York Times*, "that the universe could have been born as a doughnut."[56] In 2003, Max Tegmark, then a cosmologist at the University of Pennsylvania, now at MIT, used far more sophisticated data on the fluctuations in the cosmic background radiation, data from NASA's Wilkinson Microwave Anisotropy Probe, to consider toroidal models in articles in *Science*[57] and in one of the top journals in physics, the American Physical Society's *Physical Review D*.[58] Tegmark's work and that of many others hit the *New York Times* in a March 11, 2003, story headlined "Universe as a Doughnut: New Data, New Debate." But in the end, Tegmark "ruled out" what even he called the "bagel" model.[59] Then the cosmic doughnut hit the headlines again in 2008, this time on the prestige British science journal *Nature*'s news site. A German team led by Frank Steiner had run the data from the Wilkinson

Microwave Anisotropy Probe through four different forms of analysis[60]—four different forms of translation—and had concluded that "the doughnut gave the best match to the Wilkinson Microwave Anisotropy Probe data."[61]

So the toroidal shape, the bagel shape, was being kicked around. Not in the form you proposed it. Not with two universes separating, then crunching together again. But, hey, at least the bagel was in play.

Then there's another aspect of your big bagel theory, your idea of two universes on two separate surfaces saying good-bye to each other and eventually getting back together again. Your idea of the matter universe climbing from the bagel's hole up its topside and the antimatter universe sliding down from the hole on the bagel's bottom side.

Several concepts arose that support the notion of two universes on different but adjacent surfaces. Surfaces like the bagel's bottom and the bagel's top. One is the idea of a Saran-Wrap®pish sort of surface that comes from string theory. It's called a brane—named for a membrane. A brane is thin, like plastic wrap. And an entire universe rides on each brane, on each Saran-Wrappish sheet. Neil Turok, the director of Perimeter Institute for Theoretical Physics in Waterloo, Canada, and two Princeton physicists, Paul McFadden and Paul Steinhardt, have a brane-based theory that's very reminiscent of the big bagel.[62] In Steinhardt and Turok's model, there are two of these plastic-wrap-thin branes. There are two universes a hair's breadth apart. They are separate universes, blithely unaware of each other's existence. Unaware except for one small fact. Dark energy is a force that pulls them together. Periodically they bump into each other. Yes, every once in a while they collide. And each time they collide, they set off a big bang whose energy sends them rushing away from each other again. So they alternate between big bangs and big crashes. Does this sound big bagelish?

And there are additional cyclic models of the cosmos.[63] Models in which the cosmos annihilates, then is reborn in a new big bang. Martin Bojowald's cosmos[64] is one of these. The Penn State loop quantum gravity cosmologist proposes a model in which "branes approach collision and bounce back without actual collision."[65] That near-head-on crash ends one universe and starts another one.

New York University's Georgi Dvali[66] even suggests that gravity may leak from branes, an idea that goes one more small step toward the idea that separate universes on separate branes may be able to communicate with each other. One small step toward a universe on the top of a bagel beckoning to a universe on the underside with gravity.

Then there's Alexander Kashlinsky, a senior staff scientist at NASA's Goddard Space Center, who has measured the motion of nearly eight hundred galaxy clusters against the backdrop of the cosmic background radiation and has spotted what he calls "dark flow"—a speed rush of galaxies that seems to defy the assumptions of what's called the "conventional model" of the cosmos. This rush of galaxies seems to be hurrying toward a goal, and, to Kashlinsky, it seems to hint at something "tugging" on them. And cosmologists like Anthony Aguirre of the University of California, Santa Cruz, believe that if dark flow is for real, it could be evidence for what Aguirre calls "other universes." Could Kashlinsky's tug come from the pull of just one other universe—an antimatter universe on the bottom of the bagel?[67] And could the antimatter cosmos on the underside of the bagel be responsible for the galaxies' unaccountable speed?

The bottom line? There are a lot of cyclic universe theories doing the rounds. But the big bagel appears to be alone in something crucial: explaining dark energy.

***

Big bagel theory was adolescent science. Comic book science. Science with a bit of topology, a bit of cosmology, and a bit of theoretical physics. What made it so primitive? It didn't have equations. And without equations, you can't have science. Right?

In 2011, you went to dinner at the house of a friend, Charles Hope, cofounder of blip.tv. Charles is a computer genius who loves math and theoretical physics. So one of his guests was an astronomer from the City University of New York, Shana Tribiano. You explained big bagel theory to her. And she said point blank that without equations, no theory is astronomy. Try telling that to John Conway or to Stephen Wolfram. They wouldn't complain about the lack of equations. They would complain about the lack of cellular automata. And even Conway and Wolfram might easily overlook the fact that both math and cellular automata are deep-structure translators, Ur pattern grabbers. Both math and cellular automata are metaphors in disguise.

What does big bagel theory have to do with the themes of this book? First off, in a book that touches so often on the evolution of the cosmos, it's nice to wave good-bye with an explanation of the cosmos's beginning, middle, and end. After all, an explanation of the cosmos's end—the concept of heat death—helped make entropy and the second law of thermodynamics memorable. And I'd like to make it easy for you to remember this book.

Second, big bagel theory is based on Einstein's notions of the geometric underpinnings of the cosmos. It is a batch of implications pulled from the axioms of twentieth-century science. It is the epitome of differentiation— two universes parting like twins from a singularity, exploding from what Georges Lemaître calls a "cosmic egg," and going on their own two paths. It is opposites joined at the hip personified. It's time the translator at work. It is the ultimate in stimulus and response—two universes going through a period of repulsion, then beckoning each other with an attractive force, gravity. Opening the fortune cookie and doing what the message says. In fact, it may be one of the biggest examples of communication we will ever have. Not to mention meaning.

WILL SILICON AXIOMS FLY?

Axioms began twenty-three hundred years ago with Aristotle. They started as truths that Aristotle said we could all take for granted. Assumptions Aristotle thought were so basic that none of us could quibble about them. With Euclid, axioms began a journey. A journey that would turn them into the foundation stones on which you could build entire mathematical systems. Foundation stones on which you could build by unfolding, unpacking, and extracting implicit properties. Unpacking implicit properties with the raw force of reason.

But you didn't unpack implicit properties with just one man's or woman's reason. You unpacked the implicit properties of axioms via a reasoning process that went on for generation after generation. For century after century and for millennium after millennium. A reasoning process that had its own identity and that sustained itself no matter what humans were in its grip. A multigenerational reasoning process that was a hungry form. A recruitment strategy. A recruitment strategy that turned its participants into components of a search engine. A search engine feeling out the distant corners of possibility space.

Then the non-Euclideans—Karl Friedrich Gauss, János Bólyai, and Nikolai Lobachevsky—made something else clear: if you flip just one axiom, if you change just one of your foundation stones, the structure you extract will be very different. Instead of the geometry of a flat surface, you will get the geometry of curved surfaces. Curved surfaces that are sometimes weird as hell. But this left a big question.

Was abstract reasoning about the implications of axioms merely a useless way to keep overwrought intellectuals entertained? Did axiom flipping produce abstract monsters that only a math addict with his head in the clouds could love? Did mathematical oddities like curved geometries have anything to do with the world that you and I live in?

Then came Albert Einstein. Einstein claimed that he had flipped just one axiom—the axiom of time. But in reality, Einstein had pulled a first. He had not just flipped one axiom. He had flipped many. He had flipped the ideas we take for granted about time, space, matter, solidity, speed, and you name it. He'd also helped nail down the notion that atoms make up matter, the idea that when those atoms move, their flit and flutter is what we perceive as heat, and the proposition that light is made up of nanobricks, photons, photons that swizzle like waves but are also particles. Einstein had used the seemingly useless geometry of the non-Euclideans to flip an entire network of interlinked axioms, a mesh whose linkage meant as much as its individual threads. A mesh of axioms that fit together like the words of a sentence. Change one word and you can change the whole thing. Like when a judge holds your fate in his hands and changes his conclusion from "I declare you guilty" to "I declare you innocent."

Einstein did what Darwin had done only forty-six years earlier. He'd changed the meaning of nearly everything in his field by putting what physicists knew into a new big picture. And he'd gone out of his way to emphasize that he'd found this big picture by using muscular comprehension, muscular metaphor. He'd done it by imagining what it would feel like to run and catch up with a wave of light. Muscular metaphor had produced something very odd. It had helped Einstein use his axiom flip plus his new worldview to wrap a new layer of meaning around the onion of physics. But Einstein had also done something else that previous axiom flippers had found impossible. He had made real-world predictions. And, it bears repeating, despite the clear insanity of Albert Einstein's axiom flip: his predictions had come true.

Then, over sixty years later, Benoît Mandelbrot and John Conway had come along. In the nineteenth century, the non-Euclideans had only flipped one axiom and had kept all the rest. But Mandelbrot and John Conway had invented a new way to extract implications from axioms. They had done it using the computer. And the axioms they'd invented—their simple rules—were brand-new. What's more, Mandelbrot and Conway had shown that astonishing things could emerge from simple rules. Large-scale patterns with lives of their own. Emergent forms that popped from the simple formulae of Mandelbrot's fractals and from the minimal social IQ of John Conway's checkerboard squares. Forms that were produced by a peculiar kind of mass behavior. A mass behavior that grabs chessboard squares or atoms, choreographs them in a whorl of ornate complexity, then abandons them, moves on, and yanks together another crew. A form that's self-sustaining. A recruitment strategy.

But this time the mathematicians doing the implication extracting, the possibility unfolding, and the reasoning from axioms had not been multi-generational armies of humans. They had been machines. Silicon stand-ins. And these digital helpers had sometimes unpacked more implicate properties in a second than humans had unpacked in centuries.

Then came Stephen Wolfram, and he changed axioms by the millions. Changed millions of them because he, too, had Conway and Mandelbrot's tool. A tool that was the equivalent of billions of mathematicians working with scratch marks on clay, rolls of papyrus, wax tablets, or sheets of paper twenty-four hours a day, seven days a week to extract the implications from axioms. Working to unpack those axioms' implicate properties. And

Wolfram had proposed that if you tried enough clusters of axioms, eventually you could find the handful from which this cosmos had started. You could find the cosmos's magic beans. In essence, Stephen Wolfram had said that if you tried enough new axioms and ran them in the computer, you could solve the God Problem. You could find the way the cosmos creates.

But was that really true?

***

Topping it all off, Mandelbrot, Conway, and Wolfram's systems had solved a problem inherent in everything from Euclid's way of proving corollaries to Kant's metaphor of the seed and David Bohm's metaphor of the ink drop in glycerin. All of these systems had started from the future and worked their way backward. None of them had proved that they could work their way forward from nothing. But working their way forward from nothing was exactly what Benoît Mandelbrot's fractals, John Conway's Game of Life, and Stephen Wolfram's cellular automata had done. Euclid, Kant, and Bohm had known in advance where they were going. They had cheated. They had not demonstrated how you could unfold a cosmos from scratch. But Mandelbrot, Conway, and Wolfram had done the very opposite. They had started with very little and had let their toy universes explode and expand, toy universes whose patterns they had not been able to predict. Universes whose patterns had surprised even their makers.

What does starting from nearly nothing and going forward into the realm of shock and surprise mean? Mandelbrot, Conway, and Wolfram had come up with far more convincing metaphors for cosmic creativity. They had come up with far more convincing clues to the God Problem—the problem of how a godless cosmos creates.

And Mandelbrot, Conway, and Wolfram had come up with something more—a form of metaphor that may be able to make the metaphors of men like Herbert Spencer—his differentiation and integration—truly scientific. Mandelbrot, Conway, and Wolfram had shown the way to computer simulations that were replicable. Simulations that may someday take fuzzy ideas, big-picture ideas, and make them precise.

But there's another bottom line here. There's one more test that cellular automata need to pass to prove that they, indeed, isomorph the real world. That they indeed reflect a deep structure of reality. That they capture Ur patterns. Cellular automata need to show that they can predict.[68]

So, like the work of Einstein in 1905, Stephen Wolfram's work awaits validation. It awaits testing in the real world. Will it prove to be the biggest advance in implication unpacking, the biggest breakthrough in axiom flipping since Euclid? That remains to be seen.

But one way or the other, the history of the axiom demonstrates one simple thing—that the creativity of the cosmos may come from unfolding the implicate properties of simple rules. The history of the axiom hints that an entire cosmos may have grown from a handful of magic beans, a handful of primal commandments. It hints that, indeed, the cosmos may be like a math student at Reed College doing her homework step by step, one Planck instant after another. It hints that your corollary generator theory may be on to something.

***

There are other questions raised by the God Problem. Many of them.

Aristotle said metaphor was unscientific. Yet at the heart of every scientific breakthrough there is a central metaphor. Why? Why does metaphor work? Because it captures a primal pattern, an Ur pattern, a pattern showing its swirl, its twitch, its dance, its shape, its strategy. Showing its swivel at an arbitrary level of emergence, a level that we can grasp . . . and grab. A level that we can use to glimpse the pattern clearly. A level at which we can anatomize its twitch. A level at which we can dissect the flick, the flutter, the form as a specimen. A level at which we can use our freeze-frame as a template and a lens. We can use that glimpse, that vivid image, to get a grip on the mystery pattern's repetition at higher and lower levels.

The swirl we see when we flush the toilet shows up in the swirls of electrons that slow down the flow of electricity in a superconductor.[69] The same swirl pops up in the pinwheel spread of a *Paenibacillus vortex* bacteria colony in a petri dish, in the whorls of your fingertip, in the spiral twist of a nautilus shell, in the spiral of seeds on the face of a sunflower, in the spiral of clouds in a hurricane seen from a satellite, in the permanent twister two Earths in size that makes the Red Spot on Jupiter, in the vortices that make the dark spots on the surface of Neptune,[70] and in the spiral arms of galaxies. Understand the spiral in the toilet and you have a key to understanding every other spiral that you see. From the submicroscopic to the unbelievably huge. What's more, you may well have a glimpse deep down into the structures that kicked off this universe. You may well have a specimen of an Ur pattern doing its thing. And through that toilet swirl, you may even be able to peek deep down to the simple laws that started it all. The axioms at the beginning of the universe. The magic beans with which the ultimate implication unpacker, the ultimate corollary generator, a universe doing her homework, started it all.

***

Next question? Why did the hunger for evolution push its way from nothingness to the surface long before Charles Darwin published *On the Origin of Species by Means of Natural Selection* in 1859? Why was there a craving for an idea that scarcely existed? Because of the obsessive-compulsive itch of recruitment strategies. Because of the hunger of the stuttering forms. Because forms like spheres, spirals, quarks, and stars seem anxious to repeat themselves. They recapitulate with intense insistence. They iterate. And they often do it with supersynchrony, performing the same act in quintillions of separate places pretty much at the same time. Sometimes this plethora of repetitions changes the very nature of the medium in which it repeats itself. Like a hundred stones dropped simultaneously into a pond change the still surface into a madman's plaid. What's more, when an old pattern repeats in this brand new medium, it occasionally becomes something new. Very new. But at heart, the old form remains the same. Why?

Because it is the manifestation of an ambition. Because a new form and a new recruitment strategy are the latest corollaries pushing their way from their hiding place in the starting axioms. Because the new guise of an old form is a corollary ripe for the picking. A corollary with what seems to be a will of its own. A corollary struggling to go from possibility to reality, from implication into being. From the implicate into the world of the everyday. But is the corollary struggling to be found or struggling to be *invented*? Struggling to be conjured from the realm of fantasy in the mind of a human being?

And what accounts for this hunger of form to sculpt reality? What accounts for this compulsion of pattern to repeat? Why does the cosmos we inhabit appear to be persistent, manic, driven, and motivated? Why does it appear to be a cosmos with a primitive precursor of will? That is just one of the many mysteries raised by the God Problem.

CONCLUSION: THE BIG BANG TANGO— QUARKING IN THE SOCIAL COSMOS

> *Scientists are explorers. They are attracted to unknown territories.*[71]
> —Mike Hansell, emeritus professor of animal architecture,
> University of Glasgow

Yes, corollary generator theory leaves you with a truckload of mysteries. If this is a universe that starts with a simple set of rules, a handful of magic beans, a tiny number of axioms, a universe that creates by doing 10^{43} homework assignments per second, how do corollaries and implications come to be? How does the complex hide inside the simple? How do the ornate and the extravagant lurk in the stripped-down nudity of simple rules?

Where do the shapes and strange behaviors of the cosmic pieces come from—the quarks, the atoms, the galaxies, the stars, the cells, and you and me? And how does their brilliant fit emerge? How does that extraordinary fit carry within it new big pictures? And how do new big pictures carry within themselves such astonishing new meanings for their parts? How does this cosmos constantly invent whole new ways of fitting in and of fleshing out something higher and more ornate? How does creativity emerge from simple rules? From attraction and repulsion? From differentiation and integration? How do emergent properties come to be?

Is there more to the mystery of why metaphor, math, and experiments work? Is there more to the magic with which a geometric proposition, an algebraic formula, a ball rolling down a grooved board in a room in Pisa, or two rings of ripples in a glass-bottomed ripple tank in a London lecture room capture the patterns of a complicated cosmos? Why can you translate the patterns of the cosmos into so many mediums, symbol sets, and substances: from the neurotransmitter flows of your brain to scratches in clay, ink on paper, the pulses of a microprocessor, and the flash of pixels on a screen? Are simple rules, deep structures, and Ur patterns mere fantasies that we use to simplify things for ourselves? Are they mere artifacts of our minds? Or are they things in the cosmos itself?

Is there yet another underlying pattern that shows itself in attraction and repulsion? Does attraction and repulsion = the fission-fusion strategy = integration and differentiation? Are all three the same things in different clothes?

And do simple rules = Ur patterns = Peano's primitives = axioms = metaphors?

Are we imposing our own experience on nature when we use anthropomorphic terms like persistence and will to describe the evolution of the cosmos? Or are we acknowledging a heritage handed down by our earliest ancestor, the big bang? Are we really instruments of a cosmos searching out her potential, instruments of a cosmos that uses her progeny to reinvent herself? Are we really communities of molecules that molecules use to make new molecules? Are we really among the search engines that the cosmos uses to feel out her next implicit properties, the next corollaries of her starting rules?

And there's more. Are we pushed ahead by the past or pulled ahead by the future? Is there more to this universe than causality? Is there also a hint of teleology?

Is time really the Great Translator, the great extractor of implicit properties, the prime mover that constantly inches the cosmos into the wilderness of possibility space? Is each tick of time an extractor of information, an interpreter, an extractor of meaning?

Then there are the mysteries of shape shock. How does the cosmos turn time and space into quarks, and light into green leaves, grasses, and shrubbery on the only planet in our solar system with liquid water?

Where do properties like Pythagorean triples and the right angles of a twelve-knot rope come from? Not to mention the electron shells around the nucleus of an atom, the slosh of liquids, and the spirals on your fingertip?

Something vital is missing from the 2,350-year-long collective project of science. That missing something is an explanation for the mysteries that George Henry Lewes called emergence. An explanation for the mysteries that Herbert Spencer called progress. An explanation for the mysteries that the Santa Fe Institute folks called complexity. We are missing an explanation for the riddles that skulk in the metaphor of Karl Ernst von Baer and Hans Driesch, the mysteries that hide in the metaphor of the embryo.

***

Remember the first two rules of science: the truth at any price including the price of your life, and look at things right under your nose as if you've never seen them before? In the spirit of rule number two—look at things that you and everyone around you take for granted, then proceed from there—you have suggested five heresies. You have proposed a modest axiom shift.

- You've proposed a reversal of Aristotle's primary axiom. You've proposed that *A* does not equal *A*. And you've suggested that opposites are joined at the hip. Which means that sometimes *A* does equal *A*. Sometimes a frog is just a frog. But only sometimes.
- You've proposed a reversal of the basic rule of arithmetic. You've proposed that one plus one does not equal two. You've suggested that one plus one often equals something far, far off the number line. Sometimes one plus one summons an emergent property.
- You've proposed a reversal of the second law of thermodynamics, a reversal of the concept of entropy. You've proposed something that seems obvious: the universe is not running down, the universe is running up.
- You've proposed that randomness is not as random as it seems. You've

proposed that randomness is rigidly constrained. Which, frankly, is just what you'd expect if the cosmos were unfolding from a handful of simple starting rules.

- And you've proposed that information theory is wrong. You've argued that the meat of the matter is something that Claude Shannon deliberately left out: meaning. Meaning comes from your place in a big picture. From your place in many big pictures at once. And most important, meaning comes from your place in a web of cosmic gossip. Meaning comes from your place in a cosmos that is profoundly "relational," profoundly social . . . and profoundly conversational.

What does all of this come down to?

We have vastly underrated the cosmos that gave us birth. We have understated her achievements, her capacities, and her creativity. We've set aside will, purpose, and persistence in a magic enclosure and have claimed that the qualities of push and stick-to-itiveness do not belong to nature, they belong solely to us human beings. Will, compulsion, drive, and unrelenting determination—these are virtues that we say belong only to conscious entities. In the process we've missed one of the most astounding things around us: the hunger of the stuttering forms. And we've made another mistake. We've been certain that we can understand the cosmos based solely on material things. But we've missed the astonishing capacity of immaterial things. We've missed the secular magic of a wave. A thing that is a no thing. An entity that is form and process all at once. A merry-go-round that masters matter, commands it, grabs it in a fist. Then lets it go. A whirl that is independent of the water or the air that it pirates, twists, and twirls. A seducer, a kidnapper, and a recruiter. A moving metabolism independent of the matter on which it feeds.

Yes, a wave is as independent of the space, air, or water that it sucks in, then tosses out, as you are of the stuff you have for lunch. Today you fuel yourself on watercress salad. Tomorrow you eat lasagna. The next you eat a steak. Yet you do not become a pasta, a cow, or leaf. Instead, the pasta, cow, or leaf becomes you.

You are a wave. Every minute you say good-bye to more than a billion combinations of postsynaptic receptors in your brain and replace them with new ones. You do the same with the cells that line your digestive tract[72] and that make up your skin. And you constantly shift your mind from one obsession to another. Yet you retain an identity. Something more puzzling than mere substance continues to impose the shifting flicker of a you. No, it is not an immortal soul. And yes, it will cease when you die. But that does not diminish its mystery. That does not reduce its astonishing ability to persist as something beyond the atoms and molecules of which it's made. Your identity presents wonders that even outshine the astonishment of cells and DNA. Wonders science must learn to explain.

Hegel said that all history is spirit becoming matter. And in a sense he was right. Your identity is a pattern holding sway over a hundred trillion cells that change constantly. Yet your "you" has a coherence, a shape, and a way of going about things that is all its own. Your self is a dance that uses matter to whisk from the invisible and the impossible into the gasses, dusts, and jellies of reality. Your "you" is spirit without the religious connotations. It is the secular equivalent to soul. It is a recruitment strategy. Where does your "you" come from? How does it come to be? Implicit orders, corollaries hidden in axioms, and emergent properties tell a bit of the story, but only the slightest bit.

We are patterns with ambition. We are big pictures on the prowl. We are spirit-in-action bursting forth in a cosmos devoid of gods, of afterlives, and of immortality. But we are not the first forms that immaterial pattern, spirit-in-action has donned. Immaterial identities also work their sorcery on quarks, quanta, atoms, stars, and galaxies. Recruitment strategies are alive in the search patterns of bacteria and bees. They are equally alive in stock markets and trees. But we are the most complex social project that protons and electrons have ever attempted to achieve. We are the repeaters of the ancient patterns of attraction and repulsion, repeaters through whom the cosmos has sketched new big pictures and woven new tapestries. We are the cosmos's tools for fantasy. We are her first vessels of dreams. And yet we are only the foothills. Only the stepping stones. Only the starting blocks for the cosmos's next big leaps.

***

What is quarking in the social cosmos all about? How does this universe do her big bang tango? In those mysteries lie the real answers to the question of how a cosmos without a bearded and bathrobed god creates. In those mysteries lie the real answer to the God Problem.

***

And never forget. Sometimes new questions are more important than new answers.

ACKNOWLEDGMENTS

Terry Jean Rosenberg, Linda Regan, Jay Kenoff, Amir Siddiqui, Derek Enlander, David Tamm, T. J. Kincaid ("The Amazing Atheist"), Mark Sklawer, Antonino Vittorio D'Accampo, Mathew Tombers, David Krebs, Bob Guccione Jr., Judy Rubin, and Jonathan Spiel.

Buzz Aldrin, Sabine Allaeys, Amara Angelica, Kate Archer, Jean-Paul Baquiast, Gary Barnhard, Jeremy Barry, Howard Baskind, Don Beck, Eshel ben-Jacob, Berel Berko, Bonnie Bernstein, the members of the Big Bang Tango Media Lab, Richard Block, Kimberly Blozie, Dennis Broe, James Burke, Alex Burns, Hank Campbell, Eric Carmen, Andrew Cohen, Peter Colen, Andrew Conrad, Troy Conrad, Suzie Conway, Ted Coons, A. J. Croce, Sus Cue-Sagman, Bruce Damer, Tom Dannheiser, Don Davis, Joseph Decuir, Jon DeLore, Nancy Ellis, Burt Feuerstein, Richard Foreman, Robin Fox, Karina Freudenthal, Peter Garretson, Danny Goldberg, Raghavan Gopalaswami, Jonathan Gordon, Chris Grayson, Noelle Pollet Greco, Gustav Grob, Dan Hancock, Deena Kristi Hays, Charles Hope, Mark Hopkins, Feng Hsu, Katherine Hulit, Ginger Ingalls, Nat Irvin, Joel Isaacson, Pamela James, Rob Jacobson, Shy'Ann Jie, Darwin Marcus Johnson, Michael Johnson, Pascal Jouxtel, Pierre Jovanovic, Elizabeth Gallager Kennick, Bob Krone, Leonard Kuker, Renée Kuker, Pavel Kurakin, Jonathan Kurtz, Jon Labore, Mark Lamonica, Ida Langsam, Mike Levine, Henry Levy, Steven Johnson Leyba, David Livingston, Lisa Lyons, Jordan Macleod, Ephraim Mann, Rhonda Markowitz, Mark Marshall, Terry Martin, Mara McCann, Rob McConnell, Chris McCulloch, David McFadzean, Michael Mendizza, Suzie Dove Miles, Edgar Mitchell, Steven L. Mitchell, Jonathan Moorehead, George Noory, Ghanem Nuseibeh, Richard O'Neill, Yuri Ozhigov, Nando Pelusi, Kaja Perina, Stephanie Phelan, Daniel Pinchbeck, Grace Piper, Ian Punnett, Stephanie Rooker, Jeff Rude, Linda Diane Scalf, Jason Schneider,

Marty Scott, Howard Shalwitz, Janet Shalwitz, Robert Shalwitz, Shirley Shalwitz, Len Sherman, Mayer Spivack, Nova Spivack, Seymour Stein, John Strickland, Michael Sullivan, David Swindle, Mike Taubleb, Matthew Tombers, Ben Tyree, Alisa Kuker Ugalde, Chuck Ugalde, David Walley, Ira Weinstock, Jondi Whitis, Joan Wilson, Nancy Bass Wyden, and Steve Zuckerman.

To Catherine Boucher, Hector Zenil, Ed Pegg Jr., Troy Schaudt, and Marcus Wynne at Wolfram Research.

To DARPA for giving us the Internet. Not to mention Google Books™ Service, Google Scholar™, *Wikipedia*, the Encyclopedia Britannica® Online, Facebook®, TurboNote®, KeyText™, Dropbox®, Carbonite®, Skype™, ABBYY® Screenshot Reader™, Amazon.com®, and Pandora®. And to the staff at the Tea Lounge!

NOTES

FOREWORD

1. Jacques Monod, *Chance and Necessity*, trans. A. Wainhouse (London: Collins, 1972), p. 180.

1. APPETIZERS, CANAPÉS, AND SNACKS

Introduction: I Dare You—The Weirdest Ride in the Universe

1. Andrew Marvell, "To His Coy Mistress," in Hartley Coleridge, *The Life of Andrew Marvell* (London: Joseph Noble, 1835), p. 58.

2. David N. Schramm, *The Big Bang and Other Explosions in Nuclear and Particle Astrophysics* (Singapore: World Scientific, 1996), p. 175; Dmitry S. Gorbunov and Valery A. Rubakov, *Introduction to the Theory of the Early Universe: Hot Big Bang Theory* (Singapore: World Scientific, 2011), pp. 20–21; David Michael Harland, *The Big Bang: A View from the 21st Century* (London: Springer, 2003), p. 233.

The Café Table at the Beginning of the Universe

3. Stephen W. Hawking and Roger Penrose, *The Nature of Space and Time* (Princeton, NJ: Princeton University Press, 1996), pp. 3, 15, 33.

4. Neil F. Comins, *Discovering the Universe: From the Stars to the Planets* (New York: W. H. Freeman, 2008), p. 345.

The Problem with God: The Tale of a Twisted Confession

5. Bertrand Russell, "Why I Am Not a Christian," in *Russell on Religion: Selections from the Writings of Bertrand Russell*, ed. Louis I. Greenspan and Stefan Andersson (London: Routledge, 1999), p. 92. Originally published as a pamphlet in 1927.

6. F. Rachel Magdalene, *On the Scales of Righteousness: Neo-Babylonian Trial Law and the Book of Job*, Brown Judaic Studies 348 (Atlanta: Society of Biblical Literature, 2007), pp. 72, 97; Stephen Mitchell, *The Book of Job* (New York: HarperCollins, 1992), p. xii; Samuel Taylor Coleridge, *The*

Collected Works of Samuel Taylor Coleridge, vol. 12, *Marginalia*, pt. 6, *Valckenaer to Zwick*, ed. H. J. Jackson and George Whalley (Princeton, NJ: Princeton University Press, 2001), p. 98.

7. Norman C. Habel, *The Book of Job: A Commentary* (Philadelphia: Westminster, 1985), p. 54; John R. Beard, *The Autobiography of Satan* (London: Williams and Norgate, 1872), p. 84.

8. Job 1:3–5; Edgar Charles Sumner Gibson, *The Book of Job* (London: Macmillan, 1899), p. 2.

9. Job 1:14–20; Gibson, *Book of Job*, p. 7.

10. Archibald MacLeish, *J. B.* (Boston: Houghton Mifflin, 1989), p. 11.

2. A TASTE OF SIN

Heresy Number One: Why *A* Does Not Equal *A*

1. Alfred Tarski, *Introduction to Logic and to the Methodology of Deductive Sciences* (New York: Oxford University Press, 1995), p. 54; Amita Chatterjee, "Identity Statements," in *Logic, Identity and Consistency: Studies in Philosophical and Non-Standard Logic II*, ed. Pranab Kumar Sen (Mumbai: Allied Publishers, 1998); A. N. Kolmogorov and A. P. Yushkevich, eds., *Mathematics of the 19th Century: Mathematical Logic, Algebra, Number Theory, Probability Theory* (Boston: Birkhäuser, 2001), p. 20.

2. Frank Ayres, *Schaum's Outline of Theory and Problems of Modern Algebra* (New York: Macmillan, 1965), p. 71; Seymour Lipschutz and Marc Lars Lipson, *2000 Solved Problems in Discrete Mathematics* (New York: McGraw-Hill, 1992), p. 19; George Lakoff and Rafael Núñez, *Where Mathematics Comes From: How the Embodied Mind Brings Mathematics into Being* (New York: Basic Books, 2000), p. 113.

3. Morris Kline, *Calculus: An Intuitive and Physical Approach* (New York: Wiley, 1967).

4. Maxime Bôcher and Harry Davis Gaylord, *Trigonometry* (New York: Henry Holt, 1914); Earl William Swokowski and Jeffery Alan Cole, *Algebra and Trigonometry with Analytic Geometry* (Belmont, CA: Brooks/Cole, 2006).

5. Linus Pauling and Edgar Bright Wilson, *Introduction to Quantum Mechanics: With Applications to Chemistry* (New York: McGraw-Hill, 1935).

6. Walter Greiner, *Relativistic Quantum Mechanics: Wave Equations* (New York: Springer, 2000).

7. Michael William Lutz and Terrence P. Kenakin, *Quantitative Molecular Pharmacology and Informatics in Drug Discovery* (West Sussex, UK: Wiley, 1999) p. xiv.

8. Peter Van Zant, *Microchip Fabrication: A Practical Guide to Semiconductor Processing* (New York: McGraw-Hill, 1990).

9. Ayn Rand, *Atlas Shrugged* (New York: Signet, 1992), p. 1016.

10. Barry Mazur, "When Is One Thing Equal to Some Other Thing?" in *Proof and Other Dilemmas: Mathematics and Philosophy*, ed. Bonnie Gold and Roger A. Simons (Washington, DC: Mathematical Association of America, 2008).

11. Terence Parsons, *Indeterminate Identity: Metaphysics and Semantics* (Oxford: Oxford University Press, 2000), p. 1, http://fds.oup.com/www.oup.co.uk/pdf/0-19-825044-4.pdf.

12. Ibid.

13. Plutarch, *Lives of Illustrious Men*, trans. John Dryden et al., ed. A. H. Clough (New York: American Book Exchange, 1881), p. 50.

14. Parsons, *Indeterminate Identity*, pp. 2–4.

15. Bertrand Russell, *The Principles of Mathematics* (Cambridge, UK: Cambridge University Press, 1903) 1: 63.

16. Ibid.

17. Brian McGuinness, *Wittgenstein: A Life; Young Ludwig 1889–1921* (Berkeley, CA: University of California Press, 1988), p. 118.

18. Ludwig Wittgenstein and Friedrich Waismann, *The Voices of Wittgenstein: The Vienna Circle*, ed. Gordon P. Baker (London: Routledge, 2003), p. 73.

When Is a Frog a River? Aristotle Wrestles Heraclitus

19. Graham Priest, J. C. Beall, Bradley P. Armour-Garb, *The Law of Non-contradiction: New Philosophical Essays* (Oxford: Oxford University Press, 2004); John Watson, *An Outline of Philosophy: With Notes, Historical and Critical* (Glasgow: James Maclehose, 1898), pp. 376–77.

20. Abraham Edel, *Aristotle and His Philosophy* (New Brunswick, NJ: Transaction, 1996), pp. 108–10.

21. Aristotle, *The Metaphysics of Aristotle*, trans. John Henry M'Mahon (London: George Bell, 1896), p. 101.

22. This quote is reported in Aristotle, *Metaphysics of Aristotle*, trans. M'Mahon, p. 101. For a discussion of Heraclitus's original words, see Heraclitus, *The Art and Thought of Heraclitus: An Edition of the Fragments with Translation and Commentary*, ed. Charles H. Kahn (Cambridge, UK: Cambridge University Press, 1979), p. 168.

23. Aristotle, *Metaphysics of Aristotle*, trans. M'Mahon, p. 101.

24. Heraclitus, *Art and Thought of Heraclitus*, p. 168.

25. Aristotle, *Metaphysics of Aristotle*, trans. M'Mahon, pp. 100–101.

26. Ibid.

27. Ibid.

28. Ibid.

29. Aristotle, *Prior Analytics*, trans. Robin Smith (Indianapolis: Hackett, 1989), p. 212.

30. Aristotle, *Metaphysics*, trans. W. D. Ross (Lawrence, KA: Digireads.com, 2006), p. 35; Edel, *Aristotle and His Philosophy*, pp. 108–10.

31. Leibniz worked for the House of Brunswick.

32. Aristotle, *Metaphysics*, trans. W. D. Ross, p. 35.

33. Gottfried Wilhelm Leibniz, *Logical Papers by Gottfried Wilhelm Leibniz*, ed. George

Henry Radcliffe Parkinson (Oxford: Oxford University Press, 1966), p. 82; Gottfried Wilhelm Leibniz, *Metaphysics and Its Foundations*, ed. R. S. Woolhouse (London: Routledge, 1994), 1:297.

34. Gottfried Wilhelm Leibniz, *Discourse on Metaphysics and Related Writings*, ed. R. Niall Martin and Stuart Brown (Manchester, UK: Manchester University Press, 1988), p. 132. Or, as Leibniz put it, "Everything is what it is."

35. Augusto Vera, *Introduction to Speculative Logic and Philosophy* (St. Louis, MO: Gray, Baker, 1875), p. 16.

36. Aristotle, *Metaphysics*, trans. Ross, p. 35.

37. Ibid.

38. Ibid.

39. Ibid.

40. Noam Chomsky, *Language and Mind* (New York: Cambridge University Press, 2006), p. 144.

41. Steven Pinker, *The Language Instinct: How the Mind Creates Language* (New York: William Morrow, 1994).

42. William James, *Text-Book of Psychology* (London: Macmillan, 1892), p. 151.

43. Stanislas Dehaene, *Reading in the Brain: The Science and Evolution of a Human Invention* (New York: Penguin, 2009).

44. Andrew Blitzer, Mitchell F. Brin, and Lorraine O. Ramig, *Neurologic Disorders of the Larynx* (New York: Thieme, 2009), p. 18.

45. George Smoot and Keay Davidson, *Wrinkles in Time: Witness to the Birth of the Universe* (New York: HarperCollins, 2007), p. 187.

46. US Department of Energy, Office of Science, "Detecting the Afterglow of the Big Bang Anisotropy in the Cosmic Microwave Background Radiation," http://www.er.doe.gov/accomplishments_awards/Decades_Discovery/41.html (accessed August 13, 2010).

Heresy Number Three: Prepare to Be Burned at the Stake: The Second Law of Thermodynamics— Why Entropy Is an Outrage

47. Paul Davies, *The Cosmic Blueprint: New Discoveries in Nature's Creative Ability to Order* (West Conshohocken, PA: Templeton Foundation, 2004), p. 139.

48. Chung-Chi Chou, *Handbook of Sugar Refining: A Manual for Design and Operation of Sugar Refining Facilities* (New York: Wiley, 2000), p. 581.

49. Christine Bolling and Nydia R. Suarez, *The Brazilian Sugar Industry: Recent Developments* (Washington, DC: US Department of Agriculture, 2001).

50. Andrew Watson, *The Quantum Quark* (Cambridge, UK: Cambridge University Press, 2004), p. 264; James Walder et al., "Inside the Proton: Investigating the Structure of

Protons through 'Deep Inelastic Scattering,'" Oxford University Department of Physics, http://www.physics.ox.ac.uk/documents/PUS/dis/index.htm (accessed April 8, 2011).

51. Michael D. Lemonick, *Echo of the Big Bang* (Princeton: Princeton University Press, 2003), p. 205.

52. Christopher J. Miller, Robert C. Nichol, and David J. Batuski, "Acoustic Oscillations in the Early Universe and Today," *Science* 292, no. 5525 (June 22, 2001): 2302–2303.

53. Daniel J. Eisenstein et al., "Detection of the Baryon Acoustic Peak in the Large-Scale Correlation Function of SDSS Luminous Red Galaxies," *Astrophysical Journal* 633 no. 2 (November 10, 2005): 560, http://iopscience.iop.org/0004-637X/633/2/560/; Sloan Digital Sky Survey, "The Cosmic Yardstick—Sloan Digital Sky Survey Astronomers Measure Role of Dark Matter, Dark energy and Gravity in the Distribution of Galaxies," press release, January 11, 2005, http://www.sdss.org/news/releases/20050111.yardstick.html (accessed September 17, 2011).

54. Charles Seife, "Breakthrough of the Year: Illuminating the Dark Universe," *Science* 302, no. 5653 (December 19, 2003): 2038–39.

55. Frank L. Lambert, "Disorder—A Cracked Crutch for Supporting Entropy Discussions," *Journal of Chemical Education* 79, no. 2 (February 2002): 187–92, http://home pages .wmich.edu/~korista/phys3300/disorder_cracked-crutch-for-entropy.pdf (accessed September 17, 2011); Kenneth W. Whitten et al., *Chemistry* (Belmont, CA: Brooks/Cole, 2010), pp. 579–83.

56. Léon Brillouin, *Science and Information Theory* (Mineola, NY: Dover, 2004), pp. 114–16, originally published in 1956; A. I. Zotin, *Thermodynamic Bases of Biological Processes: Physiological Reactions and Adaptations* (Berlin: De Gruyter, 1990), p. 44.

Heresy Number Four: Randomness Is Wrong— The Six Monkeys at Six Typewriters Error

57. Michael Polanyi and Harry Prosch, *Meaning* (Chicago: University of Chicago Press, 1975), p. 174.

58. Bertram Schwarzschild, "COBE Satellite Finds No Hint of Excess in the Cosmic Microwave Spectrum," *Physics Today* 43, no. 3 (March 1990): 17.

59. National Institute of Standards and Technology, "Electron Mass. Fundamental Physical Constants. Latest (2006) Values of the Constants," in *The NIST Reference on Constants, Units, and Uncertainty* (Washington DC: NIST, June 2011), http://physics.nist.gov/cgi-bin/cuu/Value?mpsme | search_for=proton-electron+mass+ratio (accessed April 10, 2012).

60. CERN (Conseil Européen pour la Recherche Nucléaire), "LHC—The Large Hadron Collider," http://lhc.web.cern.ch/lhc/ (accessed July 10, 2011).

61. Harald [*sic*] Fritzsch, *Elementary Particles: Building Blocks of Matter* (Singapore: World Scientific, 2005).

A Brief History of the God Problem:
Were Kepler, Galileo, and Newton Creationists?

62. John Robert Christianson et al., eds., *Tycho Brahe and Prague: Crossroads of European Science, Proceedings of the International Symposium on the History of Science in the Rudolphine Period* (Frankfurt: Harri Deutsch, 2002).

63. M. M. Woolfson, *The Formation of the Solar System: Theories Old and New* (London: Imperial College Press, 2007), p. 30.

64. Johannes Kepler, *New Astronomy*, trans. William H. Donahue (Cambridge, UK: Cambridge University Press, 1992), originally published in 1609 as *Astronomia Nova*; Johannes Kepler, *The Harmony of the World*, trans. E. J. Aiton, Alistair Matheson Duncan, and Judith Veronica Field (Philadelphia: American Philosophical Society, 1997), p. 408, originally published in 1619 as *Hamonices Mundi*.

65. Johannes Kepler, *Mysterium Cosmographicum* (Munich: C. H. Beck'sche Verlagsbuchhandlung, 1938).

66. Kepler, *Harmony of the World*, p. 304.

67. Ibid.

68. David A. Weintraub, *How Old Is the Universe?* (Princeton, NJ: Princeton University Press, 2010), p. 14.

69. Kepler, *Harmony of the World*, p. 130.

70. Ibid., p. 304.

71. Ibid.

72. Ibid.

73. Ibid.

74. Ibid., p. 491.

75. Ibid., p. 304. See also Johannes Kepler, *Concerning the More Certain Fundamentals of Astrology* (New York: Clancy 1942), p. 15.

76. Ibid.

Galileo's Nature Fetish: Poking the Pope

77. Galileo Galilei, *Discoveries and Opinions of Galileo*, trans. Stillman Drake (New York: Anchor, 1957), p. 15.

78. Maurice A. Finocchiaro, review of *The Person of the Millennium: The Unique Impact of Galileo on World History*, by Manfred Weidhorn, *Historian* 69, no. 3 (Fall 2007): 601–602.

79. Galileo Galilei, "Galileo's Letter to the Grand Duchess Christina (1615)," in *The Galileo Affair: A Documentary History*, ed. and trans. Maurice A. Finocchiaro (Berkeley: University of California Press, 1989), p. 118. Also in Galileo Galilei, *The Essential Galileo*, ed. and trans. Maurice A. Finocchiaro (Indianapolis: Hackett, 2008).

80. Ingrid D. Rowland, *Giordano Bruno: Philosopher Heretic* (Chicago: University of Chicago Press, 2008), pp. 9–10.

81. Galileo, "Galileo's Letter to the Grand Duchess."

82. Ibid.

83. Galileo Galilei, "Two New Sciences," in *The Essential Galileo*, ed. and trans. Maurice A. Finocchiaro (Indianapolis: Hackett, 2008), pp. 301, 349.

84. Galileo Galilei, *Galileo on the World Systems: A New Abridged Translation and Guide*, ed. and trans. Maurice A. Finocchiaro (Berkeley: University of California Press, 1997), pp. 146, 176; George Pólya and Leon Bowden, *Mathematical Methods in Science* (Washington, DC: Mathematical Association of America, 1977), p. 100. See also James MacLachlan, *Galileo Galilei: First Physicist* (New York: Oxford University Press, 1997), p. 38.

85. Peter Grego and David Mannion, *Galileo and 400 Years of Telescopic Astronomy* (New York: Springer, 2010), p. 79.

86. George Johnson, *The Ten Most Beautiful Experiments* (New York: Knopf, 2008), p. 10; Stillman Drake, Noel M. Swerdlow, and Trevor Harvey Levere, eds. *Essays on Galileo and the History and Philosophy of Science* (Toronto: University of Toronto Press, 1999), 1: 317.

87. Drake et al., *Essays on Galileo*, p. 318; Johnson, *Ten Most Beautiful Experiments*, pp. 3–16.

88. Carla Rita Palmerino and J. M. M. H. Thijssen, *The Reception of the Galilean Science of Motion in Seventeenth-Century Europe* (Dordrecht: Kluwer, 2004), p. 208.

89. Yuri I. Manin, *Mathematics as Metaphor: Selected Essays of Yuri I. Manin*, ed. Phillip Griffiths, Dusa McDuff, and Elias Stein (Providence, RI: American Mathematical Society, 2007).

90. Galileo, *Discoveries and Opinions of Galileo*, pp. 237–38; see also Galileo Galilei, *Thus Spoke Galileo: The Great Scientist's Ideas and Their Relevance to the Present Day*, ed. Andrea Frova and Mariapiera Marenzana (Oxford: Oxford University Press, 2006), p. 402.

91. Peter Machamer, "Galileo's Machines, His Mathematics, and His Experiments," in *The Cambridge Companion to Galileo*, ed. Peter K. Machamer (Cambridge, UK: Cambridge University Press, 1999), p. 64.

92. Galileo, "The Assayer," in Galileo, *Essential Galileo*, p. 183.

93. Florian Cajori, *A History of Mathematics* (New York: General, 2010), p. 140.

94. Galileo, "The Assayer," p. 183.

95. Galileo, *Discoveries and Opinions of Galileo*, p. 237.

96. Atle Næss, *Galileo Galilei, When the World Stood Still*, trans. James Anderson (New York: Springer, 2005), pp. 7, 48, 63.

97. Galileo, *Galileo on the World Systems*, p. 164.

98. Isaac Newton. *Principia*, ed. Stephen W. Hawking (Philadelphia: Running Press, 2002), p 427.

99. Ibid.

100. Ibid., p. 428.

101. Isaac Newton, *Newton's Revised History of Ancient Kingdoms: A Complete Chronology*, ed. Larry Pierce and Marion Pierce (Green Forest, AR: New Leaf, 2009), p. 5.

102. Isaac Newton, *Philosophiae Naturalis Principia Mathematica: Motte's Translation Revised*, ed. Florian Cajori (Berkeley: University of California Press, 1934), p. 545.

103. Ibid.

104. Ibid.

105. Newton, *Principia*, ed. Hawking, p. 426

106. Ibid.

107. Sir Isaac Newton, *Observations upon the Prophecies of Daniel, and the Apocalypse of St. John*, vol. 1 (London: J. Roberts et al., 1733), pp. 219–20, http://www.isaacnewton.ca/daniel_apocalypse/.

108. Ibid.

109. Ibid., p. 54.

110. Newton, *Principia*, ed. Hawking, p. 428.

111. Richard S. Westfall, *The Life of Isaac Newton* (Cambridge, UK: Cambridge University Press, 1993), p. 6.

112. Isaac Newton, *Newton's Principia: The Mathematical Principles of Natural Philosophy to which Is Added Newton's System of the World*, ed. N. W. Chittenden, trans. Andrew Motte (New York: Daniel Adee, 1848), p. 11; David Brewster and Isaac Newton, *Memoirs of the Life, Writings and Discoveries of Sir Isaac Newton*, vol. 1 (Boston: Adamant, 2005), p. 16.

113. Newton, *Principia*, ed. Chittenden, p. 11.

114. Nathaniel Hawthorne, "Isaac Newton," *Friends Intelligencer* (Philadelphia: Association of Friends, 1869–1870), 26: 813–14.

115. Newton, *Principia*, ed. Hawking, pp. 7, 335, 336.

116. Ibid., pp. 238–42.

117. "gear, *n.*" in *Oxford English Dictionary*. The first use of the word "gear" for a wheel with teeth appeared in 1829.

118. Newton. *Principia*, ed. Hawking, pp. 21–22

119. Ibid.

120. Hawthorne, *Isaac Newton*, pp. 813–14.

Gamow versus Hoyle—The War between Big Bang and Steady State

121. Immanuel Kant, *Kant's Cosmogony as in His Essay on the Retardation of the Rotation of the Earth and His Natural History and Theory of the Heavens*, ed. William Hastie (Glasgow: James Maclehose, 1900), p. 42.

122. *American Aviation* 22 (1958): 43; Tina Grant, *International Directory of Company Histories* (Saint James, MO: St. James Press, 1996), 13: 356–57.

123. "50 Years Ago, Sputnik Changed Everything," *Buffalo News*, Oct 4, 2007.

124. Graham Farmelo, *The Strangest Man: The Hidden Life of Paul Dirac, Mystic of the Atom* (New York: Basic Books, 2009), p. 151.

125. T. E. Allibone, "Choosing between the Hare and the Hounds, a Review of Kapitza, Rutherford, and the Kremlin," *New Scientist*, June 20, 1985, p. 31.

126. Jane Wilson, "Several Lives and More," review of George Gamow's *My World Line: An Informal Autobiography, Bulletin of the Atomic Scientists*, February 1971, p. 47.

127. Mohsen Razavy, *Quantum Theory of Tunneling* (Singapore: World Scientific, 2003), p. 53; Helge Kragh, *Quantum Generations: A History of Physics in the Twentieth Century* (Princeton, NJ: Princeton University Press, 1999), p. 183.

128. Kent A. Peacock, *The Quantum Revolution: A Historical Perspective* (Westport, CT: Greenwood, 2008), p. 107.

129. George Gamow, *The Creation of the Universe* (New York: Viking, 1952), p. 43.

130. David Michael Harland, *The Big Bang: A View from the 21st Century* (London: Springer, 2003), p. 143.

131. Richard Rhodes, *The Making of the Atomic Bomb* (New York: Simon & Schuster, 1986), p. 370.

132. Simon Mitton, *Fred Hoyle: A Life in Science* (New York: Cambridge University Press, 2011), p. 88.

133. Anne J. Kox and Jean Eisenstaedt, eds., *The Universe of General Relativity* (Boston: Center for Einstein Studies, 2005), p. 182.

134. Ken Croswell, *The Universe at Midnight: Observations Illuminating the Cosmos* (New York: Free Press, 2001), p. 47.

135. Geoffrey Burbidge and Margaret Burbridge, "Thomas Gold," in *Biographical Memoirs* (Washington, DC: National Academies Press, 2006), 88: 145.

136. Fred Hoyle, "An Assessment of the Evidence against the Steady-State Theory," in *Modern Cosmology in Retrospect*, ed. B. Bertotti et al. (Cambridge, UK: Cambridge University Press, 1991), p. 221.

137. Ibid.

138. Fred Hoyle, Geoffrey R. Burbidge, and Jayant Vishnu Narlikar, *A Different Approach to Cosmology: From a Static Universe through the Big Bang towards Reality* (Cambridge, UK: Cambridge University Press, 2000), p. 222.

139. Rem Blanchard Edwards, *What Caused the Big Bang?* (Amsterdam: Rodopi, 2001), p. 74.

140. Hoyle et al., *A Different Approach to Cosmology*, p. 317.

141. Ibid., p. 241; Fred Hoyle, *Home Is Where the Wind Blows: Chapters from a Cosmologist's Life* (Mill Valley, CA: University Science Books, 1994), p. 401.

142. Hoyle et al., *A Different Approach to Cosmology*, p. 317

143. Ibid., p. 195.

144. Hoyle, *Home Is Where the Wind Blows*, p. 405.

145. Hoyle et al., *A Different Approach to Cosmology*, p. 318.

146. Hoyle, *Home Is Where the Wind Blows*, pp. 269–71.

147. Croswell, *The Universe at Midnight*, p. 47.

148. Fred Hoyle, "The Big Bang in Astronomy," *New Scientist*, November 19, 1981, p. 521.

149. Ibid., p. 522.

150. Croswell, *The Universe at Midnight*, pp. 62–63.

151. Mitton, *Fred Hoyle: A Life in Science*, pp. 171–74.

152. George Gamow, *Mr. Tompkins in Paperback* (Cambridge, UK: Cambridge University Press, 1993), p. 64. Copyright © 1993 Cambridge University Press. Reprinted with permission of Cambridge University Press.

The Tale of the Termites

153. Sources for this account of termite behavior include: Edward O. Wilson, *The Insect Societies* (Cambridge, MA: Harvard University Press, 1971); Judith Korb, "Termite Mound Architecture, from Function to Construction," in *Biology of Termites: A Modern Synthesis*, ed. David Edward Bignell, Yves Roisin, and Nathan Lo (New York: Springer, 2011), pp. 349–73; Michael Vaughan Brian, ed., *Production Ecology of Ants and Termites* (Cambridge, UK: Cambridge University Press, 2009), pp. 80, 249, 257, 282; Helmut König and Ajit Varma, eds., *Intestinal Microorganisms of Termites and Other Invertebrates* (Berlin: Springer, 2006), pp. 203, 208; J. Scott Turner, *The Extended Organism: The Physiology of Animal-Built Structures* (Cambridge, MA: Harvard University Press, 2004); Eric Bonabeau, "Editor's Introduction: Stigmergy," *Artificial Life* 5, no. 2 (Spring 1999): 95–96; Philip Ball, "For Sustainable Architecture, Think Bug," *New Scientist*, February 22, 2010; J. C. Jones and B. P. Oldroyd, "Nest Thermoregulation in Social Insects," in *Advances in Insect Physiology*, ed. Stephen Simpson (New York: Basic Books, 1996) 33: 170; Takuya Abe, David Edward Bignell, and Masahiko Higashi, eds., *Termites: Evolution, Sociality, Symbioses, Ecology* (Dordrecht: Kluwer, 2002), p. 292; Michael Henry Hansell, *Built by Animals: The Natural History of Animal Architecture* (Oxford: Oxford University Press, 2008); Holk Cruse, Jeffrey Dean, and Helge Ritter, eds., *Prerational Intelligence: Adaptive Behavior and Intelligent Systems without Symbols and Logic*, vol. 2, *Interdisciplinary Perspectives on the Behavior of Natural and Artificial Systems* (New York: Springer, 2000), p. 526; Scott Camazine et al., *Self-Organization in Biological Systems* (Princeton, NJ: Princeton University Press, 2003), p. 404; Ajith Abraham, Crina Grosan, and Vitorino Ramos, *Stigmergic Optimization* (New York: Springer, 2010), p. 3; Russell K. Standish, Mark A. Bedau, and Hussein Abbass, *Artificial Life VIII: Proceedings of the Eighth International Conference on Artificial Life* (Cambridge, MA: MIT Press, 2002), p. 371; Adelinde Uhrmacher and Danny Weyns, *Multi-Agent Systems: Simulation and Applications* (Boca Raton: CRC, 2009), p. 247; Michael Wilson and Brian Dupuis, *From Bricks to Brains: The Embodied Cognitive Science of Lego Robots* (Vancouver: University of British

Columbia Press, 2010), p. 17; Peter J. B. Slater et al., *Advances in the Study of Behavior* (New York: Academic Press, 2004), 34: 35; J. S. Turner, "On the Mound of *Macrotermes Michaelseni* as an Organ of Respiratory Gas Exchange," *Physiological and Biochemical Zoology* 74, no. 6 (2001): 798–822; J. S. Turner, "A Superorganism's Fuzzy Boundary," *Natural History*, July-August 2002, pp. 62–67; J. S. Turner, "Extended Physiology of an Insect-Built Structure," *American Entomologist* 51, no. 1 (2005): 36–38; J. S. Turner, *The Tinkerer's Accomplice: How Design Emerges from Life Itself* (Cambridge, MA: Harvard University Press, 2007), p. 282; J. S. Turner, "Termites as Models of Swarm Cognition," *Swarm Intelligence* 5, no. 1 (2011): 19–43.

154. T. G. Wood and W. A. Sands call this obsessive cleanliness "intensive nest sanitation." T. G. Wood and W. A. Sands, "The Role of Termites in Ecosystems," in *Production Ecology of Ants and Termites*, Michael Vaughan Brian, ed. (Cambridge, UK: Cambridge University Press, 2009), p. 282.

3. THE SAGA OF A SCRATCH MARK

The Mystery of the Magic Beans: What the Hell Is an Axiom?

1. Brian Greene, *The Hidden Reality: Parallel Universes and the Deep Laws of the Cosmos* (New York: Knopf, 2011), p. 299.

2. David Layzer, *Cosmogenesis: The Growth of Order in the Universe* (Oxford: Oxford University Press, 1990), p. 42: Freeman Dyson, *Selected Papers of Freeman Dyson with Commentary* (Providence: American Mathematical Society, 1996), p. 19; John T. Roberts, *The Law-Governed Universe* (Oxford: Oxford University Press, 2009), p. 8.

3. P. Adams, K. Smith, and R. Výborný, *Introduction to Mathematics with Maple* (Singapore: World Scientific, 2004), pp. 121–22.

4. *Wikipedia*, s.v. "Axiomatization," last modified March 2, 2012, http://en.wikipedia .org/wiki/Axiomatization.

5. Lester Frank Ward, *Sociology at the Paris Exposition of 1900* (Washington, DC: US Government Printing Office, 1901), pp. 1454, 1458.

6. Ferdinand Wythe Peck, *Report of the Commissioner-General for the United States to the International Universal Exposition, Paris, 1900* (Washington, DC: US Government Printing Office: February 28, 1901), 1:127.

7. Helge Kragh, *Quantum Generations* (Princeton, NJ: Princeton University Press, 1999), p. 17.

8. "Congress of Applied Chemistry," *Popular Science*, June 1913, p. 551.

9. Peck, *Report of the Commissioner-General.*

10. André Saglio, Victor Champier, and William Walton, *Paris: Exposition Universelle, 1900* (Paris: Barrie, 1900).

11. Siobhan Chapman and Christopher Routledge, *Key Thinkers in Linguistics and the Philosophy of Language* (New York: Oxford University Press, 2005), p. 228; Fulvia Skof, *Giuseppe Peano between Mathematics and Logic: Proceeding of the International Congress in Honour of Giuseppe Peano on the 150th Anniversary of His Birth and the Centennial of the Formulario Mathematico* (New York: Springer, 2011), p. 7; Bertrand Russell, John Greer Slater, and Peter Köllner, *A Fresh Look at Empiricism: 1927–42* (East Sussex, UK: Psychology Press, 1996), p. 118.

12. Bertrand Russell, *Foundations of Logic, 1903–05*, ed. Alasdair Urquhart and Albert C. Lewis (London: Routledge, 1995), p. xiii.

13. Bertrand Russell, *Autobiography* (East Sussex, UK: Psychology Press, 1998), p. 147. Originally published in three volumes, 1967–1969.

14. Hubert Kennedy, *Peano: Life and Works of Giuseppe Peano* (San Francisco: Peremptory Publications, 2002), p. 146.

15. Bertrand Russell, *The Basic Writings of Bertrand Russell*, ed. Gregory Landini (London: Routledge, 2009), 10: 4, 16.

16. Bertrand Russell, *The Principles of Mathematics* (Cambridge, UK: Cambridge University Press, 1903), p. 125.

Barley, Bricks, and Babylonians: The Birth of Math

17. Leon Festinger, *The Human Legacy* (New York: Columbia University Press, 1983), pp. 137–38.

18. Ian Hodder et al., "Çatalhöyük: Excavations of a Neolithic Anatolian Höyük," http://www.catalhoyuk.com/index.html (accessed June 27, 2011).

19. James Mellaart, *Çatal Hüyük: A Neolithic Town in Anatolia* (New York: McGraw-Hill, 1967), p. 55.

20. J. N. Postgate, *Early Mesopotamia: Society and Economy at the Dawn of History* (London: Routledge, 1992), pp. 22–28.

21. William H. Stiebing, *Ancient Near Eastern History and Culture* (New York: Longman, 2008); Bucher Gruppe, *Vorderasien: Sumer, Elam, Hubuakia, Jordangraben, Mittelmeeranrainerstaat, Tübinger Atlas des Vorderen Orients* (Memphis: General Books, 2010), http://general-books.net/book.cfm?id=3908995, in German, originally published in *Wikipedia Deutsch*.

22. Bertrand Russell, *The History of Western Philosophy* (London: Routledge, 2004), pp. 202–203. Originally published in 1946.

23. April Holladay, "The 360-Degree Circle is 4400 Years Old," Wonder*Quest*, http://www.wonderquest.com/circle.htm (accessed June 27, 2011).

24. "Why Has Geometry Not Been 'Metricked'? Why 360 Degrees Instead of 1, 10, 100 or Even 1000?" Notes & Queries, *Guardian*, http://www.guardian.co.uk/notesandqueries/query/0,,-185569,00.html (accessed June 27, 2011).

25. Graham Faiella, *The Technology of Mesopotamia* (New York: Rosen, 2005), p. 41.

26. Jens Høyrup, *Lengths, Widths, Surfaces: A Portrait of Old Babylonian Algebra and Its Kin* (New York: Springer, 2002), pp. 227–28.

27. Jöran Friberg, *A Remarkable Collection of Babylonian Mathematical Texts* (New York: Springer, 2007), p. 1.

28. Sources for this section on Mesopotamian mathematics and astronomy include: Eleanor Robson and Jacqueline A. Stedall, eds., *The Oxford Handbook of the History of Mathematics* (Oxford: Oxford University Press, 2009); Jöran Friberg, *Unexpected Links between Egyptian and Babylonian Mathematics* (Singapore: World Scientific, 2005); Glen Van Brummelen, *The Mathematics of the Heavens and the Earth: The Early History of Trigonometry* (Princeton, NJ: Princeton University Press, 2009); Jürgen Bortfeldt and Bernhard Kramer, *Einheiten und Fundamentalkonstanten in Physik und Chemie* (Berlin: Springer, 1991); Rupert Gleadow, *The Origin of the Zodiac* (London: Jonathan Cape, 1968); Francesca Rochberg, *In the Path of the Moon: Babylonian Celestial Divination and Its Legacy* (Leiden, Netherlands: Brill, 2010).

29. Samuel Noah Kramer, *The Sumerians: Their History, Culture, and Character* (Chicago: University of Chicago Press, 1963).

30. Denise Schmandt Besserat, "Oneness, Twoness, Threeness: How Ancient Accountants Invented Numbers," *Sciences*, July/August 1987. For a refutation of Schmandt Besserat, see Jean-Jacques Glassner, Zainab Bahrani, and Marc Van de Mieroop, *The Invention of Cuneiform: Writing in Sumer* (Baltimore: Johns Hopkins University Press, 2007).

31. Karl Menninger, *Number Words and Number Symbols: A Cultural History of Numbers* (Cambridge, MA: MIT Press, 1969), p. 164.

32. Gwendolyn Leick, *The Babylonians: An Introduction* (London: Routledge, 2002), pp. 84–85.

33. For the Mesopotamian use of bags, see K. R. Veenhof, *Aspects of Old Assyrian Trade and its Terminology* (Leiden, Netherlands: Brill, 1996), p. 10. See also Peter Roger Stuart Moorey, *Ancient Mesopotamian Materials and Industries: The Archaeological Evidence* (Winona Lake, IN: Eisenbrauns, 1999), p. 106; Klaas R. Veenhof, Jesper Eidem, and Markus Wäfler, *Mesopotamia: The Old Assyrian Period* (Winona Lake, IN: Eisenbrauns, 1998), pp. 116, 159.

34. Diane Wolkstein and Samuel Noah Kramer, *Inanna, Queen of Heaven and Earth: Her Stories and Hymns from Sumer* (New York: Harper & Row, 1983), p. 116; Thomas F. X. Noble et al., *Western Civilization: Beyond Boundaries* (Belmont, CA: Wadsworth, 2010), 1: 12.

35. Tonia M. Sharlach, *Provincial Taxation and the Ur III State* (Cuneiform Monographs) (Leiden, Netherlands: Brill, 2003), p. 167; Kramer, *The Sumerians*, p. 242.

36. Jane Shuter, *Mesopotamia* (Chicago: Heinemann-Raintree, 2005), p. 38; Jane Shuter, *The Sumerians* (Chicago: Heinemann-Raintree, 2008), p. 16.

37. Sir James George Frazer, *The Golden Bough: A Study in Magic and Religion* (New York: MacMillan, 1962), p. 12.

38. Friberg, *A Remarkable Collection*, p. 109.

39. *The Pennsylvania Sumerian Dictionary* (Philadelphia: Pennsylvania Museum of

Anthropology and Archaeology), s.v. "fly," http://psd.museum.upenn.edu/epsd/nepsd -frame.html (accessed June 28, 2011).

40. Tim Murray, *Milestones in Archaeology: A Chronological Encyclopedia* (Santa Barbara, CA: ABC-CLIO, 2007), p. 483.

41. Mary Ellen Snodgrass, *Encyclopedia of Kitchen History* (London: Routledge, 2004), p. 403.

42. Martin Schøyen, "Checklist of Manuscripts," *The Schøyen Collection*, 22nd Internet edition, July 2009, http://www.schoyencollection.com/math.html (accessed June 28, 2011).

43. Postgate, *Early Mesopotamia*, p. 97. For a Mesopotamian tablet with a seven sons problem, see Friberg, *Unexpected Links*, pp. 269–72.

44. Sir James George Frazer, *The Golden Bough: A Study in Magic and Religion* (New York: MacMillan, 1962), p. 12.

45. Jöran Friberg, *Amazing Traces of a Babylonian Origin in Greek Mathematics* (Singapore: World Scientific, 2007), p. 197.

46. Sometimes the Mesopotamian reed is given as seven cubits, at other times as six.

47. Eleanor Robson, "Babylonian Mathematics, Wedges and Bull's Heads, Squares and Triangles," in *Motivate: Maths Enrichment for Schools*, University of Cambridge, 2008, http://motivate.maths.org/conferences/conf114/c114_WedgesBullshead.shtml (accessed November 11, 2010).

48. Friberg, *Amazing Traces*, pp. 27–29, 58.

49. Mary G. Houston, *Ancient Egyptian, Mesopotamian & Persian Costume* (Mineola, NY: Dover, 2002) p. 120; Jean Bottéro et al., *Everyday Life in Ancient Mesopotamia* (Baltimore: Johns Hopkins University Press, 2001), p. 175; Graham Cunningham, *Deliver Me from Evil: Mesopotamian Incantations, 2500–1500 BC* (Rome: Pontificio Istituto Biblico, 1997), p. 32; Martin Levey, "Chemistry of Tanning in Ancient Mesopotamia," *Journal of Chemical Education*, March 1957, p. 142.

50. Friberg, *Amazing Traces*, p. 271; Bartel Leendert Waerden, *Science Awakening* (Leiden, Netherlands: Noordhoff, 1975), 1: 42, 44.

51. Patricia Turner and Charles Russell Coulter, *Dictionary of Ancient Deities* (Oxford: Oxford University Press, 2001), p. 95; Stephen Bertman, *Handbook to Life in Ancient Mesopotamia* (Oxford: Oxford University Press, 2005).

52. Duncan J. Melville, "Old Babylonian Weights and Measures," Saint Lawrence University, last modified June 6, 2001, http://it.stlawu.edu/~dmelvill/mesomath/obmetrology.html (accessed September 19, 2011); Friberg, *A Remarkable Collection*, p. 118; Jay L. Bucher, *The Metrology Handbook* (Milwaukee: American Society for Quality Measurement, 2004), pp. 4–5.

53. Eleanor Robson, "Field Plans," in *Motivate: Maths Enrichment for Schools*, University of Cambridge, 2008, http://motivate.maths.org/conferences/conf114/c114_field_plans .shtml 11–11-2010 (accessed July 1, 2011).

54. Jöran Friberg, *Unexpected Links*, pp. 163–64.

55. Ibid., pp. 227–28.

56. Eleanor Robson, *Mathematics in Ancient Iraq: A Social History* (Princeton, NJ: Princeton University Press, 2008), p. 180.

57. Duncan J. Melville, "Reciprocals and Reciprocal Algorithms in Mesopotamian Mathematics," Mesopotamian Mathematics, Saint Lawrence University, last modified September 6, 2005, http://it.stlawu.edu/~dmelvill/mesomath/Recip.pdf (accessed September 19, 2011).

58. Friberg, *Unexpected Links*, pp. 163–64.

59. "Magic," *Oxford English Dictionary*, 2nd ed. (Oxford: Oxford University Press, 2004), CD-ROM.

60. Eleanor Robson and Jacqueline A. Stedall, *The Oxford Handbook of the History of Mathematics* (Oxford: Oxford University Press, 2009), pp. 201–203.

61. Høyrup, *Lengths, Widths, Surfaces*, p. 106.

62. Francis L. Brannigan, *Building Construction for the Fire Service* (Maynard, MA: Jones & Bartlett, 1992), p. 68.

63. Gwendolyn Leick, "The Babylonians: An Introduction," in *The New Schaff-Herzog Encyclopedia of Religious Knowledge*, ed. Samuel MacAuley Jackson (New York: Funk and Wagnalls, 1908), p. 288.

64. Jürgen Bortfeldt and Bernhard Kramer, *Einheiten und Fundamentalkonstanten in Physik und Chemie* (Berlin: Springer, 1991), p. 1-1.

65. Friberg, *Unexpected Links*, pp. 163–64.

Scratch Mud and You Get Mind: The Rise of a Virtual Reality

66. Wayne M. Senner, *The Origins of Writing* (Lincoln: University of Nebraska Press, 1989), p. 51; Naida Kirkpatrick, *The Sumerians* (St. Louis: San Val, 2003), p. 17.

67. Asger Aaboe, "Babylonian Mathematics, Astrology, and Astronomy," in John Boardman et al., ed. *The Cambridge Ancient History*, vol. 3, pt. 2, *The Assyrian and Babylonian Empires and Other States of the Near East, from the Eighth to the Sixth Centuries BC* (Cambridge, UK: Cambridge University Press, 1992), p. 282.

68. Ibid.

69. Francesca Rochberg, *Babylonian Horoscopes* (Philadelphia: American Philosophical Society, 1998), pp. 1–17.

70. John David North, *Cosmos: An Illustrated History of Astronomy and Cosmology* (Chicago: University of Chicago Press, 2008), p. 56.

71. Alexander Marshack, *The Roots of Civilization: The Cognitive Beginnings of Man's First Art, Symbol, and Notation* (Kingston, RI: Moyer Bell, 1991); Evan Hadingham, *Secrets of the Ice Age: The World of the Cave Artists* (Portsmouth, NH: Heinemann, 1980); Peter James and Nick

Thorpe, *Ancient Inventions* (New York: Ballantine, 2006), p. 485; David H. Kelley, Eugene F. Milone, and Anthony F. Aven, *Exploring Ancient Skies: A Survey of Ancient and Cultural Astronomy* (New York: Springer, 2004), pp. 157–58; Paul G. Bahn, ed., *An Enquiring Mind: Studies in Honor of Alexander Marshack* (Oxford: Oxbow, 2009).

The Sorcery of Corners

72. William James Hamblin, *Warfare in the Ancient Near East to 1600 BC: Holy Warriors at the Dawn of History* (London: Routledge, 2006), pp. 173–74.

73. In its prologue, Hammurabi's Code lists forty-three locations over which Hammurabi has dominion, apparently a combination of cities, suburbs, and neighborhoods; William Walter Davies, *The Codes of Hammurabi and Moses* (Cincinnati, OH: Jennings and Graham, 1905), pp. 17–20; Leila A. Langston, "The Sumerians," chap. 5 in *Explore the Ancient World* (Brea, CA: Ballard & Tighe, 2005).

74. Hammurabi, "Inscription of Hammurabi in Sumerian, Recording the Building of the Temple of Samas in Larsam," and "Inscription of Hammurabi in Sumerian, Recording the Building of a Temple of the Goddess Ninna," in *The Letters and Inscriptions of Hammurabi, King of Babylon, About B.C.E. 2200* (Ithaca: Cornell University Library, 2009), 1: xliii, lxv, lxvi, originally published in 1900; Henri Frankfort, *The Art and Architecture of the Ancient Orient* (New Haven, CT: Yale University Press, 1996), pp. 107–10.

75. Genesis 1:1–12.

76. Genesis 1:3.

77. Genesis 11:31.

78. Samuel Birch, *History of Ancient Pottery* (London: John Murray, 1858), 1: 106–23.

79. Genesis 2:15.

80. Genesis 2:7.

81. Herodotus, *History of Herodotus*, trans. George Rawlinson and Henry Creswicke Rawlinson (London: John Murray, 1859), 1: 252.

82. Robert Koldewey, *The Excavations at Babylon* (London: Macmillan, 1914), pp. 5–6.

83. Kathleen Kuiper, ed., *The Britannica Guide to Ancient Civilizations: Mesopotamia—The World's Earliest Civilization* (New York: Rosen, 2010), p. 143.

84. Genesis 11:7. The Bible gives a tip-off to this neighborhood of many gods through its constant use of the word "elohim," which means "gods." And when God gets ticked off about the Tower of Babel, he says, "Let us go down, and there confound their language." He doesn't declare that he will pull off this demolition on his own.

85. Genesis 11:6.

86. Genesis 11:4.

87. The concept of a ninety-degree angle does not appear in Pythagoras, Plato, or Aristotle. It crops up for the first time in the works of Euclid in roughly 300 BCE. See Euclid,

The Elements of Euclid: With Select Theorems out of Archimedes, ed. Andrew Tacquet and William Whiston (Dublin: S. Fuller, 1728).

88. Owen Byer, Felix Lazebnik, and Deirdre L. Smeltzer, *Methods for Euclidean Geometry* (Washington, DC: Mathematical Association of America, 2010), p. 3; Bonnie Coulter Leech, *Geometry's Great Thinkers: The History of Geometry* (New York: Rosen, 2005), p. 8.

89. Otto Neugebauer, *The Exact Sciences in Antiquity* (Providence: Brown University Press, 1957), p. 38; James Joseph Tattersall, *Elementary Number Theory in Nine Chapters* (Cambridge, UK: Cambridge University Press, 2005), p. 70.

Celebrities in the Heavens: How to Invent Astronomy

90. Otto Neugebauer, *A History of Ancient Mathematical Astronomy* (New York: Springer, 1976), p. 3. Neugebauer, the seminal explorer of Mesopotamian math and astronomy, says that the Greeks used circles and geometry but that the Mesopotamians used numbers and tic-tac-toe-like charts only—no geometry. "From the cuneiform texts we learned that ephemerides had been computed exclusively by means of intricate difference sequences which, often by the superposition of several numerical columns, gave step by step the desired coordinates of the celestial bodies—all this with no attempt of a geometrical representation."

91. James Evans, *History and Practice of Ancient Astronomy* (New York: Oxford University Press, 1998), pp. 318–19.

92. Rupert Gleadow, *The Origin of the Zodiac* (London: Jonathan Cape, 1968), pp. 163–71.

93. Ibid., p. 170.

94. Julye Bidmead, *The Akitu Festival: Religious Continuity and Royal Legitimation in Mesopotamia* (Piscataway, NJ: Gorgias Press, 2002), p. 65; Rupert Gleadow, *Origin of the Zodiac*, p. 166.

95. Gleadow, *Origin of the Zodiac*, p. 166.

96. Alexander Heidel, *The Babylonian Genesis: The Story of Creation* (Chicago: University of Chicago Press, 1963), p. 42.

97. Ibid.

98. William Hayes Ward, *The Seal Cylinders of Western Asia* (Washington, DC: Carnegie Institution of Washington, 1910), p. 94.

99. Nebuchadnezzar, "The East India House Inscription of Nebuchadnezzar II, King of Babylon (601–565 b.c.)," in *Assyrian and Babylonian Literature: Selected Translations*, trans. Robert Francis Harper (New York: D. Appleton, 1900), p. 137.

100. Robert Harry van Gent, Institute for History and Foundations of Science, Web pages on the history of astronomy, University of Utrecht, http://www.phys.uu.nl/~vgent/babylon/babybibl_fixedstars.htm (accessed July 2, 2011).

101. Francesca Rochberg, *In the Path of the Moon: Babylonian Celestial Divination and Its Legacy* (Leiden, Netherlands: Brill, 2010), pp. 358–59.

102. Jonathan Ben-Dov, *Head of All Years: Astronomy and Calendars at Qumran in Their Ancient Context* (Leiden, Netherlands: Brill, 2008).

103. Donald A. Mackenzie, *Myths of Babylonia and Assyria* (Whitefish, MT: Kessinger, 2010), p. 254.

104. Patricia Turner and Charles Russell Coulter, *Dictionary of Ancient Deities* (Oxford: Oxford University Press, 2001), p. 423.

105. Jeremy A. Black, Anthony Green, and Tessa Rickards, *Gods, Demons, and Symbols of Ancient Mesopotamia: An Illustrated Dictionary* (Austin: University of Texas Press, 1992), p. 184; Peter Roger Stuart Moorey, *Ancient Mesopotamian Materials and Industries: The Archaeological Evidence* (Winona Lake, IN: Eisenbrauns, 1999), p. 354; Daniel T. Potts, *Mesopotamian Civilization: The Material Foundations* (Ithaca, NY: Cornell University Press, 1997), p. 69. For the importance of pruning date trees, see US Department of Agriculture, *Farmers' Bulletin*, Issues 1001–1025 (1920): 17.

106. Ward, *Seal Cylinders of Western Asia*, p. 94.

107. *Oxford English Dictionary*, s.v. "zodiac"; *Online Etymology Dictionary*, s.v. "zodiac," http://www.etymonline.com/index.php?search=zodiac&searchmode=none (accessed September 23, 2011).

108. Alfred Jeremias, *The Old Testament in the Light of the Ancient East*, vol. 1 (London: Williams and Northgate, 1911), pp. 13–14.

109. Ibid., p. 13.

110. George Aaron Barton, *A Sketch of Semitic Origins: Social and Religious* (New York: Macmillan, 1902), p. 206.

111. C. Scott Littleton, *Gods, Goddesses, and Mythology* (Tarrytown, NY: Marshall Cavendish, 2005), 4: 480.

112. Hugo Radau, "The Cosmology of the Sumerians," *Monist* 13 (1902–1903): 110. Morris Jastrow, *The Religion of Babylonia and Assyria* (Boston: Ginn & Co., 1898), 2: 225.

113. Hugo Radau, *Letters to Cassite Kings from the Temple Archives of Nippur* (Philadelphia: University of Pennsylvania, 1908), p. 8. Hugo Radau, "Cosmology of the Sumerians," p. 110.

114. Jastrow, *Religion of Babylonia and Assyria*, pp. 225–26. Ward, *Seal Cylinders of Western Asia*, p. 94.

115. Høyrup, *Lengths, Widths, Surfaces*, pp. 227–28.

116. Aaboe, "Babylonian Mathematics, Astrology, and Astronomy," p. 282.

117. Jeremias, *The Old Testament in the Light of the Ancient East*, 1:13–14.

118. Hermann Hunger, David Edwin Pingree, *Astral Sciences in Mesopotamia* (Leiden, Netherlands: Brill, 1999), p. 42.

119. John M. Steele, *Observations and Predictions of Eclipse Times by Early Astronomers* (New York: Springer, 2000), pp. 24–26.

120. Ibid.

121. Linda Kalof, *Looking at Animals in Human History* (London: Reaktion Books, 2007), pp. 12, 18.

122. Steele, *Observations and Predictions of Eclipse Times*, pp. 24–26.

123. Ibid.

What's the Angle? Blindness in Babylon

124. John David North, *Cosmos: An Illustrated History of Astronomy and Cosmology* (Chicago: University of Chicago Press, 2008), p. 56.

125. Stephen Bertman, *Handbook to Life in Ancient Mesopotamia* (Oxford: Oxford University Press, 2005), p. 169.

126. Wayne Horowitz, *Mesopotamian Cosmic Geography* (Winona Lake, IN: Eisenbrauns, 1998), p. 163.

127. David H. Kelley, Eugene F. Milone, and Anthony F. Aven, *Exploring Ancient Skies: A Survey of Ancient and Cultural Astronomy* (New York: Springer, 2004), p. 299.

128. Otto Neugebauer, "The Water Clock in Babylonian Astronomy," *Isis* (May 1947): 37–43.

129. Ben-Dov, *Head of All Years*; Hunger and Pingree, *Astral Sciences in Mesopotamia*, p. 46.

130. Friberg, *Amazing Traces*, pp. 184–86.

Why Knot? The Egyptian Rope Trick

131. Rudolph Kuper and Stefan Kröpelin, "Climate-Controlled Holocene Occupation in the Sahara: Motor of Africa's Evolution," *Science*, August 11, 2006, pp. 803–807.

132. Ibid.

133. Peter Gwin, "Lost Tribes of the Green Sahara: How a Dinosaur Hunter Uncovered the Sahara's Strangest Stone Age Graveyard," *National Geographic*, September 2008, http://ngm.nationalgeographic.com/2008/09/green-sahara/gwin-text.html (accessed November 21, 2010).

134. Jamie Woodward, *The Physical Geography of the Mediterranean* (Oxford: Oxford University Press, 2009), p. 56.

135. Henri J. Dumont, ed., *The Nile: Origins, Environments, Limnology, and Human Use* (New York: Springer, 2009), p. 1.

136. Jason Thompson, *A History of Egypt: From Earliest Times to the Present* (New York: Anchor Books, 2009), pp. 2–3.

137. Oswald Ashton Wentworth Dilke, *Mathematics and Measurement* (Berkeley: University of California Press/British Museum, 1987), p. 8.

138. Euclid and Proclus, *The First Book of Euclid's Elements: With a Commentary Based Principally upon That of Proclus Diadochus*, ed. William Barrett Frankland (Cambridge, UK: Cambridge University Press, 1905), p. ix; Irene K. Fischer, "At the Dawn of Geodesy," *Journal of Geodesy* 55, no. 2 (1981): 132–42; Jay Hambidge, *Dynamic Symmetry: The Greek Vase*

(Whitefish, MT: Kessinger, 2003), p. 144, originally published 1920; Hilary Wilson, *Egyptian Food and Drink* (Buckinghamshire, UK: Shire Publications, 1998), p. 11.

139. Walter Hazen, *Everyday Life: Ancient Times* (Tucson, AZ: Good Year Books, 2006), p. 10.

140. David P. Silverman, ed., *Ancient Egypt* (New York: Oxford University Press, 2003), p. 180.

141. Paula Willard, producer, *Egypt: Secrets of an Ancient World*, National Geographic, http://www.nationalgeographic.com/pyramids/pyramids.html (accessed November 25, 2010).

142. Ibid.

143. Sneferu was a nonstop pyramid builder. He built three of them. But the angle his architects chose for the slope of his second pyramid was too ambitious. It was too steep. It had a slant of over 53 degrees. Halfway through the building process, the pyramid began to break up. First the pyramid's planners tried to save the project by building an outer casing around the pyramid at a gentler angle—like building a pyramid around a pyramid. When that didn't stop the cracking, the builders finished the top half of the pyramid with a shallower angle. The result was not exactly greeted with wonder and esteem. It was ridiculous. And it is known to history as the "Bent Pyramid."

144. Susanna Thomas, *Snefru: The Pyramid Builder* (New York: Rosen, 2003), p. 80.

145. George Hart, *The Routledge Dictionary of Egyptian Gods and Goddesses* (London: Routledge, 2005), p. 82.

146. Carl Engel, *The Music of the Most Ancient Nations with Special Reference to Recent Discoveries in Western Asia and in Egypt* (London: John Murray, 1870), p. 194.

147. Carl Engel, *A Descriptive Catalogue of the Musical Instruments in the South Kensington Museum* (London: Her Majesty's Stationery Office, 1874), p. 11; Moustafa Gadalla, *The Ancient Egyptian Culture Revealed* (Greensboro, NC: Tehuti Research, 1996), p. 152.

148. Euclid and Proclus, *The First Book of Euclid's Elements*, ed. William Barrett Frankland (Cambridge, UK: Cambridge University Press, 1905), p. 129; Marshall Clagett, *Ancient Egyptian Science, A Source Book*, vol. 3, *Ancient Egyptian Mathematics* (Philadelphia: American Philosophical Society, 1999), p. 5.

149. Hazel Muir, "Pyramid Precision," *New Scientist*, November 15, 2000, http://www.newscientist.com/article/dn174-pyramid-precision.html (accessed July 3, 2011).

150. Eric H. Cline and Jill Rubalcaba, *The Ancient Egyptian World* (New York: Oxford University Press, 2005), p. 60; George St. Clair, *Creation Records Discovered in Egypt: Studies in the Book of the Dead* (London: David Nutt, 1898), p. 64; Eleanor L. Harris, *Ancient Egyptian Divination and Magic* (York Beach, ME: Weiser, 1998), p. 44; C. Scott Littleton, *Gods, Goddesses, and Mythology*, 11: 1334; Rosemary Clark, *The Sacred Magic of Ancient Egypt: The Spiritual Practice Restored* (St. Paul, MN: Llewellyn Worldwide, 2000), pp. 103, 141.

151. Corinna Rossi, *Architecture and Mathematics in Ancient Egypt* (Cambridge, UK: Cambridge University Press, 2004), p. 153; George Sarton, *Ancient Science through the Golden*

Age of Greece (Mineola, NY: Dover, 1993), p. 117, originally published by Harvard University Press, 1952.

152. J. Norman Lockyer, "On Some Points in Ancient Egyptian Astronomy," *Nature* 45, no. 1161 (January 1892): 297.

153. Eleanor Robson, *Mathematics in Ancient Iraq: A Social History* (Princeton, NJ: Princeton University Press, 2008); Gavin White, *Babylonian Star-Lore: An Illustrated Guide to the Star-Lore and Constellations of Ancient Babylonia* (London: Solaria, 2008), pp. 71, 204.

154. E. A. Wallis Budge, *Egyptian Heaven and Hell* (London: Kegan Paul, 1905), p. 145.

How to Hypnotize a Greek: Math as a Tourist Attraction

155. Clagett, *Ancient Egyptian Science*, p. 16.

156. Euclid and Proclus, *First Book of Euclid's Elements*, p. ix.

157. Clifford A. Pickover, *The Math Book: From Pythagoras to the 57th Dimension, 250 Milestones in the History of Mathematics* (New York: Sterling, 2009), p. 36.

158. Clagett, *Ancient Egyptian Science*.

159. Euclid and Proclus, *First Book of Euclid's Elements*, pp. ix–x.

160. Clagett, *Ancient Egyptian Science*, pp. 15–17.

161. Euclid and Proclus, *First Book of Euclid's Elements*, p. ix.

162. Clagett, *Ancient Egyptian Science*, p. 1.

163. Ibid., pp. 15–17; Roger Herz-Fischler, *The Shape of the Great Pyramid* (Waterloo, Ontario: Wilfrid Laurier University Press, 2000), pp. 38–40.

164. Clagett, *Ancient Egyptian Science*, p. 20.

165. Douglas M. Campbell and John C. Higgins, *Mathematics: People, Problems, Results* (Belmont, CA: Wadsworth, 1984), 2: 248.

166. Jay Hambidge, *Dynamic Symmetry: The Greek Vase* (Whitefish, MT: Kessinger, 2003), p. 144. Originally published in 1920.

167. Christoph Riedweg, *Pythagoras: His life, Teaching, and Influence* (Ithaca, NY: Cornell University Press, 2005), p. 1.

168. Iamblichus, "The Life of Pythagoras," in *The Pythagorean Sourcebook and Library*, ed. Kenneth Sylvan Guthrie and David Fideler (Grand Rapids, MI: Phanes, 1987), p. 127.

169. Clifford A. Pickover, *The Loom of God: Tapestries of Mathematics and Mysticism* (New York: Sterling, 2009), pp. 53–54.

170. Riedweg, *Pythagoras*, p. 2.

171. Pickover, *Loom of God*, p. 55.

172. Bertrand Russell, *History of Western Philosophy* (London: Routledge, 2004), p. 45.

173. Iamblichus, "The Life of Pythagoras," p. 59.

174. Dimitra Karamanides, *Pythagoras: Pioneering Mathematician and Musical Theorist of Ancient Greece* (New York: Rosen, 2006), p. 14.

175. Thucydides, *History of the Peloponnesian War*, trans. Richard Crawley, in *Library of the Future*, 4th ed. (Irvine, CA: World Library, Inc., 1996), CD-ROM, version 5.0.

176. Plutarch, *Agis*, in *Library of the Future*, 4th ed. (Irvine, CA: World Library, Inc., 1996), CD-ROM, version 5.0.

177. Clagett, *Ancient Egyptian Science*, p. 14; Paul T. Nicholson and Ian Shaw, *Ancient Egyptian Materials and Technology* (Cambridge, UK: Cambridge University Press, 2000), p. 406.

178. G. Mokhtar and Jamāl al-Dīn Mukhtār, *Ancient Civilizations of Africa* (Berkeley: University of California Press, 1990), p. 168; Barry J. Kemp, *Ancient Egypt: Anatomy of a Civilization* (East Sussex, UK: Psychology Press, 2006), pp. 171–72.

179. George Johnston Allman, *Greek Geometry from Thales to Euclid* (Dublin: Dublin University Press, 1889), pp. 7–18.

180. Diodorus, *The Historical Library of Diodorus the Sicilian*, trans. G. Booth (London: Military Chronicle Office, 1814), vol. 10, sect. 10, para. 1.

181. Isaiah M. Burney, ed. *Chronological Tables: Comprehending the Chronology and History of the World* (London: Richard Griffin, 1856), 1: 36.

182. Iamblichus, *Life of Pythagoras*, p. 61.

183. Guthrie and Fideler, *The Pythagorean Sourcebook*, p. 20.

184. H. H. Howorth, *Pythagoras in India* (publisher unknown, 1867); V. A. Smith, "On the Civilization of Ancient India," *Journal of the Asiatic Society of Bengal* 61, no. 1 (1892): 71.

185. Iamblichus, *Life of Pythagoras*, p. 62.

186. Ibid.

187. Asa Mahan, *A Critical History of Philosophy*, ed. Richard Friederich (New York, Phillips & Hunt, 1999), 1: 241. Reprint of 1883 edition.

Seduce 'Em with Numbers: How to Do a Pythagoras

188. Robert Sherrick Brumbaugh, *The Philosophers of Greece* (Albany: State University of New York Press, 1981), p. 31; Jamie James, *The Music of the Spheres: Music, Science, and the Natural Order of the Universe* (New York: Springer, 1995), p. 21.

189. Gillian Clark, *Iamblichus, On the Pythagorean Life* (Liverpool: Liverpool University Press, 1989), pp. 29–32.

190. Quoted in George Henry Lewes, *The Biographical History of Philosophy from Its Origin in Greece to the Present Day* (New York: Appleton, 1857), 1: 34–35.

191. Aristotle, *Metaphysics*, trans. Hugh Lawson-Tancred (London: Penguin, 1998), p. 22; Aristotle, *The Metaphysics* (New York: Cosimo, 2008), p. 17, originally published in 1907; Asa Mahan, *A Critical History of Philosophy*, ed. Richard Friederich (New York, Phillips & Hunt, 1999), 1: 241, reprint of 1883 edition.

192. Aristotle, *Metaphysics*, trans. Hippocrates G. Apostle (Des Moines, IA: Peripatetic, 1979), pp. 11, 242.

193. Andrew Barker, *Greek Musical Writings: Harmonic and Acoustic Theory* (Cambridge, UK: Cambridge University Press, 2004), 2: 4.

194. Carl Huffman, "Pythagoras," in *The Stanford Encyclopedia of Philosophy*, ed. Edward N. Zalta, http://plato.stanford.edu/entries/pythagoras (accessed October 4, 2011).

195. Iamblichus, "The Life of Pythagoras," in, *The Pythagorean Sourcebook and Library*, ed. Guthrie and Fideler, pp. 86–88. See also Catherine Nolan, "Music Theory and Mathematics," in *The Cambridge History of Western Music Theory*, ed. Thomas Street Christensen (Cambridge, UK: Cambridge University Press, 2002), p. 272; Iamblichus, *Iamblichus' Life of Pythagoras, or Pythagoric Life*, trans. Thomas Taylor (Rochester, VT: Inner Traditions Press, 1986), p. 62, reprint of the 1818 edition; Raymond Bernard, *Pythagoras: The Immortal Sage* (Whitefish, MT: Kessinger, 2003), p. 4.

196. Eli Maor, *The Pythagorean Theorem: A 4,000-Year History* (Princeton, NJ: Princeton University Press, 2007), pp. 19–20.

197. Iamblichus, "Life of Pythagoras," pp. 86–88. Guthrie and Fideler warn that "while the ratios given do indeed correspond to the musical intervals described, the method of obtaining them here related, using weights, is spurious."

198. Jöran Friberg, *A Remarkable Collection of Manuscripts in the Schøyen Collection: Cuneiform Texts I* (New York: Springer, 2007), pp. 346, 350, 380, 384.

199. Marshall Clagett, *Ancient Egyptian Science*, pp. 232–34.

200. Friberg, *Unexpected Links*, p. 78.

201. James, *Music of the Spheres*, p. 38.

202. Annette Imhausen, "Traditions and Myths in the Historiography of Egyptian Mathematics," in *The Oxford Handbook of the History of Mathematics*, ed. Eleanor Robson and Jacqueline A. Stedall (Oxford: Oxford University Press, 2009), p. 789.

203. Karl Popper, *The World of Parmenides: Essays on the Presocratic Enlightenment*, ed. Arne Friemuth Petersen and Jørgen Mejer (London: Routledge, 1998), p. 36; James, *Music of the Spheres*, p. 38.

204. *Encyclopedia of Philosophy for Smartphones and Mobile Devices* (Boston: Mobile Reference, 2007). According to Themistius, a fourth-century Byzantine rhetorician.

205. James, *Music of the Spheres*, p. 38.

206. Plutarch, *Plutarch's Essays and Miscellanies Comprising All His Works Collected Under the Title of "Morals,"* ed. William W. Goodwin (Boston: Little, Brown, 1906), p. 155. With an introduction by Ralph Waldo Emerson.

207. Ibid., p. 141.

208. Alan Musgrave, *Essays on Realism and Rationalism* (Amsterdam: Rodopi, 1999), p. 21.

209. Plutarch, *Plutarch's Essays and Miscellanies*, p. 155.

210. Ibid., p. 140.

211. Henry George Liddell and Robert Scott, *A Greek-English Lexicon*, Perseus Digital Library, http://www.perseus.tufts.edu/hopper/text?doc=Perseus:text:1999.04.0057:entry%3Dsfai%3Dra^ (accessed September 24, 2011).

212. Samuel Henry Hooke, *The Siege Perilous: Essays in Biblical Anthropology and Kindred Subjects* (Norwich, UK: SCM Press, 1970), p. 36; Daniel D. McLean, Amy R. Hurd, and Nancy Brattain Rogers, *Kraus' Recreation and Leisure in Modern Society* (Sudbury, MA: Jones & Bartlett, 2012), p. 52.

213. Stephen G. Miller, *Ancient Greek Athletics* (New Haven, CT: Yale University Press, 2004), p. 174.

214. Charlie Samuels, *Ancient Science: Prehistory A.D. 500* (New York: Gareth Stevens, 2011), p. 6.

215. Agence France Presse, "Ancient Flute Oldest Instrument Found," http://www.abc.net.au/science/articles/2009/06/25/2608114.htm (accessed July 4, 2011); Bruce Bower, "Doubts Aired over Neanderthal Bone 'Flute,'" *Science News*, April 4, 1998; Robert Fink, "Neanderthal Flute: Oldest Musical Instrument Matches Notes of Do, Re, Mi," *Crosscurrents* 183 (February 1997): 38.

216. Plutarch, *Plutarch's Essays and Miscellanies*, p. 143.

217. Ibid., p. 121.

218. Nicomachus (of Gerasa), *The Manual of Harmonics of Nicomachus the Pythagorean*, ed. Flora R. Levin (Grand Rapids, MI: Phanes Press, 1994), pp. 54–56.

219. Pliny (the Elder), *The Natural History of Pliny*, vol. 1, trans. John Bostock and H. T. Riley (London: Henry G. Bohn, 1855), footnote, p. 29; Plutarch, *Plutarch's Essays and Miscellanies*, p. 155.

220. Pliny, *Natural History*, pp. 52–53.

221. Ibid.

222. Ibid.

223. Ibid.

224. Philolaus, "Fragments of Philolaus [on the life of Pythagoras]," in *Pythagorean Sourcebook and Library*, ed. Kenneth Sylvan Guthrie and David R. Fideler (Grand Rapids, MI: Phanes, 1987), p. 175.

225. James, *Music of the Spheres*, p. 29.

226. Ibid.

227. Ibid.

228. Ibid.

229. Ibid.

230. Ibid.

231. Aristotle, *Metaphysics*, trans. Thomas Taylor (London: Davis, Wilks, and Taylor, 1801), p. 9.

232. James, *Music of the Spheres*, p. 29.

233. Brumbaugh, *Philosophers of Greece*, p. 32.

234. Iamblichus, "Life of Pythagoras," p. 72.

235. Ibid.

236. Ibid.

237. Ibid., p. 28.

238. Ibid.

239. Ibid.

240. Ibid.

241. Brumbaugh, *Philosophers of Greece*, pp. 36–39.

242. Iamblichus, "Life of Pythagoras," p. 129.

243. Ibid.

244. Iamblichus, *Life of Pythagoras by Iamblichus of Syrian Chacis*, ed. Kenneth Sylvan Guthrie (Alpine, NJ: Platonist Press, 1919), p. 34.

245. Iamblichus, "Life of Pythagoras," in Guthrie and Fideler, *Pythagorean Sourcebook and Library*, p. 72.

246. Ibid.

247. Ibid.

248. Ibid.

249. Brumbaugh, *Philosophers of Greece*, pp. 36–39.

250. Edouard Schur, *Pythagoras and the Delphic Mysteries: A Biography of Pythagoras* (New York: Cosimo, 2007), p. 168. Originally published in 1906.

251. Walter Burkert, *Lore and Science in Ancient Pythagoreanism* (Cambridge, MA: Harvard University Press, 1972), pp. 115–21.

252. Brumbaugh, *Philosophers of Greece*, pp. 36–39.

253. Guthrie and Fideler, *Pythagorean Sourcebook and Library*, p. 34.

254. Timaeus Locrus, "World Soul and Nature," in Guthrie and Fideler, *Pythagorean Sourcebook*, p. 181.

255. Aristotle, *Metaphysics*, p. 65.

256. James, *Music of the Spheres*, p. 36.

257. Christopher Bamford, ed., *Homage to Pythagoras: Rediscovering Sacred Science* (Hudson, NY: Lindisfarne, 1994), p. 137.

258. Arthur Koestler, *The Sleepwalkers* (New York: Macmillan, 1968), p. 25.

Squaring Your Way to Fame: Pythagoras's Hot New Theorem

259. Tattersall, *Elementary Number Theory*, p. 71; Eleanor Robson, "Words and Pictures: New Light on Plimpton 322," in *Sherlock Holmes in Babylon: And Other Tales of Mathematical History*, ed. Marlow Anderson, Victor J. Katz, and Robin J. Wilson (Washington, DC: Mathematical Association of America, 2004), p. 25. Reinhard Laubenbacher and David Pengelley, *Mathematical Expeditions: Chronicles by the Explorers* (New York: Springer, 1999), p. 172.

260. Nicholas Purcell, "Literate Games: Roman Urban Society and the Game of Alea,"

in *Studies in Ancient Greek and Roman Society*, ed. Robin Osborne (Cambridge: Cambridge University Press, 2004), p. 200.

261. Thomas Little Heath, *A History of Greek Mathematics: From Thales to Euclid* (Oxford: Oxford University Press, 1921), 1: 48.

262. *Oxford English Dictionary*, s.v. "hypotenuse."

4. HOW ARISTOTLE INVENTED THE AXIOM

A Trip to Plato's Cave

1. Gregory Chaitin, "Metabiology: Life as Evolving Software," http://www.cs .auckland.ac.nz/~chaitin/metabiology.pdf (accessed June 2, 2011), p. 102.

2. Plato, *The Republic of Plato*, trans. Alexander Kerr (Chicago: Charles H. Kerr, 1911), p. 385.

3. Ibid.

4. Ibid.

5. Ibid.

6. Ibid., pp. 1–4.

7. Ibid., pp. 410–21.

8. Ibid., p. 414.

9. Ibid., p. 7.

10. Ibid., p. 9.

11. Plato, "Timaeus," in *The Dialogues of Plato*, trans. Benjamin Jowett (Oxford: Oxford University Press, 1871), 2: 476.

12. Ibid.

13. Ibid.

14. Plato, "Phaedo and the Phaedrus," in *The Dialogs of Plato*, trans. Benjamin Jowett (New York: Scribner Armstrong, 1873), 1: 403, 404, 428–49, 431, 557, 564; Plato, *The Republic: The Statesman of Plato*, trans. Henry Davis (Washington, DC: M. Walter Dunn, 1901), pp. 227, 321. In reality, those who comment on Plato use words like "ideas," "the theory of ideas," and "the doctrine of ideas" more often than Plato does. Why? Because Aristotle brought the word "ideas" front and center roughly twenty-five years after the glory days of Plato.

15. Aristotle, *The Metaphysics*, trans. John McMahon (London: Henry G. Bohn, 1857), p. 27.

16. Lauralee Sherwood, *Fundamentals of Human Physiology* (Belmont, CA: Brooks/Cole, 2011); N. V. Bhagavan, *Medical Biochemistry* (San Diego: Academic, 2002), p. 199.

17. Christopher R. Kitchin, *Stars, Nebulae, and the Interstellar Medium* (New York: Taylor & Francis, 1987), p. 309.

18. Claus E. Rolfs and William S. Rodney, *Cauldrons in the Cosmos: Nuclear Astrophysics* (Chicago: University of Chicago Press, 1988), p. 41.

19. Aristotle, *The Logic of Science: A Translation of the Posterior Analytics of Aristotle*, ed. Edward Poste (Oxford: Francis Macpherson, 1850), pp. 41–43, 49, 54, 55, 88, 126.

20. Peter Aubusson, Allan G. Harrison, and Steve Ritchie, eds., *Metaphor and Analogy in Science Education* (Dordrecht, Netherlands: Springer, 2006); James Buchanan, *Analogy, Considered as a Guide to Truth, and Applied as an Aid to Faith* (Edinburgh: Johnstone, Hunter, 1864).

Aristotle Fights for Attention—Or Zeroing Zeno

21. Frank J. Sulloway, *Born to Rebel: Birth Order, Family Dynamics, and Creative Lives* (New York: Vintage, 1997).

22. Ibid., pp. xiii, 157, 168.

23. Ibid., p. 452.

24. Kevin Leman, *The Birth Order Book: Why You Are the Way You Are* (Grand Rapids, MI: Revell, 2009), unnumbered page.

25. Frank J. Sulloway, "Birth Order, Sibling Competition, and Human Behavior," chap. 2 in *Conceptual Challenges in Evolutionary Psychology: Innovative Research Strategies*, ed. Harmon R. Holcomb III (Dordrecht, Netherlands: Springer, 2001), pp. 39–85, http://www.sulloway.org/Holcomb.pdf (accessed July 4, 2011).

26. Martín Aluja and Allen Lee Norrbom, *Fruit Flies (*Tephritidae*): Phylogeny and Evolution of Behavior* (Boca Raton, FL: CRC Press, 2001), pp. 869–71; Mary Jane West-Eberhard, *Developmental Plasticity and Evolution* (New York: Oxford University Press, 2003), p. 562; Ulf Dieckmann, *Adaptive Speciation* (Cambridge, UK: Cambridge University Press, 2004), p. 175; M. B. Andersson, *Sexual Selection* (Princeton, NJ: Princeton University Press, 1994), pp. 210, 223; Maurice Sabelis and Jan Bruin eds., *Trends in Acarology: Proceedings of the 12th International Congress* (Dordrecht, Netherlands: Springer, 2010), p. 290.

27. Rosemary Gillespie, "Community Assembly through Adaptive Radiation in Hawaiian Spiders," *Science,* January 16, 2004, pp. 356–59.

28. Matthias Glaubrecht, ed., *Evolution in Action: Case Studies in Adaptive Radiation, Speciation, and the Origin of Biodiversity* (Heidelberg: Springer, 2010), p. 446.

29. Kelly Kissane, personal communication, July 10, 2011.

30. Kelly Kissane, "Geographic Variation and Cryptic Species: Evidence from Natural Populations of the Fishing Spider *Dolomedes triton*" (PhD dissertation, Department of Ecology, Evolutionary, and Conservation Biology, University of Nevada, Reno, August 2007).

31. Jeff Hawkins, Sandra Blakeslee, *On Intelligence* (New York: St. Martin's, 2005).

32. E. Bruce Goldstein, *Sensation and Perception* (Belmont, CA: Wadsworth, 2010), p. 62.

33. Kevin Fox, *Barrel Cortex* (Cambridge, UK: Cambridge University Press, 2008), pp. 127, 181.

34. Daniel E. Feldman, Cara B. Allen, and Tansu Celikel, "LTD, Spike Timing, and Somatosensory Barrel Cortex Plasticity," in *Excitatory-Inhibitory Balance: Synapses, Circuits, Systems,* ed. Takao K. Hensch and Michela Fagiolini (New York: Kluwer, 2004); Edward G. Jones and Irving T. Diamond, *Cerebral Cortex: The Barrel Cortex of Rodents* (New York: Plenum, 1995), pp. 1–3.

35. David P. Silverman, ed., *Ancient Egypt* (New York: Oxford University Press, 2003), p. 180.

36. Geoffrey Stephen Kirk, John Earle Raven, and Malcolm Schofield, *The Presocratic Philosophers: A Critical History with a Selection of Texts* (Cambridge, UK: Cambridge University Press, 2003), p. 79; Simson Najovits, *Egypt, Trunk of the Tree: A Modern Survey of an Ancient Land* (New York: Algora, 2003), 2: 276.

37. Aetius, quoted in Kirk et al., *Presocratic Philosophers,* p. 79.

38. James Fredal, *Rhetorical Action in Ancient Athens: Persuasive Artistry from Solon to Demosthenes* (Carbondale, IL: Southern Illinois University Press, 2006), pp. 12, 34.

39. Ibid., p. 27; James A. Colaiaco, *Socrates against Athens: Philosophy on Trial* (New York: Routledge, 2001), p. 93.

40. Homer set the Greek pattern of striving for fame, striving for "immortal praise." Homer, *The Iliad of Homer,* trans. Alexander Pope (Dublin: J. Halpen, 1791), p. 143. See also Plutarch, *The Age of Alexander: Nine Great Men* (New York: Penguin, 1977); W. K. C. Guthrie, *Aristotle: An Encounter* (Cambridge, UK: Cambridge University Press, 1981), pp. 21, 152.

41. David Giles, *Illusions of Immortality: A Psychology of Fame and Celebrity* (London: Macmillan, 2000); Leo Braudy, *The Frenzy of Renown: Fame and Its History* (Oxford: Oxford University Press, 1986).

42. Aristotle, *Logic of Science: Translation of Posterior Analytics of Aristotle,* ed. Edward Poste (Oxford, UK: Francis Macpherson, 1850).

43. Ibid., p. 13.

44. Aristotle, *Posterior Analytics,* ed. Paolo C. Biondi, (Quebec: Les Presses De L'Université Laval, 2004), 2: 19; Aristotle, *Categories,* trans. E. M. Edghill (Whitefish MT: Kessinger, 2004); Aristotle, *Prior Analytics and Posterior Analytics,* trans. A. J. Jenkinson and G. R. G. Mure (Stilwell, KS: Digireads.com, 2006), p. 118. Aristotle did not use the word "logic." Later philosophers introduced the term, then credited its invention to Aristotle.

45. John Watson, *An Outline of Philosophy: With Notes, Historical and Critical* (Glasgow: James Maclehose, 1898), p. 375.

46. Aristotle, *Logic of Science,* pp. 131–32. Watson, *An Outline of Philosophy,* p. 375. Another formulation is, "The same thing cannot at once belong and not belong to the same object in the same respect."

47. Aristotle, *Logic of Science,* p. 131.

48. Ibid., pp. 131–32.

49. Ibid.

50. Ibid.

51. Anaxagoras, *Anaxagoras of Clazomenae: Fragments and Testimonia*, ed. Patricia Curd (Toronto: University of Toronto Press, 2007), p. 3.

52. Aristotle, *Logic of Science*, pp. 131–32.

53. Ibid.

54. Ibid., p. 132.

55. Plato, *Protagoras and Meno*, trans. Robert C. Bartlett (Ithaca, NY: Cornell University Press), p. 6.

56. Ugo Zilioli, *Protagoras and the Challenge of Relativism: Plato's Subtlest Enemy* (Aldershot, UK: Ashgate, 2007), p. 19.

57. Aristotle, *Logic of Science*, pp. 131–32.

58. Ibid.

59. Ibid.

60. Ibid.

61. Ibid.

62. Ibid.

63. Aristotle, *De Anima*, trans. Hugh Lawson-Tancred (London: Penguin, 1983); Watson, *An Outline of Philosophy*, p. 375.

64. Aristotle, *Logic of Science*, p. 55.

65. Aristotle, *Metaphysics* (Sioux Falls, SD: NuVision, 2005), p. 160.

66. David L. Hull, *Science as a Process: An Evolutionary Account of the Social and Conceptual Development of Science* (Chicago: University of Chicago Press, 1988), p. 484.

67. Aristotle, *Logic of Science*, p. 42.

68. Ibid., p. 55.

69. Plato, *The Laws: Complete Works*, trans. John Madison Cooper and D. S. Hutchinson (Indianapolis: Hackett, 1997), p. 1552. "Definition" was one of the few key words Aristotle borrowed from his predecessors. You'll find it in the works of Plato.

70. Aristotle, *Logic of Science*, pp. 44, 51, 53, 57, 59.

71. Ibid., pp. 65–126.

72. Ibid., pp. 54–104.

73. Ibid., p. 42.

74. Ibid., pp. 43–106.

75. Ibid., pp. 4–125.

76. Ibid., 46–121.

77. "Science" is a word that appears eighty-three times in Aristotle's *The Logic of Science*.

78. Aristotle, *Logic of Science*, p. 121.

79. Ibid.

80. Ibid., p. 63.

81. Ibid., p. 51.

82. Ibid., p. 62.

83. Ibid.

84. Ibid., p. 75; Aristotle, *Metaphysica*, in *The Works of Aristotle*, vol. 8, trans. William David Ross and John Alexander Smith (Oxford: Oxford University Press, 1952), 10.1.1053b.

85. Aristotle, *Logic of Science*, p. 121.

86. Aristotle, *Posterior Analytics*, trans. G. R. G. Mure (Whitefish, MT: Kessinger, 2004), p. 18.

87. Ibid., p. 64.

88. Aristotle, *The Organon, or Logical treatises, of Aristotle with the Introduction of Porphyry*, vol. 2 (London: Bell, 1902).

89. Aristotle, *Logic of Science*, p. 57.

90. Jonathan Swift, *Gulliver's Travels*, in *Gulliver's Travels: The Tale of a Tub, The Battle of the Books, Etc.* (Oxford: Oxford University Press, 1919), p. 53.

91. Aristotle, *Posterior Analytics*, p. 3.

92. Aristotle, *Logic of Science*, p. 118.

93. Ibid.

94. Aristotle, *Translations from the Organon*, ed. John Magrath (Oxford: James Thornton, 1877), p. 1.

95. Aristotle, *Logic of Science*, p. 122; Aristotle, *Posterior Analytics*, p. 71.

96. Aristotle, *Logic of Science*, p. 122.

97. Ibid.

98. Ibid., p. 126.

99. Ibid.

How Euclid Makes Aristotle's "Science" Stick

100. Jane Muir, *Of Men and Numbers: The Story of the Great Mathematicians* (Mineola, NY: Dover, 1996), p. 16; reprint of 1961 original. For the history of string, see Elizabeth Wayland Barber, *Women's Work: The First 20,000 Years: Women, Cloth, and Society in Early Times* (New York: Norton, 1995).

101. Christopher Clapham and James Nicholson, *The Concise Oxford Dictionary of Mathematics* (Oxford: Oxford University Press, 2009), s.v. "number systems."

102. Richard A. Gabriel, *Great Captains of Antiquity* (Westport, CT: Greenwood, 2001), p. 84.

103. Thomas C. Brickhouse and Nicholas D. Smith, *Plato's Socrates* (New York: Oxford University Press, 1994), pp. 3–5.

104. Debra Skelton and Pamela Dell, *Empire of Alexander the Great* (New York: Chelsea House, 2009), pp. 11–12.

105. Philip Smith, *The Ancient History of the East: From the Earliest Times to the Conquest by Alexander the Great* (London: John Murray, 1881), pp. 581–82.

106. *Wikipedia*, s.v. "Alexander the Great," http://en.wikipedia.org/wiki/Alexander_the_Great#Death_and_succession (accessed July 11, 2011).

107. Katja Mueller, *Settlements of the Ptolemies: City Foundations and New Settlement in the Hellenistic World* (Leuven, Netherlands: Peeters, 2006), p. 147.

108. Margaret Bunson, *Encyclopedia of Ancient Egypt* (New York: Facts on File, 2002), p. 212.

109. George William Cox, *Tales of Ancient Greece* (London: Longmans Green, 1868), p. 29.

110. Eugenia Salza Prina Ricotti, *Meals and Recipes from Ancient Greece* (Los Angeles: Getty Museum, 2007), p. 29.

111. Kelly Trumble and Robina MacIntyre Marshall, *The Library of Alexandria* (New York: Houghton Mifflin, 2003), p. 29.

112. Chris Hayhurst, *Euclid: The Great Geometer* (New York: Rosen, 2006), pp. 50–54.

113. "Biographical Note," in Euclid, *The Thirteen Books of Euclid's Elements*, trans. Thomas Heath (Lawrence, KA: Digireads.com, 2010). Reprint of Cambridge University Press edition of 1908.

114. Euclid, *The First Book of Euclid's Elements*, trans. William Barrett Frankland (Cambridge, UK: Cambridge University Press, 1905), pp. xi–xvi.

115. Ibid; William Barrett Frankland, *The Story of Euclid* (London: G. Newnes, 1902), p. 52.

116. Euclid, *First Book of Euclid's Elements*, pp. xi–xvi.

117. Ibid.

118. Ibid.

119. Ibid.

120. Ibid.

121. Euclid, *The Elements of Euclid: Books I to VI*, trans. John Sturgeon Mackay (Memphis: General Books, 2010), pp. 11–13, reprint of 1887 edition; Richard J. Trudeau, *The Non-Euclidean Revolution* (Boston: Birkhäuser, 2008), p. 39.

122. Aristotle, *Metaphysics*, in *The Works of Aristotle*, trans. J. A. Smith and W. D. Ross (Oxford: Oxford University Press, 1908), 8: 12–13.

123. Ibid.

124. Ibid.

125. Ibid.

126. Ibid.

127. Ibid.

128. Ibid.

129. Ibid.

130. Ibid.

131. Ibid.

132. Ibid.

133. Ibid.

134. Ibid.

135. Euclid, *The Thirteen Books of Euclid's Elements*, trans. Johan Ludvig Heiberg and Thomas Heath (Cambridge, UK: Cambridge University Press, 1908), 1: 156.

136. Euclid, *First Book of Euclid's Elements*, pp. xi–xvi.

137. Peter Barlow, "Geometry," in *A New Mathematical and Philosophical Dictionary* (London: G. and S. Robinson, 1818).

138. "Preface" and "Biographical Note," in Euclid, *Thirteen Books of Euclid's Elements*; Thomas Heath, *A History of Greek Mathematics: From Thales to Euclid* (Oxford: Oxford University Press, 1921),1: 355.

139. J. Whitaker & Sons, *The Reference Catalogue of Current Literature* (Cambridge, UK: Cambridge University Press, 1906), 1: 56.

140. Euclid, Proclus, William Barrett Frankland, *The First Book of Euclid's Elements: With a Commentary Based Principally upon That of Proclus Diadochus* (Cambridge, UK: Cambridge University Press, 1905), p. xvi.

Galileo's Dad and the Drug of Geometry

141. Claude V. Palisca, "Was Galileo's Father an Experimental Scientist?" in *Music and Science in the Age of Galileo*, ed. Victor Coelho (Dordrecht, Netherlands: Kluwer, 1992), p. 143.

142. "Vincenzo Galilei," introduction to Vincenzo Galilei's "Dialog on Ancient and Modern Music," in *Source Readings In Music History*, ed. W. Oliver Strunk and Leo Treitler (New York: Norton, 1998), p. 462.

143. Vincenzo Galilei, *Dialogue on Ancient and Modern Music*, trans. Claude V. Palisca (New Haven, CT: Yale University Press, 2003), p. 313.

144. Ibid., p. 84.

145. Galileo Galilei and Polissena Galilei, *The Private Life of Galileo Compiled Principally from His Correspondence and That of His Eldest Daughter, Sister Maria Celeste* (London: MacMillan, 1870), p. 7.

Kepler: How to Tickle the Soul of the Earth

146. The number of definitions varies depending on the translation. There are thirty-five definitions in *Euclid's Elements*, ed. Robert Potts (London: Longman, Roberts, & Green, 1865). There are twenty-three definitions in *The Thirteen Books of Euclid's Elements*, trans. Johan Ludvig Heiberg and Thomas Heath (Cambridge, UK: Cambridge University Press, 1908), 1: 153–54.

147. Johannes Kepler, *The Harmony of the World* (*Harmonices Mundi*), trans. E. J. Aiton,

Alistair Matheson Duncan, and Judith Veronica Field (Philadelphia: American Philosophical Society, 1997), p. 326.

148. Ibid.

149. Henrietta McCall, *Mesopotamian Myths* (Austin: University of Texas Press, 2000), pp. 56–57; Gavin White, *Babylonian Star-Lore: An Illustrated Guide to the Star-Lore and the Constellations of Ancient Mesopotamia* (London: Solaria, 2008), pp. 168–70.

150. White, *Babylonian Star-Lore*, p. 243.

151. Alfred Jeremias, *The Old Testament in the Light of the Ancient East* (London: Williams and Northgate, 1911), 1: 13.

152. *Oxford English Dictionary*, s.v. "zodiac"; *Online Etymology Dictionary*, s.v. "zodiac," http://www.etymonline.com/index.php?search=zodiac&searchmode=none (accessed December 23, 2011).

153. Kepler, *Harmony of the World*, p. 327.

154. Ibid.

155. Ibid.

156. Ibid.

157. Ibid.

158. Ibid.

159. Ibid.

160. Ibid., p. 364.

161. Ibid.

162. Ibid., p. 326.

163. Ibid., p. 327.

164. Plato, *Timaeus*, trans. Benjamin Jowett (Charleston, SC: Forgotten Books, 2008), p. 17.

165. Charles H. Kahn, *Pythagoras and the Pythagoreans: A Brief History* (Indianapolis: Hackett, 2001), p. 56.

166. Ibid.

167. Ibid.

168. Kepler, *Harmony of the World*, p. 329.

169. Ibid., p. 337.

170. Ibid., p. 330.

171. Ibid.

172. Ibid.

173. Ibid., p. 483.

174. Ibid., p. 354.

Kepler's Boxes and Balls: Yes, Kepler's Freaky Math

175. Ibid., p. 329.

176. Edwin Burtt, *The Metaphysical Foundations of Modern Science* (Mineola, NY: Dover, 2003), pp. 56–62. Originally published in 1924.

177. Ibid., pp. 43–46.

178. Ibid., pp. 40–41.

179. Chikara Sasaki, *Descartes's Mathematical Thought* (Dordrecht, Netherlands: Kluwer, 2003), pp. 108, 419; Geneviève Rodis-Lewis, "Descartes' Life and the Development of his Philosophy," in *The Cambridge Companion to Descartes*, ed. John Cottingham (Cambridge, UK: Cambridge University Press, 1992), p. 29.

180. Rodis-Lewis, "Descartes' Life," p. 29.

181. Stephen Gaukroger, *Descartes: An Intellectual Biography* (Oxford: Oxford University Press, 1995), p. xvi; A. C. Grayling, *Descartes: The Life of René Descartes and Its Place in His Times* (London: Simon & Schuster, 2005), p. 151; John Cottingham, *Descartes* (Malden, MA: Blackwell, 1986), p. 11.

182. René Descartes, *Discourse on the Method and the Meditations*, trans. John Veitch (New York: Cosimo, 2008), p. 84. Originally published in 1637.

183. Ibid., pp. 19–20.

184. René Descartes, *Discourse on the Method and Meditations on First Philosophy*, ed. David Weissman (New Haven, CT: Yale University Press, 1996), pp. 51–52.

185. Gaukroger, *Descartes*, p. xi.

186. Isaac Newton, *Newton's Principia: The Mathematical Principles of Natural Philosophy*, trans. Andrew Motte, ed. N. W. Chittenden (New York: Daniel Adee, 1848), pp. 31–32.

187. Isaac Newton, *Principia*, ed. Stephen Hawking (Philadelphia: Running Press, 2002), pp. 3–11.

188. Alva Walker Stamper, "A History of the Teaching of Elementary Geometry: With Reference to Present-Day Problems" (PhD philosophy dissertation, Teachers College of Columbia University, New York, 1909), pp. 31–101.

189. Jürgen Overhoff, *Hobbes's Theory of the Will: Ideological Reasons and Historical Circumstances* (Lanham, MD: Rowman and Littlefield, 2000), p. 28.

190. Bertrand Russell, *History of Western Philosophy* (London: Routledge, 2004), p. 502. Originally published in 1946.

191. Overhoff, *Hobbes's Theory of the Will*, p. 28.

192. James T. Smith, *Methods of Geometry* (New York: Wiley, 2000), pp. 26–50; Russell, *History of Western Philosophy*, p. 502.

5. EVERYBODY DO THE FLIP

Guillotining an Axiom: Severing the Neck of Parallel Lines

1. Euclid, *The Elements of Plane Geometry*, ed. Thomas Keith (London: Longman, Rees et al., 1835), p. 6.

2. John William Withers, *Euclid's Parallel Postulate: Its Nature, Validity, and Place in Geometrical Systems* (Chicago: Open Court, 1905), p. 9.

3. Albrecht Durer, *Literary Remains of Albrecht Dürer*, ed. Sir William Martin Conway (London: Cambridge University Press, 1889), p. 227.

4. Withers, *Euclid's Parallel Postulate*, p. 9.

5. Morris Kline, *Mathematical Thought from Ancient to Modern Times* (New York: Oxford University Press, 1972), 1: 290.

6. Withers, *Euclid's Parallel Postulate*, p. 11.

7. Edward Shepherd Creasy, ed., *Memoirs of Eminent Etonians* (London: Richard Bentley, 1850), p. 52.

8. William Barrett Frankland, *The Story of Euclid* (London: G. Newnes, 1902), p. 140.

9. Ibid., p. 133.

10. Ibid., pp. 143–44.

11. Ibid., p. 142; Nicholas Lobachevsky, *Geometrical Researches on the Theory of Parallels*, trans. George Bruce Halsted (Austin: University of Texas Press, 1891), p. 7.

12. Frankland, *Story of Euclid*, p. 142.

13. Withers, *Euclid's Parallel Postulate*, p. 8. See also pp. 1–16.

14. Frankland, *Story of Euclid*.

15. *Oxford English Dictionary*, s.v. "Revolution."

16. Frankland, *Story of Euclid*, p. 150.

17. Ibid.

18. Ibid.

19. Ibid.

20. Withers, *Euclid's Parallel Postulate*, p. 13.

21. M. B. W. Tent, *The Prince of Mathematics: Carl Friedrich Gauss* (Natick, MA: A. K. Peters, 2008), p. 60; Guy Waldo Dunnington, *Carl Friedrich Gauss: Titan of Science* (Washington, DC: Mathematical Association of America, 2004), p. 391.

22. Frankland, *Story of Euclid*, p. 147.

23. Tent, *Prince of Mathematics*.

24. Ibid., p. xi.

25. Tent, *Prince of Mathematics*, p. xii.

26. J. B. Calvert, "The Electromagnetic Telegraph: A Technical History of the 19th-Century Electromagnetic Telegraph," University of Denver, http://mysite.du.edu/~jcalvert/tel/morse/morse.htm (accessed July 14, 2011).

27. Carl Friedrich Gauss, *Theory of the Combination of Observations Least Subject to Error*, trans. Gilbert W. Stewart (Philadelphia: Society for Industrial and Applied Mathematics, 1995), p. 210.

28. Christa Jungnickel and Russell McCormmach, *Intellectual Mastery of Nature: Theoretical Physics from Ohm to Einstein* (Chicago: University of Chicago Press, 1986), p. 73.

29. Glynn Winskel, "Discrete Mathematics II: Set Theory for Computer Science," University of Cambridge Computer Laboratory, http://www.cl.cam.ac.uk/~gw104/Disc Math.pdf (accessed July 14, 2011).

30. John Lankford, "The Golden Age of the Refracting Telescope," in *History of Astronomy: An Encyclopedia* (New York: Garland, 1997), p. 519.

31. Thomas Carlyle, *The French Revolution: The Guillotine* (London: James Fraser, 1837), p. 148.

32. Frankland, *Story of Euclid*, p. 149.

33. Guy Waldo Dunnington, *Carl Friedrich Gauss: Titan of Science* (Washington, DC: Mathematical Association of America, 2004), pp. 420–29.

34. Ibid., p. 26.

35. Ibid., pp. 27, 30.

36. Ibid.

37. *Wikipedia*, s.v. "Carl Friedrich Gauss," http://en.wikipedia.org/wiki/Carl_Friedrich_Gauss (accessed September 25, 2011).

38. John Bólyai, *The Science Absolute of Space*, trans. George Bruce Halsted (Austin: Neomon, 1896), p. xv.

39. Frankland, *Story of Euclid*, p. 149.

40. Ibid.

41. János Bólyai, "On Non-Euclidean Geometry," in *A Source Book in Mathematics*, ed. David Eugene Smith (Mineola, NY: Dover, 1959), pp. 375–88.

42. András Prékopa, Emil Molnár, and Magyar Tudományos Akadémia, eds., *Non-Euclidean Geometries: János Bólyai Memorial Volume* (New York: Springer, 2006), pp. 33–35.

43. Ibid., p. 5.

44. Ibid., p. 10.

45. Frankland, *Story of Euclid*, p. 160.

46. Prékopa et al., *Non-Euclidean Geometries*, p. 16.

47. Marvin J. Greenberg, *Euclidean and Non-Euclidean Geometries: Development and History* (New York: W. H. Freeman, 1993), p. 177.

48. Hungarian Academy of Sciences, "About János Bólyai," János Bólyai Conference on Hyperbolic Geometry, Budapest, Hungary, July 8–12, 2002, http://www.conferences.hu//Bolyai/#About János Bolyai (accessed January 25, 2011).

"One Man Deserves the Credit, One Man Deserves the Blame, and Nicolai Ivanovich Lobachevsky Is His Name"

49. Anatole Leroy-Beaulieu, *The Empire of the Tsars and the Russians*, vol. 1 (New York: G. P. Putnam, 1898), p. 79; Robert K. Massie, *Peter the Great: His Life and World* (New York: Random House, 1981).

50. Jason Socrates Bardi, *The Fifth Postulate: How Unraveling a Two-Thousand-Year-Old Mystery Unraveled the Universe* (Hoboken, NJ: Wiley, 2008), pp. 83–94.

51. Jim Bessman, "Tom Lehrer Boxes Up His Remains for Warner/Rhino," *Billboard*, Apr 15, 2000, p. 15.

52. Gerald Nachman, *Seriously Funny: The Rebel Comedians of the 1950s and 1960s* (New York: Watson-Guptill, 2004), p. 131.

53. "One Record Holds Entire Symphony," *LIFE Magazine*, July 26, 1948, p. 39.

54. Tom Lehrer, "Lobachevsky," in *Too Many Songs by Tom Lehrer* (New York: Pantheon books, 1981).

55. Michael Proudfoot and Alan Robert Lacey, *The Routledge Dictionary of Philosophy* (Abingdon, UK: Routledge, 2010), p. 382.

56. Ibid.; Alexey Stakhov and Scott Olsen, *The Mathematics of Harmony: From Euclid to Contemporary Mathematics and Computer Science* (Singapore: World Scientific, 2009), p. 262.

57. "János Bólyai," in *The MacTutor History of Mathematics Archive*, School of Mathematics and Statistics, University of St. Andrews, Scotland, http://www-groups.dcs.st-and.ac.uk/history/Biographies/Bolyai.html (accessed May 21, 2012).

58. Roberto Torretti, *Philosophy of Geometry from Riemann to Poincaré* (New York: Springer, 1984), p. 53.

59. András Prékopa et al., *Non-Euclidean Geometries*, pp. 15–16.

60. Nicholas Lobachevsky, *Geometrical Researches on the Theory of Parallels*, trans. George Bruce Halsted (New York: Cosimo, 2007), p. 6. Originally published in 1891.

61. Leonard Berlin, "Plagiarism, Salami Slicing, and Lobachevsky," *Skeletal Radiology* 38 (2009): 1–4.

62. Roberto Torretti, *Philosophy of Geometry from Riemann to Poincare* (Dordrecht, Netherlands: D. Reidel, 1978), p. 53.

Bare-Naked Math: Peano Strips It Down

63. Hubert Kennedy, *Peano: Life and Works of Giuseppe Peano* (San Francisco: Peremptory, 2002).

64. Ibid.

65. Ibid., p. 18.

66. Giuseppe Peano, *Arithmetices Principia: Nova Methodo Exposita* (Rome: Fratres Bocca, 2001); Hubert C. Kennedy, "The Mathematical Philosophy of Giuseppe Peano," in *Twelve*

Articles on Giuseppe Peano (San Francisco: Peremptory, 2002), pp. 6–13, http://hubertkennedy. angelfire.com/TwelveArticles.pdf (accessed June 4, 2012).

67. Kennedy, "The Mathematical Philosophy of Giuseppe Peano."

68. Graham Flegg, *Numbers: Their History and Meaning* (Mineola, NY: Dover, 2002), p. 60. Flegg claims that "when the Babylonian sexagesimal system had been taken over by the Greek astronomers, a small circle was adopted to indicate zero and used along with the Greek alphabetical numerals which did not otherwise need such a symbol." But apparently that zero never made it to the heart of the Greek number system.

69. Tika Downey, *The History of Zero: Exploring Our Place-Value Number System* (New York: Rosen, 2004), p. 5.

70. Tobias Dantzig, Joseph Mazur, and Barry Mazur, *Number: The Language of Science* (New York: Penguin, 2005), p. 31.

71. Downey, *History of Zero*, p. 5.

72. Charles Seife, *Zero: The Biography of a Dangerous Idea* (New York: Penguin, 2000).

73. Robert Kaplan, *The Nothing That Is: A Natural History of Zero* (Oxford: Oxford University Press, 2000).

74. Edward Robert Harrison, *Cosmology: The Science of the Universe* (Cambridge, UK: Cambridge University Press, 2000), p. 478.

75. David Bohm, *Wholeness and the Implicate Order* (London: Routledge, 1980), p. 196.

76. Eli Maor, *The Story of a Number* (Princeton NJ: Princeton University Press, 1994), p. 44.

77. Giuseppe Peano, "The Principles of Arithmetic, Presented by a New Method (1889)," in Jean van Heijenoort, *From Frege to Gödel: A Source Book in Mathematical Logic, 1879–1931* (Cambridge, MA: Harvard University Press, 1967), pp. 83–97.

78. Kennedy, *Peano*, p. 177.

79. Tony Stankus, ed., *Biographies of Scientists for Sci-Tech Libraries: Adding Faces to the Facts* (Binghamton, NY: Haworth, 1991), p. 33.

80. Fulvia Skof, ed., *Giuseppe Peano between Mathematics and Logic* (Milan: Springer, 2011), pp. 89, 102.

81. Giuseppe Peano, *Formulaire de Mathématiques*, vol. 5 (Rome: Bocca frères, Ch. Clausen, 1908); Joseph Warren Dauben and Christoph J. Scriba, eds., *Writing the History of Mathematics: Its Historical Development*, edited on behalf of the International Commission on the History of Mathematics (Basel: Birkhäuser, 2002) p. 545.

82. Elena Marchisotto and James T. Smith, *The Legacy of Mario Pieri in Geometry and Arithmetic* (Boston: Birkhäuser, 2007), p. 364.

83. David Berlinski, *One, Two, Three: Absolutely Elementary Mathematics* (New York: Random House, 2011), p. 47.

84. Hubert Kennedy, "Peano—The Unique," in Kennedy, *Twelve Articles on Giuseppe Peano*, pp. 103–106.

85. Siobhan Chapman and Christopher Routledge, eds., *Key Thinkers in Linguistics*

and the Philosophy of Language (New York: Oxford University Press, 2005), p. 228; I. Grattan-Guinness, *The Search for Mathematical Roots, 1870–1940: Logics, Set Theories, and the Foundations of Mathematics from Russell to Gödel* (Princeton, NJ: Princeton University Press, 2000), p. 90.

86. Bertrand Russell, *The Basic Writings of Bertrand Russell* (Abingdon, UK: Routledge, 2009), 10: 16.

87. Bertrand Russell, *Autobiography* (East Sussex, UK: Psychology Press, 1998), p. 147, originally published in three volumes 1967–1969; Kennedy, *Peano*.

88. Bertrand Russell, *The Principles of Mathematics* (Cambridge, UK: Cambridge University Press, 1903), p. 429.

89. Alfred North Whitehead and Bertrand Russell, *Principia Mathematica* (Cambridge, UK: Cambridge University Press, 1997), p. 91.

90. Russell, *Principles of Mathematics*, p. 429.

Ted Coons, Dancing Wonder: A Tale of Two Translations

91. Roberto Toni and Ronald M. Lechan, "Functional Anatomy of the Hypothalamus and Pituitary," chap. 3B in *Neuroendocrinology, Hypothalamus, and Pituitary*, Endotext.com, Tufts University School of Medicine, http://www.endotext.org/neuroendo/neuroendo3b/neuroendo 3b.htm (accessed May 3, 2010).

92. A. G. Berkovich and E. M. Zhmud, *Characters of Finite Groups*, pt. 2 (Providence: American Mathematical Society, 1999), pp. 114–15.

93. E. E. Coons, personal communications, July 18, 2011.

94. Neal Miller, *Conflict, Displacement, Learned Drives, and Theory* (Piscataway, NJ: Transaction, 2008), originally published in 1971; Neal E. Miller and John Dollard, *Social Learning and Imitation* (New Haven, CT: Yale University Press, 1941).

95. Edgar E. Coons, Milena Levak, and Neal E. Miller, "Lateral Hypothalamus: Learning of Food-Seeking Response Motivated by Electrical Stimulation," *Science*, December 3, 1965, pp. 1320–21; Edgar E. Coons and Howard A. White, "Tonic Properties of Orosensation and the Modulation of Intracranial Self-Stimulation: The CNS Weighting of External and Internal Factors Governing Reward," *Annals of the New York Academy of Sciences*, vol. 290, *Tonic Functions of Sensory Systems*, April 1977, pp. 158–79.

96. *Wikipedia*, s.v. "Electric Circus" (nightclub), http://en.wikipedia.org/wiki/Electric _Circus_ (accessed July 18, 2011).

97. Ted Coons, personal communication, May 4, 2011.

98. Terrence Joseph Sejnowski, *The Computational Brain* (Cambridge, MA: MIT Press, 1996), p. 148; Stéphane Jaffard, Yves Meyer, and Robert Dean Ryan, *Wavelets: Tools for Science and Technology* (Philadelphia: Society for Industrial and Applied Mechanics, 2001), pp. 5–6.

99. V. S. Ramachandran, *The Tell-Tale Brain: A Neuroscientist's Quest for What Makes Us Human* (New York: Norton, 2011).

Presto, Change-o: Translation's Little Secret

100. "Chronological List of The Publications of Giuseppe Peano," in Kennedy, *Peano*.

101. Giuseppe Peano, *Rivista di Matematica*, vols. 3–4 (Turin: Fratelli Bocca, 1893), p. 52; Giuseppe Peano, *Aritmetica Generale e Algebra Elementare* (Turin: Paravia, 1902), p. 13.

The Day You Uploaded Your Self: Translation Saves Your Life

102. Davide Castelvecchi, "Shadow World," *Science News Online*, November 17, 2007, http://www.sciencenews.org/articles/20071117/bob9.asp (accessed November 21, 2007).

103. Richard Schulz and Scott R. Beach, "Caregiving as a Risk Factor for Mortality: The Caregiver Health Effects Study," *Journal of the American Medical Association* 282, no. 23 (1999): 2215–19.

104. David Sloan Wilson and Elliott Sober, *Unto Others: The Evolution and Psychology of Unselfish Behavior* (Cambridge, MA: Harvard University Press, 1998), p. 188; David Sloan Wilson, *Darwin's Cathedral: Evolution, Religion, and the Nature of Society* (Chicago: University of Chicago Press, 2002), p. 79.

105. David Berreby, "Enthralling or Exasperating: Select One." *New York Times*, September 24, 1996.

106. Howard Bloom, *Global Brain: The Evolution of Mass Mind from the Big Bang to the 21st Century* (New York: Wiley, 2000).

107. L. H. Hou, et al. "Confuciusornis Sanctus: A New Late Jurassic Sauriurine Bird from China," *Chinese Science Bulletin* 40 (1995): 1545–51.

108. Lianhai Hou et al., "Early Adaptive Radiation of Birds: Evidence from Fossils from Northeastern China," *Science*, November 15, 1996, pp. 1164–67; Lianhai Hou et al., "A Diapsid Skull in a New Species of the Primitive Bird Confuciusornis," *Nature*, June 17, 1999, pp. 679–82; Henry Gee, ed., *Rise of the Dragon: Readings from Nature on the Chinese Fossil Record* (Chicago: University of Chicago Press, 2001), p. 123.

109. Hou et al., "Early Adaptive Radiation of Birds," pp. 1164–67.

110. Jun John Sakurai, *Currents and Mesons* (Chicago: University of Chicago Press, 1969), p. 15; Joel Isaacson, "Steganogramic Representation of the Baryon Octet in Cellular Automata," http://www.scribd.com/doc/36327492/stegano (accessed July 19, 2011).

6. IS METAPHOR A CRIME?

The Hunger of the Stuttering Forms: Isomorphic Symbol Sets

1. C. J. Date, *Logic and Databases: The Roots of Relational Theory* (Victoria, BC: Trafford, 2007), pp. 167, 172, 247–48, 252.

2. Aristotle, *The Logic of Science: A Translation of the Posterior Analytics of Aristotle, with Notes and an Introduction by Edward Poste* (Oxford: Francis Macpherson, 1850), p. 121.

Leonardo's Stones: Why Metaphor Works

3. Leonardo da Vinci, *The Writings of Leonardo da Vinci*, trans. Francesca Romei (Beaucamps-le-Vieux, France: Douglas, 2008), p. 50; Eugène Müntz, *Leonardo da Vinci: Artist, Thinker, and Man of Science* (London: Heinemann, 1898), pp. 98–187; Leonardo da Vinci, *Leonardo da Vinci's Note-Books*, trans. Edward McCurdy (London: Duckworth, 1906), p. 27.

4. Müntz, *Leonardo da Vinci*, p. 99.

5. Da Vinci, *Leonardo da Vinci's Note-Books*, p. 201.

6. Ibid.

7. Ibid., p. 209.

8. Ibid., p. 201.

9. Ibid., p. 209.

10. Ibid., p. 74.

11. Ibid.

12. Ibid., p. 96.

13. Ibid.

14. Galileo Galilei, *Galileo on the World Systems: A New Abridged Translation and Guide*, trans. and ed. Maurice A. Finocchiaro (Berkeley: University of California Press, 1997), p. 57.

15. Da Vinci, *Leonardo da Vinci's Note-Books*, p. 99.

16. Ibid.

17. Ibid., p. 98.

18. Ibid.

19. Ibid.

20. Ibid., p. 99.

21. Galileo Galiliei, *The Essential Galileo*, ed. Maurice A. Finocchiaro (Indianapolis: Hackett, 2008), p. 86.

22. Ibid., p. 92.

23. Ibid., pp. 98–99.

24. Ibid., p. 116.

25. Ibid., p. 92.

26. Quoted from Leonardo's notebooks in Fritjof Capra, *The Science of Leonardo: Inside the Mind of the Great Genius of the Renaissance* (New York: Doubleday, 2007), pp. 229–30.

27. Ibid.

28. Da Vinci, *Leonardo Da Vinci's Note-Books*, p. 117.

29. Leonardo Da Vinci, *Leonardo's Notebooks*, ed. H. Anna Suh (New York: Black Dog & Leventhal, 2005), p. 99.

30. Da Vinci, *Leonardo Da Vinci's Note-Books*, p. 117.

31. Hammurabi, *Hammurabi's Laws*, trans. M. E. J. Richardson (London: T&T Clark, 2004).

32. Da Vinci, *Leonardo da Vinci's Note-Books*, p. 117.

33. Ibid., p. 118.

34. Ibid., p. 74.

35. Da Vinci, *Leonardo's Notebooks*, p. 103.

36. James Gleick, *Isaac Newton* (New York: Random House, 2004).

37. Ian Graham, *Military and Government Technology* (Chicago: Raintree, 2011), p. 128.

38. Kathleen Krull, *Isaac Newton* (New York: Penguin, 2008), unnumbered page: "The third law, that every action has an equal and opposition reaction, is said to have occurred to Newton while observing billiard balls in play." Billiards was an indoor variation of croquet, a good adaptation for a rainy land like England, where playing outdoors was not possible most of the year. Shakespeare mentioned the game as early as 1600 in *Antony and Cleopatra*. But the first rule book of billiards was not written until 1675, when Newton was thirty-three years old. At that point, the game was still evolving, but the rule book bragged that in England there were "few Towns of note therein which hath not a publick Billiard-Table." Billiard Congress of America, *Billiards: The Official Rules and Records Book* (Guilford, CT: Lyons Press, 2005), p. 1.

39. Isaac Newton, *Opticks: Or, a Treatise of the Reflections, Refractions, Inflections and Colours of Light*, 3rd ed. (London: Innys, 1721), pp. 335–45; Isaac Newton, *Newton's Philosophy of Nature: Selections from His Writings* (Whitefish, MT: Kessinger, 2003), pp. 150–56.

40. Ibid.

41. *Oxford English Dictionary*, s.v. "particle."

Plaid in the Pool: The Eye Doctor Who Gave You Waves

42. F. G. Healey, *The Literary Culture of Napoleon* (Geneva: Droz, 1959), p. 53.

43. William Hazlitt, *The Life of Napoleon Bonaparte* (Paris: Napoleon Society, 1895), 2: 222.

44. Sir Walter Scott, *The Life of Napoleon* (Philadelphia: E. L. Carey, 1839), p. 216.

45. E. A. Wallis Budge, *The Rosetta Stone* (Whitefish, MT: Kessinger), p. 17. Originally published in 1913.

46. Ibid., p. 21.

47. R. B. Parkinson, *The Rosetta Stone* (London: British Museum Press, 2005), p. 36; British Museum, "The Rosetta Stone: Egypt, Ptolemaic Period, 196 BC," http://www.british museum.org/explore/highlights/highlight_objects/aes/t/the_rosetta_stone.aspx (accessed September 25, 2011).

48. Budge, *The Rosetta Stone*, pp. 25–26, 59; E. A. Wallis Budge, *The Decrees of Memphis and Canopus: The Rosetta Stone*, vol. 1 (London: Kegan Paul, 1904).

49. Alexander Wood and Frank Oldham, *Thomas Young: Natural Philosopher 1773–1829* (London: Cambridge University Press, 1954), pp. 138–50. Oliver Morsch, *Quantum Bits and Quantum Secrets: How Quantum Physics Is Revolutionizing Codes and Computers* (Weinheim, Germany: Wiley, 2008), p. 11; Wayne M. Saslow, *Electricity, Magnetism, and Light* (Toronto: Thomson, 2002), p. 698.

50. Wood and Oldham, *Thomas Young*, p. 138.

51. Cutler J. Cleveland, *Concise Encyclopedia of the History of Energy* (San Diego: Elsevier, 2009), p. 91; Carol Ballard, *From Steam Engines to Nuclear Fusion: Discovering Energy* (Chicago: Heinemann, 2007), p. 4.

52. Thomas Young, "Experiments and Calculations Relative to Physical Optics," and Jean Fresnel, "Fresnel's Prize Memoir on the Diffraction of Light," in Christiaan Huygens, Thomas Young, and Augustin-Jean Fresnel, *The Wave Theory of Light: Memoirs by Huygens, Young and Fresnel*, ed. Henry Crew (New York: American Book Company, 1900), pp. 68, 101.

53. Paul Allen Tipler and Gene Mosca, *Physics for Scientists and Engineers* (New York: Freeman, 2008) p. 1131.

54. Aristotle, Porphyry, *The Organon, or Logical Treatises, of Aristotle: With the Introduction of Porphyry*, vol. 1, trans. Octavius Freire Owen (London: George Bell, 1889).

55. Euclid, *The Elements of Euclid*, ed. Isaac Todhunter (London: MacMillan, 1867).

56. Galileo Galilei, *Dialogue Concerning the Two Chief World Systems, Ptolemaic and Copernican*, with a foreword by Albert Einstein, trans. Stillman Drake (Berkeley: University of California Press, 1967).

57. Ralph Baierlein, *Newton to Einstein: The Trail of Light* (Cambridge, UK: Cambridge University Press, 1991), p. 81.

58. Keith J. Devlin, *The Language of Mathematics: Making the Invisible Visible* (New York: Henry Holt, 1998), p. 165.

59. Henry Walter De Puy, *Kossuth and His Generals* (Buffalo, NY: Phinney, 1852); D. Urquhart, "The Military Strength of Turkey," *Free Press* 14–18 (1852): 18; William Manchester, *The Arms of Krupp: 1587–1968* (Boston: Little, Brown, 1968).

How Form Goes Manic—What's an Ur Pattern?

60. Geoffrey Galt Harpham, *The Humanities and the Dream of America* (Chicago: University of Chicago Press, 2011), p. 50.

61. Torleif Elgvin, "4Q413—A Hymn and a Wisdom Instruction," in *Emanuel: Studies in Hebrew Bible, Septuagint, and Dead Sea Scrolls in Honor of Emanuel Tov*, ed. Shalom M. Paul et al. (Leiden: Brill, 2003), p. 216; John Van Seters, *The Edited Bible: The Curious History of the "Editor" in Biblical Criticism* (Winona Lake, IN: Eisenbrauns, 2006), p. 314.

62. Vladimir Vladimirovich Nabokov, *The Stories of Vladimir Nabokov* (New York: Random House, 1997), p. 548.

63. W. H. Auden, *The Age of Anxiety: A Baroque Eclogue*, ed. Alan Jacobs (Princeton, NJ: Princeton University Press, 2011), p. 37. Originally published in 1947.

64. British Broadcasting Corporation, *The Listener* 97 (1977): 416.

65. Orion D. Weiner et al., "An Actin-Based Wave Generator Organizes Cell Motility," *Public Library of Science Biology* 5, no. 9 (2007), http://www.plosbiology.org/article/info%3Adoi%2F10.1371%2Fjournal.pbio.0050221 (accessed October 30, 2011); Katsuya Shimabukuro et al., "Reconstitution of Amoeboid Motility in Vitro Identifies a Motor-Independent Mechanism for Cell Body Retraction," *Current Biology* 21, no. 20 (October 2011): 1727–31.

66. Mark S. Mooseker, Thomas D. Pollard, and Kristi A. Wharton, "Nucleated Polymerization of Actin from the Membrane-Associated Ends of Microvillar Filaments in the Intestinal Brush Border," *Journal of Cell Biology* 95, no. 1 (October 1982): 223–33.

67. Charles V. Benton, *Trends in General Relativity and Quantum Cosmology* (New York: Nova, 2006), p. 28.

68. Euclid, J. L. Berggren, and Robert S. D. Thomas, *Euclid's Phaenomena: A Translation and Study of a Hellenistic Treatise in Spherical Astronomy* (Providence: American Mathematical Society, 1996).

69. Peter Grego and David Mannion, *Galileo and 400 Years of Telescopic Astronomy* (New York: Springer, 2010), p. 51.

70. David Adams Leeming, *The Oxford Companion to World Mythology* (New York: Oxford University Press, 2005), p. 258.

71. John W. Lieb, "Leonardo Da Vinci—Natural Philosopher and Engineer," *Journal of the Franklin Institute*, June 1921, pp. 767–806; Martin Kemp and Leonardo da Vinci, *Leonardo da Vinci: The Marvellous Works of Nature and Man* (Oxford: Oxford University Press, 2006), p. 81.

Real Estate in the Embryo: Location, Location, Location— Karl Ernst von Baer and Hans Adolf Eduard Driesch

72. Paul Davies, *The Cosmic Blueprint: New Discoveries in Nature's Creative Ability to Order* (West Conshohocken, PA: Templeton Foundation Press, 2004), p. 139.

73. Karl Ernst von Baer and Anton Dohrn, *Correspondence: Karl Ernst Von Baer (1792–1876) Anton Dohrn (1840–1909)*, ed. Christiane Groeben (Philadelphia: American Philosophical Society, 1993), p. 74.

74. Kenneth M. Setton, Norman P. Zacour, and Harry W. Hazard, *A History of the Crusades: The Impact of the Crusades on the Near East* (Madison: University of Wisconsin Press, 1985), p. 312.

75. Donald J. Harreld, *High Germans in the Low Countries: German Merchants and Commerce in Golden Age Antwerp* (Leiden: Brill, 2004), p. 33.

76. Georg Hartwig, *The Polar and Tropical Worlds: A Description of Man and Nature in the Polar and Equatorial Regions of the Globe*, ed. A. H. Guernsey (Springfield, MA: Bill, Nichols & Co., 1872), p. 151.

77. Edward G. Ruestow, *The Microscope in the Dutch Republic: The Shaping of Discovery* (Cambridge, UK: Cambridge University Press, 2004), p. 297.

78. Karl Ernst von Baer, *Autobiography of Dr. Karl Ernst von Baer*, ed. Jane Marion Oppenheimer (Cambridge, UK: Science History Publications, 1986), pp. 141, 209, 314; Von Baer and Dohrn, *Correspondence*, p. 11; A. Sedgwick, "Von Baer's Law and the Significance of Ancestral Rudiments in Embryonic Development," *Journal of the Royal Microscopical Society* 14 (1894): 430; John Alexander Moore, *Science as a Way of Knowing: The Foundations of Modern Biology* (Cambridge, MA: Harvard University Press, 1993), p. 404.

79. von Baer and Dohrn, *Correspondence*, p. 73.

80. Ron Amundson, *The Changing Role of the Embryo in Evolutionary Thought: Roots of Evo-Devo* (New York: Cambridge University Press, 2005), p. 59; Dov Ospovat, *The Development of Darwin's Theory: Natural History, Natural Theology, and Natural Selection 1838–1859* (Cambridge, UK: Cambridge University Press, 1981), p. 160; Eliakim Littell and Robert S. Littell, "Autobiography of a Physiologist," in *Living Age* 93 (April–June 1867): 424.

81. von Baer, *Autobiography*, p. 318. The word "differentiation" only appears once in von Baer's autobiography.

82. Ibid., p. 264; Lois N. Magner, *A History of the Life Sciences* (New York: Marcel Dekker, 2002), pp. 192–93.

83. Stephen Jay Gould, *Ontogeny and Phylogeny* (Cambridge, UK: Harvard University Press, 1977), pp. 61, 70; Amundson, *The Changing Role of the Embryo*, p. 59.

84. *Oxford English Dictionary*, s.v. "gear."

85. Anne Harrington, *Reenchanted Science: Holism in German Culture from Wilhelm II to Hitler* (Princeton, NJ: Princeton University Press, 1996), p. 49.

86. Hans Driesch, *The Science and Philosophy of the Organism: The Gifford Lectures* (London: Adam and Charles Black, 1908), p. vii.

87. Ibid., p. 223.

88. Hans Driesch, *The History and Theory of Vitalism*, trans. Charles Kay Ogden, (London: Macmillan, 1914), pp. 208–15.

89. Ibid., p. 241.

90. Driesch, *Science and Philosophy of the Organism*, p. 294.

91. Driesch, *History and Theory of Vitalism*, p. 205.

92. Ibid.

93. Ibid., pp. 208–15.

94. Ibid., p. 223.

95. Ibid., p. 224.

96. Ibid., p. 219.

97. Ibid., p. 78.

98. Driesch uses the word "unity" twenty-four times in his *History and Theory of Vitalism.*

99. Ron Cowen, "Cosmic Revelations: Satellite Homes in the Infant Universe," *Science News*, February 15, 2003, http://www.sciencenews.org/20030215/fob1.asp (accessed February 7, 2004).

100. Philip W. Anderson, "More Is Different—One More Time," in *More Is Different: Fifty Years of Condensed Matter Physics*, ed. N. Phuan Ong and Ravin N. Bhatt (Princeton, NJ: Princeton University Press, 2001), pp. 1–8.

101. Clay Shirky, *Cognitive Surplus: Creativity and Generosity in a Connected Age* (New York: Penguin, 2010), Kindle edition, location 353–54.

102. Driesch, *History and Theory of Vitalism*, p. 224.

103. John Travis, "Eye-Opening Gene: How Many Times Did Eyes Arise?" *Science News*, May 10, 1997, http://www.sciencenews.org/sn_arc97/5_10_97/bob1.htm (accessed April 11, 2011).

104. Carl Sagan, *Cosmos* (New York: Ballantine, 1985), p. 3; Stephen Eales, *Origins: How the Planets, Stars, Galaxies, and the Universe Began* (London: Springer, 2007), p. 61. Sagan calls this figure, 10^{22}, ten billion trillion.

105. Aristotle, *The Ethics of Aristotle*, ed. Sir Alexander Grant (London: John W. Parker, 1857), p. 172.

106. Isaac Newton, *Mathematical Principles of Natural Philosophy and His System of the World*, ed. Florian Cajori (Berkeley: University of California Press, 1962), 1: 670.

107. Isaac Newton, *Principia*, ed. Stephen Hawking (Philadelphia: Running Press, 2002), p. 428.

108. James Hayden Tufts, *The Sources and Development of Kant's Teleology* (Chicago: University of Chicago Press, 1892), pp. 3–4. Tufts points out that even Newton had a teleological view.

109. Ludwig Büchner, *Force and Matter: Or Principles of the Natural Order of the Universe, with a System of Morality Based Thereon*, trans. Ludwig Büchner (New York: Peter Eckler, 1891), p. 105.

110. J. A. Zahm, "Evolution and Teleology," *Popular Science*, April 1898, p. 817; "Ludwig Büchner 1824," Freethought Almanac, http://freethoughtalmanac.com/?p=1813 (accessed July 21, 2011).

111. Büchner, *Force and Matter*, pp. 172–74.

Master of the Universe:
Herbert Spencer, Grand Unifier and Flirt

112. Christoph Cardinal Schönborn, foreword to *From Aristotle to Darwin and Back Again: A Journey in Final Causality* by Étienne Gilson (Notre Dame, IN: University of Notre Dame Press, 1984), p. xx.

113. Jay Rumney, *Herbert Spencer's Sociology* (Piscataway, NJ: Transaction, 1965), p. 359.

114. John Offer, *Herbert Spencer: Critical Assessments of Leading Sociologists* (London: Routledge, 2000), 4: 314.

115. Patrick Joseph McCormick, *History of Education: A Survey of the Development of Educational Theory and Practice in Ancient, Medieval, and Modern Times* (Washington, DC: Catholic Education Press, 1915), p. 363.

116. Herbert Spencer, *A System of Synthetic Philosophy*, vol. 1, *First Principles* (London: Williams and Norgate, 1870); Herbert Spencer, *Synthetic Philosophy* (New York: D. Appleton, 1919); Frederick Howard Collins, *An Epitome of the Synthetic Philosophy*, with preface by Herbert Spencer (London: Williams and Norgate, 1889).

117. Cornelius Brown, *Lives of Nottinghamshire Worthies and of Celebrated and Remarkable Men of the County* (London: H. Sotheran, 1882), p. 273.

118. John E. B. Mayor, Robert Forsyth Scott, and St. John's College, *Admissions to the College of St. John the Evangelist in the University of Cambridge* (Cambridge: Cambridge University Press, 1893), p. 538.

119. M. J. S. Rudwick, *The Meaning of Fossils: Episodes in the History of Palaeontology* (Chicago: University of Chicago Press, 1972), p. 86.

120. Ibid., p. 84.

121. R. T. J. Moody et al., eds., *Dinosaurs and Other Extinct Saurians: A Historical Perspective* (Bath, UK: Geological Society, 2010), p. 8.

122. Christopher Upham Murray Smith and Robert Arnott, *The Genius of Erasmus Darwin* (Aldershot, UK: Ashgate, 2005), p. 1.

123. Arja Nurmi, Minna Nevala, and Minna Palander-Collin, eds., *The Language of Daily Life in England (1400–1800)* (Amsterdam: John Benjamins, 2009), p. lxxxix.

124. Robert E. Schofield, "The Lunar Society of Birmingham; A Bicentenary Appraisal," *Notes and Records of the Royal Society of London*, December 1966, pp. 144–61; Jennifer S. Uglow, *The Lunar Men: Five Friends Whose Curiosity Changed the World* (New York: Farrar, Straus, and Giroux, 2002); Albert Edward Musson and Eric Robinson, *Science and Technology in the Industrial Revolution* (Yverdon, Switzerland: Gordon & Breach, 1989), pp. 142–43.

125. H. Carrington Bolton, "The Lunar Society, Or the Festive Philosophers of Birmingham One Hundred Years Ago," *Transactions of the New York Academy of Sciences* 5–7 (1887): 194.

126. William E. Burns, *Science in the Enlightenment: An Encyclopedia* (Santa Barbara, CA: ABC-CLIO, 2003), p. 73.

127. Samuel Smiles, *Josiah Wedgwood, F. R. S., His Personal History* (New York: Harper, 1895), pp. 304–305.

128. N. Hudson Moore, *The Old China Book: Including Staffordshire, Wedgwood, Lustre, and Other English Pottery and Porcelain* (New York: Frederick A. Stokes, 1903), p. 1.

129. Llewellyn Frederick William Jewitt, *The Wedgwoods: Being a Life of Josiah Wedgwood* (London: Virtue Bros., 1865), p. 198.

130. R. W. Cooke-Taylor, *Introduction to a History of the Factory System* (London: Richard Bentley, 1886), p. 4.

131. Jewitt, *The Wedgwoods*, pp. xiii, 179, 212.

132. "Inventory of Dr. Priestley's Laboratory, 1791" (*Birmingham Weekly Post*, March 15, 22, 29, and April 15, 1890), in Joseph Priestley, *Scientific Correspondence of Joseph Priestley: Ninety-Seven Letters*, ed. Henry Carrington Bolton (New York: privately printed, 1892), p. 221.

133. Ibid., pp. 69, 190.

134. Erasmus Darwin, *Zoonomia: Or the Laws of Organic Life* (London: J. Johnson, 1794); Erasmus Darwin, *The Botanic Garden: A Poem, in Two Parts*, pt. 1 (New York: Faculty of Physic of Columbia College, 1798), pp. 5–6.

135. Darwin, *Botanic Garden*, pp. 5–6.

136. Bolton, "The Lunar Society," p. 194.

137. George Ritzer, *Encyclopedia of Social Theory* (Thousand Oaks, CA: Sage, 2005), 1: 781.

138. Thomas Young, *A Course of Lectures on Natural Philosophy and the Mechanical Arts* (London: Joseph Johnson, 1807), 2: 308, 319, 633, 639, 680.

139. Alexander Wood, *Thomas Young: Natural Philosopher, 1773–1829* (Cambridge, UK: Cambridge University Press, 1954), p. 76.

140. von Baer and Dohrn, *Correspondence*, p. 9.

141. Aaron Wilkes and James Ball, *Industry Reform and Empire: Britain 1750–1900*, books 11–14 (Dunstable, UK: Folens, 2009), p. 10.

142. Jill Condra, ed., *The Greenwood Encyclopedia of Clothing through World History* (Westport, CT: Greenwood, 2008), p. 29; Joel Munsell, *The Every Day Book of History and Chronology* (New York: Appleton, 1858), p. 42; "The Crime of Inventing Machinery," *Scientific American*, Supplement VII, no. 178 (May 31, 1879): 2825; Howard Bloom, *The Genius of the Beast: A Radical Re-Vision of Capitalism* (Amherst, NY: Prometheus Books, 2010).

143. Francis Egerton Ellesmere and Alice Byng Strafford, *Personal Reminiscences of the Duke of Wellington* (London: J. Murray, 1904), p. 119; Charles Wilson, *The History of Unilever: A Study in Economic Growth and Social Change* (Westport, CT: Praeger, 1968); Frank Atkinson, *The Industrial Archaeology of North-East England* (Devon, UK: David & Charles, 1974), p. 170; Arthur Wellesley Wellington, *Supplementary Despatches and Memoranda of Field Marshal Arthur, Duke of Wellington, K. G.* (London: J. Murray, 1860), p. 143; Dorothy Constance Bayliff Peel, *The Stream of Time: Social and Domestic Life in England, 1805–1861* (New York: Scribner, 1932), p. 67.

144. "Life Expectancy by Age, 1850–2004," Information Please, http://www.infoplease.com/ipa/A0005140.html (accessed April 7, 2010).

145. "State of Historical Science in France," *Eclectic Magazine of Foreign Literature, Science, and Art* 1–2 (1844): 169.

146. George Henry Preble, *A Chronological History of the Origin and Development of Steam Navigation* (Philadelphia: L. R. Hamersly, 1895), pp. 42–50.

147. Francis Trevithick, *Life of Richard Trevithick, with an Account of His Inventions* (London: E. & F. N. Spon, 1872), 1: v–vi, 103.

148. Michael Reynolds, *The Model Locomotive Engineer, Fireman, and Engine-Boy* (London: Crosby Lockwood & Sons, 1896), p. 84.

149. *Wikipedia*, s.v. "Locomotive," http://en.wikipedia.org/wiki/Locomotive#Origins (accessed June 5, 2012).

150. "Railroad Transportation at the Universal Exposition: 1904. St. Louis, Missouri," *The Railway and Engineering Review*, December 31, 1904, p. 31.

151. "The Duke of Portland's Tramway," *Locomotive Magazine*, April 14, 1906, pp. 60–61.

152. W. A. Hunter, *The Railway and Canal Traffic Act, 1888* (London: Sweet & Maxwell, 1889), p. 6.

153. George G. Chisholm, *Handbook of Commercial Geography* (London: Longmans, Green & Co., 1889), pp. 73–74.

154. *Railway Locomotives and Cars* (New York: Simmons-Boardman, 1839), p. 158.

155. Charles S. Parke, Augustine B. Kellogg, *The Roller Mill*, 1893, 12: 155.

156. John Rennie, "History of Engineering, Railways," *Civil Engineer and Architect's Journal* 10 (1847): 113. Sir John Rennie was a civil engineer who built the first commercial, steam-powered passenger railway, the Stockton and Darlington Railway.

157. Lewis A. Coser, *Masters of Sociological Thought: Ideas in Historical and Social Context* (Fort Worth, TX: Harcourt Brace Jovanovich, 1977), p. 104.

158. Herbert Spencer, *An Autobiography* (New York: D. Appleton, 1904), 1: 153.

159. Francis Whishaw, *The Railways of Great Britain and Ireland* (London: John Weale, 1842).

160. The title of one of Spencer's chapters in his *Autobiography* (Appleton edition), 1: 196.

161. Spencer, *Autobiography* (Appleton edition), 1: 384.

162. Ibid., p. 378.

163. Ibid.

164. "Opening of the Session," *Blackwood's Magazine* 67 (January–June 1850): 369.

165. Walter Bagehot, "Memoir of the Right Honourable James Wilson," "published as a supplement to the *Economist* soon after Mr. Wilson's death in 1860," *Literary Studies (Miscellaneous Essays) with Additions* (London: Longman, Green, and Co., 1907), 3: 304.

166. Ruth Dudley Edwards, *The Pursuit of Reason: The Economist, 1843–1993* (Cambridge, MA: Harvard Business School, 1995), p. 3–4.

167. Spencer, *Autobiography* (Appleton edition), 1: 378.

168. Edwards, *Pursuit of Reason*, p. 8.

169. Ibid., pp. 8–10.

170. Ibid., p. 14.

171. Ibid., p. 16.

172. Spencer, *Autobiography* (Appleton edition), 1: 378.

173. Ibid., p. 379.

174. Ibid.

175. Ibid.

176. Ibid.

177. Ibid.

178. Ibid., p. 329.

179. Ibid., p. 378.

180. Shailer Mathews, "Democracy and World Politics," *Bulletin of the American Library Association,* January 1917, p. 97.

181. Michael Rapport, *1848, Year of Revolution* (New York: Basic Books, 2008), p. 4.

182. Spencer, *Autobiography* (Appleton edition), 1: 378.

183. Ibid., p. 379.

184. Herbert Spencer, *Political Writings*, ed. John Offer (Cambridge, UK: Cambridge University Press, 1994).

185. Richard J. Helmstadter, ed., *Freedom and Religion in the Nineteenth Century* (Stanford, CA: Stanford University Press, 1997), p. 90.

186. Auberon Herbert, *The Voluntaryist Creed: Being the Herbert Spencer Lecture Delivered at Oxford June 6, 1906* (Oxford: Oxford University Press, 1908).

187. Spencer, *Autobiography* (Appleton edition), 1: 380.

188. Ibid., pp. 380–81.

189. Ibid., p. 382.

190. Herbert Spencer, *An Autobiography* (London: Williams and Norgate, 1904), p. 333.

191. Ibid., pp. 382–83.

192. Ibid.

193. Rosemary Ashton, "The Smart Set," *Guardian*, November 4, 2006.

The Scandal of the Century: George Eliot and Her Ape

194. Driesch, *History and Theory of Vitalism*, p. 241.

195. Spencer, *An Autobiography* (Williams and Norgate edition), p. 348.

196. Spencer, *An Autobiography* (Appleton edition), 1: 398.

197. Gábor Boros, Herman de Dijn, and Martin Moors, eds., *The Concept of Love in 17th and 18th Century Philosophy* (Leuven, Belgium: Leuven University Press, 2007); Ann Braude, *Radical Spirits: Spiritualism and Women's Rights in Nineteenth-Century America* (Bloomington: University of Indiana Press, 2001), p. 128.

198. David Friedrich Strauss, *The Life of Jesus Critically Examined*, trans. Mary Ann Evans (London: Chapman Brothers, 1846).

199. *Saturday Review of Politics, Literature, Science and Art* 26 (October 24, 1868): 560.

200. Spencer, *Autobiography* (Appleton edition), 1: 399.

201. Ashton, "Smart Set."

202. Giuseppe Mazzini, *A Cosmopolitanism of Nations: Giuseppe Mazzini's Writings on Democracy, Nation Building, and International Relations*, ed. Stefano Recchia and Nadia Urbinati (Princeton NJ: Princeton University Press, 2009), p. vii.

203. Alexander Herzen, *My Past and Thoughts*, with an introduction by Isaiah Berlin, trans. C. Garnett (New York: Knopf, 1968), pp. 687, 694.

204. Stefano Recchia and Nadia Urbinati, "Introduction: Giuseppe Mazzini's International Political Thought," in Mazzini, *A Cosmopolitanism of Nations*, p. 1.

205. Ibid.

206. Rosemary Ashton, *142 Strand: A Radical Address in Victorian London* (London: Random House, 2008).

207. Ashton, "Smart Set."

208. Mary Hannah Deakin, *The Early Life of George Eliot* (Manchester, UK: Manchester University Press, 1913).

209. George Eliot, *The Wisdom of George Eliot*, ed. Jerret Engle (New York: Kensington, 2002), pp. xx–xxi.

210. Ashton, "Smart Set."

211. Sheila Rosenberg, "The 'Wicked Westminster': John Chapman, His Contributors and Promises Fulfilled," *Victorian Periodicals Review* 33, no. 3 (Fall 2000), pp. 225–26.

212. Ibid.

213. Spencer, *Autobiography* (Appleton edition), 1: 466.

214. Ashton, "Smart Set."

215. Rosenberg, "'Wicked Westminster.'"

216. Ibid.

217. Charles Darwin, *On the Origin of Species by Means of Natural Selection or the Preservation of Favoured Races in the Struggle for Life*, 3rd ed. (London: John Murray, 1861). Originally published in 1859.

218. Spencer, *Autobiography* (Appleton edition), 1: 457.

219. Ibid.

220. Ibid.

221. Ibid., p. 398.

222. Eliot and Engle, *Wisdom of George Eliot*, p. xxiii.

223. Spencer, *Autobiography* (Williams and Norgate edition), pp. 383, 395.

224. Ibid., p. 399.

225. Ibid., p. 348.

226. "George Henry Lewes, 1817–1878," in *The World's Best Literature*, ed. John W. Cunliffe and Ashley H. Thorndike (New York: Warner Library, 1917), 5: 9037–39.

227. Jack Kaminsky, "The Empirical Metaphysics of George Henry Lewes," *Journal of the History of Ideas*, June 1952, pp. 314–32.

228. Hock Guan Tjoa, *George Henry Lewes: A Victorian Mind* (Cambridge MA: Harvard University Press, 1977), p. 8.

229. Elizabeth Garber, *The Language of Physics: The Calculus and the Development of Theoretical Physics in Europe, 1750–1870* (Boston: Birkhäuser, 1998), p. 95.

230. Kaminsky, "Empirical Metaphysics," pp. 314–32.

231. Tjoa, *George Henry Lewes*, pp. 141–46.

232. Ibid., p. 11.

233. "The Trial of the Unitarians" in "The Twelfth Report of the British and Foreign Unitarian Association," *Church of England Quarterly Review*, 1837–1838, p. 482.

234. G. H. Lewes, "A Review of Sketches, Pickwick, and Oliver Twist," *National Magazine and Monthly Critic*, December 1837, pp. 445–49; Phillip Collins, ed., *Charles Dickens: The Critical Heritage* (New York: Taylor and Francis, 1986), p. 65.

235. William Bell Scott, *Autobiographical Notes of the Life of William Bell Scott: And Notices of His Artistic and Poetic Circle of Friends 1830 to 1882*, ed. W. Minto (New York: Harper, 1892), p. 125.

236. Thomas Carlyle, *On Heroes and Hero Worship and the Heroic in History* (London: Chapman and Hall, 1840), pp. 1–247.

237. Ibid., p. 20.

238. Thomas Carlyle, "Memoirs of the Life of Scott," in *Critical and Miscellaneous Essays* (Whitefish MT: Kessinger, 2003), p. 516. Originally published in 1847.

239. Paul Mengal, "The Concept of Emergence in the XIXth Century," in *Self-Organization and Emergence in Life Sciences*, ed. Bernard Feltz, M. Crommelinck, and Philippe Goujon (Dordrecht, Netherlands: Springer, 2006), p. 218.

240. *Wikipedia*, s.v. "Johann Wolfgang von Goethe," http://en.wikipedia.org/wiki/Johann_Wolfgang_von_Goethe (accessed May 10, 2011).

241. Renee Skelton, *Charles Darwin and the Theory of Natural Selection* (Hauppauge, NY: Barron's, 1987), p. 70; Frederick Burkhardt, Sydney Smith, *A Calendar of the Correspondence of Charles Darwin, 1821–1882* (Cambridge, UK: University of Cambridge Press, 1996), p. 1.

242. Burkhardt and Smith, *A Calendar*, p. 1.

243. A. C. Seward, *Darwin and Modern Science* (Cambridge, UK: Cambridge University Press, 1909), p. 295; Julia Voss and Lori Lantz, *Darwin's Pictures: Views of Evolutionary Theory, 1837–1874* (New Haven, CT: Yale University Press, 2010).

244. Anna Swanwick, introduction to Johann Wolfgang von Goethe, *Faust*, trans. Anna Swanwick (London: George Bell and Sons, 1838), p. xli.

245. Gerlinde Röder-Bolton, *George Eliot in Germany, 1854–55: "Cherished Memories"* (Aldershot, UK: Ashgate, 2006), p. 111.

Bulging Forth from Nothing: The Emergence of "Emergence"

246. Nicholas Capaldi, *John Stuart Mill: A Biography* (Cambridge, UK: Cambridge University Press, 2004), p. 115; Gordon S. Haight, *George Eliot's Originals and Contemporaries: Essays in Victorian Literary History and Biography* (Ann Arbor: University of Michigan Press, 1992), p. 115; John Stuart Mill, *The Autobiography of John Stuart Mill* (Minneapolis: Filiquarian Publishing, 2007—Mill wrote this authobiography in the mid-1850s); Alexander Bain, *John Stuart Mill: A Criticism with Personal Recollections* (London: Longmans Green, 1888), p. 77; Vincent Guillin, *Auguste Comte and John Stuart Mill on Sexual Equality*, (Leiden: Brill, 2009), p. 278. R. E. Ockenden, "George Henry Lewes (1817–1878)," *Isis*, July 1940, pp. 70–86.

247. Mill, *Autobiography*, p. 37.

248. John Stuart Mill and Auguste Comte, *The Correspondence of John Stuart Mill and Auguste Comte*, trans. Oscar A. Haac (New Brunswick, NJ: Transaction, 1995), pp. 77, 175.

249. Gustav Jahoda, *A History of Social Psychology: From the Eighteenth-Century Enlightenment to the Second World War* (Cambridge, UK: Cambridge University Press, 2007), p. 94.

250. Garber, *Language of Physics*, p. 95.

251. George Henry Lewes, "State of Historical Science in France," *Eclectic* 1–2 (1844): 172.

252. Sally Shuttleworth, *George Eliot and Nineteenth-Century Science* (Cambridge, UK: Cambridge University Press, 1984), p. 5.

253. Lewes, "State of Historical Science in France," p. 172.

254. Auguste Comte, *The Positive Philosophy of Auguste Comte*, trans. by Harriet Martineau (London: John Chapman, 1853), 2: 465.

255. Auguste Comte, *Auguste Comte and Positivism: The Essential Writings*, ed. Gertrud Lenzer (Piscataway, NJ: Transaction, 1998), p. xlix.

256. Comte, *Positive Philosophy*, 2: 465.

257. Ibid., p. 43.

258. Ibid., p. 470.

259. Ibid., p. 23.

260. George Henry Lewes, *Comte's Philosophy of the Sciences: Being an Exposition of the Principles of the Cours de Philosophie Positive of Auguste Comte* (London: Henry G. Bohn, 1853), p. 51.

261. Comte, *Positive Philosophy*, 2: 461.

262. Lewes, *Comte's Philosophy of the Sciences*, p. 142.

263. Spencer, *Autobiography* (Williams and Norgate edition), p. 407.

264. Henri Milne-Edwards and Achille Joseph Comte, *Elements of Entomology*, vol. 2, ed. William Samuel Waithman Ruschenberger (Philadelphia: Grigg, Elliot, 1849); F. S. Beudant, Henri Milne-Edwards, and Achille Joseph Comte, *Elements of Geology*, ed. William Samuel Waithman Ruschenberger (London: Grigg, Elliot, 1846); Henri Milne-Edwards and Achille Comte, *Ornithology: The Natural History of Birds*, ed. William Samuel Waithman Ruschenberger

(Philadelphia: Turner & Fisher, 1844); Toby A. Appel, *The Cuvier-Geoffroy Debate: French Biology in the Decades Before Darwin* (New York: Oxford University Press, 1987), p. 220.

265. Spencer, *Autobiography* (Williams and Norgate edition), p. 377.

266. For an idea of the way hydrogen, oxygen, and their combination in water were regarded in 1835, see John Laurance, *Geology in 1835* (London: Simpkin, Marshall, 1836), p. 30.

267. Spencer, *Autobiography* (Williams and Norgate edition), p. 347.

268. George Wilson, *The Life of the Hon. Henry Cavendish: Including Abstracts of his More Important Scientific Papers, and a Critical Inquiry into the Claims of All the Alleged Discoverers of the Composition of Water* (London: Cavendish Society, 1851), p. 327.

269. Mary Louise Foster, *Life of Lavoisier* (Northampton, MA: Smith College, 1926); Henry Guerlac, *Lavoisier—The Crucial Year: The Background and Origin of His First Experiments on Combustion in 1772* (Ithaca, NY: Cornell University Press, 1961).

270. Hasan Padamsee, *Unifying the Universe: The Physics of Heaven and Earth* (London: Institute of Physics Publishing, 2003), p. 92.

271. Jean-Pierre Poirier, *Lavoisier: Chemist, Biologist, Economist*, trans. Rebecca Balinski (Philadelphia: University of Pennsylvania Press, 1996), p. xv.

272. Padamsee, *Unifying the Universe*, p. 92.

273. William Stirling, *Some Apostles of Physiology: Being an Account of Their Lives and Labours* (Manchester, UK: Waterlow, 1902), p. 70.

274. Ibid.

275. Joseph Priestley, *Experiments and Observations on Different Kinds of Air* (London: J. Johnson, 1776), 2: 97.

276. Ayn Rand, *Atlas Shrugged* (New York: Signet, 1992).

277. Charles Darwin, *Journal of Researches into the Natural History and Geology of the Countries Visited during the Voyage of H. M. S. Beagle Round the World* (New York: D. Appleton and Company, 1882), p. 305.

278. Ibid., pp. 305–308.

279. "Scientific News," *English Mechanics and the World of Science* 23 (April 7, 1876): 91.

280. John Stuart Mill, *A System of Logic, Ratiocinative and Inductive: Being a Connected View of the Principles of Evidence and the Methods of Scientific Investigation* (New York: Harper, 1858), p. 256.

281. George Henry Lewes, *Problems of Life and Mind, First Series: The Foundation of a Creed* (London: Trübner, 1874), 1: 174.

282. Ibid., pp. 129–30.

283. Ibid., pp. 367–71.

284. Ibid.

285. Ibid.

286. Ibid.

287. Ibid.

288. Ibid.

Charlie Darwin Shows Up Late

289. Henry Adams, *The Education of Henry Adams: An Autobiography* (Boston: Houghton Mifflin, 1918), p. 224.

290. Auguste Comte, "Plan of Scientific Work," in Auguste Comte, *Early Political Writings*, ed. H. S. Jones (Cambridge, UK: Cambridge University Press, 1998), p. 108. In his 1824 book *Plan of Scientific Studies Necessary for the Reorganization of Society*, Comte referred to his law of evolution differently. He called it a "law of development." For Lewes's summary of Comte's philosophy, see George Henry Lewes, *The History of Philosophy from Thales to Comte*, vol. 2 (London: Longmans Green, 1867).

291. Herbert Spencer, "The Development Hypothesis," in Herbert Spencer, *Sidelights on the Synthetic Philosophy: Seven Essays, Selected from the Works of H. Spencer* (London: Watts, 1907), p. 35.

292. Michael R. Hill and Susan Hoecker-Drysdale, *Harriet Martineau: Theoretical and Methodological Perspectives* (New York: Routledge, 2002), p. 178.

293. Auguste Comte, *Auguste Comte*, vol. 2, trans. Harriet Martineau (London: John Chapman, 1853).

294. Samuel Brown, "The Atomic Theory, Before Christ and Since," *Westminster Review* 59 (1853): 168.

295. George Henry Lewes, *Comte's Philosophy of the Sciences: Being an Exposition of the Principles of the* Cours de Philosophie Positive *of Auguste Comte* (London: Henry G. Bohn, 1853).

296. Lewes, "State of Historical Science in France," p. 167.

297. William Waring Johnston, *The Ill-Health of Charles Darwin: Its Nature and Its Relation to His Work* (New York: Putnam, 1901), p. 139.

298. Darwin, *On the Origin of Species by Means of Natural Selection or the Preservation of Favoured Races in the Struggle for Life*, 3rd ed. (London: John Murray, 1861), pp. 518–19.

299. Ibid., p. 32.

300. Ibid., p. 28.

301. Ibid., p. 42.

302. The *Church of England Quarterly* in 1854 was among the first to realize that Comte was offering a "scientific religion." Unsigned review of Comte's "Philosophy of the Sciences translated by Harriett Martineau," *Church of England Quarterly Review* 35, no. 1 (1854): 241.

303. Capaldi, *John Stuart Mill*, pp. 173–74.

304. Richard Congreve, *Administration of the Positivist Sacraments: The Sacraments of the Religion of Humanity, as Administered at the Church of Humanity, 19 Chapel Street, Lamb's Conduit Street, London, W. C.* (London: Church of Humanity, 1893); Richard Olson, *Science and Scientism in Nineteenth-Century Europe* (Champaign: University of Illinois Press, 2008), p. 187; Hill and Hoecker-Drysdale, *Harriet Martineau*, p. 173; Anthony Giddens, *Profiles and Critiques in Social Theory* (Berkeley: University of California Press, 1982), p. 73.

305. Charles Darwin, *The Origin of Species: 150th Anniversary Edition*, with an introduction by Julian Huxley (New York: Signet, 1958), p. 187.

306. Ibid., pp. 32, 35, 133.

307. Spencer, *Autobiography* (Appleton edition), 1: 457.

308. Ibid.

309. Walter Troughton, "Herbert Spencer's Last Years: Some Personal Recollections," in *Herbert Spencer: Critical Assessments of Leading Sociologists*, ed. John Offer (London: Routledge, 2001), 1: 196.

310. Mark Francis, *Herbert Spencer and the Invention of Modern Life* (Durham, UK: Acumen, 2007), p. 353; Gail Rae Rosensfit, *George Eliot's* Middlemarch (Piscataway, NJ: Research and Education Association, 1996), p. 2.

311. William Archer, introduction to *George Henry Lewes, Dramatic Essays* by John Forster (London: W. Scott, 1896), 3: xxxi.

312. Tjoa, *George Henry Lewes*, pp. 29–30.

313. George Washburn Smalley, *London Letters: And Some Others* (New York: Harper, 1891), p. 244; Janet K. Ruutz-Rees, "George Eliot," *The American Magazine* 11 (1881): 486.

314. Kathleen McCormack, *George Eliot's English Travels: Composite Characters and Coded Communications* (New York: Taylor & Francis, 2005), p. 159; George Lewis Levine, ed., *The Cambridge Companion to George Eliot* (Cambridge, UK: Cambridge University Press, 2001), p. 34.

The Zygote Snabs Herbert Spencer

315. Spencer, *Autobiography* (Appleton edition), 2: 9.

316. Herbert Spencer, "Progress: Its Law and Cause (1857)," in *Seven Essays*, p. 7; Spencer, *Autobiography* (Appleton edition), 2: 8–27.

317. Spencer, *Autobiography* (Appleton edition), 2: 10.

318. Herbert Spencer, *A System of Synthetic Philosophy*, vol. 4, *The Principles of Psychology*, vol. 1 (New York: Appleton, 1876). Originally published in 1855.

319. "Doing Machine Work under Difficulties," *Railway and Locomotive Engineering* 8 (1895): 563; *Railway Age Gazette* 48 (1910): 1364.

320. Herbert Spencer, *Works: Social Statistics. Man versus the State* (New York: Appleton, 1910), p. 32.

321. Herbert Spencer, *Social Statics together with Man versus the State* (New York: D. Appleton, 1913), p. 271.

322. Driesch, *History and Theory of Vitalism*, p. 209.

323. Spencer, *Works: Social Statics*, p. 271.

324. Ibid.

325. Ibid.

326. Ibid., p. 272.

327. Herbert Spencer, *Social Statistics: Or, the Conditions Essential to Human Happiness Specified, and the First of Them Developed* (New York: D. Appleton and Company, 1890), p. 497.

328. Ibid.

329. Georg Wilhelm Friedrich Hegel, *The Science of Logic*, trans. George di Giovanni (Cambridge, UK: Cambridge University Press, 2010), p. 382.

330. Jon Bartley Stewart, *The Hegel Myths and Legends* (Evanston, IL: Northwestern University Press, 1996), p. 304.

331. Heinrich Moritz Chalybäus, *Historische Entwicklung der Speculativen Philosophie von Kant bis Hegel* (Dresden: Arnoldis, 1837).

332. Karl Marx, *The Poverty of Philosophy* (London: Martin Lawrence, 1900), pp. 38, 43, 89, 91, 100.

333 Spencer, *Autobiography* (Appleton edition), 2: 281.

334. Spencer, *Works: Social Statics* (London: John Chapman, 1851), p. 455.

335. Ibid.

336. Herbert Spencer, *Social Statics: Abridged and Revised; Together with the Man versus the State* (New York: Appleton, 1897), p. 256.

337. Ibid; Herbert Spencer, "The Development Hypothesis," in Spencer, *Seven Essays*, p. 8.

338. Spencer, *Works: Social Statistics*, p. 32.

339. Ibid., p. 272.

340. Herbert Spencer, *The Principles of Sociology* (New York: Appleton, 1882); Herbert Spencer, *The Study of Sociology* (London: Henry S. King, 1873).

341. Spencer, *Autobiography* (Williams and Norgate edition), 2: 486.

342. Charles Darwin, "Embryonic Development," in *The Descent of Man, and Selection in Relation to Sex* (New York: Appleton, 1872), 1: 14. Darwin alluded to embryology many a time. And he refers to von Baer as "the illustrious von Baer." But the embryo is not a part of Darwin's central metaphor.

343. Peter J. Bowler, *Reconciling Science and Religion: The Debate in Early-Twentieth-Century Britain* (Chicago: University of Chicago Press, 2001), pp. 13, 44, 48; Philip Clayton, "Conceptual Foundations of Emergence Theory," in *The Re-Emergence of Emergence: The Emergentist Hypothesis from Science to Religion*, ed. Philip Clayton and Paul Davies (Oxford, UK: Oxford University Press, 2006); Ursula Goodenough, *The Sacred Depths of Nature* (New York: Oxford University Press, 1998), p. 49.

344. Bowler, *Reconciling Science and Religion*, p. 44.

345. Brian Greene, *The Hidden Reality: Parallel Universes and the Deep Laws of the Cosmos* (New York: Knopf, 2011), p. 33.

The Embryo Goes Cosmic

346. Carole L. Palmer, *Work at the Boundaries of Science: Information and the Interdisciplinary Research Process* (New York: Springer, 2001), p. 106.

347. Brian Clegg, *Before the Big Bang: The Prehistory of Our Universe* (New York: St. Martins, 2009), p. 3; David E. Newton, *Chemistry of Space* (New York: Facts on File, 2007), p. 3.

348. George Gamow, *The Creation of the Universe* (New York: Viking Press, 1961), p. 2.

349. E. V. Pinneker, D. E. Howard, and J. C. Harvey, *General Hydrogeology* (New York: Cambridge University Press, 1983), pp. 32–35.

350. Joseph Silk, *The Big Bang* (New York: Henry Holt, 2001), p. 107.

7. EINSTEIN TURNS AN AXIOM INSIDE OUT

The Man Who Gave *Star Trek* Its Space: Bernhard Riemann

1. Stephen W. Hawking and Leonard Mlodinow, *The Grand Design* (New York: Random House, 2010), pp. 139, 142, 184.

2. John Stillwell, *Mathematics and Its History* (New York: Springer, 2010), p. 365.

3. Herbert Spencer, *An Autobiography* (London: Williams and Norgate, 1904), p. 294.

4. Anne H. Weaver, *The Voyage of the Beetle: A Journey around the World with Charles Darwin* (Albuquerque: University of New Mexico Press, 2004), p. 71.

5. Michael Monastyrsky, *Riemann, Topology, and Physics* (Boston: Birkhäuser, 2008), pp. 9–10.

6. Andreĭ Nikolaevich Kolmogorov and A. P. Yushkevich, eds., *Mathematics of the 19th Century: Geometry, Analytic Function Theory* (Basel: Birkhäuser, 2001), p. 58.

7. Valentin I. Ivanov and Michael K. Trubetskov, *Handbook of Conformal Mapping with Computer-Aided Visualization* (Boca Raton, FL: CRC, 1995), pp. 1–3.

8. Bernhard Riemann, "Posthumous Thesis on the Hypotheses which Lie at the Foundation of Geometry (1867)," in *Landmark Writings in Western Mathematics 1640–1940*, ed. I. Grattan-Guinness (Amsterdam: Elsevier, 2005), p. 506; Detlef Laugwitz, *Bernhard Riemann 1826–1866: Turning Points in the Conception of Mathematics* (Boston: Birkhäuser, 2008), pp. 16–24.

9. Bernhard Riemann, "On the Hypotheses which Lie at the Bases of Geometry," trans. William Kingdon Clifford, in David R. Wilkins, *Mathematicians and Philosophers of Mathematics* (Dublin: School of Mathematics, Trinity College), http://www.maths.tcd.ie/pub/HistMath/People/Riemann/Geom/WKCGeom.html (accessed February 1, 2011). Originally published in *Nature* in 1873.

10. Ibid.

11. Ibid.

12. Ibid.

13. Ibid.

14. Ibid.

15. Ibid.

16. Ibid.

17. Ibid.

18. Ibid.

19. Ibid.

20. Barton Zwiebach, *A First Course in String Theory* (Cambridge, UK: Cambridge University Press, 2004), p. 344.

21. Edward Witten, "String Theory Dynamics in Various Dimensions," in *The World in Eleven Dimensions: Supergravity, Supermembranes, and M-Theory*, ed. M. J. Duff (Philadelphia: Institute of Physics Publishing, 1999), p. 333.

22. Ivor Grattan-Guinness, ed., *Companion Encyclopedia of the History and Philosophy of the Mathematical Sciences* (Baltimore: Johns Hopkins University Press, 1994) 1: 336. Cambridge University's Arthur Cayley also introduced the term "(*n*) dimensions" in his 1844 *Chapters in the Analytical Geometry of (n) Dimensions*. See A. J. Crilly, *Arthur Cayley: Mathematician Laureate of the Victorian Age* (Baltimore: Johns Hopkins University Press, 2006), pp. 82–83. Nonetheless, it's Riemann who usually gets the credit for introducing what Ivor Gratton-Guinness calls "the new concept of an *n*-dimensional manifold."

23. Manfredo Perdigão do Carmo, *Riemannian Geometry* (Boston: Birkhäuser, 1992), p. 1.

24. Detlef Laugwitz, *Bernhard Riemann*, p. 272.

25. Richard Dedekind, *Theory of Algebraic Integers* (Cambridge, UK: Cambridge University Press, 1996), p. 46. Originally published in 1877.

26. William Barrett Frankland, *The Story of Euclid* (London: G. Newnes, 1902), pp. 147–73.

Albert Einstein's Pajamas

27. Sadri Hassani, *From Atoms to Galaxies: A Conceptual Physics Approach to Scientific Awareness* (Boca Raton, FL: CRC Press, 2010), p. 362.

28. Albert Einstein, *Selections from the Principle of Relativity*, ed. Stephen Hawking (Philadelphia: Running Press, 2002), p. xiii.

29. Krista Tippett, *Einstein's God: Conversations about Science and the Human Spirit* (New York: Penguin, 2010).

30. Albert Einstein, *Works of Albert Einstein: On the Electrodynamics of Moving Bodies, Relativity; The Special and General Theory, Sidelights on Relativity, Dialog about Objections against the Theory of Relativity & More*, trans. Meghnad Saha (Boston: MobileReference, 2010), Kindle edition, location 2792.

31. Albert Einstein, "Relativity: The Special and General Theory, Appendix III—The Experimental Confirmation of the General Theory of Relativity," in *Works of Albert Einstein*, trans. Robert W. Lawson (Boston: MobileReference, 2010), Kindle edition, location 1763.

32. Gregory Scott Charak, "Between Soul and Precision: Ernst Mach's Biological Empiricism and the Social Democratic Philosophy of Science" (PhD dissertation, University of California, San Diego, 2007), p. 72; H. Gutfreund and G. Toulouse, eds., *Biology and Computation: A Physicist's Choice* (Singapore: World Scientific, 1994), p. 315.

33. Paul Pojman, "Ernst Mach," *Stanford Encyclopedia of Philosophy*, ed. Edward N. Zalta (Metaphysics Research Lab, Center for the Study of Language and Information, Stanford University, Winter 2011), http://plato.stanford.edu/entries/ernst-mach/ (accessed March 8, 2011).

34. Ernst Mach, *The Science of Mechanics: A Critical and Historical Account of Its Development*, trans. T. J. McCormack (Seaside, OR: Watchmaker Publishing, 2010). Originally published in 1883.

35. John T. Blackmore, *Ernst Mach: His Work, Life, and Influence* (Berkeley, CA: University of California Press, 1972), p. x. Mach resisted the use of his concept of relativity for the physical universe. And he attacked Einstein's relativity with all his might.

36. Kolmogorov and Yushkevich, *Mathematics of the 19th Century*, p. 57; András Prékopa, "The Revolution of Janos Bólyai," in *Non-Euclidean Geometries: János Bólyai Memorial Volume*, ed. András Prékopa and Emil Molnár (New York: Springer, 2006), pp. 3–61.

37. Nikolai I. Lobachevsky, *Pangeometry*, ed. and trans. Athanase Papadopoulos (Zurich: European Mathematical Society, 2010), pp. 57–58.

38. Frank Washington Very, *The Luminiferous Ether: (I) Its Relation to the Electron and to a Universal Interstellar Medium; (II) Its Relation to the Atom* (Boston: Four Seas Co., 1919); Samuel Lawrence Bigelow, *Theoretical and Physical Chemistry* (New York: Century, 1917), pp. 110–13.

39. Nikhilendu Bandyopadhyay, *Theory of Special Relativity* (Calcutta: Academic Publishers, 2000), pp. 4–6.

40. Vidwan Singh Soni, *Mechanics and Relativity* (New Delhi: PHI Learning, 2009), pp. 285–90; Richard P. Olenick, Tom M. Apostol, and David L. Goodstein, *Beyond the Mechanical Universe: From Electricity to Modern Physics* (Cambridge, UK: Cambridge University Press, 1986), pp. 360–64.

41. George Johnson, *The Ten Most Beautiful Experiments* (New York: Random House, 2008), p. 113.

42. Raymond A. Serway and John W. Jewett, *Principles of Physics: A Calculus-Based Text*, vol. 1 (Belmont, CA: Brooks-Cole, 2006), p. 262.

43. Johnson, *Ten Most Beautiful Experiments*, p. 113.

44. Grant R. Fowles, *Introduction to Modern Optics* (New York: Holt, Rinehart & Winston, 1968), p. 308. The Michelson-Morley apparatus was floated on a bed of mercury to make turning easy.

45. Max Planck, *The Theory of Heat Radiation*, trans. Morton Masius (Philadelphia: Blakiston, 1914), p. vii; Albert Einstein, *Ideas and Opinions*, ed. Carl Seelig (New York: Three Rivers Press, 1982).

46. Manjit Kumar, *Quantum: Einstein, Bohr, and the Great Debate about the Nature of Reality* (New York: Norton, 2011), p. 1.

47. Max Planck, *Eight Lectures on Theoretical Physics*, trans. A. P. Wills (New York: Columbia University Press, 1915), p. ix.

48. Eugene A. Sharkov, *Passive Microwave Remote Sensing of the Earth: Physical Foundations* (Berlin: Springer, 2003), pp. 208–13.

49. Nouredine Zettili, *Quantum Mechanics: Concepts and Applications* (Chichester, UK: John Wiley, 2009), p. 4.

50. Nicholas J. Turro, V. Ramamurthy, and Juan C. Scaiano, *Principles of Molecular Photochemistry* (South Orange, NJ: University Science Books, 2009), p. 172.

51. Zettili, *Quantum Mechanics*, pp. 4–7.

52. Bernhard Riemann, *Oeuvres Mathématiques de Riemann* (Paris: Gauthier-Villars, 1898), p. 282.

53. Kumar, *Quantum*, pp. 21–22, 46.

54. Robert J. A. Lambourne, *Relativity, Gravitation, and Cosmology* (Cambridge, UK: Cambridge University Press, 2010), p. 18; Kenneth R. Lang, *Astrophysical Formulae: Space, Time, Matter, and Cosmology* (Berlin: Springer, 1999), 2: 150.

55. Einstein, *Works of Albert Einstein*, Kindle edition, location 730.

56. Ibid.

57. Hendrik Lorentz, "Electromagnetic Phenomena in a System Moving with Any Velocity Smaller than That of Light (1904)," *Proceedings of the Royal Netherlands Academy of Arts and Sciences*, 1904, 6: 809–31, http://www.dwc.knaw.nl/DL/publications/PU00014148 .pdf; Michel Le Bellac, "The 1905 Articles and the Lorentz Group," in *The Scientific Legacy of Poincaré*, ed. Éric Charpentier, Étienne Ghys, and Annick Lesne (Providence: American Mathematical Society, 2010), p. 331.

58. Ş. Selçuk Bayin, *Mathematical Methods in Science and Engineering* (Hoboken, NJ: Wiley, 2006), p. 201.

59. Dennis D. McCarthy and P. Kenneth Seidelmann, *Time: From Earth Rotation to Atomic Physics* (Weinheim, Germany: Wiley-VCH, 2009), p. 97.

60. H. A. Lorentz, "Electromagnetic Phenomena in a System Moving with Any Velocity Less than That of Light," in Hendrik Lorentz et al., *The Principle of Relativity: A Collection of Original Papers on the Special and General Theory of Relativity* (London: Methuen, 1923), pp. 11–35.

61. Lorentz, "Electromagnetic Phenomena," pp. 11–35.

62. Wayne M. Saslow, *Electricity, Magnetism, and Light* (Toronto: Thomson Learning, 2002), p. 698.

63. Galileo uses the word "energy" only six times in his *Dialogues Concerning Two New Sciences* (New York: Macmillan, 1914).

64. Einstein, *Works of Albert Einstein*, Kindle edition, locations 15, 241, 251, 1024, 1869.

65. Ibid., location 934.

Einstein Gives Seven Ugly Ducklings a Home: The Year of Miracles

66. Dudley Herschbach, "Einstein as a Student," in *Einstein for the 21st Century: His Legacy in Science, Art, and Modern Culture*, ed. Peter Galison, Gerald James Holton, and Silvan S. Schweber (Princeton, NJ: Princeton University Press, 2008); see also Dudley Herschbach, "Einstein as a Student," Department of Chemistry and Chemical Biology, Harvard University, http://www.chem.harvard.edu/herschbach/Einstein_Student.pdf (accessed March 11, 2011), p. 18. Dudley Herschbach is a Nobel Prize winner.

67. Arthur I. Miller, *Einstein, Picasso: Space, Time, and the Beauty that Causes Havoc* (New York: Basic Books, 2001), p. 193.

68. Jürgen Neffe, *Einstein: A Biography* (New York: Farrar, Strauss & Giroux, 2007), p. 125.

69. Herschbach, "Einstein as a Student," p. 18.

70. Jürgen Renn, "Einstein in *Annalen der Physik*," Max Planck Institute for the History of Science, 2005, http://einstein-annalen.mpiwg-berlin.mpg.de/home (accessed September 28, 2011).

71. Princeton University Press, promotional copy for Albert Einstein, *The Collected Papers of Albert Einstein*, vol. 1, *The Early Years, 1879–1902*, ed. John Stachel, David C. Cassidy, and Robert Schulmann (Princeton, NJ: Princeton University Press, 1987), http://press.princeton.edu/titles/2515.html (accessed March 10, 2011).

72. Herschbach, "Einstein as a Student."

73. Ronald W. Clark, *Einstein: The Life and Times* (New York: Avon, 1972), p. 67.

74. Ibid., pp. 67–68.

75. Walter C. Mih, *The Fascinating Life and Theory of Albert Einstein* (Commack, NY: Kroshka Books, 2000), p. 9.

76. Walter Isaacson, *Einstein: His Life and Universe* (New York: Simon & Schuster, 2007), p. 84.

77. Herschbach, "Einstein as a Student."

78. Albert Einstein, *Einstein's Annalen Papers: The Complete Collection 1901–1922*, ed. Jurgen Renn (Weinheim, Germany: Wiley-VCH, 2005), p. 10.

79. Herschbach, "Einstein as a Student," p. 4.

80. Peter Galison, *Einstein's Clocks, Poincaré's Maps: Empires of Time* (New York: Norton, 2003), p. 250.

81. Edmund Blair Bolles, *Einstein Defiant: Genius versus Genius in the Quantum Revolution* (Washington, DC: Joseph Henry Press, 2004), p. 141.

82. Herschbach, "Einstein as a Student," p. 3; Isaacson, *Einstein*, p. 17. Dudley Herschbach says this incident occurred when Einstein was ten. Walter Isaacson pegs it as happening when Einstein was eleven.

83. Herschbach, "Einstein as a Student," p. 3.

84. A. Bernstein, *Popular Books for Practical Use in Every Household, for Readers of all Classes* (New York: Chr. Schmidt, 1869).

85. Marie Hammontree, *Albert Einstein: Young Thinker* (New York: Simon & Schuster, 1988), p. 86.

86. Albert Einstein, *A Stubbornly Persistent Illusion: The Essential Scientific Works of Albert Einstein*, ed. Stephen Hawking (Philadelphia: Running Press, 2007), p. 337.

87. Herschbach, "Einstein as a Student," p. 3; Galison et al., *Einstein for the 21st Century*, pp. 2, 218.

88. Isaacson, *Einstein*, p. 20.

89. Ibid., p. 17.

90. Herschbach, "Einstein as a Student," p. 3.

91. Isaacson, *Einstein*, p. 20

92. Ibid.

93. Ibid.; John J. Stachel, *Einstein from "B" to "Z"* (Boston: Birkhäuser, 2002), p.13; Herschbach, "Einstein as a Student."

94. Don Howard and John J. Stachel, eds., *Einstein: The Formative Years, 1879–1909* (Boston: Birkhäuser, 2000), 8: 23–41.

95. Isaacson, *Einstein*, p. 20.

96. Stachel, *Einstein from "B" to "Z,"* p. 22.

97. Ibid., pp. 13–14.

98. John W. Klooster, *Icons of Invention: The Makers of the Modern World from Gutenberg to Gates* (Santa Barbara, CA: ABC-CLIO, 2009), pp. 158–59; Gavin Weightman, *Signor Marconi's Magic Box: The Most Remarkable Invention of the 19th Century* (Cambridge, MA: Da Capo Press, 2009), p. 96.

99. Fulvia Skof, ed., *Giuseppe Peano between Mathematics and Logic* (Milan: Springer, 2011), p. 80; Roberto Torretti, *Philosophy of Geometry from Riemann to Poincaré* (Dordrecht, Netherlands: D. Reidel, 1984), p. 218.

100. Robert Cwiklik, *Albert Einstein and the Theory of Relativity* (Hauppauge, NY: Barron's, 1987), p. 36.

101. Herschbach, "Einstein as a Student."

102. Albert Einstein, *The Collected Papers of Albert Einstein*, vol. 1, *The Early Years, 1879–1902*, ed. John Stachel, David C. Cassidy, and Robert Schulmann (Princeton, NJ: Princeton University Press, 1987), p. 6.

103. Patrick J. Keane, *Emily Dickinson's Approving God: Divine Design and the Problem of Suffering* (Columbia: University of Missouri Press, 2008), p. 53.

104. Herschbach, "Einstein as a Student," p. 3; Isaacson, *Einstein*, p. 26; Peter A. Bucky and Allen G. Weakland, *The Private Albert Einstein* (Riverside, NJ: Andrews McMeel, 1992), p. 26; Hassani, *From Atoms to Galaxies*, p. 362.

105. Stachel, *Einstein from "B" to "Z,"* p. 23.

106. Renn, *Einstein's Annalen Papers*, p. 10.

107. Roger Highfield, "Einstein When He's at Home," in John Brockman, *My Einstein: Essays by Twenty-Four of the World's Leading Thinkers on the Man, His Work, and His Legacy* (New York: Random House Digital, 2006).

108. Ibid.

109. Renn, *Einstein's Annalen Papers*.

110. Albert Einstein, "On a Heuristic Point of View Concerning the Production and Transformation of Light," *Annalen der Physik* 17 (1905): 132–48, in Albert Einstein, *The Collected Papers of Albert Einstein: The Swiss Years, Writings, 1900–1909*, trans. Anna Beck, ed. Peter Havas (Princeton NJ: Princeton University Press, 1989), p. 86.

111. J. L. Heilbron, *The Dilemmas of an Upright Man: Max Planck and the Fortunes of German Science* (Boston: Harvard University Press, 1986), pp. 35, 98. In 1905 and 1906 Max Planck was president of the German Physical Society, the Deutsche Physikalische Gesellschaft, the organization that published *the Annalen der Physik*.

112. Max Planck, *Max Planck: Annalen Papers*, ed. Dieter Hoffmann (Weinheim, Germany: Wiley-VCH, 2008), p. 7.

113. Einstein, *Ideas and Opinions*.

114. The phenomena that puzzled Einstein came from the experiments of the Hungarian Nobel Prize–winning physicist Philipp Lenard. For details see Satya Prakash, *Physics* (New Delhi: VK [India] Enterprises, 2009), pp. 1151–52; Joy Manners, *Quantum Physics: An Introduction* (Milton Keynes, UK: Open University, 2000), p. 14; Per F. Dahl, *Flash of the Cathode Rays: A History of J. J. Thomson's Electron* (London: Institute of Physics Publishing, 1997), pp. 2–3.

115. Einstein, "On a Heuristic Point of View," p. 101; Mauro Dardo, *Nobel Laureates and Twentieth-Century Physics* (Cambridge, UK: Cambridge University Press, 2004), p. 51.

116. Einstein, "On a Heuristic Point of View," p. 87.

117. Ibid., p. 86.

118. Hugh Cahill, "Review of *Einstein's Miracle Year: The* Annalen der Physik *Papers of 1905*," Information Services and Systems, University of London, March 2005.

119. Ibid.

120. Albert Einstein, "On the Movement of Small Particles Suspended in Stationary Liquids Required by the Molecular-Kinetic Theory of Heat," *Annalen der Physik* 17 (1905): 549–60, in Einstein, *Collected Papers of Albert Einstein*, p. 123.

121. For a previous attempt to show that Brownian movement was caused by the jostle

of "molecules," see R. Meade Bache, "The Secret of the Brownian Movements," *Proceedings of the American Philosophical Society*, June 1894, pp. 163–77.

122. Robert M. Mazo, *Brownian Motion: Fluctuations, Dynamics, and Applications* (Oxford: Oxford University Press, 2002), pp. 1–3.

123. James Clerk Maxwell, *Theory of Heat* (London: Longmans, Green, 1872). Thomas Preston, *The Theory of Heat* (London: Macmillan, 1894).

124. John S. Rigden, *Einstein 1905: The Standard of Greatness* (Cambridge, MA: Harvard University Press, 2006), p. 67; Wesley C. Salmon, *Reality and Rationality* (Oxford, UK: Oxford University Press, 2005), p. 37.

125. Albert Einstein, "On the Electrodynamics of Moving Bodies," in Einstein, *Works of Albert Einstein*.

126. Albert Einstein, *Relativity: The Special and General Theory* (New York: Henry Holt, 1920), pp. 30–37.

127. Einstein, "On the Electrodynamics of Moving Bodies."

128. "Caoutchouc and its Gatherers," *Appletons' Journal*, July 3, 1875, p. 2.

129. Albert Einstein, "On the Electrodynamics of Moving Bodies," translated from "Zur Elektrodynamik bewegter Körper," *Annalen der Physik* 17 (1905), in Einstein, *A Stubbornly Persistent Illusion*, p. 7.

130. Albert Einstein, *Investigations on the Theory of the Brownian Movement* (Mineola, NY: Courier Dover Publications, 1956), p. 17. Reprint of Methuen edition of 1926.

131. Albert Einstein, "Does the Inertia of a Body Depend upon Its Energy-Content?" translated from "Ist die Trägheit eines Körpers von Seinem Energieinhalt Abhängig?" *Annalen der Physik* 17 (1905), in Einstein, *Selections from the Principle of Relativity*.

132. Ibid., p. 26.

133. Einstein, *Relativity*, p. xi.

134. Einstein, *Collected Papers of Albert Einstein*, p. 104.

135. Cahill, "Review of *Einstein's Miracle Year*."

136. Abraham A. Ungar, *Analytic Hyperbolic Geometry: Mathematical Foundations and Applications* (Singapore: World Scientific, 2005), p. 349.

137. Stephen Hawking, in Einstein, *A Stubbornly Persistent Illusion*, p. 235.

138. "Space acts on matter, telling it how to move. In turn, matter reacts back on space, telling it how to curve." See Charles W. Misner, Kip S. Thorne, and John Archibald Wheeler, *Gravitation* (New York: W. H. Freeman, 1973), p. 5.

139. Krzysztof Maurin, *The Riemann Legacy: Riemannian Ideas in Mathematics and Physics* (Dordrecht, Netherlands: Kluwer, 1997), p. xv; Rainer Kurt Sachs, *General Relativity and Cosmology* (New York: Taylor & Francis, 1971).

140. Moshe Carmeli, *Relativity: Modern Large-Scale Spacetime Structure of the Cosmos* (Singapore: World Scientific, 2008), p. 92.

141. Einstein, *A Stubbornly Persistent Illusion*.

Einstein's Secret Weapon: Aristotle's Invention

142. I. Bernard Cohen, *Revolution in Science* (Cambridge, MA: Harvard University Press, 1985), p. 435.

143. Albert Einstein, *A Stubbornly Persistent Illusion*, p. 339.

144. Ibid., p. 342.

145. Ibid., p. 238.

146. Ibid., p. 251.

147. Ibid., pp. 250–51.

148. Ibid., p. 363.

149. Ibid.

150. Quoted in Gerald Holton and Yehuda Elkana, *Albert Einstein: Historical and Cultural Perspectives* (Princeton, NJ: Princeton University Press, 1982), p. 62.

151. Albert Einstein, "Geometry and Experience: An Expanded Form of an Address to the Prussian Academy of Sciences in Berlin on January 27, 1921," reprinted online in Eric Baird, *Relativity in Curved Space-Time, 2007–2009*, Relativity Resources, http://relativitybook.com/resources/Einstein_geometry.html (accessed August 8, 2011).

152. Einstein," Geometry and Experience: An Expanded Form of an Address to the Prussian Academy of Sciences in Berlin on January 27, 1921," in Einstein, Hawking, *A Stubbornly Persistent Illusion*, p. 251.

The Adventures of Einstein's Predictions

153. Albert Einstein, "Geometry and Experience," in Albert Einstein, *Works of Albert Einstein*, ed. John Walker (Boston: MobileReference, 2010), Kindle edition, location 215.

154. Kenneth R. Lang and Charles Allen Whitney, *Wanderers in Space: Exploration and Discovery in the Solar System* (Cambridge, UK: Cambridge University Press, 1991), p. 22; Richard H. Enns, *It's a Nonlinear World* (New York: Springer, 2011), pp. 155–57; Theo Koupelis, *In Quest of the Universe* (Sudbury, MA: Jones & Bartlett, 2011), p. 90.

155. Jürgen Renn, Max-Planck-Institut für Wissenschaftsgeschichte, *Albert Einstein: Chief Engineer of the Universe*, vol. 1 (Berlin: Wiley, 2005).

156. Donald Ray Smith, *Singular-Perturbation Theory: An Introduction with Applications* (Cambridge, UK: Cambridge University Press, 1985), p. 30.

157. Spencer, *An Autobiography* (Appleton edition), 1: 196.

158. Herbert Spencer, *An Autobiography* (Whitefish, MT: Kessinger, 2005), 1: 301.

159. Mark Francis, *Herbert Spencer and the Invention of Modern Life* (Ithaca, NY: Cornell University Press, 2007), p. 26; David Duncan, *Life and Letters of Herbert Spencer* (London: Methuen, 1908), 1: 67–70; Spencer, *An Autobiography* (Kessinger edition), 1: 312.

160. George Eliot, *George Eliot's Life as Related in Her Letters and Journals: Arranged and Edited by Her Husband, J. W. Cross* (London: Harper, 1903), pp. 92–98, 269, 275, 298.

161. Walter William Rouse Ball, *A Short Account of the History of Mathematics* (London: Macmillan, 1888), p. 439.

162. "The Paris Academy of Sciences, June 4," *Living Age* 10 (1846): 245; Patrick Moore and Robin Rees, *Patrick Moore's Data Book of Astronomy* (Cambridge, UK: Cambridge University Press, 2011), p. 92.

163. David Blair and Geoff McNamara, *Ripples on a Cosmic Sea: The Search for Gravitational Waves* (New York: Perseus, 1997), p. 21.

164. Asaph Hall, *Reports on Telescopic Observations of the Transit of Mercury, May 5–6, 1878* (Washington DC: Government Printing Office, 1879), p. 65. This is a report Hall submitted to the United States Naval Observatory.

165. Milton A. Rothman, *Discovering the Natural Laws: The Experimental Basis of Physics* (Mineola, NY: Courier-Dover, 1989), p. 78; Jong-Ping Hsu and Dana Fine, *100 Years of Gravity and Accelerated Frames: The Deepest Insights of Einstein and Yang-Mills* (Singapore: World Scientific, 2005), p. 480; John Snygg, *Clifford Algebra: A Computational Tool for Physicists* (Oxford: Oxford University Press, 1997), p. 127. See also Einstein, *Relativity*, pp. 150–52. Milton Rothman gives a figure of 42.56. Jon-Ping Hsu and Dana Fine cite the 1882 figure of Simon Newcomb, 42.98. And John Snygg gives the figure as "41.24 ± 2.09 per century." Einstein himself cites an 1895 work by Simon Newcomb, but doesn't give the exact figure. For Simon Newcomb's calculations, see Simon Newcomb, "Tables of the Heliocentric Motion of Mercury," in *Astronomical Papers Prepared for the Use of the American Ephemeris*, vol. 6 (Washington, DC: United States Naval Observatory, Nautical Almanac Office, 1898).

166. Hubert Goenner, ed. *The Expanding Worlds of General Relativity* (Boston: Center for Einstein Studies, Birkhäuser, 1999), pp. 90–95.

167. Jeroen van Dongen, *Einstein's Unification* (Cambridge, UK: Cambridge University Press, 2010), p. 23.

168. John Earman, Michel Janssen, and John D. Norton, *The Attraction of Gravitation: New Studies in the History of General Relativity* (Boston: Center for Einstein Studies, Birkhäuser, 1993), p. 136.

169. Paul Davies, *The New Physics* (Cambridge, UK: Cambridge University Press, 1989), p. 33.

170. András Prékopa, "The Revolution of János Bólyai," in *Non-Euclidean Geometries: János Bólyai Memorial Volume*, ed. Magyar Tudományos and Emil Molnár (New York: Springer, 2006), p. 40; Donald Goldsmith and Marcia Bartusiak, *E = Einstein: His Life, His Thought, and His Influence on Our Culture* (New York: Sterling, 2008), p. 125.

171. Sir Arthur Stanley Eddington, *Space, Time, and Gravitation: An Outline of the General Relativity Theory* (Cambridge, UK: Cambridge University Press, 1921), pp. 123–35.

172. Einstein, *Relativity*, p. 152.

173. Jürgen Renn and Tilman Sauer, "Heuristics and Mathematical Representation in Einstein's Search for a Gravitational Field Equation," in Goenner, *Expanding Worlds of General Relativity*, pp. 87–123.

174. Albert Einstein, "On the Influence of Gravity on the Propagation of Light," in Einstein, *Selections from the Principle of Relativity*, p. 27.

175. Ibid.

176. Leonardo da Vinci, "Fourth Book on Light and Shade," in *The Literary Works of Leonardo da Vinci* (London: Sampson Low, Marston, Searle & Rivington, 1883), 1: 111.

177. Govert Schilling, *Atlas of Astronomical Discoveries* (New York: Springer, 2011), pp. 103–104.

178. Christopher M. Linton, *From Eudoxus to Einstein: A History of Mathematical Astronomy* (Cambridge, UK: Cambridge University Press, 2004), p. 471.

179. S. Chandrasekhar, *Eddington: The Most Distinguished Astrophysicist of His Time* (Cambridge, UK: Cambridge University Press, 1983); Clive William Kilmister, *Eddington's Search for a Fundamental Theory: A Key to the Universe* (Cambridge, UK: Cambridge University Press, 1994), p. 34

180. Kilmister, *Eddington's Search*, p. 18.

181. Chandrasekhar, *Eddington*, p. 28.

182. Hubert F. M. Goenner, "The Reception of the Theory of Relativity in Germany as Reflected by Books Published between 1908 and 1945," in *Studies in the History of General Relativity*, ed. Jean Eisenstaedt and Anne J. Kox (Boston: Center for Einstein Studies, 1992), p. 37.

183. Kilmister, *Eddington's Search*, p. 36.

184. S. Chandrasekhar, "Of Some Famous Men: Verifying the Theory of Relativity," *Bulletin of the Atomic Scientists*, June 1975, p. 17.

185. Linton, *From Eudoxus to Einstein*, p. 471.

186. John Clayton Taylor, *Hidden Unity in Nature's Laws* (Cambridge, UK: Cambridge University Press, 2001), pp. 209–10; Jayant Vishnu Narlikar, *The Lighter Side of Gravity* (Cambridge, UK: Cambridge University Press, 1996), pp. 89–90.

187. Eisenstaedt and Kox, *Studies in the History of General Relativity*, p. 77; Linton, *From Eudoxus to Einstein*, p. 471.

188. Robert P. Crease, *The Great Equations: Breakthroughs in Science from Pythagoras to Heisenberg* (New York: W. W. Norton, 2008), p. 203.

189. Eddington, *Space, Time, and Gravitation*, p. 115.

190. F. W. Dyson, A. S. Eddington, and C. Davidson, "A Determination of the Deflection of Light by the Sun's Gravitational Field, from Observations Made at the Total Eclipse of May 29, 1919," *Philosophical Transactions of the Royal Society of London, Series A* 220 (1920): 291–333.

191. Ibid., p. 118.

192. Ibid; A. C. D. Crommelin and C. R. Davidson, "Corona and Prominences at Eclipse of 1919, May 29," in *Science Abstracts* (Institution of Electrical Engineers, 1920), 23: 118; Carnegie Institution of Washington, "Report of the Department of Terrestrial Magnetism,"

in *Year Book* 18 (1920): 297; "Relativity," in *The Engineering Index* (New York: American Society of Mechanical Engineers, 1921), p. 472.

193. Ernest Rutherford, paraphrased in Kilmister, *Eddington's Search*, p. 36.

194. Elisabeth T. Crawford, *The Beginnings of the Nobel Institution: The Science Prizes, 1901–1915* (Cambridge, UK: Cambridge University Press, 1984), p. 124.

195. Richard Staley, *Einstein's Generation: The Origins of the Relativity Revolution* (Chicago: University of Chicago Press, 2008), p. 307.

196. Quote from an article in a contemporary newspaper. Though the clipping appears scanned, its source and date are not given. See H. A. Lorentz, *The Einstein Theory of Relativity* (Boston: MobileReference, 2010); reprint of Brentano's 1920 print edition.

197. Lorentz, *The Einstein Theory of Relativity* (New York: Brentano's, 1920).

198. Arthur Eddington, *Report on the Relativity Theory of Gravitation* (London: Fleetway Press, 1920); Eddington, *Space, Time, and Gravitation*; Arthur Eddington, *The Theory of Relativity and its Influence on Scientific Thought* (Oxford: Oxford University Press, 1922); Arthur Eddington, *The Mathematical Theory of Relativity* (Cambridge, UK: Cambridge University Press, 1923); Arthur Eddington, *Relativity Theory of Protons and Electrons* (Cambridge, UK: Cambridge University Press, 1936). These are Eddington's five books on relativity. Then there's a semi-sixth: Arthur Eddington, "The Downfall of Classical Physics and Relativity," in *The Nature of the Physical World*, The Gifford Lectures (New York: Macmillan, 1928), extracted as a complete book by Kessinger Publishing (Whitefish, MT), 2005.

199. Thomas F. Glick, ed., *The Comparative Reception of Relativity* (Dordrecht, Netherlands: Reidel, 1987), p. 195.

200. "Albert Einstein," in *Time 100: Heroes & Icons: Person of the Century* (New York: Time-Life Books, 2000), pp. 98–104.

201. Richard C. Tolman, *Relativity, Thermodynamics, and Cosmology* (Oxford, UK: Oxford University Press, 1934), p. 211; Mendel Sachs, *Physics of the Universe* (London: Imperial College Press, 2010), p. 24.

202. Ronald W. Clark, *Einstein: The Life and Times* (New York: Avon, 1972), p. 260.

203. Albert Einstein, "On the Influence of Gravity."

204. Albert Einstein, "The Fundamentals of Theoretical Physics," *Science*, May 24, 1940, in Einstein, *Ideas and Opinions*; Albert Einstein, *The Theory of Relativity, and Other Essays* (Secaucus, NJ: Citadel Press, 1996), pp. 8–15, 60; Fouad G. Major, *The Quantum Beat: Principles and Applications of Atomic Clocks* (New York: Springer, 2007), p. 447; Abhay Ashtekar, *One Hundred Years of Relativity—Space-Time Structure: Einstein and Beyond* (Singapore: World Scientific, 2005), p. 207.

205. Einstein, *A Stubbornly Persistent Illusion*, p. 442.

206. Thibault Damour et al., eds, *Einstein, 1905–2005: Poincaré Seminar 2005* (Basel: Birkhäuser, 2006), p. 44.

207. Paul Fleisher, *Objects in Motion: Principles of Classical Mechanics* (Minneapolis:

Lerner, 2002), p. 18; Joseph Mazur, *Zeno's Paradox: Unraveling the Ancient Mystery behind the Science of Space and Time* (New York: Plume/Penguin, 2007).

208. Stefano Bregni, *Synchronization of Digital Telecommunications Networks* (Chichester, UK: Wiley, 2002), p. 284.

209. Thomas C. McKay, *Physical Measurements in Sound, Light, Electricity, and Magnetism* (Berkeley: University of California Press, 1908), p. 47.

210. Clark, *Einstein*, p. 260.

211. "Early History of the Department," Harvard University Department of Physics, http://www.physics.harvard.edu/about/history.html (accessed September 29, 2011).

212. Marianne J. Dyson, *Space and Astronomy: Decade by Decade* (New York: Facts on File, 2007), p. 40.

213. Anthony J. G. Hey and Patrick Walters, *Einstein's Mirror* (Cambridge, UK: University of Cambridge Press, 1997), p. 180.

214. Rusty L. Myer, *The Basics of Physics* (Westport, CT: Greenwood, 2006), p. 292.

215. Dyson, *Space and Astronomy*, p. 40.

216. Chandrasekhar, "Of Some Famous Men," p. 20.

217. Eddington, *Space, Time, and Gravitation.*

218. Silvia Mollerach and Esteban Roulet, *Gravitational Lensing and Microlensing* (Singapore: World Scientific, 2002); Peter Schneider, C. S. Kochanek, and Joachim Wambsganss, *Gravitational Lensing: Strong, Weak, and Micro* (Berlin: Springer, 2006).

219. Mollerach and Roulet, *Gravitational Lensing and Microlensing*, pp. 2–3.

220. Eddington, *Space, Time, and Gravitation*, p. 112; Schneider et al., *Gravitational Lensing*, pp. 1–5; Mollerach and Roulet, *Gravitational Lensing and Microlensing*, pp. 1–3; Govert Schilling, *Atlas of Astronomical Discoveries* (New York: Springer, 2011), pp. 177–78.

221. Lambourne, *Relativity, Gravitation and Cosmology*, p. 145; Vladimir B. Ginzburg, *Prime Elements of Ordinary Matter, Dark Matter & Dark Energy: Beyond Standard Model & String Theory* (Boca Raton, FL: Universal, 2007), p. 237.

222. Brian Greene, *The Hidden Reality: Parallel Universes and the Deep Laws of the Cosmos* (New York: Knopf, 2011), p. 240; Dennis Overbye, *Einstein in Love: A Scientific Romance* (New York: Penguin, 2001).

223. Moshe Carmeli, *Relativity: Modern Large-Scale Spacetime Structure of the Cosmos* (Singapore: World Scientific, 2008), p. 133.

224. "Schwarzschild," The MacTutor History of Mathematics Archive, School of Mathematics and Statistics, University of St. Andrews, Scotland, http://www-history.mcs.st-andrews.ac.uk/Biographies/Schwarzschild.html (accessed August 17, 2011).

225. Ibid.

226. Aaron J. Barth, "Black Holes in Active Galaxies," in *Coevolution of Black Holes and Galaxies*, ed. Luis C. Ho (Cambridge, UK: Cambridge University Press, 2004), p. 225.

227. Frank H. Shu, *The Physical Universe: An Introduction to Astronomy* (Sausalito, CA: University Science Books, 1982), p. 203.

228. Robert H. Keyserlingk, *Austria in World War II: An Anglo-American Dilemma* (Quebec: McGill-Queen's Press, 1988), p. 31.

229. Tamra Orr, *The Atom Bomb: Creating and Exploding the First Nuclear Weapon* (New York: Rosen, 2005), p. 17.

230. Kati Marton, *The Great Escape: Nine Jews Who Fled Hitler and Changed the World* (New York: Simon & Schuster, 2007), pp. 1–4.

231. Jeff A. Hughes, *The Manhattan Project: Big Science and the Atom Bomb* (New York: Columbia University Press, 2002); F. G. Gosling, *The Manhattan Project: Making the Atomic Bomb* (Washington, DC: United States Department of Energy, 1999), p. 144; J. Poolos, *The Atomic Bombings of Hiroshima and Nagasaki* (New York: Infobase Publishing, 2008), p. 114.

232. Donald E. Schmidt, *The Folly of War: American Foreign Policy, 1898–2005* (New York: Algora, 2005), pp. 185–86.

233. Richard Rhodes, *The Making of the Atomic Bomb* (New York: Simon & Schuster, 1986), p. 924; Frank Barnaby, "The Continuing Body Count at Hiroshima and Nagasaki," *Bulletin of the Atomic Scientists*, December 1977, pp. 48–49.

234. Konrad Hugo Jarausch, *After Hitler: Recivilizing Germans, 1945–1995* (Oxford: Oxford University Press, 2006), pp. 1–25.

235. Little Boy carried one hundred pounds of uranium 235, but "less than two pounds actually underwent fission." Richard Wolfson, *Nuclear Choices: A Citizen's Guide to Nuclear Technology* (Cambridge: Massachusetts Institute of Technology Press, 1993), p. 299.

236. Rhodes, *Making of the Atomic Bomb*, p. 737.

237. Ibid.

238. Gar Alperovitz, *The Decision to Use the Atomic Bomb* (New York: Random House, 1995); Wilson Miscamble, *The Most Controversial Decision: Truman, the Atomic Bombs, and the Defeat of Japan* (New York: Cambridge University Press, 2011).

239. Steven Weinberg, "Einstein's Mistakes," *Physics Today*, November 2005, p. 31.

240. Sources for this account of the cosmological constant include: Albert Einstein, *Relativity: The Special and General Theory*, trans. Robert W. Lawson (New York: Penguin/Plume, 2006); Spiros Cotsakis and Gary W. Gibbons, eds., *Mathematical and Quantum Aspects of Relativity and Cosmology: Proceedings* (Berlin: Springer, 2000), p. 143; Maurice H. P. M. Van Putten, *Gravitational Radiation, Luminous Black Holes, and Gamma-Ray Burst Supernovae* (Cambridge, UK: Cambridge University Press, 2005), p. 55; Theo Koupelis, *In Quest of the Universe* (Sudbury, MA: Jones & Bartlett, 2011), p. 532; Marc Leslie Kutner, *Astronomy: A Physical Perspective* (Cambridge, UK: Cambridge University Press, 2003), pp. 385–89; Jerzy Plebański and Andrzej Krasiński, *An Introduction to General Relativity and Cosmology* (Cambridge, UK: Cambridge University Press, 2006), p. 262.

241. Ian Ridpath, *Astronomy* (New York: DK, 2006), p. 57.

242. Thibault Damour, "Cosmological Singularities. BKL Conjecture," in *General Relativity and the Einstein Equations*, ed. Yvonne Choquet-Bruhat (Oxford: Oxford University Press, 2009).

243. Jayant V. Narlikar, *Elements of Cosmology* (Hyderabad: Universities Press, 1996), p. 22.

244. Alexander Heidel, *The Babylonian Genesis: The Story of Creation* (Chicago: University of Chicago Press, 1951), p. 42.

245. Roger Penrose, introduction to Albert Einstein, *Relativity: The Special and General Theory*, ed. Roger Penrose and Robert Geroch (New York: Pearson, 2005), p. xxvi.

246. Brian P. Schmidt et al., "The High-Z Supernova Search: Measuring Cosmic Deceleration and Global Curvature of the Universe Using Type IA Supernovae," *Astronomical Journal*, November 1998, pp. 46–63; Adam G. Reiss et al., "Observational Evidence from Supernovae for an Accelerating Universe and a Cosmological Constant," *Astrophysical Journal*, September 1998; Yun Wang, *Dark Energy* (Weinheim, Germany: Wiley-VCH, 2010), p. 219; L. Bergstrom and A. Goobar, "Particle Astrophysics and the Dark Sector of the Universe," in *Astrophysics Update*, ed. John W. Mason (Berlin: Springer, 2004), 1: 113.

247. Joshua S. Bloom, *What Are Gamma-Ray Bursts?* (Princeton NJ: Princeton University Press, 2011), p. 195.

248. Catherine Amoroso Leslie, *Needlework through History: An Encyclopedia* (Westport, CT: Greenwood, 2007), pp. xv–xviii.

8. THE AMAZING REPETITION MACHINE

Forget Information: Or How Claude Shannon Got It Wrong

1. John L. Bell, "Hermann Weyl on Intuition and the Continuum," *Philosophia Mathematica* 8, no. 3 (2000): 3. Available on Publish Web Server, University of Western Canada, http://publish.uwo.ca/~jbell/Hermann%20Weyl.pdf (accessed April 3, 2011).

2. Vlatko Vedral, *Decoding Reality: The Universe as Quantum Information* (New York: Oxford University Press, 2010), Kindle edition, location 324.

3. Thomas A. Bass, *The Eudaemonic Pie: The Bizarre True Story of How a Band of Physicists and Computer Wizards Took On Las Vegas* (Boston: Houghton Mifflin, 1986), p. 128.

4. National Endowment for the Arts, "Westbeth: At Home in the Arts," http://www.nea.gov/about/40th/westbeth.html (accessed August 19, 2011); Westbeth Center for the Arts, "Our History," http://www.westbetharts.org/our-history/ (accessed August 19, 2011).

5. Marcus Du Sautoy, *Symmetry: A Mathematical Journey* (New York: HarperCollins e-books, 2009), Kindle edition, location 4; James Gleick, *The Information: A History, a Theory, a Flood* (New York: Pantheon, 2011), Kindle edition, location 4837.

6. David G. Luenberger, *Information Science* (Princeton NJ: Princeton University Press, 2006), p. 18.

7. Gleick, *Information*, Kindle location 71.

8. Ibid., location 84.

9. Govert Schilling, *Atlas of Astronomical Discoveries* (New York: Springer, 2011), pp. 151–52.

10. Michigan Board of State Auditors, *Annual Report of the Board of State Auditors for the State of Michigan for the Year 1918* (Lansing, MI: State Printers, 1918), p. 30; Robert Slater, *Portraits in Silicon* (Cambridge MA: MIT Press, 1989), p. 33.

11. Anthony Debons, *Information Science 101* (Lanham MD: Rowman & Littlefield, 2008), pp. 18–19.

12. Alan R. Earls and Robert E. Edwards, *Raytheon Company: The First Sixty Years* (Charleston, SC: Arcadia, 2005), p. 9.

13. Alan Seaburg, *Cambridge on the Charles* (Cambridge, MA: Anne Miniver Press, 2001), p. 120.

14. Gleick, *Information*, Kindle location 3073.

15. Claude Shannon, "A Symbolic Analysis of Relay and Switching Circuits," in *Great Papers in Computer Science*, ed. Phillip A. Laplante (New York: IEEE Press, 1996), pp. 219–45.

16. George Boole, *George Boole: Selected Manuscripts on Logic and Its Philosophy*, ed. I. Grattan-Guinness and Gérard Bornet (Basel: Birkhäuser, 1997), pp. xiv, lviii; Alan D. Solomon, *Boolean Algebra Essentials* (Piscataway, NJ: Research and Education Association, 1990).

17. Bertrand Russell, *The Basic Writings of Bertrand Russell*, vol. 10 (Oxon, UK: Routledge, 2009), p. 177.

18. Gottfried Wilhelm Leibniz, *Philosophical Papers and Letters by Gottfried Wilhelm Leibniz*, trans. and ed. Leroy E. Loemker (Dordrecht, Netherlands: Kluwer, 1989), p. 59.

19. H. P. Alesso and Craig Forsythe Smith, *Connections: Patterns of Discovery* (New York: Wiley, 2008), p. 81.

20. William Poundstone, *Fortune's Formula: The Untold Story of the Scientific Betting System that Beat the Casinos and Wall Street* (New York: Hill & Wang, 2005), p. 23.

21. Philip Mirowski, *Machine Dreams: Economics Becomes a Cyborg Science* (Cambridge, UK: Cambridge University Press, 2002), p. 68.

22. Richard W. Dillman, "HFCL FOCUS Shannon's Formula for the Power of a Code," http://www.rdillman.com/HFCL/FOCUS/Information/formula1/formula1.00.html (accessed June 11, 2012).

23. Ibid.

24. Stephen Wolfram, *A New Kind of Science* (Champaign, IL: Wolfram Media, 2002), p. 1069.

25. J. S. Chitode, *Information Theory & Coding* (Pune, India: Technical Publications, 2009), p. B-8.

26. Saeed V. Vaseghi, *Advanced Digital Signal Processing and Noise Reduction* (Chichester, UK: Wiley, 2008), p. 52.

27. Vlatko Vedral, *Decoding Reality: The Universe as Quantum Information* (Oxford: Oxford University Press, 2010), pp. 34–35.

28. Claude E. Shannon, "A Mathematical Theory of Communication," *Bell System Technical Journal*, July 1948, pp. 379–423, October 1948, pp. 623–56; Jorge Reina Schement and Brent D. Ruben, eds., *Between Communication and Information*, vol. 4 (New Brunswick, NJ: Transaction, 1993), p. 39.

29. Quoted in Steve Jones, ed., *Encyclopedia of New Media: An Essential Reference to Communication and Technology* (Thousand Oaks, CA: Sage, 2003), p. 406.

30. Debons, *Information Science 101*, pp. 18–19. The nonsense string in Debons is erroneously expressed with 13 instead of 14 characters; for clarity of illustration, I've added a fourteenth character to the end of the string.

31. Gleick, *Information*, Kindle location 3897.

32. Warren Weaver, "The Mathematics of Communication," *Scientific American*, July 1949, pp. 11–15.

33. Claude Elwood Shannon and Warren Weaver, *The Mathematical Theory of Communication* (Champaign: University of Illinois Press, 1964), p. 99.

34. Shannon and Weaver, *Mathematical Theory of Communication*, p. 99. Also quoted in John Impagliazzo, James Glimm, and Isadore Manuel Singer, eds., *The Legacy of John Von Neumann* (Providence: American Mathematical Association, 2000).

35. Gleick, *Information*, Kindle location 4409.

36. Ibid.

37. Ibid., location 4422.

38. Gartner Inc., "Gartner Says Worldwide IT Services Revenue Declined 5.3 Percent in 2009," press release, May 4, 2010, http://www.gartner.com/it/page.jsp?id=1363713 (accessed March 30, 2011).

39. Peter H. Fraser, Harry Massey, and Joan Parisi Wilcox, *Decoding the Human Body-Field: The New Science of Information as Medicine* (Rochester, VT: Healing Arts, 2008).

40. Evgueni A. Haroutunian, Mariam E. Haroutunian, and Ashot N. Harutyunyan, *Reliability Criteria in Information Theory and in Statistical Hypothesis Testing* (Hanover, MA: Now Publishers, 2008), p. 1–2.

41. Tim Wu, *The Master Switch: The Rise and Fall of Information Empires* (New York: Borzoi Books, 2010).

The Case of the Conversational Cosmos

42. Andrew Watson, *The Quantum Quark* (Cambridge, UK: Cambridge University Press, 2004), p. 264.

43. James Walder et al., "Inside the Proton: Investigating the Structure of Protons through 'Deep Inelastic Scattering,'" Oxford University Department of Physics, http://www.physics.ox.ac.uk/documents/PUS/dis/fundam.htm (accessed April 8, 2011).

44. Robert H. Sanders, *The Dark Matter Problem: A Historical Perspective* (Cambridge, UK: Cambridge University Press, 2010), p. 82.

45. William T. O'Donohue and Kyle E. Ferguson, *The Psychology of B. F. Skinner* (Thousand Oaks, CA: Sage, 2001), p. 18.

46. B. F. Skinner, *Science and Human Behavior* (Cambridge, MA: B. F. Skinner Foundation, 2005), http://www.bfskinner.org/BFSkinner/Society_files/Science_and_Human_Behavior .pdf (accessed October 12, 2011). Originally published in 1953.

47. A. Charles Catania, Steven Harnad, and B. F. Skinner, *The Selection of Behavior: The Operant Behaviorism of B. F. Skinner: Comments and Consequences* (Cambridge, UK: Cambridge University Press, 1988), p. 458.

48. Ernst Niedermeyer and F. H. Lopes da Silva, *Electroencephalography: Basic Principles, Clinical Applications, and Related Fields* (Philadelphia: Lippincott, 2005), pp. 1–5. The first electroencephalographs appeared in the years between 1880 and 1913.

49. Nandini K. Jog, *Electronics in Medicine and Biomedical Instrumentation* (New Delhi: Prentice-Hall of India, 2006), pp. 7.2, 7.3.7.

50. Russell A. Poldrack, Jeanette Mumford, and Thomas Nichols, *Handbook of Functional MRI Data Analysis* (New York: Cambridge University Press, 2011), pp. 5–6.

51. Skinner, *Science and Human Behavior*, pp. 48, 54, 65, 117, 121, 124.

52. B. F. Skinner, "Can Psychology Be a Science of Mind?" *American Psychologist*, November 1990, pp. 1206–10.

53. Ibid.

54. Ta-you Wu and W-Y Pauchy Hwang, *Relativistic Quantum Mechanics and Quantum Fields* (Singapore: World Scientific, 1991), p. 321.

55. Paul Davies, *The New Physics* (Cambridge, UK: Cambridge University Press, 1989), p. 406.

56. Jonathan Allday, *Quarks, Leptons, and the Big Bang* (London: Institute of Physics Publishing, 2002), p. 122.

57. Galileo Galilei, "Letter to the Grand Duchess Christina (1615)," in Galileo Galilei, *The Essential Galileo*, ed. Maurice A. Finocchiaro (Indianapolis: Hackett, 2008), p. 118.

58. Valerius Geist, *Life Strategies, Human Evolution, Environmental Design: Toward a Biological Theory of Health* (New York: Springer, 1978); Valerius Geist, personal communications, 1997–2000.

59. Lee Smolin, "The Relational Idea in Physics and Cosmology," keynote lecture for the Physics Graduate Student Association, Waterloo, Canada, March 3, 2005, later renamed "The Case for Background Independence," in *Structural Realism and Quantum Gravity*, ed. Dean Rickles, Steven French, and Juha Saatsi (Oxford: Oxford University Press, 2006); Lee Smolin, *The Life of the Cosmos* (New York: Oxford University Press, 1997); Lee Smolin, *Three Roads to Quantum Gravity* (New York: Basic Books, 2002); Lee Smolin, *The Trouble with Physics: The Rise of String Theory, the Fall of a Science, and What Comes Next* (New York: Houghton Mifflin Harcourt, 2007).

60. John Archibald Wheeler, *At Home in the Universe* (Melville, NY: American Institute of Physics, 1996), pp. 25, 291–92.

61. Ibid., p. 291.

62. This influential Wheeler quote is cited in at least forty-six books. For an example, see Mark Burgin, *Theory of Information: Fundamentality, Diversity, and Unification* (Singapore: World Scientific, 2010), p. 34.

63. Smolin, "Case for Background Independence"; Smolin, *Life of the Cosmos*; Smolin, *Three Roads*; Smolin, *Trouble with Physics*.

How Gossip Grows the Universe

64. Adrienne Mayor, *The First Fossil Hunters: Paleontology in Greek and Roman Times* (Princeton, NJ: Princeton University Press, 2001), p. 5.

65. R. T. J. Moody et al., eds., *Dinosaurs and Other Extinct Saurians: A Historical Perspective* (Bath, UK: Geological Society of London, 2010), p. 8.

66. J. William Schopf and Cornelius Klein, *The Proterozoic Biosphere: A Multidisciplinary Study* (New York: Cambridge University Press, 1996), p. 360.

67. Rafael Palacios and William Edward Newton, *Genomes and Genomics of Nitrogen-Fixing Organisms* (Dordrecht, Netherlands: Springer, 2005), p. 41.

68. Reinhard Krämer and Kirsten Jung, eds., *Bacterial Signaling* (Weinheim, Germany: Wiley-VCH, 2010), pp. 7, 23–24.

69. Paul G. Bahn and Jean Vertut, *Journey through the Ice Age* (Berkeley: University of California Press, 1997), p. 31; Bryan E. Penprase, *The Power of Stars: How Celestial Observations Have Shaped Civilization* (New York: Springer, 2011), p. 134.

70. Peter James and Nick Thorpe, *Ancient Inventions* (New York: Ballantine, 1994), p. 485; Evan Hadingham, *Early Man and the Cosmos* (New York: Walker, 1985), pp. 85–88.

71. Alexander Marshack, *The Roots of Civilization: The Cognitive Beginnings of Man's First Art, Symbol, and Notation* (Kingston, RI: Moyer Bell, 1991); David H. Kelley, Eugene F. Milone, and Anthony F. Aven, *Exploring Ancient Skies: A Survey of Ancient and Cultural Astronomy* (New York: Springer, 2004), pp. 157–58; Paul G. Bahn, ed., *An Enquiring Mind: Studies in Honor of Alexander Marshack* (Oxford: Oxbow, 2009).

72. A. Thom, "Megalithic Astronomy: Indications in Standing Stones," *Vistas in Astronomy* 7 (1966): 1–56; Clive Ruggles, "The Stone Alignments of Argyll and Mull: A Perspective on the Statistical Approach in Archaeoastronomy," in *Records in Stone: Papers in Memory of Alexander Thom*, ed. Clive Ruggles (Cambridge, UK: Cambridge University Press, 1988), p. 233.

73. Penprase, *The Power of Stars*, pp. 11, 68, 71, 74–76, 91–92, 123–24.

74. Kenneth R. Lang, *The Sun from Space* (Berlin: Springer, 2009), p. 385.

75. J. Edward Wright, *The Early History of Heaven* (Oxford: Oxford University Press, 2000), p. 31.

76. Lorna Oakes, *Mesopotamia* (New York: Rosen, 2009), p. 54.

77. Tonia Sharlach, "Taxes in Ancient Mesopotamia," *University of Pennsylvania Almanac* 48, no. 28, April 2, 2002, http://www.upenn.edu/almanac/v48/n28/AncientTaxes.html#meso (accessed June 28, 2011); Louise Roug, "Cuneiform Bits Become History Bytes," *Los Angeles Times*, May 27, 2003, http://articles.latimes.com/2003/may/27/entertainment/et-roug27 (accessed October 12, 2011).

78. Robert W. Smith, *The Expanding Universe: Astronomy's "Great Debate," 1900–1931* (Cambridge, UK: Cambridge University Press, 1988).

The Magic Onion of Meaning

79. Bernard E. J. Pagel, *Nucleosynthesis and Chemical Evolution of Galaxies* (Cambridge, UK: Cambridge University Press, 1997); Nivaldo J. Tro and Don Neu, *Chemistry in Focus: A Molecular View of Our World* (Belmont, CA: Brooks/Cole, 2007), p. 62.

80. Valerie Ahl and T. F. H. Allen, *Hierarchy Theory: A Vision, Vocabulary, and Epistemology* (New York: Columbia University Press, 1996), pp. 107–12.

81. Henry Stephens Randall, *Sheep Husbandry: With an Account of the Different Breeds, and General Directions in Regard to Summer and Winter Management, Breeding, and the Treatment of Diseases* (New York: C. M. Saxton, 1856), p. 173.

82. Colin G. Brown, Scott A. Waldron, and John William Longworth, *Modernizing China's Industries: Lessons from Wool and Wool Textiles* (Cheltenham, UK: Edward Elgar, 2005), p. 23.

Doing the Glycerin Twist: David Bohm

83. John Archibald Wheeler and Kenneth W. Ford, *Geons, Black Holes, and Quantum Foam: A Life in Physics* (New York: W. W. Norton, 2000), p. 216.

84. F. David Peat, *Infinite Potential: The Life and Times of David Bohm* (New York: Basic Books, 1997), p. 256.

85. L. Pocasangrer et al., "Survey of Banana Endophytic Fungi from Central America and Screening for Biological Control of the Burrowing Nematode (*Radopholus similis*)," *Infomusa: The International Magazine on Banana and Plantain*, June 2000, p. 3.

86. Steven Levy, *In the Plex: How Google Thinks, Works, and Shapes Our Lives* (New York: Simon and Schuster, 2011), p. 48.

87. Kai Bird and Martin J. Sherwin, *American Prometheus: The Triumph and Tragedy of J. Robert Oppenheimer* (New York: Random House, 2005). Toney Allman, *J. Robert Oppenheimer: Theoretical Physicist, Atomic Pioneer* (Farmington Hills, MI: Gale, 2005).

88. Robert Eugene Wyatt and Corey J. Trahan, *Quantum Dynamics with Trajectories: Introduction to Quantum Hydrodynamics* (New York: Springer, 2005), pp. 40–42.

89. Mathew Chandrankunnel, *Philosophy of Quantum Mechanics—Quantum Holism to Cosmic Holism: The Physics and Metaphysics of Bohm* (New Delhi: Global Vision, 2008), p. 11.

90. Peat, *Infinite Potential*, pp. 58–64.

91. Vincent C. Jones, *Manhattan, the Army, and the Atomic Bomb* (Washington, DC: US Army Center of Military History, 1985), p. 74.

92. Bird and Sherwin, *American Prometheus*, p. 185.

93. Ibid., p. 193.

94. Ibid., p. 393.

95. Walter Isaacson, *Einstein: His Life and Universe* (New York: Simon & Schuster, 2007), p. 20.

96. Ibid., pp. 393–95.

97. Peat, *Infinite Potential*, p. 98.

98. David Bohm and Lee Nichol, *The Essential David Bohm* (London: Routledge, 2003), p. 192.

99. David Bohm and F. David Peat, *Science, Order, and Creativity* (Oxon, UK: Routledge, 2011), p. 172. Originally published in 1987.

100. David Bohm, "Hidden Variables and the Implicate Order," in *Quantum Implications: Essays in Honour of David Bohm*, ed. Basil J. Hiley and F. David Peat (London: Routledge, 1991), pp. 40–41.

101. Bohm and Peat, *Science, Order, and Creativity*, p. 174.

102. Bohm, "Hidden Variables," pp. 40–41.

103. Paavo Pylkkänen, *Mind, Matter, and the Implicate Order* (Berlin: Springer, 2007), p. 82.

104. Bohm and Nichol, *Essential David Bohm*, pp. 99–100.

105. David Bohm, *Wholeness and the Implicate Order* (London: Routledge, 1980), p. 242.

106. Ibid.

107. David Bohm and Basil J. Hiley, *The Undivided Universe: An Ontological Interpretation of Quantum Theory* (Oxon, UK: Routledge, 1995), pp. 270–71; Dipankar Home, *Conceptual Foundations of Quantum Physics: An Overview from Modern Perspectives* (New York: Plenum, 1997), pp. 50–55.

108. Bohm and Hiley, *Undivided Universe*, p. 40.

109. Roel Snieder, *A Guided Tour of Mathematical Methods for the Physical Sciences* (Cambridge, UK: Cambridge University Press, 2004), p. 107. Meinard Kuhlmann, Holger Lyre, and Andrew Wayne, *Ontological Aspects of Quantum Field Theory* (Singapore: World Scientific, 2004), p. 298.

110. Akira Tonomura, *The Quantum World Unveiled by Electron Waves* (Singapore: World Scientific, 1998), p. 84.

111. Chandrankunnel, *Philosophy of Quantum Mechanics*, p. 8.

112. Ibid., p. 13.

113. Jiddu Krishnamurti and David Bohm, *The Ending of Time* (New York: Harper, 1985).

114. Jiddu Krishnamurti and David Bohm, *The Future of Humanity: Two Dialogues between J. Krishnamurti and David Bohm* (Bramdean, UK: Krishnamurti Foundation Trust Ltd., 1986); Jiddu Krishnamurti and David Bohm, *The Limits of Thought: Discussions* (London: Routledge, 1999); Susunaga Weeraperuma, *Jiddu Krishnamurti: A Bibliographical Guide* (Delhi: Motilal Banarsidass, 1996).

115. William Arntz, Betsy Chasse, and Mark Vicente, directors, *What the Bleep Do We Know!?* (Captured Light Industries, Lord of the Wind Films, 2004) http://www.whatthebleep.com/ (accessed October 13, 2011).

116. Bohm, *Essential David Bohm*, p. 143.

117. Immanuel Kant, *Kant's Cosmogony as in His Essay on the Retardation of the Rotation of the Earth and His Natural History and Theory of the Heavens*, ed. William Hastie (Glasgow: James Maclehose and Sons, 1900), p. 186.

118. Robyn Arianrhod, *Einstein's Heroes: Imagining the World through the Language of Mathematics* (Oxford: Oxford University Press, 2006), p. 187; Marcia Bartusiak, *The Day We Found the Universe* (New York: Random House, 2010), p. 257.

119. Jeff Buzby, "DNA Uncoiled Length," Newton: Ask a Scientist (Argonne National Laboratory and US Department of Energy), http://www.newton.dep.anl.gov/askasci/mole00/mole00413.htm (accessed August 27, 2011).

120. D. O. Hall and K. K. Rao, *Photosynthesis* (Cambridge, UK: Cambridge University Press, 1999).

121. Jeff L. Bennetzen and Sarah Hake, *Handbook of Maize: Genetics and Genomics* (New York: Springer, 2009), p. 84.

Benoît Mandelbrot Zigs and Zags

122. G. Julia, "Mémoire sur l'itération des fonctions rationnelles," *Journal de Mathématiques Pures et Appliquées*, 1918; Michèle Audin, *Fatou, Julia, Montel: The Great Prize of Mathematical Sciences of 1918, and Beyond* (Springer: Berlin, 2011), p. 1.

123. "Benoît Mandelbrot," interview with Benoît Mandelbrot in "Math Marvels" (East Setauket, NY: Three Village Central School District, Math Department), http://www.3villagecsd.k12.ny.us/wmhs/Departments/Math/OBrien/mandlebrot.html (accessed January 19, 2004).

124. Maurice Mashaal, *Bourbaki: A Secret Society of Mathematicians* (Providence: American Mathematical Society, 2006), p. 130.

125. Benoît B. Mandelbrot and Richard L. Hudson, *The (Mis)Behavior of Markets: A Fractal View of Risk, Ruin, and Reward* (New York: Basic Books, 2004), p. 150.

126. Ibid.

127. Ibid.

128. Bertrand Russell, *Pacifism and Revolution, 1916–18*, ed. Richard A. Rempel et al. (London: Routledge, 1995), p. lv; Bertrand Russell, *The Selected Letters of Bertrand Russell: The Public Years, 1914–1970*, ed. Nicholas Griffin (London: Routledge, 2001), p. 140.

129. Michael Frame and Benoît B. Mandelbrot, *Fractals, Graphics, and Mathematics Education* (Washington, DC: Mathematical Association of America, 2002), p. 30.

130. Ibid.

131. M. H. A. Newman, "Mathematics: Gateway or Barrier? Review of *Mathematics and the Physical World* by Morris Kline," *New Scientist*, March 30, 1961, p. 830; William Aspray and Philip Kitcher, *History and Philosophy of Modern Mathematics* (Minneapolis: University of Minnesota Press, 1998), p. 12; Eleanor Robson and Jacqueline A. Stedall, eds., *The Oxford Handbook of the History of Mathematics* (Oxford: Oxford University Press, 2009), pp. 119, 266; Elizabeth Garber, *The Language of Physics: The Calculus and the Development of Theoretical Physics in Europe, 1750–1914* (Boston: Birkhäuser, 1999), p. 350; Paolo Mancosu, Klaus Frovin Jørgensen, and Stig Andur Pedersen, *Visualization, Explanation, and Reasoning Styles in Mathematics* (Dordrecht, Netherlands: Springer, 2005), pp. 13–16; Jean-Marie Laborde, ed., *Intelligent Learning Environments: The Case of Geometry* (Grenoble: NATO-ASI Series, 1989), pp. 95–96; Siobhan Roberts, *King of Infinite Space: Donald Coxeter, the Man Who Saved Geometry* (New York: Walker, 2006), p. 155.

132. G. H. Hardy, *Integration of Functions* (Cambridge, UK: Cambridge University Press, 1916).

133. Eric D. Beinhocker, *The Origin of Wealth: Evolution, Complexity, and the Radical Remaking of Economics* (Boston: Harvard Business School Press, 2006), p. 388.

134. "Benoît Mandelbrot," interview with Benoît Mandelbrot, Three Village Central School District.

9. IT'S FROM BITS: THE TWO-BIT TARANTELLA

How Math Lost Its Pictures . . .
and How It Got Them Back Again

1. Dan E. Tamil et al., "Electro-Optical DSP of Tera Operations per Second and Beyond," in *Optical Supercomputing: First International Workshop*, ed. Shlomi Dolev, Tobias Haist, and Mihai Oltean (Berlin: Springer, 2008), p. 56.

2. Benoît B. Mandelbrot, *Fractals and Scaling in Finance: Discontinuity, Concentration, Risk* (New York: Springer, 1997), pp. 363, 468; Steven Holtzman, *Digital Mosaics: The Aesthetics of Cyberspace* (New York: Simon & Schuster, 1997), p. 49; Donald A. MacKenzie, *An Engine, Not a Camera: How Financial Models Shape Markets* (Cambridge MA: MIT, 2006), p. 107.

3. Ulf Hashagen, Reinhard Keil-Slawik, and Arthur Lawrence Norberg, *History of Computing: Software Issues; International Conference on the History of Computing* (Berlin: Springer 2002), p. 20.

4. Pavel Kurakin, personal communication, March 29, 2011.

5. Jane Muir, *Of Men and Numbers: The Story of the Great Mathematicians* (Mineola, NY: Dover, 1996), p. 16, reprint of 1961 original; Elizabeth Wayland Barber, *Women's Work: The First 20,000 Years: Women, Cloth, and Society in Early Times* (New York: Norton, 1994).

6. René Descartes, *Discourse on Method, Optics, Geometry, and Meteorology*, trans. Norman Kemp Smith (Indianapolis: Hackett, 2001). Originally published in 1637.

7. Benoît B. Mandelbrot and Richard L. Hudson, *The (Mis)Behavior of Markets: A Fractal View of Risk, Ruin, and Reward* (New York: Basic Books, 2004), p. 150.

8. Ibid.

Fuse and Fizz, Thou Shalt Bud: Fractals and the Bounce from Boom to Bust

9. Gregory Chaitin, "Metabiology: Life as Evolving Software—Course Notes," draft, University of Auckland, New Zealand, October 1, 2010, pp. 89–90, http://www.cs.auckland .ac.nz/~chaitin/metabiology.pdf (accessed June 2, 2011),

10. Dr. Seuss, *If I Ran the Zoo* (New York: Random House, 1950).

11. Jennifer Anne Weghorst, "Behavioral Ecology and Fission-Fusion Dynamics of Spider Monkeys in Lowland Wet Forest" (PhD dissertation, Washington University, St. Louis, MO); F. P. G. Aldrich-Blake et al., "Observations on Baboons, *Papio anubis*, in an Arid Region in Ethiopia," *Folia Primatologica* 15 (1971):1–35; "Fission-Fusion Societies and Cognitive Evolution," workshop held in Siena, Italy, August 28–30, 2004, http://www.ethoikos.it/ FisFus2004.html (accessed October 13, 2011); F. Aureli et al., "Fission-Fusion Dynamics: New Research Frameworks," *Current Anthropology*, August 2008, pp. 627–54; Janet Mann et al., *Cetacean Societies, Field Studies of Dolphins and Whales* (Chicago: University of Chicago Press, 2000).

12. Howard Bloom, *The Genius of the Beast: A Radical Re-Vision of Capitalism* (Amherst, NY: Prometheus Books, 2009).

13. K. R. L. Hall. "Experiment and Quantification in the Study of Baboon Behavior in Its Natural Habitat," in *Primates: Studies in Adaptation and Variability*, ed. Phyllis C. Jay (New York: Holt, Rinehart, and Winston, 1968), pp. 120–30.

14. Piyapas Tharavanij, "Capital Market Development, Frequency of Recession, and Fraction of Time the Economy in Recession," MPRA Paper No. 4954, September 9, 2007, p. 15, Munich Personal RePEc Archive, http://mpra.ub.uni-muenchen.de/4954/1/MPRA_ paper_4954.pdf (accessed December 28, 2008).

15. James West Davidson, William E. Gienapp, and Christine Leigh Heyrman, *Nation*

of Nations: A Narrative History of the American Republic (New York: McGraw-Hill, 1998), p. 320; Willard Wesley Cochrane, *The Development of American Agriculture: A Historical Analysis* (Minneapolis: University of Minnesota Press, 1993), pp. 59–60.

16. "Nashville Land for Sale," landandfarm.com, http://www.landandfarm.com/search/TN/Nashville-land-for-sale/ (accessed August 29, 2011).

17. $127 million per acre is the rough price of real estate in Chicago's toniest residential neighborhoods—the Gold Coast and Streeterville.

18. Rufus Blanchard, *Discovery and Conquests of the North-west, with the History of Chicago* (Wheaton, IL: R. Blanchard & Co., 1881), p. 340.

19. Wolfgang Schivelbusch, *The Railway Journey: The Industrialization of Time and Space in the 19th Century* (Berkeley: University of California Press, 1986), p. 96.

20. James William Putnam, *The Illinois and Michigan Canal: A Study in Economic History* (Chicago: University of Chicago Press, 1918), pp. xviii–44.

21. Charles Moreau Harger, "The Revival in Western Land Values," *American Monthly Review of Reviews* 35 (1907): 63.

22. "The Homestead Act of 1862," in *A History of Us: Sourcebook and Index: Documents That Shaped the American Nation*, ed. Steven Mintz (Oxford: Oxford University Press, 2003), p. 163.

23. Nathaniel Wright Stephenson, *Abraham Lincoln and the Union: A Chronicle of the Embattled North* (New Haven, CT: Yale University Press, 1918), p. 210.

24. Dennis M. Welch, "Blake, the Famine of 1795, and the Economics of Vision," *European Romantic Review*, December 2007, pp. 597–622; Leslie A. Clarkson and E. Margaret Crawford, *Feast and Famine: Food and Nutrition in Ireland, 1500–1920* (Oxford: Oxford University Press, 2001), p. 131.

25. "The Failure of the Russian Harvest," *Speaker*, August 22, 1891, p. 218.

26. Archer Butler Hulbert, *Historic Highways of America: The Great American Canals* (Cleveland: Arthur H. Clark, 1904), p. 212; State of New York, "Report of the Joint Legislative Committee on the Barge Canal," Legislative Document 1961, March 21, 1961, in Morris Pierce, *History of the Erie Canal*, Department of History, University of Rochester, http://www.history.rochester.edu/canal/bib/nys1961/historyc.htm (accessed January 17, 2009).

The Sorcery of Simple Rules

27. Lewis Fry Richardson, *Collected Papers of Lewis Fry Richardson*, vol. 1, *Meteorology and Numerical Analysis*, ed. Oliver M. Asford and P. G. Drazin (New York: Cambridge University Press, 1993), p. 11.

The Japanese Sword Maker and the Alchemy of Iteration

28. Yumei Dang, Louis H. Kauffman, and Daniel J. Sandin, *Hypercomplex Iterations: Distance Estimation and Higher Dimensional Fractals*, vol. 1 (Singapore: World Scientific, 2002), p. 97.

29. Ian G. Peirce and Ewart Oakeshott, *Swords of the Viking Age* (Woodbridge, UK: Boydell, 2002), p. 36.

30. Nick Evangelista, *The Encyclopedia of the Sword* (Westport, CT: Greenwood, 1995), p. 612.

31. A. Guillaume, *The Life of Muhammad: A Translation of Ibn Ishaq's Sirat Rasul Allah* (New York: Oxford University Press, 1955), p. 469.

32. Egerton Castle, *Schools and Masters of Fence: From the Middle Ages to the Eighteenth Century* (London: G. Bell, 1885), pp. 227–28.

33. DK Publishing, *Weapon: A Visual History of Arms and Armor* (London: DK, 2006), p. 121.

34. "Iron and the Smith," *Van Nostrand's Eclectic Engineering Magazine* 12 (1875): 144.

35. John M. Yumoto, *The Samurai Sword: A Handbook* (Boston: Tuttle, 1958), p. 28.

36. Ibid., p. 26.

37. Ibid.

38. Christopher Ross, *Mishima's Sword: Travels in Search of a Samurai Legend* (Cambridge, MA: Da Capo, 2006), p. 184.

39. Leon Kapp, Hiroko Kapp, and Yoshindo Yoshihara, *The Craft of the Japanese Sword* (Tokyo: Kodansha, 1987), p. 32.

40. Yumoto, *Samurai Sword*, p. 98.

41. Stanford D. Carman, *A Book of Five Swords and a Scroll* (self-published via Lulu.com, 2004), pp. 51–52.

42. National Geographic Channel, *Samurai Sword*, http://natgeotv.com/asia/samurai-sword/about (accessed September 2, 2011).

43. Yumoto, *Samurai Sword*, p. 26.

44. Leonid Ivanovich Ponomarev, *The Quantum Dice* (London: Institute of Physics Publishing, 1993), p. 83.

45. Ludwig Wittgenstein, *Wittgenstein's Lectures on Philosophical Psychology, 1946–47* (Hemel Hempstead, UK: Harvester Wheatsheaf, 1988), p. 56.

Gaming Your Way to Fame: John Conway Enters the Scene

46. Benoît Mandelbrot, *Les Objets Fractals, Forme, Hasard et Dimension* (Paris: Flammarion, 1975).

47. Fred Hoyle, *Home Is Where the Wind Blows: Chapters from a Cosmologist's Life* (Mill Valley, CA: University Science Books, 1994), p. 341.

48. Benoît B. Mandelbrot, *Selecta (Old or New): Selected Works of Benoît B. Mandelbrot* (New York: Springer, 2002), pp. 218–25.

49. Marcus Du Sautoy, *Symmetry: A Mathematical Journey* (New York: HarperCollins e-books, 2009), Kindle edition, locations 5133–5135.

50. Michael John Bradley, *Mathematics Frontiers: 1950 to the Present* (New York: Infobase, 2006) p. 37.

51. Du Sautoy, *Symmetry*, Kindle location 5108.

52. Ibid., locations 5104–5105.

53. John O'Connor and Edmund Robertson, "John Conway," in The MacTutor History of Mathematics Archive, School of Mathematics and Statistics, University of St. Andrews, Scotland, http://www-history.mcs.st-andrews.ac.uk/Biographies/Conway.html (accessed February 23, 2011).

54. Elizabeth Adkins-Regan, *Hormones and Animal Social Behavior* (Princeton, NJ: Princeton University Press, 2005), p. 96; Kikunori Shinohara et al., "Physiological Changes in Pachinko Players; Beta-Endorphin, Catecholamines, Immune System Substances, and Heart Rate," *Applied Human Science* 18, no. 2 (1999): 37–42.

55. Ayako Onzo and Ken Mogi, "Cognitive Process of Emotion under Uncertainty," in *Neural Information Processing: 11th International Conference*, ed. Nikhil R. Pal et al., International Conference on Neural Information Processing (ICONIP), Calcutta, India, November 2004 (Berlin: Springer, 2004), p. 301; Wolfram Schultz, "Midbrain Dopamine Neurons: A Retina of the Reward System?" in *Neuroeconomics: Decision Making and the Brain*, ed. Paul W. Glimcher et al. (London: Academic Press, 2008), p. 326.

56. Michael A. Hogg and Joel Cooper, *The Sage Handbook of Social Psychology* (London: Sage, 2003), p. 312.

57. Mikal J. Aasved, *The Biology of Gambling* (Springfield, IL: Charles C. Thomas, 2003), p. 234.

58. Du Sautoy, *Symmetry*, Kindle locations 5153–5154.

Axioms in Silicon: Conway's Game of Life

59. Martin Gardner, "The Fantastic Combinations of John Conway's New Solitaire Game 'Life,'" *Scientific American* 223 (1970): 120–23.

60. Dan E. Tamil et al., "Electro-Optical DSP of Tera Operations per Second and Beyond," in *Optical Supercomputing: First International Workshop*, Vienna, Austria, August 26, 2008 (Berlin: Springer, 2008), p. 56.

61. Gardner, "The Fantastic Combinations."

Good-Bye to Equations:
Stephen Wolfram's New Kind of Science

62. Penny Le Couteur and Jay Burreson, *Napoleon's Buttons: 17 Molecules that Changed History* (New York: Tarcher/Penguin 2004), Kindle locations 2461–63.

63. Quoted in Ernest H. Lindley, "A Study of Puzzles with Special Reference to the Psychology of Mental Adaptation," *American Journal of Psychology* 8 (July 1897): 473.

64. Freeman J. Dyson, *Selected Papers of Freeman Dyson with Commentary* (Providence: American Mathematical Society, 1996), p. 19.

65. Gladwin Hill, "Physicist Awarded 'Genius' Prize Finds Reality in Invisible World," *New York Times*, Sunday, May 24, 1981.

66. Steven Levy, "The Man Who Cracked the Code to Everything," *Wired*, June 2002.

67. "Stephen Wolfram," NNDP, http://www.nndb.com/people/325/000022259/ (accessed February 27, 2011).

68. David C. Stork, "Computers, Science, and Extraterrestrials: An Interview with Stephen Wolfram," in *HAL's Legacy: 2001's Computer as Dream and Reality*, ed. David G. Stork (Cambridge, MA: MIT, 1997), pp. 333–48.

69. Stephen Wolfram, "My Hobby: Hunting for Our Universe," *Wolfram Blog*, September 11, 2007, http://blog.wolfram.com/?year=2007&monthnum=09&name=my-hobby -hunting-for-our-universe#more (accessed October 2, 2011).

70. "Stephen Wolfram," NNDP.

71. Robert Lee Hotz, "A Math Genius Who Decided Not to Play It by the Numbers," *Los Angeles Times*, September 30, 1996.

72. "Stephen Wolfram," NNDP.

73. Stephen Wolfram, "Statistical Mechanics of Cellular Automata," *Reviews of Modern Physics* 55, no. 3 (1983): 601–44; Stephen Wolfram, "Universality and Complexity in Cellular Automata," *Physica D: Nonlinear Phenomena* 10, no. 1–2 (January 1984): 1–35; Stephen Wolfram, "Cellular Automata as Models of Complexity," *Nature*, October 4, 1984, pp. 419–25; Stephen Wolfram, *Cellular Automata and Complexity: Collected Papers* (Boulder, CO: Westview Press, 1994).

74. "Stephen Wolfram," NNDP.

75. *Complex Systems* home page, http://www.complex-systems.com/index.html (accessed October 2, 2011).

76. "Stephen Wolfram," NNDP.

77. Stork, *HAL's Legacy*, pp. 333–48.

78. Stephen Wolfram, "Some Modern Perspectives on the Quest for Ultimate Knowledge," in *Randomness and Complexity: From Leibniz to Chaitin*, ed. Cristian Calude (Singapore: World Scientific, 2007), pp. 367–79.

79. Ibid.

80. Jennifer Speake and John Simpson, *The Oxford Dictionary of Proverbs* (Oxford: Oxford University Press, 2008).

81. René Descartes, *Discourse on the Method and the Meditations*, trans. John Veitch (New York: Cosimo Books, 2008), originally published by J. M. Dent in 1924; Isaac Newton, *The Mathematical Papers of Isaac Newton: 1664–1666*, ed. D. T. Whiteside (Cambridge, UK: Cambridge University Press, 1967). Descartes helped introduce the equation in 1637 when he turned geometry into algebra. Then Isaac Newton, from the 1670s onward, injected equations into the mainstream of science.

82. Stork, *HAL's Legacy*, p. 340.

83. Wolfram, "Some Modern Perspectives."

84. Ibid.

85. Ibid.

86. Ibid.

87. Ibid.

88. Ibid.

89. Ibid.

90. Ibid.

91. Ibid.

92. Ibid.

93. Stork, *HAL's Legacy*, p. 340.

94. Wolfram, "Some Modern Perspectives."

95. Ibid.

96. Dennis Bray, *Wetware: A Computer in Every Living Cell* (New Haven, CT: Yale University Press, 2009), p. 103.

97. Wolfram, "Some Modern Perspectives."

98. Stork, *HAL's Legacy*, p. 340.

99. Ibid., pp. 333–48.

100. Wolfram, "Some Modern Perspectives."

101. "Cellular Automata and the Mechanisms of Nature Based on Chapter 2: The Crucial Experiment, from *A New Kind of Science* by Stephen Wolfram," wolframscience.com, http://www.wolframscience.com/downloads/artwork/CAandNature.pdf (accessed September 5, 2011).

102. Stephen Wolfram, "Evolution of a Continuous Cellular Automaton with Rule Based on Addition," in Stephen Wolfram, *A New Kind of Science* (Champaign, IL: Wolfram Media, 2002), p. 60, http://www.wolframscience.com/downloads/colorimages.html (accessed September 5, 2011).

103. Bray, *Wetware*, p. 103.

104. Hector Zenil, Senior Research Associate, Wolfram Research, personal communications, September 30, 2011, and October 1, 2011.

105. Andrew Adamatzky, *Game of Life Cellular Automata* (London: Springer, 2010), p. 72.

106. Stephen Wolfram, "Statistical Mechanics of Cellular Automata," *Reviews of Modern Physics* 55 (1983): 601–44.

107. Stephen Wolfram, *A New Kind of Science* (Champaign, IL: Wolfram Media, 2002), pp. 261–66.

108. Wolfram, "Some Modern Perspectives."

109. Michael J. Behe, *The Edge of Evolution: The Search for the Limits of Darwinism* (New York: Simon & Schuster, 2008), p. 120.

110. Zenil, personal communication.

111. Stork, *HAL's Legacy.*

112. Wolfram, "Some Modern Perspectives."

113. Stork, *HAL's Legacy*, pp. 333–48.

114. Ibid.

115. Ibid., p. 346.

116. Ibid.

117. Ibid.

118. Eric Weisstein, "Universal Turing Machine," Wolfram MathWorld (website), http://mathworld.wolfram.com/UniversalTuringMachine.html (accessed October 3, 2011).

119. Stephen Wolfram, "My Hobby."

120. Ibid.

121. Ibid.

122. Ibid.

123. Ibid.

124. Ibid.

125. Ibid.

126. Ibid.

127. Ibid.

128. Ibid; Wolfram, *A New Kind of Science*, pp. 486–88.

129. Wolfram, "My Hobby."

130. Ibid.

131. Ibid.

132. Ibid.

133. Ibid.

134. Ibid.

135. Ibid.

136. Ibid.

137. Ibid.

138. Ibid.

139. Stork, *HAL's Legacy.*

10. WHAT ARE THE RULES OF THE UNIVERSE?

The Case of the Obsessive-Compulsive Cosmos

1. Aristotle, *The Logic of Science: A Translation of the Posterior Analytics of Aristotle*, with notes and an introduction by Edward Poste (Oxford: Francis Macpherson, 1850).

2. Thomas C. McKay, *Physical Measurements in Sound, Light, Electricity, and Magnetism* (Berkeley: University of California Press, 1908), p. 47.

3. J. C. Polkinghorne, *Quantum Theory: A Very Short Introduction* (New York: Oxford University Press, 2002).

4. Freeman Dyson, "Could Atomic Science Explain Free Will?" BigThink.com, http://bigthink.com/ideas/19295 (accessed September 6, 2011).

5. Stuart Kauffman, "Physics and Five Problems in the Philosophy of Mind," July 15, 2009, arXiv.org, http://arxiv.org/abs/0907.2494 (accessed September 30, 2011); Stuart A. Kauffman, "Five Problems in the Philosophy of Mind," Edge.org, August 7, 2009, http://www .edge.org/3rd_culture/kauffman09/kauffman09_index.html (accessed September 7, 2011); Robert Kane, *The Oxford Handbook of Free Will* (New York: Oxford University Press, 2011).

6. John Conway and Simon Kochen, "The Free Will Theorem," April 11, 2006, http://arxiv.org/pdf/quant-ph/0604079 (accessed September 7, 2011).

7. Dyson, "Could Atomic Science Explain Free Will?"

8. Kauffman, "Five Problems in the Philosophy of Mind."

9. Conway and Kochen, "Free Will Theorem."

10. Reinhold Blümel, *Foundations of Quantum Mechanics: From Photons to Quantum Computers* (Sudbury, MA: Jones and Bartlett, 2010), pp. 15, 32.

11. Robert L. Cooper, "The Radiative Decay Mode of the Free Neutron" (PhD dissertation, University of Michigan, 2008), pp. 4–5; Detlef Filges and Frank Goldenbaum, *Handbook of Spallation Research: Theory, Experiments, and Applications* (Weinheim, Germany: Wiley-VCH, 2009), p. 648.

12. Maximilian A. Schlosshauer, *Decoherence and the Quantum-to-Classical Transition* (Berlin: Springer, 2008), p. 8.

13. Karl Popper, *Quantum Theory and the Schism in Physics: From the Postscript to the Logic of Scientific Discovery* (London: Routledge, 2000), pp. 86–88. Originally published 1982.

14. Walter Pötz, Jaroslav Fabian, and Ulrich Hohenester, *Quantum Coherence: From Quarks to Solids* (Berlin: Springer, 2006), p. 28.

15. For the way the environment of the early universe "measures" the particles within it, see Dennis Dieks et al., eds., *Explanation, Prediction, and Confirmation* (Dordrecht, Netherlands: Springer, 2011), p. 421.

16. Kohsuke Yagi, Tetsuo Hatsuda, and Yasuo Miake, *Quark-Gluon Plasma: From Big Bang to Little Bang* (Cambridge, UK: Cambridge University Press, 2005), p. 12.

17. Paola A. Zizzi, "Emergence of Universe from a Quantum Network," in *Physics of Emergence and Organization*, ed. Ignazio Licata and Ammar Sakaji (Singapore: World Scientific, 2008), pp. 314–15.

18. Martin Bojowald, *Once before Time: A Whole Story of the Universe* (New York: Knopf 2010), Kindle edition, locations 2966–67.

19. Ibid.

20. National Institute of Standards and Technology, "The NIST Reference on Constants, Units, and Uncertainty," http://physics.nist.gov/cuu/Constants/index.html (accessed October 1, 2011).

21. WordNet Search-3.1, s.v. "dominance," http://wordnetweb.princeton.edu/perl/webwn?s=dominance (accessed February 22, 2011).

22. Michael Waller, personal communication, 1997.

23. Peter H. Bodenheimer, *Principles of Star Formation* (Heidelberg: Springer, 2011), p. 251.

Time, the Great Translator: An Information Theory of Time

24. Sean M. Carroll, *From Eternity to Here: The Quest for the Ultimate Theory of Time* (New York: Penguin, 2010).

25. Vladislav Čápek and Daniel Peter Sheehan, *Challenges to the Second Law of Thermodynamics: Theory and Experiment* (Dordrecht, Netherlands: Springer, 2005), p. xiii.

26. Ibid.

27. *Wikipedia*, s.v. "stair riser," http://en.wikipedia.org/wiki/Stair_riser (accessed April 4, 2011).

28. Sources for this account of bees include: Thomas D. Seeley, *Honeybee Democracy* (Princeton, NJ: Princeton University Press, 2010); Thomas D. Seeley, *Honeybee Ecology: A Study of Adaptation in Social Life* (Princeton NJ: Princeton University Press, 1985); Thomas D. Seeley, *The Wisdom of the Hive: The Social Physiology of Honey Bee Colonies* (Cambridge MA: Harvard University Press, 1995); Thomas D. Seeley, "Research Interests," Thomas D. Seeley faculty web page, Cornell University Department of Neurobiology and Behavior, http://www.nbb.cornell.edu/Faculty/seeley/research2.html (accessed April 15, 2008); Thomas D. Seeley and Royce A. Levien, "A Colony of Mind: The Beehive as Thinking Machine," *Sciences*, July/August 1987; E. O. Wilson, *The Insect Societies* (Cambridge, MA: Harvard University Press, 1971); E. O. Wilson, *Sociobiology: The New Synthesis* (Cambridge, MA: Harvard University Press, 1975); P. K. Visscher, "Collective Decisions and Cognition in Bees," *Nature*, February 4, 1999; Karl von Frisch, *Bees: Their Vision, Chemical Senses, and Language* (Ithaca, NY: Cornell University Press, 1950); Karl von Frisch, "Decoding the Language of the Bee," *Nobel Lectures*, December 12, 1973, http://nobelprize.org/nobel_prizes/medicine/laureates/1973/frisch-lecture.pdf (accessed September 30, 2008); Eugenia Alumot, Y. Lensky,

and Pia Holstein, "Sugars and Trehalase in the Reproductive Organs and Hemolymph of the Queen and Drone Honey Bees (*Apis mellifica* L. var. *Ligustica* spin)," *Comparative Biochemistry and Physiology*, March 1969, pp. 1419–25; Robin L . Foster et al., "Reproductive Physiology, Dominance Interactions, and Division of Labour among Bumble Bee Workers," *Physiological Entomology* 29 (2004): 327–34; M. Gries and N. Koeniger, "Straight Forward to the Queen: Pursuing Honeybee Drones (*Apis mellifera* L.) Adjust Their Body Axis to the Direction of the Queen," *Journal of Comparative Physiology A: Neuroethology, Sensory, Neural, and Behavioral Physiology*, October 1996, pp. 539–44; Jon F. Harrison, Orley R. Taylor Jr., and H. Glenn Hall, "The Flight Physiology of Reproductives of Africanized, European, and Hybrid Honeybees (*Apis mellifera*)," *Physiological and Biochemical Zoology*, March–April 2005, pp. 153–62; E. R. Hoover, Heather A. Higo, and Mark L. Winston, "Worker Honey Bee Ovary Development: Seasonal Variation and the Influence of Larval and Adult Nutrition," *Journal of Comparative Physiology B: Biochemical, Systemic, and Environmental Physiology*, January 2006; Helge Schlüns et al., "Multiple Nuptial Flights, Sperm Transfer, and the Evolution of Extreme Polyandry in Honeybee Queens," *Animal Behaviour*, July 2005, pp. 125–31; Charles W. Whitfield, Anne-Marie Cziko, and Gene E. Robinson, "Gene Expression Profiles in the Brain Predict Behavior in Individual Honey Bees," *Science*, October 10, 2003, pp. 296–99; Charles W. Whitfield, "Molecular Mechanisms and Molecular Evolution of Social Behavior, Using Social Insects as a Model," Charlie Whitfield Lab home page, University of California, Davis, http://www.life.uiuc.edu/cwwhitfield (accessed May 18, 2008).

29. N. K. Franks, "On Optimal Decision Making in Brains and Social Insect Colonies," *Interface: Journal of the Royal Society*, November 2009, pp. 1065–74; Seeley, *Honeybee Democracy*, pp. 215–17.

30. Seeley, *Wisdom of the Hive*, p. 124.

31. Ibid., p. 90.

32. Seeley, *Honeybee Democracy*, p. 41.

33. George Malinetskii, "Synergetics and High Technologies," http://spkurdyumov.narod.ru/Malinetskiy/Malinetskiy.htm (accessed September 9, 2011).

34. Pavel V. Kurakin, George G. Malinetskii, and Howard Bloom. "Conversational (Dialogue) Model of Quantum Transitions," arXiv.org, http://arxiv.org/ftp/abs/quant-ph/0504088 (accessed October 1, 2011).

35. Yuri Ozhigov, home page, http://qi.cs.msu.su/home_pages/ozhigov_home_page.html (accessed September 9, 2011); see also http://qi.cs.msu.su/ru/teachers/ozhigov (accessed May 2, 2012).

36. Yuri Ozhigov, "Constructive Physics," submitted May 19, 2008 (v1), last revised September 16, 2008 (v2), arXiv.org, http://arxiv.org/abs/0805.2859 (accessed November 8, 2011).

37. Yuri Ozhigov, personal communication, March 17, 2011.

Wrap Yourself in String: Iteration and Emergent Properties

38. Elizabeth Wayland Barber, *Women's Work: The First 20,000 Years: Women, Cloth, and Society in Early Times* (New York: Norton, 1995).

39. T. Morii, C. S. Lim, and S. N. Mukherjee, *The Physics of the Standard Model and Beyond* (Singapore: World Scientific, 2004); Quang Ho-Kim and Xuân-Yêm Phạm, *Elementary Particles and Their Interactions: Concepts and Phenomena* (Berlin: Springer, 1998), pp. 1–10; "The Particle World," US/LHC: Particle Physics at Discovery's Horizon, National Science Foundation and US Department of Energy, http://www.uslhc.us/LHC_Science/Questions_for_the_Universe/Particles (accessed September 9, 2011).

40. Peter H. Bodenheimer, *Principles of Star Formation* (Heidelberg: Springer, 2011), p. 251.

41. Pieter G. van Dokkum and Charlie Conroy, "A Substantial Population of Low-Mass Stars in Luminous Elliptical Galaxies," *Nature*, December 16, 2010, pp. 940–42.

Baking the Big Bagel: How to Start and End a Universe

42. Roswell Park Cancer Institute, "About Roswell Park Cancer Institute," http://www.roswellpark.org/about-us (accessed September 10, 2011).

43. Graham Farmelo, *The Strangest Man: The Hidden Life of Paul Dirac, Mystic of the Atom* (New York: Basic Books, 2009); Helen R. Quinn and Yossi Nir, *The Mystery of the Missing Antimatter* (Princeton, NJ: Princeton University Press, 2008), p. 42; F. E. Close, *Antimatter* (Oxford: Oxford University Press, 2009).

44. Helge Kragh, *Dirac: A Scientific Biography* (Cambridge, UK: Cambridge University Press, 1990), p. 116.

45. Jagdish Mehra and Helmut Rechenberg, *The Formulation of Matrix Mechanics and Its Modifications 1925–1926* (New York: Springer, 1982), p. 5; Leonid Ivanovich Ponomarev, *The Quantum Dice* (London: Institute of Physics Publishing, 1993), pp. 83–84.

46. Carl D. Anderson, "The Production and Properties of Positrons," *Nobel Lectures*, December 12, 1936, http://www.nobelprize.org/nobel_prizes/physics/laureates/1936/anderson-lecture.pdf (accessed September 10, 2011).

47. V. K. Mittal and R. C. Verma, *Introduction to Nuclear and Particle Physics* (New Delhi: PHI Learning, 2009), p. 308.

48. Ibid.

49. George Gamow, *One, Two, Three—Infinity: Facts and Speculations of Science* (Mineola, NY: Dover, 1988). Originally published in 1947.

50. For a similar use of steep curves in a topologically depicted universe, see Martin Bojowald's cyclic loop-quantum-gravity cosmos, whose structure "drives a short period of super-inflation during which the inflation is pushed up its potential hill." Martin Bojowald,

Roy Maartens, and Parampreet Singh, "Loop Quantum Gravity and the Cyclic Universe," arXiv.org, http://arxiv.org/abs/hep-th/0407115 (accessed April 18, 2011).

51. Alan H. Guth, *Inflation* (Cambridge, MA: Massachusetts Institute of Technology, Center for Theoretical Physics, 1992); Alan H. Guth, *The Inflationary Universe: The Quest for a New Theory of Cosmic Origins* (New York: Basic Books, 1998).

52. Brian P. Schmidt et al., "The High-Z Supernova Search: Measuring Cosmic Deceleration and Global Curvature of the Universe Using Type IA Supernovae," *Astronomical Journal*, November 1998, pp. 46–63; Adam G. Reiss et al., "Observational Evidence from Supernovae for an Accelerating Universe and a Cosmological Constant," *Astrophysical Journal*, September 1998.

53. Mario Livio, *The Accelerating Universe: Infinite Expansion, the Cosmological Constant, and the Beauty of the Cosmos* (New York: John Wiley and Sons, 1999).

54. Adam G. Riess and Michael S. Turner, "The Expanding Universe: From Slowdown to Speed Up," Scientific American, September 23, 2008, http://www.scientificamerican.com/article.cfm?id=expanding-universe-slows-then-speeds (accessed September 10, 2011).

55. Salvatore Capozziello, Valerio Faraoni, *Beyond Einstein Gravity: A Survey of Gravitational Theories for Cosmology and Astrophysics* (Dordrecht, Netherlands: Springer, 2010), p. 327; Michael A. Seeds and Dana E. Backman, *Foundations of Astronomy* (Boston, MA: Brooks/Cole, 2011), p. 407.

56. Dennis Overbye, "Universe as Doughnut: New Data, New Debate," *New York Times*, March 11, 2003, http://www.nytimes.com/2003/03/11/science/universe-as-doughnut-new-data-new-debate.html (accessed April 16, 2011).

57. M. Tegmark, "Measuring Spacetime: From the Big Bang to Black Holes," *Science*, May 24, 2002, pp. 1427–33.

58. A. de Oliveira-Costa, M. Tegmark, M. Zaldarriaga, Andrew Hamilton, "Significance of the Largest Scale CMB Fluctuations in WMAP," *Physical Review D* 69, no. 6 (March 25, 2004).

59. Ibid.

60. Ralf Aurich et al., "Do We Live in a 'Small Universe'?" in *Classical and Quantum Gravity*, June 21, 2008.

61. Zeeya Merali, "Doughnut-Shaped Universe Bites Back: Astronomers Say Universe Is Small and Finite," *Nature*, May 23, 2008.

62. Paul L. McFadden, Neil Turok, and Paul J. Steinhardt, "Solution of a Braneworld Big Crunch/Big Bang Cosmology," *Physical Review D*, 76, 104038 (2007); Ron Cowen, "Pre-Bang Branes and Bubbles: What Happened before the Big Bang?" *Science News*, April 23, 2011, p. 22, http://www.sciencenews.org/view/feature/id/72325/title/Pre-Bang_branes_and_bubbles (accessed October 15, 2011).

63. Roger Penrose, *Cycles of Time: An Extraordinary New View of the Universe* (New York: Random House, 2011); Theo Koupelis, *In Quest of the Universe* (Sudbury, MA: Jones & Bartlett, 2011), p. 532.

64. Martin Bojowald, *Once before Time: A Whole Story of the Universe* (New York: Knopf, 2010), Kindle edition.

65. Bojowald, Maartens, and Singh, "Loop Quantum Gravity and the Cyclic Universe."

66. Cédric Deffayet, Gia Dvali, and Gregory Gabadadze, "Accelerated Universe from Gravity Leaking to Extra Dimensions," *Physical Review D*, 65 (2002), 044023; Ron Cowen, "Dark Doings Searching for Signs of a Force that May Be Everywhere ... or Nowhere," *Science News Online*, May 22, 2004.

67. Amanda Gefter, "Dark Flow: Proof of Another Universe?" *New Scientist*, January 23, 2009, pp. 50–53.

Will Silicon Axioms Fly?

68. Stephen Wolfram, *A New Kind of Science* (Champaign, IL: Wolfram Media, 2002), p. 739, http://www.wolframscience.com/nksonline/page-739 (accessed September 12, 2011). Wolfram dodges the challenge of prediction. He proposes that the sort of systems he studies can only be run in the computer, run as many times as it takes to see the system evolve. The result? The computer simulation may take as long to run as the phenomenon it models. Wolfram calls this "computational irreducibility." And Wolfram states bluntly, "Indeed, whenever computational irreducibility exists in a system it means that in effect there can be no way to predict how the system will behave except by going through almost as many steps of computation as the evolution of the system itself." For more on how Wolfram avoids the test of prediction, see Lawrence Gray, "A Mathematician Looks at Wolfram's *New Kind of Science*," *Notices of the American Mathematical Society*, February 2003, pp. 200–12.

69. Takeshi Kobayashi, Hisao Hayakawa, and Masayoshi Tonouchi, *Vortex Electronics and SQUIDs* (Berlin: Springer, 2003), p. 2.

70. Robert Penrose Pearce, Royal Meteorological Society (Great Britain), *Meteorology at the Millennium* (London: Academic Press, 2002), p. 309.

Conclusion: The Big Bang Tango— Quarking in the Social Cosmos

71. Michael Henry Hansell, *Built by Animals: The Natural History of Animal Architecture* (Oxford, UK: Oxford Universit Press, 2007), p. 146.

72. M. Sue Houston, Jeffrey Holly, and Eva Feldman, eds., *IGF in Health and Disease* (Totowa, NJ: Humana Press, 2005), p. 272.

INDEX

Abraham, 102

abstraction, 25–26, 28, 33, 56, 85, 97, 130, 131, 133, 146, 167, 180, 185, 217, 222, 233, 238, 281, 284, 354–55, 384, 386, 389, 404, 406, 453, 455, 464, 497, 533, 544, 553

Academy. *See* Plato's Academy

acceleration, 276, 394–97, 406, 546–48

actin, 278

Adam (the Bible's first human), 50, 102

Adams, Henry, 329

addition (mathematics), 9, 75, 85, 87, 234, 256, 272, 476

a = *a*, 23, 29, 31–33, 37–38, 88, 138, 152, 167, 175–181, 188, 232, 255, 324, 462, 560. *See also* Aristotle's law of identity; Aristotle's law of noncontradiction; equating, equality, equal sign; identity

Africa, 72, 171, 185, 250, 392–93, 470

agriculture. *See* farms

Aguirre, Anthony, 551

Aharonov-Bohm Effect, 449

Ahmose, 126

Alexander the Great, 186

Alexandria, Egypt, 50, 186–87, 191, 212, 217, 268–69, 277, 532

algebra, 25, 55, 62, 127, 179, 211, 225, 235–36, 244, 247–48, 255, 372, 412–13, 464, 496, 505, 559

algorithms, 24, 85–86, 422, 489, 539. *See also* axioms; rules, simple rules

alphabet, alphabetic letters, 33–5, 38, 47, 184–84, 187, 269, 434, 453, 463, 484,

532

alternating current vs. direct current, 371, 373. *See also* electric

Amakuni, 479

Amenemhet III (king of Egypt), 126

American. *See* United States

American Revolution, 31, 216, 219

"America the Beautiful" (Bates), 474

amplitude, 510

Amsterdam, 209–10, 250

Attempt to Introduce Youth to the Fundamentals of Pure Science, Elementary and Advanced, by a Clear and Proper Method (Bólyai), 221

analogy vs. metaphor, 169

analytic geometry, 352, 372

Anaxagoras of Clazomenae, 169, 176–77, 189

Anaximander, 140–44, 169, 176

Anderson, Carl, 544

Anderson, Philip, 292–93. *See also* more is different

angles, 81–82, 95, 98, 101, 103, 105–109, 114, 116, 118, 122–27, 130, 134, 138, 155–57, 161, 171, 188, 193–203, 212, 226, 236, 249, 256, 261, 272, 284, 322, 362, 380, 560. *See also* right angles; protractor; degree

Annalen der Physik, 356, 369–70, 374–75

Annus Mirabilis (year of miracles, 1905), 369, 380, 391. *See also* Einstein, Albert

anthropocentrism, 509

anthropomorphism, 57, 110, 116, 130, 143,

ABOUT THE AUTHOR

"I know a lot of people. A lot. And I ask a lot of prying questions. But I've never run into a more intriguing biography than Howard Bloom's in all my born days."
—Paul Solman, business and economics correspondent, *PBS NewsHour*

Howard Bloom has been called "next in a lineage of seminal thinkers that includes Newton, Darwin, Einstein, [and] Freud" by Britain's Channel 4 TV; "the next Stephen Hawking" by *Gear* magazine; and "the Buckminster Fuller and Arthur C. Clarke of the new millennium" by Buckminster Fuller's archivist.

Bloom's second book, *Global Brain*, was the subject of an Office of the Secretary of Defense symposium in 2010, with participants from the State Department, the Energy Department, DARPA, IBM, and MIT. Bloom is currently co-designing a multi-planetary mission and an energy infrastructure for the solar system at Caltech under the sponsorship of the Keck Institute for Space Studies. Bloom is founder and head of the Space Development Steering Committee, a group that includes astronauts Buzz Aldrin, Edgar Mitchell (the sixth man on the moon), and members from the National Science Foundation, NASA, and the National Space Society.

Bloom's specialty is mass behavior, from the mass behavior of quarks to the mass behavior of human beings. He has lectured at Yale, Stanford, and Columbia University's Department of Neuroscience. He has published on theoretical physics, cosmology, and evolutionary biology. His scientific work has appeared in arXiv.org, the leading pre-print site in advanced theoretical physics and math; *PhysicaPlus*; *Across-Species Comparisons and Psychopathology*; *New Ideas in Psychology*; the *Journal of Space Philosophy*; and in the book series Research in Biopolitics. He lectured at an international conference of quantum physicists in Moscow—Quantum Informatics 2006—on why everything we know about quantum physics is wrong, and the concepts Bloom introduced were later used in a book proposing a new approach to quantum physics, *Constructive Physics*, by Moscow University's Yuri Ozhigov. Bloom is serious about understanding the sweep of mass behavior from elementary particles to humans. He has worked with Michael Jackson, Prince, Bob Marley, Bette Midler, AC/DC, Kiss, Queen, Aerosmith, Billy Joel, Paul Simon, Billy Idol, Joan Jett, David Byrne, Peter Gabriel, Run–D.M.C., Amnesty International, Farm Aid, the NAACP, and the United Negro College Fund.

Bloom's writing has appeared in the *Washington Post*, the *Wall Street Journal*, *Wired*, the *Village Voice*, and *Cosmopolitan*; in various publications via the Knight-Ridder Financial News Service; and in the *Scientific American*'s online edition.

Bloom is the author of six books: *The Lucifer Principle: A Scientific Expedition into the Forces of History* ("Mesmerizing." —*Washington Post*); *Global Brain: The Evolution of Mass Mind from the Big Bang to the 21st Century* ("Reassuring and sobering." —*New Yorker*); *The Genius of the Beast: A Radical Re-Vision of Capitalism* ("Impressive, stimulating, and tremendously enjoyable." —James Fallows, national correspondent, *Atlantic*); *How I Accidentally Started the Sixties* ("Wow! Whew! Wild! Wonderful!" —Timothy Leary), *The Mohammed Code* ("A terrifying book. ... The best book I've read on Islam." —David Swindle, *PJ Media*); and this book, *The God Problem: How a Godless Cosmos Creates* ("Bloom's argument will rock your world." —Barbara Ehrenreich).

Bloom has debated one-one-one with senior officials from Egypt's Muslim Brotherhood and Gaza's Hamas on Iran's global Arab-language al-Alam News Network. He has also dissected headline issues and new scientific findings over forty times on Saudi Arabia's KSA 2-TV, Al Ekhbariya-TV, and on Iran's global English-language Press TV. Interestingly, Sheikh Mohammed bin Rashid Al Maktoum, Dubai's ruler, who doubles as the prime minister of the United Arab Emirates, has named a racehorse after one of Bloom's books. Bloom has probed the untold story of the Syrian Civil War with Nancy Kissinger. And India's eleventh president, Dr. A. P. J. Kalam, has called Bloom's work a "visionary creation."

Bloom also founded the Group Selection Squad (1995), which gained acceptance for the concept of group selection in evolutionary biology; and the International Paleopsychology Project (1997), which created a new multidisciplinary synthesis between cosmology, paleontology, evolutionary biology, and history.

Says Berkley neuroscientist Walter J. Freeman of Bloom's work, "I am speechless with admiration, overwhelmed by virtuosity."

31901056934799